Kitchen and Herb Gardener

Kitchen and Herb Gardener

RICHARD BIRD AND JESSICA HOUDRET

with special photography by
Jonathan Buckley and Andrea Jones

LORENZ BOOKS

First published in 2000 by Lorenz Books

Lorenz Books is an imprint of
Anness Publishing Limited
Hermes House
88–89 Blackfriars Road
London SE1 8HA

Published in the USA by Lorenz Books
Anness Publishing Inc.
27 West 20th Street, New York
NY 10011; (800) 354-9657

This edition distributed in Canada by
Raincoast Books
8680 Cambie Street
Vancouver
British Columbia V6P 6M9

A CIP catalogue record for this book is available from the British Library

Publisher: Joanna Lorenz
Senior Editor: Doreen Palamartschuk
Editor: Caroline Davison
Designers: Ruth Hope, Lilian Lindblom, Patrick McLeavey and Ian Sandom
Illustrators: Liz Pepperell and Madeleine David
Photographers: Andrea Jones and Jonathan Buckley
Indexer: Janet Smy
Production Controller: Ben Worley

Previously published in two separate volumes, **The Kitchen Garden Book** and **The Ultimate Book of Herbs and Herb Gardening**

10 9 8 7 6 5 4 3 2 1

Page One **A bay tree clipped into a spiral.**
Page Two **Herb plots can be decorative as well as productive.**
Page Four **Brick paths divide up this large informal vegetable garden.**

Publisher's notes

This book is intended as a source of information on herbs and their uses, not as a practical guide to self-medication. Neither the authors nor the publisher can be held responsible for any specific individual's reactions, harmful effects or claims arising from the use of the general data and suggestions it contains, whether in recipe form or otherwise. Nor is any responsibility taken for mistaken identity of any of the plants. Many plants are poisonous, all can be toxic if used inappropriately, and the advice of a qualified medical practitioner should always be sought before using any herbal treatments or remedies. The use of any information contained in this book is entirely at the reader's own risk. In the United States, the burning of plants or bulbs (if they are diseased, for example) is prohibited.

contents

introduction

In the 21st century, gardens will increasingly become our most valuable contact with nature. To be able to come home and relax in an oasis of green, with plants that attract birds, butterflies and other wild life, adds a quality to our lives that would otherwise be missing, except on special trips to the countryside and parks.

One step beyond the idea of a simple refuge of decorative plants is to grow some of your own vegetables and herbs. Even just a few will add greatly to both your enjoyment of the garden and also your food. With space and time, growing enough to be self-sufficient in vegetables and herbs is most cooks' ultimate dream.

One of the greatest pleasures of growing your own vegetables and herbs is the freshness and the flavour of the produce, neither of which can be had from any greengrocer. The fact that you can go from garden to pot to plate in a matter of minutes means that little taste is lost. Allied to this is the knowledge of how your vegetables have been grown. You are able to choose the varieties you like most as well as keep them free of chemicals and other pollutants.

Growing your own vegetables and herbs

In this age it may seem a bit of an anachronism that people in the modern world should still be growing their own vegetables and herbs. Not only are they readily available from shops but we also have so much else to do with our time. But take a look at the people who grow their own produce and you will usually find healthy, happy souls who enjoy good food; there is more to it than saving a little money.

Once upon a time, growing vegetables was the cheap option; a few pence (cents) on seed saved pounds at the greengrocers. This is not now necessarily so, especially if you adopt the modern habit of costing your own time. Now vegetables are grown for many other reasons. Fresh herbs, on the other hand, were difficult to find in shops, so growing your own was the only option. Now the common ones are much more readily available, but they are still well worth growing, much for the same reasons as vegetables.

The order of priority of these reasons depends very much on the individual, but nearly all vegetable gardeners would say that the crops you grow yourself are far superior to those that you buy in the shops. While there is a little one-upmanship evident here, this is far from the whole story.

ABOVE **Retaining a kitchen garden with dwarf box hedging is the ideal way to keep the area neat and tidy. Here, sunflowers add the perfect decorative touch to the garden.**

Commercial crops versus home-grown produce

Above all, vegetables and herbs from your own garden are fresh: they can be in the ground one minute and in the pot the next. Once you have tasted fresh vegetables you realize the vast difference between them and the glossy, but days-old ones in the shops. Mass-produced vegetables have been bred to a different set of criteria to those that we grow in the garden. Greengrocers and supermarkets want fruit that will arrive at the shops looking fresh and undamaged, and so the produce is bred to have tough skins to help them travel well. This will also help give them a long shelf life. Fruit and vegetables from the garden do not have to travel and can have soft, succulent, tastier skins.

BELOW **These terracotta forcers are used to hurry vegetables such as rhubarb into growth. They also serve an ornamental purpose, dressing up what can be a dull vegetable plot.**

The farmer wants to harvest the crop all at once, so it is important that all the peas, for example, are ready for picking on the same day. This, therefore, is another quality bred into farmed crops. The gardener, on the other hand, wants as long a season as possible, and so the crops can retain their natural fruiting cycle. The supermarket wants all the vegetables to be the same size and look the same – gardeners are not so fussy, unless they exhibit, and so are happy to have produce that has not had uniformity bred into them in preference to taste. At the bottom of the list of qualities demanded by the shop, or frequently not on the list at all, is taste. Customers go back to buy carrots week after week without any thought to what the last batch tasted like. The gardener, however, has a wide choice of carrot seed, many selected for flavour, and can choose the variety that tastes the best. To those that have never tasted it, it cannot be over-emphasized that the quality of fresh vegetables is second to none.

ABOVE **Here, pink-flowered chives, red lettuce and purple cabbage as well as fennel and parsley create an informal vegetable garden.**

Advantages of growing your own crops

Another advantage, allied to taste, is that the gardener knows what has been put on the food. Most use few chemical sprays and powders, but shop-bought crops have been doused in an ever increasing number of compounds, that ensure, among other things, that they come to the shops in a totally unblemished state. In addition, many vegetables and fruits, such as apples and peppers, have their skins waxed to make them look shiny and much more attractive to the buyer. None of these chemicals are necessary; they are related to marketing rather than any aspect of growing. Time alone will tell what effect such unnecessary chemicals will have on us. The gardener can be sure that his or her food is completely untainted and all the better for it. A few slug holes in a lettuce or a few brown leaves on the parsley is a small price to pay for having vegetables and herbs in their natural state.

Garden vegetables, herbs and fruit are the ultimate in convenience food. Admittedly, you have to wash them, but they sit there just waiting to be harvested when you want them.This gives you the freedom to decide at the last minute what you want to include in a soup, for example. It also allows you to choose the exact quantity. You may only need one stick (stalk) of celery, so why go and buy a whole root when you can quickly cut one stem from the garden? This is much more economical and saves you going to the shops. Excess can be

ABOVE **Different thymes make a marvellous patchwork of colour and texture, as these plants illustrate.**

frozen or otherwise stored and used when you need it.

Herbs have a much broader use than vegetables. These days they are mainly used for culinary purposes, but many are still used in one way or another for their scented qualities. More and more people have discovered the advantages of using fresh herbs in cooking, and probably more people than ever before now grow at least a few, even if it is only a pot on the windowsill. In the past, herbs also played a very important part in the cure of various ailments. Although not used to the same extent by the average householder, they still play an important and increasing role in modern healthcare, not only in their use in alternative medicines, but also in the preparation of modern drugs. In recent years herbs have had a resurgence in popularity and are here to stay as a vital element in any garden.

Fruit is not as commonly grown as herbs and vegetables, but once again, fruit straight from the bush or tree is second to none. You can pick it when it is exactly ripe and at its best, which is something that supermarket fruit rarely is. It is surprising how much fruit you can grow, even in a small garden. Strawberries can be grown in containers, fruit trees placed against walls and perhaps a row of cordons can be used as a space divider rather than a hedge or fence.

Kitchen gardens can be very decorative. Even a simple garden with everything grown in rows or blocks is likely to be attractive, but designed as a potager, vegetables can be arranged in even more decorative ways. Herb gardens can be separate or part of the vegetable garden. Either way, they are frequently decorative features that are well worth having in any garden, over and above the value of the herbs produced. A desirable element of any herb garden, and of any vegetable garden for that matter, is to have a seat in it so that you can sit and relax and enjoy the feeling of the place.

BELOW **Beans can form part of an attractive kitchen garden. Both the pod and the bean are appealing when mottled with distinctive crimson markings.**

Benefits of gardening

Finally, as well as having healthy food, the gardener gets plenty of exercise and fresh air, which is no bad thing. Then there is the interaction with nature. A cliché perhaps, but there is still something very fundamental about getting your hands dirty and listening to the birds or watching a toad as you work. Not all these benefits of gardening come free, you do have to work and often work quite hard, but the effort is well worth it.

That is the end of the philosophy of the kitchen garden. From this point, the book becomes a practical one. We concentrate on describing all the techniques required to produce attractive and productive kitchen and herb gardens.

ABOVE **A fig tree can easily be grown in a pot, which is ideal as the trees need to have their roots contained. The best position is against a warm wall, facing the sun.**

Planning your garden

To place the kitchen and herb gardens in their context we start off with a brief history of both and then move on to the details of the kitchen garden. We outline the design of the garden both from the point of aesthetics and from the more practical aspect of growing the plants. This is followed by the important subject of crop planning. While the growing techniques are no doubt the most important aspect of the vegetable garden, thorough planning will help you to produce the best of crops. There is something undeniably pleasant about sitting indoors on a winter's evening planning what and where you are going to grow the crops during the coming season.

The soil is the most important commodity that any gardener has at his or her disposal. Its preparation, improvement and maintenance are the most vital of all the techniques that a gardener must learn. We are not all blessed with the best of soils in our gardens, especially those with plots not cultivated before, but with time and a little effort even the most barren of gardens can be made to produce very acceptable crops.

ABOVE **Sunflowers and nasturtiums provide brilliant colour in the garden when flowering. They seeds are also edible and suitable for salads.**

Other techniques, such as sowing, planting, maintenance and harvesting are obviously important and are considered in detail, often shown in step-by-step photographs taken specially for the book. Once the basic groundwork has been covered, it is time to look at the individual vegetables in depth.

All the information that you require to grow and harvest them is given, as well as lists of recommended varieties and synopses of cultivation requirements. This information will serve as a constant source of reference for years to come.

Fruit is then looked at in the same detail; including special techniques such as pruning and shaping trees and bushes. Again, a detailed directory follows, containing all the fruit you are likely to want to grow.

The section of fruit is followed by that other mainstay of the kitchen: herbs. A detailed account of propagating and growing herbs is given, both indoors and out. Attention is given to the important aspect of planting herbs as well as harvesting and preserving them. Then comes the directory of herbs with a comprehensive list of plants to choose from. Each herb's history and place in tradition and mythology is detailed, as well as a description, how to grow it and its uses. The list covers those herbs used in medicine as well as in cooking.

BELOW **In early autumn, harvest apples when ripe and collect them before strong winds blow them off the trees. If you have a glut of fruit, make jams, jellies and preserves from the fruit.**

Developing your skills

With this book as a guide you will soon not only be growing your own produce, but also acquiring traditional skills, many of which have been handed down over the centuries. Such skills are often thought only to belong to those with green fingers (thumbs), but anybody can grow vegetables and herbs.

A visit to a group of allotments will soon reveal the wide range of people able to do so. As a beginner you may be in awe of them and their crops, but by getting on with it and getting your hands dirty you will soon learn the few basic techniques required, and once these have been added to common sense you will be in a position to grow anything.

Joining local horticultural societies is a good way of gaining knowledge. Most have regular lectures by experts on various aspects of gardening, including vegetable, herb and fruit growing. More valuable is the opportunity to meet like-minded people who live locally, enabling you the to discuss growing plants as well as visit each other's gardens. Such friendships not only provide a wealth of information and help, but invariably lead to the swapping of seeds and plants. Many old varieties of vegetable have been continued in this way, long after they have disappeared from commercial sources. The really keen members exhibit their vegetables and fruit at the annual or biannual shows. These are not as frightening as they may seem at first glance, and a great deal of fun and friendly rivalry is to be had. It certainly helps to hone your gardening techniques if you are able to produce vegetables and fruit to a high standard.

ABOVE **Fruit can be grown in containers, such as this dwarf apple tree and strawberry pots.**

ABOVE **Ornamental cabbages are at their best in autumn, in gorgeous shades of blue-green and purple.**

Producing your own vegetables, fruit and herbs is, then, not a difficult task, but it is one with lots of benefits, the most important of which is the produce itself. One thing that will doubtless surprise the beginner is the sheer excitement of seeing things grow, and taking that first crop of vegetables or handful of herbs into the kitchen. Fortunately, that excitement never seems to dwindle. Give it a try.

history
of kitchen and herb gardens

While it is not necessary to know anything about the history of either the vegetable garden or the herb garden, it certainly adds to their fascination. The interesting thing is that there is surprisingly little history as such. A monk in his medieval herb garden would not only recognize a modern herb garden, but would also understand the processes the modern gardener used to achieve it.

The same is true of the vegetable garden. Not only have the techniques and tools changed very little over the centuries, but the plants have remained remarkably similar too. With the exception of Asian vegetables, virtually all those that we grow in a modern garden were already grown by late Elizabethan times. The varieties may be different but the basic plant has changed very little. The same applies to fruit, except that here, there have been advances on the type of rootstock that trees can be grown from, giving us much more scope for growing them in small gardens. Herbs have changed even less – many of them are species and hence in many cases are still the same native plants that have been used for generations.

However, herb and herb gardens have been in existence for thousands of years, and some changes have been seen during this time.

ABOVE **A careful selection and arrangement of food crops helps to make the cottage kitchen garden both productive and ornamental. The beans in the background are as beautiful in flower as they are later fruitful.**

BELOW **The bland foliage of the cabbage family in the garden can be relieved by interplanting with herbs. Here, lavender and parsley make a colourful border along the pathway without too much growing space being sacrificed.**

History of the kitchen garden

Even since people ceased to be hunter-gatherers and settled down to growing their own food and shepherding their own animals, vegetable gardens of one sort or another have existed.

From farm to garden

To start with, the difference between farming and gardening would have been difficult to establish, as the former would probably have only been on a small scale to supply a single family. Farming went on for many centuries before gardens began to be developed, especially around towns where there was need to supply the inhabitants who had no space to grow their own produce. Some of the first gardeners were monks supplying the inmates of their monasteries. In this way gardening skills developed and were eventually passed on down the generations. After the Middle Ages there was a general increase in the number of people having their own gardens, especially in the country.

Initially vegetables were grown in blocks rather than rows, as can be seen in the many illustrations of early gardens. Sometimes these were dug straight into the earth and sometimes contained in raised beds. In the 18th century a revolution took place in agriculture when Jethro Tull invented the seed drill. Up until then, seed had been broadcast by hand over an area, whereas the seed drill enabled seed to be sown in even rows. This had many advantages, among them the ability to move between the rows to hoe and tend the plants. This development was taken up by gardeners and soon many were sowing their seed in rows that are still seen today in most vegetable gardens. In some parts of Europe, gardeners still broadcast their seed in blocks, and it is becoming a popular method, once again, among modern gardeners, especially those with small gardens where such techniques allow maximum cropping.

The cottage garden tradition

The modern kitchen garden owes many of its traditions to the old cottage gardens rather than the enormous kitchen gardens of the larger house. However, many of the basic techniques were the same – the differences lay in the scale and the expense of the more exotic vegetables and fruit that were grown in heated glass houses.

ABOVE **An old-fashioned kitchen garden can be both productive and decorative.**

Within the cottage garden tradition, the distinctions between the flower garden and the vegetable garden were often blurred. This may be because many original flower gardens developed out of a patch of herbs grown for culinary or medicinal purposes. Even today, in some rural areas, the two types of garden are indistinct, with vegetables being grown among the flowers. This has been taken up by garden designers, and now many kitchen gardens are planned as visual entities as well as being somewhere to grow produce for the kitchen. Potagers were originally just the French equivalent of the kitchen garden, but slowly the term has changed to imply a decorative vegetable garden, in which not only are the vegetables laid out in an attractive manner but flowers and herbs are also integrated into the design.

Looking at some of the old paintings and etchings of very early gardens, the people working in them are employed in very familiar tasks and use familiar tools. New techniques have evolved, particularly with regard to pesticides and the use of machinery to lighten various tasks, but it is still possible to garden in a medieval way, and the resulting garden and its produce would look and taste much the same as any other kitchen garden.

ABOVE **In an ornamental kitchen garden, colour combinations, although incidental to the main objective of raising food, are nonetheless important. Whether by design or accident, these dark-leaved brassicas make a fine contrast with lettuces and beans.**

Old varieties of vegetables and fruit

One of the unexpected aspects of vegetable gardening is that nearly all the vegetables we grow today have been around for centuries. Apart from the modern introduction of Asian vegetables, themselves grown for thousands of years, there have been very few modern introductions.

The origin of vegetables

The Mediterranean basin has always been the centre of vegetable introductions, many of them going back thousands of years. Few of the vegetables that we grow did not either start there or pass through (often from the Far East) on the way to the rest of Europe and eventually to the Americas. The last large influx of important vegetables, such as tomatoes, potatoes, and many of the beans, were brought back from the Americas by the conquistadors in the 16th century. These were slow to spread to northern Europe, and it was a couple of centuries later before potatoes, for example, became popular amongst cottage gardeners in Britain, although the gentry had been eating them from their first introduction.

It is difficult to track the origins of vegetables and the course of the spread. Many, such as garlic, go so far back in time that their origins are virtually lost, especially as there is no equivalent growing anywhere in the wild today. We have a rough idea where they might have come from but that is as far as it goes. The other interesting thing about garlic is that no seed-bearing plants are known, and so apart from a few mutations all the varieties of garlic in existence go back thousands of years.

BELOW **The "Victoria" plum is one of the finest of the old-fashioned breeds with its rosy skin, golden flesh and subtle flavour.**

The earliest introductions to northern Europe were made by the Romans who took their favourite vegetables throughout their empire, including the British Isles. Some disappeared during the Middle Ages only to be reintroduced soon afterwards. By Elizabethan times virtually all our modern vegetables had been introduced in their modern form, with the exception of those that originated in the Americas. These were soon included so that by the 18th century all the vegetables we grow were in existence. A notable exception is the courgette (zucchini) which was not introduced to Britain from

America until the mid-19th century, but even this is a form of the marrow (squash) which had been in England for centuries.

A few vegetables have disappeared from our diet, but even these are still grown by some gardeners. Some root vegetables, in particular, are not as common as they once were. Scorzonera and salsify are two such vegetables, but seed is still generally available. On the other hand, another root, skirret, is much more difficult to find and is not often grown. The surprising thing is that so few vegetables have disappeared.

ABOVE **Gardeners in the past grew a wide range of fruit and vegetables without the use of chemical fertilizers or blanket insecticides.**

Vanishing varieties

What has disappeared are many of the older varieties. European regulations are such that seed cannot be sold without first being on a register of allowable cultivars. Unless someone is able to pay the expensive fees for keeping it on the register it cannot be sold. The big seed merchants are the only companies that can afford this, and they like to keep introducing new varieties in order to entice and keep the gardener's interest.

The new introductions are not necessarily better than those they replace, but novelty sells. This has meant that many good varieties have all but disappeared. The variety of broad bean "The Sutton", for example, was awarded the Royal Horticultural Society's highest award for excellence in the same year as it was dropped from the British list of available seed by all the seed merchants, thus, theoretically at least, making it unattainable.

Fortunately, many gardeners have collected and used their own seed over the years. Now societies such as the Henry Doubleday Research Association have started seed libraries where these old varieties are maintained by a number of gardeners growing them every year. They are not allowed to sell the seed but a great deal of swapping goes on, so that anyone interested in the older, and often better, varieties can get hold of them. Gardeners can try these older varieties alongside their modern counterparts to see which really are the best.

Herbs in History

There is ample evidence of the herbal use of plants by the civilizations of ancient Egypt, over a period from 3000 BC to the reign of Cleopatra, which began in 48 BC. Papyri dating from 2800 BC record the medicinal use of some familiar herbs, including juniper, mint and marjoram. The wall paintings of tombs and temples reveal the use of aromatic plants, spices and gums in religious and funerary rites and on social occasions. Also an inscription in the temple of Karnak relates Ramses III's plea to the god Amun for victory in battle, reminding him of the pharaoh's generous sacrifice of 30,000 oxen, quantities of "sweet-smelling herbs and the finest perfume". Archaeologists have also found the physical remains of plants, flowers and seeds used for food and flavouring, as votive garlands and in cosmetic and embalming ointments.

Offerings made to the sun god Ra, at Heliopolis, included a concoction of 16 herbs and resins. Known as *kyphi* or *khepri*, it was adopted by the Greeks, and then the Romans, and was described by Dioscorides. Later analysis confirmed that it contained among its ingredients *Acorus calamus*, cassia, cinnamon, peppermint, juniper, acacia and henna.

The Greeks, the great period of whose culture overlapped with the end of the Egyptian dynasties, adopted Egyptian skills in making ointments from aromatic plants, as their literature often confirms. The cosmetic use of plants was a frequently described theme:

He really bathes
In a large gilded tub, and steeps his feet
And legs in rich Egyptian unguents;
His jaw and breasts he rubs with thick palm oil,
And both his arms with extract of sweet mint;
His eyebrows and his hair with marjoram,
His knees and neck with essence of ground thyme.
– Antiphanes

Above *Plants being ground in a mortar, from a 10th-century French herbal.*

Above *A relief at the Temple of Karnak in Luxor, Egypt, depicting a botanical garden showing plants brought from Syria by Pharaoh Tutmosis III.*

The Romans have left many records of their use of herbs for flavouring food, in perfumery, for decoration and strewing at social events. Medicinal uses are discussed in the works of writers such as Pliny. The vast spread of their empire also meant that the Romans took Mediterranean plants to northern areas that had never known them before and where many became naturalized.

After the fall of Rome, in the period sometimes known as the Dark Ages, AD 476–*c.*1000, herbal knowledge was nurtured and kept alive in Christian monasteries. In Britain during this time, Anglo-Saxon writings show a wide knowledge of herbs and evidence of correspondence with centres in Europe.

The Eastern Connection

During the 10th century a great Muslim empire stretched from the eastern Mediterranean, taking in Arabia, Persia, parts of Spain and North Africa. Arab academics were paramount in the medicinal practice of the time and Avicenna, born in Persia, AD 980, was one of the most famous. He was the first to describe the making of attar of roses by distillation, was instrumental in the discovery of plant essential oils, and his *Canon* became a standard medical text. Crusaders from Britain, who set out to destroy the Muslim influence, brought home the new plants and exotic spices from the Near East.

In India, where so many medicinal and scented plants grow, there is a long tradition of using spices and aromatic herbs in cookery, for perfumes and cosmetics. An 18th-century Italian traveller wrote that "nowhere do the women pay greater attention to their cleanliness than in the East, bathing frequently and massaging all parts of their body with perfumed oils". Ayurvedic medicine, practised in India, is an ancient system based on herbs and shares many similarities of concept with Chinese herbal medicine, whose longest unbroken tradition of practice is often considered to be the most ancient in origin. The Yellow Emperor, Huang Ti, born *c.* 2000 BC, wrote a medical treatise which is often cited as the earliest herbal on record. Chinese herbalism is currently enjoying a revival in the West.

The Renaissance and the Discovery of the New World

With the Renaissance, the great revival of learning marking the birth of modern Europe, came advances in medicine and the study of the healing properties of plants. The 16th and 17th centuries were the age of great herbalists and herbals: Turner, Gerard and Parkinson in Britain; Brunfels, Fuchs and Bock in Germany; Clusius, L'Obel and Dodoens in the Netherlands; Mattioli and Porta in Italy.

Above *A man and woman harvesting sap, from* Le Livre des Simples Médecines, *a 15th-century French herbal.*

Above *Collecting herbs to use in the stillroom.* Spring *by Lucas van Valkenborch, 1595.*

At the same time the use of herbs in cookery, perfumery and for cosmetics was widespread and well documented in many books on household skills, such as Sir Hugh Platt's *Delights for Ladies*, 1594, and T. Dawson's *The Good Housewife's Jewel*, 1585. It should be remembered, however, that the line between perfumery for pleasure and health was a narrow one. It was generally accepted that a fragrant smell was in itself proof against infection and many recipes in the stillroom books for perfumed powders and pot-pourris, which would now be considered fripperies, had a serious underlying purpose.

In the 16th and 17th centuries a huge quantity of new plants, many of which were used by the Native Americans in their traditional medicine, were brought to Europe from the Americas. Seeds were taken the opposite way by the early colonists keen to establish, in their new country, gardens stocked with the familiar herbs of home – including parsley, savory and thyme.

The Modern Era

Up until the 18th century, botany and medicine were closely allied, but with the rise of modern scientific enquiry they drew apart as separate disciplines. During the 19th century the medical establishment turned away from plant-based remedies, and synthetic drugs, produced in the laboratory, began their ascendancy. This is not to say that old herbal remedies and culinary and cosmetic recipes disappeared: traditions were kept alive in many country districts and in some countries never fell from use. In Europe the day-to-day use of herbs remained more widely practised than it did in Britain.

Mrs Grieve, whose famous herbal was published in 1931, did much to promote the renewed interest in herbs in Britain in the 20th century, as did Eleanour Sinclair Rohde, who wrote many books on herbs and became a popular lecturer on the subject in the United States, following World War II.

With the dawn of the 21st century the revival of interest in all things herbal continues. Emigration and accessibility of travel have spread the use of culinary herbs and spices across many countries and cultures. There is wide recognition among scientists today of the value of plants as the basis for drugs to combat major diseases, such as cancer and AIDS, and much research is being carried out. However, the drugs under development depend on isolating and copying active plant compounds. This takes a different direction from the use of the whole plant as practised in traditional herbal medicine.

Old Herbals

Old herbal manuscripts make fascinating reading. They give an insight into how herbs were used in the past and increase our general understanding of the subject. Not all are readily available and are kept in specialist libraries, but some have been reissued in modern editions and facsimiles and many are widely quoted from by modern authors. The following are some of the more important works on herbs written in the West.

Early Manuscript Herbals

c. **320 BC** *Historia Plantarum* and *De Causis Plantarum* – by Theophrastus, *c.* 370–286 BC, Greek philosopher and pupil of Aristotle. (Edited and translated as *The History of Plants* and *The Causes of Plants* by Sir A.F. Hort, Loeb Library, 1916.)

c. **AD 60** *De Materia Medica* – written by Dioscorides, a Greek physician, living in Rome. Describes 600 herbs and their healing properties. It became the standard work on medicine, influencing most herbals that followed for over 1,500 years. (English translation by John Goodyer, 1655.)

c. **AD 77** *Naturalis Historia* – by Pliny the Elder, contemporary of Dioscorides. A massive, 37-volume work, 16 concern trees, plants and medicines.

AD 400 *The Herbal of Apuleius* – Author unknown. Originally written in Latin it drew quite heavily on Dioscorides and Pliny, adding pagan prayers and superstitions. It was much copied over the years. (Anglo-Saxon translation made in 11th century.)

c. **AD 900** *The Leech Book of Bald* – compiled by a Saxon physician. Reveals a wide knowledge of native plants and includes prescriptions sent by the Patriarch of Jerusalem to King Alfred.

c. **1150** *Physica* – by Hildegard of Bingen. Unique as a book on the medicinal properties of plants by a woman and had great influence on the famous German "fathers of botany", Brunfels, Fuchs and Hieronymus Bock.

c. **1248–1260** *De Proprietatibus Rerum* by Bartholomaeus Anglicus, an Englishman living in Paris, then Saxony. A huge encyclopedia in 19 sections, number 17 being on plants and trees and their herbal properties.

Above *Collecting herbs for the Apothecary's preparations, from a Latin manuscript version of the Herbal of Apuleius.*

Printed Herbals

1491 *Hortus Sanitatis* – compiled by publisher Jacob Meydenbach of Mainz. The last of the medieval works on herbs.

1500 *Liber de Arte Distillandi de Simplicibus* – by Hieronymous Braunschweig. The first major work on the techniques of distillation "of the waters of all manner of herbes". (English translation by L. Andrewes 1527.)

1525 *Banckes's Herbal* – anonymous, a quarto volume published by Richard Banckes. Earliest English printed herbal, based on earlier manuscript herbals.

1530 *Herbarum Vivae Eicones* – by Otto Brunfels, a former monk, Lutheran preacher, botanist and also physician. Published in Strasbourg, with realistic illustrations, it began the movement towards a more scientific mindset.

1539 *Kräuter Buch* – by Hieronymus Bock. Rather than repeat Dioscorides, Bock wrote about native plants and was the first to attempt a system of plant classification.

1542 *De Historia Stirpium* – written by Leonhard Fuchs. A scholarly work, which sought to clarify identification of medicinal plants mentioned by Dioscorides, through carefully observed illustrations. Records many new plants introduced to Germany from other parts of the world.

1551–68 *The New Herball* – by William Turner, credited as the "father of English botany". Based on his own observations of native plants but using many of the woodcuts from Fuchs' work.

1554 *Cruydeboeck* – by Rembert Dodoens, physician to the Holy Roman Emperor Maximilian II and professor of botany at Leyden University. A work of botanical importance, which borrowed Fuchs' pictures. (Many English editions, *A Niewe Herbal or History of Plants*, by Henry Lyte in 1578.)

1563 *Coloquios dos Simples* – by Garcia de Orta, a Portuguese doctor who spent time in Goa and produced a book on the plants and medicines of India.

Above *Frontispiece to* The Herball, *1597, by John Gerard.*

1569 *Dos libros, el uno que trata de todas las cosas que traen de nuestras Indias Occidentales* – by Nicholas Monardes, a Spaniard, who never himself visited America. His book on the plants of the "New World" became better known by the title of the first English edition: *Joyfull Newes Out of the Newe Founde Worlde*, 1577.

1597 *The Herball or Generall Historie of Plantes* – by John Gerard, gardener and botanist. Based on Dodoens' work, it remains one of the most popular, widely quoted from herbals of all time for the grace of its Elizabethan language.

1629 *Paradisi in Sole Paradisus Terrestris*; **1640** *Theatrum Botanicum* – by John Parkinson. The emphasis in the first is on ornamental planting, the second lists 3,800 plants and their medicinal properties.

1652 *The English Physician* – by Nicholas Culpeper, an astrologer, considered a charlatan by the medical establishment of his day. His book is one of the most popular herbals of all time.

1656 *The Art of Simpling*; **1657** *Adam in Eden* – by William Coles. Less popular, but more readable than Culpeper, who Coles thought was "ignorant". Includes much herb lore.

Later Herbals

With the break between botany and medicine, few great medicinal herbals appeared after the 17th century. Those of note included:

1710 *Botanologia, The English Herbal or History of Plants* – by William Salmon.

1838 *Flora Medica* – written by John Lindley, botanist and lecturer to the Society of Apothecaries, who wrote several important horticultural works.

1931 *A Modern Herbal* – by Mrs M. Grieve. Seminal work on herbs of the 20th century.

Stillroom Books

As well as the learned tomes, written by the medical men of their day, there is a long tradition of more homely recipe (usually spelled "receipt") books, which include instructions on the culinary and cosmetic uses of herbs as well as medicinal remedies. They are sometimes known as "stillroom books". Throughout the 17th and 18th centuries all the big country houses had their own stillroom and women were supposed to be fully conversant in the art of making herbal and culinary preparations.

1585 *The Good Housewife's Jewel and Rare Conceits in Cookery* – by T. Dawson. A comprehensive, informative compilation of herbal recipes.

1594 *Delights for Ladies* – by Sir Hugh Platt. A book to fit in the palm of the hand, subtitled "to adorne their Persons, Tables, Closets & Distillatories with Beauties, Banquets, Perfumes & Waters".

1654 *The Art of Cookery* – by Joseph Cooper, recipes of Charles I's head chef.

1655 *The Queen's Closet Opened* – by W. M. (cook to Queen Henrietta Maria). Includes perfumed, culinary and medicinal preparations.

1668 *Choice and Experimental Receipts* – by Sir Kenelm Digby, Stuart diplomat, with a side interest in cookery, alchemy and herbalism. **1669** *The Closet of Sir Kenelm Digby Opened*. Many medicinal and fragrance recipes.

1719 *Acetaria* – written by John Evelyn. Cookery book by the prolific author and diarist, with a large section on the virtues of salad herbs, picked from the garden.

1719 *The Accomplished Lady's Delight* – by Mrs Mary Eales (confectioner to Queen Anne). Includes recipes for candying many flowers and fruits as well as for perfumes and scented waters.

1723 *The Receipt Book of John Nott* – competent, often workable recipes of the cook to the Duke of Bolton.

1732 *Country Housewife and Ladies Directory* – by R. Bradley. Intriguing cookery recipes.

1775 *The Toilet of Flora* – Anonymous. The title page states: "The Chief Intention of this performance is to point out, and explain to the Fair-Sex, the Methods by which they may preserve and add to their charms." But it is also for "Domestic Economy" and gives methods of preparing herbal baths, essences, pomatums, powders, perfumes, sweet-scented waters and opiates for preserving and whitening teeth.

1784 *The Art of Cooking* – by Mrs Glasse.

1845 *Miss Leslie's Directions for Cookery* – by Eliza Leslie (published USA). Primarily culinary recipes, but also contains directions for making oil of flowers, sweet jars, perfumes and scented bags.

Above *A medieval garden from* Rustican de Cultivement des Terres, *also known as* Les Livres des Prouffits. *British Library.*

Traditional Herb Gardens

Herbs have been grown in gardens since ancient times, as evidenced in Egyptian frescoes and descriptions of the Roman *Hortus*. However, it is really the monastery gardens of the early Christian era, following the fall of Rome, which begin the Western tradition of the herb garden.

A plan of the Benedictine monastery of St Gall in Switzerland, dating from AD 812, provided a blueprint of the style of garden attached to religious houses and which became central to their life and ministry. There were three distinct areas in this early plan: A physic garden of medicinal plants, which included sage, rosemary, rue and roses, was close to the infirmary. On the other side of this building was the vegetable garden, divided into 18 plots, each designated a single species of plant, many of which we would call herbs. There were cabbages, lettuce, onions, celery, coriander, dill, poppy, radish, garlic, parsley, chervil and fennel. The orchard adjoined, with a large, cross-shaped path at the centre, and included burial plots. At the centre of the enclosed cloister garden was an area of lilies, roses and scented flowers for decorating the church, often known as a "paradise garden".

Above *Reconstruction of a Tudor garden, with a central "knot", at Southampton, England.*

Above *An elaborate 17th-century garden, from a painting by Johan Walter, 1660.*

Monastery gardens were by their nature enclosed. This was a feature, too, of privy gardens belonging to a palace or castle in the medieval period. However, the emphasis here was on enjoyment, with scents, seats and arbours.

Another characteristic of the monastic gardens, which was carried into the designs of the Renaissance period beginning in the 16th century, is the rectangular layout of symmetrical paths, with the cross as a central motif. It has often been noted, however, that the Islamic and Persian tradition of a garden on a grid pattern (probably set out this way for ease of watering by irrigation channels) was also an influence.

In England the fashion for knot gardens began at the outset of the reign of Henry VIII, in the early 16th century, and was popular for over 200 years. Some of the patterns, depicting interlaced ribbons, were extremely complicated and set out in clipped hedges of wall germander, hyssop, cotton lavender and box, infilled with coloured stones or scented herbs and flowers. By the 17th century the more expansive and open French parterre, with its elaborate swirls of curls and loops, became fashionable.

It was during the 17th century that a host of new plants arrived in Europe, brought back by explorers and traders. Many of the new arrivals were from North America, including nasturtiums and sunflowers. They were planted in physic gardens and the gardens of the great houses, as well as in large botanical gardens throughout Europe, where the study of botany and medicine still went hand in hand. It was a two-way traffic as plants from the "old world" were also taken to North America.

The landscape movement and "natural" school of garden design in the 18th century swept away the intricate knots and parterres; and physic gardens declined in importance as medicine moved apart from botany. Herbs were still grown, of course, but retreated to the cottage garden. Here, they largely remained until the early 20th century when Vita Sackville-West and Gertrude Jekyll started the fashion for informal planting of old-fashioned species, and restored herbs to centre stage.

Herb Gardens for Today

When planning a herb garden today there is a vast choice of styles and influences to choose from. As herbs and plants cover such a wide range, they are often grown throughout the garden in ornamental beds and borders or among vegetable plots. But a designated herb garden with a range of medicinal, culinary and aromatic plants and its own boundaries always makes a rewarding feature. In a very small garden, of course, it may well be designed to take up the whole area.

Historical precedents provide much inspiration for a herb garden in the formal style, with rectangular beds, straight paths and edgings of clipped box. It could be based on the medieval garden, with narrow, raised beds filled with a single species, divided by wide alleys. Or you could draw inspiration from the romantic enclave of a castle garden; or a cloister or paradise garden. And, the striking pattern of a knot garden or parterre is always effective.

Informal designs based on curves and irregular shapes give scope for imaginative planting schemes with a bold use of colour and texture; and the cottage-garden style, with its profusion of plants crammed into a small space, is another option.

In any scheme a place to sit, either a simple bench or intricate covered arbour, is a must. A sundial or urn as a centrepiece provides a good focal point.

Whatever the style, some kind of enclosure adds an extra dimension, setting the herb garden apart. It could be a low fence or herbal hedge or, for a larger area, high trelliswork or a wall may be more appropriate. Herbs may be practical plants, for particular purposes, but they also add a little mystery and magic to the world and deserve a special place of their own.

Above *A beautiful, scented cloister garden at Château de Vandrimare in France.*

Left *A sundial makes a traditional focal point in an informal planting of herbs and roses, with a statue in the background.*

designing a kitchen garden

Before you even contemplate putting a spade in the soil, it is a very useful exercise to sit down and think about what you are trying to achieve in your kitchen garden. Firstly, you need to consider whether you have the time, space and conditions to achieve what you want.

The design of a kitchen garden can then be approached in two ways. It can be either purely functional, in which case you simply have to ensure that the layout and planting of the garden will produce the largest possible volume of produce. Alternatively, you might like to adopt a more decorative approach, orchestrating the design so that the garden is pleasing to look at as well as productive.

There is also a variety of more technical considerations to take into account. For example, how you are going to get the best out of your plot? Will there be any limitations to your plans caused by lack of space, problem soils and difficult weather conditions, and how can the overall layout help to prevent the influx of pests and diseases? Once you have thought through questions such as these, you can start having fun and planning your garden in greater detail.

RIGHT **This is a traditional kitchen garden, with vegetables neatly lined up in rows. Although it is autumn, there will be plenty of vegetables in season over the next few months.**

There are several factors to consider when planning the overall design of a kitchen garden. Many of these relate to more specific issues and are dealt with later in more detail but are mentioned here in a general context.

What do you want?

The first priority is to work out what you want. Do you want a productive garden that will provide food for a large family or for selling or giving away? If so, you will probably be planting varieties of vegetables in bulk, which reduces the possibility of using intricate patterns. If, however, you are thinking in terms of a decorative feature, with the vegetable crops as a secondary consideration, you are going to need a different approach to laying out the kitchen garden. What do you want to include? Are you hoping to grow fruit and herbs as well as vegetables? This kind of decision will influence how much space you need and how you use it.

Do you want a greenhouse? If so, is it going to be within your kitchen garden or will it be tucked away, out of sight in a corner of the garden? What are you going to do with items such as sheds, cold frames and compost bins? Someone with a working kitchen garden is likely to position these where they are convenient. If you want a decorative kitchen garden, you may well consider that these structures are eyesores and better located in a separate area, perhaps screened by a hedge.

How much time?

If you are going to do it properly, a kitchen garden takes up a tremendous amount of time. If you have help in the garden this may not be a problem, but if you do it all yourself, at weekends for example, you may find that time runs short during a critical period if there are two

LEFT **This is a highly decorative kitchen garden, in which a selection of flowering plants grows among the vegetables.**

wet weekends followed by one when you are away from home. In other words, design the garden to suit the amount of time available. A large kitchen garden that has been neglected is a sad sight.

ABOVE A well-ordered garden is attractive in its own way. Many gardeners take great pride in keeping everything neat and tidy, which not only looks good, but also increases productivity.

How much space?

It may not be a question of deciding how much space you want to devote to vegetables; this may already be decided by the amount of space actually available. Do not try and squeeze too much into a small space. Remember that there may be a call on the space for other purposes – children playing, for example.

Suitability of the space?

An important point to consider is whether the space you want to use is suitable for vegetables or whether you will have to modify the design to allow for problem areas. For example, there is no point in trying to grow vegetables under trees. Nor can they be grown on swamp-like ground. Removing the trees or, at least, reducing the shade they cast is possible, but it may be undesirable or too expensive. Wet ground can be drained, of course, but this, again, may be too expensive, and it may be better to turn that part of the garden into a pond.

What's the weather like?

Although it is not a serious problem for the design of the garden, the weather does play a part in your plans. A vegetable garden should have plenty of sunshine, so if you want to reserve the sunny part of the garden for relaxation and sunbathing, there may well be nowhere to grow vegetables. If the bottom of the garden is a frost hollow, growth will be delayed there, and this may upset the overall decorative balance of your garden even if it does not affect its productivity. Prevailing dry, wet, cold or warm climates may affect what you can grow and therefore limit the productive or decorative qualities of your intended garden.

The Vegetable Plot

In the working vegetable garden, the overall visual design may not be important. Vegetables are, of course, decorative in their own right, and even the most regimented plot, where everything is grown in rows, usually has some visual appeal. With this type of garden, however, the design is subordinate to convenience and output, with rectangular blocks composed of rows or blocks of crops.

ABOVE **Lack of space is not a problem if you want to grow your own vegetables. Even this small border functions as a working vegetable garden.**

Permanent structures

The first consideration is the position of more permanent items, such as greenhouses, cold frames, sheds and compost bins. The greenhouse needs plenty of light and should be away from cold winds. It should also be near the house because it often needs attention in the winter and at night. This also applies to cold frames. The shed and the compost bins can be more or less anywhere, although not too far away. If the compost bin is a long way away, you may be tempted to leave rotting vegetation lying around rather than clearing up.

All these structures need access paths, which again will dictate their position. A compost bin on the far side of a bed may fill a space, but it will be of little use if you have to walk over the bed to get to it. Putting in a path to it, however, will take up valuable growing space.

Bed design

The positioning of the beds should have prime consideration. Practice varies considerably on the shape and method employed. Most gardeners prefer to have large rectangular plots, 3.6m/12ft wide and as long as the garden allows. Typically, there are two such plots, one each side of a central path. Within these plots rows of vegetables are set out across the beds, with temporary narrow paths between each row.

Recent years have seen the reintroduction of a different method, which had fallen out of favour. This is the use of deep beds, only 1.2m/4ft wide. Such beds, can, in fact, be easily superimposed on the old system by dividing up the long plot into any number of 1.2 x 3.6m/4 x 12ft beds. The significance of the 1.2m/4ft width is that the whole bed can be reached from either side. These smaller beds have permanent paths on each side, which can be paved or left as bare earth.

Permanent planting

Most planting in the kitchen garden is done on an annual basis and changes every year, but there are some plants that stay in the same position for several, if not many, years. Vegetables such as rhubarb, globe artichokes and asparagus need a permanent base. Most fruit is permanent or is moved only every few years. Tree fruit, in particular, must be considered as a long-term addition to the garden. These types of plants are usually kept together, partly for convenience and partly because they can all be protected against birds by being included in one fruit cage.

Paths

Paths in a productive kitchen garden tend to be for access purposes and not seen as part of a decorative pattern.

RIGHT **This large traditional vegetable garden contains a great variety of foliage, which can be highly decorative.**

A Walled Vegetable Garden

A vegetable garden is basically a utilitarian space for growing vegetables, but it frequently becomes much more than that. Vegetables are decorative in their own right and a well-planned vegetable plot can usually become a very attractive part of the garden.

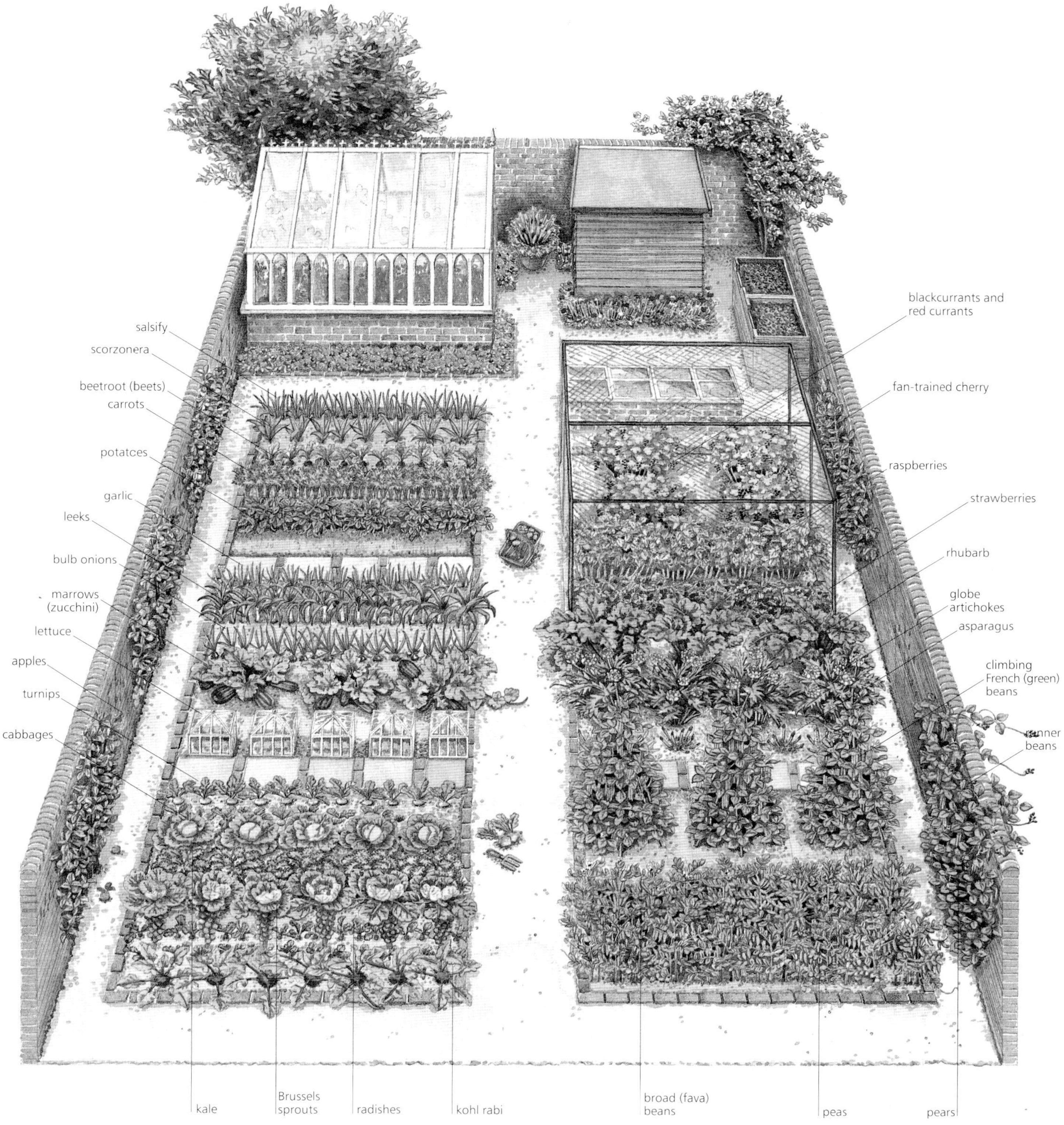

Decorative Fruit and Vegetables

One tends to think of vegetables and fruit as being grown either in special gardens or in beds within gardens that are devoted solely to them. There is, however, no reason why they should not be mixed with plants that are grown for decorative purposes. Most gardens have flowering and foliage plants, so why not mix a few vegetables in with them?

ABOVE **Many vegetables are decorative in their own right. Both the flowers and foliage of these climbing beans are purple.**

Decorative vegetables

Some vegetables seem to have been created for inclusion in decorative schemes. Ruby chard, also known as red-stemmed Swiss chard or rhubarb chard, is a perfect example. Although it is good to eat, its vivid red stems and deep purple foliage make it an ideal border plant, particularly in a position where a touch of bright colour is required. Beetroot (beets), while perhaps not quite as colourful, can be used in the same way.

Colour is not all. The foliage of carrots may not be particularly unusual in colour, but it has a wonderful filigree shape and soft texture. These qualities can be used to soften or link two neighbouring colours, or to break up an area of rather solid foliage.

Climbing plants, such as beans, peas, marrows (zucchini) and squashes, can be used to cover arbours and pergolas. Colourful squashes and marrows hanging down in a walkway can be an attractive, if unexpected, sight.

Decorative fruit

Fruit is even more adaptable than vegetables. Apple or plum trees create a dappled shade that is perfect for sitting under or for creating beds in which to grow shade-loving plants. They can be grown against walls as cordons, espaliers or fans, where they create beautiful two-dimensional patterns that can be even more attractive than conventional climbers. In addition to the shape, there are the blossom and the fruit to enjoy, and the leaves of some varieties of pears have wonderful autumn colours.

Walls are not the only way to display trained fruit trees. They can be used to decorate arbours, pergolas and arches. Grapes can also be used in this type of position, rather than training them in a regimented way against wirework in a fruit garden.

Some bush fruit, red currants and gooseberries in particular, can be grown as tree-form standards – that is, they have a thin, unbranched trunk with the "bush" sitting on top. These can look extremely attractive in borders and beds, especially

LEFT **Many vegetables, such as these purple-leaved Brussels sprouts, have dramatic leaves that make a vegetable plot look very striking.**

An Ornamental Fruit Garden

Fruit gardens should be laid out in the most productive way possible, ensuring that each plant has sufficient space to grow and develop as well as plenty of air and light. However, this does not prevent a fruit garden from being designed in an attractive way that makes the most of the natural beauty of the fruit trees and bushes.

if they are the centrepiece. Naturally, they look best when they are in full fruit.

Even strawberries can be used in a decorative manner. Alpine strawberries make good edging plants for borders. A single line between the border and a path, for example, can be extremely effective, especially as they have a long flowering season. They work really well around the edge of herb gardens but can be used in any type of border.

Decorative herbs

Although herbs can be kept together in a separate garden, they do lend themselves particularly well to being spread around the garden in the decorative borders. Shrubby plants, such as rosemary, sage and thyme, have an obvious decorative function, but so do many of the herbaceous varieties. The thin, grass-like leaves of chives, for example, contrast well with the bolder shapes of hostas, and they are also particularly good for edging paths. The frothy leaves of parsley can be used in much the same way.

Many herbs can be grown in decorative borders for their flowers rather than their leaves. The leaves of bergamot (*Monarda*), for example, are used as a herb, but the flowers, which are a bright bold red, are exceptionally decorative, making this a superb border plant.

Potagers

Strictly speaking, a potager is simply a kitchen garden, but it has taken on romantic overtones and is now taken to mean those kitchen gardens that have a decorative as well as productive function.

ABOVE **Flowers are often mixed in with the vegetables in a potager. Sweet peas are one of the most popular choices among gardeners.**

Overall design

The simplest design for a potager is a square or circle, and in many ways these take a lot of beating. Many gardeners, however, enjoy having much more complicated patterns than this, going on to divide the basic shape like the spokes of a wheel or creating four squares, perhaps. Much more intricate patterns can be created, with circles within squares or squares within circles. And so the list of design ideas expands.

The patterns do not have to be geometric. Some gardeners prefer more free-flowing plots, divided with swirls and curved lines. Although these can be extremely attractive, they can be difficult to plant effectively.

Sources of inspiration for such gardens may be visits to actual gardens or pictures in magazines or books. Other useful sources which are often overlooked are arts and crafts that use similar patterns. A book on patchwork, for example, can highlight all kinds of design ideas that can be mixed and matched with further ideas from other gardens.

The shapes of the beds are usually delineated by paths, which are both decorative in their own right and also useful in that they provide access to the beds. These can be paved with brick or stone, or covered with gravel. Although properly laid paths are ultimately best, it is possible to lay them in a temporary fashion until you are certain that you like the layout, or if you want to change the overall plan every few years. Simply lay paving stones, for example, directly onto the levelled soil.

A further way to delineate the beds is to surround them with low box hedging. This creates a permanent structure but it increases its attraction. The box plants will take a few years to become established but the effort and wait are worth it.

Other structural elements are more three-dimensional. Arches, for example, can be used, particularly in the centre of the garden, perhaps covered with fruit. Small trees and standard fruit bushes can be used as centrepieces for individual beds. All add to the shape and texture of the garden.

LEFT **Here, the flowers are situated close enough to the fruit and vegetables to become an integrated part of the potager.**

Designing with plants

The vegetables are the least permanent part of the garden. Just planting them out in lines or blocks will produce an attractive effect, but more interest can be generated by consciously

A Potager Garden

A potager is simply a kitchen garden, but it is used, increasingly, to mean a kitchen garden that has been laid out in a decorative manner. Instead of plants filling more or less random rows, a more complex and involved plan is drawn up, and the garden takes on a new dimension.

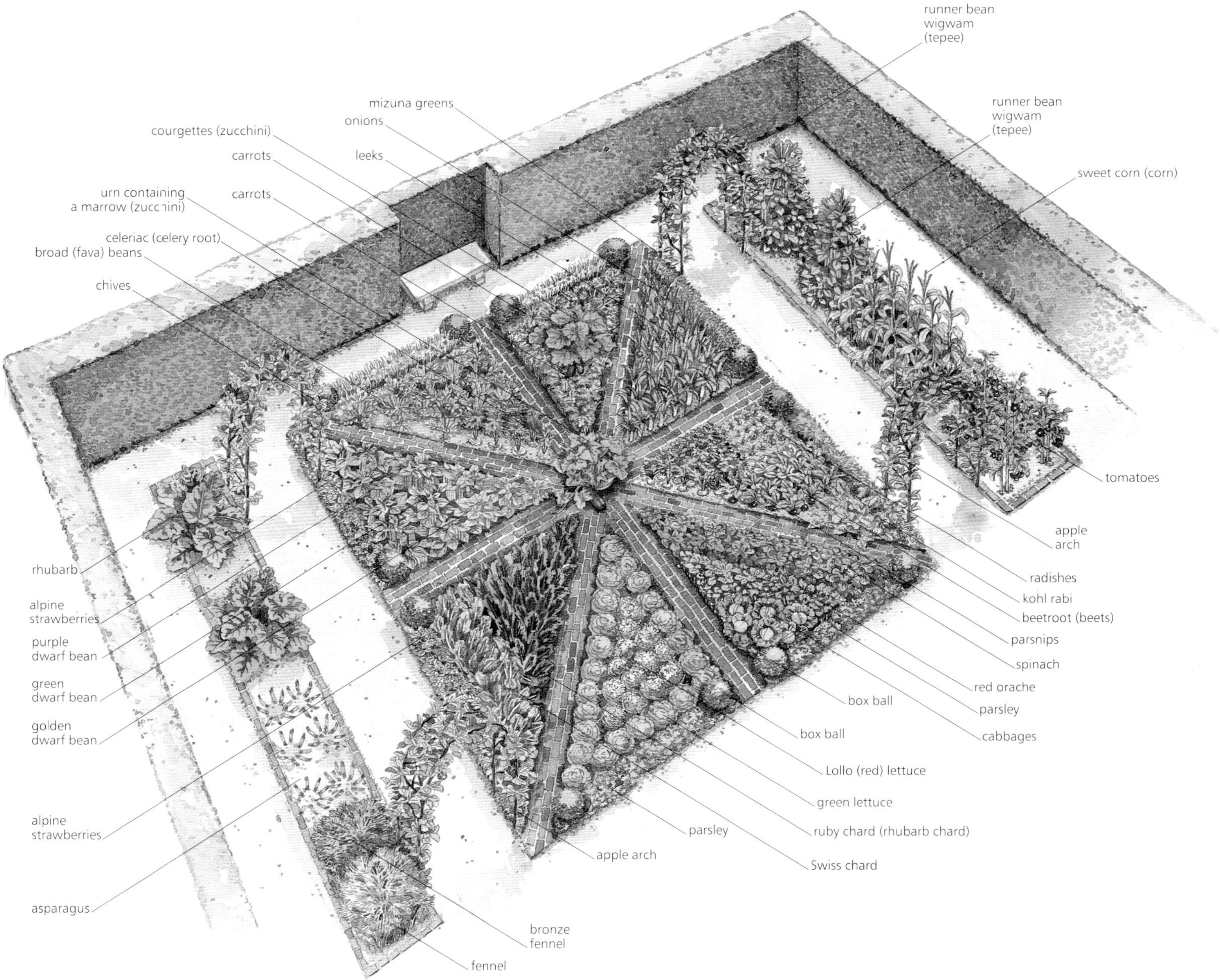

planning each bed, thinking about the plants' colours and textures. Red-leaved lettuces, for example, can be used as winding threads through green vegetables. Parsley can be used as edging, or as a boundary between groups of vegetables. Rows of beans growing up canes can divide beds into sections or they can be grown over archways. Plants need not be planted in blocks, they can be laid out in circles with other plants growing in the middle or around the outside.

However, there is a serious problem with such designs and that is whether to eat the vegetables or not! A meticulous design with every plant in its place is utterly ruined if one is taken off for use in the kitchen. This is something that you must plan for and a less formal style may be the answer.

Another factor to be borne in mind is that it is bad gardening practice to grow the same plants on the same ground each year. Because crops should be rotated, it is not possible to use the same pattern each year unless you create it using different plants.

Containers

Increasing interest is being shown in containers as a method of growing a few vegetables in a small space, perhaps on the patio or possibly even on a balcony or roof garden. This interest is fuelled by the range of beautiful containers that is now available from garden centres and nurseries.

ABOVE **A surprising amount can be grown in a relatively small space, as can be seen from this collection of herbs and vegetables in pots.**

The containers

Virtually any container can be used to grow vegetables, but success is more likely if it is reasonably large – the bigger the better, in fact. Most vegetables do not like to dry out and the greater the volume of compost (soil mix) that is available, the less chance there is of this occurring. A larger amount of space also allows you to grow several different plants in the same container, which is much more decorative than using just one type.

Terracotta pots are extremely attractive, but the porous nature of the material allows water to evaporate more quickly through the sides of the pot than through, say, a glazed one. Most pots are heavy even without compost (soil mix), so make sure you position them before you fill them. Large, black plastic buckets are practical and can be used successfully, although they are not as attractive as ceramic pots.

ABOVE LEFT **More than just a taste of peas can be grown in a container. However, it is important not to let the tub dry out.**

LEFT **Cabbage may not be the first planting idea that springs to mind when thinking of containers, but here four good specimens are growing happily in a plastic tub.**

Growing bags

If you do not mind their utilitarian appearance, growing bags – plastic sacks filled with a formulated growing medium – are an inexpensive way of growing vegetables. They are particularly useful for tomatoes, but they can be used for many other vegetables as well. They were originally developed for use in the greenhouse (where their appearance does not matter), but they can be used outside just as well. A warm corner, against a wall, is the ideal location.

Hanging baskets

Hanging baskets are not ideal for growing vegetables, mainly because they are too small, but a basket of decorative lettuces, perhaps a mixture of green and bronze varieties, can be eye-catching. Some varieties of tomato are trailing, producing tiny, bite-sized fruit, and these are ideal for baskets. A little imagination should allow you to create something productive as well as attractive.

The position

Containers of vegetables can be placed together with purely decorative containers, although they should not be grown in shade. Although plants such as aubergines (eggplants) and peppers are better grown in a warm situation, most other vegetables prefer not to get too hot, and you should bear in mind that plants grown in pots do not have the solid mass of earth around their roots to keep them cool during the day and it is possible that the roots can become too hot.

A Courtyard Kitchen Garden

You do not need a garden in order to grow vegetables. A patio, courtyard or even a balcony is sufficient to produce a few crops. With care, an attractive arrangement can be made which makes an original alternative to most container plantings. There is less weeding involved than in a conventional plot, but a container garden requires a great deal of watering.

Another problem with siting the containers in a warm place is that they will need watering several times a day.

You should, therefore, choose a warm but not hot place, preferably one where there is plenty of air circulating, but not causing a draught (draft).

From a decorative point of view, vegetables can be grown wherever they will fit in. A group of containers can make an attractive feature. You could include a tripod of beans and a tub of golden courgettes (zucchini) and tomatoes, with yellow as well as red ones to vary the scheme. Other pots might contain sweet or bell peppers or aubergines (eggplants), both of which are decorative. It is a question of using your imagination as well as checking growing times and choosing your favourite tastes that should determine what you do. If you do not like the results, you can always try something different next year.

designing
a herb garden

Herb gardens are not just expected to be productive these days, they are also expected to look good. A carefully considered design in the herb garden also has a practical advantage. It will help you plan your herb growing so that you will benefit from crops throughout the year. A clear layout will also help you to decide what varieties to grow and how much seed you will need. Most of the designs for herb gardens in the past were clearly laid out with such things in mind, and also provided scope for ornamental features.

This chapter looks at traditional herb gardens and their influence on styles for today, followed by comprehensive information on choosing a design for your plot and whether to opt for a formal or informal approach. There are practical projects with step-by-step instructions on making a knot garden, a raised bed and herb wheel. There are also examples of themed gardens for inspiration, with detailed plans.

Herb Gardens

Herb gardens tend to fulfil two functions. The first, and obvious one, is to provide herbs. The second arises from the fact that herbs can be highly decorative, making an attractive garden on their own.

Herbs as herbs

Although we grow almost as many herbs as our ancestors, they are primarily included in our gardens for romantic reasons. The number of herbs that most gardeners use in the kitchen is relatively small. But small as this number is, those we do use regularly are important. When you are designing a herb garden, make certain that these herbs are readily accessible from the path, and put those that are never or rarely used in the more inaccessible parts of the border.

The most frequently used herbs should be placed as near to the kitchen door as possible so that the cook can grab a handful when necessary. This means that either the herb garden should be located here or the important herbs should be mixed in with other plants in a decorative border. Another solution is to grow these particular herbs in a container or containers, which can then be placed near the kitchen door for easy access.

Herbs for atmosphere

Although many people regularly use a large number of herbs, most of the gardeners who maintain herb gardens do so because of their romantic associations. And there is no doubt that herbs are romantic. This is partly the atmosphere they create in the garden. Herbs tend to be gentle plants, and only occasionally do we come across brash ones. The colours are muted and soft, the atmosphere they create is hazy. On sunny days the garden is perfumed by their scents and is drowsy with the sound of bees. This is the perfect garden in which to sit and relax, so you should remember to include a seat in your design.

Above *Coriander (cilantro) is a popular herb with a pungent taste. Its delicate flowers and leaves are also decorative.*

Herbs by design

The layout of a herb garden depends largely on the space available, of course, but also on the time you can spend in it. It is possible to create small gardens, and the herb wheel is one of the most popular plans. A cartwheel is laid out on prepared ground and the spaces between the spokes are filled with herbs. When real wheels are not available, the same design can be created from bricks.

Left *Box hedges associate very well with herb gardens. They add order to what, at times, can be an untidy collection of herbs.*

Important culinary herbs

Basil	Marjoram
Bay	Mint
Chives	Parsley
Dill	Rosemary
French tarragon	Sage
Lovage	Thyme

Choosing a Design

Working out the design of a new herb garden is an exciting project. But before you begin there are several questions you need to answer to ensure that the end result is a success. Space is the first consideration. How much room are you prepared to devote to herbs? Do you have a large enough area to make a garden within a garden? Perhaps you would like to turn most, or all, of your existing space over to herbs? Or would a bed or border of herbs be more appropriate?

Plan how the design is going to fit in with your surroundings. Think about your house and current garden, as this will dictate the overall style you choose; formal, informal, old-fashioned or state-of-the-art or of the 21st century.

Consider how much time and energy you have for upkeep. Beware of choosing a large and complicated scheme if from a practical point of view your needs are for a low-maintenance garden. A simple knot of box hedging, filled in with gravel needs clipping only twice a year. But be wary of putting in other traditional clipped herbs, such as santolina and germander, unless you are prepared to trim the plants frequently. A formal potager, which needs constant replanting and tending to keep it in shape, can be very time-consuming. But a carefully thought-out border of shrubby herbs and perennials needs little upkeep. Containers of herbs can provide extra space and variety.

Consider which category of herbs is your chief interest – culinary, medicinal or scented and aromatic? Your preference here may dictate size, layout and planting plans. If your main aim is to produce a good supply of culinary herbs, a small, formal patch may be sufficient. But if your ambition is to include as many species as possible, a more extensive scheme is inevitable.

Left *A colourful archway and large containers of pelargoniums mark the entrance to an inviting garden bounded by a high hedge.*

Below *Topiary and architectural plants of contrasting foliage lend height and interest to a mixed scheme of herbs.*

Formal Gardens

Taking their inspiration from the Renaissance gardens of France and Italy, formal designs depend on straight lines and geometric shapes, on symmetry and regularity. Balance is the key, with elements arranged around a central axis. The strict pattern of paths, which form the structure, is all-important. Paths may be of brick, stone, gravel or grass, but make sure they are wide enough to walk on comfortably and to take a wheelbarrow. A metre (about three feet) is a minimum width for straight sections, with some wider areas to create a feeling of spaciousness and for extra manoeuvrability. Planting schemes echo the geometry of the layout, with corresponding blocks of colour filling the beds. Foliage plants, especially those with a dense habit of growth such as thyme, are often more suitable than those with a profusion of flowers and a tendency to sprawl.

Large pots and ornaments or statues provide focal points at the ends of vistas. If placed to line a path edge or in a regular pattern they will provide visual links, drawing the scheme together and reinforcing the regularity. Topiary and plants growing over a shaped framework are used in much the same way. They also introduce a theatrical element which underlines the style. But beware of cramming in too much – for this look to be successful, understatement and simplicity are best.

Above *Silver thyme in a geometric design.*

Opposite *A bird bath is a focal point here.*

This plan is for a garden about 11 x 9.50 m (36 x 31 ft), enclosed by a brick wall to one side and trelliswork at each corner supporting a scented, white-flowered jasmine. If you do not have a site where a wall can be used as one boundary, the trellis can be extended. An archway, clothed in the coppery pink climbing rose, 'Albertine', forms the main entrance, with a bench seat under a jasmine arbour on the opposite side, against the wall. Topiary in pots – box trees clipped in spheres and rosemary globes – mark the points of entry, add height to the scheme and increase the sense of regularity.

A sundial surrounded by a chamomile lawn, of the non-flowering cultivar *Chamaemelum nobile* 'Treneague', makes a focal point at the centre, emphasized by the square beds of creeping thymes, bronze-purple 'Russetings' and the white-flowering *Thymus serpyllum* var. 'albus'. Chamomile is quite difficult to establish as a lawn and needs constant weeding, so is best kept on a small scale, as it is here. Paths are of stone slabs with brick or tiling edges to the beds.

The emphasis of the planting is on scented herbs with a purple, silver and white colour scheme predominating. Dark-green hyssop, which has blue flower spikes in summer, along with feathery bronze fennel, provide contrast and texture. Golden hops, trained against the wall, echoed by golden sage, lend brightness. Each of the main beds is edged with a low-growing lavender and has a standard rose at the centre.

Plan of a brick enclosed garden

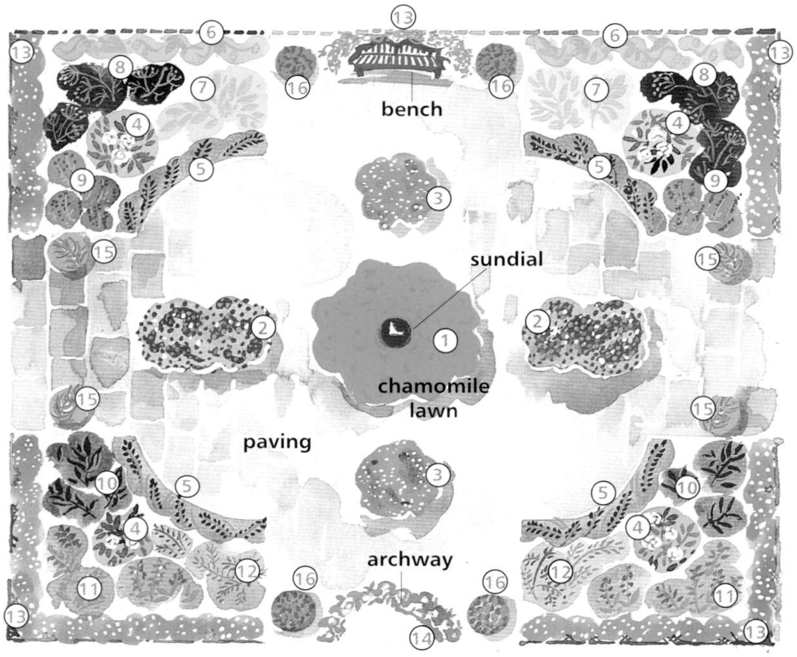

Key to planting plan

1. *Chamaemelum nobile* 'Treneague' – non-flowering chamomile
2. *Thymus serpyllum* 'Russetings' – creeping thyme (mauve-flowering)
3. *Thymus serpyllum* var. 'albus' – creeping thyme (white-flowering)
4. *Rosa* 'Félicité Perpétue' – as a weeping standard
5. *Lavandula angustifolia* 'Hidcote' – low-growing lavender
6. *Humulus lupulus* 'Aureus' – golden hops
7. *Salvia officinalis* 'Icterina' – golden sage
8. *Foeniculum vulgare* 'Purpureum' – bronze fennel
9. *Hyssopus officinalis* – hyssop
10. *Salvia officinalis* Purpurascens Group – purple sage
11. *Salvia sclarea* – clary sage
12. *Artemisia absinthum* – wormwood
13. *Jasminum officinale* – jasmine
14. *Rosa* 'Albertine' – rose 'Albertine'
15. *Rosmarinus officinalis* – rosemary trained over a globe frame
16. *Buxus sempervirens* – box trained as a "lollipop"

A Formal Herb Garden

Herb gardens need to be carefully planned if they are to be attractive. Primarily a herb garden is a place for growing herbs for the kitchen, but it should also be a peaceful haven where the scents and colours of the plants can be enjoyed. However, it is worth remembering that a well maintained herb garden needs more attention than a vegetable plot.

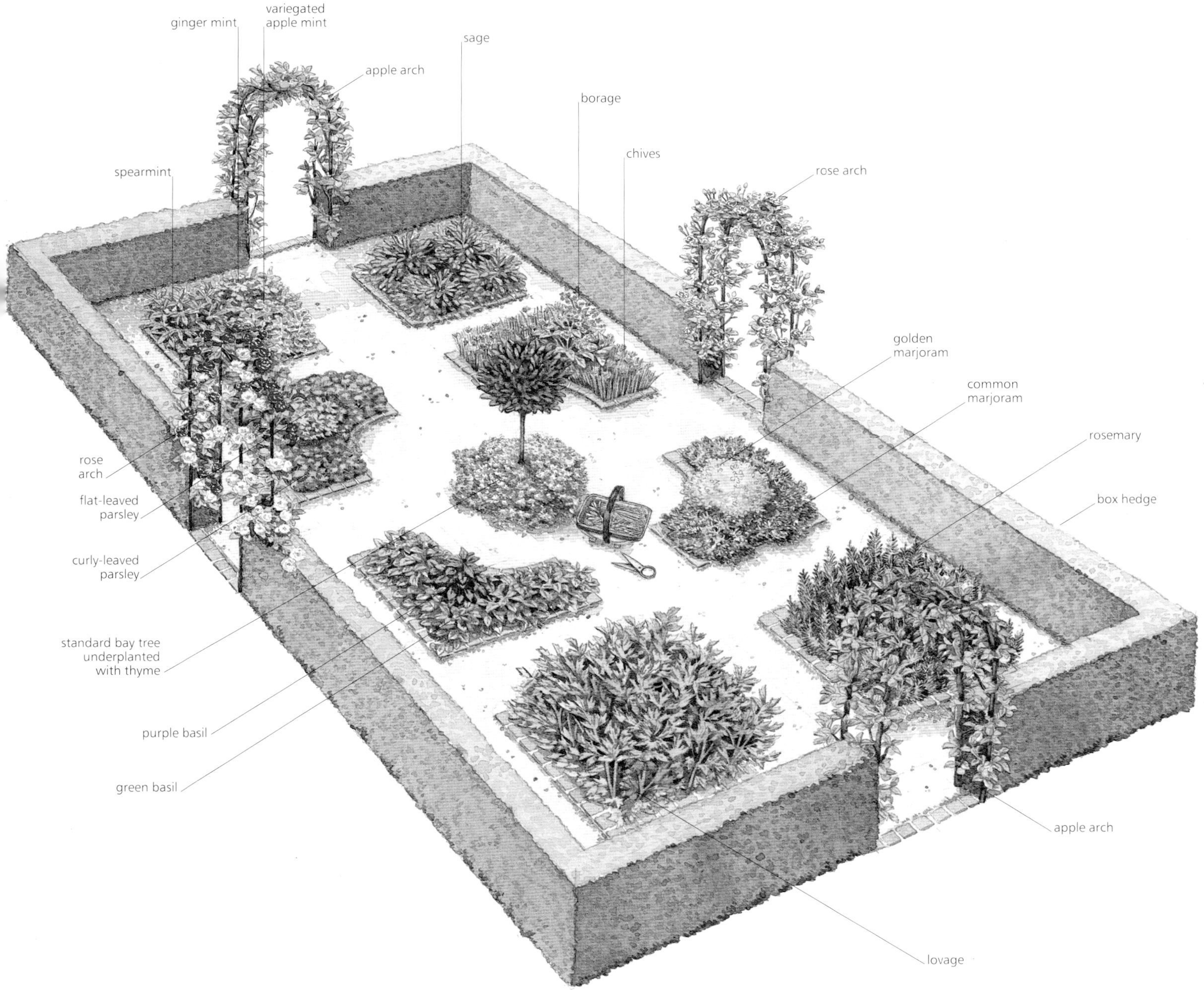

In herb gardens, remember not to use herbs that are too rampant. If you want to use the more vigorous plants in a small area, regularly dig them out and replace them. It is worth mentioning that the only time of year when the internal divisions of the garden will be clearly seen is in the winter when the vegetation has died back. During the growing seasons, the lush growth will be such that the outlines of the beds are not easily seen. If you want to see the demarcations, edge the beds with low box hedges, which will also give good definition to the design.

Opposite *An old-fashioned garden can produce far more aromatic herbs and fragrances than even a large household could possibly use.*

Formal Beds and Borders

Beds edged with low hedges of clipped, dwarf box are a sure way of providing a formal, structured look. This works well for several beds, each being one element of a larger, overall design, or for a single herb border to stand alone.

A large border may also be subdivided by a pattern of internal hedges for a more interesting effect. The spaces in between construct individual planting areas for different species of herb. Timber or tiling edges are another way to give beds a neat finish in a formal scheme.

Right *Tightly clipped box hedging provides an orderly framework for herbs.*

Left *Various designs for long, rectangular borders which are sub-divided by low, internal hedges. Diamonds and squares create satisfying patterns as border divisions and can be filled with a variety of other herbs.*

Above *Pyramids of box and tiling edges give beds a neat finish in a formal scheme.*

Clipped Mounds

Clipped mounds of plants such as cotton lavender, or golden or variegated dwarf box, may be used to great effect, either as edgings or to infill a whole bed. This kind of scheme has more impact if punctuated by clipped plants of a contrasting shape and colour: such as a large bed filled with mounds of silvery santolina, set against pyramids of dark-green box bordering a path.

A formal effect can also be achieved by planting blocks of herbs to make up a simple pattern of squares or triangular shapes, which can be repeated. This works most successfully for herbs of contrasting foliage colour and similar heights and habits: silver posie thyme, perhaps, with the dark green of wall germander, or golden and purple sage.

Topiary Herbs

Standard "mop-head" box or bay trees, pyramids or spiral shapes are an instant way to add formality. If you have time and patience you can train your own to shape, but it may be easier to buy them ready-grown. Topiary and citrus fruit trees in tubs were a popular feature in Tudor and Renaissance gardens, and can still work well in a modern scheme. Placed at strategic points in a geometric scheme, they add an old-fashioned touch and increase the sense of order and regularity. They can also be very useful for introducing the all-important dimension of height and visually linking the various elements of a garden.

Effective herbs for potted topiary include: bay, wall germander, mintbush (*Prostanthera rotundifolia*), rosemary, scented-leaf pelargoniums – especially *P. crispum* – myrtle and box.

Right *A bay tree clipped into a spiral emerges from a sea of lavender.*

Below *Box hedging punctuated by finials, tall clipped shapes in the beds and the trim, rounded heads of an avenue of* Quercus ilex *add up to topiary on a grand scale.*

Knot Gardens

Pattern is very satisfying to the eye and a knot garden always makes a stunning feature. The historic ideal consisted of four elements, each of a different pattern, but it would be as well to start with something simpler.

An area 3–4 m (10–13 ft) square will be large enough to contain an interesting, interwoven pattern. If possible it should be sited where it can be viewed from above – an upstairs window, neighbouring mound or raised level in the garden. It could also form an attractive centrepiece of a sunken garden. A sunny position and well-drained soil will suit it best. The old pattern books include a wide variety of hedging plants for knot gardens. To do the job effectively the plants need to be evergreens with small leaves, dense growth and an ability to withstand close clipping. Although they all have attractive flowers and are not as neat and compact as box, excellent results can be obtained with the following herbs:

Teucrium chamaedrys has glossy, dark-green foliage, shaped like oak leaves. It is fully hardy and tolerates hard trimming, and is easy to grow from cuttings. Plant 23 cm (9 in) apart.

Santolina chamaecyparissus has silvery foliage. This responds well to close clipping and regenerates from old wood. Plant cuttings approximately 23 cm (9 in) apart. *Santolina rosmarinifolia* and *Santolina viridis* have acid-green leaves, treat these as *S. chamaecyparissus*.

Hyssopus officinalis has dark green foliage and is semi-evergreen. This often loses its leaves where winters are hard, but regenerates from old wood. Clip it regularly to avoid straggling and replace plants every four or five years. Plant 23 cm (9 in) apart.

Lavandula angustifolia 'Hidcote' – A low-growing lavender with silvery foliage. Immediately after flowering clip back to shape. However, do not cut into any old wood.

Using box for knot gardens

Box is ideal for knot gardens as its neat habit of growth means that it retains a clipped shape better than most plants. However, it is relatively slow-growing, and an instant finished effect is not easy to achieve.

Buxus sempervirens 'Suffruticosa' has bright-green leaves and is a compact plant, ideal for all edging work.

Buxus sempervirens 'Elegantissima' with small, silver-edged, olive-green leaves is slow-growing and makes a good contrast for darker leaves. *Buxus microphylla* 'Koreana' is low-growing and has dense, dark-green leaves.

It is best to choose compact varieties of box such as these, or the garden will soon grow unwieldy. Using all box makes a more manageable scheme than interspersing other knot garden plants, with different rates of growth and heights when mature.

'Elegantissima'

'Suffruticosa'

'Koreana'

Above *This striking pattern in the form of a foot maze at Hatfield House, England, symbolizes the complexities of following the Christian path through life.*

Right *A stunning and colourful knot garden of clipped box, with spaces between hedges filled with roses, lavender and scented herbs.*

To make a simple knot garden

YOU WILL NEED

Knot garden design (shown); tape measure; string; short lengths of cane with pointed ends; builder's set square (in proportions 3:4:5); plastic bottle and fine sand; box plants

Tips for success:

- Prepare the site well. Dig in some garden compost or manure, as it will be difficult to add organic matter once the plants are established.
- Make sure the area is completely level – use boards and a carpenter's spirit level.
- Accuracy of measuring out the design and putting in the plants is essential. A large set square, made of lengths of wood nailed together in the proportion of 3:4:5, ensures accurate 90° angles at the corners.

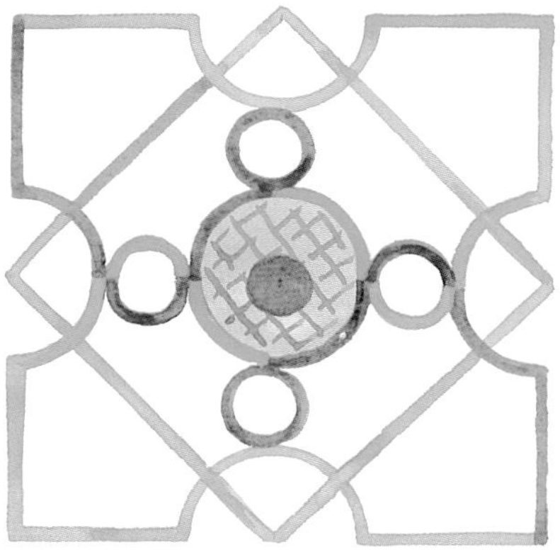

1 Draw the plan out on graph paper in measurements to suit your plot (3–4 m or 10–13 sq ft). Colour in the design to represent the plants to be used to achieve the effect of interwoven ribbons.

2 Using the plan as a guide, mark out the squares on the ground using the tape measure, string and short lengths of cane. A builder's square will ensure accurate right angles.

3 Find the centre point of each side of the outer square and mark the semi-circles by drawing arcs with string attached to a cane. The string should be the length of the radius of the semi-circles.

4 Mark out the semi-circle with the pointed canes and attach the string tautly to define the curve. This provides an accurate guide to follow when delineating the design in sand.

5 Mark out the rest of the design with string and canes, measuring everything carefully. To define the pattern, fill a plastic bottle with fine sand and pour it out evenly along the lines of the string and all markings. Remove the string and canes.

6 Put in the plants, spacing them evenly, 15 cm (6 in) apart and keeping accurately to the markings. Follow the colour code on the plan, making sure the interwoven effect is achieved by putting the right colour plant at the intersections.

7 It will take two to three years for the plants to develop and close the gaps. In the second year, pinch out the centres and trim lightly to encourage growth. Once filled out, clip twice a year (late spring and early autumn). Avoid clipping if there is any danger of frost, as the new soft growth will be damaged by it.

Informal Gardens

Designs based on fluid shapes and an irregular layout give plenty of scope for growing a variety of herbs. They often fit better than formal schemes with the style of a contemporary house and surroundings. Paths may be offset and gently curving, with beds and borders placed seemingly at random. Areas of hard material are often broken by greenery and flowers. Plants spill over on to the paths and spring up among the pea shingle; gaps are left among the paving stones of a terrace to be filled with creeping, aromatic herbs. Bare expanses of plant-free gravel are not in keeping with this style of garden.

Planting should be exuberant: forests of poppies, stands of valerian, a vibrant jumble of flowers and foliage. Pruning and trimming are, of course, essential, but the close-clipped look is less acceptable here.

This is not to say that the structure of the informal garden has to be completely irregular. A relaxed look is frequently achieved by the planting schemes as much as by the layout of beds and paths. This has its roots in the cottage garden genre of gardening, where a central path divided two rectangular areas, and lack of space forced an eclectic mix of plants.

In many informal gardens a regular framework works well. But it has to be simple – four rectangular beds, divided by intersecting paths, perhaps. There is little room for complex patterns and rigid symmetry.

Above *Exuberant planting in a cottage garden style.*

Above *Irregular circular shapes and a gently winding path in a display garden at the National Herb Centre, England.*

Plan for an informal herb garden

This has been designed as a peaceful, rustic retreat as well as being an all-purpose herb garden containing a wide variety of plants. A path of circular logs, laid at the side of the central sweep of gravel, leads around the edge of a pond to a wooden decking area for seating and a table. Creeping thymes are planted in pockets among the log paving, and architectural spires of mullein, *Verbascum thapsus*, spring up at random in the gravel.

The borders at either side are planted for colour and to provide a selection of culinary herbs as well. A further collection of culinary herbs in containers is sited near the seating area, and an olive tree in a tub (so that it can be moved to a protected area for winter) is near the entrance. This is surrounded by shrubby herbs: thyme, sage, prostrate rosemary and winter savory in a gravel mulch, which echoes the main area of gravel.

For early summer colour there are swathes of red and white valerian and opium poppies, to be followed later in the season by brilliant red bergamot, *Monarda didyma* 'Cambridge Scarlet'. A broad band of blue catmint, *Nepeta* x *faassenii*, leads the eye up to the pond, where the fine mossy growth of Corsican mint, *Mentha requienii*, spills over the logs, with clumps of chives and gold and green variegated gingermint nearby. An ornamental form of sweet flag, *Acorus gramineus* 'Variegatus', which does not grow as large as the more authentic sweet flag, *Acorus calamus*, is planted in the pond with some water lilies.

Behind the pond, the spearmint is planted in a bucket with no base to prevent it spreading. Angelica, lovage and fennel provide height and texture as well as being valuable culinary herbs. At the top of the garden, just on its boundaries, is a common elder, with golden and fern-leafed varieties for extra interest.

To complete the countryside feel of the garden and continue the timber theme the boundary could be further defined by traditional wicker screening.

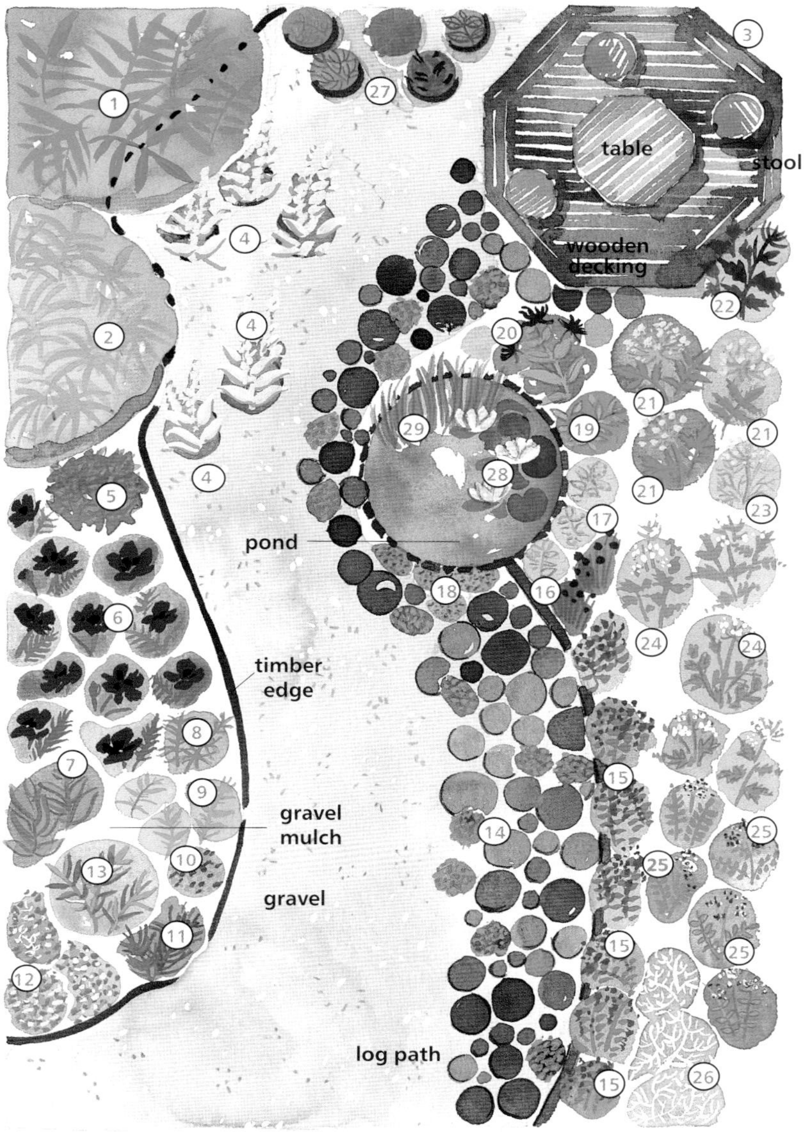

Key to planting plan

1. *Sambucus nigra* – common elder
2. *Sambucus nigra* 'Aurea' – golden elder
3. *Sambucus nigra* f. *laciniata* – fern-leafed elder
4. *Verbascum thapsus* – mullein
5. *Origanum onites* – pot marjoram
6. *Papaver somniferum* – opium poppy has white or lilac flowers, but there are many attractive cultivars in reds and pinks
7. *Salvia officinalis* – common sage
8. *Artemisia dracunculus* – tarragon
9. *Satureja montana* – winter savory
10. *Thymus vulgaris* – common thyme
11. *Rosmarinus officinalis* – prostratus group – prostrate rosemary
12. *Thymus vulgaris* 'Silver Posie' – silver posie thyme
13. *Olea europaea* – olive tree
14. *Thymus serpyllum* 'Bressingham Pink' – creeping thymes and *T. serpyllum Coccineus*
15. *Nepeta* x *faassenii* – catmint
16. *Allium schoenoprasum* – chives
17. *Mentha* x *gracilis* 'Variegata' – gingermint
18. *Mentha requienii* – Corsican mint
19. *Mentha spicata* – spearmint
20. *Monarda didyma* 'Cambridge Scarlet' – bergamot, red flowering
21. *Angelica archangelica* – angelica
22. *Levisticum officinale* – lovage
23. *Foeniculum vulgare* – fennel
24. *Valeriana officinalis* – white valerian
25. *Centranthus ruber* – red valerian
26. *Helichrysum italicum* – curry plant
27. A selection of culinary herbs in pots
28. *Nymphaea odorata* – white water lily
29. *Acorus gramineus* 'Variegatus' – variegated sweet flag

Herbal Beds and Borders

Island beds or long borders can make gratifying small herb gardens where space is limited. They are ideal for providing a supply of herbs for cooking, or a colourful medley of medicinal and aromatic herbs for general household use. In larger beds, paths or narrow brick divisions may be appropriate as visual separations and to prevent invasive species from growing into each other. Stepping stones, placed in a random pattern, provide easy access to the plants for picking or weeding.

When planting island beds, tall subjects, such as angelica and lovage, may be placed at the centre, with lower growing plants surrounding them. In a border against a wall or hedge, plant heights look best graduated, with the tallest at the back and dwarf and creeping plants at the front. Introducing height with statuesque plants adds interest. Standards, especially of plants with irregular growth patterns – olive trees, lemon verbena, old-fashioned roses – also add extra height. Scented climbing plants, such as jasmine, hops or honeysuckle, trained over tepees of canes or wooden sticks, make unusual punctuation marks in a large border.

Above *A simple, rectangular border with paved divisions, set in a gravel surround, makes a self-contained herb garden.*

Left *Bronze fennel contrasts well with white-flowering* Galega officinalis *'Alba'.*

Below *A river of creeping thymes, flanked at right by gallica roses (*R.g. *var.* officinalis *and* R.g. *'Versicolor'), makes an imaginative and decorative feature.*

Above *Closely-packed herbs provide a riot of midsummer colour.*

Right *Alternating clumps of purple and green-leafed sage,* Salvia officinalis.

Below *A pocket of mixed thymes, set in golden stone.*

Raised Beds

These have many advantages. They can be used to provide ideal conditions where garden soil is unsuitable. If your garden is on heavy clay, which most herbs dislike, especially the shrubby, Mediterranean varieties, a raised bed can offer the requisite free-draining environment. Where soil is poor and dry, a raised bed can be filled with a good moisture-retentive growing medium for herbs that need damp ground. Beds at a higher level can also make gardening easier and more rewarding for the disabled or elderly. For everyone, they allow plants to be seen from a new perspective so that flowers, foliage and scents can all be appreciated more closely.

Heights of raised beds may be varied according to intended purpose or preference. Old illustrations reveal the popularity from medieval times into the age of the Renaissance garden, of beds raised from the surrounding paths by no more than a few inches. For old-style physic gardens and formal potagers, low raised beds, edged with timber, are both practical and decorative.

Above *A brick-built raised bed provides a free-draining environment, which suits many herbs, especially those of Mediterranean origin.*

There are various materials that can be used for constructing raised beds:

Timber – use planks that are wide enough to sink into the ground. Screw or nail together securely at the corners and treat with wood preservative suitable for plants.

Railway sleepers (railroad ties) can be used for a rustic, informal look. Clean off any tar and preservatives, which are toxic to plants, with solvent. A plastic membrane may be necessary for heavily impregnated sleepers. No foundations are necessary as their weight makes them stable. Lay them flat, rather than on edge, for stability and fix together at the corners with steel rods, driven through them and into the ground.

Bricks are durable and attractive in a variety of settings (especially old bricks). Check they are frostproof as ordinary housebricks may not be suitable.

Above *A raised bed made of timber with feverfew and grasses.*

Above *Marjorams growing in a bed walled with stone.*

Above *Herbs flourish in a brick-built raised bed.*

Making a raised bed

Raised beds can be laid out as functional squares and rectangles, in decorative shapes or made to fit a corner of the garden such as this bed for culinary herbs.

YOU WILL NEED

Short stakes or dowel; string; builder's set square; fine sand or line-marker paint; tape measure; cement; ballast; builder's sand; pointing trowel; approximately 90 bricks; spirit level; waterproof paint; paintbrush; rubble; gravel or pea shingle (pea stone); 3 bags of topsoil; potting medium; a selection of herbs

1 Mark out the shape of the bed on the ground, using a short, pointed stake or dowel and string. Use a builder's set square to ensure correct right angles. Define the lines with a dribble of fine sand, or use line-marker paint.

2 Dig out the soil along the markings to a depth and width of 15 cm (6 in). Fill in with concrete to within 5 cm (2 in) of the top. Firm down, level and leave for 24 hours to set completely. For concrete, use one part cement to four parts ballast.

3 Build up four or five courses of bricks, and set into mortar, carefully checking with a spirit level at each stage. (Mortar is one part cement to four parts sharp or builder's sand.)

4 Clean up the mortar, while it is still wet, with a pointing trowel. Leave it to harden.

5 Before filling with soil, coat the inside of the wall with a waterproof paint.

6 Put in a layer of rubble, topped with gravel or pea shingle for drainage. Fill in with bought topsoil and stir in a top layer of a good potting medium.

7 Plant up the raised bed with your chosen herbs.

8 The completed raised bed planted with a selection of culinary herbs and wild strawberries.

Herb Wheels

These were a feature of numerous Victorian gardens, when old cartwheels (wagon wheels) were plentiful. They provided frameworks of little beds containing kitchen herbs, the spokes prevented the different varieties from encroaching on each other. If you are using an old cartwheel, it must be treated with a plant-friendly preservative to prevent the timber from rotting. The spokes may also be a little close together to be practical, so consider removing some of them.

A brick-built wheel is long-lasting and the sections can be more effectively allocated. Choose a location in full sun if possible, and if it is for culinary herbs, put it near the kitchen.

Above *Nasturtiums are good in salads.*

Above *Pot marigolds add bright colour to a herb garden.*

Above *Chives and golden marjoram.*

Above *An intriguing design for a herb wheel at the Henry Doubleday Research Association.*

Herbs for a cook's herb wheel

Medium- to low-growing herbs of similar heights make for a balanced effect.

Perennial selection:

Allium schoenoprasum – Chives. Mild onion flavour herb with attractive, purple flowers.

Origanum onites – Pot marjoram. Warm-flavoured leaves, with pinkish-purple flowers.

Satureja montana – Winter savory. Makes an aromatic, neat pillow of dark-green foliage with white flowers.

Thymus x *citriodorus* – Thyme. Delicious, lemon-scented thyme.

Salvia officinalis Purpurascens Group – Purple sage. Bold purple and green foliage; strong, savoury taste.

Foeniculum vulgare – Fennel. Tall, feathery plant with an aniseed flavour for central pot.

Petroselinum crispum – Parsley. Biennial. It is also suitable for growing as an annual.

Annual selection to sow from seed:

Calendula officinalis – Pot marigold. Well worth including for the brilliance of its flowers. Self-seeds.

Anthriscus cerefolium – Chervil. A delicately flavoured herb, which is fully hardy and can be sown successionally for a continuous supply. Self-seeds.

Coriandrum sativum – Coriander (Cilantro). Spicy flavour. Thin out seedlings and keep moist.

Tropaeolum majus – Nasturtium. Grow it for the bright flowers and use them in salads.

Ocimum basilicum 'Purple Ruffles' – Purple basil. The foliage provides a foil for other green herbs. Good basil flavour.

Satureja hortensis – Summer savory. This is more subtly flavoured than the perennial variety and it goes very well with beans.

Anethum graveolens – Dill. Plant in the central pot for its feathery foliage and delicate taste.

Making a raised brick herb wheel

1 *Using a length of string equal to the radius of the bed, attached to a piece of pointed cane, mark out a circle on the ground. Then shorten the string and mark a small inner circle at the centre. Sink a length of earthenware (clay) sewage pipe (from builder's merchants or building supply stores) in the centre. Then measure off equal points on the circumference to form the spokes, marking them out with canes and string.*

2 *Trace over the whole design with fine sand or line-marker paint.*

3 *Dig a trench for the bricks and fill with sharp or builder's sand.*

4 *Construct as for the raised bed (steps 3–5), putting in one or two layers of bricks, set in mortar, to form the outer circle and spokes.*

5 *Fill in the sections of the wheel and the earthenware pipe with rubble, then gravel or pea shingle, topsoil and compost (soil mix).*

YOU WILL NEED

String; short canes or dowel; earthenware (clay) sewage pipe; fine sand or line-marker paint; tape measure; sharp sand; approximately 90 bricks; cement; builder's sand; ballast; pointing trowel; spirit level; waterproof paint; rubble; gravel or pea shingle; 3 bags of topsoil; compost (soil mix); a selection of culinary herbs

6 *Plant the herb wheel with a selection of culinary herbs such as wild strawberry, thyme, sage, rosemary and lemon verbena.*

Themed Gardens

A themed garden can make a vibrant and colourful display for herbs. In the following section there are plans for various styles of gardens – an old-fashioned medieval garden, a decorative Shakespearean garden with a small knot garden of clipped box, and a pot-pourri garden with many different fragrant herbs and scented flowers. The cook's or kitchen garden is not only productive but will look good too.

The potager is intended mainly for culinary use but with bold use of colour, it makes an excellent ornamental layout. The plan for a traditional apothecary's garden with small, individual plots of medicinal herbs shows how to make a functional, but very eye-catching, herb garden, that needs the bare minimum of maintenance.

Right *A re-creation of a medieval pleasure garden with scented herbs, at Tretower Court, Wales.*

Medieval Garden

Above *Herbs such as valerian and feverfew grow in the raised beds of this medieval-style garden. When gardens like this were laid out, beauty was not a consideration, but with their symmetry, and the colours and shapes of the plants, the effect is delightful.*

In gardens of the Middle Ages herbs were often grown in small beds, each devoted to a single species. This made it easy to tend and harvest the plants, as well as to identify them, and was the chosen style of monastery and physic gardens, whose primary purpose was practical.

By the 12th and 13th centuries pleasure gardens, based on cloister gardens, became a feature of palaces and castles. These usually took the form of a small enclosed "privy" garden, for the benefit of the lady of the house and her attendants. King Henry III installed one for his queen, stipulating that it should have a pleasant herbery and high walls so that no one should enter except the Queen. There are narrow beds at the side, and a seat or an arbour is standard, and often there is a fountain splashing in the corner.

Plan for a medieval garden

This small garden, designed to take up approximately 6 x 8 m (19 x 26 ft), is surrounded by a trellis, with a low fence on one side and a Gothic arch as entranceway. Since a "flowery mead" would be an impractical proposition in this space, the path is made of gravel, with a central bed of pot marigolds, surrounded by a chamomile lawn.

Two chamomile seats, made as raised beds, are separated by a gallica rose, with further gallica roses at opposite corners. *Rosa eglanteria*, the eglantine rose of Chaucer's day, climbs over the trellis, but a compromise has been made with the other climbing rose, 'Noisette Carnée'. This rose, unlike the others, is not ancient enough to be a true medieval rose, but has a delicate old-fashioned form and the great benefit of repeat flowering to provide interest over a longer period.

Narrow beds against the perimeter are planted with a froth of lady's mantle, flax (with its profusion of dainty blue flowers), feverfew, wild strawberries and other plants common at the time – though a modern cultivar, *Achillea millefolium* 'Moonshine', has been substituted for wild yarrow, which would be too invasive for the area and not very attractive. There is a small fountain and shallow pond in one corner, with the moisture-loving *Iris versicolor* planted at its margins. White Madonna lilies, popular in the medieval era as a symbol of purity and associated with the Virgin Mary, are planted in pots.

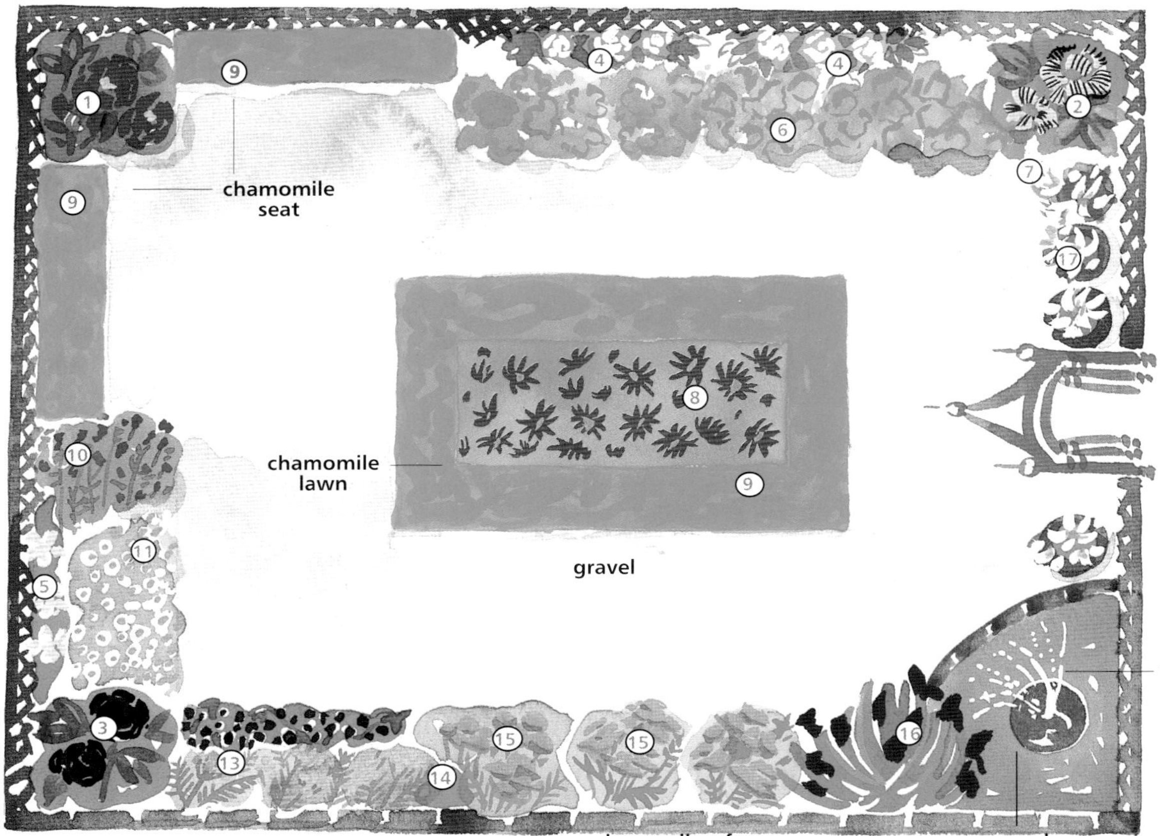

Key to planting plan

1. *Rosa gallica* var. *officinalis* – the fuschia-pink apothecary's rose
2. *Rosa gallica* var. *officinalis* 'Versicolor' – pink-and-white-striped gallica rose
3. *Rosa gallica* var. *officinalis* 'Tuscany Superb' – dark-crimson, double gallica
4. *Rosa* 'Noisette Carnée' (syn. 'Blush Noisette') – pale-pink repeat-flowering climber
5. *Rosa eglanteria* – sweet briar rose, a vigorous climber with simple, palest pink blooms.
6. *Alchemilla mollis* – lady's mantle
7. *Thymus vulgaris* 'Silver Posie' – thyme with silver-variegated foliage
8. *Calendula officinalis* – pot marigold
9. *Chamaemelum nobile* 'Treneague' – a non-flowering chamomile
10. *Linum usitatissimum* – flax
11. *Tanacetum parthenium* – feverfew
12. *Fragaria vesca* – wild strawberry
13. *Tanacetum vulgare* – tansy
14. *Thymus vulgaris* – thyme
15. *Achillea millefolium* 'Moonshine'
16. *Iris versicolor* – blue flag
17. *Lilium candidum* – Madonna lily

Shakespearean Garden

For those with a literary bent, a garden based on the herbs and flowers included in the works of Shakespeare makes an exciting project. No other poet and playwright can have made so many references to these plants, nor indicated such a delight in them and knowledge of their uses and characteristics. There is also scope for a comprehensive selection, as over 130 plants are mentioned, some under two or three different names.

Culinary herbs include "saffron to colour the warden pies", "a dish of caraways" (caraway seeds) to eat with apples and "parsley to stuff a rabbit". Garlic gets several mentions, usually in connection with its odour on the breath, and onions are linked with tears.

Medicinal uses of plants make frequent entrances – though the portrait of the downtrodden apothecary (in *Romeo and Juliet*) with his "old cakes of roses" and other accoutrements "thinly scattered to make up a show" is hardly a flattering one. The narcotic properties of poppies and mandrake are referred to several times and the myth that mandrakes scream when uprooted is perpetuated. The power of the witch's brew is noted, with its deadly "root of hemlock digged i' the dark". The symbolic associations of herbs are acknowledged such as wormwood for bitterness, and also rosemary for remembrance.

Household uses of herbs include polishing chairs with juice of balm in *The Merry Wives of Windsor*; and the soothing power of scented flowers is memorably evoked in Oberon's description of Titania's bower in *A Midsummer Night's Dream*:

I know a bank whereon the wild
thyme blows,
Where oxlips and the nodding
violet grows
Quite over-canopied with luscious
woodbine [honeysuckle],
With sweet musk-roses, and with
eglantine.

Who could resist re-creating this for themselves? For researching the full extent of Shakespeare's references to herbs, *Shakespeare Concordance* by A. Bartlett, 1894, is a great help.

Other works include: *The Plant-lore and Garden Craft of Shakespeare* – by Rev. Henry N. Ellacombe, 1884; *The Flora and Folklore of Shakespeare* – by F.G. Savage (Shakespeare Press, 1923); *The Shakespeare Garden* – by Esther Singleton (William Farquhar Payson, New York, 1931); *Shakespeare's Wild Flowers* – by Eleanour Sinclair Rohde (the Medici Society 1935); *The Flowers of Shakespeare* – by Doris Hunt (Webb and Bower, 1980).

Above *Box and cotton lavender form intertwining ribbons in a garden edging.*

Top *The flower stems of silvery blue* Sempervivums *create an intricate pattern.*

Above *Lavender grows very well in the free-draining soil of a bed with raised timber edge.*

Opposite *An Elizabethan knot garden, closely planted with colourful flowers for a richly embroidered effect, at Stratford-upon-Avon, England.*

Plan for a Shakespearean garden

The plan is for a garden approximately 9 x 13 m (29 x 43 ft) in the formal style that was popular in Shakespeare's day. At the centre is a small knot garden of clipped box, surrounded by narrow borders of lavender and pinks. Three spacious steps lead to an arbour on a higher level, so that the knot can be viewed from above. Creeping thyme is planted in pockets on the stone slabs in front of the seat, and over the steps. The arbour is clad in honeysuckle and roses and surrounded by the 'wild thyme' and other flowers and herbs of Titania's bower. Raised beds, with brick-retaining walls, form the boundaries and topiary trees in tubs visually link the garden and mark the entrance points. Poisonous plants such as hemlock, henbane, aconitum and others have not been included in this garden for safety reasons. The two rue bushes are at the back of the border, where they are least likely to be accidentally brushed. Rue can cause blistering on contact, but has long been a popular aromatic plant.

Key to planting plan

1. *Thymus serpyllum* – wild thyme
2. *Viola odorata/Viola tricolor* violets and heartsease
3. *Primula veris/Primula vulgaris* – cowslips/primrose
4. *Lilium candidum* – Madonna lily
5. *Rosa moschata* – musk rose
6. *Rosa eglanteria* – sweet briar rose
7. *Lonicera periclymenum* – honeysuckle
8. *Dianthus caesius/Dianthus deltoides* – pinks
9. *Lavandula angustifolia* 'Hidcote' – lavender
10. *Satureja montana* – winter savory
11. *Consolida ajacis* – larkspur
12. *Papaver somniferum* – opium poppies
13. *Calendula officinalis* – pot marigold
14. *Rosa* x *alba* – white rose of York
15. *Rosa gallica* var. *officinalis* – red rose of Lancaster
16. *Ruta graveolens* – rue
17. *Artemisia absinthum* – wormwood
18. *Hyssopus officinalis* – hyssop
19. *Origanum onites* – marjoram
20. *Mentha* spp. – mint
21. *Carum carvi* – caraway
22. *Foeniculum vulgare* – fennel
23. *Borago officinalis* – borage
24. *Melissa officinalis* 'Aurea' – variegated lemon balm
25. *Petroselinum crispum* – parsley
26. *Sanguisorba minor* – salad burnet
27. *Laurus nobilis* – standard bay
28. *Buxus sempervirens* – standard box
29. *Rosmarinus officinalis* – rosemary (trained as topiary)
30. *Buxus sempervirens* 'Suffruticosa' – dwarf box
31. *Myrtus communis* subsp. *tarentina* – dwarf myrtle

Pot-pourri Garden

There is a long tradition of drying scented flowers and aromatic herbs for sweetening the air. Stillroom books of the 17th and 18th centuries include many recipes for scented powders and "perfumes" as pot-pourri was more usually known then. The term as currently used to describe a mixture of dried fragrant petals and leaves did not become common until the 19th century. It comes from the name of a Spanish stew, *olla podrida* (literally meaning "rotten pot"), and the French translation of pot-pourri came to mean any medley or mixture.

An area of scented herbs and flowers, which can be picked for pot-pourri, makes a rewarding garden feature. Stock it with plenty of roses – pink and red ones are best as they retain good colour when dried.

"Rose-leaves ... were gathered even as they fell to make into a pot-pourri for someone who had no garden." (*Cranford* by Mrs Gaskell).

Above *A pergola covered in old-fashioned roses provides plenty of petals for drying.*

Plan for a pot-pourri garden

This plan would fit into an area about 8 m (26 ft) square to make a scented garden with plenty of material to cut for making pot-pourri. The four corner beds, set in a grass path, are edged with dwarf box and filled with colourful flowers and fragrant herbs. The central circular area is brick-paved, with pockets for a low-growing double chamomile and vivid caraway thyme. The gazebo supports a richly perfumed, dark crimson 'Ena Harkness' climbing rose and a cloud of jasmine. There is room beneath it for a seat, or a small table and some stools, and it is surrounded by pots of colourful, scented pelargoniums, pineapple sage and lemon verbena.

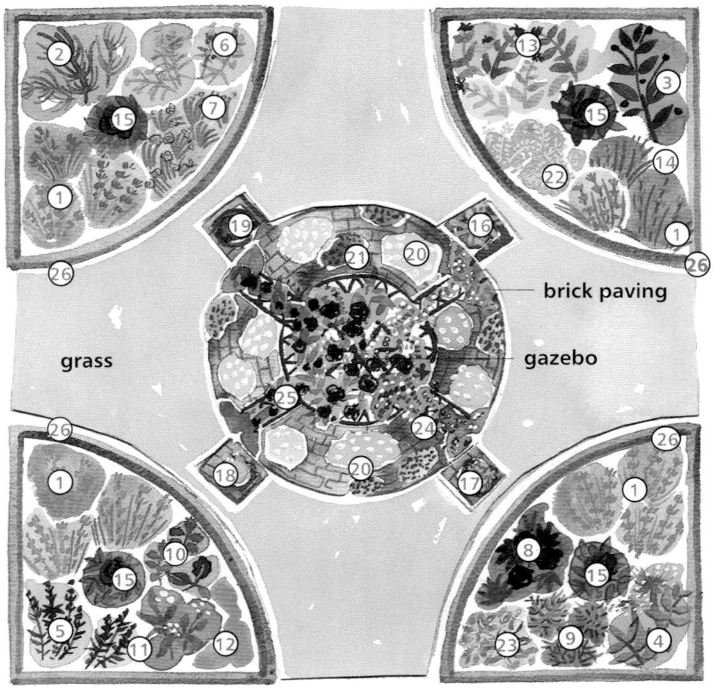

Key to planting plan

1. *Lavandula angustifolia* 'Munstead' – dark blue, low-growing lavender
2. *Rosmarinus officinalis* – rosemary
3. *Myrtus communis* – myrtle
4. *Angelica archangelica* – angelica
5. *Agastache foeniculum* – anise hyssop
6. *Hyssopus officinalis* – hyssop
7. *Dianthus* 'London Delight' – an old-fashioned pink
8. *Paeonia officinalis* 'Rubra Plena' – a rich red paeony
9. *Artemisia abrotanum* – southernwood
10. *Coriandrum sativum* – coriander (cilantro)
11. *Tanacetum balsamita* – alecost
12. *Consolida ajacis* – larkspur
13. *Monarda* 'Croftway Pink' – a pink bergamot
14. *Iris germanica* var. *florentina* – Orris
15. *Rosa* 'François Juranville' – a gold-pink rose, as a weeping standard
16. *Aloysia triphylla* – lemon verbena
17. *Pelargonium tomentosum* – peppermint scented
18. *Pelargonium* 'Lady Plymouth' – scented-leaf geranium, with cream margins
19. *Salvia elegans* – pineapple sage
20. *Chamaemelum nobile* 'Flore Pleno' – dwarf, double-flowered chamomile
21. *Thymus herba-barona* – caraway-scented thyme
22. *Thymus vulgaris* 'Silver Posie' – a silver-leafed thyme
23. *Mentha* x *gracilis* 'Variegata' – gingermint
24. *Jasminum officinale* –the white-flowering jasmine
25. *Rosa* 'Ena Harkness' – dark-red climbing rose
26. *Buxus sempervirens* 'Suffruticosa' – dwarf box

To make a rose pot-pourri

Making your own pot-pourri is a rewarding and creative experience. The results will have individuality and a more pleasant fragrance than shop-bought.

YOU WILL NEED

3 cups dried rose petals; 2 cups mixed dried flowers; 15 ml (1 tbsp) dried lavender; 1 cup mixed dried herbs: mint, marjoram, thyme and angelica; 5 ml (1 tsp) cloves; 2.5 ml/½ tsp) ground allspice; 10 ml (2 tsp) ground orris root; 5–10 drops rose essential oil

1 *To dry the plant material, pick everything on a dry day. Spread out on newspaper and leave in a warm, airy place (out of direct sunlight) for 5–7 days, until papery to the touch.*

2 *To make the pot-pourri, combine all the ingredients, mix thoroughly and put them in an airtight container. Leave in a dry, warm place for 2–3 weeks, shaking the container occasionally.*

Above *A traditional rose garden in full bloom and (right) a garden of scented herbs and flowers for making pot-pourri.*

Cook's Garden

A small border or bed can provide a surprisingly good selection of herbs to meet basic culinary needs, especially if supplemented by a few tubs and containers. A sunny location is important as the herbs will thrive and have a better flavour. For convenience the kitchen garden should be sited as close to the kitchen door as possible so that herbs can be harvested without you having to trudge too far.

Plan for a cook's garden of herbs

A semicircular-shaped bed against a wall allows space for 13 useful herbs, with bay, basil and mint in containers: tender basil is much easier to grow in a pot, and mint is inclined to spread into its neighbours. A narrow brick path divides the space and makes it easier to reach the plants when tending or picking them.

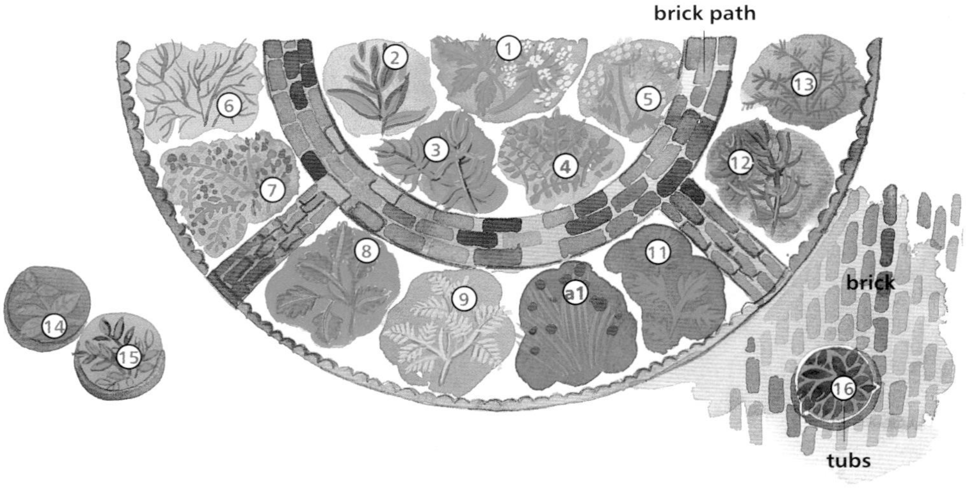

Key to planting plan

1. *Angelica archangelica* – angelica
2. *Salvia officinalis* – sage
3. *Artemisia dracunculus* – tarragon
4. *Origanum onites* – pot marjoram
5. *Levisticum officinale* – lovage
6. *Anethum graveolens* – dill
7. *Thymus vulgaris* or *Thymus* x *citriodorus* – thyme or lemon thyme
8. *Coriandrum sativum* – coriander (cilantro)
9. *Anthriscus cerefolium* – chervil
10. *Allium schoenoprasum* – chives
11. *Petroselinum crispum* – parsley
12. *Rosmarinus officinalis Prostratus* Group – prostrate rosemary
13. *Satureja montana* – winter savory
14. *Ocimum basilicum* – sweet basil
15. *Mentha spicata* – spearmint
16. *Laurus nobilis* – bay

Above left *An informal kitchen herb garden with nasturtiums and coriander (cilantro).*

Far left *A pot of golden and purple sage provides a ready source of leaves for cooking.*

Left *Sweet basil is a traditional complementary flavour for tomatoes and is frequently used in culinary dishes.*

Potager

A potager is a garden where vegetables and herbs are grown together in an ornamental layout. Early cooks' gardens contained as many herbs as "vegetables" – as we now call them – with little distinction being made between the two. "Sallet"(salad) herbs in Elizabethan times included a wide variety of unusual leaves and colourful flowers. They were also made into stuffings and uncooked sweet and savoury sauces: flower petals pulverized with ground almonds and sugar, or potent mixtures of green herbs pounded together in vinegar.

Growing herbs and vegetables together is practical and ornamental at the same time. Mixed plantings of this nature suffer less from pests because the bright flowers of many herbs attract beneficial insects, such as lacewings and ladybirds (bugs). At the same time, aromatic plants deter aphids and other insects. If vegetables are intermingled with strong-smelling herbs, rather than planted in huge blocks on their own, they become a less obvious target for the pests normally attracted to them.

As with all vegetable growing, allowance must be made for rotation of crops and there will inevitably be bare patches at intervals to accommodate this. But the garden is afforded a permanent structure by the framework of paths and perennial herbs.

Paths may be of gravel, brick, stone or any hard material. The central one should be at least 1 m (3 ft) wide and the divisions between the beds no less than 0.5 m (20 in). Beds should be no more than 1.5 m (5 ft) wide so that they are easy to reach; timber or tiling edges give them a neat finish and link the elements of the garden together.

Archways for climbing plants at the entrance or at the centre of the garden add height and visual appeal. Espaliered fruit trees at the perimeter make a practical and decorative screen. A tunnelled archway of apples or pears is a traditional feature.

Plan for a potager garden

This potager is both practical and ornamental, with beds about 1.5 m (5 ft) in length and paths 0.5 m(20 in) wide. The plan below allows for perennial herbs, such as lavender, rosemary and sage, to be planted at the ends of each bed.

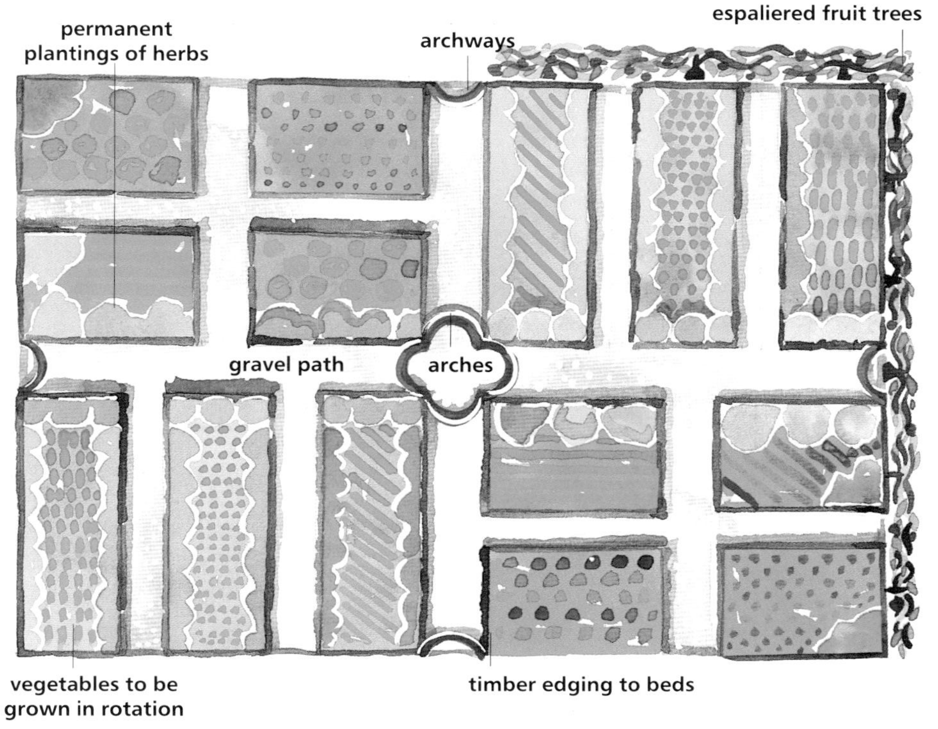

Above *A formal potager of box-edged beds, packed with sturdy vegetables, ruby chard (foreground), sweetcorn, marrow and beans, interspersed with aromatic rosemary.*

Apothecary's Garden

Also known as a "physic garden", the apothecary's garden was the source of raw materials for making medicines to heal the sick.

In the tradition of the monasteries, a range of "simples", or medicinal plants, were grown in their own little plots. These were sometimes prescribed to be used on their own, or, more frequently, the apothecary concocted compounds from them, consisting of several ingredients. The advantage of keeping each herb in its separate bed in this way was to make identification easier when it came to picking, as well as being an efficient method of cultivation on a small scale. It also provided easy access for planting, weeding and watering.

When making their remedies, the apothecaries were guided by a variety of herbals: the earliest of which was written in China nearly 5,000 years ago. They also studied the works of the great physicians of ancient Greece – Hippocrates, Galen, Theophrastrus and Dioscorides – and the texts from the Dark Ages which were copied by generations of monks, and given a new lease of life by the invention of printing in the mid-15th century.

The role and influence of the apothecary began to wane during the 16th century as European herbalists started to base their work on empirical observations of plants. John Gerard's *Herball or Generall Historie of Plantes* was in this tradition of enquiry and was first published in England in 1597. Apothecaries established their own society at the beginning of the 16th century and were the pharmacists of the time, dispensing drugs for the physicians and giving out medical advice to patients.

Above *Herbs growing in little beds, created by gaps in paving slabs, make an attractive and practical medicinal garden.*

Left *A collection of herbs in sunken pots, carefully labelled to ensure correct identification.*

A modern garden of herbs for making home remedies, which draws on the best of these traditions, has understated charm and is a low-maintenance way to grow herbs. Filled with traditional herbs, such as bright gold pot marigolds (*Calendula officinalis*), neatly patterned houseleek (*Sempervivum tectorum*), aromatic lavender, rosemary, thyme and sage, laid out in a simple configuration of beds, it will be both functional and eye-catching.

Top *Houseleek is a useful plant for soothing skin irritations.*

Above *Pot marigolds are picked for drying before they have a chance to go over.*

Plan for an apothecary's garden

This garden of medicinal plants is based on the old idea of individual plots for each herb, but simplified and brought up to date by setting the herbs among paving slabs. The plan is uncomplicated by the need to lay paths, or put in edgings. All that is required is a level, completely weed-free site, some paving slabs and a base of sand and cement to bed them into. The design will fit a space of 4.5 x 6 m (15 x 19 ft).

Key to planting plan

1. *Calendula officinalis* – pot marigold – for soothing creams
2. *Sempervivum tectorum* – houseleek – for chapped skin and insect bites
3. *Myrtus communis* – myrtle – for sinusitis and bronchial infections
4. *Foeniculum officinalis* – fennel – for indigestion
5. *Marrubium vulgare* – horehound – for coughs
6. *Tanacetum parthenium* – feverfew – for migraines
7. *Salvia officinalis* – sage – for mouth and gum infections
8. *Lavandula stoechas* – lavender – for tension headaches
9. *Rosmarinus officinalis* – rosemary - for colds and depression
10. *Thymus vulgaris* – thyme – for sore throats
11. *Origanum onites* – pot marjoram – for arthritis
12. *Allium sativum* – garlic – for warding off colds
13. *Valeriana officinalis* – valerian – for insomnia
14. *Hypericum perforatum* – St John's wort – for anxiety and nervous tension

Boundaries

A herb garden with its own distinct boundaries becomes a secluded retreat, a place to sit and relax away from the pressures of the outside world. The key point is that the enclosing wall, fence or hedge does not have to be very solid, or even high – so as not to cast too much shade, which is usually better for gardens. It is the illusion of a place apart that counts, which can be achieved just as effectively with a low balustrade fence or plant-clothed pergola. And even a low division still provides some shelter, reduces the wind-chill factor and helps to retain and intensify the fragrance of the plants.

Above *A simple construction of posts and cross-rails divides areas of a kitchen garden.*

Above *Trelliswork, in the foreground, makes an effective internal division in a secluded garden bounded by a wall and plant-clothed walkway.*

A garden entirely enclosed by high brick walls enjoys its own warm microclimate. But in order not to be overpowering it has to cover a reasonably large area, as in the walled kitchen gardens of the grand houses of the past. In the smaller gardens of today, it is sometimes possible to make use of a high brick wall as one boundary, but other internal walls are best kept to a height of about 60 cm–1 m (2–3 ft).

Fences are a useful way to provide an instant screen and come in a wide range of materials. Choose one that is sympathetic to the overall style of your herb garden. A simple balustrade fence can work very well, or a traditional picket fence, popular in many American herb gardens: these are often painted white, but also look good with a green or blue finish. Wattle or wicker screens, as used in medieval enclosures, are another congenial fencing material.

Trelliswork, also known as treillage, makes a versatile boundary. It adds elegance and romance and works in formal or informal settings. Trellis comes in different patterns, may be painted in a range of colours and provides a frame for climbing plants. It is important, as for all fences, that the support posts are solid and firmly installed. The easiest and longest- lasting method of securing posts is to bed them into a custom-made pointed metal base set into the ground, or set them into a rubble and concrete base. Timber posts should be treated with preservative – choose one that does not harm plants. (If you use creosote, planting must be delayed for a year, as it can harm plants.)

Pergolas are another way of making a visual boundary, rather than a solid screen, and will suit a small garden as well as a large one. A covered or semi-covered walkway, clothed in plants, was a traditional feature of many 17th-century gardens and it was usually called an "arbour" or "herber". Strictly speaking a pergola should be constructed as a double row to form an arched walkway with a curved or rectangular top. But it can also be made as a single row of posts and cross-rails, to act as a support for climbers and to make an internal fence or division.

Espaliered fruit trees trained flat against a system of posts with wires strained horizontally between them provide an openwork, living screen as a boundary or division. They can be planted in a single row or a double one to form a walk. They also look good trained against a wall. Plant as young trees, removing any side shoots and training the branches along the wires as they grow.

Hedging Plants

Hedges make the ideal boundary for many herb gardens. They divide different areas and delineate paths. They may be formally clipped, or left to a more natural pattern of growth, and reach different heights to provide a high dense screen or a low division. Low, clipped hedges form knot-garden patterns. Choose from a selection of the following:

- *Taxus baccata* – Yew. Slow-growing, but makes a superb screen and its dark green provides a foil for many plants.
- *Buxus sempervirens* – Box. Makes an excellent hedge for a neat, clipped finish. Formal hedges – low to medium height.
- *Buxus sempervirens* 'Suffruticosa' – Dwarf box. Much more compact than the common box, ideal for knot gardens.
- *Santolina chamaecyparissus* – Cotton lavender. A silver plant which responds well to clipping into mounds or low hedges.
- *Teucrium chamaedrys* – Wall germander. The dark-green foliage needs frequent trimming to keep it in shape. Can be grown as an informal hedge and left to flower.
- *Origanum vulgare* 'Aureum' – Golden marjoram. Although it can be clipped to form mounds, its relaxed habit of growth makes it less suitable as a conventional formal hedge.
- *Rosmarinus officinalis* – Rosemary. Can be clipped to a squared-off hedge shape, or trimmed as an informal hedge.
- *Rosa rugosa* – Rose. This forms a dense, impenetrable barrier of medium to full height.
- *Artemisia abrotanum* – Southernwood. Light-green, feathery foliage makes a delightful informal hedge that needs trimming only once or twice a year.
- *Hyssopus officinalis* – Hyssop. It is possible to clip this to a formal shape, but the blue flower spikes make it worth growing in its natural form, lightly trimmed. Cut back in the spring.
- *Lavandula* spp. – Lavender. There are different heights to choose from. Makes a fragrant hedge, needing little attention, apart from cutting back firmly (but not into old wood) after flowering.

Planting a hedge

1 Dig out a shallow trench along the line of the proposed hedge and fork over the soil at the base of it to ensure good drainage.

2 Add plenty of garden compost, digging it lightly into the soil, and just before planting, fork in a sprinkling of blood, fish and bone organic fertilizer, wearing gloves and a respirator mask.

3 Mark the centre line of the hedge with string and pegs, put in the plants, spacing them evenly by using a measured length of wood – 23 cm (9 in) apart is suitable for most. Fill in the soil, firming it around each plant, and water.

4 The hedge will soon become established, ready for its first trim in the second year. Give it a mulch of compost in subsequent years or add a little organic fertilizer to the soil, watering it in.

Above *Rosemary forms a good hedge-like boundary in this enclosed herb garden.*

Focal Points

The design of the herb garden will be stronger and have more impact with the inclusion of focal points to draw the eye. They may be in a central position or at the end of a path or vista. A sundial is a traditional feature in many herb gardens. Birdbaths and fountains introduce the soothing element of water. A stone urn overflowing with trailing or flowering herbs is always a simple but effective centrepiece, and standard topiary trees in tubs make versatile and movable points of interest.

An arbour, in the sense of a covered seat or shelter, strikes just the right note in an ornamental herb garden. It provides a focal point as well as being a frame for climbing plants, and introduces the all-important dimension of height. At the same time it adds a hint of mystery and makes a secluded place to sit and enjoy the sights and scents of the surroundings. Sited at the end of a walk, in a far corner or high vantage point, it becomes an inevitable attraction that has to be visited. Arbours may be constructed from many types of materials including posts and rails, trellis, metal frames, or, for a more rustic look, wickerwork.

Archways can be sited to emphasize an important feature, such as a statue, within the garden itself, or to frame a distant view .

Right *The elegant façade of a distant house is framed by an archway of roses.*

Opposite *A fountain makes an attractive centrepiece in a sheltered garden.*

Below *A water-lily pond provides the focal point in the centre of a cloister herb garden.*

planning
the crops

For most vegetable growers, the ultimate goal is their produce: they want to grow the best possible vegetables. In order to achieve this, the gardener needs to plan his or her crops very carefully, especially if lack of time and the size of garden are possible limitations. There is little point in taking on a large kitchen garden if you cannot maintain it and, similarly, it is inadvisable to expect large harvests from a small plot of ground.

However, with planning and a careful use of space and time, a surprising amount can be grown. Some parts of the planning stage are largely aesthetic, but others will influence the quantity and quality of your crops. Techniques such as crop rotation, successional cropping and intercropping are particularly important in this context.

One of the first decisions to be made is whether to grow the vegetables in rows or in blocks. There are advantages and disadvantages to both systems, and in the end it is really a question of personal choice.

The consideration of all these factors will eventually become second nature to you. The experienced gardener does not have to think twice about them, but if you are approaching kitchen gardening for the first time, it is important to think about them carefully.

RIGHT This kitchen garden has been packed with vegetables. No rows are left unfilled and the spaces between them have been mulched with grass clippings to keep the weeds at bay and to prevent the evaporation of water.

While it is important to get pleasure out of a vegetable garden by arranging it in a pleasing and attractive style, it is equally important to remember that there is a range of practical considerations to be borne in mind when you are planning how to group your crops.

What do you want to grow?

The first factor is, of course, deciding what crops you want to grow. If no one in the family likes beetroot (beets), do you really want to grow them, even if they do look attractive? If space is short should you be growing something else that will be eaten? Potatoes are comparatively inexpensive from greengrocers and farm shops, and, since they take up a lot of space, is it worth your while growing them? If you really want to grow potatoes, perhaps you could compromise and grow a few earlies for that wonderful flavour that only potatoes cooked straight from the soil have, but buy in your maincrop, which will probably not taste all that different from those you would grow yourself.

It is also worth thinking carefully about how much of each crop you need to grow. Go by what you need and not by the quantity of seed in the packet. It is easy, for example, to plant out all the runner bean seeds you have bought only to find that the plants that result will produce far more beans than you could ever eat. Balance the space available against what you want to grow and the quantities that you will require of each. This leads on to the fact that you

BELOW Rows of spring onions (scallions) have been alternated here with rows of carrots. This is a traditional way of deterring carrot root fly and is effective because the strong smell of the onions masks that of the carrots.

should sow only to meet your immediate requirements. There really is no point in sowing a whole row of lettuce if you get round to eating only a few of them before they have bolted (run to seed). It is better to sow a third of a row now and another third in a couple of week's time and so on, in order to get a succession of vegetables rather than a glut which you probably won't be able to consume.

ABOVE **This small raised bed is not only decorative but very productive, and demonstrates just how much can be grown in a small garden.**

Designing the beds

Once you have decided what to grow, there is the layout to consider. Most gardeners use the traditional way of growing their plants in rows, but blocks are becoming more popular. One of the advantages of this method is that more plants can be grown in a single area, and it is thus ideal for a garden where space is limited.

Crop rotation is another important consideration. Gardeners have long known that it is not a good idea to grow the same crop on the same ground in successive years, and so the crops are "rotated". This is not difficult to achieve, but it does mean that if you are designing a decorative garden you cannot use the same design for two consecutive years unless you use different plants.

Allowing for more permanent plants

A point to consider when planning the layout is that some crops will remain in the ground over winter. It is rare to start off with a completely bare plot each spring. Sprouting broccoli, for example, will still be growing until late spring, while plants such as garlic and broad (fava) beans, planted in late autumn or early winter, will be there until summer. Remember to allow for these crops when you draw up your plan. Fruit trees and bushes also need a permanent position, as do some vegetables such as rhubarb that are not moved for years.

Crop Rotation

Crop rotation has been practised by farmers and gardeners for generations as a simple and effective precaution against pests and diseases. The basic idea is that if you grow the same type of plant on the same patch of ground every year, the soil will harbour pests and diseases from one season to the next. If you move the crop to another piece of ground, the pests and diseases will lose their host and will die out.

ABOVE **In a four-year rotation, courgettes (zucchini) would be grown in plot three. Alternatively, they can be grown on a compost heap.**

The practical side of this philosophy is the division of the vegetable garden into four or five areas. The different types of crops – brassicas, beans and so on – are moved from one plot to another so that they return to the same piece of ground only every fourth year.

For four-year crop rotation, the crops are divided into four groups – the fifth bed is used for the permanent plants, which obviously do not move. Look at the list of vegetables that you wish to grow for the coming year and divide them into their various groups. Allocate planting areas to each. Do the same for the following year, but move all the crops to another plot. If space is limited, a three-year rotation is better than nothing.

BELOW **Globe artichokes stay in the ground for several years, so they are grown in a permanent plot and do not form part of the rotation plan.**

Four-Year Crop Rotation

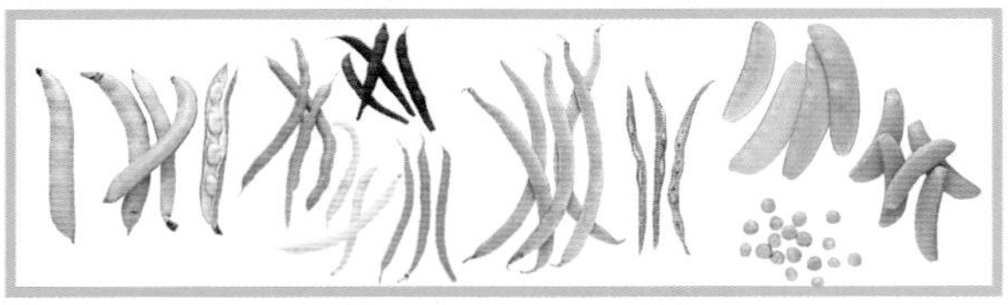

Plot 1
Peas
Broad (fava) beans
French (green) beans
Runner beans

Plot 2
Cabbages
Brussels sprouts
Calabrese (Italian sprouting broccoli)
Broccoli
Kale
Radishes
Swedes (rutabaga or yellow turnips)
Turnips
Kohl rabi

Plot 3
Bulb onions
Spring onions (scallions)
Shallots
Leeks
Garlic
Sweet corn (corn)
Marrows (zucchini), squashes and pumpkins
Lettuce

Plot 4
Potatoes
Parsnips
Beetroot (beets)
Carrots
Salsify
Scorzonera
Celery
Celeriac (celery root)
Tomatoes

Plot 5 (permanent)
Rhubarb
Asparagus
Perennial herbs
Globe artichokes
Jerusalem artichokes
Seakale

Four-Year Crop Rotation

In many gardens, the differentiation between the plots is hardly discernible, but it makes life easier to split the garden into individual plots.

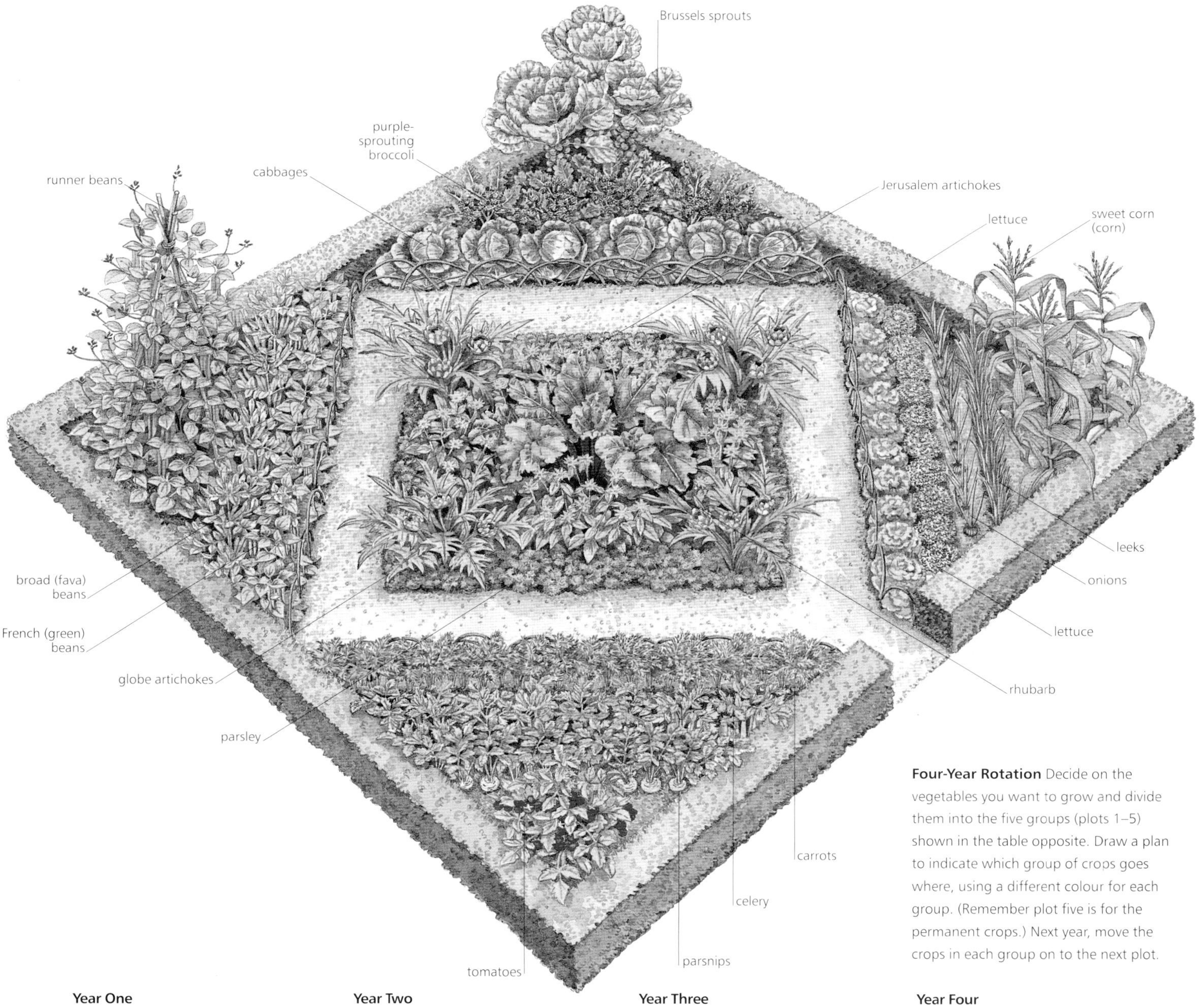

Four-Year Rotation Decide on the vegetables you want to grow and divide them into the five groups (plots 1–5) shown in the table opposite. Draw a plan to indicate which group of crops goes where, using a different colour for each group. (Remember plot five is for the permanent crops.) Next year, move the crops in each group on to the next plot.

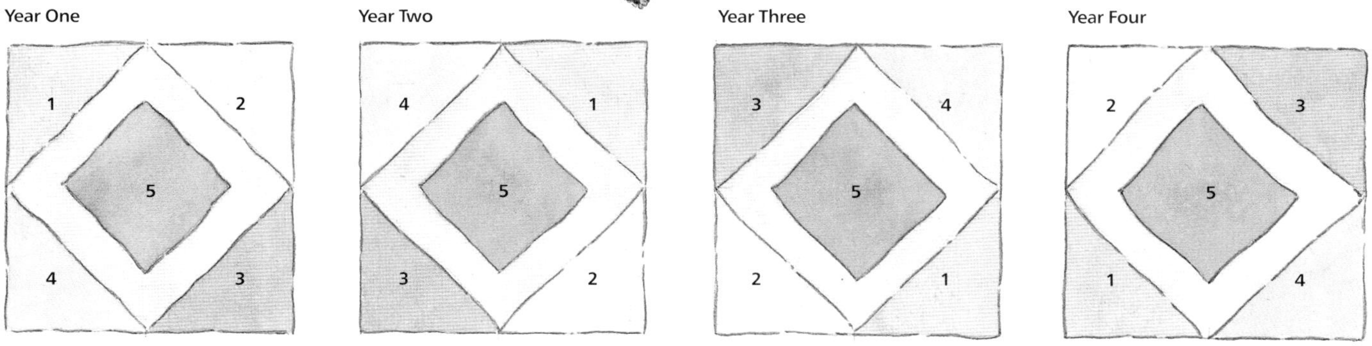

Three-Year Crop Rotation

This is a more conventional method of dividing up the garden into separate plots, keeping each group of plants together for rotating.

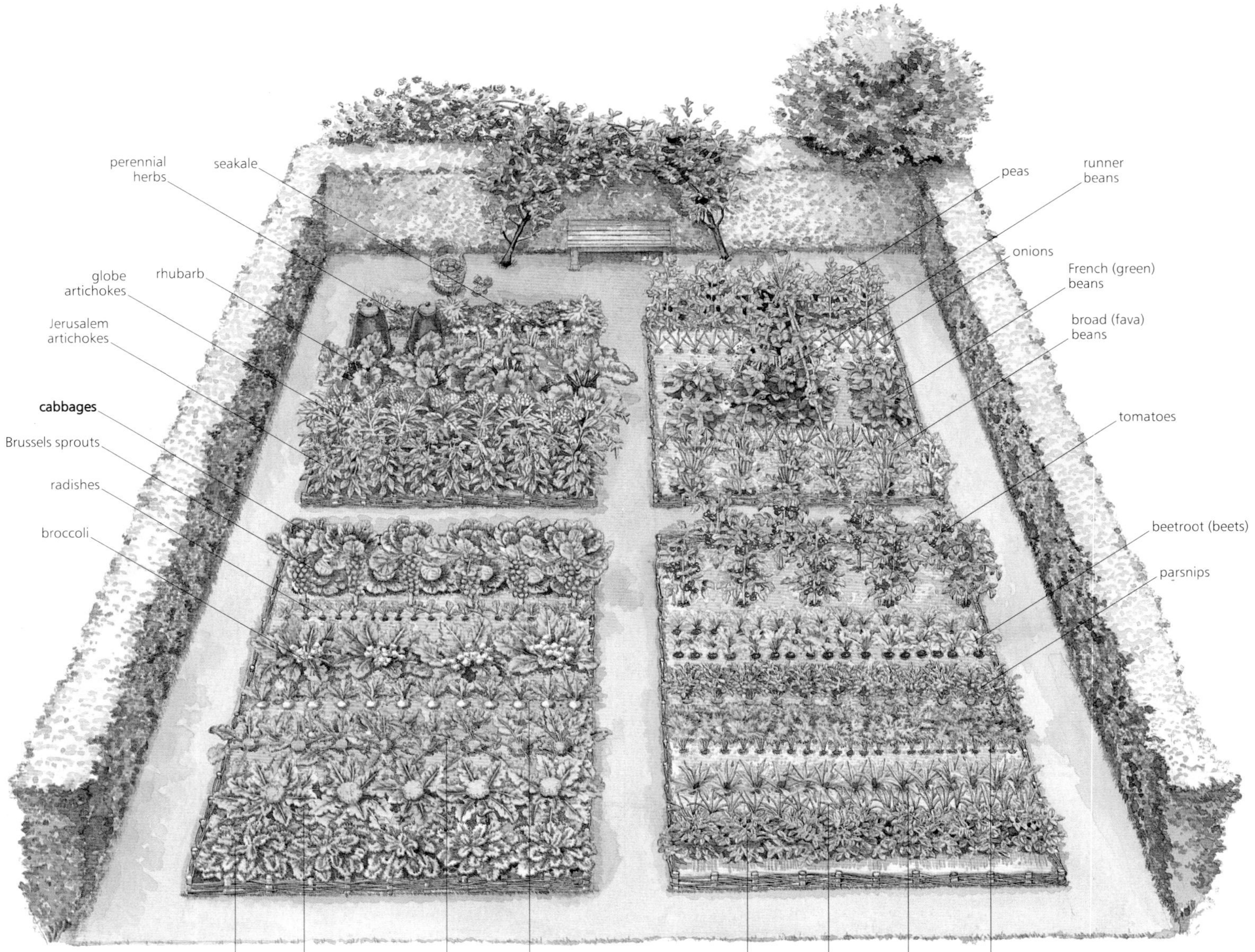

Three-Year Rotation
Decide on the vegetables you want to grow and divide into the four groups (plots 1–4) shown in the table opposite. Draw a plan to indicate which group of crops goes where, using a different colour for each group. (Remember plot four is for permanent crops.) Move the crops in each group to the next plot the following year.

Year One

Year Two

Year Three

Three-Year Crop Rotation

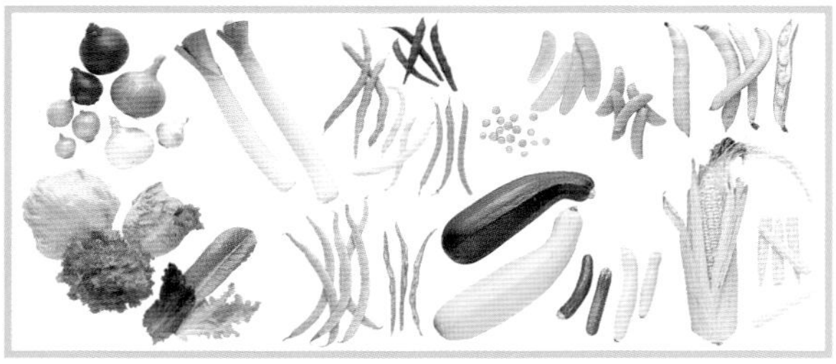

Plot 1
- Peas
- Broad (fava) beans
- French (green) beans
- Runner beans
- Bulb onions
- Leeks
- Sweet corn (corn)
- Marrows (zucchini), squashes and pumpkins
- Lettuce

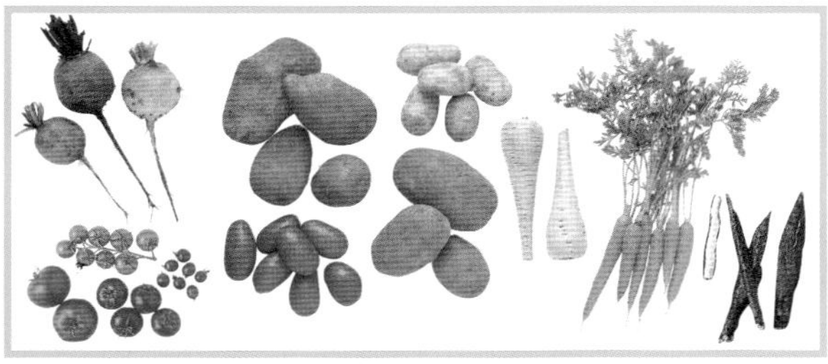

Plot 2
- Potatoes
- Parsnips
- Beetroot (beets)
- Carrots
- Salsify
- Scorzonera
- Tomatoes

Plot 3
- Cabbages
- Brussels sprouts
- Calabrese (Italian sprouting broccoli)
- Broccoli
- Kale
- Swede (rutabaga or yellow turnips)
- Turnips
- Kohl rabi
- Radishes

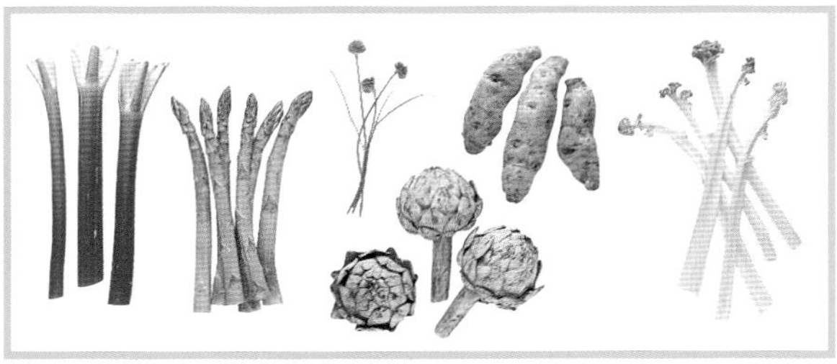

Plot 4 (permanent)
- Rhubarb
- Asparagus
- Perennial herbs
- Globe artichokes
- Jerusalem artichokes
- Seakale

ABOVE **In a three-year crop rotation, tomatoes are grown in plot two, along with root crops such as parsnips and carrots.**

ABOVE **Rhubarb is planted in the permanent bed when crops are rotated, and can stay in the same position for up to 25 years.**

As well as having advantages in terms of pests and diseases, there are other reasons for moving crops around. Some crops will tolerate newly manured ground while others cannot. Thus, one plot can be heavily manured when it is dug in the autumn during the first year and cabbages and related plants can be planted in it in spring. In the following year the plot is simply dug, and the root crops, which do not like the soil too rich, are planted there.

Strict crop rotation is not the easiest of things to maintain. Many gardeners start off with good intentions and manage it for a few years, but gradually things begin to slip. Some brassicas that have been left in the ground over winter may block the space that is required for some other plants, or perhaps a few plants have been slipped in to fill a gap. Leaving plants in the ground until the following year so that you can collect your own seeds also plays havoc with rotation if you have only a small amount of space. If you find this happening, there is no need to worry.

In a small kitchen garden, crop rotation, although it is admirable in theory, is not that important in practice. One of the main difficulties is the amount of space required to put strict rotation into effect. In agricultural situations the crops are fields apart; even in a large garden, the distances involved can be quite large. In a small garden, however, it is often impossible to get the plots far enough apart for the pests or diseases not to be able to find their host plant. The other problem is that, in practice, four years is not always long enough to kill off all the diseases anyway.

This does not mean that crop rotation is unimportant, however, because it still has some effect. Yet it does mean that you should not lose any sleep if you are not able to follow the sequence to the exact letter. Most gardeners do not grow the same crop on the same ground for two years running in any case – with the exception of plants such as runner beans – but they do not follow strict crop rotation.

Rows

Vegetables have traditionally been grown in rows. Although some gardeners challenge the claims made for this method, suggesting that blocks and deep beds are better, rows are probably still the most widely used system.

The basic idea is simple: the vegetables are grown in a single line, with some crops, such as beans and peas, being grown in a double line. The lines or rows are separated by a distance somewhat wider than the breadth of the plants, so that there is bare earth between the rows. This bare earth acts as a path, allowing access for maintenance, such as weeding and watering, as well as for harvesting.

Growing vegetables in rows is an attractive way of producing them. The varying heights, shapes, textures and colours all show up well, with the rows looking like decorative ribbons stretched across the garden. Their appearance is not, however, the principal reason for growing vegetables in this way. There are practical considerations, too.

Access is one of the important benefits provided by individual rows. The paths between the rows allow the gardener to move freely among the plants without having to stretch. Each plant can be examined for condition as well as for pests and diseases. Pests have less chance of being overlooked if the plant can be clearly seen from at least two sides, and individual plants can be tended to if necessary. The bases of the plants can be easily seen for inspection, weeding and watering.

Another advantage is that there is plenty of air circulating among the plants, which helps considerably to reduce mildew-type diseases. The plants generally have plenty of space in which to develop, and the leaves are able to open out to receive the maximum amount of light. Finally, rows are easy to cover with the majority of cloches available.

Needless to say there are also disadvantages. The use of so many "paths" means that a lot of space is unproductive when you look at the plot as a whole, an important factor in a small garden, where space is limited. Another disadvantage is that the paths allow light to reach the soil, so increasing the number of weeds that germinate, although this is offset to some extent by the ease with which it is possible to hoe. With constant use, the paths become compacted, which does not help the soil structure. Although the whole bed will be dug each year, because it is so large it is necessary to walk over it

LEFT **Traditional rows of vegetables, filling all the available space, can be very decorative.**

while the ground is being prepared, again adding a certain degree of compaction. Constant hoeing will help overcome this by breaking up the soil and keeping it aerated. However, in dry weather, hoeing should be avoided as it encourages water loss. An alternative is to lay planks of wood between the rows. This not only helps to prevent soil compaction but also acts as a mulch which will help retain the moisture in the soil as well as keep weeds down.

ABOVE **The decorative quality of vegetables can be clearly seen in these rows. All the leaves are green and yet the variety of greens and the shapes of the leaves form a very attractive picture over a long season.**

LEFT **It is important to leave plenty of space for young plants to fill out. Rows with plenty of space between them also allow for access and easy weeding.**

Blocks and Deep Beds

Growing vegetables in blocks as opposed to rows is an old method that more or less dropped out of use in many countries but that has been reintroduced in recent years. The basic idea is to grow the plants in a square or rectangle, say five plants wide by five plants deep, rather than in a single row.

ABOVE **These blocks of contrasting lettuces have been planted in deep beds that are almost flush with the ground. The beds have been dug deeply rather than built up.**

RIGHT **Each of these blocks of vegetables and herbs is about 1.2m/4ft wide, which allows access from the paths running across the plot.**

The vegetable plot is divided into smaller plots, each about 1.2m/4ft across and spanning the width of the main plot. These smaller beds are permanent, unlike rows, and between each is a path, either trodden earth or more substantial paving slabs or bricks. The width of the smaller beds is determined by the gardener's reach – 1.2m/4ft should allow access of about 60cm/24in from each side so that the entire bed can be reached without compacting the soil. Keeping off the beds means that the soil structure is always kept in top condition.

Some gardeners simply dig the soil in the existing plot, adding organic material to it as they go. Others prefer to create a deep bed system, either by digging deeper, using a double digging method, or by raising the height of the bed with boards or a low wall and then adding a mixture of good loam and organic material. The bed is worked from the path so that the soil is never compacted.

The advantage of a rich soil in good condition is that it will support more plants, and so most gardeners plant much more closely than in the conventional rows. This means that productivity is improved considerably, and many more plants can be raised from the same area of ground. As well as being productive, close planting also means that weed seeds have little chance of germinating.

A solid block of plants, however, makes it more difficult to get at any weeds, as well as making it harder to see if there are any pests and diseases lurking below the leaves. Because the plants are close together, there is likely to be less air circulating than around vegetables grown in rows, and this increases the possibility of diseases that like damp conditions with stagnant air. It is also not as easy to water the base of individual plants. Watering can, in fact, become erratic, with some areas ending up drier than others as water runs off the leaves. Another disadvantage is that it is not as easy to cover the vegetables with cloches, and although it is, of course, possible to construct a cover, this will not be as mobile as individual cloches.

You can take advantage of both methods by using deep beds, with their rich soil conditions, and planting short rows across the beds instead of blocks. This method works well for those gardeners who feel that digging destroys the structure of the soil. They dig the soil initially, adding plenty of organic material, but thereafter only top-dress the surface with more organic material, perhaps hoeing it in or allowing the worms to move it below the surface. Although this benefits the soil, most gardeners prefer the more traditional method of digging at least once a year because this has other advantages.

LEFT **Boards create a greater depth of fertile soil, so vegetables can be planted much closer together.**

Intercropping

There can be few gardeners who have enough space to grow everything they wish, and this is particularly true of those with small gardens. One way partly to overcome the problem is to make sure that every available piece of land is in use and to avoid letting ground lie idle.

There are two main ways to ensure that the land is used efficiently. The first is to plant quick-growing crops among slower ones so that the former have been harvested before the latter have grown sufficiently to fill the space. Brussels sprouts, for example, are planted at anything up to 75cm/30in apart, depending on the size of the variety. For several weeks after they have been planted there is a lot of empty space around each plant. This can be filled with a crop such as lettuce or radishes that takes only a short while to come to maturity.

Some plants, however, cannot be planted out in the early part of the season, and rather than leave the ground empty, it can be filled with a temporary crop. For example, a bed of lettuces can be planted and the first ones to be harvested can be replaced by young sweet corn (corn), the rest of the lettuces being harvested as the corn develops.

A similar idea can be used with station-sown seeds. For example, parsnip seeds can be sown in groups of three at, say, 23cm/9in intervals. In between each group a few radishes can be sown. This method has advantages in that not only will the quick-growing radishes make use of the ground before the parsnips need it, but, because parsnips are slow to germinate, the radishes will actually mark the row, making it easier to hoe off any weeds without disturbing the parsnips, which are still below ground.

Another aspect of intercropping is purely decorative. A simple example is to intercrop red-leaved lettuces with green ones. To create these effects, it is best to raise the plants in trays or modules and plant them out in a pattern when they are large enough.

When you are intercropping for visual effects, take care in the choice of neighbours. There is little point in planting decorative lettuces next to potatoes, which will eventually flop over and smother them. However, from the productive point of view it is a good idea to plant lettuces between rows of potatoes before the latter have emerged or have reached any height, because the lettuces will be cropped before the ground is smothered by the potato leaves.

BELOW **Intercropping carrots with lettuces – here a tinted variety known as 'Nelson' – makes for a very decorative effect.**

ABOVE **Here, a short row of radishes is being sown between individual cabbages. They will crop long before the cabbages have grown large enough to cover them.**

ABOVE **As an alternative to sowing, individual lettuces can be planted between slow-growing plants such as cabbages.**

Successional Crops

Closely related to the question of intercropping is that of successional sowing and planting. The idea behind this is to phase the crops so that your plot provides a continuous stream of produce and not a series of sudden gluts. In other words, this is another method of ensuring that you get the most out of your ground.

Many gardeners have a tendency to sow a complete row right across their plot, whether they need that amount of produce or not, simply because a whole row looks better than a short one. This can be wasteful, because two-thirds of the row may bolt before you have consumed it and then you are left with nothing. It is far better to sow a third of a row of, say, spinach, wait two or three weeks and then sow another third and finally the last section two or three weeks later still. This means that the crops will reach maturity at two- to three-week intervals, spreading out so that you have spinach for two months or more rather than for the two to three weeks that would have been the case if you had sown the whole row at once.

Another way of securing a succession of crops is to choose varieties that mature at different times. Peas, for example, are classified into first earlies and maincrop types, and within these groups some varieties produce peas sooner than others. Choosing several different varieties rather than just one will provide a much longer harvesting season.

The same principle is true of fruit. Choosing different varieties of raspberries, for example, will enable you to harvest fruit from early summer right through to late autumn. This also applies to strawberries, apples and many other types of fruit.

There may, of course, be times when you do not want to spread the harvesting. For example, if you like to freeze vegetables for winter use it is easier if, for example, all your peas mature at once so that you can quickly freeze them and replant the ground with another crop of something else – late turnips perhaps. Vegetables that all crop at once are usually marked in the seed catalogues as being suitable for freezing.

If you are creating a vegetable garden as a decorative feature as well as a productive one, successional sowing and planting becomes doubly important. Any crop removed, whether it is a single lettuce or a row or a wigwam (tepee) of peas will leave a gap and the sooner it is filled the better the garden will look.

Both from the productive and the visual point of view it is always worthwhile having a few plants coming along in pots ready to plant out. Lettuce, Swiss chard and parsley, for example, can be sown at two-week intervals in modules to provide a good supply of plants to fill the gaps.

Another aspect of successional cropping is replacing one crop with another as soon as it is finished. Thus, replant the ground occupied by broad (fava) beans with a late crop of leeks as the beans are finished or plant out spring cabbage in the space that becomes available when the onions are harvested. Keep the ground producing for you even if you only sow green manure, which is dug back into the soil later in the year.

RIGHT **Some crops are better planted at intervals so that they do not all mature at the same time. To facilitate this, it is often easier to fill long rows with several different types of vegetables rather than leave gaps to be sown later.**

greenhouses

sheds and equipment

Considering the large number of tools and equipment that is now available from the average garden centre, the gardener can actually get by with buying surprisingly few of them, as long as they are chosen carefully and with a view to what is actually needed. Starting a vegetable garden need not be a costly business.

You do not, for example, have to invest in a large greenhouse or in cold frames, although a shed will prove useful if you do not want to perform unhygienic gardening tasks in the kitchen. A wheelbarrow is the only mechanical device that most gardeners will require although many may use a rotavator (rototiller) for digging larger plots. There are also many excellent second-hand tools to be had, very often at a fraction of the price of new ones that may be of an inferior quality, so it is worth spending a little time on finding the best tools.

ABOVE **Greenhouses are available in a variety of shapes and sizes, which means that you should be able to find one to suit your garden.**

In many ways gardening is a very personal hobby and no more so than in the choice of tools and other equipment. Everybody has their favourite selection of tools and feels lost if, for example, they are working in someone else's garden without these items.

What do you really need?

Life is much easier in the garden if you have items such as a wheelbarrow, but bear in mind that, in a small garden, you can grow an extra couple of plants in the space needed to store it. Indeed, most things, such as weeds and compost, can be carried in a bucket in small-scale gardening.

One of the problems with owning a lot of tools and equipment is that you need somewhere to keep them, and that means there is even less garden for growing once you have erected the requisite shed. The advantage of having just a few hand tools is that they will usually fit into the back of the garage or even under the stairs in the house. Once you own a large rotavator (rototiller), no one will be pleased when it is trundled across the carpet to put it away or its sharp tines scratch the side of the car as you try to manoeuvre it into and out of a tightly packed garage.

Once you start to use a rotavator (rototiller) your gardening will be on a scale that usually means having a shed devoted to tools, and you may want to consider having a combined tool and potting shed – it should be a simple matter to put a bench down one side of a tool shed. Having a potting shed may seem to be rather an old-fashioned idea, but once you have had one you will find it difficult to manage without. However, it is not essential, and many successful gardeners manage quite well without one.

Do you need a greenhouse or cold frame?

Just as a handful of tools are all that you need to get started, it is also not essential to have a greenhouse and cold frames. There is no doubt that such structures are useful and will make your life much easier in many ways, but they are expensive in terms of both cost and space – and also in terms of the

time you will spend in them if you have only a limited number of hours available for gardening. In any case, most of the things that you will do in a greenhouse can be carried out elsewhere. Any propagation, for example, that is necessary can be done on the kitchen windowsill (as long as the cook is sympathetic), while tomatoes and cucumbers, which are the most common greenhouse crops, can be grown in the open, even if it means they crop later.

If, however, you intend to garden on a large scale and do wish to invest in a greenhouse, then bear in mind that the design is very much a matter of personal preference. Often your choice of greenhouse will be dictated by what you can comfortably fit into the available space in your garden as much as by its aesthetic appeal. In spite of the wide variety of greenhouses now on the market, there is still ample scope for the keen amateur to design and build a greenhouse suited to his or her own specifications and requirements. If you are not that practically minded, however, and do not want to go to the expense of buying a greenhouse, you might like to consider using polythene (plastic) tunnels instead. Although not very attractive, these tunnels are a cheap and practical alternative to the traditional greenhouse.

ABOVE **A small vegetable and herb garden such as this does not require a large battery of tools.**

BELOW **Terracotta pots, which are used for blanching seakale and other vegetables, such as endives, make striking ornaments in the garden.**

Greenhouses

The ultimate goal of most gardeners is to have a greenhouse, for it extends the possibilities of the garden tremendously. Such a structure can be used for propagation, for growing tender or winter crops and for overwintering plants that cannot be safely left outside. There is a fourth, often unspoken, use and that is to keep the gardener dry and warm in winter.

Most of the horticultural operations that are done in a greenhouse can be achieved perfectly satisfactorily in cold frames. Most gardeners, however, prefer to carry them out in the warmth and comfort of the greenhouse, rather than bending over a cold frame in a cold or wet wind.

Choosing a greenhouse

As with any equipment, the first thing to consider are your reasons for making the purchase. Why do you want a greenhouse? What are you going to do with it? This is an important stage, because answering these questions will help to determine the size. Cost and the available space will also obviously influence the size, but if possible, make use the prime consideration. Most gardeners, slightly tongue in cheek, will tell you to work out the size and then double it. There is some truth in this old saw, and many, if not most, gardeners wish that they had bought a larger greenhouse than the one they did. So buy larger rather than smaller if you possibly can.

Material

These days the choice is mainly between wood and aluminium, although it is still possible to find old0 wood. For most gardeners the choice is simply an aluminium frame, because it is the cheapest style available, but there are other factors to be taken into consideration. For example, wooden greenhouses are far more attractive than aluminium ones. However, although they usually fit more sympathetically into the garden, they are more expensive and the upkeep is more time-consuming. Wooden greenhouses are slightly warmer in winter. It is possible to make your own, working to your own design and dimensions.

Aluminium greenhouses are cheap and easy to maintain. The cheaper ones may, however, be rather flimsy, and in exposed positions the sides may flex and the glass fall out! They normally come in standard sizes, but because they are modular, there is a choice of the number of windows and their position. Some companies will build to your specifications, but this is obviously a more expensive option. It is now possible to buy aluminium greenhouses where the frame is painted, which partially disguises the aluminium.

Glass can now be replaced with plastic. Most gardeners prefer the traditional material, but if there are children around it is often more sensible to go for plastic on safety grounds.

Digging in

The old-fashioned idea of sinking the green-

ABOVE **The marigolds planted with a row of tomatoes in this greenhouse will ward off potential pests, a technique known as companion planting.**

BELOW **This standard straight-sided greenhouse is made of aluminium, but it has been painted green, rather than being left silver, so that it blends in better with the colours of the garden.**

RIGHT **An unusually shaped greenhouse with a steeply pitched roof that not only looks different from conventional greenhouses, but has the added advantage that the steep sides absorb the low winter sun more easily.**

IMPERIAL GREENHOUSE
ROBINSONS
FIRST AVENUE

LEFT It is vital not to let greenhouses over-heat. Opening the windows at the right time is not always possible if you are not at home during the hottest part of the day, but automatic window-openers will do the job for you.

house into the ground is a good one as long as you can overcome any drainage problems. Steps lead down to the door, and on to a central aisle, dug out of the soil. The side benches are laid on the natural soil level and the roof springs from a low wall on the ground. The advantage of this system, apart from the fact that it is relatively cheap, is that the soil acts as a vast storage heater. Gardeners using such a greenhouse find that as long as they provide some form of insulation, no heat is required to overwinter tender plants. Traditionally, a wooden framework would have been used for the roof, but aluminium would do just as well.

Shape

The shape of the greenhouse is a matter of personal preference. Traditional styles have vertical sides, but some new ones have sloping sides, which allow in more light – especially useful during winter when the sun is low or if you have trays of seedlings on the floor.

Octagonal greenhouses are suitable for small sites, and many people find them more decorative than the traditional shapes. Because they are almost round, the "aisle" is just a central standing area, thus saving a lot of wasted space. However, the amount of useful space is still quite small.

Lean-to greenhouses can be built against walls, which not only saves space but also makes use of the warmth that is usually found in the wall, especially house walls. These are obviously much cheaper than a full greenhouse, but the amount of useful space within them is limited because the light does not come from all directions and plants can get drawn. Painting the wall white helps because more light is reflected back onto the plants.

Ventilation

When you buy a greenhouse, make sure that it has as many opening windows as you can afford because the free passage of air through the structure is of the utmost importance. Stagnant air in a greenhouse is a killer, as all kinds of fungal diseases are

ABOVE Insulating the greenhouse is important during the cold winter months, helping to keep heating costs down as well as preventing any violent fluctuations in temperature. Polythene (plastic) bubble insulation is cheap and efficient.

LEFT Some plants, such as peppers, grow better in a greenhouse than they do outside in the open air. In a greenhouse, they are assured of a constant temperature and humidity.

LEFT **It is important to keep the sun out of the greenhouse during the hottest part of the year. Shading helps to keep the temperature down and also protects the plants from the scorching effects of the sun.**

likely to develop very quickly. Openings can either be covered with conventional windows or with louvres. If you are away during daylight hours in summer, the time when windows need to be opened on hot days, automatic openers can be used. The mechanism opens the windows as soon as a specified pre-set temperature is reached. Having a door at each end helps on larger houses. In winter, windows should be left open as much as possible, and, when it is necessary to close them, use a fan to keep the air circulating.

Heating

There are various methods of heating a greenhouse, but one of the most versatile is with electricity. Although the cost per unit of heat may be greater, the control of its output through the use of thermostats is such that no heat (or money) is wasted, because the appliance comes on only when the temperature drops below a certain point. Thermostatically controlled gas heaters are also now becoming available. Paraffin heaters are cheap, but they need to be regularly filled and maintained and they produce large amounts of water vapour, which encourages disease unless the greenhouse is ventilated.

Heating bills can be reduced by insulating the greenhouse. Double glazing is the ultimate but is expensive. A cheaper alternative is to line the house with sheets of clear polythene (plastic), preferably containing air bubbles. If you have only a few plants that need protecting, it is cheaper to close off one end of the greenhouse with polythene and heat just this area. If the number of plants is small enough, a heated propagator or a cloche over a heated bench may be sufficient.

Shading

Greenhouses need to be as light as possible, especially during the winter, but at the same time bright sunshine should be kept out as this will raise the temperature too much. It is possible to buy shade netting, which can be draped over the outside or clipped to the inside of the glass. This is easy to remove in overcast periods. An opaque wash applied to the glass reduces the effect of the sun considerably, but it is time-consuming to keep removing it during dull weather, so it is usually left in place from early summer to mid-autumn. There is one form of wash that becomes transparent when it rains, thus letting in more light.

Fittings

The full height of the greenhouse is needed for tomatoes and cucumbers, which can be grown in growing bags on the floor. Benching or staging is a useful addition, at least down one side, and can be made of wood or longer-lasting aluminium.

If the staging has raised sides it can be filled with sand. This is useful for sinking pots in to help keep them warm and moist. Heating cables can also be used to keep the bench warm, and building a polythene (plastic) or glass cabinet or lid on top will turn it into an effective propagating bench.

Polytunnels

Polythene (plastic) tunnels are a cheap alternative to greenhouses. They are ideal for growing winter and early spring vegetables and for housing and propagating plants until they are ready to plant out. They are, however, rather ugly and can get very cold, and the polythene will need replacing every three years or so.

RIGHT **Electric fan heaters are very efficient. When equipped with thermostats, they only come on when extra heat is required. They can also be used to circulate the air on still, damp days.**

Tools and Equipment

To look in the average garden centre you would imagine that you need a tremendous battery of tools and equipment before you could ever consider gardening, but in fact you can start (and continue) gardening with relatively few tools and no equipment at all.

Tools are personal things, so one gardener may always use a spade for digging, no matter how soft the ground, whereas another would always use a fork as long as the ground was not too heavy. The type of hoe for certain jobs is another subject on which gardeners hold widely different opinions.

Buying tools

It is not necessary to buy a vast armoury of tools when you first start gardening. Most of the jobs can be done with a small basic kit. When you are buying, always choose the best you can afford. Many of the cheaper tools are made of pressed steel, which soon becomes blunt, will often bend and may even break. Stainless steel is undoubtedly the best, but tools made of this tend to be expensive. Ordinary steel implements can be almost as good, especially if you keep them clean. Avoid tools that are made of aluminium. Trowels and hand forks especially are often made of aluminium, but they wear down and blunt quickly and are not good value for money.

Soil Testers

The chemical composition of the soil can be tested by the gardener by using one of a range of soil testers. The most commonly used checks the acidity/alkalinity of the soil. It is chemical based and involves mixing soil samples with water and checking the colour against a chart. More complicated tests indicate whether there is a shortage of minerals or trace elements. The balance can then be adjusted by adding lime or fertilizers to the soil.

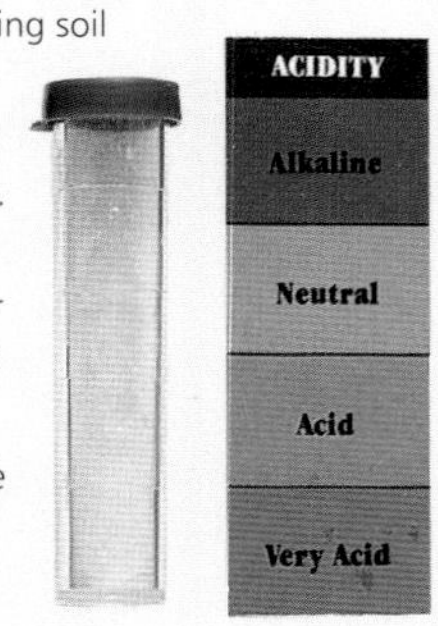

Second-hand

A good way to acquire a collection of tools is to buy them second-hand. There are advantages to this. One is that they are usually much cheaper than new ones. Frequently, too, they are made of much better steel than cheap, modern ones and still retain a keen edge, even after many years' use. In the past gardening tools were made with a much greater variation in design and size. If you go to buy a modern spade, for example, you will probably find that the sizes in the shop are all the same – designed for the "average" gardener. Old tools come in all shapes and

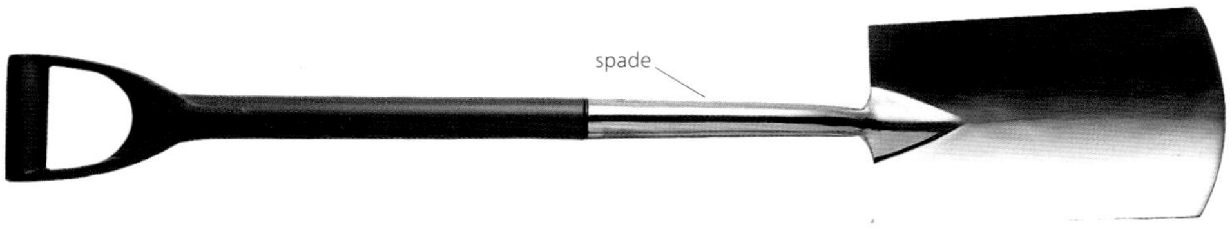

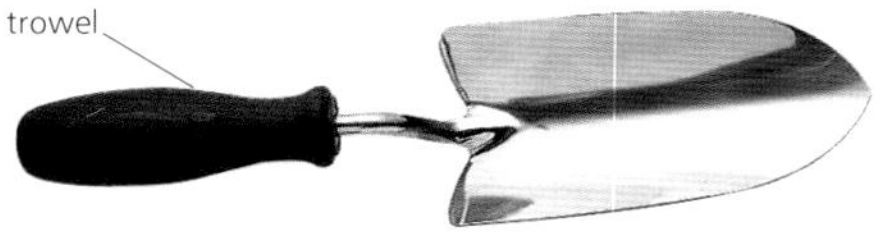

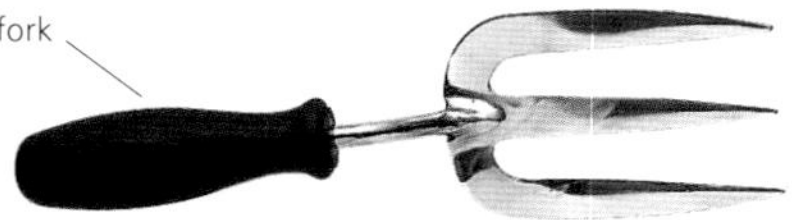

Labelling and Tying

When working in the garden, it is useful to have a tray of odds and ends, such as string, raffia, plant ties and labels. You never know when you might need them. For example, it is always difficult to remember what has been planted or sown where – it may be weeks before seed you have sown is visible above ground.

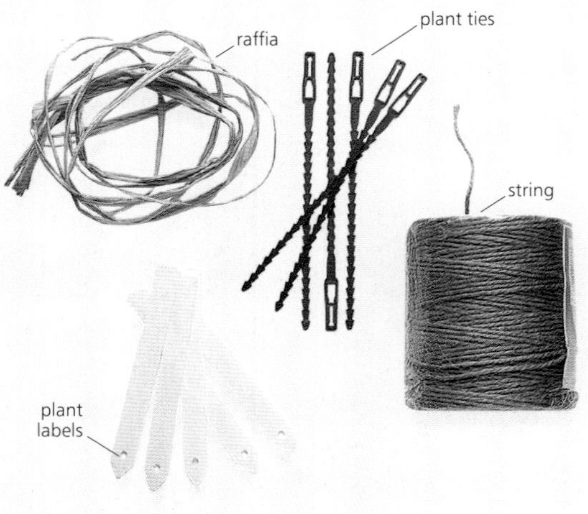

sizes, and if you find modern tools uncomfortable to use you are more likely to find an old one that is made just for you.

Not all old tools are good by any means, of course, but by keeping an eye out and buying only good quality ones you will end up with tools that will more than see you through your gardening career and at a relatively modest price. Car boot fairs (garage sales) and rural junk shops (second-hand stores) are the places to look out for them. Avoid antique shops where such tools are sold at inflated prices to be hung as decorations on the wall rather than to be used.

Care and maintenance

Look after your tools. If you do this they will not only always be in tip-top working condition but will last a lifetime. Scrape all the mud and any vegetation off the tools as soon as you have used them. Once they are clean, run an oily rag lightly over the metal parts. The thin film of oil will stop the metal from corroding. This not only makes the tools last longer but also makes them easier to use because less effort is needed to use a clean spade than one with a rough surface of rust.

In addition, keep the wooden parts clean, wiping them over with linseed oil if the wood becomes too dry.

Keep all blades sharp. Hang tools up if possible. Standing spades and hoes on the ground, especially if it is concrete, will blunt them over time. Keep them away from children.

Equipment

It is possible to run a vegetable and fruit garden with no mechanical aids at all. However, if you have grass paths, a lawn mower will, obviously, be more than useful – it will be essential. Hedge cutters, too, are useful, although hedges can be cut by hand much more easily than grass paths.

In the vegetable garden itself the only mechanical device that you may require is a rotavator (rototiller), which can be used for digging and breaking up the soil. Unless you have a large garden, however, this is not absolutely necessary, although it does make life easier if you want to break down a heavy soil into a fine tilth.

Keep all your equipment maintained. There is nothing worse than wanting a piece of machinery to use in a hurry only to find that it will not start. After the weather, machinery is the most stressful part of gardening.

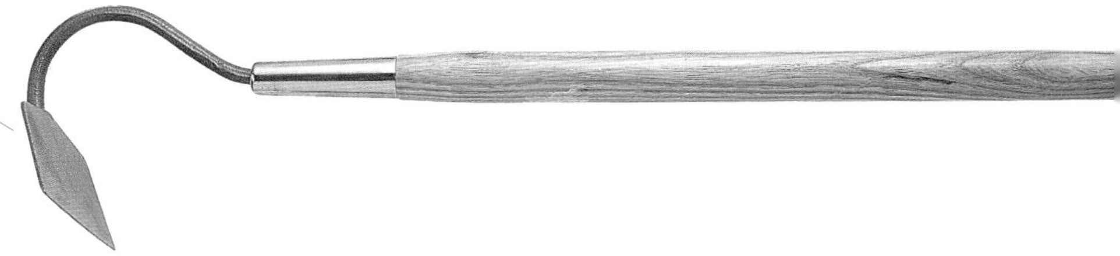

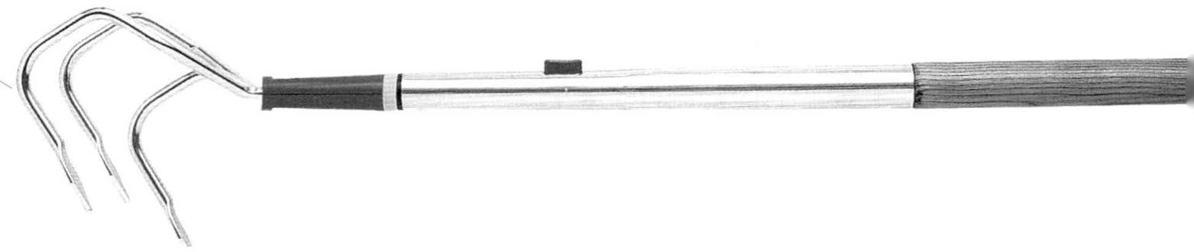

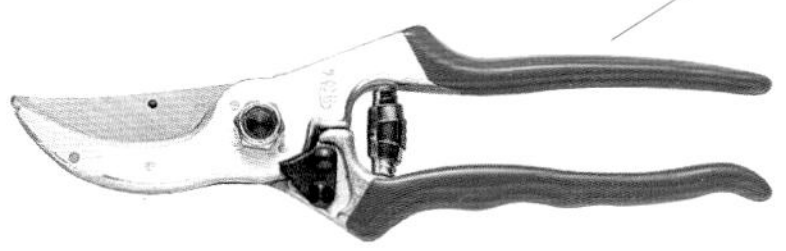

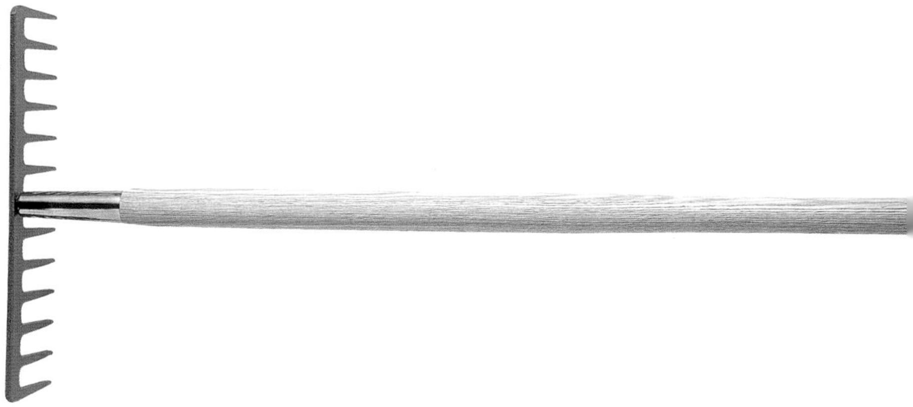

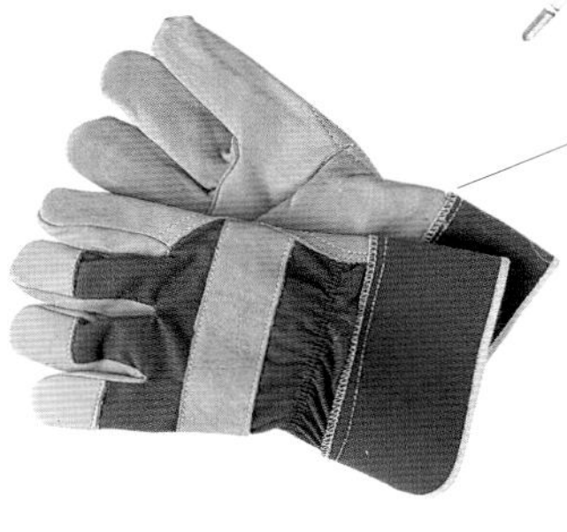

Tool Sheds

The larger the garden and the more tools you have, the bigger the problem you will have in storing them. It is possible to keep a handful of items in a cupboard in the house or hanging on the garage wall. Gradually, however, more and more space is required.

When gardening, you will accumulate bags of compost (soil mix) to be stored as well as a multitude of pots, and, depending on where you live, the wheelbarrow might be best stored under cover. The ultimate solution to these problems is to get a tool shed.

Buying

As with a greenhouse, whenever you buy a shed it always seems to be too small soon after you get it, so think carefully before you buy. What do you need it for? If it is just to store tools, then it is possible to buy a small shed that is no more than a cupboard. This might have just enough space to hang tools and stand a couple of sacks of compost (soil mix) and some pots on the floor, but there will not be enough room to walk into it.

If you want to keep non-gardening things in there as well – a couple of bicycles, perhaps, as well as the garden furniture – you are obviously going to need far more space.

BELOW **Although it is not absolutely essential, a potting shed is a useful place to work, especially on a wet day.**

It is worth considering whether you want to use it as a combined tool and potting shed, and this would obviously require yet more space. Ultimately, the decision is likely to depend on how much money you want to spend and the amount of room available.

Materials

Most tool sheds are made out of wood, and they are usually purchased in prefabricated sections that are bolted together on site. The cheaper softwoods will last for years if they are treated with preservatives at regular intervals. The more expensive cedar sheds will last much longer, although they, too, benefit from treatment with preservatives. Cheap plastic and sheet metal sheds are also available, but they generally look cheap and do not last long. If that is all you can afford, tuck it out of sight – behind a hedge or screen, for example.

There is no reason why you should not make your own shed. This would not necessarily work out cheaper than buying one, but at least it can be tailor-made to the site and to your requirements. Wooden structures can be dismantled and moved elsewhere, but for a more robust and warmer building, it could be made from brick. Remember to check local planning laws before you begin work on it.

Cheaper sheds are supplied without floors and are simply set on the ground – but it is preferable to have a concrete base. Concrete is cold and unyielding to feet if you have to stand on it for any length of time – while potting, for example. A wooden floor, set above the earth or concrete, is warmer, but unless it is well supported from below, it flexes as you walk on it and in some cases the whole shed may rock. Windows take up valuable wall space, but if your shed is a reasonable size or if you are using it for potting, they are essential to let in light.

ABOVE **As well as being the ideal place to store your tools, equipment and other gardening materials, a tool shed can be attractive in its own dusty way.**

Organization

Most hand tools can be hung on the walls using ready-made racks or by using wooden dowel pegs set into a strip of wood. If there is space it is a good idea to build a potting bench along one wall, preferably under a window. Equipment or bags of compost (soil mix) can be stored below the bench, while shelves above it can carry pots or smaller tools. An old bathroom cabinet or a similar small cupboard with a child-proof lock is useful for keeping chemicals in if you use them. Open bags of compost tend to get spilt, so it is a good idea to store them in plastic dustbins (containers) that fit under the bench.

RIGHT **This selection of tools is still in working order, even after many years' work. Clean and well oiled, they should give many more years' good service.**

Cold Frames

Cold frames are rather underrated by many gardeners. They are not only useful in their own right but they can also be used for most of the jobs that are undertaken in the greenhouse. They are less expensive than greenhouses, take up less space and are cheaper to keep warm. Their main disadvantage is that the gardener works outside and not inside in the warm and dry as with a greenhouse.

Uses

In the vegetable garden, cold frames are frequently used for producing winter or early crops of such vegetables as carrots. The frame can be in a permanent position in the garden or moved, rather like a large cloche, onto the vegetable bed itself. The vegetables can be grown either directly in the soil or in growing bags. Later in the year, the cold frame can be used for growing cucumbers or melons.

Another basic use is to afford protection and warmth to trays of seeds or seedlings. Once the plants are ready to go out, the lights can be opened over a period of a week or two to harden off the plants before they are planted out.

Materials

As with greenhouses, the cheaper cold frames are made from aluminium. Their advantage is that they are light enough to move around, but they are not good at retaining heat. Wooden ones are better at this, and cold frames with solid walls made from brick, concrete or even old railway sleepers (ties) provide much better protection during the winter.

Aluminium-framed cold frames can be designed to include glass in the sides, which allows in more light. Solid-sided ones are much warmer but light can enter only through the glass above. It is a good idea to paint the inside of the walls white to reflect some of the light.

Lights (lids) that are glazed with glass are generally preferable, but plastic can be used where there is danger of accidents – if children or elderly people are in the garden, for example.

Heating

Most cold frames, as their name suggests, are not heated. However, it is easier and cheaper to provide some warmth than in a greenhouse, and if you want to propagate or overwinter tender plants it may be possible to supply some form of heat. Electric heating cables installed in the sand below the pots and around the walls of the frame is the easiest method. It is also the most efficient if the cables are connected to a thermostat that switches the electricity on only when heat is required.

Hotbeds

A traditional way to heat cold frames is to set them on a pile of farmyard manure, usually horse dung. As the dung breaks down it releases more than enough heat to keep the frames warm. Soil can be laid on top of the manure and a wide range of vegetables grown in it during the winter. The manure should be fresh, and once it has rotted down and no longer generates heat, it can be spread on the garden and dug in.

Insulation

It is easy to insulate cold frames because they are small. The simplest way is to throw an old carpet over the frame on cold nights.

LEFT **When the seedlings are fully acclimatized and ready to be planted out, the lights (lids) can be left off altogether.**

This may be sufficient to hold in the residual heat, so no extra heating is required to keep the frame above freezing. More efficient methods would be to cover the frames with bubble polythene (plastic) or even to line the inside of the lights with it.

Ventilation

When it is not necessary to keep the frames tightly shut to avoid heat loss, it is sensible to open them slightly, even if it is just a crack, to let air circulate among the plants. This helps prevent various fungal diseases, especially botrytis, which cause seedlings to die through rotting.

RIGHT **A cold frame with a partially opened light (lid) so that the greenhouse-grown seedlings gradually become acclimatized to the outside conditions.**

BELOW **A brick cold frame with a soil bed for growing winter and early spring vegetables.**

Cloches

Cloches are portable forms of protection, rather like miniature cold frames. They are mainly employed during the winter and early spring, but they can be used at any time of year to bring on a crop or to protect it.

Uses

There are frequently times when you want to cosset a few plants. They may need protection from the cold or it may be that they are not particularly worried by the cold but need a little warmth to make them grow faster. One row of strawberries, for example, can be covered with cloches to make them fruit one or even two weeks earlier than they would if uncovered. During the winter, broad (fava) beans will come on better if they are protected not only from the cold but also the extremes of rain and wind. Cloches can also be used to protect plants from predators.

In wet and cold areas cloches can be used to cover the ground so that it both dries out and warms up ready for sowing. This will often enable the gardener to sow several weeks earlier than the weather would otherwise allow in the unprotected garden.

In autumn, cloches can be used to cover ripening or harvested vegetables. For example, cordon tomatoes can be lowered to the ground onto straw and allowed to ripen under cloches, while onions that have been harvested in a wet summer can be placed under cloches to "harden off" before storing.

Materials

Some of the earliest cloches were glass bell jars – like upside-down glass vases – which were placed over individual plants. Other traditional cloches were made from sheets of glass, and the earliest types were held in iron frameworks, and resembled miniature greenhouses. Later, cloches became simpler, and the glass was held together by metal or, more recently, plastic or rubber clips. These were known as barn or tent cloches because of their shapes, and could cover a single plant or a whole row when arranged in a line.

Glass is still used, but most cloches are made of polythene (sheet vinyl or plastic) or rigid plastic. There are two main types. One is made up of individual units, which link up in some way, and the other is like a miniature polytunnel, with a single sheet of polythene stretched along the length of the row.

ABOVE **A rigid plastic cloche is easy to use. The sections butt up against each other and can be pegged into the soil. Endpieces are also available.**

All cloches will do the job they are designed to do. Glass should last the longest, unless you are careless. Although plastics and polythene (sheet vinyl) have a more limited lifespan, they are generally cheaper to replace and are usually lighter and easier to store.

Making your own

Bought cloches may not fit the length or width of the rows in your garden, especially if you are growing in deep beds or blocks. It is relatively simple to make your own. For smaller rows, several hoops of galvanized wire are pushed into the earth at intervals of 60cm/24in and a sheet of polythene (plastic) is laid over them. Place more wire hoops over the first, so that the polythene is trapped between them and held securely. For real security the sides and the two ends of the polythene can be buried in the earth.

For larger beds hoops can be made from lengths of plastic water pipe. Place a stick or iron stake in the ground on each side of the block or row and place the end of the pipe over the stake, forming a hoop. Proceed as before, using more hoops to hold the polythene (plastic) in place, or use strings stretched over the polythene next to the hoops and attached to wire hooks sunk into the ground.

LEFT **Glass bell jars are simple cloches for covering one plant. They are expensive, but plastic sweet jars make a good, if not as attractive, alternative.**

RIGHT **Old-fashioned cloches are particularly good for decorative vegetable gardens. However, they are also very expensive.**

soil

The soil in your garden is your most valuable asset, and it should be cared for accordingly. Some gardeners are lucky and inherit soil in good condition, others find that their soil was once good but is now a little tired and in need of attention. Unlucky gardeners start with virgin soil, often a heavy clay and filled with builder's rubble. Even good soil needs care, while the other two types of soil, especially the heavy soil, need plenty of attention. However, given time and energy even a heavy soil will become fertile and workable, and produce good vegetables.

The main tool in the gardener's armoury is organic material: farmyard manure, garden compost and many other well-rotted forms of humus. It is never possible to have too much of this if you want good soil. Gravel and sharp sand can also be used in the battle against heavy soil. When added to clay, these fine crushed stones separate the particles of clay and allow water to drain through.

Once you have improved your soil, you will find that there is nothing more satisfying than turning a barren soil into a fertile one.

RIGHT A soil that is well worked is ideal for growing vegetables as long as its structure and fertility are maintained by the addition of well-rotted organic material.

Know your soil

All soils are different, and even in a single garden the soil may vary from place to place. Look at your soil: notice how it absorbs water, how well plants grow, what does well and what does not. Check several sites around the garden with a soil test kit – small kits are available from garden centres. The more you study and get to know your soil, the better gardener you will become and the better crops you will grow. The two main aspects to consider are its structure and its fertility. If you can get these right, the rest of your gardening should be easy.

Working the soil

Some people are lucky: they take over a garden that has been well worked. Others are not so fortunate: they inherit a new site that is little more than pure clay. However, although the people who have a well-worked garden may think they can relax, it is important that they keep on treating the ground with respect. If they neglect to feed the soil, it will become tired and infertile; if they stomp around on it after heavy rain, the soil will become compacted and the beautiful structure that has been built up over the years will be lost.

Those with a new garden will have to work hard, especially if it is heavy clay, but gradually, season by season, the soil will improve until eventually it will be unrecognizable. I remember my father moving to a garden in which the soil was nothing but solid yellow clay; by the time he hung up his boots for the last time, it was possible to dig the ground with a fork in midwinter, such was the extent to which its condition had been improved. It does not take a lifetime to improve the soil, however, and even a few seasons will make a real difference.

There are few soils that the average householder will encounter in which it is impossible to grow vegetables. Simply digging and sowing will produce results – not necessarily good results, especially if you do just that every year, but nonetheless, it will produce results. However, if it is fed with organic material the soil will soon not only be easier to work but will also produce better crops.

BELOW Using raised beds is one method of creating a controlled medium, away from the influence of the native soil. For example, a fertile loam can be imported and used in a bed on top of a heavy clay, thus providing an "instant" garden.

Better crops

By better crops we mean bigger and tastier vegetables. Vegetables that are half-starved or that grow in dry soils are often tough and bitter tasting. Compost and similar materials help to retain moisture in the soil, releasing it to the plants over a long period, thus reducing the risk of drought and dry soil. Quantity is also improved, because a richer soil will support more plants. It is worth remembering, too, that undernourished, struggling plants are more susceptible to pests and diseases, and providing good soil is, therefore, a way of protecting your plants and reducing the need for chemicals.

There's nothing like muck

The greatest soil improver of them all is well-rotted organic material of some sort. This is relatively cheap, especially if bought in quantity, and in some areas stables give horse manure away free to anyone prepared to collect it – a bargain that should never be overlooked. There is also a great deal of garden and kitchen waste that can be recycled.

BELOW **Working from wooden planks is a useful way of avoiding walking directly on the soil, which can cause it to compact. This precaution is especially important when the soil is wet.**

Types of Soil

Vegetables can, within reason, be grown on most soils, but, as one would expect, there is an optimum soil in which the best vegetables can be grown. Most soils can be persuaded, with varying degrees of effort, to move towards that optimum, but the starting point is often different.

ABOVE **The better the soil, the better the crops will be. Keeping the soil in good condition is the key to successful kitchen gardening.**

Clay

When they work well clay soils can be fertile, but their structure is the despair of most gardeners. Clay is heavy and the particles cling together, making the soil sticky. Clay soil compacts easily, forming a solid lump that roots find hard to penetrate and that is difficult to dig. Try not to walk on clay soils when they are wet. This tendency to become compacted and sticky means that clay soils are slow to drain, but, once drained, they "set" like concrete, becoming a hard mass. They also tend to be cold and slow to warm up, making them unsuitable for early crops.

Clay soil is not, one would think, a good basis for growing vegetables, yet many of the best gardens are on clay. Clay soils are usually rich, and all the hard effort needed in the initial stages to improve the soil will pay off in the long term.

BELOW **Soil that has been well worked, as the soil in this garden clearly has, is essential to the production of good crops of vegetables.**

Sandy soils

Soils that are made up of sand and silts are quite different. They have few of the sticky clay particles but are made up of individual grains that allow the water to pass through quickly. This quick passage of water through the soil tends to leach (wash) out nutrients, so the soils are often poor. But they also tend to be much warmer in winter and are quicker to warm in spring, thus making it easier to get early crops. Silts contain particles that are a bit more clay-like in texture than those found in sandy soils, and they hold more moisture and nutrients.

Both types of soil are easy to improve and are not difficult to work. Sand does not compact like clay does (although it is still not good practice to walk on beds), but silty soils are more susceptible to the impact of feet and wheelbarrows. Adding organic material can temper their insatiable thirst.

Loams

The soil of most gardeners' dreams is loam. This is a combination of clay and sandy soils, with the best elements of both. They tend to be free draining, but at the same time

COMMON TYPES OF SOIL

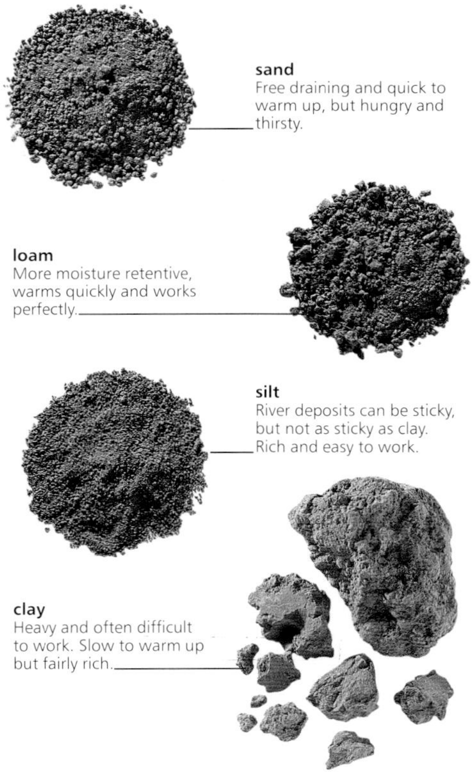

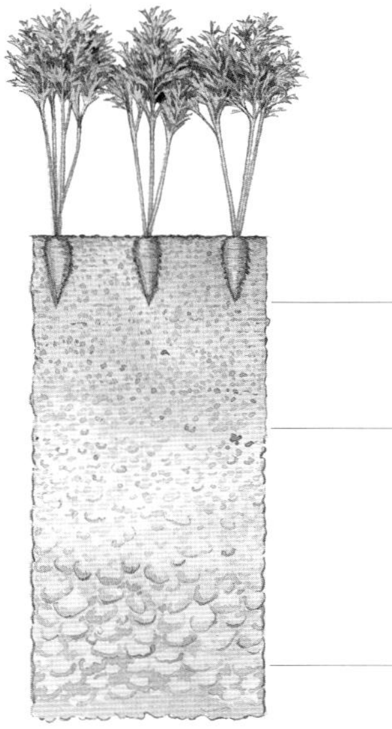

Soil profile A typical soil profile usually consists of three main elements: an upper layer of dark, fertile topsoil; a middle layer of lighter, infertile subsoil; and a lower layer of bedrock, which ranges from a few to hundreds of metres (yards) deep.

moisture retentive. This description – free draining and moisture retentive – is often used of soils and potting mixes and it may seem a contradiction. It means that the soil is sufficiently free draining to allow excess moisture to drain away, but enough moisture is retained for the plant without it standing in stagnant water. Such soils are easy to work at any time of the year, and they warm up well in spring and are thus good for early crops.

Acid and alkaline soils

Another way of classifying soils is by their acidity or alkalinity. Those that are based on peat (peat moss) are acid; those that include chalk or limestone are alkaline. Gardeners use a scale of pH levels to indicate the degree of acidity or alkalinity. Very acid is 1, neutral is 7 and very alkaline is 14, although soils rarely have values at the extremes of the scale. Although they can be grown on a wider range of soils, vegetables are usually grown in soils with a pH of 5.5–7.5, with the optimum conditions being around 6.5. So, the best pH for growing vegetables is slightly on the acid side of neutral. A test with a soil kit will show the rating in your own garden. You can adjust the acid soils of a garden, but it is more difficult to alter alkaline ones.

pH values

1.0	extremely acid
4.0	maximum acidity tolerated by most plants
5.5	maximum acidity for reasonable vegetables
6.0	maximum acidity for good vegetables
6.5	optimum for the best vegetables
7.0	neutral, maximum alkalinity for good vegetables
7.5	maximum alkalinity for reasonable vegetables
8.0	maximum tolerated by most plants
14.0	extremely alkaline

TESTING THE SOIL FOR NUTRIENTS

1 Collect the soil sample 5–8cm/2–3in below the surface. Take a number of samples, but test each one separately.

2 With this kit, mix one part of soil with five parts of water. Shake well in a jar, then allow the water to settle.

3 Draw off some of the settled liquid from the top few centimetres (about an inch) for your test.

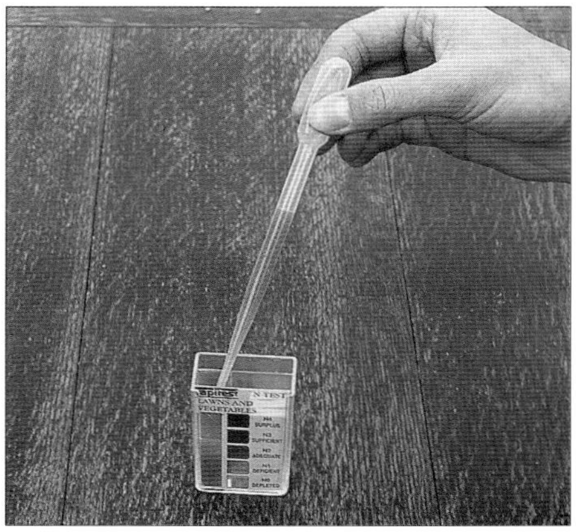

4 Carefully transfer the solution to the test chamber in the plastic container, using the pipette.

5 Select a colour-coded capsule (one for each nutrient). Put the powder in the chamber, replace the cap and shake well.

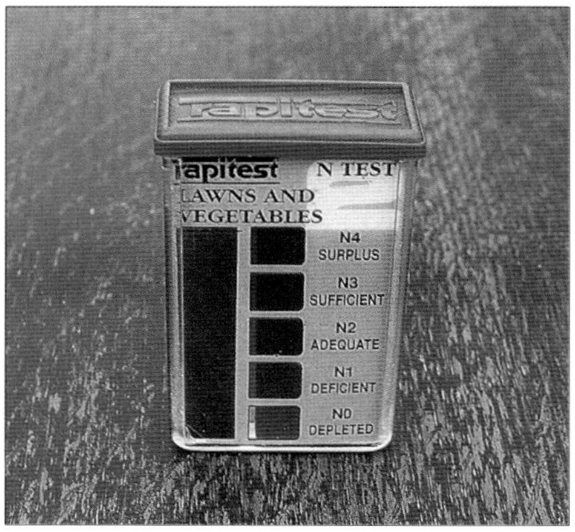

6 After a few minutes, compare the colour of the liquid with the shade panel of the container.

Improving Drainage

Few garden plants, and certainly no vegetables, like to sit in stagnant water – watercress, of course, likes water, but it must be running. A free-draining soil is of the utmost importance if you want to grow decent crops. In the majority of gardens this simply means improving the soil, but in a few gardens, where the problem is serious, it will mean installing a drainage system first.

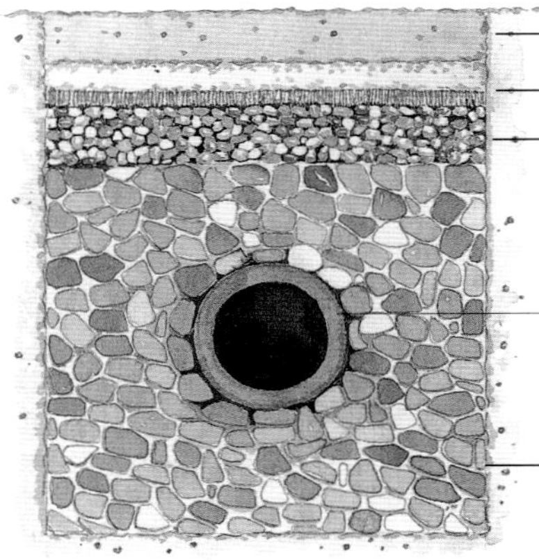

Section through a land drain This cross-section of a typical land drain shows the various layers of materials from which it is constructed, including the topsoil, an inverted turf or perforated plastic membrane, gravel, peabeach or crushed stone, and the land-drain pipe.

Working the soil

In many gardens wet soil can be improved simply by improving the soil itself so that the water drains away. One way to achieve this is to add organic material to improve the soil's fertility. The fibrous material contained in the organic matter helps to break up the clay particles, allowing water to pass through. This material eventually breaks down and so it should be added every time the soil is dug.

The other method is to add gravel or grit to the soil. The best material for this is what used to be known as horticultural grit – that is, grit up to about 5mm/¼in in diameter. Flint grit that has been crushed is best because the angular faces allow water to drain away better than the rounded surfaces of the uncrushed grits, such as peabeach. It may seem sacrilege to add stones to soil, but these fine gravels will make all the difference.

Drainage systems

Of course, it is no good improving the soil if the water still does not have anywhere to go. In fact, the situation could become worse because the well-drained soil in the bed could become a sump, with water running off adjacent paths and lawns into it. If water lies in the garden, then there is nothing for it but to install proper drainage. This can be a big undertaking, and many gardeners may prefer to get professional help.

The basic idea is to channel the water away from the garden. It may be possible to send it into a ditch, but under no circumstances should you connect it to the main drainage system from the house because this is bound to be breaking all kinds of local laws and regulations. If you do not have a ditch, there are two possible solutions. The first is to dig a soakaway. This is a deep hole, usually at least 2m/6ft deep, filled with clean rubble. Water runs out of the drainage pipes into the hole from which it slowly soaks away into the surrounding soil, well below the level of the beds. Alternatively, if the lay of the land allows it, excess water can be piped into a decorative pond, along with other surface water – such as that from the roof of the house, for example.

The drainage system that removes the water from the land is constructed by digging a series of trenches about 60cm/24in deep. There is one main trench, and the others join it at an angle. The trenches should slope towards the soakaway if the

LEFT **Good drainage ensures that this garden is able to support a diverse array of flowers and vegetables, including cabbages and sunflowers.**

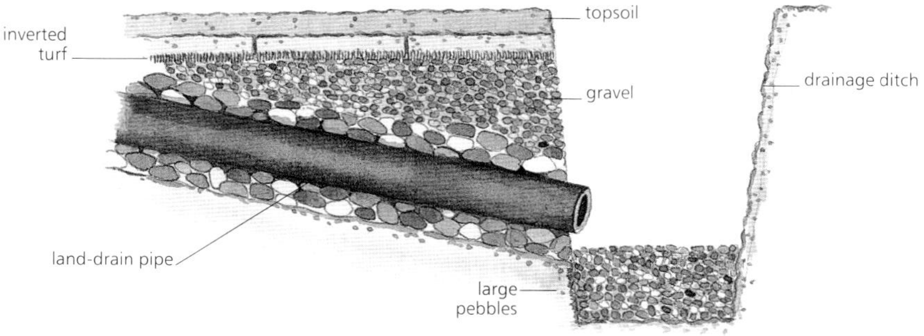

Land drain on a flat site This is a section through a land drain on a flat site, showing the fall of the pipe – in this case the angle is exaggerated – which slopes down into a drainage ditch. The water percolates through the soil and pebbles and into the pipe, which then delivers it to the drainage ditch.

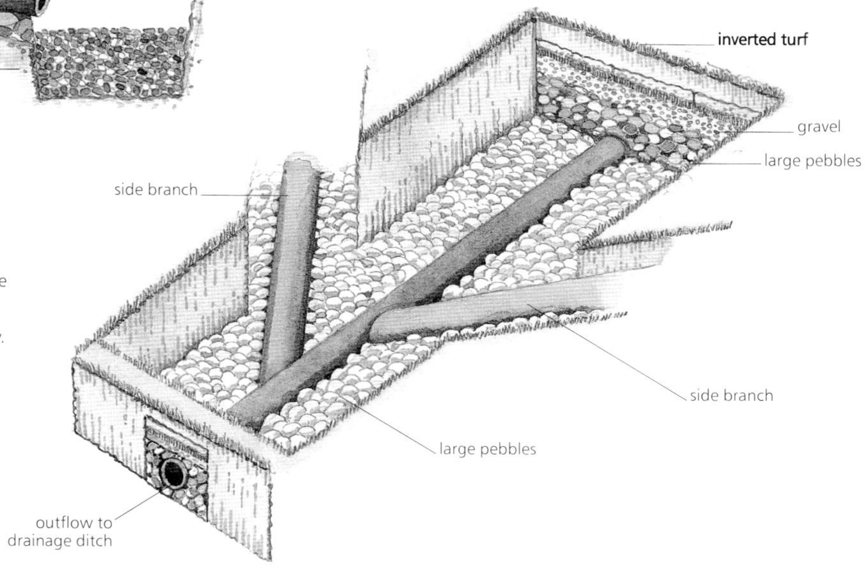

Land drain on a sloping site An aerial view of the drainage system, showing the side branches, which are constructed in the same way as the main pipe. When the ground slopes, the pipes are laid parallel to the ground, so that the water can drain away.

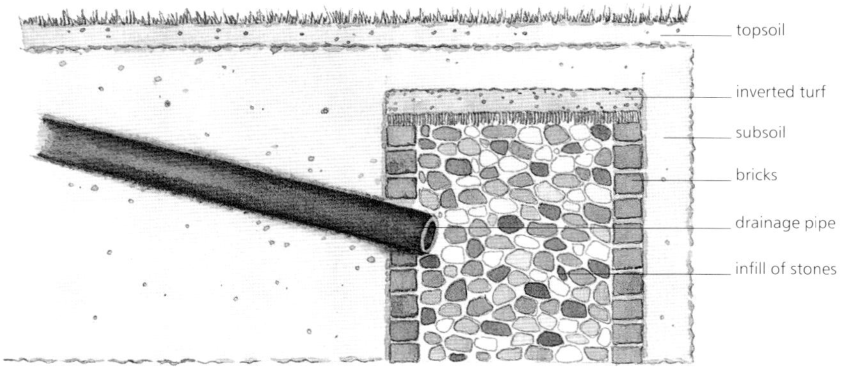

Laying a soakaway If there is no ditch or drain available, then the water must be directed into a soakaway. This is a large hole filled with clean rubble or large stones. In lighter soils, it should be lined with bricks to prevent it filling with soil.

ground is flat, but should run parallel to the surface if the ground slopes. Perforated plastic tubing that comes in a continuous reel is the cheapest form of piping. This is laid on gravel with more gravel laid on top. Upturned turves are then laid on the top of the gravel (to prevent soil from washing into the gravel and blocking the drainage) and the topsoil is replaced. If turf is not available, a pervious plastic membrane can be used.

As an alternative to plastic piping, traditional tile drains can be used. These are short lengths of ceramic pipe laid with a small gap between each. A less efficient, but traditional, method is to use French drains – fill a trench with rubble and top it off with upturned turves and topsoil.

WORKING IN ORGANIC MATTER

1 Soil that has been dug in the autumn can have more organic matter worked into the top layer in the spring. Spread the organic matter over the surface.

2 Lightly work the organic material into the top layer of soil with a fork. There is no need for full-scale digging.

Soil Structure

Perhaps the most important task in any garden is to improve and maintain the quality of the soil. Good-quality soil should be the aim of any gardener who wants to grow vegetables or fruit. To ignore the soil is to ignore one of the garden's most important assets.

ABOVE **Green manure helps to improve both the structure and fertility of the soil. Sow it when the ground is not being used for anything else and then dig it in before it flowers and seeds.**

Organic material

The key to improving the soil in your garden is organic material. This is an all-embracing term that covers any vegetable matter that has been broken down into an odourless, fibrous compost. It includes such things as rotted garden waste, kitchen vegetable waste, farmyard manures (which are plant materials that have passed through animals) and other plant waste material.

It is important that any such material should be well-rotted. If it is still in the process of breaking down, it will need nitrogen to complete the process and will extract it from the soil. This, of course, is the reverse of what the gardener wants – the gardener's aim is, in fact, to add nitrogen to the soil. If you are unsure, a good indicator that the material has broken down sufficiently is that it becomes odourless. Even horse manure is free from odour once it has rotted down, and manuring a garden should not be the smelly occupation it is often depicted as being.

Some substances contain undesirable chemicals, but these will be removed if the material is stacked and allowed to weather. Bark and other shredded woody materials may contain resins, for example, while animal and bird manures may contain ammonia from urea. These chemicals will evaporate or be converted by weathering.

Digging in

The best way to apply organic material to the vegetable garden is to dig it in. In this way it becomes incorporated into the soil. If possible, double dig the bed, adding material all the way to the bottom of both spits. This will help to retain moisture and supply nutrients where they are needed, which is down by the roots. It will also encourage roots to delve deeply rather than remaining on the surface where easy water can be obtained from the odd rain shower or watering can. The deeper the roots go the more stable will be the plant's water supply and the plant will grow at a regular pace rather than in unproductive fits and starts. This will produce much better plants.

Top-dressing

Once the ground has been planted, especially with permanent vegetables and fruit, it is impossible to dig in organic material to anything more than a couple of inches. The damage done by disturbing roots makes it pointless to attempt to go any deeper. The answer here is to top-dress with well-rotted matter. A 10cm/4in layer of, say farmyard manure, will be slowly worked into the soil by the earthworms. As well as being taken into the soil, such a dressing will also act as a mulch, protecting the ground from drying out as well as preventing any weed seeds from germinating.

The top-dressing should also be free from any weed seeds or you will be creating problems rather than solving them. Properly made compost and the other types of material that can be used should always be weed free and suitable for use in this way.

Fruit and permanent plantings

For any type of plant that will be in position for several if not many years, it is important that the soil is in the best possible condition before planting begins. Once planted it will be impossible to dig in more material, and

IMPROVING SOIL FERTILITY

The fertility of the soil is much improved by the addition of organic material, but a quick boost can also be achieved by adding an organic fertilizer, spreading it over the surface and then raking it in.

REDUCING SOIL ACIDITY

The acidity of the soil can be reduced by adding lime some weeks before planting and working it in with a rake. Check the soil with a soil testing kit to see how much lime is required.

LEFT **A garden in which the soil is well cared for will reward the gardener with a plentiful harvest. In this large walled kitchen garden, rows of brassicas and espaliered fruit bushes nestle between beds planted with cosmos and marigolds.**

you will have to depend on top-dressing. Although this is a good supplement, it is not an alternative to proper preparation in the first place. The ground should be double dug if possible, and you should add as much organic matter as you can get, especially in the lower layers of soil.

Improving the soil's pH

The other aspect of improving soil is to improve the pH level. For vegetables, as we have noted, the level to aim at is pH6.5, but anything between 6 and 7 is still good, while 5.5–7.5 is acceptable.

If the soil is too acid, the pH can be adjusted somewhat by adding lime to the soil. Three types of lime can be used for reducing soil acidity. Ordinary lime (calcium carbonate) is the safest to use. Quicklime (calcium oxide) is the strongest and most caustic, but it may cause damage. Slaked lime (calcium hydroxide) is quicklime with water added; it is not as strong as quicklime and is therefore less dangerous. Always take safety precautions when you are applying lime and follow the quantities recommended by the manufacturer on the packet. Do not add lime at the same time as manure, because this will release ammonia, which can damage the plants. Spread the lime over the soil at the rate prescribed on the packet and rake it in. Do not sow or plant in the ground for at least a month. Do not over-lime.

It is not as easy to reduce the alkalinity of soil. Peat (peat moss) used to be recommended for this purpose, but not only is collecting peat environmentally unsound, it breaks down quickly and needs to be constantly replaced. Most organic manures are on the acid side and help to bring down the levels. Leafmould, especially that from pine trees, is also acid.

Spent mushroom compost contains lime and is useful for reducing acidity, but it should not be used on chalky (alkaline) soils.

When not to add manure

Not all crops like to be grown in soil that has been freshly manured. Root crops, such as parsnips, for example, tend to "fork" when the soil is too rich. This means that, instead of the single, long, tapering roots, they have short stubby roots with several branches. The parsnip may taste the same, but it is not so convenient to clean and peel.

The way to prevent this happening is to avoid manuring before planting. Either use soil that has been manured from a previous crop – follow the brassicas, for example – or add the organic material during the previous autumn so that it has had a chance to break down before the root crops germinate and start to grow.

IMPROVING SOIL STRUCTURE

1 One of the best ways to improve the structure of the soil is to add as much organic material as you can, preferably when the soil is dug. For heavy soils, this is best done in the autumn.

2 If the soil has already been dug, then well-rotted organic material can be worked into the surface of the soil with a fork. The worms will complete the task of working it into the soil.

WORKING ON WET SOIL

It is best to avoid working on wet soil, but sometimes it is necessary. To ensure that the soil is not compacted and its structure destroyed, it is advisable to work from a plank of wood.

Soil Conditioners

Quite a range of organic conditioners is available to the gardener. Some are free – if you do not count the time taken in working and carting them. Others are relatively cheap, and some, usually those bought by the bag, can be quite expensive. However, not everyone has a stable nearby or enough space to store large quantities of material, and these gardeners will therefore need to buy it as required.

ABOVE **Farmyard manure should be left stacked in a heap until it has lost its smell and has finished rotting down.**

Farmyard manure

A traditional material and still much used by many country gardeners, farmyard manure has the advantage of adding bulk to the soil as well as supplying valuable nutrients. The manure can come from any form of livestock, although the most commonly available is horse manure. It can be obtained from most stables, and many are so glad to get rid of it that they will supply it free if you fetch it yourself. There are often stables situated around the edge of towns, so manure is usually available to town gardeners as well as to those in the country.

Some gardeners do not like the manure when it is mixed with wood shavings rather than with straw, but it is worth bearing in mind that the former is often less likely to contain weed seeds, and as long as it is stacked and allowed to rot down it is excellent for adding to the soil as well as for use as a top-dressing.

All manures should be stacked for a period of at least six months before they are used. When it is ready, it will have lost its dungy smell.

Garden compost

All gardeners should try to recycle as much of their garden and kitchen vegetable waste as possible. In essence, this is simply following nature's pattern, where leaves and stems are formed in the spring and die back in the autumn, falling to the ground and eventually rotting and returning to the plants as nutrients. In the garden some things are removed from the cycle, notably vegetables and fruit, but as much as possible should be recirculated.

Compost is not difficult to make, and, of course, it is absolutely free. If you have the space, use several bins so there is always some available for use.

Unless weeds that are in seed or diseased plants have been used, compost should be safe to use as a soil conditioner and as a mulch.

Leafmould

Leafmould is a natural soil conditioner. It is easy to make and should not cost anything. Only use leafmould made by yourself; never go down to the local woods and help yourself because this will disturb the wood's own cycle and will impoverish the soil there.

SOME ORGANIC MATERIALS

Four stakes knocked into the ground with a piece of wire-netting stretched around them will make the perfect compound for making leafmould. Simply add the leaves as they fall from the trees. It will take a couple of years for them to break down and what was a huge heap will shrink to a small layer by the time the process is complete.

Add leafmould to the soil or use it as a top-dressing. It is usually acid and can be used to reduce the pH of alkaline soil. Leafmould from pine needles is particularly acid.

Peat (peat moss)

This is expensive and does little for the soil because it breaks down too quickly and has little nutritive content. It is also ecologically unsound to use it.

Spent mushroom compost

Often available locally from mushroom farms, the spent compost is relatively cheap, especially if purchased in bulk. It is mainly used in the ornamental part of the garden, but it is still useful in the vegetable garden if it is allowed to rot down. It is particularly useful if the soil is on the acid side because it contains chalk.

Vegetable industrial waste

Several industries produce organic waste material that can be useful in the garden. Spent hop waste from the brewing industry has always been a favourite among those who can obtain it. Coco shells are now imported, although these are better used as a mulch than as a soil conditioner. Several other products are locally available. Allow them to rot well before using.

Green manure

Some crops can be grown simply to be dug back into the ground to improve the soil condition and to add nutrients. They are particularly useful on light soils that are left vacant for any length of time, such as over winter.

Green manures
Broad (fava) beans nitrogen fixing
Italian ryegrass quick growing
Lupins nitrogen fixing
Mustard quick growing
Phacelia quick growing
Red clover nitrogen fixing
Winter tare nitrogen fixing

Green manures can be sown in early autumn and dug in during spring. Alternatively, if you plant fast-growing varieties, you can use them whenever land becomes available during the growing season.

Avoid letting the green manure flower and seed, otherwise it will self-seed. Most of the foliage and stems can be used in the compost bin.

BELOW **Green manure can be grown as a separate crop or it can be grown between existing crops. Here, clover is grown amongst cabbages, where it not only fixes nitrogen in the soil, but also provides a ground cover, keeping the weeds down.**

Making Compost

Compost is a valuable material for any garden, but it is especially useful in the vegetable garden. It is free, apart from any capital required in installing compost bins, but these should last a lifetime and the overall cost should be negligible. A little bit of effort is required, but this is a small price to pay for the resulting gold-dust.

ABOVE **A range of organic materials can be used, but avoid cooked kitchen waste or any weeds that have seed in them. *Clockwise from top left:* kitchen waste, weeds, shreddings and grass clippings.**

The principle

The idea behind compost-making is to emulate the process in which a plant takes nutrients from the soil, dies and then rots, putting the nutrients back into the ground. In the garden, waste plant material is collected, piled in a heap and allowed to rot down before being returned to the soil as crumbly, sweet-smelling, fibrous material.

Because it is in a heap the rotting material generates heat, which encourages it to break down even more quickly. The heat also helps to kill pests and diseases as well as any weed seed in the compost. If the rotting material is to break down properly, a certain amount of moisture is needed, as well as air. If there is too much water, however, the process is slowed down; if there is insufficient air, the heap will go slimy and smell bad.

The process should take up to about three months, but many old-fashioned gardeners like to retain the heap for much longer than that, growing marrows and courgettes (zucchini) on it before they break it up for use in the garden.

The compost bin

Gardeners always seem to generate more garden waste than they ever thought possible and never to have enough compost space, so when planning your bins, make sure you have enough. The overall aim is to have three: one to hold new waste, one that is in the process of breaking down, and the third that is ready for use.

The bins are traditionally made from wood (often scrap wood), and because these can be hand-made to fit your space and the amount of material available, this is still the best option. Sheet materials, such as corrugated iron, can also be used. Most ready-made bins are made of plastic, and although these work perfectly well, they may be a bit on the small side in a busy garden.

A bin should contain at least a cubic metre/3.5 cubic feet of compost for it to heat up adequately. If you have a large garden, a bin double this size would be even more efficient. The simplest bin can be made by nailing together four wooden pallets to form a box. If the front is made so that the slats are

RIGHT **Only a small proportion of the vegetables and flowers for cutting in this plot will be used. This means that most of the foliage and stems can be put in the compost bin.**

slotted in to form the wall, they can be removed as the bin is emptied, making the job of removing the compost easier. This is a refinement, however, and not essential.

Materials

Any plant garden waste can be used for composting as long as it does not contain weed seeds. (In fact, it is useful to have a separate bin for anything that contains seeds, because the compost can be used for permanent plantings such as trees. Compost used for this purpose will never come to the surface, and any seeds will be prevented from germinating.) You should also avoid including perennial weeds. Woody material, such as hedge clippings, can be used, but shred it first.

Kitchen vegetable waste, such as peelings and cores, can be used but avoid cooked vegetables, and do not include meat, which will attract rats and other vermin.

Technique

Placing a few branches or twiggy material in the bottom of the bin will help to keep the contents aerated. Put in the material as it becomes available but avoid building up deep layers of any one material, especially grass cuttings. Mix them with other materials.

To help keep the heap warm, cover it with an old carpet or sheet of polythene (plastic). This also prevents excess water from chilling the contents as well as swamping all the air spaces. The lid should be kept on until the compost is required.

Every so often, add a layer of farmyard manure if you can get it because it will provide extra nitrogen to speed things up. Failing this, you can buy special compost accelerators. It is not essential to add manure or an accelerator, however – it just means waiting a couple of weeks longer for your compost.

Air is important, and this usually percolates through the side of the bin, so leave a few gaps between the timbers. If you use old pallets, these are usually crudely made, with plenty of gaps. The colder material around the edges takes longer to break down than that in the centre of the heap, so turn the compost around every so often. This also loosens the pile and allows air to circulate.

MAKING COMPOST

1 A simple compost bin, which should be about 1m/3ft square, can be made by nailing four flat pallets together. These bins are usually roughly made, which means that there will be plenty of air holes between the slats.

2 Pile the waste into the compost bin, making certain that there are no thick layers of the same material. Grass clippings, for example, will not rot down if the layer is too thick because the air cannot penetrate.

3 It is important to keep the compost bin covered with an old mat or a sheet of polythene (sheet vinyl or plastic). This will help to keep in the heat generated by the rotting process and it will also prevent the compost bin from getting too wet in bad weather.

4 Every so often turn the contents of the bin with a fork, partly to let in air and partly to move the outside material, which is slow to rot, into the centre so that the rotting process speeds up. It is easier if you have several bins and turn the compost from one bin into another.

5 When the bin is full, cover the surface with a layer of soil and use it to grow marrows (zucchini), pumpkins or cucumbers. If you want to use the contents as soon as possible, omit the soil and keep covered with polythene. The finished product *(inset, below)* is dark brown, crumbly and has a sweet, earthy smell, not a rotting one. It can be used straight away or left covered until required.

Fertilizers

You cannot go on taking things out of the soil without putting anything back. In nature plants return the nutrients they have taken from the soil when they die. In the garden the vegetables are removed and eaten, and the chain is broken. Compost and other organic materials help to redress the balance, but there may not be enough available to do the job properly and then fertilizers are needed.

ABOVE **The most natural way of adding nutrients to the soil is to rot down old plant material in a compost bin, and then return it to the soil.**

What plants require

The main foods required by plants are nitrogen (N), phosphorus (P) and potassium (K), with smaller quantities of magnesium (Mg), calcium (Ca) and sulphur (S). They also require small amounts of what are known as trace elements, including iron (Fe) and manganese (Mn).

Each of the main nutrients tends to be used by the plant for one specific function. Thus nitrogen is concerned with plant growth and is used for promoting the rapid growth of the green parts of the plant. You should, therefore, add nitrogen to help leafy plants such as cabbage but cut back on it with plants such as runner beans, because you do not want to promote lush leaves at the expense of flowers and beans. Phosphorus, usually in the form of phosphates, is used to create good root growth as well as helping with the ripening of fruits, while potassium, in the form of potash, which is used to promote flowering and formation of good fruit, is, for example, the main ingredient in tomato feed.

The natural way

The most natural way to add nutrients to the soil is to use compost and other organic matter. As we have already seen, such materials are important to the general structure of the soil, but they also feed it. Well-rotted farmyard manure and garden compost have been the main way that gardeners have traditionally fed their gardens. However, some of today's gardeners are unhappy with this method because they claim that you cannot know which fertilizer you are adding and in what quantity, because the quality of organic materials varies so much. Although they concede that organic material is useful for adding bulk, they prefer to use bought fertilizers to feed the soil.

Organic material normally contains less of the main nutrients than concentrated fertilizers, but it is often strong in trace elements, and although they may not contain such a strong concentration of nitrogen, they do release it over a longer period which is of great benefit. Because of its other benefits, farmyard manure and garden compost are still the best way of treating the soil.

INORGANIC FERTILIZERS

Organic fertilizers

Synthetic, concentrated fertilizers are broken down into two groups: organic and inorganic. Organic fertilizers are made up of chemicals derived from naturally occurring organic materials. So bonemeal (ground-up bones) is quite strong in nitrogen and phosphates, making it a good fertilizer to promote growth, especially at the start of a plant's life. Bonemeal also has the advantage in that it breaks down slowly, gradually releasing the fertilizer over a long period. When you apply bonemeal, you may want to wear gloves. Other organic fertilizers include fish, blood and bone; hoof and horn; and seaweed meal.

Because they are derived from natural products without any modification, they are deemed "safe" by organic growers.

Inorganic fertilizers

These are fertilizers that have been made artificially, although they are frequently derived from natural rocks and minerals and the process may just involve crushing. They are concentrated and are usually soluble in water. This means that they are instantly available for the plant and are useful for giving a plant a push when it is required. They do, however, tend to wash out of the soil quickly and need to be replaced.

Some are general fertilizers, and might contain equal proportions of nitrogen, phosphorus and potassium, for example. Others are much more specific. Superphosphate, for example, is entirely used for supplying phosphorus, while potassium sulphate is added to the soil when potassium is required.

ORGANIC FERTILIZERS

Increasing numbers of gardeners are turning against inorganic fertilizers, unaware that they are not as artificial as is generally believed. Many are not classified as organic simply because they are not derived from living things. Nevertheless, it is their concentrated form and the fact that they can be readily washed from the soil that lead many gardeners to object to their use.

Slow-release fertilizers

A modern trend is to coat the fertilizers so that they are released slowly into the soil. These are expensive in the short term, but because they do not leach away and do not need to be replaced as frequently, they can be considered more economic in the longer term. They are particularly useful for container planting, where constant watering is necessary (with its attendant rapid nutrient leaching).

LEFT **This kitchen garden is planted with a delightful mixture of herbs, vegetables and flowers, growing in well-fed beds.**

Digging and Breaking Down

Although it is a technique that is now being questioned by some gardeners, digging is still one of the main garden activities. It breaks up the soil, allowing the ingress of water and air, which are both important for plant growth. In addition, it also allows organic material to be incorporated deep down in the soil, right where the roots need it.

All weeds and their roots can be removed during digging, which also brings pests to the surface so that they can be destroyed. Also and importantly, it allows the gardener to keep an eye on the condition of the soil.

Single digging

The most frequently carried out method is single digging, of which there are two ways, one informal and the other formal. In the informal method the ground is usually already quite loose, and the gardener simply forks it over, turning it over and replacing it in the same position, hardly using any trench at all. This process is more frequently carried out on light or sandy soils.

Formal single digging is necessary on heavier soils and when there is organic material to be incorporated. First, a trench is dug across the width of the plot, and the earth taken from the trench is taken – in a wheelbarrow – to the other end of the bed. Compost or farmyard manure is put into the bottom of the trench and then another trench is dug. This time, the earth removed from the trench is put into the first trench to cover the organic material. This procedure is repeated down the length of the plot. When the final trench has been dug and organic material placed in it, it is refilled with the pile of soil taken from the first trench.

Further refinements can be applied. For example, the first trench can be dug so that it is two trenches wide. Dung is put in the bottom as usual, and then the next trench is dug but the soil is spread over the bottom of the previous two trenches, only half-filling them. This is then covered with another layer of dung and then the fourth trench dug, filling up the first. Trenches three and four are treated in the same way, being filled first with the soil from trench five and then from trench six. This method makes a better distribution of the organic material through the soil.

ABOVE **After a winter exposed to the weather, most soils will readily break down into a fine tilth by using a rake. More recently turned soil, may need to be broken down with a heavier hoe first.**

Double digging

Double digging is the method that is employed to break up the subsoil, and it is useful on any new plot of ground as well as when deep beds are being prepared.

Dig the trench as before, taking the earth to the end of the plot. Then dig the soil in the bottom of the trench to the depth of a fork or spade, adding in organic material. Add more organic material on top and then dig the next trench, placing the soil into the first. Repeat until the end of the plot is reached. Take care that you do not bring any subsoil up to the top.

SINGLE DIGGING

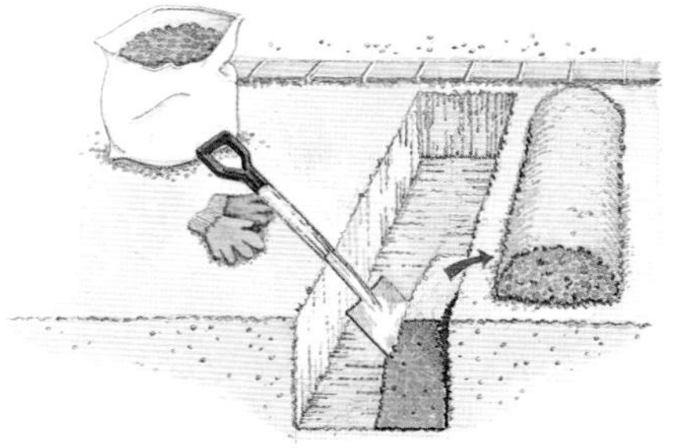

1 Start by digging a trench across the plot, putting the soil from the first trench to one side to be used later in the final trench.

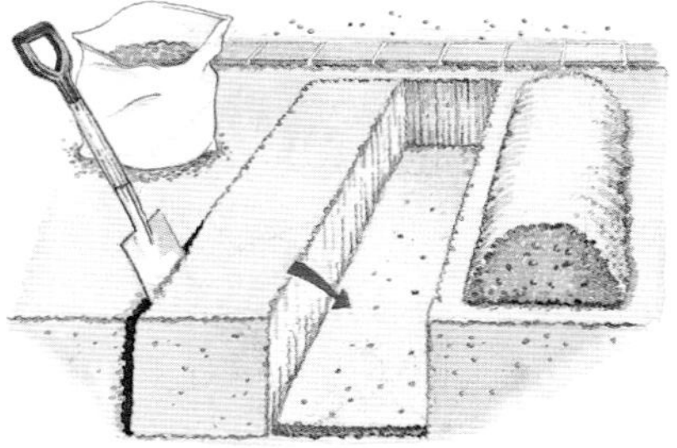

2 Put a layer of manure in the bottom of the trench. Dig out the next trench and cover over the manure in the first trench with earth taken from the second trench.

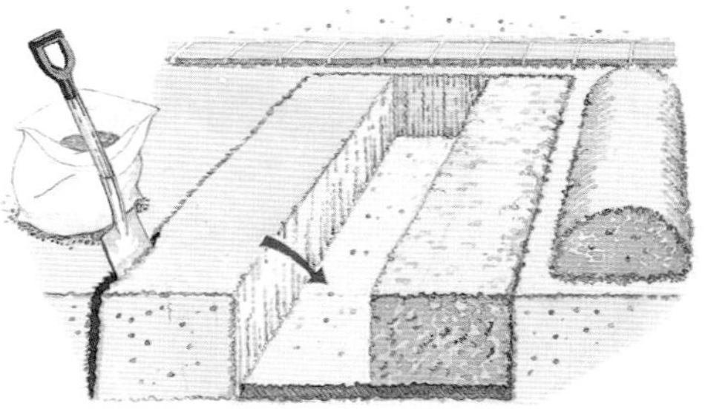

3 Repeat this process of adding manure to each trench and filling in with earth from the next, breaking up the soil as you go and keeping the surface as even as possible.

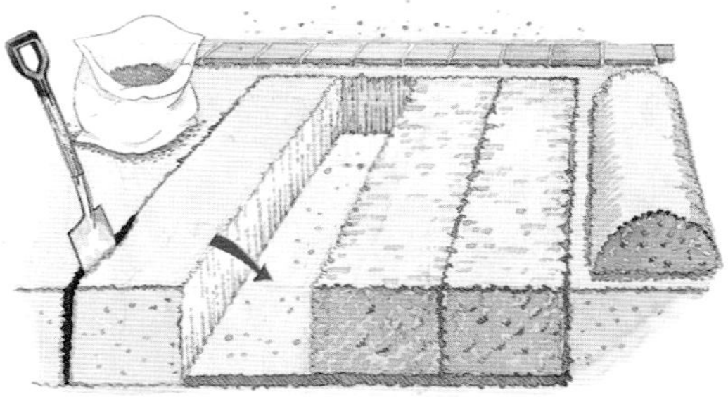

4 Continue down the length of the plot until you reach the final trench. This should be filled in with the earth taken from the first trench, which was set to one side.

DOUBLE DIGGING, METHOD ONE

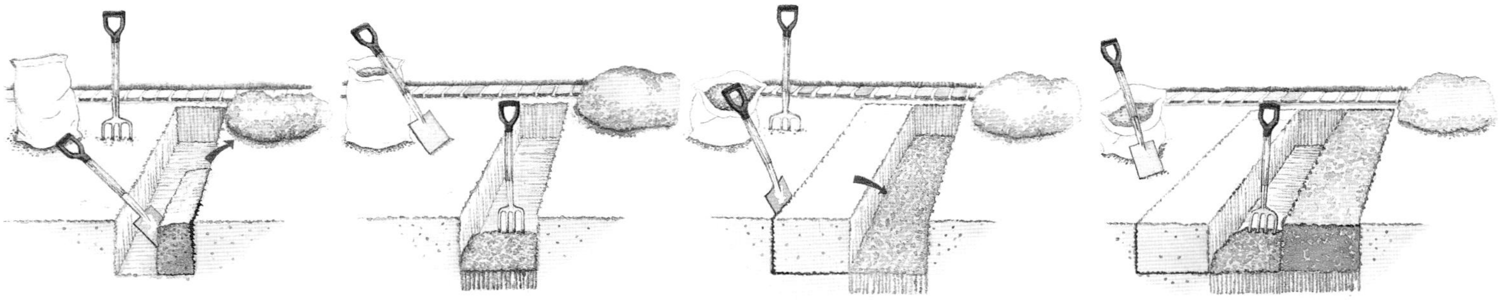

1 Dig a wide trench, placing the soil to one side to be used later when filling in the final trench.

2 Break up the soil at the bottom of the trench, adding manure to the soil as you proceed.

3 Dig the next trench, turning the soil over on top of the broken soil in the first trench.

4 Continue down the plot, ensuring that subsoil from the lower trench is not mixed with topsoil of the upper.

A method requiring more energy but giving better results is to dig out the first trench and then dig another below it, keeping the two soils separate. Dig out the top spit of the next trench and also put this to one side. Add organic material to the first double trench and dig the bottom spit of the second trench into it. Add more dung and then take the top spit of the third trench and place this on top of the new soil in the bottom of the first trench. Repeat down the plot and then fill in the remaining trenches with the reserved soil from the first ones.

Mechanical digging

It is possible to dig the soil using a mechanical rotavator (rototiller). These are, however, best used on large plots. One disadvantage of using a mechanical digger is that it cuts up weed roots into small pieces, and they are more difficult to remove by hand than with conventional digging.

Breaking down into a fine tilth

The best time to dig a heavy soil is in the autumn, then the winter frosts and rain will break it down for you. If clay soils are dug in the spring and allowed to dry out too much, they are difficult to break down because the clods set like concrete. A mechanical rotavator makes breaking the soil down easier, especially if the plot is large. For smaller plots, work on the soil when it is neither too wet nor too dry (experience will show you when), breaking it down, first with a large hoe and then with a rake. Shuffling along the surface with your feet will also help considerably, but do not do this if the ground is wet.

It is better to leave sandy soils until the spring because these do not need much breaking down. Raking the surface is usually all that is required.

Occasionally, the soil becomes too hard to break down. If this happens, water the soil with a sprinkler, leave it to dry slightly – so that it is no longer muddy – and then break it down. Alternatively, draw out a deep sowing row in the rough soil and fill it with potting compost (soil mix) and dig this in.

ABOVE **For larger gardens with heavy soil, a rotavator (rototiller) will break down the soil into a fine tilth. Even a small one saves a lot of time, especially if the soil is too dry to break down with a rake.**

DOUBLE DIGGING, METHOD TWO

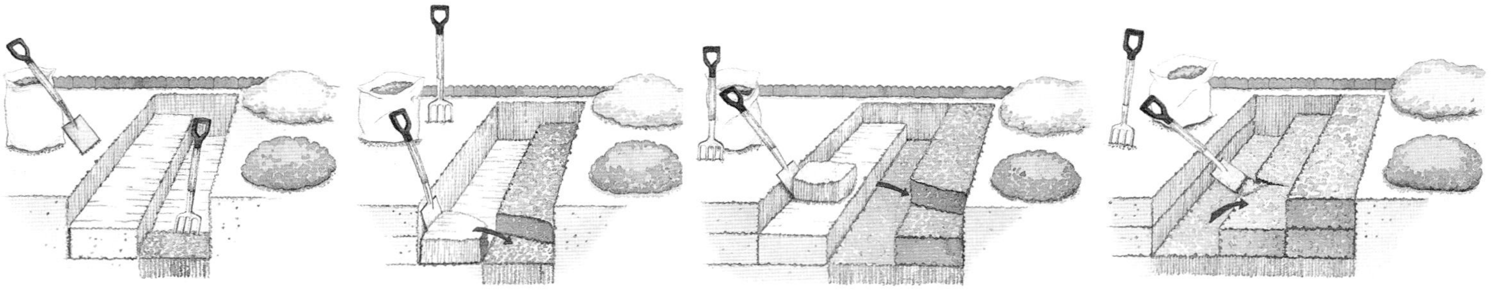

1 Keeping soil from each level separate, dig first trench two spits deep. Fork over trench. Dig second trench one spit deep.

2 Add organic material to the first double trench and dig the lower spit of the second trench into it.

3 Dig an upper third trench one spit deep, and place the soil on top of that already placed in the first trench.

4 Continue, ensuring topsoil and subsoil do not mix. Fill in remaining trenches with soil taken from first ones.

common problems

Nothing is ever straightforward in the garden – perhaps if it were, many gardeners would give up through sheer boredom. Nature always throws in a few problems just to keep us on our toes. The weather is rarely consistent: it is either too wet or too dry, too hot or too cold. You turn your back for a few moments, and weeds seem to sprout up everywhere. Just when everything looks perfect, plagues of pests and diseases arrive. The gardener has a lot to contend with.

On the other hand, the situation is rarely as bad as many chemical companies would have you believe. Many of the problems are such that you can probably live with them, while others need only minor attention. Chemicals are only usually needed as a last resort.

RIGHT This informal vegetable garden, with its rows of onions, carrots, marrows (zucchini), spinach and beans, is a tribute to good garden hygiene.

Getting it in perspective

If the problems encountered by gardeners were insurmountable, no one would ever grow any vegetables at all. It cannot be denied that there are problems, but they often seem worse than they really are, particularly if you believe the literature issued by the chemical companies. Most of the problems that occur in the garden can be overcome by simple means that cost little in terms of either time or money. Many of the difficulties are insignificant and can, unless you are fastidious to the extreme, be ignored. A bit of rust on the leeks in a wet year doesn't look nice but it will not do a great deal of harm. A few minutes' contemplative hoeing will see off most of the weeds, and a sudden outbreak of caterpillars can soon be picked off by hand.

Do not let the thought of pests and diseases put you off in any way. An occurrence of either to the extent that serious action is needed is rare. Most gardeners find they survive season after season without any trouble. Anyway, if the worst comes to the worst, you can always give up and start afresh next year.

ABOVE Mulching with a layer of grass cuttings helps to preserve the moisture in the soil. You will need to water the ground before applying the mulch.

Be prepared

If you exercise a little forethought and adopt a good routine, you will be able to pre-empt many of the problems that might occur. Always practise good hygiene. Never leave rotten vegetables on the plants or in the ground. Remove them to the compost heap. Don't leave piles of weeds lying about, but put them on the compost heap or, if they are pernicious, burn them. Keep a close eye on your crops and take action as soon as possible if you see problems beginning to appear. Take out the tips of broad (fava) beans, for example, before they can be infested with blackfly. Cover your brassicas with fleece to keep off butterflies, and hence the caterpillars. If you notice one or two greenfly, crush them with your fingers before they can start breeding. Don't wait until they have multiplied and you have to resort to chemicals to control them.

ABOVE **Weeds use up a great deal of moisture and nutrients, and crowd out young plants, making them drawn and sickly. Weeds can also harbour disease.**

Hoe as part of a regular routine. If you allow weeds to get too large, they will take longer to remove. Make your compost in such as way that it gets hot enough to destroy all weed seeds and fungal spores.

Stake peas and beans early, rather than leaving them until they are a tangled mass. Put up windbreaks in exposed areas, instead of waiting for things to blow over. Mulch to preserve moisture so that the soil does not dry out and you have to water. Foresight saves a lot of time and frustration.

Chemical control

An increasing number of gardeners are becoming aware of the benefits of organic gardening and are avoiding the use of chemicals. There are times when chemicals can be useful, but these are less frequent than the large companies that manufacture them would have us believe. A weed-infested garden can probably only be cleared with chemicals, but if this is carried out properly, it should need to be done only once, and all subsequent control can be done by hand. Using chemicals on just one occasion will probably do no permanent harm to the soil, but do not become dependent on herbicides and reach for the spray every time you see a weed – that is not what gardening is about. You will end up creating a desert and a polluted one at that.

BELOW **A good mixed garden, with plenty of varieties of flowers and vegetables, is less likely to have problems than one restricted to a monoculture.**

If you do use chemicals make sure that you follow the manufacturer's instructions. Take the necessary safety precautions and thoroughly wash all equipment. Never leave chemicals or associated equipment where children can get at them.

Weather Problems

We cannot control the weather; we simply have to take what nature throws at us. Nevertheless, there are some ways in which we can limit the worst of its effects.

Wind

Winds can be destructive. Not only can they knock over and break plants, but also wind-rock can cause a plant to move about so that it becomes loose in the soil or it can create a hole around the point at which the plant enters the soil. This fills with stagnant water, and the plant can rot. A dry or hot wind can remove moisture from leaves, making them wilt. Cold winds can create wind-burn, which shrivels leaves. Winds can also make it unpleasant to work in the garden, frequently making the gardener not only uncomfortable but also irritable – not the best of moods to produce a good vegetable garden.

A long catalogue of woes, but the wind can be tamed to a large degree by creating windbreaks of some sort. By far the best defence is a hedge, which filters the wind, cutting down its speed considerably but at the same time not creating turbulence. A wall, on the other hand, stops the wind dead, but it escapes over the top and creates turbulence on the far side, and this can be more destructive than the wind itself. An alternative to a hedge is a form of plastic netting that is designed especially to be used as a windbreak. This is not the most beautiful of materials, but it is extremely functional.

ABOVE **A maximum/minimum thermometer is ideal for keeping track of the temperature both in the open garden and inside a greenhouse.**

BELOW **A hedge provides excellent protection from the wind. It allows some air to filter through, thus reducing the turbulence that occurs with solid features such as walls.**

TOP **Newspaper makes an excellent temporary insulation against sudden frosts in spring. Drop several layers, one on top of the other, to create air pockets. Do not leave on during the day.**

ABOVE **Fleece has a similar function to newspaper. It is very light and will not harm the plants. Unlike newspaper, it can be left on during the day as light penetrates though it.**

RIGHT **If a frost pocket is caused by a thick hedge, stopping cold air rolling down a hill, cut a hole in the base so that the air can pass through and continue down the hill away from the garden.**

Make sure that the poles supporting it are anchored securely because the netting will act as a sail and exert enormous pressure on its supports.

As a rule, a hedge or windbreak netting will create a "wind shadow" of about ten times the height of the barrier. In other words, a hedge 2m/6ft high will create a relatively wind-free area of about 20m/60ft from its base. The degree of protection decreases the further you get from the hedge, and at 20m/60ft from the hedge the decrease in wind speed is minimal.

Turbulence is reduced considerably by the use of double hedges or two rows of windbreak. Set a few yards apart, these give far greater protection than a single barrier.

Frost

There are two aspects to frost. The first is general winter cold; the second is those sudden unseasonable frosts that can wreak havoc among tender, newly put-out plants.

Winter cold is not generally too much of a problem in the vegetable garden because most of the things left in the garden are hardy. In particularly cold areas or in very cold spells, it is a good idea to give protection to some of the permanent crops, such as globe artichokes, by covering them with straw.

There is more of a problem if the garden is a cold one and the soil does not warm up until late in the spring. If your garden is like this, you will find it impossible to start gardening until then, and this makes early crops difficult to grow. There are several things you can do to help, however. If your vegetable garden is in a frost hollow – caused by cold air being trapped within it – it may be possible to "drain" it. Make a hole in the hedge or fence at the lowest point of the garden so that the air can flow through and continue down the slope. Alternatively, hedges may be placed higher up the slope to deflect the cold air as it moves downhill. Covering the soil with black polythene (plastic) or cloches will help warm up and dry out the soil so that you can start work on it earlier.

Sudden frosts can be a nightmare, especially if they are preceded by a warm spell that brings plants into early growth. Keep an ear or eye on the weather forecasts and cover tender plants if frost threatens. Use cloches, fleece or even newspaper.

ABOVE **Some plants, such as globe artichokes, are hardy but can be damaged by severe weather. They can be covered with straw to give them extra protection.**

ABOVE **Filling a box with straw makes a good form of insulation that can be removed and replaced. It also prevents the straw being blown about.**

ABOVE **Cloches produce longer-term protection than straw. They can be used to protect crops through the winter or as temporary cover in spring whenever frosts threaten.**

Drought

Few vegetables and fruit will grow without adequate moisture. Many plants will grow in dry conditions, but they quickly bolt (run to seed) and tend to be tough and often taste bitter. A constant supply of water is necessary so that growth is steady and uninterrupted. Irregular supplies of water will lead to irregular growth and many vegetables and fruit, in particular, will split.

Maintaining reserves

Throughout this book there is an emphasis on adding as much organic material as possible to the soil. Once again, this advice has to be repeated. Any free moisture in ordinary soil is likely to drain away or evaporate from the surface. However, fibrous material around the plant's roots will hold moisture in the same way as a cloth or a sponge. If there is excess moisture it will drain away, so that the plant is not standing in stagnant water, but enough will be retained to supply the plant's roots over a considerable time. Even if the water supply depends on irregular rain showers, the slow release will help to mitigate the dry periods.

Working as much organic material as possible into the soil is one way of pre-empting a dry summer. Add it to the soil when it is dug or, if you are using a non-digging, deep-bed system, add it as a top-dressing. Do this every year so that the water-retaining quality of the soil improves.

ABOVE **The best way to water a vegetable garden is with a watering can. Water can then be applied to exactly the right spot and in the right quantity with little water being wasted. However, watering by hand is both time-consuming and heavy work.**

Keeping water in

One way that moisture is lost from the soil is through evaporation from the surface. Hot sun and drying winds quickly take their toll on the soil and can dry it to a surprising depth, simply because more is drawn upwards to replace what has been lost nearer the surface. Covering the soil with a mulch helps to preserve this moisture.

ABOVE **A dribble hose is a good watering method because the hose is laid along the row of plants and it only waters the immediate area. The water slowly seeps out of the pipe, which means that it does not flood the area, but sinks well into the soil.**

LEFT **Place water butts beneath as many rooves as possible to catch the water as it runs off. It is the purest form of water to use and, being at ambient temperature, it does not chill the plants. It will also save water and, in most gardens, the money spent on water bills.**

RIGHT **Mulching with a layer of grass cuttings helps to preserve the moisture in the soil. Water before mulching and do not use too thick a layer as this may heat up and burn the plant – 7.5cm/3in is sufficient.**

Organic mulches are the best ones to use because they not only act as a barrier, but also eventually break down and are taken into the soil, much to its benefit. A mulch acts as a barrier partly because moisture does not evaporate from it quite as quickly as it does from ordinary soil, and partly because it acts as a thermal barrier, preventing the soil from getting too warm and thus speeding up the drying process.

Non-organic mulches – polythene (plastic), for example – prevent even greater loss as little moisture finds its way through, but, of course, it is not as easy for water to penetrate in the first place. Those to whom the aesthetic qualities of the kitchen garden are important may find that polythene looks ugly and will prefer to use an organic mulch.

It is important that the ground is thoroughly watered before any mulch is applied. If the ground is left dry the mulch will prevent it from getting wet unless a very large quantity of water is supplied.

Watering

Water is an expensive commodity – and becoming increasingly expensive in some areas – so you should use it only where and when it is really needed. Avoid, if possible, using sprinklers that waste large quantities of water on paths and other non-productive ground. If you have the time and strength use a watering can, supplying water to the base of individual plants. If you do this, you can be sure that the water goes where it is most needed. Sprinklers are especially useful when there is a large area of produce to cover or if watering by hand is difficult for physical reasons.

One efficient way of supplying water is to use a drip hose. This is a hosepipe (garden hose) with holes in it. It is laid along the line of plants and water constantly dribbles out. There is not enough water to flood the soil, but there is sufficient to provide a constant supply to the plants. If the ground is mulched, lay the pipe under the mulch. These hoses are best left on for several hours until the soil has taken up sufficient moisture, and then turned off, but there are gardens where they can be left on permanently. The system works best with permanent plantings, such as fruit bushes.

Whatever method you use, make certain that the ground is thoroughly soaked. A sprinkling of water on the surface will do little other than lay the dust. To be effective, a watering should supply at least the equivalent of 2.5cm/1in of rain.

LEFT **Black polythene (plastic) mulch is not attractive, but it is effective in reducing the water lost through evaporation. Special horticultural mulch can also be bought which allows water to pass through into the ground but prevents it escaping again.**

Weed Control

Many people are put off gardening simply because they do not like the idea of weeding. However, there are two points that they probably never consider. The first is that in a well-maintained garden there is far less weeding to do than they might think, and, second, weeding can be a rather relaxing, even therapeutic, task.

ABOVE **Avoid using chemical weedkillers in the vegetable garden. If necessary, use them to kill persistent weeds when initially preparing the plot. Always follow the instructions on the packet.**

Keep it clean

Weeds in the right place can be a good thing, but the right place is not the vegetable garden. Weeds take nutrients and moisture from the soil, depriving the vegetables of their share. They can grow tall, smothering or drawing up the vegetables so that they do not grow properly. Many weeds harbour diseases, particularly rusts, and pass these on to your crops. So keep your kitchen garden clear of weeds if you want to produce the best crops.

Good preparation

One way to reduce the amount of weeding is to prepare the ground thoroughly in the first place. If all perennial weeds are removed, either by hand or with weedkillers, the only problem to cope with are new perennial and annual weeds that germinate from seeds. These are not much of a problem as long as they are hoed off soon after they have appeared. If you remove them before they can run to seed, gradually the number of seeds left in the soil – and hence the number of germinating weeds – will be reduced.

Keeping on top

As long as you keep on top of weeds they are not a problem. It is when you let things slip that it all becomes a chore. Hoe off weed seedlings as they appear and it will only take a few minutes of your time. Allow them to become fully grown and it will take hours to sort things out.

Hoeing

The method of hoeing is often a matter of personal preference. If you have a draw or swan-neck hoe, you scrape the weeds off by drawing the hoe towards you. If you have a plate or Dutch hoe, you push it forwards, slicing off the weeds. If you have a three-pronged cultivator, you pull it through the top layer of soil, disturbing the roots of the weeds. In dry weather a hoe of either kind is best because you do not want to open the soil too much or water will evaporate. In wetter weather, however, the cultivator can be extremely useful because it opens the soil and allows the water to drain through.

Close work

Weeds do not always conveniently grow between the rows; they also grow in them where it is not as easy to hoe. With well-spaced

BELOW **For delicate hoeing around plants that may be easily damaged, a small one-handed hoe, known as an onion hoe, can be used. It is a form of draw hoe.**

ABOVE **It is not always possible to hoe without damaging the vegetables, or because the weeds are too well advanced. Weeding with a hand fork is then the best alternative.**

TOP **A push, plate or Dutch hoe is pushed forward, slicing either on or just below the surface, cutting off the weeds.**

ABOVE **A cultivator is a form of three-pronged hoe that is drawn between the rows of vegetables. This loosens the earth and with it any seedlings that have just germinated. As their roots are loose in the soil they cannot pick up moisture, and so die. This method is not as good in wet weather because the rain replants the weeds.**

LEFT **Hoeing is the traditional way of keeping a vegetable garden free of weeds. A draw hoe or swan-neck hoe is pulled towards the gardener in a series of chopping movements.**

crops, such as cabbages, it is possible to hoe around them, but this is impossible with vegetables such as carrots, and here you will have to weed by hand. Sometimes there is space to use an onion hoe, a small hoe with a short handle, which is held in one hand.

When you are working close to vegetables be careful not to disturb them. If a vegetable is disturbed when weeding nearby, firm down the soil and water in afterwards.

Non-digging methods

Gardening lore says that one year's weed seed means seven years' hard work, spent removing the resulting seedlings. What actually happens is that the seeds get mixed with the soil and germinate only when they come to the surface – one year's worth of weed seeds, therefore, will continue to be a nuisance until they have all been used up. However, if you do not bring the seeds to the surface in the first place they cannot germinate, and in non-digging methods only the surface layer is disturbed and the store of weed seeds is quickly used up. In consequence, if you regularly scrape off any weeds that appear, then the amount of work will soon be reduced because the only new weeds will be those blown in on the wind – the rest will be left underground, out of harm's way.

Pests and Diseases

Some gardeners get terribly worried about pests and diseases, but in reality they are rarely a real problem. Common sense and good management mean that you should be able to go for years without feeling the need to reach for the spray gun.

Gardening books always include long lists of pests and diseases and make it look as if these problems are lurking around every corner, just waiting to burst in on your garden and ruin your crops. In fact, it is unlikely that most gardeners will ever see a fraction of these during his or her lifetime, and, if they do, they are probably not really worth worrying about.

A mixed garden

One of the best ways of keeping the garden pest free is to grow a wide range of crops. If you only grow carrots and carrot root fly turns up and devastates your crop, you have nothing left. However, if you grow 20 different types of vegetables, you are only going to lose a twentieth of your total crop, which is relatively insignificant.

A mixed garden, which contains plenty of flowers – particularly the old-fashioned varieties – will attract a host of wildlife such as ladybirds, hoverflies and plenty of other predators, which will attack any pests that arrive in the garden. I have a large cottage garden with several large flower gardens within it and I am rarely troubled by even such common pests as aphids. Indeed, I cannot actually remember the last time any chemicals were used on my garden, not because I am against using chemical treatments, but because it has just not been necessary to do so.

ABOVE **Rabbits can devastate a garden overnight, leaving nothing but chewed off stumps as a result of their visit.**

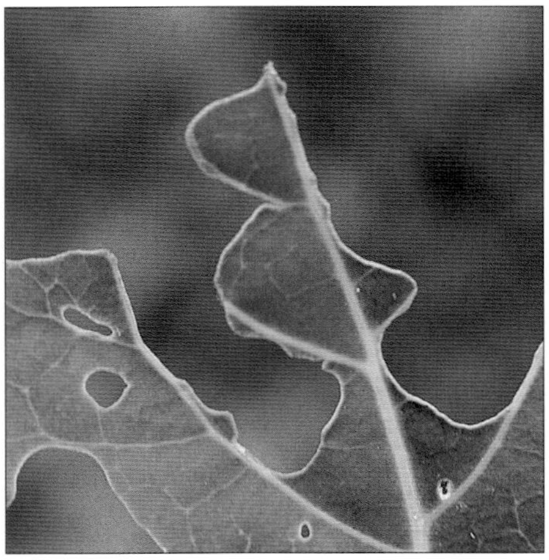

ABOVE **Birds are one of the worst pests in the garden. Here large bites have been taken out of a brassica.**

LEFT **Nets can be used to guard your crops against rabbits and rodents.**

Animals

There is one type of pest that is very difficult to control – mammals. They can rarely be killed and are difficult to deter. The only real action that you can take is preventative, and this means building a barricade around your garden. Wire netting, which will keep out most animals, should be partially buried in the ground to prevent burrowing species, such as rabbits, getting underneath. For the more athletic species, such as deer, the barrier will need to be at least 2.4m/8ft high if you are to prevent them from jumping over it. Fortunately, there is no need to take action unless you live in an area where these pests are a problem. You will rarely be troubled, for example, if you garden in a town.

Birds

While only relatively few gardeners have deer to contend with, birds are everywhere, and even if things are quiet one day, a large flock of pigeons can appear the next, even in a town. The only real recourse against pigeons is to net everything. A fruit cage that is tall enough to allow the gardener in is the best,

ABOVE **Damage to trees can be prevented by using wire guards.**

RIGHT **Birds and butterflies can be kept at bay with fine-meshed nets.**

ABOVE **Insect damage can cause a wide range of problems. Aphids, like these, not only distort and kill plants by sucking the sap from leaves and stems, but can also introduce diseases.**

ABOVE **The caterpillar stage in the development of butterflies and moths causes a great deal of damage to leaves, especially to members of the cabbage family.**

ABOVE **Mechanical methods are often easier and cause less harm than using chemicals. Here, fleece is used to cover brassicas to prevent butterflies from laying eggs.**

but this is expensive. Low level netting can be used as temporary protection when crops are at their most vulnerable.

Bird scarers are also a possibility, but they are not especially effective. Humming tapes are probably the most effective solution, but they do not always work.

In addition to eating fruit, buds and leaf vegetables, birds can also cause damage to crops by dust-bathing in the seedbeds of the garden. These can be covered with netting as a deterrent. The birds are usually also deterred if several pea-sticks are laid temporarily on the bed.

LEFT **Biological controls are an increasingly successful way to fight pests. They are mainly used in greenhouses, but others are now becoming available for the open garden. The control insects are released, here from a sachet, in order to attack the pests.**

LEFT **Sticky traps are another form of non-spray control that is becoming popular for a wide range of pests. Here, pheromones attract insect pests to the trap, where they get stuck. Other sticky traps consist of sheets of yellow plastic covered with a non-drying glue. These are mainly used in greenhouses.**

Insects

A wide range of insect pests can attack vegetables. Some of these, such as aphids, attack virtually anything; others, such as carrot fly, restrict themselves to one type of crop. Many pests can be deterred by taking simple precautions. Cabbage root fly, for example, can be deterred by placing a piece of roofing felt or plastic on the ground around the plant to prevent the adults from laying their eggs next to the stem. Black fly can be a pest of broad (fava) beans, but if you remove their favourite part of the plant, the succulent tips, before they appear, the blackfly usually do not stop. Small outbreaks of insects can usually be removed by hand before they get out of control.

If the worst comes to the worst, you can use a chemical control. There are types that are safe to use with vegetables, but it is essential to read the instructions on the packaging, especially any advice about safety. Use chemicals only when and where they are needed; do not automatically drench everything. Make sure that spray or powder does not drift onto other plants, especially those that may be ready to be harvested.

Caterpillars

There are three ways of dealing with caterpillars. The first is preventative. Cover the plants with fleece or small-mesh netting so that butterflies and moths cannot lay their

LEFT **Slugs and snails have few friends among gardeners. They make holes in just about any part of a plant, often leaving it useless or even dead.**

eggs. The second is to check susceptible plants regularly and remove any eggs or caterpillars by hand. You may miss a few, but this usually keeps the problem within reasonable bounds. The third is to use chemicals. Again, be certain that they are suitable for vegetables and follow the instructions scrupulously.

Slugs and snails

Mollusc are probably the gardener's worst enemy. There are many traditional ways of ridding the garden of them, including using containers of beer sunk into the beds, but one of the most effective ways is to go out after dark with a torch (flashlight) and round up as many as you can see – and you will be surprised how many you will find. Kill them by putting them in a container of water with added washing-up liquid, or capture and release them on waste ground away from your garden. Doing this for a few nights should help to keep the problem under control.

If you must, you can use slug bait. There are organic baits available if you prefer, but they do not seem to be as effective as the non-organic type. Always follow the manufacturer's instructions to the letter and do not leave either bait or dead slugs around because they may be eaten by wildlife. Biological control is available, but it is expensive, the supply is erratic, and it does not always work; but things should improve on this front.

Diseases

Good housekeeping can prevent many diseases. Remove diseased or rotting material as soon as you see it. Deter aphids, which are often the carriers of disease, and, as a matter of practice, do not use the same ground two years running for the same crop. Wet, ill-drained soil may be the cause of some diseases, so improving the condition of the soil can be an important factor in keeping disease at bay. Healthy, well-fed and watered plants are less likely to fall prey to disease. Never buy, or accept as gifts, diseased plants.

Many modern hybrids are less susceptible to certain diseases than some of the older ones, so choose your varieties with care, if you are worried about possible diseases.

Some diseases can be treated with chemicals, but if there is any doubt, dig up the affected plants and burn them as soon as possible. If you do use chemicals, be careful and follow all instructions, especially the safety ones. Store chemicals well out of the reach of young children.

Burning is the only solution for plants suffering from viral diseases, such as mosaic virus on marrows (zucchini) and cucumbers or on spinach, because there is no known cure. Burning vegetables may seem a waste, but it is far better to safeguard the unaffected plants as well as to prevent spores from getting into the soil. If this does happen, next year's plants might be affected as well. To avoid this, use a rotational system of growing crops.

Remember not to put diseased plants on the compost heap. In theory, the compost should get hot enough to kill off any spores, but you can never be quite certain that all parts of the heap are sufficiently hot, and you might end up spreading the disease over the whole garden.

BELOW **Many of the diseases that affect vegetables are fungal ones, such as this rust on leeks.**

Herb Pests and Diseases

Herbs in general do not suffer greatly from pests and diseases. As predominantly wild plants, they have health and vigour and many are highly aromatic, which gives them inherent protection from insects, which do not like the strong smell. But bacterial and fungal diseases do occasionally strike and no garden is without its share of insect pests. They are, after all, part of a chain, providing food for predators: hedgehogs, birds, mice and other insects.

Above *Damage from red spider mites.*

Top *Scale insect on a bay leaf.*

Above *The damage caused by a scale insect.*

Pests

Aphids: Blackfly and greenfly, which suck the sap of a plant, weakening it, checking growth and often transmitting viral diseases. Greenfly are attracted to roses and the various species of black aphid to the new soft growth of many green plants. Encourage natural predators such as ladybirds (ladybugs), spray with soapy water, hose with plain water, or spray with derris dust or rotenone. (Black aphids, commonly known as blackfly, should not be confused with American bloodsucking black flies, which are a true fly, rather than an aphid.)

Whitefly: These are small winged insects which usually live on brassicas but can be a problem in the greenhouse. Spray with soft soap, hang up sticky traps (yellow attracts whitefly) or introduce *Encarsia formosa*, a parasitic wasp.

Red spider mite: Flourishes in hot, dry conditions, especially the greenhouse in summer. Difficult to detect without a magnifying glass – watch for bronzed or withered leaves and a fine cobweb mesh on the plants. Cut off badly affected leaves, hose off with plenty of water and spray with soft soap, or introduce a biological predator, another even smaller mite *Phytoseiulus persimilis*.

Scale insects: Flat, brownish insects which attach themselves to the undersides of leaves, suck the sap and spread a sticky substance, followed by a sooty mould. Bay is especially prone to attack. Cut off affected leaves and burn them, spray with insecticidal soap or introduce predatory wasp, *Metaphycus helvolus*, as a control.

Slugs: These do most damage in early spring and appear in the evenings. Pick them off by hand or sink jars filled with beer into the soil to attract and trap them.

Above *Greenfly suck the sap of a rose.*

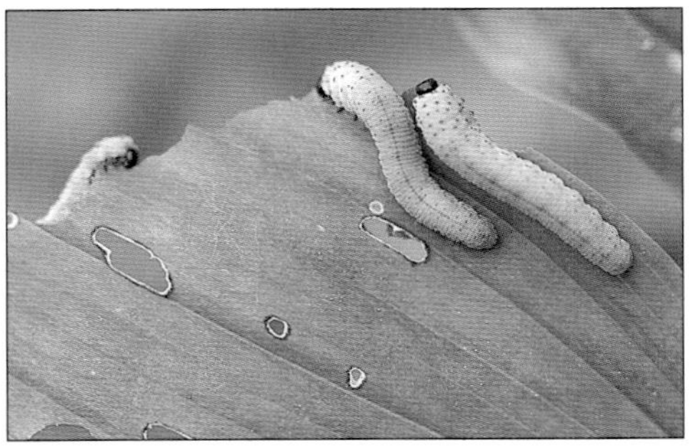

Above *Caterpillars on* Polygonatum odoratum.

Diseases

Powdery mildew: A fungal disease which thrives in high humidity. Bergamot, *Monarda didyma*, is prone to it. Don't overwater or overfertilize plants. Spray with Bordeaux mixture.

Botrytis: A fungus which attacks many plants, especially if grown under glass, including tomatoes, strawberries, roses and sunflowers. Seen as a grey mould, it thrives in high humidity. Spray with Bordeaux mixture, following the manufacturer's instructions.

Rust: Brownish-red pustules appear on the leaves and the plant wilts. It affects mint. Dig up and destroy plants if severely affected. Dust with a proprietary sulphur powder following manufacturer's instructions.

Damping-off disease: A fungal disease, it affects seedlings grown under glass. Prevention is best – sow seeds thinly, as overcrowding will encourage the condition, do not overwater, and provide adequate ventilation.

Prevention

Healthy plants depend on good gardening practice. They should not be overcrowded, which deprives them of light and air. Keep them free of weeds and prune regularly – always using clean secateurs (pruners) and other cutting tools so that you do not pass diseases from one plant to another by mistake.

Vigilance is important – try to remove insect infestations before they build up, and cut out diseased leaves as soon as you see them and burn them. Overfeeding plants with chemical fertilizers will only weaken them and make for fresh, sappy growth which attracts insect pests, but an organic seaweed fertilizer, applied as a spray, helps to build up their resistance.

Correct watering, especially for greenhouse and indoor plants, is also a vital factor. Overwatering tends to lead to rotting plants and inadequate ventilation encourages mildews and botrytis.

Beneficial Insects

Lacewings, ladybirds (ladybugs) and the larvae of the hoverfly all prey on aphids. Grow plants to attract them.

Lacewings: These are attracted by yarrow (*Achillea millefolium*), golden rod (*Solidago virgaurea*) and chamomile (*Chamaemelum nobile*).

Ladybirds (ladybugs): These are attracted by yarrow (*Achillea millefolium*) and pot marigolds (*Calendula officinalis*).

Hoverflies: These are attracted by yarrow (*Achillea millefolium*), lovage (*Levisticum officinale*), dill (*Anethum graveolens*), sweet cicely (*Myrrhis odorata*), fennel (*Foeniculum officinale*), golden rod (*Solidago virgaurea*) and centaury (*Centaurium erythraea*).

Other insects which prey on specific pests can be bought in.

Encarsia formosa: Small parasitic wasps that control whitefly infestations.

Phytoseiulus persimilis: A Chilean mite smaller than its red spider mite prey.

Metaphycus helvolus: Predatory wasp for scale insects.

Aphidoletes aphidimyza: A parasitic midge which preys on aphids.

Above *Yellow sticky traps used for catching whitefly in a commercial greenhouse.*

Organic Pesticides

Sometimes sprays are the only way to control a situation. But the problem with chemical sprays is that they destroy all the beneficial insects as well as pests. They also upset the balance of nature as the predatory insects are less numerous, multiply less enthusiastically than their prey and do not recover. Therefore, the next generation of pests multiplies unchecked and the problem is compounded.

It is best to use organic sprays where possible, but the most effective of these destroy insects, not just pests.

Soap is the least harmful method. A household liquid soap is suitable. Horticultural insecticidal soaps are even more effective. Derris is made from a tropical plant, and available in liquid or powder form. It kills beneficial insects as well as pests so use with great discretion. Bordeaux mixture is an inorganic chemical fungicide, but not harmful to human or animal life.

Companion Planting

The insect-repellent properties of many herbs, owing to the high concentration of aromatic oils they contain, makes them ideal companions for protecting vulnerable plants such as roses, fruit and vegetables from insect attack. Plant them in a potager garden. Rue (*Ruta graveolens*), cotton lavender (*Santolina chamaecyparissus*), curry plant (*Helichrysum angustifolia*), tansy (*Tanacetum vulgare*) and southernwood (*Artemisia abrotanum*) are all strongly aromatic and can discourage many types of pests.

Chives and garlic are beneficial to roses. They give off an odour which discourages aphids and may help cut the incidence of the disease, blackspot.

Chamomile, once known as "the plants' physician", has a reputation for improving the health and vigour of those plants and herbs surrounding it.

Pennyroyal (*Mentha pulegium*) helps to keep ants away, planted among paving. Summer savory (*Satureja hortensis*), planted in rows next to broad beans (fava beans), provides some protection from blackfly.

French marigolds, *Tagetes*, are excellent at discouraging whitefly, especially in the greenhouse.

Nicotiana sylvestris works on a trap principle. It attracts whitefly, which are then caught by the sticky stems and leaves and can be disposed of.

growing vegetables

There are almost as many different ways of doing things in the garden as there are gardeners. In truth, no one way is better than any other – it depends very much on who is doing what and where it is being done. Something that works for you may not help a gardener just a few doors away down the road.

Having said that, there is a certain amount of common ground in most of the techniques used in the vegetable garden, and the procedures we discuss here should stand you in good stead, even if you eventually develop your own methods. In this section you will find helpful advice on general kitchen gardening techniques, including sowing seed, both outdoors and under glass; thinning and transplanting seedlings; and harvesting and storing.

Detailed advice on the techniques to master for individual crops are covered in the later chapters on specific vegetables, herbs and fruit.

Timing

There is an optimum time for most of the activities that are carried out in the garden, but precise timing is rarely crucial, and it does not matter if you cannot do something one week and have put it off to the next – or even later. Clay soils, for example, are best dug in autumn, but many gardeners never get around to it until spring.

Apart from social and business pressures that might upset your schedule, the weather and general garden conditions are likely to vary from year to year. When it comes to digging, for instance, a wet autumn may make it impossible for you to get onto the ground to dig it, and so you will have to wait until spring. When spring comes, you may want to get on with it and sow your carrots, but there is little point in doing this if the ground is still too cold, because carrots will not germinate until it has warmed up and any attempt to do so will end with wasted seeds.

It is, of course, wise to stick to the best timing if possible, particularly as there often comes a point when it is too late to do something. For example, there is little point in sowing most seeds after midsummer because they will not come to anything before autumn and winter set in.

Remember, though, that there is always another year. If things do go awry one year, there is always the next to look forward to.

ABOVE **Greenhouses need more care and attention than the open garden. Factors such as good hygiene and the control of pests and diseases must be borne in mind.**

Effort

Gardening can be strenuous, especially if you are elderly or not particularly fit. Do not overdo things, especially heavy tasks such as digging. Build up gradually, particularly after an idle winter. Many techniques and tools can be adapted for the disabled and elderly, but if things do become difficult, there is no shame in getting help of one sort or another.

Keeping tidy

When you are working in the garden, try to keep things tidy. Thinnings and weeds should always be removed from the beds to prevent the waste material promoting or harbouring disease. When you are harvesting produce, cut off and discard any fruit or vegetables that are rotten or diseased and do not leave them there to spread their problems. Many difficulties in the garden can be avoided by adopting techniques that result in a neat and tidy garden.

RIGHT **Most techniques involve working with nature, but a few are inevitably artificial. Terracotta rhubarb forcers, for example, are used to bring rhubarb crops to maturity faster than they would normally.**

Sowing in the Open

Most vegetables and herbs can be sown directly into the open ground. The two main advantages of doing this are that no indoor facilities are required and the plants' growth is not delayed when they are planted out. Some plants also resent their roots being disturbed.

ABOVE **Some seed, beetroot (beets) in particular, benefits from an hour's soaking in tepid water before sowing.**

Soil requirements

The main requirement is that the soil should be broken down into a fine tilth – in other words, the soil crumbs should be small. The soil should be neither too wet nor too dry. If it is wet, cover it with cloches or polythene (plastic) to prevent it being further wetted and wait until it dries out a little before sowing. If the soil is too dry, then water the ground a short time before sowing; there should be sufficient water to soak in but not leave a sticky surface. The ground should also be warm. Seeds sown in cold ground will frequently just sit there until they rot. Ideally, the soil should be at a temperature of at least 7°C/45°F.

LEFT **Vegetables that are usually planted out, rather than sown where they are to grow, such as these cabbages, can still be sown in the open and then transplanted when they are large enough.**

Seed requirements

Most of the seed that is available these days is of a high quality, especially when it comes from the major suppliers. The germination rate is usually good, although occasionally one gets an unsatisfactory batch. Non-germination, however, is usually due to some other factor, such as cold conditions. It is possible to keep your own seed, but only do this for non-F1 hybrids because F1s will not come true to type. Most seed is sold loose in packets, but seeds can be bought in other forms, and one of the most common is pelleted, when the seeds are coated with clay. The coating makes the seeds easier to handle and to sow. Increasingly, pre-germinated seeds and young seedlings are also becoming available. For most purposes, however, ordinary seeds will be suitable and certainly the cheapest.

Sowing in rows

The conventional way of sowing seeds is to do so in rows. Using a garden line for guidance, draw out a shallow drill in the fine soil with the corner of a hoe. If the ground is dry, water along the drill with a fine-rose watering can. Sow the seeds thinly. Mark the ends of the row with a label and a stick and draw the soil back over the drill with a rake. The

SOWING SEED

1 Draw out a shallow drill with the corner of a draw hoe, using a garden line to ensure that it is straight.

2 If the soil is dry, water along the length of the drill and allow it to drain before sowing seed.

3 Sow the seed along the drill, sowing it as thinly as

4 Put a label at the end of the row clearly showing what is in the row. Put a stick or another label at the far end. Do this before filling in the drill.

5 Rake the soil into the drill over the seed. Gently tamp down the soil along the row with the flat of the rake and then lightly rake over.

6 If the soil is heavy and is difficult to break into a fine tilth, draw out the drill and then line it with potting compost (soil mix).

depth of the drill depends on the size of the seeds, but most finer seeds should be sown at a depth of 1cm/½in. The seed packet usually gives the depth required.

Station sowing

With plants that grow quite large and therefore need to be spaced out in the row, it is wasteful to sow a continuous line of seeds. Station sowing involves sowing three seeds at distances that will be the eventual gap between plants – parsnip seeds, therefore, are sown at 20cm/8in intervals.

Wide rows

Some seeds, mainly peas and beans, are sown in wide rows – in effect, two rows are sown at once. A wide drill, 15cm/6in across, is made with the flat of the hoe. Two rows of peas or beans are sown, one down each side of the drill, and the soil is carefully raked back over the seeds so that they are not disturbed.

Broadcasting

This is the best method for sowing seeds in blocks. Rake the area to a fine tilth and scatter the seeds thinly but evenly over the surface. If the soil is dry, gently rake the seeds in and water with a fine-rose watering can.

Protecting

Fine earth is attractive to both birds and animals as a dust bath as well as a litter tray, and when it is used the seeds will be scattered far and wide. In addition, some birds find emerging seedlings an irresistible source of food. Protect the seeds by placing wire-netting guards along the rows. Alternatively, a few pea-sticks can be laid across the surface of the soil. Another possibility is to place short sticks in the ground and to twine cotton between them. This last method is the least convenient because the protection cannot be quickly removed and replaced to permit for hoeing and weeding.

Labelling

Before covering the seed with soil, mark the end of the rows with pegs and a label. Once the drill is filled in, it is difficult to see where it is. It may be some time before the seedlings emerge and the row can be easily disturbed by, for example, accidentally hoeing through it. Similarly, it is important to know what is sown where, so a label bearing the name and variety of the vegetable is important. Traditionally, many gardeners spike the seed packet on a peg but these quickly deteriorate and often blow away.

Sowing under Glass

Germinating seeds under glass is more tedious and time-consuming than sowing direct into the ground, but raising plants in this way has its advantages. It allows the gardener to grow reasonably sized plants that are ready to set out as soon as the weather allows, stealing a march on those sown in the soil by about two weeks. If there are pest problems, such as slugs or birds, the plants are better able to resist them if they are well grown when they are planted out than if they have to fight for their life as soon as they emerge through the soil.

ABOVE **There is a range of pots and trays now available that are suitable for sowing vegetable and herb seed. *Clockwise from top left*: individual cells or modules, a half tray, plastic pots, a fibrous pot and fibrous modules.**

Containers

Seeds can be sown in a variety of containers. Traditionally they were sown in wooden trays or flats. Some gardeners prefer to make their own, claiming that they are warmer and that they can be made deeper than the purchased equivalents. Plastic trays have, however, generally replaced the wooden varieties. They can be made of rigid plastic for multiple use or thin, flimsy plastic, and these are used only once before being thrown away.

Often, only a few plants may be required, and it is rather wasteful to sow a whole or half tray. A 9cm/3½in pot is usually sufficient.

More and more gardeners are using modular or cellular trays, in which one or two seeds are sown in a small cell. If both germinate, one is removed and the remaining seedling is allowed to develop without having to be pricked out. This method avoids a lot of root disturbance.

Even less root disturbance occurs if the seeds are sown in biodegradable fibrous modules. As soon as the seedling is big enough to be planted out, both pot and plant are inserted into the ground, and the pot allows the roots to grow through its sides into the surrounding earth.

Propagators

Propagators are glass or plastic boxes that help to keep the seed tray moist and in a warm atmosphere. The more expensive models have heating cables in them so that the temperature can be controlled. Although they are desirable, they are by no means absolutely necessary. Cheap alternatives can also be made simply by slipping the tray into a polythene (plastic) bag and removing it as soon as the seeds have germinated. Plastic jars can also be cut down to fit over trays or pots.

SOWING IN BLOCKS

Fill the cellular block with compost (soil mix) and tap it on the table to firm it down. Sow one or two seeds in each cell. Cover with a light dusting of compost. Remove the weaker of the two seedlings after germination.

SOWING IN POTS

Fill the pot with a good seed compost (soil mix), tap it on the bench and sow one to three seeds in each pot. Once germinated, the weaker seedlings will be removed, leaving one to grow on.

SOWING IN TRAYS

1 Fill the seed tray with seed compost (soil mix) and tamp down the compost lightly to produce a level surface. Sow the seed thinly across the compost.

2 Cover with a thin layer of compost (soil mix), lightly firm down and label. Labelling is very important because the seedlings of many vegetables look the same.

WATERING IN

Water the trays or pots by standing them in a shallow tray or bowl of water so that the water comes halfway up the container. Remove the tray or pot as soon as the surface of the compost (soil mix) begins to moisten.

USING A PROPAGATOR

1 Place the seeds in a propagator. You can adjust the temperature of heated propagators like this. Seed packets should indicate the best temperature, but you may need to compromise if different seeds need different temperatures.

2 This propagator is unheated and should be kept in a warm position in a greenhouse or within the house. Start opening the vents once the seeds have germinated to begin the hardening-off process.

Heat

A source of heat is useful for the rapid germination of seeds. It can be provided in the form of a heated propagator, but most seeds will germinate in the ambient temperature of a warm greenhouse or conservatory, or even within the house.

Sowing seed

Fill the seed tray with a good quality seed or potting compost (soil mix). Gently firm down and sow the seeds thinly on the surface. Spread a thin layer of potting compost over the seeds so that they are just covered. Again, firm down lightly. Water by placing the seed tray in a shallow bowl of water, so that the level of the water comes halfway up the sides of the seed tray. Once the surface of the compost shows signs of dampness, remove the tray and place it in a propagator or in a polythene (plastic) bag. A traditional alternative – and one that still works well – is to place a sheet of glass over the tray.

Subsequent treatment

As soon as the seeds begin to germinate, remove the lid from the propagator – or open the bag, depending on the method you are using – to let in air and after a couple of days remove the tray altogether. If you are using a propagator, turn off the heat and open the vents over a few days and then remove the tray.

Once the seedlings are large enough to handle, prick them out into trays, individual pots or modules. Hold the seedlings by the seed-leaves and not by the stem or roots. Make sure they are well spaced in the trays – at least 5cm/2in apart – and keep them warm and watered.

As the time approaches to plant them out, gradually harden them off by exposing them to outdoor conditions for a little longer each day until they can be safely left out overnight. They are then ready to plant out.

USING A COLD FRAME

1 Once the trays of seedlings or pricked-out seedlings are ready to plant out, harden them off by placing in a cold frame which is opened a little wider each day to let in more air.

2 Finally leave the lights of the cold frame off altogether so that the plants become accustomed to outside light.

Thinning and Transplanting

Outdoor-sown seedlings inevitably grow too thickly, no matter how thinly you try to sow them. In order to grow properly, they will need thinning. Seeds are often sown in a row that will not be their ultimate cropping position. Leeks, for example, are grown in a seed row and later transplanted to their final positions.

Why thin?

It is important that vegetables have enough space in which to develop. Plants that are too close together become drawn as they try to move to the light. In addition to not having room to develop, they become undernourished as they compete with their neighbours for moisture, nutrients and light. Crops that are too tightly planted are more susceptible to disease because air cannot circulate freely around them, allowing fungal diseases, such as mildew, to get a hold. Half-starved plants are also more prone to disease than fully nourished ones. A little attention at this stage will pay dividends in producing healthy plants.

THINNING AND TRANSPLANTING SEEDLINGS

1 Water the row of seedlings, the night before if possible, but at least a few hours before transplanting.

2 Using a hand fork, dig up, rather than pull out, the excess plants. Only dig up the plants as you need them; do not dig them up all at once and leave them lying around.

3 Using a garden line to keep the row straight, and a measuring stick to get the distances equal, replant the seedlings using a trowel.

4 Gently firm in each plant and water around them. Rake the soil around the plants in order to tidy it up and to remove footprints and uneven soil.

Thinning distances

Beetroot (beets) 7.5–10cm/3–4in
Broad (fava) beans 23cm/9in
Carrots 7.5cm/3in
Dwarf French (bush green) beans 20cm/8in
Florence fennel 25cm/10in
Kohl rabi 20cm/8in
Lettuce 23cm/9in
Parsley 15cm/6in
Peas 5cm/2in
Parsnips 15–20cm/6–8in
Radishes 2.5–5cm/1–2in
Runner beans 25–30cm/10–12in
Salsify 15cm/6in
Scorzonera 15cm/6in
Spinach 15cm/6in
Spring onions (scallions) 5cm/2in
Swedes (rutabagas or yellow turnips) 30cm/12in
Swiss chard 30cm/12in
Turnips 15cm/6in

Thinning

The idea behind thinning is to remove all unwanted plants, leaving the best at regular intervals. Before you begin to thin, water the row to soften the earth and to make sure that the remaining plants have taken up enough water in case their roots are accidentally disturbed. Allow the water to soak in and the plants to take it up. If possible, water the evening before you plan to thin.

Go along the row, with a measuring stick if you are uncertain about the distances between the plants, removing the weaker seedlings and leaving one strong one at the correct planting distance for that variety – 15–20cm/6–8in for parsnips, for example. When you pull out the unwanted seedlings, gently press the ground around the one that is left so that the pulling motion does not disturb that one as well.

When the row is complete, gently water along its length so that soil is washed back around the roots of the remaining plants that may have been disturbed. Dispose of the unwanted seedlings on the compost heap.

Avoid thinning during hot or windy conditions because the remaining plants may become desiccated before their roots can become re-established if they have been disturbed. A slightly damp, overcast day is ideal.

In hot dry weather, you can snip the unwanted seedlings off with a pair of scissors so you do not disturb their neighbours' roots.

RIGHT **Thinning vegetables to the correct distances ensures healthy, full-sized plants: shown are rows of onions, beetroot (beets), potatoes, carrots, spinach.**

Transplanting

Plants for transplanting can either be grown from seed sown in pots or trays, or from seed sown directly in the open ground. Seedlings that have been grown in containers should be pricked out first into individual pots, or widely spaced trays, so that each plant has room to develop. Harden them off if they have been grown under glass before transplanting them into the open ground.

Damp, overcast weather conditions are ideal for transplanting seedlings because the plants will not dry out quickly in a muggy atmosphere. Again, as with thinning, it is essential to water the plants first before transplanting them. This will give them sufficient moisture to keep them going until they have re-established their root systems.

Dig up just a few plants at a time – there is no point in leaving plants lying around on the ground where they can dry out. Discard any that are weak or undernourished, and never use any that are diseased. Using a line to make sure that the row is straight and a measuring stick in order to get the planting distances correct, plant at the same depth as in the seed bed, except where stated under individual vegetables – leeks, for example, are planted deeper. Gently firm in around each plant and water in.

THINNING SEEDLINGS IN SITU

When thinning a row of seedlings that have been sown in situ, water the row the night before or at least a few hours before. Remove the unwanted plants, leaving the recommended gap between each retained plant. Try not to disturb the plants that are left. Water the seedlings after thinning and remove all the discarded seedlings to the compost heap.

USING A DIBBER

Cabbages (shown here), onions and leeks are planted out using a dibber. This makes a hole in the ground into which the plant is slipped before the earth is firmed in around it.

Planting distances

Asparagus 30–38cm/12–15in
Aubergines (eggplants) 60cm/24in
Broccoli 60cm/24in
Brussels sprouts 50–75cm/20–30in
Cabbages 30–50cm/12–20in
Calabrese (Italian sprouting broccoli) 15–23cm/6–9in
Cauliflowers 50–75cm/20–30in
Celeriac (celery root) 30–38cm/12–15in
Celery 23–30cm/9–12in
Courgettes (zucchini) 60cm/24in
Cucumbers 60cm/24in
Garlic 15cm/6in
Globe artichokes 75cm/30in
Jerusalem artichokes 30cm/12in
Kale 60cm/24in
Leeks 15cm/6in
Marrows (zucchini) 60cm/24in
Onion sets 10cm/4in
Peppers 45–60cm/18–24in
Potatoes 30–38cm/12–15in
Pumpkins 90–180cm/36–72in
Rhubarb 75–90cm/30–36in
Runner beans 25–30cm/10–12in
Seakale 30cm/12in
Shallots 15–18cm/6–7in
Sweet corn (corn) 30cm/12in
Tomatoes 60cm/24in

Greenhouse Vegetables

Use a greenhouse to grow tender vegetables and plants that do best under glass in cooler climates – such as aubergines (eggplant) and certain varieties of tomatoes and cucumber – and use the warmth of the greenhouse to produce early vegetables while it is still too cold to plant out in the open garden.

ABOVE **Greenhouses, popular since the 18th century, are important for providing an artificially warm environment, not only for producing plants out of season, but also for propagating seedlings.**

Growing summer vegetables

Most vegetables benefit from being grown outside in the open ground, but there are a handful that are best grown under glass in cooler regions, even in the summer, because they prefer an even temperature that does not dip too low at night. Some plants, such as aubergines (eggplant) are usually always best grown under cover except in hot places. Others, such as tomatoes, cucumber and peppers can be grown outside in warmer areas but they have a much shorter season than when grown under glass.

It is possible to grow vegetables directly in the soil in greenhouse beds, but this soil soon becomes tired and crops begin to dwindle after a few years with an increase in disease. The laborious remedy is to dig the soil out and replace it with fresh, but the most common method is to grow the plants in containers that are renewed each season.

The simplest and most commonly used container is the growing bag, a large plastic sack filled with a compost (soil mix) especially formulated for growing plants under these conditions. These can be laid on the floor of the greenhouse for tall plants such as tomatoes, or on the benches for shorter subjects such as peppers. They are often too shallow to take a stake to support the plant and so either a special frame has to be used or strings are tied from the roof of the house down under the bags. The size of bags varies but most will accommodate up to three plants in a row. An alternative is to grow each plant in a large pot using a good quality general-purpose potting compost.

The key to growing any plants under these conditions is to keep them well watered; they must never be allowed to dry out. Under glass the plants get through a surprising amount of water and it is essential to water at least once a day and often twice.

LEFT **The cold frame is used not only to raise fruit and vegetables which need protection, but also as a means of nursing young stock through its tender weeks by giving shelter and, later, by allowing a gradual hardening-off.**

The temperature should never be allowed to get too hot. There should be plenty of air passing through the house, not only to keep the temperature down but also to prevent the air becoming stagnant, which makes it an ideal breeding ground for diseases. A light sun screen will also help reduce the temperature. This can either be applied as a wash to the glass or as netting. The advantage of the latter is that it can be removed during dull weather.

The plants can be planted much earlier than those outside – tomatoes can be planted under heat in April or even March. This means they will be in fruit before outdoor varieties have even been established. When selecting varieties, check the packets to ensure that they are for growing under glass rather than outside types.

Winter and spring vegetables

The greenhouse can be used to produce vegetables long before they can be grown in the open ground. Lettuce, carrots and French beans are all candidates. They can be grown in open beds on the base of the greenhouse if the soil is changed every other year, or they can be grown in growing bags.

Some plants, such as lettuce and spinach can be sown in the late summer or autumn for growing on through the winter, but others should be sown in the early spring just one or two weeks before sowing outside. There is no point in sowing earlier than this because although the temperature can be raised to keep the plants warm, they also need longer hours of daylight than late winter provides. They can be sown and treated in the same way as those growing outside except that they should be kept well watered, as obviously there is no rain to do it for you. It is advisable to space them further apart so that there is plenty of air circulating around them to prevent the onset of disease. Most of this type of vegetable does better growing outside, except for an early crop. Most can also be grown in a coldframe or under a cloche instead of in the greenhouse.

RIGHT **Glasshouse production of mixed crops needs expert management. On a smaller scale, it is best to stick to one or two items, or to grow plants with similar needs: tomatoes with green peppers and aubergines (eggplant) might be a useful combination.**

BELOW **Ripening the fruit of lemon trees in the greenhouse.**

Summer vegetables for under glass

Aubergines (eggplants)
Chilli peppers
Cucumbers
Melons
Okra
Sweet peppers
Tomatoes

Winter and spring vegetables for under glass

Carrots
Spinach
Lettuce
Oriental greens
Salad leaves
French beans
Radishes

Harvesting and Storing

The great moment comes when the vegetables are ready to harvest; nothing tastes quite like fresh vegetables that you have grown for yourself. However, not all the produce can be eaten at once and it is prudent to store some, especially for the winter months when fresh vegetables are at a premium.

ABOVE **Harvest root crops by levering up the root with a fork and pulling on the stems or leaves.**

Harvesting

Try to resist the temptation to harvest vegetables too soon. Until they have developed fully, their taste might not be matured and some might even be bitter. Traditionally, parsnips, celery and Brussels sprouts should not be harvested until they have experienced at least one frost, which makes them taste sweeter. There are some plants that can be harvested prematurely, however, in particular leafy crops. For example, young turnip tops are worth eating, while the tips of broad (fava) bean shoots can be tasty, long before the beans themselves have matured.

When you are harvesting do not simply pick the best vegetables. If you also come across any that are diseased or rotting, harvest these as well and compost them. Do not leave rotting vegetables on the plant or in the ground because they will spread their problems to healthy fruit or the spores may remain in the ground until the following year.

ABOVE **Some vegetables are harvested by cutting through the stems as and when they are required. Swiss chard, shown here, is a good example of this method of harvesting. The stem is cut close to the base. Some gardeners prefer to twist or snap the stems off at the base rather than cutting them.**

RIGHT **Quite a number of vegetables are picked. This usually entails snapping or cutting the stem just above the vegetable so that either part of the stalk remains or there is a complete break at the junction between vegetable and stalk. Here, runner beans are being harvested.**

There is no hard and fast rule about when or at what time of day to harvest, although taking the vegetable straight from the garden to the pot does, of course, give the freshest tasting dish. If possible, try to harvest when you want a vegetable, rather than leaving it lying around for a few days before using.

Storing

There are several ways of storing vegetables for later use. If you pick or dig up a vegetable and are unable to use it right away, it can usually be kept a few days before use. The best way of keeping these is to store them in a cool, dark place, preferably a cellar or cold shed. However, this is not always possible and a refrigerator is the next best thing.

The traditional way of storing root crops throughout winter is to dig them up, clean off any dirt and remove the leaves. Then they can be placed in trays of just-moist peat (peat moss or peat substitute) or sand. The vegetables are covered with more peat and, if the tray is deep enough, another layer of root crops is placed on top and again covered in peat. Carrots, beetroot (beets), celeriac (celery root), turnips, swedes (rutabagas or yellow turnips) and parsnips can all be stored in this way.

STORING ROOT CROPS

1 Most root crops can be stored in trays of just-moist sand or peat (peat moss or peat substitute). Place a layer of peat in the bottom of the tray and then lay a row of carrots on top. Cover these with more peat.

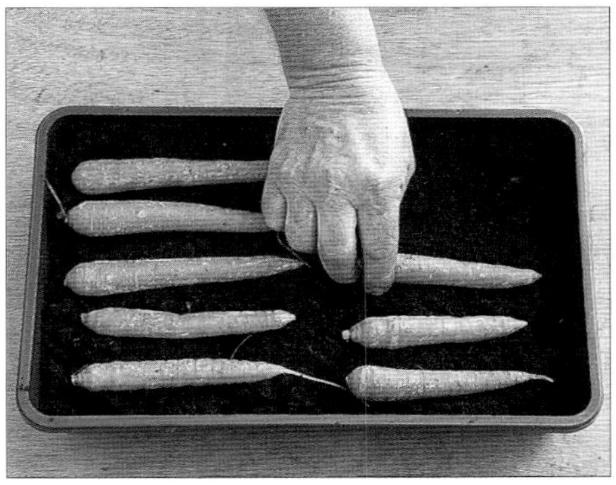

2 Place another layer of carrots on top and cover these with more peat. Repeat with more layers until the tray is full, topping off with a layer of peat.

Unless the weather is extremely cold, parsnips, celeriac (celery root), swedes (rutabagas or yellow turnips), carrots and beetroot (beets) can simply be left in the ground until they are required. However, if a deep frost is likely to occur, it is best to lift at least a few and store them inside because it is difficult to get them out of the ground once it has frozen. Although not strictly a root crop, leeks can also be left in the ground until they are needed.

Trays of root crops should be stored in a cool, but frost-free, shed or cellar. This is also one of the best places to store many other vegetables. Squashes, pumpkins and marrows (zucchini) can be stored on shelves or wire racks. Bulbous onions, shallots and garlic can be kept in trays or in net sacks. The important thing about storing all these vegetables is that they should not touch one another and that air should be able to circulate freely around them.

Brassicas are not so easy to store, but some of the solid cabbages can be harvested and hung in nets or placed on shelves in the same cool, frost-free shed until they are required. Stored in this way, they will stay sound for several months. Some brassicas are winter hardy and can be left where they are until required. Brussels sprouts are a good example of this.

Many vegetables will freeze reasonably well. To maintain good flavour they should first be blanched (placed in boiling water) for a few minutes, the length of time depending on the type of vegetable. Details can be found in good cookery books.

Although some vegetables do not freeze well this way, many can still be frozen, simply by cooking them first – Florence fennel, for example, can be cooked and puréed before freezing.

Another, more traditional way to store vegetables and fruit is to turn them into chutneys, pickles or some other sort of preserve. Fruit is delicious when bottled.

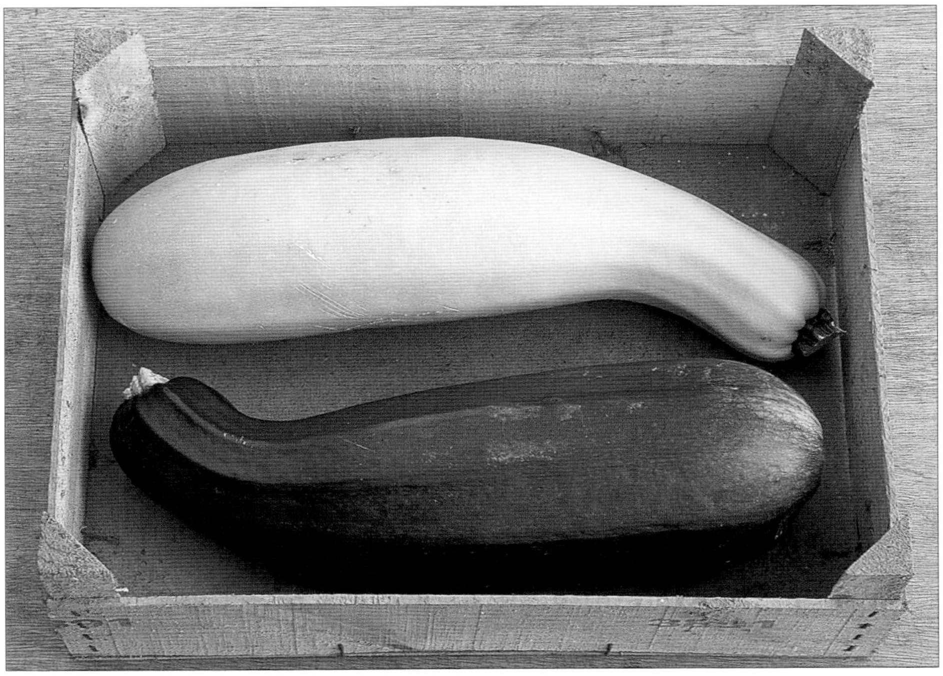

LEFT **Many vegetables, such as these marrows (zucchini), can be stored in trays. It is best if they are not touching one another.**

Freezing Vegetables

One advantage we have over our medieval predecessors is our ability to store vegetables by freezing them. This can be time-consuming but the small effort required ensures that there are fresh vegetables the year round.

ABOVE **Blanch carrots before freezing and serve them with herb butter.**

Winter vegetables

On the whole, vegetables are best either eaten fresh or stored in their natural state. Most of the vegetables that mature late in the season, such as root crops and some of the hard cabbages, can either be left in the ground or stored for several months. Bulbous types such as onions, garlic and leeks also store well, as it is in their nature to overwinter, ready for growing again the next season. However, there are many of the summer crops, such as beans and peas, that although they can be dried, are otherwise difficult to store. On the whole the joy of such crops is to eat them fresh while they last and then look forward to their next season. However, it seems a shame when there is a glut of such vegetables not to be able to store them. This is possible now that home freezers are widely available. The taste is different from when the vegetables were fresh, but they still make a welcome change in the winter months.

Suitable vegetables

There is no point in freezing vegetables that can be stored in the normal way. Root crops, for example, are best left in their natural condition. Only those that cannot be stored naturally should be frozen, although there are exceptions to this. Brussels sprouts, for example, can be left on the plants until required, but they can be frozen for out of season use if there is a glut.

Most seed catalogues mark those varieties that are most suitable for freezing. In some cases this mark indicates little more than the fact that the crop tends to mature all at the same time (having originally been bred for commercial use where this is important). In others it genuinely indicates those that do freeze better. Experiment to know which are the best vegetables for your purposes.

LEFT **Savoy cabbage, cauliflower, broccoli, spinach leaves and Brussels sprouts are all suitable vegetables for freezing. They can be all be boiled or steamed after freezing.**

Methods of freezing

There are many ways of freezing vegetables. Some can be frozen whole or sliced and will return to their former selves when unfrozen (peas and beans, for example), and can be used as if they were freshly picked. Others can be frozen as they are but will never return to their previous solid state, such as tomatoes and soft fruit. These can be used in casseroles and other cooked dishes where the vegetable would naturally go soft and lose its shape. Finally, there are those that are best cooked first and puréed before being frozen. Tomatoes can be treated in this way, as well as fruit such as apples.

Of those vegetables that are cooked whole, most benefit from being blanched first before being frozen. This involves a brief immersion in boiling water before being plunged into cold water to stop them cooking any further. You do not have to bother with this, but the storage life and taste is improved if it is carried out.

Larger plants, such as cabbages and celery, are best cut up into smaller pieces, especially if (as with celery) they are going to lose their crunchiness and can only be used in cooked dishes such as casseroles, where they would naturally become soft.

You could spread the vegetables on a tray to freeze them, putting them into a bag once they are frozen. In this way they will remain separate and you can take as many from the bag as you want. Alternatively, put them all in the bag and freeze together, although they will generally come out as a lump and you will have to use them all at once.

Frozen life-span

The storage life of frozen vegetables varies from type to type, some lasting a couple of months, and others up to a year. Generally it is the flavour that deteriorates rather than the vegetable going bad. The shorter the time they are frozen, the better they will taste. The presence of many ice crystals inside the bag indicates that a lot of moisture has been removed from the vegetables and they are less likely to taste good. If you are in doubt, throw them away.

mixed Swiss chard

kale

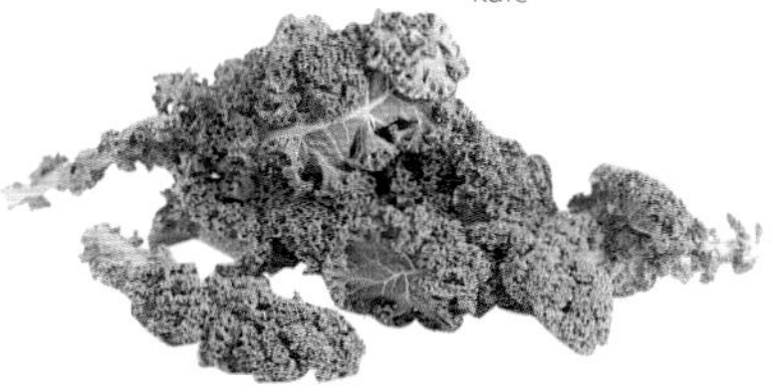

Some vegetables for freezing

b = blanche
p = purée
s = shred or chop
() = a choice

Broad (fava) beans b
Broccoli b
Brussels sprouts b
Calabrese b
Cauliflower b/s
Cabbages b/s
Celery s
Courgettes (zucchini) b
French beans b
Kale b
Marrow (squash) b/s
Peas b
Pumpkin p
Rhubarb p/s
Runner (green) beans b/s
Spinach b
Sweet corn (corn) b/(s)
Swiss chard b/s
Tomatoes b/(p)

RIGHT **Runner beans, fine green beans, mange touts (snow peas), broad beans, peas and corn on the cob all freeze well and taste almost as good as when freshly picked.**

directory
of vegetables

Vegetables are the mainstay of any kitchen garden. The quantities and varieties as well as the way in which the crops are laid out will be determined by the preferences of the gardener. However, there are a few principles that apply to the growing of each type of vegetable, and these are described in this section of the book.

The gardener is spoilt for choice when it comes to the range of varieties available. At first it will be a question of experimenting to find the varieties whose taste you prefer as well as those that are best suited to the soil and climate in your garden. Once they have identified these varieties, many gardeners tend to stick with them. There is no harm in this, although it pays to be adventurous and to try not only a few new varieties, but also some types of vegetable that you have not grown before.

As well as buying seed, many gardeners collect their own. In this way they are certain to continue using the varieties that do well in their garden, especially if they collect seed from the best plants each time. F1 hybrids will not come true and it is not worth collecting seed from them, but it is worth experimenting with ordinary open-pollinated seed. Some plant seeds, like beans and peas, are easy to collect, but other plants, such as carrots, are biennial and do not set seed until the second year. Leaving plants in the ground for two years takes up valuable space and so it may not be worth it for these. Experiment, it will add to the fun of gardening, especially if you end up with your own strain of vegetables.

BULB VEGETABLES

Onions

Allium cepa

Onions are one of the oldest vegetables. They were grown by the Ancient Egyptians over 5,000 years ago and were probably eaten long before that. Their actual origins are not known, but they probably first grew in the mountainous regions of Central Asia. As well as adding flavour to food, they have long been known for their health-giving properties.

Traditionally, the large, round onions that are mainly used for cooking are grown from sets, which are small bulbs that have started their life during the previous season when they were sown as seed by seed merchants. They are harvested at the end of their first season, when they are approximately 1–2.5cm/½–1in in diameter. They are then either sold loose or, as is more frequently the case these days, they are pre-packaged and bought by weight or, less often, by number.

Some varieties can be grown from seed as long as they are sown early enough, and this usually means sowing under glass in midwinter in order to get a sufficiently long growing season. Another group, known as Japanese onions, has been developed for sowing as seed or for planting out as sets in autumn for harvesting earlier than sets planted out in spring.

Smaller bulb onions are either shallots or pickling onions. Pickling onions are small, round onions that are grown from seed.

There are over one hundred different varieties of onion available. They can be broken down into three basic types according to colour: golden-brown, red and white. Most are round, but some varieties are torpedo-shaped. The main criteria – unless you are growing for showing, when uniformity and appearance are important – are taste and storage qualities. Golden varieties are generally best for storing, but the reds and whites provide, respectively, sweeter and milder flavours.

ABOVE **A good crop of onions growing in a block in a raised bed.**

Cultivation

Onions should be planted in an open position in a light soil that has been manured during the previous autumn. Plant the sets out in early spring.

Some varieties are heat treated, which prevents them from bolting, and they can be planted out later, in mid- to late spring when the soil is warmer. Plant them at 10cm/4in intervals in rows that are spaced about 30cm/12in apart. Plant with a dibber and cover the bulbs so that only the tips are showing.

Spring-sown seed can be sown in trays under glass in midwinter. Harden off and plant out in rows in mid-spring. Sow Japanese onions directly in beds in late summer or plant out as sets in early autumn.

Keep the plants weed free. There is generally no need to water unless the summer is particularly dry.

LEFT **The leaves of these onions are beginning to brown and have been moved to one side in order to speed up this process. This also allows maximum sunlight to reach the bulbs. Although not necessary, arranging the leaves in this way gives a satisfying beauty to a practical task.**

Cultivation

Sets
Planting time early spring (most varieties); early summer (overwintering varieties)
Planting distance 10cm/4in
Distance between rows 25–30cm/10–12in
Harvesting late summer (most varieties); midsummer (overwintering varieties)

Seed
Sowing time midwinter (under glass)
Sowing distance sow thinly
Sowing depth 1cm/½in
Distance between rows 25–30cm/10–12in
Thinning distance 5–10cm/2–4in
Harvesting late summer

RIGHT **Onions should be stored in trays in a frost-free shed.**

Harvesting

Onion bulbs can be lifted at any point in their growth for immediate use. However, for storage they must be fully developed, and the foliage should be beginning to die back. This is usually in late summer (midsummer for Japanese onions). As the foliage begins to turn yellow, lift each bulb slightly with a fork so that the roots start to break. Two weeks later carefully lift the bulbs. Clean off any soil and place them in a sunny, dry place to finish drying. A greenhouse is ideal, but if they are placed outside, move them under cover at night or if rain threatens.

Storage

Tie the onions into ropes or place them in net bags or on trays. Store them in a cool but frost-free place, such as a cellar, garage or shed. Check regularly, throwing out any that show signs of rotting.

Pests and diseases

The main pest is onion fly, whose maggots eat the onions, turning the leaves yellow and eventually killing them. Sets are less susceptible to onion fly than seed-grown onions are. Burn or destroy any affected bulbs. Onion eelworm produce distorted leaves. Again, burn or destroy affected plants.

Various fungal diseases, such as neck rot and white rot, can affect the bulbs. Destroy all infected bulbs.

Varieties

Bulb onion
'Ailsa Craig' spring- to late-summer-sown seed, golden skinned
'Albion' spring-sown seed, white skinned
'Autumn Gold' sets, golden skinned
'Bedfordshire Champion' spring-sown seed, golden skinned
'Buffalo' autumn-sown seed, golden skinned
'Dobie's All Rounder' sets, golden skinned
'Giant Fen Globe' sets, golden skinned
'Hygro' spring-sown seed, golden skinned
'Mammoth Red' winter-sown seed, red skinned
'Red Baron' sets, red skin and flesh
'Red Torpedo' late-summer sown, red skinned
'Rocardo' sets, red skinned
'Sturon' sets, golden skinned
'Stuttgart Giant' sets, golden skinned
'White Prince' sets, white skinned

Pickling onions
'Barletta'
'Giant Zittau'
'Paris Silver Skin'
'The Queen'

large and small red onions

brown onion

small brown onions

white onions

Shallots

Allium cepa Aggregatum Group

Shallots have been grown for almost as long as onions. They were originally named scallions after Ascalon (Ashqelon) in Israel, the place from where the Greeks thought the vegetable originated, but shallots probably originally came from Central Asia.

Shallots are widely used in cooking, especially in France, where small onions are preferred. Although they lack the strong smell of onions and do not make your eyes water, the taste is often more intense yet sweeter than that of onions, and they are used where delicate flavours are needed. The leaves are sometimes used as a substitute for chives, and in country areas shallots are often used as a substitute for pickling onions.

Shallots are a small form of onion, but instead of growing as single bulbs they tend to grow in bunches or clusters. The shapes and colours of shallots vary considerably, and France in particular has a great number of cultivars. Some are torpedo-shaped, others are rounded. The colour varies from yellows through browns to reds, and flavours range from delicate to strong.

Cultivation

An open, sunny position is required for growing shallots, and a light soil, which has been dug and manured during the previous autumn, is preferable. In the northern hemisphere the traditional day for planting shallots in many regions is Boxing Day, but this is too early for most areas, and late winter or early spring is a better time. Set them out in rows, planting the individual bulbs at 15–18cm/6–7in intervals. Use a dibber or trowel, and bury the bulbs so that only the tips are showing. The rows should be 30cm/12in apart.

Keep weeded. Water in early summer if necessary.

Harvesting

When the foliage shrivels in midsummer, ease the shallots from the soil with a fork. Place them on staging in a greenhouse or on racks of wire netting to dry. Once the leaves have completely dried, remove any

PLANTING

Plant the shallot bulbs in rows at 15–18cm/6–7in intervals with 30cm/12in between each row. Using a dibber or trowel, bury the bulbs so that only the tips are showing.

LEFT **Rows of shallots with garlic growing in the background.**

BELOW **Shallots drying on netting in the sunshine before being stored.**

ABOVE **A vigorous crop of young shallots with the individual bulbs just beginning to form.**

dirt and dead foliage and break them up into individual bulbs before leaving to dry further.

Storage

Place shallots on wire racks or trays or in netting bags. Store them in a dark, cool but frost-free place, such as a cellar or garage. They should keep through the winter. Check on them regularly and throw out any that show signs of rotting.

Pests and diseases

On the whole, shallots are relatively trouble free, but they may succumb to the same problems in terms of pests and diseases as onions. The main pest is likely to be onion eelworm, which produces distorted leaves. Onion fly may also be a problem. They lay their eggs in the bulbs, and the maggots then go on to eat the shallots, turning the leaves yellow and eventually killing them. Companion planting with parsley is a traditional deterrent. In both cases you will have to burn or destroy any infected bulbs.

Various fungal diseases, such as neck rot and white rot, can affect shallots. Burn or destroy all infected bulbs.

Cultivation

Planting time late winter to early spring
Planting distance 15–18cm/6–7in
Planting depth just below the surface
Distance between rows 30cm/12in
Harvesting midsummer

'Atlantic' yellow skinned
'Delicato' red skinned
'Dutch Red' red skinned
'Dutch Yellow' yellow skinned
'Giant Red' red skinned
'Giant Yellow' yellow skinned
'Golden Gourmet' yellow skinned
'Hâtive de Niort' brown skinned
'Pikant' yellow skinned
'Sante' yellow skinned
'Success' red-brown skinned
'Topper' yellow skinned

shallots

Garlic

Allium sativum

Garlic is a very individual form of onion, characterized by its distinctive smell and flavour. It is widely used throughout the world for cooking and medicinal purposes and has been so for thousands of years. It is thought to have originated in Central Asia, but it can no longer be found in the wild. Even in cultivation it has ceased to set seed, and existing cultivars are thought to be very old indeed.

Garlic forms a bulb made up of numerous individual cloves. There are several different cultivars available worldwide, but they are very similar, the main differences being taste and pungency. The skins are usually white but can be tinged to a lesser or greater extent with purple. The only other differences are the size and number of cloves, hardiness and storage qualities. Garden-grown garlic is often bigger and more pungent than purchased bulbs.

Most seed merchants sell one or two varieties, sometimes just listed as "garlic bulbs". It is possible to plant bulbs purchased through a greengrocer or supermarket, but sometimes these have been "treated" and fail to sprout or, if they do sprout, produce distorted leaves. It is, however, worth trying if you find a variety you particularly like.

BELOW **This is a healthy crop of garlic plants. Unlike onions, the garlic bulbs form out of sight below the ground.**

ABOVE **Young garlic in spring before the bulbs begin to form.**

PLANTING

1 Use a dibber to make holes in the ground for each clove, at 10–15cm/ 4–6in intervals. A line of string will help you to keep the row straight.

2 Plant the cloves just below the surface, firming them in so that they are covered to their own height with soil.

RIGHT **Garlic can be started off by planting the cloves in individual pots.**

Cultivation

A sunny open position is required and, as with other members of the onion family, a light soil is preferred. Use soil that has been manured for a previous crop or, if you are planting in spring, dig in the manure in the preceding autumn.

If possible plant in mid- to late autumn. In colder districts, however, and in heavy cold soils it is better to wait until spring. Remove the outer skin and break the bulbs into individual cloves. Use a dibber to plant the cloves at 10–15cm/4–6in intervals, burying them so that they are covered to about their own height with soil. Alternatively, draw out a drill about 5cm/2in deep and plant the cloves in this at 10–15cm/4–6in intervals. Allow 30cm/12in between each row.

Keep well weeded, but avoid damaging the bulbs with the hoe.

Harvesting

Lift the bulbs when the leaves have turned yellow. Spread them out in a sunny place, preferably under cover – on greenhouse staging is ideal. When they have dried out thoroughly, remove any dirt and any long roots. If you are plaiting them or tying them in bunches, the leaves will need to be left on. If you are keeping them in net bags or trays, remove the dead foliage, leaving about 2.5cm/1in of stem.

Storage

Tie the stems together so that the garlic can be hung in bunches. A more sophisticated method is to plait the leaves together so that a chain of garlic is formed. Although these ropes of garlic are decorative, resist the temptation to hang them in the kitchen because the warmth and moist air will soon bring them into growth. Hang them in a cool, but frost-free, shed or cellar. Alternatively, place the garlic in trays and keep them in a similar position.

Pests and diseases

Garlic is relatively pest free. It can, however, suffer from various fungal or viral diseases. If the problem is a minor attack of rust, it can be ignored. If it is anything else, you will have to remove the bulbs, and burn or destroy them.

LEFT **A simple way of "stringing" garlic is to thread a stiff wire through the dry necks of the bulbs. The bulbs can also be tied on string.**

Varieties

Frequently just listed as garlic.
'Long Keeper'
'Long Keeper Improved'
'Marshall's Mediterranean'

Cultivation

Planting time mid-autumn (milder areas); early spring (cold areas)
Planting distance 10–15cm/4–6in
Planting depth twice height of the clove
Distance between rows 30cm/12in
Harvesting mid- to late summer

garlic

Spring Onions (Scallions)

Allium cepa

Spring onions (scallions) are small onions that are eaten fresh; they are not dried. They produce small bulbs that are little more than a slight swelling at the base of the stem. The bulb and the base of the stem is white; the cylindrical leaves are green. A young form of large, bulbous onions, they originate from the same part of the world, Central Asia. They are called spring onions (scallions) because they are ready to eat in spring, unlike other onions, which do not mature until later in the year.

ABOVE **Spring onions (scallions) can be pencil-slim or have a slight swelling at the base, forming a small bulb.**

The Welsh onion is similar to spring onions (scallions) but derives from a different species, *Allium fistulosum*. It has little to do with Wales, since it has been introduced to the West only relatively recently, although it has been in cultivation in China since prehistoric times. It found its way westwards through Russia in the early 17th century, possibly picking up its name from the German *welsche* (foreign) on the way. Welsh onions are somewhat coarser in appearance than spring onions. They are perennials, rather like coarse chives, and the foliage can be used in the same way as that of chives.

Bunching onions are similar again and have been derived from Welsh onions. These can be used as annuals, like spring onions (scallions), or as perennials, like Welsh onions.

Spring onions (scallions) can be used in cooking but they are more frequently eaten raw, especially in salads. The leaves can be used as a substitute for chives, and the onions themselves are often used as a garnish. Welsh and bunching onions are used in much the same ways.

Many gardeners use shallots for pickling. However, there is also a special type of pickling onion (also called a cocktail onion) that can be grown. These are similar to spring onions (scallions) except that the bulb develops more fully. They are small, white-skinned onions. Like spring onions, they are grown from seed sown in the spring and are usually ready for harvesting after two months. They are treated in the same manner as spring onions and can be left unthinned for smaller bulbs or thinned for larger ones. The smaller ones can be used as a substitute for bulbous spring onions. Although usually pickled they can be stored like other bulbous onions.

THINNING

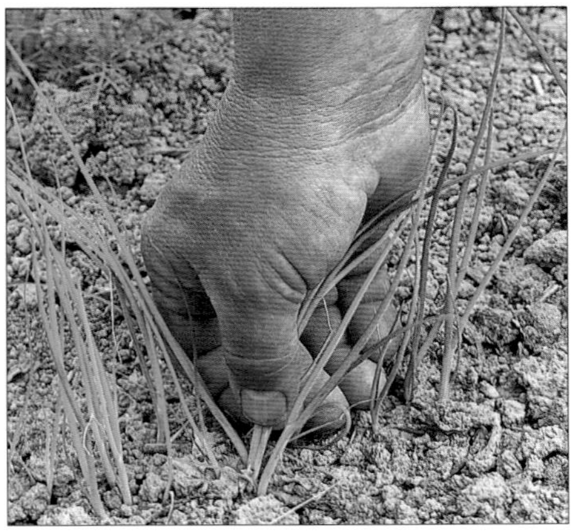

Although it is advisable to avoid thinning spring onions (scallions) where possible, it is often necessary to thin out congested rows.

Cultivation

Like the rest of the family, spring onions (scallions) need an open, sunny site. The soil should preferably be light, but they will grow in most soils as long as they are manured. Dig in manure in autumn for spring sowing. Sow the seed in spring and then at three-week intervals for a succession. Late summer sowings can be overwintered under cloches for an early spring crop.

Sow thinly in drills 1cm/½in deep and 15–20cm/6–8in apart. If sown thinly enough, there should be no need to thin. This is important because the smell of bruised plants that is caused by thinning attracts onion fly.

Spring onions (scallions) should be grown quickly or they become tough, so they will need watering in dry weather. Welsh onions are grown in the same way but should be left in situ – only the leaves are cropped. Lift and divide every few years when the clumps get congested.

Harvesting

Spring onions (scallions) are ready for use at about eight weeks from sowing. Simply pull them from the ground. If the soil is compacted, they can be eased out with a hand fork.

Storage

Spring onions (scallions) cannot be stored for more than a few days. Keep in a cool place or in a refrigerator. The leaves can be chopped

HARVESTING

Spring onions (scallions) can be harvested either by pulling them from the ground by hand or, as is shown here, by gently forking them out.

ABOVE **Spring onions (scallions) that have been newly harvested.**

and frozen, either in bags or in ice cubes, for use in winter in the same way as chives.

Pests and diseases

The main pest is onion fly, whose maggots eat the onions, turning the leaves yellow and eventually killing them. The dangerous period is when the onions are damaged by thinning or weeding because the flies smell the odour that is given off. Burn or destroy any affected onions. Onion eelworm produces distorted leaves. Again, burn or destroy affected plants.

Various fungal diseases can affect spring onions (scallions) but because their life is so short any diseased plants should be destroyed and a fresh start made in a new position in the garden.

Cultivation

Sowing time early spring
Sowing distance sow thinly
Sowing depth 1cm/½in
Distance between rows 15–20cm/6–8in
Thinning distance avoid thinning if possible
Successional sowing three-week intervals
Harvesting eight weeks after sowing

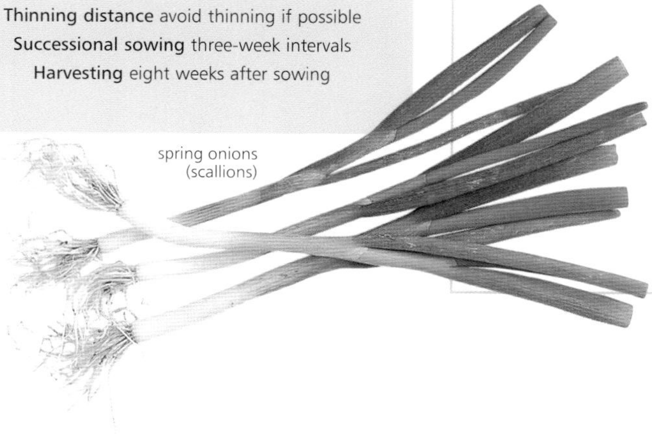

spring onions (scallions)

Varieties

'Guardsman' for summer use
'Hikari Bunching' for summer use
'Ishikura' for summer use
'North Holland Blood Red' red skinned, for summer use
'Santa Claus' red skinned, for summer use
'Savel' for summer use
'White Knight' for overwintering
'White Lisbon' for summer use and overwintering
'Winter White Bunching' for overwintering

Leeks

Allium porrum

Like most forms of onion, leeks have been grown since ancient times. They were probably derived from **Allium ampeloprasum*****, which grows in the Near East and in countries of the Mediterranean littoral. Its traditional connection with Wales arose because Welshmen were said to have worn leeks in their hats in a battle against the Saxons in AD640 to distinguish them from their enemies.***

Although leeks belong to the onion family, they do not have such a pronounced basal swelling nor the pungent flavour and smell of the other culinary members of the genus. They consist of cylinders of tightly wrapped leaves, white where they have been blanched and green above soil level. It is the white section that is mainly used. Unlike the other culinary onions, which are mainly used as flavourings, leeks are used as a vegetable in their own right in a wide range of dishes and soups. They can also be used, of course, as a simple vegetable accompaniment.

A wide range of varieties is available, some are hardier than others (those with bluer leaves tend to be hardier), and some are ready earlier, while others stand better until spring. Some varieties have been bred specifically for their appearance on the show bench.

BELOW **A good block of leeks, with their rich green leaves, looks decorative in its own right.**

PLANTING

1 Make a hole with a dibber and drop the plant in. Do not fill in the hole.

2 Fill each hole along the row with water.

Cultivation

Leeks like an open, sunny position and a rich, fertile soil that is reasonably free draining. Dig well-rotted organic compost into the soil in autumn for planting in spring. Leeks like a long growing season, so start them off by sowing in nursery-bed rows in early to mid-spring. Sow thinly in drills 1cm/½in deep and 15cm/6in apart if you need more than one row. Transplant

Cultivation

Sowing time early to mid-spring
Sowing distance sow thinly
Sowing depth 1cm/½in
Distance between sown rows 15cm/6in
Planting distance 15cm/6in
Distance between planted rows 30cm/12in
Harvesting early autumn to late spring

when the seedlings are 15–20cm/6–8in high, which will be two or three months after sowing. Water the row the day before lifting and then dig out in batches with a hand fork. Plant into their permanent rows using a dibber. The plants should be 15cm/6in apart and the rows should be 30cm/12in apart. Make a hole about 15cm/6in deep and drop the leek in so that about 5cm/2in of the leaves show above the soil. Do not fill in the hole with soil, but fill it with water. This will wash sufficient soil around the roots.

As the leeks grow, earth (hill) them up by pulling soil up around the stems to blanch them. Alternatively, plant the leeks in the bottom of a trench and gradually fill the trench as the leeks grow. Keep weeded and watered in the early stages of growth.

Harvesting

Leeks can be lifted for use at any time between early autumn and late spring. Dig them out with a fork. Autumn varieties are not as hardy and should be harvested before midwinter.

Storage

Leeks are generally hardy and can be left in the ground until they are required. In cold areas they can be covered over with a cloche. They are best used fresh from the ground, but they can be dug several days before use and kept in a cool place. There is no method of storing leeks out of the ground. If the piece of ground they occupy is needed for some other purpose in the spring, then they can be lifted and heeled in elsewhere until they are needed. Simply dig a trench and insert the leeks to the same depth as they were in their original planting position. Dig them up as and when they are required.

EARTHING (HILLING) UP

Earth up the plants as they grow in order to blanch the stems. Alternatively, plant the leeks in a trench and fill it in as the plants grow.

HARVESTING

Harvest the leeks by digging under them with a fork. As you do this, pull them from the ground with the other hand.

Pests and diseases

Leeks are not usually troubled by pests and diseases. Rust is the most likely problem. Infected plants can be burned or destroyed; if the rust is not too severe it can be ignored, although it is best to plant leeks elsewhere for the next year. Other onion pests and diseases may occasionally be a problem; destroy any affected plants.

Varieties

Autumn
'Albinstar'
'Autumn Giant Startrack'
'Autumn Mammoth-Argenta'
'Elephant'
'Pancho'
Mid-season
'Carentan'
'Cortina'
'Grenvilliers-Splendid'
'King Richard'
Winter
'Alaska'
'Giant Winter-Cantalina'
'Giant Winter-Royal Favourite'
'Giant Winter-3'
'Kajak'
'Musselburgh'
'Wila'
'Yates Empire'

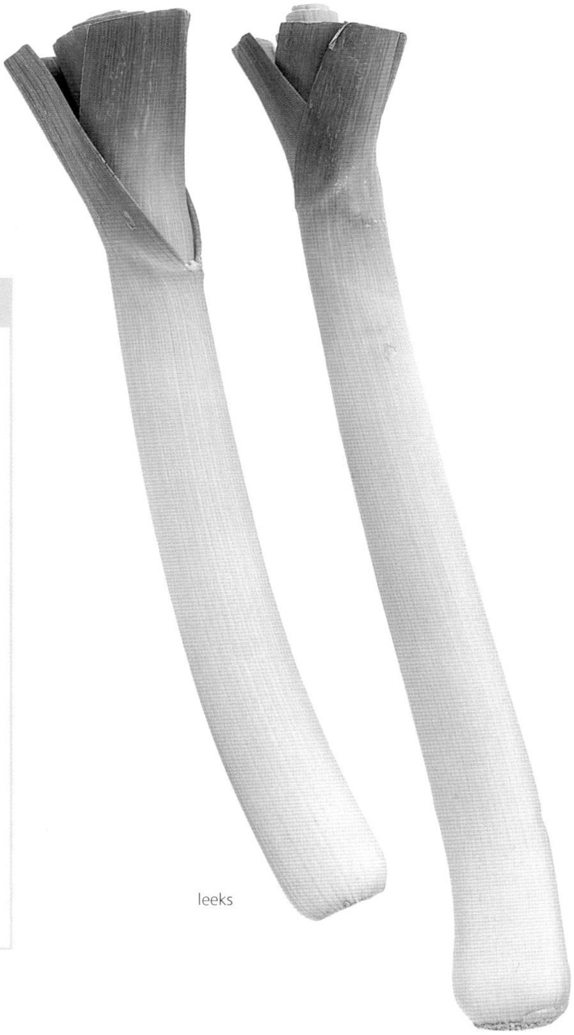

leeks

LEAF VEGETABLES

Cabbages

Brassica oleracea Capitata Group

Cabbage has been in cultivation for 3,000 years or so, but the cabbage as we know it today is a comparatively recent development, probably dating from the Middle Ages. Cabbage can be found growing in the wild throughout Europe, from Britain to Spain, but the wild form is more akin to broccoli than the hearted varieties with which we are now familiar.

ABOVE **This is a very well-grown specimen that would do as well on the show bench as it will on the kitchen table.**

Cabbages come in various forms, mainly depending on the time of year they are harvested – spring, summer, autumn and winter varieties are self-evidently named. These are all hearting cabbages, although spring cabbage is also available as "greens", which are loose heads of green leaves, unlike the typical tight heads of blanched leaves. There are also a few other winter varieties, which are sometimes considered separately, such as the savoys (with their distinctive, crinkly leaves), hybrids between the savoys and winter cabbages and 'January King'. The most distinctive of this group of cabbages is the red cabbage.

Some people have been put off cabbage by having to eat overcooked leaves, but it has always remained a staple winter vegetable for gardeners, especially in country areas, and nowadays it is enjoying a revival in popularity as people increasingly appreciate its culinary potential.

PROTECTING YOUNG CABBAGES

Young cabbages need protecting from birds. Wire guards are light and easy to erect. They are also easy to store if they are made in short sections.

Cultivation

Cabbages do best in an open, sunny site in a soil that is fertile but reasonably free draining. They do not like a soil that is too acid, and acid soil may need liming to bring it to pH6.5–7. This should be done immediately after digging and before planting. Most gardeners sow cabbages in nursery beds and transplant them; others prefer to sow them in trays under glass; still others buy them as young plants from nurseries and garden centres. The methods are basically the same for all types; it is just the timing that varies.

Thinly sow seed in shallow drills about 1cm/½in deep. Thin seedlings if necessary to prevent them from becoming drawn. After about five weeks, when they have four or five leaves, transplant them to their final position. Final spacing depends on the type and size (see Cultivation). Plant using a dibber or trowel and firm the soil in well around the roots. Water well and keep watered until they have become established.

Spring cabbages can be sown in situ and initially thinned to 10cm/4in. In spring thin again to 30–38cm/12–15in.

Hoe regularly and keep free of weeds. Draw up some soil around the stems of overwintering varieties. Remove any dead leaves.

Harvesting

Cut the hearting cabbages when they have become firm. Use a knife to cut through the stem, just below the firm head but inside any loose leaves. Savoy cabbages taste better if they are harvested after they have experienced at least one frost. The leaves of spring cabbages are cut as required, a few being left to heart up if required.

Storage

Most cabbages are winter hardy and can be left where they are until required. Those with solid heads can be cut and stored in a cool place, where they will keep for a couple of months. Some varieties of red cabbages may not be as hardy and can be harvested in early winter and stored.

PREVENTING CABBAGE ROOT FLY

Cabbage root fly can be kept at bay by placing a felt or plastic collar around the base of the cabbage in order to stop the fly laying its eggs.

Cultivation

Spring cabbage
Sowing time late summer
Sowing distance sow thinly
Sowing depth 1cm/½in
Distance between sown rows 15cm/6in
Planting distance 30–38cm/12–15in
Distance between planted rows 50–60cm/20–24in
Harvesting spring

Summer cabbage
Sowing time early to mid-spring
Sowing distance sow thinly
Sowing depth 1cm/½in
Distance between sown rows 15cm/6in
Planting distance 35cm/14in
Distance between planted rows 60cm/24in
Harvesting midsummer onwards

Autumn cabbage
Sowing time late spring
Sowing distance sow thinly
Sowing depth 1cm/½in
Distance between sown rows 15cm/6in
Planting distance 50cm/20in
Distance between planted rows 60–75cm/24–30in
Harvesting autumn

Winter cabbage
Sowing time late spring
Sowing distance sow thinly
Sowing depth 1cm/½in
Distance between sown rows 15cm/6in
Planting distance 50cm/20in
Distance between planted rows 60–75cm/24–30in
Harvesting winter

Varieties

Spring cabbage
'April'
'Durham Early'
'Greensleeves'
'January King'
'Offenham 1-Myatt's'
'Offenham Compacta'
'Pixie'
'Spring Hero'

Summer cabbage
'Castello'
'Derby Day'
'Hispi'
'Minicole'
'Primo'
'Quickstep'

Autumn cabbage
'Autoro'
'Bingo'
'Castello'
'Minnicole'
'Rapier'
'Winnigstadt'

Winter cabbage and savoys
'Best of All'
'Capriccio'
'Celtic'
'Christmas Drumhead'
'Duncan'
'Hidena'
'Ice Queen'
'January King'
'Novusa'
'Ormskirk 1-Ormskirk Late'
'Tundra'
'Wivoy'

Red cabbage
'Kissendrup'
'Metro'
'Red Drumhead'
'Red Dutch'
'Ruby Ball'
'Vesta'

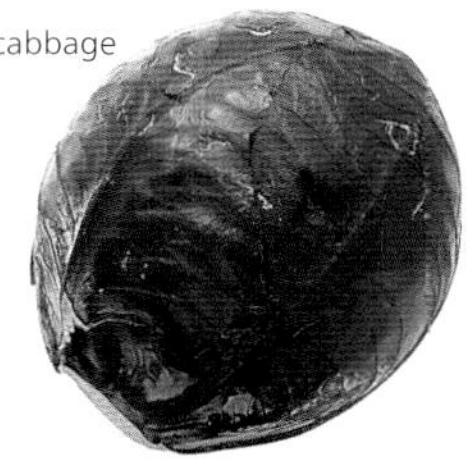
red cabbage

loose-leaf cabbage

Pests and diseases

Cabbage root fly are a nuisance, but they can be deterred by placing a collar of roofing felt or a similar material around the plant's stem. This prevents the adults from laying their eggs near the plant. Caterpillars are another problem. Cover the plants with netting or fleece to stop butterflies laying their eggs. Caterpillars can be removed by hand, but if you decide to spray, follow the manufacturer's instructions. Flea beetles make small holes in young leaves and should be prevented by dusting with the appropriate chemical. Slugs and snails should be controlled. The most serious disease is club root, which causes the roots to swell up. Any affected plants should be burned or destroyed. Liming helps to deter club root, as does growing cabbages in a different bed each year.

RIGHT **A block of cabbages in very good condition.**

Brussels Sprouts

Brassica oleracea Gemmifera Group

Brussels sprouts are so called because they are thought to have originated in Belgium, where they are recorded as growing in the mid-18th century. By the beginning of the 19th century they had spread to France and Britain. Even after 200 years of cultivation, Brussels sprouts still seem to be an acquired taste. Not everybody likes them, and children in particular seem to find that they have too strong a taste. When cooked properly, however, they are a very tasty and valuable part of winter meals, and few would consider their Christmas dinner complete without a bowl of them.

Cultivation

Sowing time early to mid-spring
Sowing distance sow thinly
Sowing depth 1cm/½in
Distance between sown rows 15cm/6in
Planting-out time when 13cm/5in high
Planting distance 50-75cm/20-30in
Distance between planted rows 75cm/30in
Harvesting mid-autumn to spring

Brussels sprouts are usually categorized according to season: early, mid and late. If plants are grown from each group, there can be a continuous crop from autumn right through to spring.

The sprouts themselves are the tight buds that form where the leaves join the main stem. As well as the sprouts, the succulent tops of the plants can be harvested once the sprouts are finished. The size of the plant varies according to cultivar, and some that have been bred as dwarf or compact plants are best suited to smaller gardens where space is at a premium. Another intriguing type is the red-leaved variety, 'Rubine', which is ideal for decorative kitchen gardens.

ABOVE **These Brussels sprouts are just beginning to develop. Soon the lower leaves will be removed, exposing the sprouts.**

Cultivation

An open position is required, but it should be protected from strong winds. The ground should be manured in autumn and limed if necessary to bring the acidity to within pH6.5–7. The seed can be sown in the open ground or started in trays under cover. For a late-summer picking, the seed should be sown in late winter or early spring – soil and weather conditions would generally mean that these seeds should be sown inside. For the more usual autumn-onwards harvest, sow in the open in early to mid-spring. Sow the earliest varieties first and the latest a few weeks later to make sure that they crop successionally. Sow thinly in shallow drills (see Cultivation). Plant out in the final position about five weeks after sowing, when the plants are about 13cm/5in tall. Plant the taller varieties at 75cm/30in intervals and the dwarfer forms at 50cm/20in intervals, with 75cm/30in between rows. Use a dibber or a trowel and firm the soil lightly around the plant. Water well.

Keep the plants well watered until they are established. Because there is such a large amount of space between plants they can be intercropped with a fast-growing crop such as radishes or lettuces. Keep the weeds down. If the site is exposed, stake the plants against the wind, and drawing soil up around the stems also helps. Remove the bottom leaves as they turn yellow.

Harvesting

Harvest when the Brussels sprouts are large enough to pick but while they are still tight. Start at the bottom of the plant, picking a few off each plant and snapping off each one with a downward twist. Move up the stems as the sprouts fill out. When all the sprouts are removed, pick the loose heads or tops and cook them as greens. Most gardeners prefer not to start harvesting until after the first frosts because this improves the flavour. As you harvest, remove any sprouts that have "blown" – that is, those that have not formed tight sprouts but are just a loose collection of leaves – and put them on the compost heap.

BELOW **Here, purple-leaved Brussels sprouts make an impromptu, but striking, combination with *Dahlia* 'Bishop of Llandaff' on the other side of the fence.**

ABOVE **This healthy block of Brussels sprouts has been planted with red cabbages to create a highly decorative effect.**

Storage

Brussels sprouts are hardy and can be left on the stems until they are required. They cannot be stored after picking for any length of time unless they are frozen. Freeze early maturing varieties before the weather damages the outer leaves. Choose only good quality, uniform sprouts for freezing.

Varieties	
Early	'Mallard'
'Lancelot'	'Roger'
'Oliver'	**Late**
'Peer Gynt'	'Fortress'
Mid-season	'Icarus'
'Bedford Fillbasket'	'Sheriff'
'Citadel'	'Trafalgar'
'Evesham Special'	'Widgeon'

Pests and diseases

Brussels sprouts are prone to the same problems as cabbages. The worst problem is clubroot. Aphids will also take shelter in the tightly packed sprouts.

Brussels sprouts

Broccoli

Brassica oleracea Cymosa Group

Broccoli was developed from the wild cabbage in the 17th century in Italy, from where it spread through the rest of Europe. It is also known as sprouting broccoli or purple sprouting broccoli. Calabrese (Italian sprouting broccoli) and romanesco (Roman broccoli) are very closely related, but in the garden and kitchen they are considered separately because they grow at a different time of year and are cultivated in a slightly different way. In the past, gardeners also referred to winter cauliflowers as broccoli, and in some areas they may still do so.

Cultivation

Sowing time mid-spring
Sowing distance sow thinly
Sowing depth 1cm/½in
Distance between sown rows 15cm/6in
Planting-out time when 13cm/5in high
Planting distance 60cm/24in
Distance between planted rows 60–75cm/24–30in
Harvesting late winter to mid-spring

It is the flower shoots of broccoli that are gathered and eaten, just as the buds are forming and before the yellow of the opening flowers is seen. The flower-heads appear both at the top of the plant and as side shoots. In most varieties the flower-buds are purple – hence one of the alternative names, purple sprouting – but there are also creamy-white varieties, on which the flower-buds appear like miniature cauliflowers. The purple varieties are generally considered to be hardier than the white forms. There is one variety – 'Nine Star Perennial' – which, as its name suggests, is perennial in habit. If all the heads are picked each year it should last up to about five years, producing white heads each year.

In addition to the flower-heads, the stalk just below the buds and their associated leaves can also be eaten. Even more stalk may be eaten if the tougher outside is first removed.

The harvesting period for broccoli varies slightly, but it fills the "hungry" gap between late winter – 'Rudolph' is one of the earliest varieties – and mid-spring, when fresh vegetables are at a premium. The problem is that they are large plants and occupy the land for the best part of the year. Use the space between plants when they are first planted out for cultivating catch crops such as radishes. Each plant usually produces plenty of shoots and if space is very limited, it is worth growing just a couple of plants.

Cultivation

An open position is required, preferably one not buffeted by strong winds. The ground should be reasonably rich as well as manured in autumn and limed if necessary to bring the acidity to pH6.5–7. The seed can be sown in spring in the open ground or started in modules or trays under cover. Sow thinly in shallow drills 1cm/½in deep. If necessary, thin to 5cm/2in apart. Transplant the young broccoli when they are about 13cm/5in high. Water the row of plants the day before transplanting. Plant out the young broccoli at 60cm/24in intervals with the same distance between rows, using a dibber or trowel. Firm them in well with your heel and water. Keep watered until they are established. Remove any weeds as soon as you notice them. In windy areas it may be necessary to stake the plants to prevent wind-rock. Earthing (hilling) up the stems will also help.

LEFT **This purple-sprouting broccoli is now ready for cutting.**

Harvesting

Depending on variety, harvesting starts in late winter to mid-spring. Snap or cut off the shoots as they begin to bud up but before they come into flower. Shoots should be about 15cm/6in long. Pick the shoots from all parts of the plant. Do not allow any to come into flower, or they will quickly run to seed and exhaust the plant.

Storage

Broccoli is perfectly hardy and should be left on the plant until required. It will not keep for more than a few days after picking, although it can be stood in a jug of water to keep it fresh or placed in a cool place such as a refrigerator. It can be stored for longer periods by freezing, a good way of coping with excess heads, which should always be picked and not left on the plant to flower.

Pests and diseases

Broccoli is susceptible to the same problems as cabbages.

Varieties

'Claret' late season
'Early Purple Sprouting' early to late season
'Nine Star Perennial' mid-season
'Purple Sprouting' mid- to late season
'Rudolph' early season
'White Sprouting' mid- to late season

broccoli

Calabrese (Italian Sprouting Broccoli)

Brassica oleracea Italica Group

Although calabrese (Italian sprouting broccoli) is in many ways very similar to broccoli, it is usually considered as a separate vegetable. Its origins are the same: it originated in the countries of the eastern Mediterranean littoral and in Italy, before moving to the rest of Europe. It is sometimes known as Italian broccoli or American broccoli. A similar vegetable, which is usually bracketed with calabrese, is Romanesco (Roman broccoli).

Unlike broccoli, calabrese (Italian sprouting broccoli) is quick growing but not very hardy, and it is grown so that the edible heads, which are much larger than those of broccoli, are produced in late summer and autumn. Calabrese forms a large central head, rather like a loose cauliflower, and when this is picked, side shoots develop, each carrying a slightly smaller head. Not all varieties seem capable of producing side shoots, however, and these varieties are finished once the main head is picked. The colour is different from broccoli in that it has a blue-green tinge. Another major difference to broccoli is that it is important that growth should not be checked so it is sown where it is to grow and not transplanted.

Romanesco (Roman broccoli), which is sometimes known as green cauliflower, is similar to calabrese (Italian sprouting broccoli) and is, in fact, often listed as a variety of calabrese. The main difference is that it is hardier and can be grown to produce heads from late autumn into early winter, covering at least part of the gap between calabrese and broccoli. Unlike calabrese and broccoli, romancesco only produces a single head and is then finished. The shape of the head is also different. It is distinctly conical-shaped, with little eruptions over the surface, creating further small whorls or pinnacles. It is an attractive plant, with yellowish, lime-green buds.

STATION SOWING

Calabrese (Italian sprouting broccoli) needs to be sown where it is to grow. Station sow the seed at intervals of 30cm/12in.

Cultivation

Sow in an open site in a fertile soil that has either been manured for a previous crop or manured during autumn digging. It is important to sow calabrese (Italian sprouting broccoli) and romanesco (Roman broccoli) where they are to mature, because they do not transplant well. Station sow in shallow drills about 1cm/½in deep at 30cm/12in intervals. Sow three seeds at each station. Rows should be 30cm/12in apart. Seeds can be sown closer together but this results in smaller heads. After germination, remove surplus seedlings so that only one, the strongest, remains at each station.

Keep well watered, especially in dry spells, so that the plants' growth is not checked. Keep them free of weeds.

Harvesting

Depending on variety, calabrese (Italian sprouting broccoli) is ready for harvesting from summer until well into autumn, usually 10–12 weeks after sowing. Romanesco (Roman broccoli) is ready from late autumn to the turn of the year or even later if protected with cloches.

Calabrese (Italian sprouting broccoli) first produces a single head, which should be cut while it is still tightly closed. Some varieties will subsequently produce side shoots with smaller heads. Romanesco (Roman broccoli) produces only one head, and when this is harvested the plant can be disposed of.

Cultivation

Calabrese (Italian sprouting broccoli)
Sowing time successional sowings from mid- to early summer
Sowing distance station sow at 30cm/12in
Sowing depth 1cm/½in
Distance between sown rows 30cm/12in
Harvesting late summer to autumn

Romanesco (Roman broccoli)
Sowing time early summer
Sowing distance station sow at 30cm/12in
Sowing depth 1cm/½in
Distance between sown rows 30cm/12in
Harvesting late autumn early winter (later if protected)

Storage

Neither calabrese (Italian sprouting broccoli) nor romanesco (Roman broccoli) keeps for more than a few days in a cool place and both are best eaten straight from the plant. They can be preserved for longer by freezing.

Pests and diseases

Both vegetables are susceptible to the same problems as cabbages.

Varieties

Calabrese (Italian sprouting broccoli)
'Caravel'
'Corvet'
'Green Comet'
'Mercedes'
'Ramosa'
'Trixie'

Romanesco (Roman broccoli)
'Romanesco'
'Temple'

calabrese (Italian sprouting broccoli)

Kale

Brassica oleracea Acephala Group

Because kale is a leafy, rather than a headed, brassica, it is much closer than many of the others to the original wild cabbage, and it is, therefore, probably one of the oldest forms. There are several different types, because the name is used to refer to any leafy brassica, including a whole group of coloured varieties that are used purely as ornamental plants. The main edible group is the curly kales, which are also known as borecoles. Another group, particularly popular in the southern United States, is the plain-leaved collards.

Although kale is one of the least favourite of brassicas as far as culinary uses are concerned, it does fill the period in midwinter when there are very few fresh vegetables around. Kales are very hardy and withstand winter weather well, and they will also tolerate wet and even poor soil conditions.

The edible varieties are decorative and are often grown for that attribute rather than for their flavour. The leaves of the traditional curly kale are so curled that they look like froth. In recent times the dark, narrow-leaved 'Nero di Toscana' (palm-tree cabbage) has become very popular for its visual qualities, and it is frequently seen in decorative potagers. In addition, there are some non-edible forms that are used purely as decoration both in the kitchen garden and in flower borders. Ornamental kales come in a wonderful range of purple, pinks, reds and creamy-whites. They are at their best in the winter when there is very little else of interest in the garden.

The leaves of kale are eaten, especially the young leaves from the centre of the plant. Some of the resistance to eating kale arises from the fact that some kales are used as cattle and sheep fodder in winter. Some people dislike its strong flavour, which can be rather bitter if the leaves are not cooked properly. Cooked well, however, kale makes a very good winter dish and is well worth growing.

WATERING

It is important that kale plants are kept growing, so make sure that you do not let the soil dry out. Water well, as and when required.

BELOW **This informal vegetable garden includes a block of young curly kale plants.**

Cultivation

Kale needs an open situation in which to grow. Although it prefers a fertile soil, it will grow in poorer soils than most other cabbages. If possible, however, incorporate manure when digging in autumn. Thinly sow the seed in late spring in the open ground in drills that are about 1cm/½in deep and 20cm/8in apart. Thin if necessary so that the young plants are about 5cm/2in apart. Transplant to their final positions when they are about 13cm/5in high. The final planting distances vary depending on the variety – for smaller varieties 45cm/18in will do, but the largest may need to be 60cm/24in apart. Allow 60cm/24in between the rows.

Kale needs to be kept steadily growing because it is slow to recover from any checks. It is, therefore, necessary to water during dry spells, especially when the plants are young. Weed regularly and remove any yellowing leaves.

Harvesting

With early varieties, harvesting can begin in autumn and continue through winter and into spring. Pick the young leaves but do not strip plants, which will take time to recover. It is better to remove just a few leaves from each plant. In spring pick the emerging shoots before they come into flower. Leaves and shoots are picked simply by snapping them off.

Storage

Kale is extremely hardy, and the leaves can be left on the plants until required. It cannot be stored for any length of time, although it can be frozen for use between spring and the first of the summer vegetables.

Pests and diseases

Kale is generally the most pest free of all the brassicas, but it is still prone to the same problems as cabbages. Caterpillars can be a particular problem with autumn-picked varieties, especially because they hide within the curly leaves. Treatment with a spray or powder may help if it gets into the creases. Soaking the leaves in salted water before you cook them is a good way to remove caterpillars.

Cultivation

Sowing time late spring
Sowing distance sow thinly
Sowing depth 1cm/½in
Distance between sown rows 20cm/8in
Planting-out time when 13cm/5in high
Planting distance 45–60cm/18–24in
Distance between planted rows 60cm/24in
Harvesting autumn to mid-spring

curly kale

HARVESTING

Narrow-leaved black kale is being harvested here by removing the younger, more succulent leaves.

Varieties

'Cottagers'
'Dwarf Blue Curled Scotch'
'Dwarf Green Curled'
'Fribor'
'Frosty'
'Hungry Gap'
'Nero di Toscana'
'Pentland Brig'
'Tall Green Curled'
'Thousandhead'

Cauliflowers

Brassica oleracea Botrytis Group

Cauliflowers are not the easiest of crops to grow, but they are one of the most rewarding, both in a sense of achievement and in the eating. Like so many of our vegetables, their origins are rather obscure. The Romans are thought to have cultivated a type of cauliflower, but the vegetable as we know it today originated in the countries at the eastern end of the Mediterranean at a much later date. It was introduced into Italy in the late 15th century and finally reached Britain about a hundred years later. However it was another two hundred years before it came to be widely grown.

Cauliflowers are characterized by their large, dome-shaped heads of creamy-white flowers (which are generally known as "curds"). When well-grown, these should be tight, evenly shaped and unblemished. The typical cauliflower has creamy-white curds, but there are also other colours for those who want something a bit different. Purple is the most common alternative colour, but there are also various shades of green and orange, although most of these are not true cauliflowers but hybrids, often produced using broccoli. The heads are usually 15–20cm/6–8in across, but there are now modern hybrids, often known as mini-cauliflowers, which develop very quickly and have heads to only 10cm/4in or less across.

PLANTING

Cauliflowers must be firmed in well when they are planted. Plants in loose soil run to seed quickly.

For those with the space to grow them there are cauliflowers for almost every season of the year. The only gap comes in winter, because most of the so-called winter cauliflower are not, in fact, ready until spring.

Cauliflowers can be awkward to grow, but, with care and attention, all gardeners should be able to produce good-quality crops. The main factor is to make sure that the plants' growth is not checked, because this causes irregular and undersized curds. An irregular water supply can be one cause. Late transplanting may be another. The one aspect that is difficult for the gardener to control is high summer temperatures, which are not conducive to growing good cauliflowers, since they prefer cool conditions. In hot areas you may have to abandon the idea of summer cauliflowers and concentrate on winter varieties.

Cultivation

Cauliflowers should be planted in an open, sunny position. To grow cauliflowers well it is essential that you have a fertile soil, preferably manured during digging in autumn. The manure is important, because the soil should be moisture-retentive so that the plants are not checked during dry

LEFT **Harvest the cauliflower by cutting the stem with a sharp knife just below the first ring of leaves.**

periods. The soil must not be too acid; if possible adjust the pH level to 6.5–7 by liming in autumn.

Cauliflowers can be sown in the open ground or in modules or trays. They should be sown thinly in shallow drills about 1cm/½in deep and 20cm/8in apart. For the timing for the various seasons, check the Cultivation box. If necessary, thin the seedlings to about 5cm/2in apart. Transplant them when they have five leaves, which should be about six weeks after sowing. Water the rows of seedlings on the day and then transplant them using a dibber or trowel. Firm the soil around the plant down well with your heel. The planting distances vary from 50–75cm/20–30in, depending on the variety: compare Varieties with Cultivation box.

Keep cauliflowers well watered, especially in warm, dry spells. Once the curds begin to form, snap the larger outside leaves down over them to protect them. This will prevent discoloration.

Harvesting

The curds are ready when they form an even dome shape. Summer and autumn varieties mature in about 16 weeks from sowing and winter ones in about 40 weeks. Mini varieties are ready in about 15 weeks. When they are ready, cut through the stem with a sharp knife just below the head, leaving one or two leaves around the curd to protect it on its way to the kitchen. If you are storing them for a while, cut them so that they have a short length of stem from which you can hang them. If the leaves are occasionally sprayed with water, they will keep for several weeks in cool conditions.

PREVENTING SUN SCORCH

Protect the curds from discoloration by the sun by covering them with the inner leaves.

Storage

In general, it is best to leave the cauliflowers on the plants until they are required, but they can be cut and placed in a cool place for up to three weeks. They store best if they are hung upside down, otherwise cauliflowers will freeze well.

Pests and diseases

Cauliflowers are susceptible to the same problems as cabbages.

cauliflower

Cultivation

Early summer
Sowing time midwinter
Sowing position under glass
Planting-out time spring, when 13cm/5in high
Planting distance 50cm/20in
Distance between planted rows 60cm/24in
Harvesting early to midsummer

Summer
Sowing time mid-spring
Sowing distance sow thinly
Sowing depth 1cm/½in
Distance between sown rows 20cm/8in
Planting-out time early summer, when 13cm/5in high
Planting distance 60cm/24in
Distance between planted rows 60–75cm/24–30in
Harvesting late summer

Autumn
Sowing time late spring
Sowing distance sow thinly
Sowing depth 1cm/½in
Distance between sown rows 20cm/8in
Planting-out time early summer, when 13cm/5in high
Planting distance 60cm/24in
Distance between planted rows 60–75cm/24–30in
Harvesting autumn

Winter
Sowing time late spring
Sowing distance sow thinly
Sowing depth 1cm/½in
Distance between sown rows 20cm/8in
Planting-out time summer, when 13cm/5in high
Planting distance 70–75cm/28–30in
Distance between planted rows 60–75cm/24–30in
Harvesting late winter to early spring

Mini-cauliflowers
Sowing time spring
Sowing distance station sow 15cm/6in
Sowing depth 1cm/½in
Distance between sown rows 45cm/18in
Harvesting late summer to autumn

Varieties

Early summer and summer
'All Year Round'
'Alpha'
'Mayflower'
'Montana'
'Snow Crown'
'Snowball A'
'White Summer'

Late summer and autumn
'All Year Round'
'Autumn Glory'
'Castlegrant'
'Dok Elgon'
'Plana'
'Violet Queen'
'Wallaby'

Winter
'Arcade'
'Cappacio'
'Early Feltham'
'Jerome'
'Purple Cape'

Mini-cauliflowers
'Candid Charm'
'Mini-Cauliflower King'

Spinach

Spinacia oleracea

Spinach is the bane of most children and many adults, and yet when it is cooked properly it is a magnificent vegetable and a key ingredient in many classic and modern dishes. Spinach is related to the beetroots (beets) and chards and not to the cabbages or lettuces, to which it bears a superficial resemblance. It was first cultivated in Asia by the Persians, and it spread along the trade routes to China and eventually to Spain by the 11th century. It was five centuries later that it arrived in Britain.

Spinach is really a plant for a cool climate. It dislikes hot, dry summers, when it will very quickly go to seed, often before it is fully developed and ready to harvest. However, if you make sure that your plants are properly watered and that you select cultivars that suit your area, you can produce a crop that should last for two or three weeks and, with successional cropping, this can be extended considerably.

The plants look rather like a loose lettuce, with stalked leaves rising from a central stem. When the plant bolts, this stem quickly elongates. Supplying the plant with plenty of moisture and nourishment can postpone the tendency to bolt.

Alternatives to spinach

Spinach has a relatively short life, especially in hot, dry summers, when it is likely to bolt, and so many gardeners (erroneously one can't help feeling) think it is not worth growing. There are other vegetables that are cooked in the same way as spinach and have the advantage of having a longer season. These are generally known as "perpetual spinach", and the chief of them is Swiss chard. Another good alternative is New Zealand spinach (*Tetragonia tetragonioides*), which is not related botanically to spinach but makes a good substitute, both in the garden and kitchen. It is grown as an annual, but unlike true spinach it can be picked throughout the summer months and also way into autumn. Sow in trays or modules under glass and plant out after the danger of frosts has passed. Alternatively, station sow at 45cm/18in intervals in shallow drills, 1cm/½in deep, where they are to grow, again after the last frosts. It is more tolerant of drought than spinach but it does best if

Cultivation

Summer
Sowing time successional sowings from early to late spring
Sowing distance thinly
Sowing depth 1cm/½in
Thinning distance 15cm/6in
Distance between sown rows 30cm/12in
Harvesting early to late summer

Winter
Sowing time late summer to early autumn
Sowing distance thinly
Sowing depth 1cm/½in
Thinning distance 15cm/6in
Distance between sown rows 30cm/12in
Harvesting winter and spring

LEFT **This beautifully maintained walled potager includes a healthy crop of spinach.**

HARVESTING

Spinach is a very easy crop to harvest. When you require some, simply cut away the young leaves with a pair of sharp scissors.

RIGHT **This row of healthy looking spinach is now ready for harvesting.**

watered during dry periods. Pinch out the tip to make it bush out and harvest the leaves when they are big enough. Carry on doing this for as long as the plants last. Do not allow them to set seed or they may self-sow and possibly keep coming up for several years.

The young leaves of red orache or red mountain spinach (*Atriplex hortensis*) can also be used in the same way. In spring, sow seed where they are to grow either in shallow drills or by broadcasting. Thin to 30cm/12in apart. It is worth growing in a potager for its decorative qualities alone.

Cultivation

Grow spinach in an open, sunny position but preferably one that does not get too hot. The soil should be fertile and contain as much organic material as possible so that it is moisture retentive. Permanently wet soils should be avoided, however. Dig in manure or compost in autumn.

Thinly sow the seed in early spring, with successional sowings at two-week intervals through to late spring. It is better to sow several short or part-rows at intervals than one long one if there is the possibility that most of the plants will run to seed before they are harvested. Sow in shallow drills, about 1cm/½in deep and 30cm/12in apart. As soon as the seedlings are big enough to handle, thin them out to 15cm/6in apart. Keep well watered and keep weeds under control.

A crop for overwintering can be sown in late summer or early autumn. This will benefit from being covered with cloches from autumn onwards. The cloches will not only protect the plants, but will keep the leaves tender.

Harvesting

Start harvesting as soon as the leaves are big enough, which is usually 8–12 weeks after sowing. Don't strip the plant, but just take a few leaves to start with and until the plants are mature. Break or cut the stems, but avoid pulling because this may loosen the plant and precipitate bolting. Continue harvesting until the plants start to run to seed – when the central stem starts to elongate. When harvesting winter spinach, do not overpick.

Storage

Spinach should be picked and used as fresh as possible because it does not store. The leaves can, however, be frozen.

Pests and diseases

Spinach should be grown so fast that there can be few problems (apart from bolting) and, in any case, there is little time for the gardener to satisfactorily correct any problems that do occur. The best solution in this case is to scrap the affected plants and start again.

To avoid slug damage, clear the ground of slugs before sowing and at regular intervals thereafter.

The most likely diseases to affect spinach are downy mildew (choose resistant varieties) and spinach blight. Destroy the affected plants.

Varieties

Summer	Winter
'Bloomsdale'	'Broad-leafed Prickly'
'King of Denmark'	'Norvak'
'Long Standing'	'Sigmaleaf'
'Medana'	'Symphony'
'Monopa'	
'Melody'	
'Triathlon'	

spinach

Swiss Chard

Beta vulgaris Cicla Group

ABOVE **The vibrant colour of the stems of Swiss chard can be relied upon to make a strong decorative statement in the kitchen garden.**

Swiss chard has a number of alternative names, including chard and seakale beet. The red-stemmed forms are additionally known as rhubarb chard, red chard or ruby chard. Spinach beet or perpetual spinach is essentially the same but has thinner stems. Although it is called Swiss chard, the plant originates from around the Mediterranean and dates back long before the modern state of Switzerland was thought of. Both the Greeks and Romans grew chard including red-stemmed forms. Although not grown much in England until recently, it has been around since at least the 16th century.

Swiss chard has large, glossy, dark green leaves on wide creamy-white stalks. Both parts can be eaten, although they are often cooked separately, because the stems take much longer than the leaves. Ruby chard is similar, but the stems are a brilliant red and the leaves are a deep purple-green in some varieties and green in others. A third variant are those with striped stems, which can be in a range of colours, including red, yellow and orange. All three versions are very decorative and can be used in any ornamental scheme. Unlike some other brightly coloured vegetables – ornamental kale, for example – these chards are eminently edible as well as being decorative.

Perpetual spinach is relatively dull in comparison. It has smaller, less shiny leaves and stems that have no ornamental value at all. However, it makes a very good alternative to spinach. Both are easy to grow and maintain and produce an abundance of leaves for harvesting over a long period. Both can be used as a straightforward vegetable dish or combined with ingredients to make something a bit more special.

WINTER PROTECTION

In cold areas Swiss chard needs some form of winter protection. Any form of cloche or portable cold frame can be used.

Cultivation

Swiss chard and perpetual spinach need an open site and a fertile soil. Manure the soil while digging it in the autumn. Station sow the chard in spring in shallow drills 1cm/½in deep and 38cm/15in apart. The stations should be 45cm/18in apart for larger plants, although for smaller plants they can be closer together. For perpetual spinach the intervals should be 30cm/12in. Germination is rapid, within a few days. Thin out unwanted seedlings at each station. A sowing can be made in late summer to provide a crop that goes on until the following summer, thus together with the spring sowing, providing leaves all year round.

Water and keep weed free. Both can be sown in trays or modules and planted out when they have reached an adequate size, at the same intervals as above. In very cold areas it may be necessary to give the plants protection of cloches or fleece, but they are generally hardy enough to need no protection.

Harvesting

Both forms, the Swiss chard and perpetual spinach, are perpetual in that once they have matured (usually 8–12 weeks after sowing) leaves can be cut from them as you wish, right through from summer until the following spring when they are likely to start running to seed (Swiss chard in seed is a very decorative vegetable indeed, so do not be in too much of a hurry to get rid of it unless you desperately need the space). Snap or cut off the leaves at the

HARVESTING

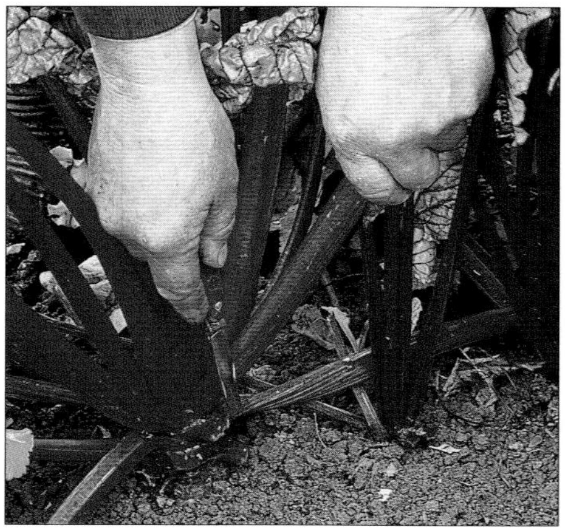

Swiss chard is harvested by cutting the stalks at the base with a sharp knife. Like perpetual spinach, it can be harvested from summer until the following spring.

Cultivation

Swiss chard
Sowing time late spring
Sowing distance station sow at 45cm/18in
Sowing depth 1cm/½in
Distance between sown rows 38cm/15in
Harvesting late summer to spring

Perpetual spinach
Sowing time mid spring
Sowing distance station sow at 30cm/12in
Sowing depth 1cm (½in)
Distance between sown rows 38cm/15in
Harvesting late summer to spring

base of the plant. Take the leaves as soon as they are big enough and continue to harvest them so that the outer leaves do not get too large and coarse.

Storage

Neither Swiss chard nor perpetual spinach stores well and should be cooked straight from the plant. Both can be frozen if necessary.

Pests and diseases

On the whole, both Swiss chard and perpetual spinach are pest and disease free. However, it is difficult to grow perfect Swiss chard (the leaves always seem to have holes in them), but while this may be a problem on the show bench, once cut up in the kitchen, no one will notice, so it isn't something to worry too much about. Slugs, earwigs, caterpillars, flea beetles and birds may all be to blame, but apart from getting rid of the slugs there is little need for action. If planted too close together they may suffer from downy mildew, especially in a damp season.

ABOVE **This row of mixed colour Swiss chard is ready for harvesting.**

ABOVE **A perfect specimen of Swiss chard, clearly showing the white ribs that can be cooked separately from the leaves.**

Varieties

Swiss chard

'Argentata' deep green leaves, silvery white stems
'Bright Lights' dark green leaves, red, pink, orange, creamy silver and yellow stems
'Charlotte' purple-red leaves, bright red stems
'Feurio' red leaves, red stems
'Fordhook Giant' deep green leaves, white stems
'Lucullus' pale green, ruffled leaves, white stems
'Rainbow Chard' red, pink, orange, creamy silver or yellow stems.
Sometimes listed simply as "Swiss Chard" (with white stems) or "Rhubarb Chard" (with red stems) with no varietal name given.

Perpetual spinach

No varieties normally simply listed as "Perpetual Spinach" or "Leaf Beet".

Chinese Cabbage

Brassica rapa var. pekinensis

Chinese cabbage is rather like a cos (romaine) lettuce, with crisp, crunchy leaves that can be eaten either raw or cooked. It is also a convenient name under which to group several other oriental greens, such as pak choi (bok choy) and mizuna, in which gardeners are becoming increasingly interested.

ABOVE **Young pak choi (bok choy) planted in a block, ready for harvesting. They can be cut on a cut-and-come-again basis.**

Chinese cabbage has been developed over centuries, particulary in China, since it was first recorded in the 5th century. It had reached America by the end of the 19th century but had to wait until the last decades of the 20th century before it arrived in Europe.

The original Chinese cabbages were loose headed, but the varieties we grow today are mainly hard headed and mostly derive from cultivars raised in Japan. They are tightly packed with dense leaves, which are a very pale creamy-yellow, blanched through lack of light, and sweet tasting. They last well if kept cool after harvesting, and one head seems to last several days of liberal helpings as a salad leaf. It can also be cooked, but its delicate flavour can be lost or overpowered by stronger flavours if the cook is not careful. Not many new vegetables have been introduced into gardens in the last couple of hundred years, but this one is most welcome.

Other new introductions have also appeared from the Far East, although they are perhaps not as popular as Chinese cabbage. Pak choi (bok choy; *Brassica rapa* var. *chinensis*) is one such. The common varieties are looser headed than the more commonly grown forms of Chinese cabbage and look more like a small Swiss chard, with dark green leaves and wide white stems. There is more flavour in pak choi (bok choy) than in Chinese leaves. They can be used raw or cooked.

Another plant that is creating increasing interest is mizuna (*Brassica rapa* var. *nipposinica*), which originated in Japan. This is unlike other greens in that the leaves are feathery, which makes them useful for the decorative kitchen garden as well as the purely productive one. They, too, can be cooked or used in salads.

LEFT **Like the original Chinese cabbages, this specimen is loose-headed.**

Cultivation

As with most vegetables, Chinese cabbage and other oriental greens like an open position and a fertile soil that is moisture retentive. Dig in plenty of well-rotted organic material during autumn digging. They do not do well on poor soils. Sowing in the open is best because they resent disturbance, which may cause bolting. They will also bolt if sown too early. Sow in early to midsummer in shallow drills 1cm/½in deep and 25cm/10in apart. Station sow the seed at 30cm/12in intervals, or sow thinly and thin to that distance. Take care not to disturb the roots too much when transplanting, and to avoid this, seed can be sown in modules. Keep weeded and well watered at all times.

Cultivation

Chinese cabbage
Sowing time early summer
Sowing distance station sow at 30cm/12in
Sowing depth 1cm/½in
Distance between sown rows 25cm/10in
Harvesting late summer to late autumn

Pak choi (bok choy)
Sowing time late spring
Sowing distance thinly
Sowing depth 1cm/½in
Distance between sown rows 15cm/8in–45cm/18in
Harvesting summer to late autumn

Mizuna
Sowing time spring
Sowing distance thinly
Sowing depth 1cm/½in
Distance between sown rows 38cm/15in
Thinning distance 15–45cm/6–18in
Harvesting summer to winter

RIGHT **The hard-headed Chinese cabbage is derived mainly from cultivars raised in Japan.**

Similar sowing conditions prevail for pak choi (bok choy), which can be sown a bit earlier as it is slightly less prone to bolt. Sowing distances vary from about 15cm/6in for smaller varieties to 45cm/18in for the larger. Mizuna, which does not bolt, can be sown at any time during the season, and it can be easily transplanted from seed trays if so desired. The spacing is the same as for pak choi. It can be harvested in winter from a late summer sowing, although it does best with some form of winter protection.

Harvesting

Chinese cabbage is ready to harvest after about seven weeks and can be cut as required through until late autumn. It can also be cut on a cut-and-come-again basis at a much earlier stage. However, it is more usual to remove the whole head by cutting just below the lowest leaves. If the stump is left in the ground, more leaves may develop, and these can be harvested as required.

Leaves of pak choi (bok choy) can be cut at any stage once they are big enough, usually after about three weeks. Whole heads can be removed when ready and the stumps left to reshoot. Flower-heads can also be eaten. Mizuna leaves can be cut at any stage from three weeks onwards, although the older leaves are not as succulent. The flower stalks can be eaten.

Storage

Chinese cabbage and other oriental greens should be used fresh from the garden.

Pests and diseases

The main pests are likely to be slugs, snails and caterpillars. Apart from these, there are usually not too many problems, although Chinese cabbage and the other oriental greens can be prone to any of the cabbage diseases.

Varieties

Chinese cabbage
'China Express'
'Eskimo'
'Harmony'
'Jade Pagoda'
'Kasumi'
'Mariko'
'Michihili'
'Tip Top'

Pak choi (bok choy)
Frequently listed simply as pak choi/bok choy.
'Joi Choi'
'Mei Quing'
'Shanghei'
'Tai-Sai'

Mizuna
Usually listed simply as mizuna greens.

Chinese cabbage

Lettuce

Latuca sativa

Lettuce is an odd vegetable, which is as often used for decorative purposes as for taste and nutrition. Shop-bought lettuces have much to answer for in this respect, as are the oft-repeated scare stories about their being full of chemicals. Home-grown lettuces not only have flavour, but you also know what they have been fed on. Another advantage of growing your own lettuces is that you can grow several different types and colours so that you can make a really attractive salad – and, of course, they are fresh. You can pick just as many leaves as you want right at the last minute.

Lettuces have been popular for a long time and were even depicted in carvings and paintings in Ancient Egypt. They were popular among the Romans, who are reputed to have introduced them to Britain. The original lettuces were probably quite bitter and needed blanching to make them palatable, much like endives today.

Modern gardeners are fortunate in having so many different types as well as a wide range of varieties. The main type is the cabbage or headed lettuce. These are either loose balls of soft leaves – butterhead lettuces – or those with much firmer, crinkly-edged leaves – crispheads. Cos or romaine lettuces are more upright and have long, crisp leaves and a succulent heart. Then there are the loose-leaved or non-heading varieties, which do not produce a heart but just a mass of loose, individual leaves. These lettuces are very good when you want to be able to take leaves as and when you require them. There has recently been a great deal of interest in these cut-and-come-again lettuces, and many new varieties have appeared. This method of growing lettuces is far from new, however.

HARVESTING

Harvest lettuces when the "heart" feels firm.

The mainstay of salads, lettuce is usually eaten raw, although an increasing number of recipes include cooked lettuce. Lettuce leaves are also widely used as a garnish, for which the coloured forms of the loose-leaved varieties are particularly useful. There is now quite a wide range of red- and bronze-leaved forms, as well as green forms with decorative leaves.

Lettuces are not difficult to grow and, in theory, can be harvested all year round, but some type of protection is required for winter varieties. They grow relatively quickly and will be ready from 5 to 12 weeks after sowing, depending on the variety. This means that they can be grown among slower growing crops or used to replace another crop that has already been harvested.

Cultivation

Lettuces need an open, sunny position, although light, partial shade during the heat of the day can be an advantage in hot areas or during hot summers. The soil needs to be fertile and, preferably, moisture retentive, and this is best achieved by incorporating plenty of manure during the autumn dig. Lettuces can be sown straight in the ground or grown in trays and transplanted. It is a good idea to sow a short row of lettuces and then, instead of throwing away the thinnings, to transplant them to make up the rest of the row. The advantage of this is that the transplants will take a few days to settle down and will produce a slightly later crop than the sown plants. If the whole row is sown at once, the lettuces will mature at the same time, which will probably mean that many are wasted.

ABOVE **A block of developing lettuces shows how decorative this varied crop can be.**

Transplanting is difficult after midsummer, because lettuces often rapidly run to seed.

Start early sowings in trays or modules under glass in late winter or early spring. Plant these out under cloches or in cold frames to get an early crop. Seed can be sown directly in the soil from early spring onwards. Sow in shallow drills 1cm/½in deep, each row about 30cm/12in apart. Thin the lettuces to 15–30cm/6–12in apart, depending on the size of the variety. Transplanted lettuces should be planted at the same distances. Keep the soil moist and do not allow the plants' growth to be checked or they will rapidly run to seed. Sowings after midsummer will provide lettuces for autumn and early winter, but cover them with cloches when necessary from around mid-autumn. Special winter varieties can be overwintered under cloches or grown in greenhouses or in cold frames.

Harvesting

Lettuces can be harvested whole or leaves can be taken from the plants as required. The loose-leaved varieties are usually picked leaf by leaf, but cabbage-type varieties can be picked in the same way if you wish. Hearted varieties are usually ready for harvesting as soon as they feel plump and firm. Do not leave them too long in the

ABOVE **A block of decorative lettuces, showing the rich variety of colours available.**

ground after maturing or they may bolt. Pull the whole lettuce from the ground or cut below the bottom leaves if you want the plant to resprout. Loose-leaved varieties mature earlier, and leaves can be picked as soon as they are large enough, which is usually from about seven weeks after sowing.

Storage

Whole lettuces can be kept in a refrigerator for a short time, but they are best used straight from the garden.

Pests and diseases

Slugs and greenfly (aphids) are two of the worst problems and should be dealt with by your preferred methods. Other pests can include root aphids and cutworms.

The main disease is downy mildew, and lettuces also tend to suffer from a few other fungal diseases. These occur mainly in wet seasons and are best avoided by making sure that individual lettuces are not planted too close together. This will ensure that there is plenty of air movement around the plants. If pests or diseases do get out of control, do not spend a lot of time and money on chemical control. Simply get rid of the plants and start again.

Cultivation

Sowing time late winter (under glass) to early spring onwards
Sowing distance thinly
Sowing depth 1cm/½in
Distance between sown rows 30cm/12in
Thinning distance 15–30cm/6–12in
Harvesting early summer onwards

Varieties

Butterhead
'Avondefiance'
'Buttercrunch'
'Continuity'
'Dolly'
'Hilde II'
'Musette'
'Sabine'
'Tom Thumb'

Crisphead
'Avoncrisp'
'Beatrice'
'Iceberg'
'Lake Nayah'
'Malika'
'Minetto'
'Saladin'
'Warpath'
'Webb's Wonderful'

Cos
'Balloon'
'Bubbles'
'Corsair'
'Little Gem'
'Lobjoits Green Cos'
'Paris White'
'Wallop'

Loose-leaved
'Cerise'
'Cocarde'
'Frisby'
'Lollo Rosso'
'Red Fire'
'Red Sails'
'Redina'
'Salad Bowl'

Winter
'Arctic King'
'Kellys'
'Novita'
'Valdor'
'Winter Density'

Salad Leaves

Although lettuces, perhaps supplemented by leaves such as endives and chicory, provide the traditional greenery for most salads, there is an increasing number of small leaves that play their part. Some are available during the winter months, when lettuce from the garden may be scarce, and as well as adding bulk, each adds an individual flavour to pep up the overall interest of the salad. The two most important of these salad leaves are rocket (arugula; Eruca vesicaria*), which is also known as salad rocket, rucola and Italian cress, and lamb's lettuce (mâche;* Valerianella locusta*), which is also known as corn salad.*

ABOVE **Chinese leaf mustard, in this case the variety is 'Red Giant', will add a zing to any salad with its pungent flavour.**

Neither rocket (arugula) nor lamb's lettuce (mâche) is new – indeed, both have been eaten for centuries – but their popularity seems to be on the increase, particularly in the United States, where numerous varieties are available. The choice is also increasing in Europe, where it has always been particularly popular in France, from where many of the varieties come.

Young rocket (arugula) leaves have a sharp taste, and the older the leaves, the hotter and spicier the taste. They are usually eaten raw in salads, but older leaves are sometimes cooked, and the flowers can be eaten too. They make an excellent winter crop. Lamb's lettuce (mâche) is also used as a winter crop. The leaves are milder than those of rocket, and it is also much slower growing, taking up to 12 weeks before being ready to cut, compared with three weeks for rocket.

Several other leaves can be grown, each needing similar cultivation to rocket (arugula) and lamb's lettuce (mâche). The leaves of land cress (*Barbarea verna*) have a similar flavour to watercress. Mustard (*Brassica hirta*) and the similar tasting salad rape (*Brassica napus*) are also worth growing. Cress (*Lepidium sativum*), also known as garden or curly cress, can be grown to complement the other leaves, and winter purslane (*Claytonia perfoliata*) is another mild leaf for the salad bowl.

Cultivation

All these salad leaves are plants for a cool climate and will rapidly run to seed in hotter areas. Because of this and because other salad materials are scarce at that time, they are mainly grown for autumn and winter use. In cooler areas they can be sown in spring for summer use. Although they are hardy, they need to be protected by cloches to be at their best.

Both rocket (arugula) and lamb's lettuce (mâche) are sown in late summer; rocket can also be sown in early autumn. Sow in drills 1cm/½in deep and 30cm/12in apart. Thin the resulting seedlings to 15cm/6in apart for rocket and 10cm/4in for lamb's lettuce. Keep lettuces watered if the weather is dry. Cover with cloches in late autumn or early winter.

LEFT **Land cress, often known as upland cress, is similar in taste to watercress and is often used as a land-grown substitute. This makes a welcome contribution to most salads.**

Cultivation

Rocket (arugula)
Sowing time late summer to early autumn
Sowing distance thinly
Sowing depth 1cm/½in
Distance between sown rows 30cm/12in
Thinning distance 15cm/6in
Harvesting late autumn onwards

Lamb's lettuce (mâche)
Sowing time late summer
Sowing distance thinly
Sowing depth 1cm/½in
Distance between sown rows 30cm/12in
Thinning distance 10cm/4in
Harvesting winter

ABOVE **Curled cress, or simply cress, is grown for its sprouts, but can also be used when fully grown, as is the case here.**

Harvesting

Either pick individual leaves or cut off the lot as soon as they are large enough. They will sprout again.

Storage

Both plants should be picked as required because they will not store.

Pests and diseases

Both plants should be free of both pests and diseases, although rocket (arugula) may be attacked by flea beetle. If the tell-tale marks appear on the leaves, dust with derris.

LEFT **Lamb's lettuce or mâche is a mild-flavoured leaf that is useful in autumn and winter salads.**

Varieties

Rocket (arugula)
Sold under one or other of its common names – rocket (arugula), rucola, salad rocket – rather than as varieties.
'Jade'
'Verte de Cambrai'
'Volhart'

Lamb's lettuce (mâche)
Frequently sold simply under its common name.
'Cavallo'
'Grote Noordhollandse'

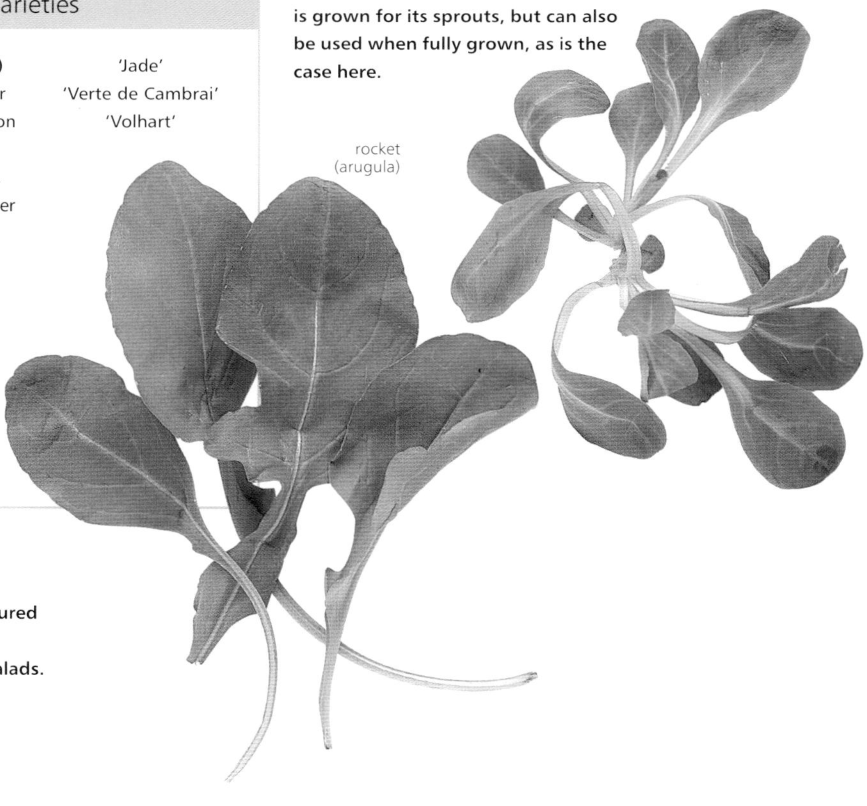

Endives

Cichorium endivia

ABOVE **These curly-leaved endives, whose foliage creates a textured effect, have been grown in a block rather than in rows.**

*Endives and chicory (*Cichorium intybus*) are very closely related. So close, in fact that they can often be confused. The confusion is not helped by the fact that in France endive refers to what an English-speaking gardener would call chicory, while chicorée frisée is, in fact, the frilly-leaved form of endive. When it comes to growing them in the garden, however, there is rarely any confusion.*

There are two main types of endive. Curly endive is a flat-growing plant with frilly leaves; it is not very hardy and is mainly grown as a summer salad vegetable. Batavian endive or escarole is a more upright plant, with broad, wavy (rather than frilly) leaves. It is much hardier than curly endive and is, therefore, the type to choose for winter growing, although in milder areas both can be grown. Both types are annuals, unlike chicory which is a perennial.

Endives have been used as a salad vegetable for many centuries – in fact, civilizations as far back as the Ancient Egyptians are known to have enjoyed them. They are thought to have originated somewhere in the Near East but have long been grown in southern Europe, before eventually moving northwards. They are still not cultivated as widely as lettuces, probably because they have a rather bitter taste, which deters many people from growing them. The flavour can be dramatically improved, however, by blanching the leaves and the bitterness is more intense in hot conditions, so it is worth remembering that summer varieties are likely to have a sharper taste than the winter ones. This bitter taste contrasts well with other flavours in a mixed leaf salad.

One advantage that endives have over lettuce is that some varieties can be used in winter when lettuces are scarce. In summer, particularly in late summer, endives have the added advantage that they are less likely to bolt in dry weather, and they are also less prone to diseases, making them a reliable choice all the year round for the vegetable garden.

LEFT **Broad-leaved endives or escaroles are more cold-tolerant than the curly-leaved varieties.**

Cultivation

Endives generally prefer an open, sunny position, but in very hot areas they will benefit from a little light shade. The soil should be fertile and moisture retentive. Both curly-leaved and broad-leaved forms can be sown in open soil from spring onwards, and broad-leaved forms can also be sown in late summer for winter cropping. Sow in shallow drills 1cm/½in deep and 38cm/15in apart. When the seedlings appear, thin them to 25cm/10in apart for curly varieties and 38cm/15in for broad-leaved forms. Make sure that the soil does not dry out because it is very important not to check their growth.

Cultivation

Curly-leaved
Sowing time spring to summer
Sowing distance thinly
Sowing depth 1cm/½in
Distance between sown rows 38cm/15in
Thinning distance 25cm/10in
Harvesting summer

Broad-leaved
Sowing time spring to late summer
Sowing distance thinly
Sowing depth 1cm/½in
Distance between sown rows 38cm/15in
Thinning distance 38cm/15in
Harvesting summer, autumn and winter

Cover the winter varieties with cloches at the onset of winter. Alternatively, they can be grown in a greenhouse or covered cold frame.

Curly-leaved forms can be blanched by slipping a porous pot (terracotta is best) over the plant for about a week in summer or for up to three weeks in the colder weather of autumn and winter. Cover only a few plants at a time because they do not keep for long under these conditions. Place the cover over them when the leaves of the plant are dry. The taller broad-leaved varieties can also be covered, but it is often enough simply to tie the plant with raffia or soft string so that the outer leaves exclude the light from the inner ones.

Harvesting

Cut the blanched plants as required. Both can either be cut complete or just a few leaves can be used. The cut stalks will reshoot.

Storage

Neither form stores well and should be cut as required.

Pests and diseases

On the whole both forms of endive are trouble free. The most likely problem to occur will be attacks from slugs and snails, especially during the blanching process. Place a few slug pellets under the cover or lift it regularly and remove any slugs or snails that you find.

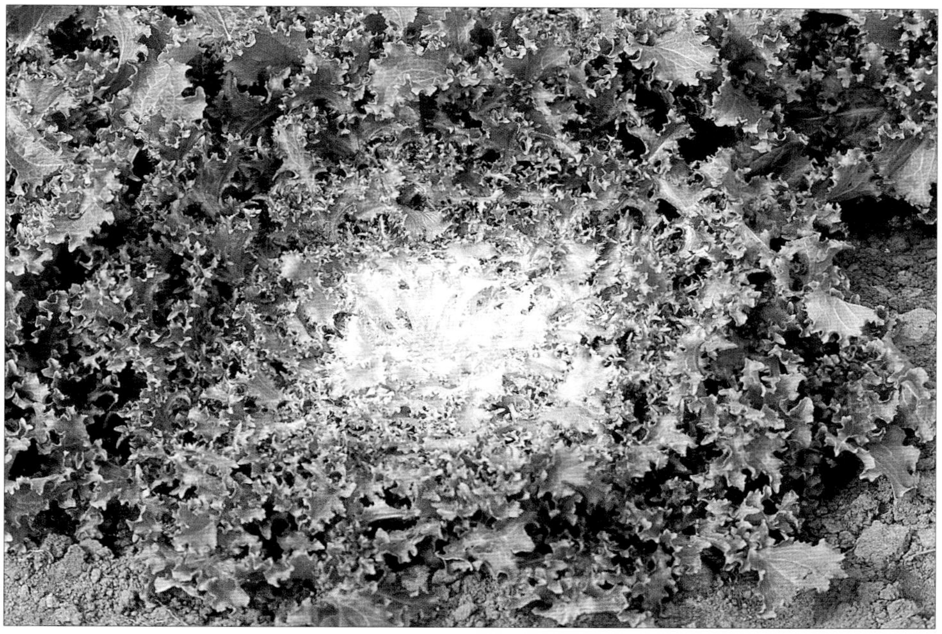

TOP **The leaves of endives can be used in salads or cooked. Unblanched leaves like these are more bitter than blanched ones.**

ABOVE **Blanching makes the leaves of endives taste sweeter. A plate laid over the centre of the plant is one way to achieve this.**

Varieties

Curly-leaved	Broad-leaved
'De Ruffec'	'Batavian Broad-leaved'
'Frisée de Namur'	'Batavian Green'
'Green Curled'	'Cornet de Bordeaux'
'Monaco'	'Full Heart Italian'
'Moss Curled'	'Golda'
'Riccia Pancalieri'	'Stratego'
'Wallone'	

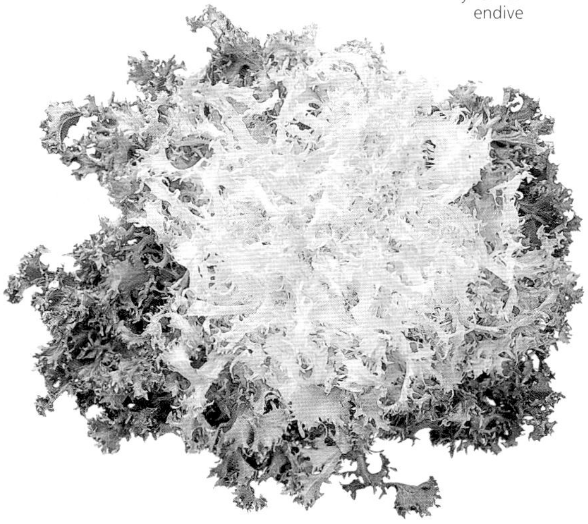

Chicory

Cichorium intybus

Although it is very closely related to the endive, chicory is quite distinct, both in the kitchen and the garden. Both vegetables are salad leaves, both can be bitter and both are useful as winter vegetables, but whereas endive is an annual, chicory is a perennial, even though it is often grown as an annual.

ABOVE **The Witloof or Belgian chicories are mainly grown for their chicons, but the leaves can also be eaten.**

Chicory dates from at least Roman times, when it was eaten as a salad leaf and a cooked vegetable. It has always been most widely used in Italy, which still grows more varieties than most countries. Left unharvested, chicory produces blue dandelion-like flowers, which set plenty of seed. The seeds spread easily, and chicory has become naturalized in many places, including North America, where it did not formerly grow.

As with endive and lettuce, the name chicory is, in fact, used to describe several distinct types. The best known is probably Witloof or Belgian chicory, which has green edible leaves but is grown mainly for the tight-leaved shoot or "chicon". This is produced in winter by blanching and can be used raw in salads or cooked.

Another type is the sugar loaf chicory, which has an upright head, looking rather like a cos (romaine) lettuce. Its large outer leaves envelop the inner ones, so that these are blanched naturally and thus lose some of their bitterness. Sugar loaf chicory is usually harvested from late summer onwards and can be used as a winter crop if given protection.

Radicchio or red-leaved chicory is another group. Unlike the sugar loaf type, this is a low-growing plant, but again, the outer leaves protect the tight, crisp heart, thus blanching it naturally and improving the taste. As well as flavour, radicchio adds colour to winter salads. It is harvested in the autumn and on through winter if given protection.

Traditionally, chicory has also been grown for its root, which has been used, roasted and ground, to bulk up coffee. Today few gardeners grow chicory for this purpose, although there is no reason why they should not.

Although it is not a chicory, dandelion (*Taraxacum officinale*) is often treated and eaten in exactly the same way, with the blanched leaves providing salad material. Sow in spring, removing any flower-heads that subsequently appear. Early in the following spring, cover and blanch the leaves. Keep the plants for another year or discard and start again.

Cultivation

Grow chicory in an open, sunny position. Although it will grow in any soil, it does best in fertile ground, into which manure has been incorporated during the previous autumn. Sow Witloof chicory in late spring or early summer in drills 1cm/½in deep and 30cm/12in apart. Thin the subsequent seedlings to about 15cm/6in. Remove any flowering stems.

To blanch chicory cut off all the leaves in late autumn and cover the remaining stumps with 15cm/6in of free-draining soil or compost (soil mix). The chicons are ready to pick as they appear. To blanch them indoors, lift a few roots from late autumn onwards. Cut off the leaves and trim back the base of the roots so that they fit into a 23cm/9in pot. Put three or four roots in the pot and fill with damp compost so that just the tops show. Cover with another pot or a bucket and place in a dark, preferably warm place. The chicons should be ready in about three weeks. Cut and cover again to get a second crop.

Sow sugar loaf from spring to late summer in 1cm/½in drills set 30cm/12in apart. Thin to 25cm/10in. Do not allow soil to dry out.

Radicchio can be sown in a similar way from early to midsummer. Thinning should be the same, although some of the larger

LEFT **Radicchio or red-leaved chicory produces a tight, self-blanching head that can be eaten like a lettuce.**

ABOVE **Radicchio chicories do not need the same care as Witloof or Belgian chicories.**

varieties may need more space. Protect with cloches once winter arrives.

Harvesting

Chicons should be cut complete when they are about 15cm/6in long. Harvest individual leaves of other forms as required or remove the complete head. The inner leaves are always the sweetest.

Storage

Chicory does not store well, so cut as needed. They can be kept for a few days in a refrigerator but wrap them so that no light reaches them or they will turn green and become bitter.

Pests and diseases

Slugs and snails are likely to be the only problem.

Cultivation

Witloof
Sowing time spring to early summer
Sowing distance thinly
Sowing depth 1cm/½in
Distance between sown rows 30cm/12in
Thinning distance 15cm/6in
Harvesting late autumn and winter

Sugar loaf
Sowing time spring to summer
Sowing distance thinly
Sowing depth 1cm/½in
Distance between sown rows 30cm/12in
Thinning distance 25cm/10in
Harvesting autumn

Radicchio
Sowing time early to midsummer
Sowing distance thinly
Sowing depth 1cm/½in
Distance between sown rows 38cm/15in
Thinning distance 25–30cm/10–12in
Harvesting late autumn to winter

Varieties

Witloof
'Normato'
'Witloof'
'Witloof Zoom'

Sugar loaf
'Bianca di Milano'
'Crystal Head'
'Poncho'
'Snowflake'
'Sugar Loaf'
'Winter Fare'

Radicchio
'Cesare'
'Medusa'
'Palla Rossa Zorzi Precoce'
'Rossa di Treviso'
'Rossa di Verona'

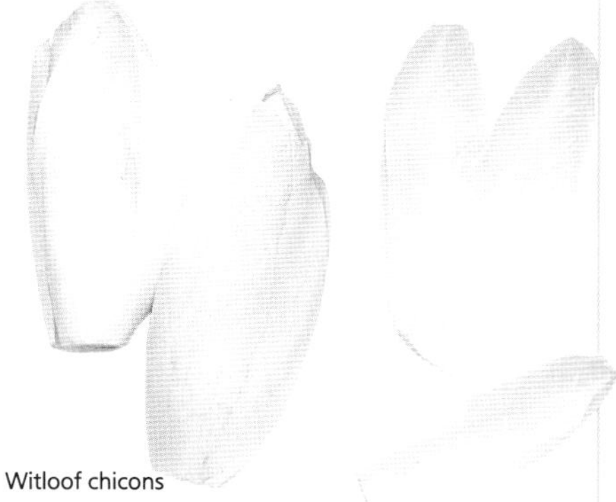

Witloof chicons

ROOT CROPS

Parsnips

Pastinaca sativa

Parsnips were developed in Europe from the widespread wild parsnip. It is possible that the Greeks and Romans cultivated them, but there is confusion over whether they were referring to parsnips or carrots in their writings. However, parsnips were certainly being eaten in Europe in the Middle Ages, although they subsequently went into something of a decline (except as cattle food), and it is principally in Britain where they remain popular. Parsnips have always been part of country fare, but they are now regaining a rightful place as vegetables for discerning palates.

ABOVE **Parsnips can be left in the ground until they are required.**

There is not much to see of the parsnip above ground, except for its inedible leaves. It is the large, swollen root that is the part that is eaten. Some varieties, especially when they are in light, fertile soil, can grow very big, to 45cm/18in or even longer. For most purposes, however, smaller roots are more than adequate.

There are more than 30 different varieties of parsnip. They differ little from each other, although some are more resistant to canker, while others have less hard cores. Certainly, none is more decorative than any other, either in the garden or on the plate. Ultimately, your choice of variety will be based on which grows best for you and which taste you prefer, although, in truth, there is not a great deal of difference.

Cultivation

An open, sunny position is required. Parsnips can be grown in heavy soils, but they prefer light ones, and although they do best in a fertile soil, do not sow them on freshly manured ground (the parsnips fork). Sow in soil that was manured the previous season or dug in the autumn. Always use fresh seed; last year's is unlikely to germinate. The seed should be station sown at 15–20cm/6–8in intervals in 1cm/½in drills. The rows should be 30cm/12in apart. Do not sow too early – the soil should be at least 7°C/45°F – but they do need a long growing season, so sow as soon as you can. Parsnips are slow to germinate so sow a few radishes between the stations of parsnips. These will appear quickly and mark the line of the rows, making it easier to hoe without accidentally disturbing the germinating parsnips.

In heavy or stony soils the parsnips may fork and produce stunted growth, rather than the desired conical shape. To avoid this, make holes with a crowbar at each sowing station, moving it in a circle to make an inverted conical hole in the ground. Fill this with potting compost (soil mix) or good loam and sow the seeds in this.

Thin the seeds to one to each station as soon as they are big enough to handle. Keep

PLANTING IN STONY GROUND

1 At the required sowing intervals, make an inverted conical hole with a crowbar.

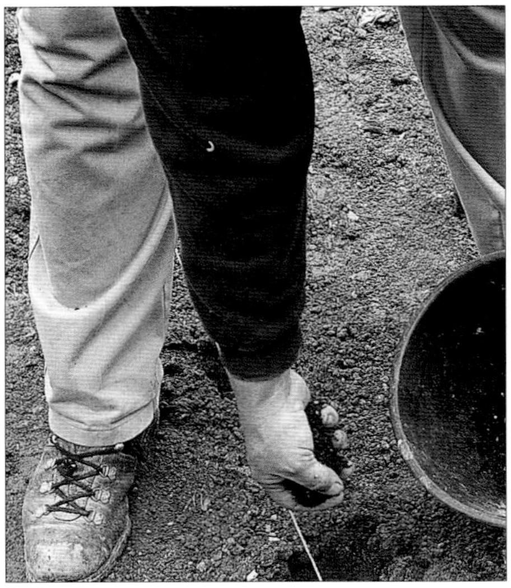

2 Fill the hole with potting compost (soil mix) and sow in the centre, covering the seed with more compost.

Cultivation

Sowing time early spring
Sowing distance station sow at 15–20cm/6–8in
Sowing depth 1cm/½in
Distance between sown rows 30cm/12in
Harvesting late autumn until spring

free from weeds. Water in dry spells because sudden rain after a prolonged dry spell may cause the roots to split. In very cold climates cover the rows of parsnips with straw during the winter.

Harvesting

Parsnips can be harvested from autumn onwards. Although they can be harvested before the leaves die back, most gardeners wait for this. Many gardeners also wait until after the first frosts, because these make parsnips taste sweeter. Dig the roots from the ground with a fork. In heavy soil or if the parsnips have deep roots, take care or the fork may slash through the flesh rather than lifting it out of the ground.

Storage

Parsnips are very hardy and should be left in the ground until they are required. If a frosty spell is forecast, however, it can be a good idea to lift a few while you can still get them out of the ground, and place them in trays of just-moist peat (peat moss) or sand until they are required. They are a late crop and may be harvested in spring well beyond the time that the ground may require preparing for the next crops. The parsnips can be dug up and temporarily heeled into another piece of ground or stored in sand or peat as described.

Varieties

'**Avonresister**' small, some canker resistance
'**Bayonet**' long-rooted, some canker resistance
'**Cobham Improved Marrow**' medium
'**Gladiator**' long-rooted, some canker resistance
'**Hollow Crown Improved**' long-rooted
'**Intermediate**' small
'**Tender and True**' long-rooted, some canker resistance
'**White Gem**' medium, long-rooted
'**White Spear**' long-rooted

ABOVE **Harvest parsnips by digging a fork well under the root and levering them out.**

Pests and diseases

Parsnips can be attacked by such pests as celery fly or carrot flies, but on the whole they are usually pest free.

Parsnips are also prone to canker, but you can help reduce the chances of this occurring by choosing one of the increasing number of varieties that have been grown with a resistance to this problem.

SOWING

Parsnips are best station sown in groups of three, eventually reducing the seedlings to one by thinning out the weakest.

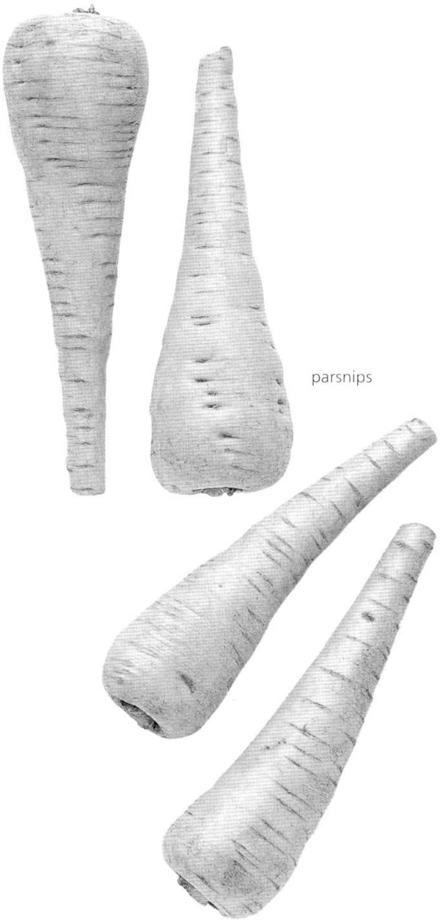

parsnips

Carrots

Daucus carota

Many people may wonder if it is worth growing carrots when they are so cheap to buy. The answer must be an emphatic "yes". Fresh carrots, whether old or young, that are taken straight from the ground before being cooked taste infinitely better than shop-bought ones; there is no comparison. You may have to put up with them being covered in mud and perhaps with slug and carrot fly holes in them, but this is a minor consideration compared with the superior taste.

Wild carrots appear throughout Europe and well into Asia. The exact origin of domestic carrots is rather obscure, but they probably originated in the countries of the eastern Mediterranean, possibly even in Afghanistan. The original domesticated ones were various colours, including white, yellow, purple and red, and carrots of these colours are currently being re-bred and will soon be re-introduced by seed merchants. The orange ones, with which we are all familiar, were developed in Holland and France at a much later date.

The edible part of the carrot is below ground, while above are the attractive filigree leaves. Although mainly grown for the kitchen, they are well worth growing as purely decorative plants.

Although carrots bought in supermarkets are more or less identical, there is a lot of variety available to the gardener. Not only are there early carrots (often grown in frames) that are round, looking almost like radishes, there are some that are long and tapered. Others are just as long but are cylindrical, with parallel sides and a rounded end. Shorter varieties are best for immediate use, while the longer ones are better for storing over winter. Although the other colours are being bred, the majority of carrots are the familiar orange, but there are a few pale yellow and creamy-white forms available.

THINNING

Thin the carrots only if necessary. Do so on a still, muggy evening to prevent the smell of the carrots travelling and betraying their presence to carrot root flies. Water after thinning.

Cultivation

Choose an open, sunny position. Carrots will grow in heavier soils, but they do best in light ground – sandy soils are perfect. The soil should be free from stones and fresh manure because both will cause the carrots to fork. If the soil is stony, make individual holes with a crowbar, fill them with compost (soil mix) and sow into these. Avoid freshly manured soil by using a plot that was manured for a previous crop or by manuring in the autumn. Sow very thinly in drills 1cm/½in deep and set 15–20cm/6–8in apart. Sow under cloches in late winter or in the open from early spring, but not before the soil has warmed up to at least 7°C/45°F. Sow successionally, with the last sowing in early summer.

When the seedlings appear, thin the earliest to 8cm/3in and the maincrop to 5–8cm/2–3in apart, depending on the size of carrot required. It is best to thin on a muggy, windless evening in order to avoid attracting carrot fly. For the same reason, remove all thinnings and bury them in the compost heap. Weed regularly but avoid disturbing the young carrots – a mulch of grass cuttings will help keep weeds down. It will also help to keep the soil moist. Water in dry weather.

SOWING WITH SAND

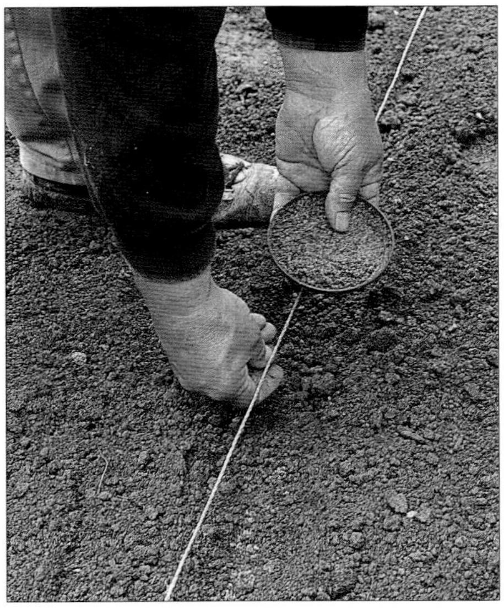

Carrots must be sown thinly. To help with this mix the seed with a little silver sand and "sow" the mixture.

Harvesting

Harvesting can begin at a very early stage as the thinnings can be very delicious, although they are rather tedious to clean. Early carrots can be dug up from late spring onwards, approximately seven weeks after sowing. Maincrop carrots take a bit longer and are ready from ten weeks onwards. Shorter varieties can be pulled, but longer ones and those that have been grown in heavier soils will need digging out with a fork.

HARVESTING

Shorter varieties can be pulled out by hand, but longer ones and those grown on heavier soils will need digging out with a fork. Try to avoid piercing the roots with the tines of the fork.

Storage

Carrots are usually left in the ground until they are required. They may even be left in the ground over winter unless there are a lot of slugs or the winter is very harsh. Instead, they can be lifted, cleaned and placed in a tray of just-moist sand or peat (peat moss).

Pests and diseases

The worst pest is undoubtedly carrot fly, the maggots of which burrow into the carrots. There are an increasing number of varieties that are resistant to this pest and these may be worth trying. Be careful when thinning, because the flies are attracted by smell, and the bruising of any part of the carrot will release the tell-tale odour. Planting garlic nearby is a traditional way of disguising the smell. Another, cumbersome but successful, method is to erect a fine mesh barrier, up to 90cm/3ft high, around the carrots. This deflects the flies, which fly quite close to the ground.

The principal disease from which carrots are likely to suffer is violet root rot, in which, as its name suggests, the root rots, becoming a violet colour. Burn or destroy all affected plants and make sure that you do not use the same ground for carrots for at least a couple of years.

ABOVE **A flourishing row of carrots, coming to maturity. These will be ready for harvesting a few at a time, whenever required for the kitchen.**

Cultivation

Sowing time early spring and successionally to early summer
Sowing distance very thinly
Sowing depth 1cm/½in
Distance between sown rows 15–20cm/6–8in
Thinning distance 5–8cm/2–3in
Harvesting late spring onwards

Varieties

Early
'Amsterdam Forcing 3' cylindrical
'Amsterdam Sweetheart' cylindrical
'Early Nantes' stump-rooted
'Rondo' round

Maincrop
'Autumn King' cylindrical
'Chantenay Red Cored' tapered
'Favourite' stump-rooted
'Fly Away' cylindrical
'Ingot' cylindrica
'James Scarlet Intermediate' tapered
'Nantes' stump-rooted
'Nantes Express' stump-rooted
'St Valery' tapered

Beetroot (Beets)

Beta vulgaris

Beetroot (beets) originated around the shores of the Mediterranean and was spread northwards into the rest of Europe by the Romans. Once the Romans reached northern and eastern Europe, the vegetable seems to have been taken to heart, and many of the recipes in use today come from these areas.

Beetroot (beets) is related closely to Swiss chard and shares its distinctive bright red coloration. This is not only manifest in the leaves and stems of the plant but also in the roots themselves, and when they are cut or bruised they exude a wonderfully deep red juice. When it is cooked, the flesh is still a very deep colour, even though it loses a lot of colour in the water if it is boiled (baking preserves it). Not everyone likes this coloration, because it has a tendency to stain not only other food, but lips and clothes as well.

However, although you never see them in greengrocers, there are also white and golden varieties, which are equally delicious but do not cause the staining. There are also a few fancy ones in which the roots are made up of concentric rings of white and red flesh. The general shape is round or near round, but cylindrical or even tapered varieties are available.

The green or reddish-green leaves can also be eaten when they are young, either in salads or cooked.

Unlike parsnips and carrots, the bulk of the vegetable's swollen root sits on top of the ground so that you can watch its progress and easily determine when it is ready to harvest.

Many of the older varieties have a tendency to bolt, particularly if they are sown early, but there are now ample alternatives that have had this characteristic bred out of them. Another aspect of choosing varieties is related to germination. Most seed is, in fact, made up of a cluster of seeds, which means that when they germinate they produce several seedlings close together. However, if you find that thinning these is fiddly, look out for monogerm varieties, which usually have the word "mono" somewhere in their name.

BELOW **Beetroot growing in a block in a raised bed. This method enables you to control the growing medium and grow crops unsuited to your soil.**

Cultivation

Sowing time early spring and successionally to early summer
Sowing distance thinly or in stations at 8cm/3in intervals
Sowing depth 1cm/½in
Distance between sown rows 20cm/8in
Thinning distance 8cm/3in
Harvesting early summer onwards

Cultivation

Beetroot (beets) needs an open, sunny position. They will grow in heavy soils, but do best in light ones. The soil should be fertile but not freshly manured. Use a plot that was manured for the previous crop or one into which manure was dug during the

HARVESTING

Harvest beetroot by pulling it by hand from the ground. In heavier soils a fork may be needed to loosen the roots.

PREPARING FOR COOKING

Remove the leaves by twisting them off, 3–5cm/1–2in from the root. This prevents the beetroot (beets) losing their colour by "bleeding" when they are cooked.

previous autumn. Sow directly into the open soil into shallow drills 1cm/½in deep and set 20cm/8in apart. The seed should be station sown at 8cm/3in intervals or sown thinly and thinned to that distance when they have germinated. Beetroot (beet) seed is slow to germinate but it can be speeded up by soaking for an hour in warm water before sowing. Seed can be sown in early spring, once the soil has warmed up to 7°C/45°F, and successionally sown at two-week intervals until early summer. An earlier sowing can be made under cloches.

Keep beetroot (beet) weed free but avoid damaging them with a hoe. Keep them supplied with constant moisture. Avoid alternating dry and wet periods, or they may split.

ABOVE **Even a small garden such as this can accommodate a selection of crops, including onions and beetroot (beets).**

Harvesting

Pull the young beetroot (beets) from the ground while they are still quite small. This will be about seven weeks after sowing. Continue to pull as required. You may need to use a fork to help ease later crops or those in heavy soils from the ground. If possible, do not break the thin root attached to the bottom of the globe, because this will "bleed", causing the beetroot to lose a lot of its colour. For a similar reason do not cut off the leaves; instead, twist them off, leaving about 5cm/2in on the beet.

Storage

Beetroot (beets) can be left in the ground until they are required, except in cold districts, where they can be lifted, cleaned and placed in trays of just-moist sand or peat (peat moss). Store these trays in a cool, frost-free shed or garage.

Pests and diseases

On the whole, beetroot (beets) are reasonably trouble free in terms of possible pests and diseases. Birds may eat the young seedlings when they first appear, so keep these off with netting of some sort. If any diseases occur, burn or destroy the affected plants and re-sow them elsewhere.

Varieties

'Action' miniature
'Albina Vereduna' white flesh
'Boltardy' round
'Burpee's Golden' gold flesh
'Cheltenham Green Top' cylindrical
'Cheltenham Mono' monogerm
'Chioggia Pink' pink and white stripes
'Cylindra' cylindrical
'Detroit-Little Ball' miniature
'Dorée' golden
'Forono' cylindrical
'Moneta' monogerm
'Monodet' monogerm
'Monogram' monogerm
'Monopoly' monogerm
'Red Ace' cylindrical
'Tardel' miniature

Swedes (Rutabagas or Yellow Turnips)

Brassica napus

Swedes are one of those vegetables that never seem to get into ready-prepared, convenience dishes and yet are still popular with cooks who prepare their own food. They belong, perhaps, to what one might call the category of "wholesome food" (such as stews) rather than high cuisine, but they are increasingly used in a wide range of dishes, including delicate soups. Swedes are convenience food in their own right – it takes only a matter of seconds to pull one from the ground, peel, chop and put it to cook.

Swedes (rutabagas or yellow turnips) are not very old as vegetables go, although no one is certain about their origins. It seems likely that they appeared in Europe as a random cross between turnips and cabbages sometime in the Middle Ages. They did not find their way to Britain until the latter part of the 18th century, and it is thought that they were introduced from Sweden, hence the name. The American name "rutabaga" also has Swedish origins, being derived from *rotbagga*, which is Swedish for "ram's foot", an apt visual description of small or immature swedes.

LEFT **This is a typical swede, with lots of spreading leaves. This plant should stand in the ground throughout the winter.**

Cultivation

Sowing time late spring to early summer
Sowing distance thinly
Sowing depth 1cm/½in
Distance between sown rows 38cm/15in
Thinning distance 23cm/9in
Harvesting autumn onwards

Although they are usually considered a rootcrop, swedes (rutabagas or yellow turnips) actually belong to the cabbage family and, as such, suffer from similar pests and diseases. For this reason, they should be included with the cabbages when you are planning a rotational system. The swollen root of the swede is mainly above ground, with just a small amount being buried. In the better garden varieties, the top of the globe is usually purple, while the lower section, which is hidden from the light, is white. The flesh is a creamy-yellow, usually deepening during cooking. The appearance of the foliage clearly shows its close alliance to the cabbage.

Many gardeners used to sow a later crop of swedes (rutabagas or yellow turnips) around midsummer in order to provide "tops", or the leaves, which can be used as greens during spring. These can be grown closer together than suggested above for conventional use.

Cultivation

An open site is required. Like most root crops, swedes (rutabagas or yellow turnips) prefer a light soil, although they can be grown on heavier ground. As with most brassicas, the soil should not be too acid. Lime if necessary to bring it to about pH6.5. The ground should not be freshly manured, but it is important that it contains as much organic material as possible because the soil should be moisture retentive. Add manure during autumn digging. Sow thinly in late spring or early summer into drills that are 38cm/15in apart and 1cm/½in deep. Thin the swedes

ABOVE **These healthy looking swedes have just been harvested. The spreading stems can be clearly seen. This variety is 'Acme'.**

RIGHT **Swedes are generally round, but can vary in shape depending on the growing conditions. This variety, 'Marian', has become elongated.**

to 23cm/9in apart, preferably doing this in stages. Make sure that the soil is kept moist throughout summer, otherwise any check in the growth may result in woody or split globes. Keep the weeds down.

Harvesting

Swedes (rutabagas or yellow turnips) can be harvested from autumn onwards, throughout the winter, once they are large enough to use. Lift the globes as they are required. In most soils they can simply be pulled from the soil, but in heavier ones they may need loosening with a fork first.

Storage

Swedes (rutabagas or yellow turnips) are completely hardy and can be left in the soil as long as necessary. Some varieties become woody if they are left in the ground beyond the turn of the year, however, so these should be lifted and stored in trays of just-moist sand or peat (peat moss) and placed in a cool, frost-free shed or garage.

Pests and diseases

Being brassicas, swedes are prone to the same diseases as the rest of the cabbage family. Flea beetles are a particular scourge and the leaves should be dusted with derris as soon as they are spotted. Mildew can also be a problem, but there are now varieties that are resistant. Club root is another problem to look out for.

Varieties

'Best of All'	'Marian'
'Brora'	'Ruby'
'Devon Champion'	'Western Perfection'

purple-topped swedes (rutabagas or yellow turnips)

Turnips

Brassica napa Rapifera Group

Like swedes (rutabagas or yellow turnips), turnips are members of the cabbage family. The origins of the turnip go back so far that they are obscure, but the wild plant from which it is derived is still commonly found throughout Europe and Asia and is thought to have been cultivated as far back as prehistoric times. The long history has meant that many forms have appeared in cultivation, particularly in China and Japan. The popularity of the turnip has waned in the West, and with it a number of different forms, although there are still some 30 varieties from which to choose.

The Western form of the turnip is round, sometimes an almost perfect globe, sometimes slightly flattened. It has one thickish root or several roots emerging from the base. The skins are a creamy-white, and the top of the globe can be green, purple, white or creamy-yellow. The flesh is white or yellowish. The globe is partly sunk into the ground, but most of it is above ground. In Asia long-rooted varieties are also grown, and seed of this form is sometimes available in the West. It is also possible sometimes to find old European varieties with long roots.

The fleshy ball is cooked and eaten, but many gardeners also enjoy the young leaves, which are cooked as spring greens. Summer turnips are more succulent and lend themselves to a range of dishes. Those that are overwintered are generally not quite as tender, but they are useful in casseroles, stews and soups. In Japan they are often eaten raw.

BELOW **A well-shaped, purple-topped turnip. It is advisable to keep turnips moist so that they will grow quickly.**

Cultivation

Because turnips are a member of the brassica family, they should be included with cabbages in the rotational sequence. They need an open, sunny situation and, preferably, a light soil, although they can be grown in heavier ground. There must be plenty of organic material in the soil so that it does not dry out. The manure should either be left from a previous crop or be dug in during the previous autumn.

Cultivation

Summer
Sowing time late winter (under cloches) to early spring
Sowing distance thinly
Sowing depth 1cm/½in
Distance between sown rows 23cm/9in
Thinning distance 13cm/5in
Harvesting summer

Autumn and winter
Sowing time mid- to late summer
Sowing distance thinly
Sowing depth 1cm/½in
Distance between sown rows 30cm/12in
Thinning distance 20cm/8in
Harvesting autumn and winter

Greens
Sowing time late summer
Sowing distance thinly
Sowing depth 1cm/½in
Distance between sown rows 8–10cm/3–4in
Thinning distance none
Harvesting spring and early summer

Sow early varieties of turnip under cloches in late winter for early crops or in open ground from early spring onwards. Sow seed 1cm/½in deep in drills 23cm/9in apart. When the seedlings are big enough to handle, thin them to about 13cm/5in apart. Continue to sow at two- to three-week intervals for a continuous

HARVESTING

Turnips can be harvested by simply pulling them from the ground.

ABOVE **These turnips – a variety known as 'Tokyo Cross' – have just been harvested and will grace any dining table.**

ABOVE **The distance between the plants in this row of red-topped turnips is just right for growing them successfully.**

supply of small, tender turnips throughout the summer. For varieties to be harvested from the autumn and winter, sow in midsummer. They should be at the same depth, but rows should be about 30cm/12in apart. Thin the seedlings to 20cm/8in.

If you want to grow turnips just as "greens", sow thinly in late summer and there should be no need to thin. Rows can be as close as 8–10cm/3–4in.

The secret of growing good turnips is to keep them moist so that they can grow quickly. Keep them weeded.

Varieties

- 'Golden Ball'
- 'Green Top Stone'
- 'Hakutaka'
- 'Imperial Green Globe'
- 'Jersey Navet'
- 'Manchester Market'
- 'Market Express'
- 'Milan Early White Top'
- 'Milan Purple Top Forcing'
- 'Milan White Forcing'
- 'Orange Perfection'
- 'Presto'
- 'Purple Top Milan'
- 'Red Milan'
- 'Snowball'
- 'Stanis'
- 'Stone'
- 'Tokyo Cross'
- 'Tyfon'
- 'Veitch's Red Globe'

Harvesting

Harvest the early and summer varieties as soon as they are the size of golf balls. They can be eaten when they are slightly larger, but they are at their best at this size. Larger and older turnips become woody, so rather than sowing one long row, it is better to sow short rows at different times to provide a steady supply of young turnips. Varieties sown in midsummer can be harvested from autumn onwards as they are required. The "greens" can be harvested as young leaves from spring into summer.

Storage

Turnips can be left in the ground until they are required. In very cold areas or if they are likely to be frozen in the ground and impossible to extract, they can be lifted, the tops removed and the globes stored in trays of just-moist sand or peat (peat moss), and kept in a frost-free place.

Pests and diseases

Turnips suffer from the same problems as cabbages. Flea beetle, which is likely to be the worst pest, should be treated with derris dust.

Diseases can include violet root rot and club root. Destroy any affected plants.

green-topped turnips

Kohl Rabi

Brassica oleracea Gongylodes Group

Although it is not strictly a root vegetable, kohl rabi is placed in this group because of its similarity to the turnip. In reality, it is a short-stemmed cabbage, but the stem has swollen into a round ball. The fact that it is a stem can be seen from the cabbage-like leaves that sprout out from all around the swelling, unlike those of a turnip, which grow on top. The skin is either green or purple, depending on variety, and the flesh is white. Because it is a stem, kohl rabi sits on or just above the ground, with a taproot descending into the soil.

This curious vegetable is a relative newcomer to gardens, and it is thought to have originated in Europe as late as the 15th or 16th century, although it may have developed earlier – Pliny describes a similar type of vegetable being grown by the Romans in the 1st century AD. No matter when it originated, kohl rabi is not as popular today as it should be. Even after four centuries it is still considered something of a rarity in France and Britain, although it is more widely grown in Germany and Austria – as is testified by varieties such as 'Purple Vienna' and 'White Vienna' – as well as in Eastern Europe.

Kohl rabi has a fresh, mild taste, which is somewhat similar to that of turnips, and it is useful in a wide range of dishes, including soups, as well as being eaten as a vegetable in its own right. It can also be eaten raw – in salads, for example. From the gardener's point of view it has the advantage over the turnip in that it can be grown in drier conditions yet still retain its succulence. Most varieties should be harvested while they are still quite small – about the size of a tennis ball – but some varieties, such as 'Gigante', which comes from the Czech Republic, usually grow to 4.5kg/10lb or more but remain succulent. Unfortunately, 'Gigante' is not an easy variety to get hold of, but it is definitely worth growing if you come across any seed. Purple-skinned varieties of kohl rabi are slightly hardier than white-skinned forms.

ABOVE **The leaves of these healthy looking kohl rabi are in perfect condition. The kohl rabi have been planted in a block.**

Cultivation

Kohl rabi needs an open, sunny situation, preferably with light soil, but they will grow on heavier ground. The soil should be well manured, ideally from an earlier crop or during the previous autumn. The seed should be sown thinly in drills, about 1cm/½in deep and 30cm/12in apart. Sowing can start under cloches in late winter for an early crop or early spring in the open ground. Continue to sow at three-week intervals until late summer for a continuous crop of tender roots. Thin to about 15cm/6in for earlier crops and to 20cm/8in for later ones. Watering is not as crucial as for turnips, but they are less likely to split if the moisture supply to the roots is constant. Keep weeded, but avoid damaging the roots with the hoe.

Harvesting

The stems are best harvested when they are about the size of tennis balls. Most varieties get rather woody after that. Later crops can be left in the ground until early winter and

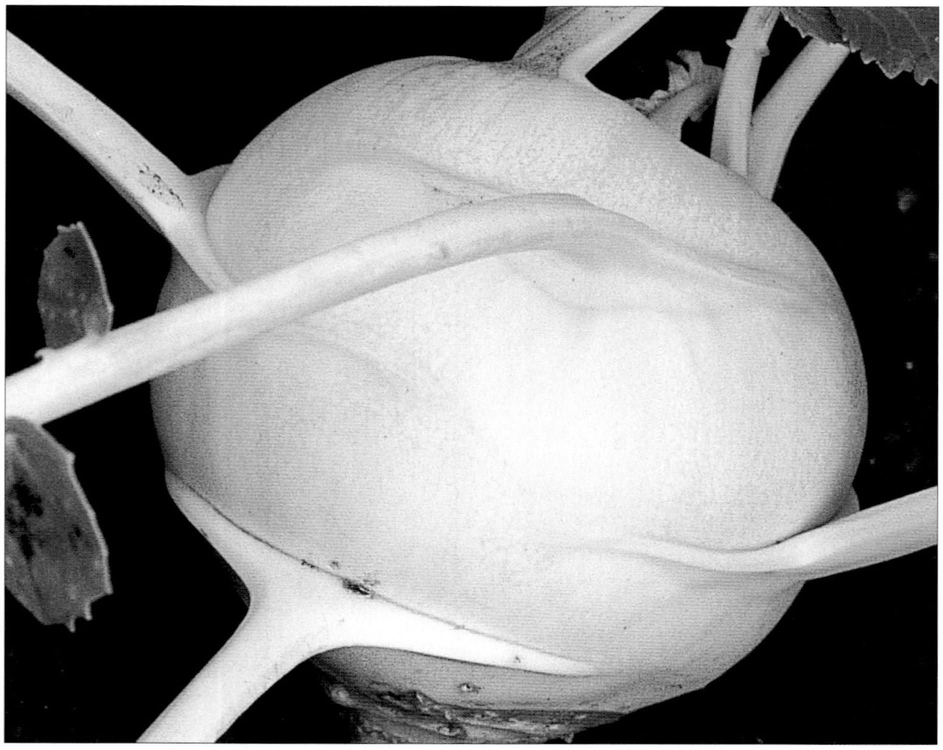

LEFT **This is a perfect specimen of kohl rabi, which is ready for harvesting. Use in soups, for example, or eat as a vegetable in its own right.**

Cultivation

Sowing time late winter (under cloches) and early spring to late summer
Sowing distance thinly
Sowing depth 1cm/½in
Distance between sown rows 30cm/12in
Thinning distance 15–20cm/6–8in
Harvesting summer onwards

possibly even later in milder areas. They are very easy to harvest as they can be simply pulled from the ground. When harvesting, shorten the root and cut back the leaves, leaving short stems before taking them into the kitchen for preparation.

Storage

There is no need to store kohl rabi because they should be pulled from the ground as required. In colder areas the last crop can be pulled, cleaned and stored in trays of just-damp sand or peat (peat moss), but they do not keep as well as other root crops as they tend to shrivel.

Pests and diseases

Kohl rabi suffers from the same kind of pests and diseases as cabbage. Flea beetles can be one of the worst pests, and leaves should be dusted with derris if an infestation occurs.

ABOVE **A purple-skinned kohl rabi, showing the soft bloom that appears on the skin.**

LEFT **Grow kohl rabi quickly, with plenty of moisture. This one was grown in conditions that were too dry.**

white-skinned kohl rabi

Varieties

'Adriana'	'Purple Vienna'
'Gigante'	'Quickstar'
'Green Early Ball'	'Rapidstar'
'Kolpak'	'Roblau'
'Kongo'	'Rowel'
'Lanro'	'Trero'
'Purple Danube'	'White Danube'
'Purple Early Ball'	'White Vienna'

Salsify and Scorzonera

Tragopogon porrifolius and *Scorzonera hispanica*

ABOVE **A basket of salsify just after the crop has been harvested, showing the small side roots that make the roots "hairy" and difficult to clean.**

Although salsify and scorzonera are different plants, they are closely related, not only botanically but also in the manner in which they are grown and used. Neither is in the mainstream of vegetables, which is surprising because both are delicious. Salsify is, in fact, also known as vegetable oyster or oyster plant because of its taste. The roots are, however, not among the easiest to prepare – they are relatively narrow with plenty of smaller roots, which makes peeling difficult. In addition, they discolour very quickly once they have been peeled. In the kitchen, despite the fine taste, they are not very versatile since they are usually used as vegetables in their own right rather than as part of other dishes.

Salsify originated from the countries around the Mediterranean, although garden escapees have naturalized over a large part of Europe and North America. Scorzonera is not quite as rampant and is still restricted to Europe, from the warm Mediterranean countries to the arctic wastes. As with most vegetables their history is rather uncertain, but salsify is thought to have been first cultivated in Italy in the 16th century, while scorzonera was grown in Spain and Italy even earlier.

Both vegetables have long, narrow tap-roots, which are covered in thinner side roots. Salsify has a yellowish skin, rather like that of a parsnip, and scorzonera has a dark brown or black skin. They are grown mainly for the roots, but the young shoots and flower-buds can also be eaten. Salsify is also grown as an ornamental plant for its attractive purple flowers, although the leaves can be rather untidy. The flowers produce copious amounts of seed, which soon drifts away and germinates. Scorzonera has inconspicuous yellow flowers.

These vegetables are usually sold by their name rather than under the name of a cultivar, since few of the latter have been bred. However, one variety of salsify is well known – 'Sandwich Island'.

LEFT **This block of salsify shows clearly how untidy and unattractive the foliage is. The resulting crop, however, is its own reward.**

Cultivation

Choose a site that is sunny and open. As with most root crops, both vegetables like a light soil, although they will grow in heavier conditions. The soil should be deeply dug and have humus added well in advance of sowing because they do not like freshly manured ground. To be sure of having a sufficiently large crop, both must be sown as early as possible to give a long growing season, although scorzonera should not be sown too early or it will run to seed. Seed should be sown by mid-spring, 1cm/½in deep in drills set 25cm/ 10in apart. Use fresh seed rather than any left from a previous season. Thin the seedlings to 15cm/6in apart. Although they can be grown closer together, they are more difficult to dig up individually.

Neither vegetable needs a great deal of attention, apart from being kept weeded. On the whole, they will not require watering, although if there is a prolonged drought, give them a good soaking once a week.

Harvesting

Like parsnips, salsify and scorzonera taste best after they have experienced a frost. This is not to say that you cannot harvest earlier, and they are usually ready from mid-autumn onwards. Dig the roots

Cultivation

Sowing time early to mid-spring
Sowing distance thinly
Sowing depth 1cm/½in
Distance between sown rows 25cm/10in
Thinning distance 15cm/6in
Harvesting autumn and winter

ABOVE **Scorzonera leaves are wider and more glossy than those of salsify, which are quite untidy in appearance.**

RIGHT **Salsify is worth growing for its flowers alone.**

up with a fork as required, taking care not to bruise or damage them. Salsify should be harvested and used during the first winter because it is a biennial. Scorzonera, however, is a perennial and can be left in the ground and harvested in the following autumn and winter, which gives the roots the chance to get larger.

Storage

Both plants are very hardy and can be left in the ground until needed, although it can be a good idea to lift a few and store them in trays of just moist sand if a hard frost is forecast, because it may then be difficult to get them out of the ground.

Pests and diseases

Neither salsify nor scorzonera tends to suffer from pests or diseases.

Varieties

Salsify
Most are listed simply as salsify or vegetable oyster.
'Mammoth'
'Sandwich Island'
Scorzonera
Most are listed simply as scorzonera.
'Duplex'
'Lange Jan'
'Maxima'
'Russian Giant'

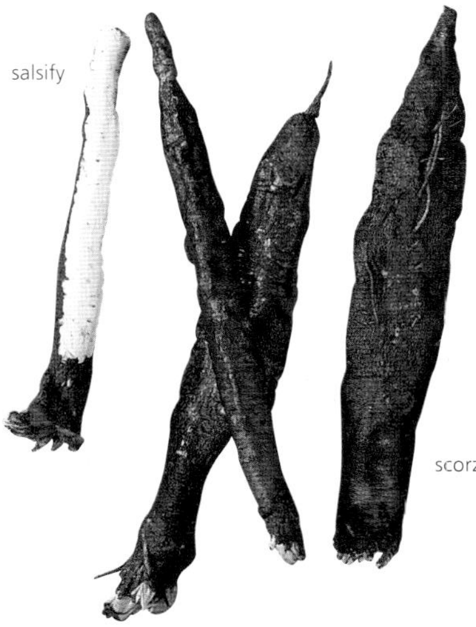

Potatoes

Solanum tuberosum

The potato is one of the most important food crops in the world. The family to which it belongs, Solanaceae, is found worldwide, although the potato itself originates from a fairly restricted area in the Andes, spreading up into Mexico. There are many species involved in the botanical development of the potato, which is very complicated, and the history of the potato in cultivation is almost as complicated as its botanical history.

ABOVE **Potatoes have attractive flowers. In early crops, the opening of the flowers is an indication that the tubers are ready.**

The potato has been grown as a vegetable in the Andes for thousands of years, and the Incas were discovered to be eating it by the conquering Spanish in the late 16th century. Taken to Italy, it eventually spread to the rest of Europe. The original cultivars were not particularly hardy, and it took a long time for the potato to catch on in northern Europe and two centuries before it was widespread in Britain.

The tubers – that is, the swellings on the roots – are eaten. All other parts, including the leaves and the fruit, are poisonous. If the potatoes themselves are exposed to light for any length of time, they turn green, and this, too, is poisonous unless cooked.

Potatoes are grown from "seed potatoes". These are not seeds in the conventional sense, but potato tubers that have been selected for growing. Once they have been planted, the seed potatoes start to sprout, producing roots and leaves. As the roots grow, new tubers are formed on them, and these are harvested when they are large enough.

Because potatoes are so widely distributed, there are hundreds of varieties from which to choose. Many are suited to particular climates, and different types will be found in different countries. The varieties differ in a number of respects. The first main difference is the timing of the crop, and there are two main groups, earlies and maincrop, which are further subdivided into first earlies and so on. The next main difference is use. Some are better for baking or roasting; others are better for boiling or frying; others are suitable for salads.

Finally, and in some respects the most important criterion, is flavour. Most varieties taste quite different from each other, and many gardeners have their own favourites, although this does not stop them from experimenting with different ones.

Given these characteristics, it might be supposed that gardeners would grow several cultivars. However, potatoes can

LEFT **This row of potatoes shows the earth drawn up around the stems.**

BELOW **A crop of newly dug salad potatoes, "drying" in the sun.**

Cultivation

First earlies
Planting time early spring
Planting distance 30cm/12in
Planting depth 10–15cm/4–6in
Distance between rows 45cm/18in
Harvesting early summer

Second earlies
Planting time mid-spring
Planting distance 38cm/15in
Planting depth 10–15cm/4–6in
Distance between rows 60cm/24in
Harvesting summer onwards

Maincrop
Planting time mid- to late spring
Planting distance 38cm/15in
Planting depth 10–15cm/4–6in
Distance between rows 75cm/30in
Harvesting autumn

ABOVE **This large kitchen plot contains rows of neatly earthed- (hilled-) up potatoes. Frosts can be a problem for the emerging foliage.**

take up a lot of space in the garden and they are relatively inexpensive to buy. Many gardeners, therefore, prefer to restrict themselves to growing a few earlies, which have an incomparable flavour when taken straight from the ground to the kitchen, and to go to the greengrocer for the rest of the year. The ground on which the earlies were grown can be used for later crops, such as cabbages or leeks.

There are so many varieties that it could take more than one gardening lifetime to get through them all by sowing one or two varieties each year. One way of trying as wide a range as possible is to get together with two other gardeners and to buy bags of, say, three potatoes each and to divide them up between yourselves so that each of you can grow a small number of nine varieties rather than a large number of three varieties. Keep a note of those you like best and make them your maincrop for the following year.

It is possible to enjoy new potatoes at Christmas too by planting a few in large pots in early autumn and keeping these in the greenhouse.

LEFT **A recently harvested uprooting of red-skinned potatoes, all evenly shaped and with good-quality skin.**

Cultivation

Potatoes are best grown in an open, sunny position. As earlies are likely to emerge through the ground before the last of the frosts, try to choose a warm, protected spot away from frost pockets. They will grow on most soils, although they prefer slightly acid conditions. The soil should be fertile but avoid planting potatoes on newly manured grounds.

Earlies should be chitted. This involves standing the seed potatoes on a tray so that the eyes are facing upwards. Place the tray in a cool but frost-free place that is in the light although out of direct sunlight. Short shoots will appear, and this gets the crop off to a good start. Maincrop can be treated in the same way, although it is not essential.

First earlies are planted in early spring followed by second earlies two weeks later. Draw out a row with a hoe about 10cm/4in deep and place potatoes at 30cm/12in intervals. Rows should be 45cm/18in apart.

ABOVE **This harvesting of early potatoes is now ready for transferring to the kitchen. They will make delicious "new potatoes".**

Alternatively, the potatoes can be planted in holes dug with a trowel or with a special potato planter. Whichever method you use, cover the potatoes with soil and then draw up more soil to form a low ridge above them. When the shoots reach heights of 23–25cm/9–10in, draw earth up around them along the rows to make certain that all the tubers are well covered; otherwise they turn green. Continue to do this until the foliage touches across the rows.

Second earlies and maincrop are treated in the same way, except that they are planted in the second half of spring and the potatoes are set 38cm/15in apart and in rows 60cm/24in apart for second earlies and 75cm/30in apart for maincrop.

Keep an eye on weather reports, and if frost is forecast cover any shoots with newspaper or horticultural fleece. Keep all potatoes, especially earlies, watered if there is a prolonged dry spell forecast.

CHITTING POTATOES

Before planting, place the potatoes in a tray in a light place (but out of direct sunlight) in order to "chit". This means that the potatoes produce shoots.

PLANTING

Hoe out a trench 10cm/4in deep and lay the tubers about 30–40cm/12–15in apart, depending on the type. Cover with soil and earth (hill) up into a low ridge.

EARTHING UP

When the shoots reach 23–25cm/9–10in long, draw the soil around them along the rows.

An alternative method of growing potatoes is to plant them under a sheet of black polythene (plastic). Place the polythene along the row and anchor it by burying the edges in the soil. Cut slits at the relevant intervals and plant potatoes through them.

FROST PROTECTION

Once the potato shoots have emerged through the soil, it is important to take note of any frost forecasts. The shoots will need protecting from possible frost damage. Cover them over with horticultural fleece or even with newspaper.

HARVESTING

To harvest, dig a fork well under the potatoes and draw it up through the soil, bringing the tubers up with the earth.

Varieties

First earlies
'Arran Pilot' white skin, early
'Epicure' white skin, early
'Foremost' white skin, waxy yellow flesh
'Maris Bard' white skin, waxy texture, very early
'Pentland Javelin' white skin, waxy flesh last of the earlies to crop
'Ulster Chieftain' white skin, floury texture

Second earlies
'Estima' white skin, waxy yellow flesh, good boiler
'Kondor' red skin, yellow flesh, good boiler
'Marfona' white skin, heavy cropper, good for baking
'Maris Peer' white skin, waxy texture, good boiler
'Wilja' white skin, waxy yellow flesh, good salad potato

Maincrop
'Cara' pink skin, white floury flesh, late
'Desiree' pinkish red skin, waxy yellow flesh, good for baking and for fries
'King Edward' pink and white skin, creamy floury texture, good for baking and roasting
'Maris Piper' white skin, floury texture, heavy cropper, good for baking
'Pentland Dell' white skin, floury texture, heavy cropper, good for baking and roasting
'Pink Fir Apple' pink skin, yellow waxy flesh, wonderful salad potato
'Ratte' white skin, yellow waxy flesh, excellent salad potato
'Romano' red skin, firm white flesh, good boiler

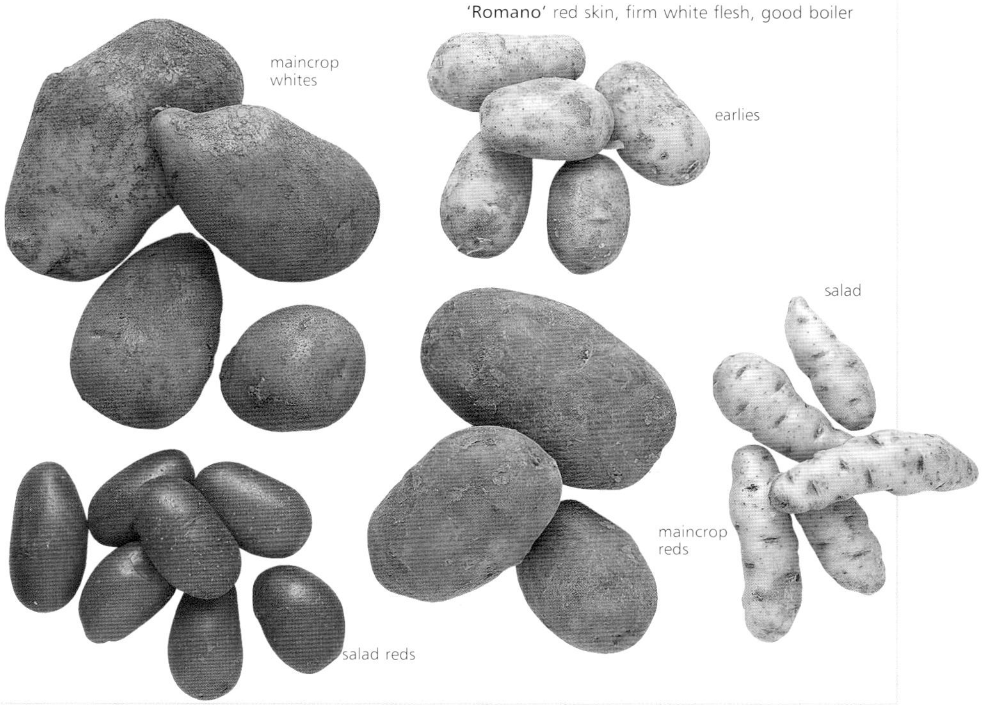

Harvesting

Early potatoes are harvested in early summer, usually just as their flowers are opening, which should be about 12 weeks after planting. They are usually lifted as they are required. Maincrop are left in the soil until the autumn and are usually all lifted at once and stored. To harvest earlies, dig a fork in well below the potatoes and lever them out of the soil, at the same time pulling on the haulm (stems and leaves). For maincrop, remove the haulm about two weeks before harvesting so that the skins on the potatoes harden. Lift the maincrop on a dry, warm day and leave them lying in the sun for an hour or two to let them dry and to harden the skins.

Storing

Do not leave potatoes in the light for too long. Pack them into hessian (burlap) or paper sacks and store them in a dark, cool but frost-free place. Alternatively, they can be stored in trays as long as no light gets to the tubers. Regularly check all potatoes and remove any that have started to rot.

Pests and diseases

The worst problem that can occur is blight, which is particularly prevalent in wet years. The leaves go yellow and brown and start to curl. Eventually the haulm seems to fall to pieces. The potatoes develop black patches, which eventually turn into a slimy, evil-smelling rot. Do not plant potatoes on ground that was affected the year before (either from potato or tomato blight). Earth (hill) them up well to keep the spores from the tubers. If necessary, spray with the appropriate copper-based fungicide, preferably in wet years before blight appears. Look out for resistant varieties.

Another common disease is potato scab, which disfigures the surface of the tubers. To avoid it occurring, do not grow potatoes on ground that has been recently limed or manured. Other diseases include spraing, violet root rot and blackleg.

The main pests are slugs and wire-worms, both of which eat holes in the tubers. Other pests can include cutworms and potato cyst eelworms.

Jerusalem Artichokes

Helianthus tuberosus

Surprisingly, these potato-like tubers are grown on plants that are sunflowers. Unlike the dinner-plate-sized flowers of its relative, however, the flowers of the Jerusalem artichoke are small, but borne on equally tall stems. The knobbly tubers are found below ground, and they can used as a vegetable in their own right and cooked in the same way as potatoes or parsnips – roasting is a particularly good way of cooking them. They have a lovely distinct flavour but also combine well in other dishes, especially soups, and can be eaten raw. The tubers should be about the size of a chicken's egg; larger ones can be cut into pieces.

ABOVE **Here, an uprooted Jerusalem artichoke plant clearly shows the tubers that are now ready for harvesting.**

Jerusalem artichokes have no connection with Jerusalem nor with globe artichokes. They originated in North America and were brought to Europe in the 16th century, eventually finding their way to Britain via Holland in the early 17th century. The name Jerusalem could be a corruption of the Italian word for sunflower, *girasole*, or it may be derived from the name of the town in Holland, Terneuzen, from where they were sent to Britain.

This is a very easy vegetable to grow. It is not particular about the soil and it is troubled by few pests and diseases. The only real problem is getting rid of it if you decide to stop growing it at any stage. A single piece of one of the many tubers left in the ground will resprout to produce a new plant, and it is, unfortunately, easy to miss one or more pieces. The regrowth normally appears in the row, however, and it will not spread throughout the garden unless you are careless enough to distribute the tubers about.

Although Jerusalem artichokes are grown primarily as a vegetable, they can also be grown to provide a temporary windbreak. They grow rapidly, sometimes to 3m/10ft, and make a dense hedge of wiry stems that needs no support except in exposed sites.

The mature plants make excellent windbreaks within the kitchen garden, as well as creating visual screens that can be used to divide up the garden.

LEFT **A basket of recently harvested Jerusalem artichokes. These are perfect easy-to-peel specimens that are not too knobbly.**

Cultivation

Unlike most vegetables, Jerusalem artichokes are tolerant of light shade. They are also tolerant of a range of soils, even growing in poor ones, although best results will be obtained from ground that has been manured during the previous autumn. Do not overfeed because this may result in lush vegetation at the expense of tubers.

Try to purchase named varieties but, if you cannot find them, tubers from the greengrocer can be used. The planting time is not critical – any time in spring will do. Plant the tubers 10–13cm/4–5in deep in holes made with a trowel. They should be about 38cm/15in apart and the rows should be 90cm/3ft apart.

They need little attention apart from being kept weed free. If they are likely to be rocked by the wind, draw earth up around the stems to help stabilize them so that the tubers are not disturbed. In very windy sites, individual stems may need to be supported with canes. The stems can be cut off in summer at about 1.8m/6ft to lessen the chance of wind damage – this is necessary not so much because the

RIGHT **The top growth of Jerusalem artichokes shows its relationship with the sunflower. Unfortunately, all this lush growth is of no use except for making compost.**

plants will be flattened but because the tubers will be disturbed by the movement of the plants and not develop properly.

Harvesting

The tubers can be lifted once the leaves start to wither in autumn. The skins should be pale brown, without any soft patches.

Cut off the stems, then lift the tubers with a fork, digging right under them. Sift through the soil to check that all the pieces are removed. Any piece of tuber remaining in the soil will grow again in the following year. This is all right if you plan to plant in the same place next year, but a nuisance if you do not. They can be quite difficult to eradicate, especially in heavy soils where it is easy to miss tubers, so harvest carefully.

Storing

Jerusalem artichokes are frost hardy and are best stored in the ground and dug only as they are required. A few can be dug if frost threatens to freeze the soil, making digging impossible, and stored in trays of just-moist sand or peat (peat moss) in a frost-free shed or garage.

Pests and diseases

Jerusalem artichokes do not attract pests and diseases.

Jerusalem artichokes

Cultivation

Sowing time spring
Sowing distance 38cm/15in
Sowing depth 10–13cm/4–5in
Distance between sown rows 90cm/3ft
Harvesting summer onwards

Varieties

Often listed simply as Jerusalem artichokes.
'Boston Red'
'Dwarf Sunray'
'Fuseau'

Radishes

Raphanus sativus

Radishes are one of the easiest and quickest of all crops to grow. The rapidity with which they appear through the soil makes them suitable for children to grow, because little patience is required, and, indeed, many gardeners' first experience of growing vegetables was with this humble plant. However, the wide range of types and varieties that are available make this a vegetable that is of as much interest to the mature gardener as to the embryonic one.

The radish has a long history as far as cultivation is concerned, having been known in Ancient Egypt. Its origins are obscure, but it probably derived from native plants found growing in Mediterranean countries. At first, varieties had long, tapering roots, originally black, later white, and these larger rooted forms are still cultivated in Europe. By the 18th century, however, the more familiar round ones with red skins began to appear.

Today the small, red-skinned radishes are the most frequently grown, and these are mainly used in salads or as a decorative garnish. In China and Japan, where the large varieties are still common, they are eaten both raw and cooked, and the large-rooted types are becoming more widely grown in the West, especially new varieties imported from China. These larger varieties have the advantage that they can be left in the ground for longer and so make a valuable contribution to the selection of winter crops.

One of the advantages of the short life-cycle of the radish is that it can be grown among slower growing crops, thus making the best use of the available ground. Radishes make good markers if they are sown along with a vegetable that is slow to germinate, such as parsnips. Because

ABOVE **These round radishes are suffering from slug damage (top) and from cracking due to irregular watering (middle).**

BELOW **These neat rows of radishes have been planted in abundance. You will have to consume large quantities to grow so many at once.**

HARVESTING

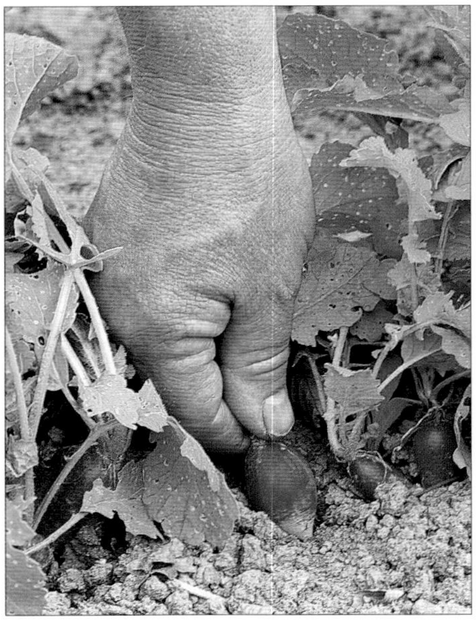

Radishes are harvested simply by pulling them from the ground by hand. They should be harvested when they are large enough to eat.

Cultivation

Summer
Sowing time late winter (under cloches) to early spring onwards
Sowing distance thinly
Sowing depth 1cm/½in
Distance between sown rows 15cm/6in
Thinning distance 2.5cm/1in
Harvesting late spring onwards

Winter
Sowing time midsummer
Sowing distance thinly
Sowing depth 1cm/½in
Distance between sown rows 25cm/10in
Thinning distance 13cm/5in
Harvesting autumn onwards

radishes appear quickly they will indicate the position of the row so that the parsnip seeds are not accidentally disturbed by hoeing or weeding.

Cultivation

Ordinary summer radishes do not need either a deep or particularly rich soil. They prefer one that does not dry out or they will quickly run to seed. Slow-growing radishes also tend to be woody and over-hot to the taste. They should be grown in an open, sunny position.

Sowing can start under cloches in late winter or in early spring in the open soil. Sow in shallow drills about 1cm/½in deep, set about 15cm/6in apart. Water the soil along the row if it is dry at the time of sowing. Sow thinly so that little thinning is required, then thin to about 2.5cm/1in. Do not sow too much at once because radishes are rapidly past their best, and it is better to sow short rows every two weeks to obtain a succession of crops than one long one in which many of the roots will be wasted. Do not let them dry out.

Sow the larger winter radishes at about midsummer. Do not sow too early or they may run to seed. These should be sown in drills set 25cm/10in apart. When they are large enough to handle, thin to about 13cm/5in apart.

Varieties

Summer
'Cherry Belle' globe
'Crystal Ball' globe
'Flamboyant Sabina' cylindrical
'French Breakfast' cylindrical
'Juliette' globe
'Long White Icicle' tapering
'Prinz Rotin' globe
'Saxa' globe
'Scarlet Globe' globe
'Sparkler 3' globe

Winter
'Black Spanish Long'
'Black Spanish Round'
'China Rose'
'Mino Early'
'Minowase'
'Violet de Gournay'

Harvesting

Summer radishes should be pulled when they are large enough to eat. Discard any that have become large or old because these will be too woody as well as too hot to eat. Winter radishes can be dug up from autumn onwards.

ABOVE **A bunch of recently harvested cylindrical radishes. They should not be allowed to grow too large, or they become woody and very hot.**

Storage

Summer radishes quickly shrivel once they are out of the ground and should be used as soon as possible after harvesting. Long-rooted winter varieties can be left in the ground until they are required. In very cold areas or if severe frosts are threatened, which would make digging them from the ground impossible, dig the roots and store them under cover in trays of just-moist peat (peat moss) or sand.

Pests and diseases

Although they may not look like it, radishes are related to cabbages and so suffer from the same pests and diseases. Flea beetle is likely to be the worst problem, and should they appear, young plants should be dusted with derris. Slugs are also partial to radishes and can leave unsightly holes in the roots. If anything worse than this happens, scrap the plants and re-sow elsewhere in the garden.

PEAS AND BEANS

Peas

Pisum sativum

Of all vegetables, peas are perhaps the best reason for growing one's own: it is impossible to buy peas that taste anything like those that are picked straight from the garden. However, the difficulty is that if you want to grow a succession of crops to give you peas throughout the summer, you will have to devote quite a large area to them. This is not the problem it once was, however, because the majority of peas are now much shorter, and even if you have space to grow only a few in a large bucket, the effort is worth it for the taste alone.

Peas are one of the oldest vegetables cultivated by man. They have been found in settlements from the Late Stone Age onwards – that is, nearly 8000 years ago. One of the advantages of peas has always been that not only can they be eaten fresh, either raw or cooked, but they can also be dried and stored for later use.

The Romans, in particular, spread the cultivation of peas, probably introducing them to Britain. Surprisingly, they seem to have vanished from cultivation in Britain and were reintroduced from mainland Europe only in the 16th century. The wild pea, from which the cultivated form was developed, is still found growing in Turkey, and it is thought that this is where they probably originated, especially as some of the earliest archaeological finds come from that area.

Until about 50 years ago, peas grew to 1.8m/6ft or more and had to be supported with pea-sticks. Modern varieties are generally quite short, however, and can be easily supported with low wire netting or even a couple of strings stretched horizontally. Some varieties need no support at all.

Although the peas themselves are generally regarded as the "vegetable", from surprisingly early – certainly before the end of the 16th century in Britain – there have been forms with edible pods. There are various types of pea. First earlies are the earliest of the year. Those that are overwintered have smooth skins, but there are less hardy varieties, which are planted in early spring, and these have wrinkled skins. Although they are less hardy, they taste sweeter. Second earlies and maincrop all have wrinkled skins.

Mangetout (snow) peas, also known as sugar peas, can be eaten whole when the peas are still immature. Snap peas also have edible pods but can be eaten when they are more mature. Asparagus peas have winged pods and an asparagus-like taste. Petit pois are small, sweet-tasting peas.

SOWING

Peas can be sown in a double row along a shallow trench, in an open, sunny position.

ABOVE **Pea-sticks can be used to support tall varieties of peas.**

Cultivation

Peas like an open, sunny site. The soil should be fertile, with manure or compost incorporated during the previous autumn. First earlies can be sown in late autumn and then overwintered; remember to cover the plants with cloches in colder areas. Alternatively, they can be sown in the late winter or early

PROTECTING AGAINST BIRDS

Covering the plant with a wire netting guard will keep the birds away.

Cultivation

Earlies
Sowing time late autumn, late winter or early spring
Sowing distance 5cm/2in
Sowing depth 5cm/2in
Distance between sown rows 60–90cm/2–3ft
Thinning distance no need to thin
Harvesting early summer

Second earlies
Sowing time early spring
Sowing distance 5cm/2in
Sowing depth 5cm/2in
Distance between sown rows 60–90cm/2–3ft
Thinning distance no need to thin
Harvesting early summer

Maincrop
Sowing time early spring to early summer
Sowing distance 5cm/2in
Sowing depth 5cm/2in
Distance between sown rows 60–90cm/2–3ft
Thinning distance no need to thin
Harvesting summer to early autumn

ABOVE **Wire netting can be used to support shorter varieties of peas.**

spring. They can also be grown under cloches if necessary. Crops can then be sown at intervals until the early summer.

The easiest way to sow peas is to pull out a flat-bottomed trench with a hoe, about 15–20cm/6–8in wide and 5cm/2in deep. The peas are then sown in pairs, one on each side of the trench with the seeds at 5cm/2in intervals. Alternatively, they can be sown in a single drill at the same intervals. The distance between rows varies between 60–90cm (2–3ft), depending on the height of the peas. Add supports when the peas reach 5–8cm/2–3in high and the tendrils start to form. Use plastic pea netting, which is sold specially for the purpose, wire netting or pea-sticks. Once the flowers start to appear, keep the peas watered during dry weather.

Harvesting

Pick the pods as soon as the peas have swollen and are large enough to eat. Mangetout (snow) peas and similar types should be picked before the pods get tough. Keep picking the peas as they mature. The peas of many modern varieties, which have been created for agricultural needs, mature at the same time, and this can be a problem for the gardener.

Storage

Peas are best picked straight from the plant, although they can be frozen, which is one way of coping with a glut so that they are available through the whole year. Although it is not common now, they can also be kept by drying.

Pests and diseases

Unfortunately, peas are prone to quite a number of pests and diseases. At an early stage both mice and birds can eat the seed. Birds will also strip the emerging seedlings, and it may be necessary to protect them with wire netting. Aphids and pea thrips can also be a problem.

Mildew is something that affects crops most years, especially later in the season. It can normally be ignored, but you may prefer to use varieties that are less prone to mildew.

Varieties

Round
'Bountiful' early, tall
'Douce Provence' early, short
'Feltham First' early, short
'Meteor' early, short
'Pilot' early, medium

Wrinkled
'Alderman' maincrop, tall
'Banff' early, short
'Early Onward' early, tall
'Hurst Beagle' early, short
'Hurst Greenshaft' maincrop, short
'Little Marvel' maincrop, short
'Miracle' maincrop, tall
'Onward' maincrop, short
'Top Pod' maincrop, medium

Petit pois
'Darfon' maincrop, short
'Minnow' maincrop, short

Mangetout
'Herault' early, tall
'Honey Pod' early, short
'Nofila' early, short
'Norli' early, short
'Oregon Sugar Pod' maincrop, medium
'Sugar Short Sweet Green' maincrop, medium

Asparagus pea
Usually listed by its name rather than by variety.

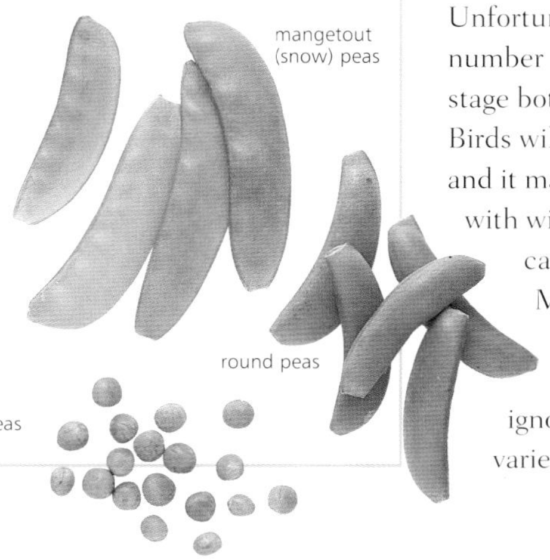

Runner Beans

Phaseolus coccineus

Although many gardeners have given up growing peas because they feel they take up too much space, very few seem to have given up runner beans for the same reason. Possibly it is because they are seen as better value for money and space because they continue to crop over a long period and it is possible to freeze any excess for later use. As with peas, fresh runner beans are far better than those you buy in the shops, so the effort is certainly worthwhile.

ABOVE **This is a good crop of runner beans which is accompanied by the flowers to produce more.**

Runner beans originated in Mexico, where they have been grown for more than 2,000 years, long before the Spanish conquistadors arrived. They were introduced to Europe in the 16th century but were at first grown more for their decorative qualities than for their culinary ones. Even today their presence in a kitchen garden is notably ornamental, although the beans are usually eaten as well as admired.

Runner beans usually grow up to about 1.8m/6ft, although in good soil they will grow to 2.4m/8ft or more. There is, however, little to be gained from growing them so tall because it is difficult to harvest the topmost beans. Dwarf varieties are available for those who want them, but they have never become very popular, partly because yields are lower and partly because all the beans tend to mature at the same time. The pods are long and rather coarse in texture, much coarser than the equivalent French (green) beans. This coarseness also applies to the texture, and it is important to pick the pods young – once they age they become very stringy. Some varieties are less stringy than others.

The pods are usually eaten along with the young beans, but they can be allowed to mature and the fully grown beans dried and eaten later in the year.

The general colour of the flowers is red, hence the old name of scarlet runner beans, but there are now other colours, including white and mauve. These are very useful in decorative schemes, and they still produce a good crop of beans.

HARVESTING

Harvest the beans when they are large enough, but avoid the older, tougher beans.

Cultivation

Beans do best in an open, sunny position; in more exposed areas they should be protected from winds, partly to prevent them from blowing over and partly because pollination is more difficult in such conditions. They will grow in quite poor soil but do best in a soil that has been well manured during the previous autumn. The traditional method is to dig a deep trench and bury plenty of compost and manure, even old newspaper. The idea is not so much to provide nutrients, although this is obviously important, but to create an area around the roots that retains plenty of moisture.

Beans must not appear above ground before the last frost has passed, so early summer is usually the earliest one can begin planting. To get them off to a good start, sow beans individually in pots or modules and plant out when the weather is right. Alternatively, sow directly into the soil. If you are able to make an early start, it is often a good idea to sow again some three weeks later so that there is a continuous crop until the first frosts of winter.

Before sowing or planting you will need to construct some form of support up which the beans will climb. This can be in the form of a single or double row (double is usually preferable) of poles, canes or strings for them to climb up, or it can be a wigwam or tepee – that is, a circle of poles or canes, pulled together at the top with string to form a cone. The distance between the poles or strings should be about 25cm/10in, for although they will grow closer together, it is easier to pick the beans if the plants are not too close.

Plant or sow one bean at each pole. Many gardeners sow two or three beans at each position – "one for the crow, one for the slug and one for the kitchen" – and remove the weaker seedlings, leaving just one. The beans are self-clinging but may need help to go up the right pole or string, as they often seem to prefer their neighbour's. Make sure that the soil is always moist, especially in dry periods.

Cultivation

Runner beans
Sowing time late spring (under glass) to early summer
Sowing or planting distance 25cm/10in
Sowing depth 5cm/2in
Distance between sown rows 90cm/3ft
Thinning distance no need to thin
Harvesting late summer until first frosts

Dwarf runner beans
Sowing time late spring (under glass) to early summer
Sowing or planting distance 15cm/6in
Sowing depth 5cm/2in
Distance between sown rows 45cm/18in
Thinning distance no need to thin
Harvesting late summer until first frosts

RIGHT **A wigwam or tepee of runner beans supported by long bamboo canes.**

Sow or plant dwarf varieties at 15cm/6in intervals in a single row with 45cm/18in between rows. Pinch out any long shoots that develop. After harvesting, cut down the beans but leave the roots to rot in the ground; they contain stores of valuable nitrogen.

Harvesting

Pick the pods as soon as the beans begin to swell, which is usually when the beans are about 15cm/6in long. Some varieties, especially those developed for exhibition, can be considerably longer than this. A larger crop can be encouraged by picking regularly, putting any excess in the freezer. It is also important to pick regularly because old beans become stringy and inedible.

Storage

Beans do not keep well and should be eaten as they are harvested. The only storage method used today is freezing, although in the past they were often preserved in salt.

Pests and diseases

Slugs and snails are always a problem when the plants first emerge, and they can easily kill the entire planting. Runner beans are otherwise generally problem free, apart from possible attacks of blackfly.

Powdery mildew and chocolate spot may also occur.

Varieties

Runner beans
'Achievement' long pods
'Butler' stringless, medium-length pods
'Czar' white seeds, long pods
'Desirée' stringless, long pods
'Enorma' long pods
'Ivanhoe' stringless, lilac seeds, long pods
'Kelvedon Wonder' early, short pods
'Lady Di' long pods
'Painted Lady' medium-length pods
'Polestar' early, stringless, medium-length pods
'Prizewinner' medium-length pods
'Red Knight' stringless
'Red Rum' early, short pods
'Royal Standard' stringless, long pods
'Scarlet Emperor' early, long pods
'Streamline' long pods
'White Emergo' white seeds, long pods

Dwarf runner beans
'Gulliver'
'Hammond's Dwarf Scarlet'
'Pickwick'

French (Green) Beans

Phaseolus vulgaris

French (green) beans are among the oldest type of cultivated bean. They originated in Central and South America, where evidence suggests that they were being grown at least 8,000 years ago. They did not reach Europe until the 16th century, when they were introduced by the returning Spanish. The English name "French beans" presumably derives from the fact that the beans were introduced into Britain from France.

There are several distinct forms of French (green) beans, the most obvious distinction being between the dwarf and climbing varieties. Recently, climbing varieties have become a popular alternative to runner beans and this makes them seem to be a modern development, but, in fact, they are the older of the two types, dwarf beans not having been widely grown until the 18th century.

French (green) beans are either eaten whole, while the seeds are still immature, or grown on and the seeds dried and used as haricot (navy) beans. Some varieties are better for drying than others. Pods vary: they can be green, purple or yellow, and they can be round or flat. The flat varieties tend to be more succulent, and the flat ones often become rather stringy when they become old.

Like runner beans, French (green) beans are frost tender and need to be sown or planted out after the last frosts. They also need warm soil in which to germinate and thrive. They are, however, quicker to mature than runner beans and so provide a valuable early crop. They also have a quite different flavour and so bring welcome variety to the kitchen.

Dwarf varieties are still the most popular, especially as they do not take up much room and are useful in small gardens. In addition, the yield is high and the season for each sowing is relatively long. The climbers or pole varieties are a useful alternative to runner beans because of their different taste and earlier harvest and also because they do not become so stringy. The variety of coloured pods makes them valuable in the ornamental kitchen garden.

SOWING

Sow the beans in a single or double trench, once the threat of frosts has passed.

Cultivation

French (green) beans, both dwarf and climbing, need a sunny, open site. The soil should be fertile but free-draining, preferably manured during the previous autumn. An early start can be made by sowing the beans in pots or modules under glass in late spring and planting out after the threat of frost has passed. Alternatively, they can be sown directly into the soil and covered with cloches. Most gardeners, however, tend to wait until early summer and sow directly into the soil, when the conditions should be perfect. Sow in a single or double row, spacing the beans about 8cm/3in apart in rows set 45cm/18in apart. They should be planted about 4cm/1½in deep. Climbing or pole varieties should be treated in the same way as runner beans. Keep watered in dry weather.

Harvesting

Harvesting can usually begin seven or eight weeks after sowing. Pick while the seeds are still immature and go on picking for as long as the beans cook and eat well. Leave those that you want to treat as haricot (navy) beans until the pods have swollen and turned yellow. Cut the whole plants and hang them up in a dry place to complete the drying. Shell and store.

Cultivation

Dwarf beans

Sowing time late spring (under glass) to early summer
Sowing or planting distance 8cm/3in
Sowing depth 4cm/1½in
Distance between sown rows 45cm/18in
Thinning distance no need to thin
Harvesting late summer until first frosts

Climbing beans

Sowing time late spring (under glass) to early summer
Sowing or planting distance 15–25cm/6–10in
Sowing depth 4cm/1½in
Distance between sown rows 90cm/3ft
Thinning distance no need to thin
Harvesting late summer until first frosts

Storage

French (green) beans are best used fresh from the plant, but they can be frozen, which is a good way of dealing with a glut. Haricot (navy) beans should be dried and stored in airtight jars.

Pests and diseases

On the whole French (green) beans are not prone to many problems. Slugs and snails are the most likely nuisance, especially when the plants are first emerging, but they can also eat the pods as well. Blackfly and fungal diseases may also be a problem.

HARVESTING

Do not to pull too hard when harvesting French (green) beans because the plants may be pulled from the ground.

ABOVE **These climbing French (green) beans are being supported by a bamboo cane.**

ABOVE **These striking purple French (green) beans are now ready for harvesting. It seems a shame to pick such a decorative crop.**

Varieties

Dwarf beans
'Annabel' green, slim pods, stringless
'Canadian Wonder' green, flat pods
'Daisy' green, long pods, stringless
'Delinel' green, slim pods, stringless
'Golddukat' yellow waxpod, pencil pods
'Golden Sands' yellow waxpod, stringless
'Masai' green, very slim pods
'Mont d'Or' yellow waxpod
'Purple Queen' purple, round pods, stringless
'Purple Tepee' purple, round pods, stringless
'Radar' round pods, stringless
'Royalty' purple, stringless
'Sprite' green, round pods, stringless
'Tendergreen' green, pencil pods, stringless
'The Prince' green, flat pods, early

Haricot (navy) beans
'Brown Dutch'
'Chevrier Vert'
'Comtessa de Chambord'

Climbing beans
'Blue Lake' green, round pods, stringless, white seeded
'Hunter' flat pods, stringless
'Kentucky Blue' round pods
'Largo' round pods, stringless
'Mont d'Or' golden, slightly flat pods, near-black beans
'Veitch's Climbing' green, flat pods

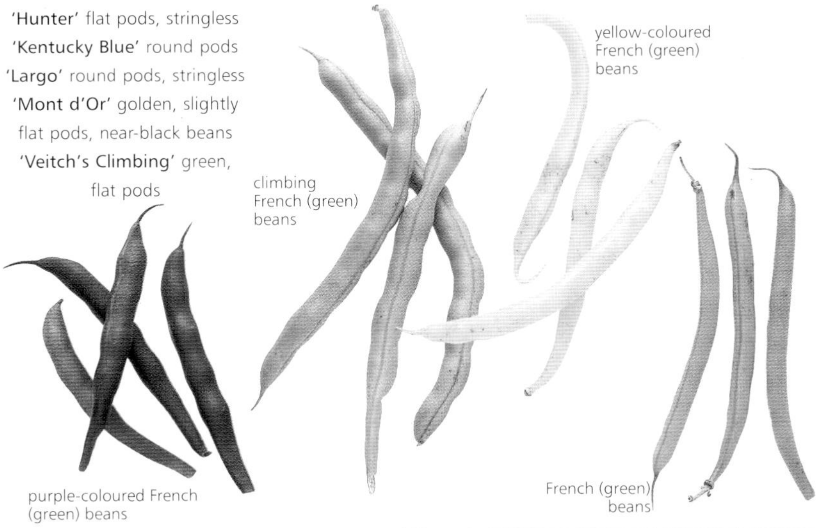

Broad (Fava) Beans

Vicia faba

Unlike other forms of bean, broad (fava) beans can be an acquired taste; not everybody likes them. However, when they are cooked straight from the plant, home-grown beans have a flavour that is never found in bought ones, so if you have not enjoyed them in the past, grow some and try them again – you may be pleasantly surprised. These beans also have the advantage of being one of the first vegetables of the year to mature. While the other two main forms of garden bean come from the Americas, the broad (fava) bean is native to the Old World, probably originating in the Near East. Like the pea, it has been grown since Neolithic times, and, also like the pea, it can be eaten fresh or it can be dried and stored, which is a valuable attribute that has been appreciated right up to the advent of the freezer.

ABOVE **A row of healthy young beans at an early stage of their growth.**

Broad (fava) beans are categorized in various ways. Sometimes it is by length of pod. The long-pods have up to eight kidney-shaped beans in each pod, whereas the Windsors, the short-podded form, have only half that number of seeds, each of which is rounded. They can also be categorized by the colour of the seeds, which can be green, white (pale green, really) or mahogany-red; green seeds are better for freezing. They are also categorized as dwarf or tall forms, the former being better for the small garden. Finally, they can be divided into those that can be overwintered and those that are best sown in spring; this generally corresponds to the divisions between long-pods and Windsors, as the long-pods tend to be hardier.

PINCHING OUT

Pinching out the tops of the beans is a good practice because it discourages blackfly. The tops can then be boiled and eaten.

Cultivation

These beans need an open, sunny site, which is protected from strong winds, especially if you are growing overwintering types. A reasonably fertile soil is required, and this is best achieved by incorporating manure or compost during the autumn dig. Over-wintering varieties can be sown in late autumn. Other types should be sown in late winter or early spring. Although new varieties have extended the sowing season until early summer, most varieties need to be sown before the end of spring.

Sow in double rows in a shallow trench, 23cm/9in wide and 4cm/1½in deep. Alternatively, sow each seed individually with a dibber. In both cases, the seeds should be about 23cm/9in apart, and the rows should be 60cm/24in apart. Seeds can also be raised in pots or modules in late winter under glass and planted out in spring.

Taller varieties will need to be supported with string tied to canes that are set at intervals along each side of the double row. When the beans are in full flower, pinch out the tender top by 8cm/3in to reduce the chance of blackfly infestation and to make the pods fill out. Water during dry periods.

Harvesting

Pick the pods when the beans inside them have swollen. Some can be picked at an earlier stage for cooking whole. Do not allow the beans to become too old – that is, when they are leathery and pliable – or they will be tough and too floury. Some people like to cook and eat the young tops when they are removed.

Storage

These beans are undoubtedly best when picked straight from the plant, but any excess can be frozen for future use. They can also be dried.

Pests and diseases

The most serious problem is blackfly, but this can often be avoided by removing the tips of the plant (see left). On the whole, these beans are reasonably trouble free, although chocolate spot can be a problem. This can usually be ignored, but burn or destroy the affected plants when they are finished with rather than put them on the compost heap.

STAKING

Taller varieties of broad (fava) beans will need supporting with string tied to canes that are set at intervals along the rows.

ABOVE **This row of broad (fava) beans is being supported with canes and string.**

Varieties

'Aquadulce Claudia' long-pod, white seeds
'Bunyards Exhibition' long-pod, white seeds
'Express' pale green seeds
'Hylon' long-pod, white seeds
'Imperial Green Longpod' long-pod, green seeds
'Jade' long-pod, green
'Jubilee Hysor' white seeds
'Jumbo' large green seeds
'Masterpiece Green Longpod' long-pod, green seeds
'Meteor Vroma' green seeds
'Red Epicure' red seeds
'Relon' long-pod, green seeds
'The Sutton' dwarf, pale green seeds
'White Windsor' white seeds

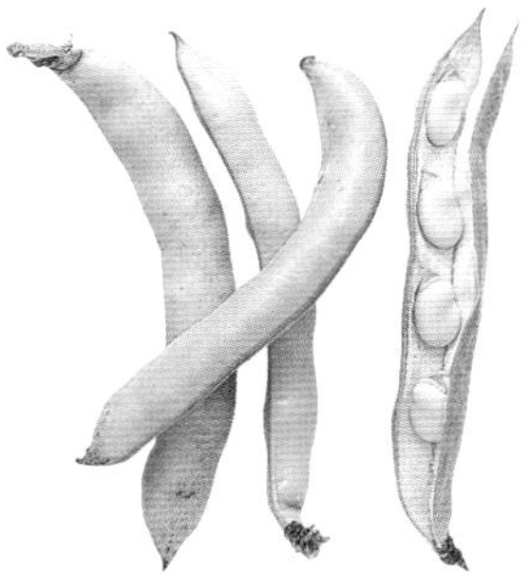

broad (fava) beans

Cultivation

Sowing time late autumn, late winter to late spring
Sowing or planting distance 23cm/9in
Sowing depth 4cm/1½in
Distance between sown rows 60cm/24in
Thinning distance no need to thin
Harvesting early to late summer

MARROWS & SQUASH CROPS

Marrows and Courgettes (Zucchini)

Cucurbita pepo

Although marrows (zucchini), pumpkins and squashes are essentially the same plant, they are dealt with separately because they are usually considered differently in the garden and kitchen. First, it is important to consider the difference between marrows and courgettes (zucchini). In fact, there is no real difference: courgettes are an immature form of marrow, and, if left to grow, will turn into marrows. However, some varieties are best grown as one or the other.

ABOVE **A female flower on a developing courgette (zucchini). The male flowers are often picked before they are open and used in cooking.**

The history of the marrow (zucchini) is not really known, and although they came to Europe from North America, there are no longer any native species that correspond to the plants we grow today. The marrow reached Europe in the 16th century and has been grown ever since. The idea of eating immature marrows as courgettes (zucchini) is a relatively recent development.

There are two types of marrows (zucchini): trailing and bush. The trailing forms throw out long stems that cover a great deal of space, and can be trained over a trellis or archway. The fruits appear at intervals along the stems. Bush varieties are much more compact, and the fruits grow from the central cluster of stems. They take up less space and are far better plants for small gardens. Courgettes (zucchini) are usually only grown as bushes; marrows are grown as either type.

In recent years courgettes (zucchini) have become much more popular than marrows (zucchini), partly because many people find that marrows are watery and bland and partly because, as families have become smaller, a whole marrow is difficult to dispose of in one sitting. However, marrows still have their devotees, and there are some very tasty ways of cooking them.

Courgettes (zucchini), on the other hand, are not only a more convenient size but, being immature, they do not dissolve into pulp quite so readily when they are cooked. They also have a more positive flavour. Nearly everybody who grows courgettes accidentally leaves at least one on the plant, which develops into a marrow (zucchini), so there is every opportunity of trying both. The flowers can also be eaten, either raw or cooked. Marrows (zucchini) were traditionally grown on compost heaps. The heaps or bins were made up during winter and spring, topped with earth and left until the following autumn before being spread. The high concentration of rich, fibrous material meant that moisture and nutrients were in abundant supply, creating the ideal conditions for these plants during the summer growing season. They can, of course, be grown in ordinary vegetable plots, but using the compost heap does save space, which can be used for other crops.

LEFT **Do not plant courgettes (zucchini) too close together; leave space to harvest the fruit.**

Cultivation

Marrows and courgettes (zucchini) like an open, sunny situation and a rich, moisture-retentive soil. As noted above, they can be grown on the compost heap or in a bed that has been heavily manured during the previous autumn. They are frost tender, so plants should not be put outside before the last frosts have passed, unless they are protected with cloches.

Plants can be raised under glass by sowing the flat seed edgeways in individual pots or in modules in late spring or sown directly in the

PLANTING OUT

This marrow (zucchini) is being planted in its fibre pot. It has been grown like this to prevent disturbing the roots.

soil in early summer. Germination is speeded up by soaking the seed in water overnight. Keep seed that has been planted in the open warm by covering the soil with a jamjar or cloche until the seed has germinated. Sow two seeds at each position and remove the weaker if both germinate. Even if you sow in the open, sow a few in pots as insurance against sudden cold weather or the ravages of slugs.

Bush types can be left to develop by themselves but trailing varieties may need to be trimmed back if they get too vigorous. They can be left to trail outwards, like the spokes of a wheel, if there is enough space or they can be trained round in a circle, if

HARVESTING

Harvest a marrow (zucchini) by cutting it off at the base with a sharp knife.

Cultivation

Bush
Sowing time late spring (under glass) to early summer
Sowing or planting distance 90cm/3ft
Sowing depth 4cm/1½in
Distance between sown rows 90cm/3ft
Thinning distance no need to thin
Harvesting midsummer onwards

Trailing
Sowing time late spring (under glass) to early summer
Sowing or planting distance 1.2–1.8m/4–6ft
Sowing depth 4cm/1½in
Distance between sown rows 1.8m/6ft
Thinning distance no need to thin
Harvesting midsummer onwards

the stems are pegged down as they grow. If they are grown up a trellis or some other support, the shoots must be tied in regularly. Towards the end of summer remove the tips of each shoot. Keep well watered.

Harvesting

Courgettes (zucchini) are best harvested while they are still young – that is, when they are about 10cm/4in long – but in practice they can be harvested at any time, and circumstances usually dictate that they are picked at any stage between being a courgette and a small marrow (zucchini). If they are left on the plant, courgettes will eventually develop into full marrows and can be cut at any time until the first frosts. Whatever the size of the crop, cut through the stem 2cm/¾in or more away from the fruit.

Storage

Courgettes (zucchini) are difficult to store for more than a few days and are best eaten fresh from the plant. They can be frozen, although they become less firm. Marrows (zucchini), in contrast, will last for several weeks after picking, especially if they have been left to mature and ripen. Pick marrows at the end of the season, before the first frosts, and then store them in a frost-free place for several weeks, on trays or hanging in net bags.

Pests and diseases

Although generally trouble free, slugs are the most severe problem, eating right through the stem if not checked.

Cucumber mosaic virus is the most common disease, causing mottled leaves and distorted fruit. The plant should be burned or destroyed. In some years powdery mildew is also a problem; rightly or wrongly gardeners tend to ignore it.

Varieties

Bush
'All Green Bush'
'Badger Cross'
'Green Bush'
'Long Green Bush'
'Long White Bush'
'Minipak'

Trailing
'Long Green Trailing'
'Long White Trailing'
'Table Dainty'
'Tender and True'

Courgettes (Zucchini)
'Ambassador'
'Burpee Golden Zucchini'
'Bush Champion'
'Defender'
'Early Gem'
'Gold Rush'
'Greyzini'
'Tondo di Nizza'
'Zucchini'

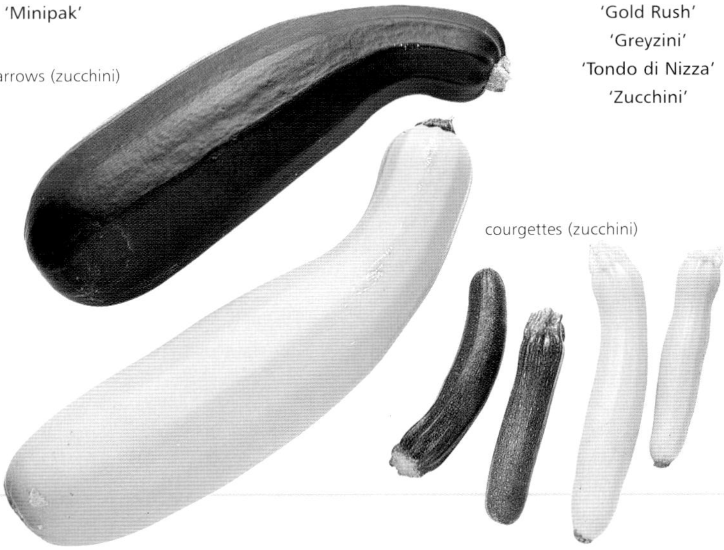

Pumpkins

Cucurbita maxima

The pumpkin is a curious vegetable. In some arable areas it is treated seriously and grown for the kitchen; in other areas it is planted for fun, to see who can grow the biggest, or it is grown to be carved and hollowed out for a Hallowe'en lantern or mask. Whether for decorative or culinary use, pumpkins are definitely worth growing if you have the space.

ABOVE **The skins of pumpkins should be hardened in the sunshine.**

LEFT **A healthy crop of pumpkins.**

Originally from South America, where they have been part of the staple diet for centuries, pumpkins are extremely popular in North America, and it is from there that their recent revival in Britain has come. They are, in fact, winter squashes but are frequently separated from the other members of the family simply on grounds of their size and uses. The distinctive name of pumpkin is usually given to the large, round winter squashes.

Some people consider pumpkins rather too large for consumption, but not all pumpkins need be big. The smaller ones, no more than 30cm/12in across, have usually been bred for taste rather than appearance and there is plenty of flesh on them for most purposes. Similarly, not all are the golden colour of Hallowe'en and show-bench pumpkins. 'Crown Prince' for example, has a bluish-grey skin and is only 30cm/12in across. The dense flesh, a deep old-gold colour, tastes delicious when cooked, and 'Crown Prince' will store much better than its big brash cousins.

Although pumpkins take time and patience, they are good plants with which to encourage young gardeners. The prospect of growing a huge vegetable that will weigh several hundred pounds – so heavy that even their parents can't lift it – seems to appeal to children, although what the cook does with so much pumpkin flesh defies thought – there is a limit to the amount of pumpkin soup and pies one can consume.

PLANTING

Pumpkins are rich feeders and appreciate moisture near their roots, so add plenty of organic material to the soil when planting.

Cultivation

Pumpkins need a sunny site that is open and yet protected from strong winds, which can soon tear the large leaves to shreds. The soil should be rich in well-rotted organic material, not only to feed the pumpkins but also to hold plenty of moisture in the soil. At each site, dig a pit 45cm/18in deep and 60cm/24in square and half-fill it with manure before replacing the top soil. In late spring start the pumpkins off in the greenhouse in modules or fibre pots. They do not need such a high temperature as cucumbers – a gentle heat of 15–18°C/59–64°F will be adequate. You can speed up germination by soaking the seed in water overnight.

HARVESTING

Harvest pumpkins when they have reached their mature colour by cutting through the stem at the top with a sharp knife.

Cultivation

Sowing time late spring under glass
Sowing or planting distance 1.8m/6ft
Sowing depth 4cm/1½in
Distance between sown rows 1.8m/6ft
Thinning distance no need to thin
Harvesting autumn

RIGHT **This is a large bed of pumpkins and squashes. Such close planting makes harvesting difficult, unless they are all harvested at once.**

When the threat of frost is passed, plant in the prepared ground at distances of 1.8m/6ft or further apart for more vigorous varieties. Keep the plant within bounds by training the stems in a spiral around the plant, pinning them down with wire pegs. If you want to grow giant specimens, reduce the number of young fruit to between one and three. Water regularly and apply a high-potash liquid feed at least once every two weeks and more frequently for giant fruit. Towards the end of summer, pinch out the tips of the shoots. Stop watering and feeding once the fruit is mature.

Harvesting

Harvest the pumpkins when they have reached their mature colour: deep orange or blue-grey. A good indicator that they are ready is that the stems begin to split. Cut them with a stem of about 5cm/2in. Make sure that they are all picked before the first frosts. Place them in a sunny position for about a week so that the skins fully harden.

Storage

Orange-skinned pumpkins will store for several weeks in a frost-free position. Blue-grey ones will last much longer, sometimes up to several months.

Pests and diseases

On the whole, pumpkins are trouble free. Slugs are probably the most severe problem and will eat right through the stem if not checked.

Cucumber mosaic virus is the most troublesome disease. The leaves become mottled and the fruit distorted. Destroy the entire plant.

Varieties

'Atlantic Giant' very large, orange skin
'Crown Prince' medium-sized, grey-blue skin, stores well
'Hundred Weight' large variety, yellow skin, stores well
'Jack Be Little' very small, orange skin, stores well
'Jackpot' medium- to large-sized, mottled orange and green skin
'Janne Gros de Paris' large, rough pink skin, stores well
'Mammoth' large, orange skin
'Small Sugar' small- to medium-sized, orange skin
'Spellbound' medium-sized, orange skin, stores well
'Spirit' medium-sized, orange skin
'Tom Fox' medium-sized, orange skin

pumpkins

Squashes

Cucurbita maxima

When it comes to definitions, squashes can be a confusing group of plants. In the broadest sense of the word, squashes include marrows (zucchini) and pumpkins as well as what are known as winter and summer squashes, because they all belong to the same botanical grouping and because their cultivation is broadly the same. However, many gardeners distinguish among squashes, marrows and pumpkins, because not only do they look different but they are grown and used in slightly different ways.

ABOVE **Harvest squashes by cutting through the stem with a sharp knife.**

There are two types of squash: summer squashes and winter squashes. The main difference is that winter squashes will store for long periods in winter, whereas summer squashes are for more immediate use, although they will keep for a few weeks. Marrows (zucchini) are types of summer squash; many pumpkins are types of winter squash. Pumpkins and squashes tend to merge together, and it is sometimes difficult to know if a specific variety is one or the other. In reality, it does not matter: it is only a name, and the growing and the eating are the same.

Squashes are a diverse group of plants, and many of them exhibit weird shapes – some have crooked necks or look like a Turkish turban or even a flying saucer – while others have ribbed or warty surfaces. The flesh ranges in colour from almost white to deep orange. The taste also varies, but, like marrows (zucchini), the flavour is not particularly intense. Although they undoubtedly do have culinary value, they are often grown for their appearance, the wide range of shapes and colours making them not only attractive but also intriguing.

Originally from South America, squashes were introduced to Europe by returning conquistadors and explorers in the 16th century. The majority of the vast range of varieties have been developed in South and North America, and it is only recently that they have regained popularity in Britain.

Cultivation

The cultivation for both summer and winter squashes is basically the same, it is only in their storage that there is any real difference. They need an open, sunny site that is protected from strong winds. Squashes like a soil that is rich in organic matter, both to provide them with nutrients and to hold an ample supply of moisture. Dig in plenty of manure or compost in the autumn.

Sow squashes under glass in a medium temperature of about 18°C/64°F. Because they do not like root disturbance, grow them individually in modules or fibre pots. Once the frosts have passed, they can be planted out, setting them at least 1.8m/6ft apart. Alternatively, they can be sown where they are to grow. Sow two seeds at each station, removing the weaker seedling once they have germinated. Sowing should be in early summer, after the frosts have passed. As the stems grow, they can be trained around in a spiral to save space and pinned down with wire pegs. Many types of squash can be grown as climbing plants and trained up a trellis or netting. Keep the plants well watered, and feed with a high-potash liquid fertilizer about once every ten days.

Harvesting

Squashes are ready to harvest when the stems begin to split. Cut the summer squashes when they are large enough to eat and while the skin is still soft (your finger-nail should easily sink into the skin). Cut

LEFT **If necessary, reduce the size of squash plants by cutting off the trailing stems, two leaves above a fruit.**

Cultivation

Summer
Sowing time late spring (under glass) to early summer
Sowing or planting distance 1.8m/6ft
Sowing depth 4cm/1½in
Distance between sown rows 1.8m/6ft
Thinning distance no need to thin
Harvesting late summer and autumn

Winter
Sowing time late spring (under glass) to early summer
Sowing or planting distance 1.8m/6ft
Sowing depth 4cm/1½in
Distance between sown rows 1.8m/6ft
Thinning distance no need to thin
Harvesting autumn

them with a short length of stem attached. Winter squashes can be cut in the same way if they are to be used straightaway; for winter storage leave them on the plants for as long as possible, but harvest before the first frosts. If possible, leave in the sun for a few days before storing to harden the skin.

Storage

Summer squashes can be stored for a short while – two weeks or so, but generally not much longer. They are best used straight from the plant. If the skins of the winter squashes have been hardened, they will keep for several weeks in a frost-free place. They can be stored in nets or in trays, each squash placed so that it is not touching its neighbour.

PROVIDING SUPPORT

Support growing squashes on straw to prevent them from being damaged.

ABOVE **A terracotta saucer can be used to protect squashes instead of a layer of straw.**

Pests and diseases

On the whole, squashes are usually trouble free. Slugs are once again the most severe problem and they will quickly eat straight through the stem if they are not checked in time.

Cucumber mosaic virus is the most troublesome of the potential diseases. The leaves become mottled and the fruit distorted. The whole plant should be destroyed if it is affected. In some years powdery mildew can also be a possible problem; rightly or wrongly, most gardeners find that its occurrence can usually be safely ignored.

Varieties

Summer
'Custard White' round, white skin, scalloped edges
'Dawn' yellow skin, crooked neck
'Little Gem' round, dark green skin, pale flesh
'Orangetti' cylindrical, orange skin, spaghetti-like flesh
'Scallopini' discus-shaped, green skin, scalloped edges
'Table Ace' small and acorn-shaped, dark green skin, orange flesh
'Vegetable Spaghetti' cylindrical, sphagetti-like flesh

Winter
'Butternut' cylindrical, cream skin, orange flesh
'Cobnut' cylindrical, cream skin, cream flesh
'Cream of the Crop' ribbed oval fruit, cream skin, cream flesh
'Early Acorn' oval-shaped, dark green skin, orange flesh
'Golden Hubbard' oval, yellow knobbly skin
'Green Hubbard' oval, green knobbly skin
'Sweet Dumpling' ribbed and rounded fruit, cream and dark green skin, orange flesh
'Turk's Turban' turban-shaped, green, cream and orange skin

winter squashes

Cucumbers

Cucumis sativus

One of the quickest ways to prepare a meal is to pop into the garden, grab a lettuce, some tomatoes and a cucumber. Add some fresh, crusty bread – and there you are. Most gardeners grow lettuces and tomatoes, but fewer grow cucumbers, perhaps because they think they require a greenhouse or they are difficult to grow. They need not be either. Outdoor cucumbers can be grown as easily as courgettes (zucchini), which few gardeners find a problem.

Cucumbers have been used as a vegetable for the best part of 5,000 years. They were first grown and eaten in India, where they were developed from a native species, and from there they spread north-east into China and north-west into Greece and Rome.

There are several colours and shapes. In the West we are more used to long cucumbers with green skins, but they can also be oval or even round, and colours can range from white to yellow.

As far as the gardener is concerned, there are two types of cucumber: the climbing varieties with long fruit that are grown under glass and the ridge varieties that are much shorter and are grown in the open. The advantage of greenhouse varieties is that they can be started earlier and are not as dependent on the weather. Ridge varieties, on the other hand, need less looking after and are less prone to attack by pests and diseases, which thrive in the warmth of the greenhouse. From the culinary point of view, the greenhouse forms are often preferred, mainly because outdoor cucumbers have tough, often prickly, skins and do not look quite as elegant as their indoor cousins. Until recently, many outdoor varieties tended to taste bitter, but this is now no longer generally the case.

Gherkins are a form of ridge cucumber, which are used for pickling. Any immature ridge cucumber can be used, but some varieties have been specially bred for the purpose. Like courgettes and marrows (zucchini), there is no difference in cultivation technique other than the time of picking.

LEFT **A ridge or outdoor cucumber, with its attractive yellow flowers and tough, prickly skin clearly on display.**

Cultivation

Greenhouse cucumbers need a high temperature in which to germinate and a high temperature in which to grow. Using seed of all-female varieties – they are less likely to be bitter – sow two seeds, edgeways, in pots or modules and place in a propagator at 24°C/75°F. When they germinate, remove the weaker seedling and reduce the temperature to 21°C/70°F. Plant the young plants with as little root disturbance as possible into growing bags, two per bag depending on the size. Use square-meshed netting or a system of poles and horizontal wires as supports, and tie in the shoots as they grow. Pinch out the tip of the shoot when it reaches the roof. Tie the laterals to horizontal wires and pinch out the tips two leaves beyond the first fruit to form. Water to keep the soil constantly moist and throw some water on the floor of the greenhouse to keep the atmosphere humid. Keep the house shaded. Once the fruit start to develop, feed them with a high-potash liquid feed once every two weeks.

ABOVE **Ridge or outdoor cucumbers growing in the open need a sunny spot that is sheltered from the wind.**

Ridge or outdoor cucumbers need a sunny spot sheltered from the wind. Add plenty of well-rotted manure to the soil before sowing. Sow ridge cucumbers either inside in pots or outdoors where they are to grow. If sown directly, cover them with a glass jamjar or cloche to raise the temperature. Do not sow until after the threat of frost has passed and the soil has warmed up. Sow, leaving about 75cm/30in in each direction between plants. If the seed is germinated in pots, ensure that the roots are not disturbed when they are transplanted. Fibre pots can help with this,

Cultivation

Greenhouse
Sowing time late winter onwards
Sowing or planting distance 60cm/24in
Sowing depth 2.5cm/1in
Thinning distance no need to thin
Harvesting midsummer onwards

Ridge
Sowing time late spring (under glass) to early summer
Sowing or planting distance 75cm/30in
Sowing depth 2.5cm/1in
Distance between sown rows 75cm/30in
Thinning distance no need to thin
Harvesting midsummer onwards

ABOVE **This ridge or outdoor cucumber has been trained up a cane tripod. The large leaves and fruits have a pleasing architectural quality.**

because the cucumbers can be planted without removing them from the pots. Pinch out the tip of the main shoot after six leaves have formed so that the plant bushes out. Water freely. Once the fruit start to develop, feed with a high-potash liquid feed once every two weeks.

Harvesting

Cut the fruit with a short length of stalk as soon as they are large enough to eat. Pick frequently and more fruit will develop. Harvest gherkins when they are 5–8cm/2–3in long.

ABOVE **Climbing varieties of cucumber are grown under glass. They have smooth skins and are longer than ridge varieties.**

Varieties

Ridge
'Burpless Tasty Green'
'Bush Champion'
'Crystal Apple'
'Long Green Ridge'
'Masterpiece'

Greenhouse
'Birgit'
'Fenumex'
'Pepinex'
'Petita'
'Telegraph'
'Telegraph Improved'

Gherkins
'Bestal'
'Venlo Pickling'

Storage

Keep for no more more than a few days; they are best eaten fresh.

Pests and diseases

Slugs and snails can quickly eat through a stem, killing the plant; remove by your preferred method. In the greenhouse, red spider mite and whitefly may be a problem.

SHOOT CROPS

ABOVE **Harvest asparagus by cutting the stems below the ground.**

Asparagus

Asparagus officinalis

Asparagus was once the food of the wealthy – if you didn't have your own garden, you couldn't grow it. Nowadays it is much more widely available, but shoots cut straight from the garden and cooked immediately still taste best. Asparagus is not only good to eat, but the decorative foliage has a wonderful filmy quality about it. A great uncle of mine grew asparagus all his long life, not to eat it, but so that he could use the cut foliage with his sweet peas. In a potager or decorative kitchen garden, the great plumes of finely cut foliage make a fine display.

The tender shoot of asparagus is the part of the plant that is eaten. The shoot emerges from below ground in late spring and early summer. Once it gets above approximately 15–20cm/6–8in long it becomes tough-skinned and rather chewy and is then best left, the remaining shoots developing into tall foliage stems with inconspicuous flowers and, eventually, orange-red berries.

Asparagus grows wild throughout Europe and has been eaten and possibly cultivated from at least the time of the Ancient Greeks. It has long been grown in gardens, but the main disadvantage is that it takes up quite a lot of space. If you have a small garden but want to grow asparagus, try planting one or two crowns in the flower borders, picking the spikes in early summer and then leaving them in the border as a decorative foliage plant.

One of the attractive features of creating an asparagus bed is that it lasts for at least 20 years, and apart from a little maintenance, not much effort is required to produce a wonderful feast each year. Asparagus plants are either male or female. Male plants have the advantage of being more productive and not producing seed (which readily self-sows). Asparagus can be raised from seed, but the results can be disappointing if you use your own collected seed; it is better to buy named varieties on which you can rely. An increasing number of F1 hybrids is available, and these produce very good all-male plants.

APPLYING A SPRING MULCH

In the spring, before growth starts, apply a deep mulch of manure over the rows of asparagus.

Cultivation

Asparagus needs an open, sunny site, and it likes a light, preferably sandy soil, although it can be grown in any soil as long as it is free-draining and reasonably fertile. In heavy soils it can be grown by raising the level of the soil or by making a raised bed. In the autumn before planting, dig the bed, removing all traces of perennial weeds and incorporating plenty of well-rotted manure or compost. In the spring dig out a trench 20cm/8in deep with an 8cm/3in ridge running down the centre. If more than one row is required, set the trenches 90cm/3ft apart. Set each asparagus crown on the ridge, spreading out its roots around it. Each crown should be 45cm/18in apart. Cover them with soil to a depth of 8–10cm/3–4in.

If you are growing from seed, soak them overnight in water and sow in a drill 1cm/½in deep. Do this in spring. Thin to 15cm/6in and transplant the following spring in the same manner as for bought crowns above. As the plants grow, draw in more earth from the side of the trench until it is filled.

Do not cut any spears in the first year and only one or two from each plant during the next year. Each spring, cover the trench with a layer of manure or compost, leaving it slightly heaped up so that over the years the row becomes earthed (hilled) up in the

CUTTING DOWN IN AUTUMN

In the autumn, as the asparagus fronds are turning brown, cut them down to the ground.

same way you treat potatoes. Keep the ground weeded. Cut down the ferns as they begin to turn yellow and, if possible, before the berries begin to ripen; alternatively, pick all the berries. If they are left on the plants the birds will eat them and before long asparagus will be appearing all over the garden. For the same reason, avoid putting berried stems on the compost heap.

Cultivation

Sowing
Sowing time spring
Sowing depth 1cm/½in
Distance between sown rows 30cm/12in
Thinning distance 15cm/6in
Transplanting following spring
Planting
Planting time early spring
Planting distance 45cm/18in
Planting depth initially 8–10cm/3–4in
Distance between sown rows 90cm/3ft
Harvesting in late spring for six weeks (third year onwards)

Harvesting

In late spring, when the shoots that have emerged are 10–15cm/4–6in long, cut them by inserting a knife 5cm/2in below the surface of the soil. Only cut through the stem, do not thrash around below the soil level or you may damage spears that have not yet emerged. Make a slanting cut. After the third year cutting can take place over about six weeks.

Storage

Asparagus is best used fresh from the plant, but it can be stored for a couple of days if it is stood in a jug of cold water in the refrigerator.

Varieties

'Accell'	'Giant Mammoth'
'Boonlim'	'Limbras'
'Cito'	'Lucullus'
'Connover's Colossal'	'Martha Washington'
'Franklin'	

ABOVE **Once the harvesting season is over, the asparagus is left to grow to its full height.**

Pests and diseases

Asparagus is usually pest and disease free. Slugs, as usual, are likely to be the worst problem, making holes in the spears. Asparagus beetle can also be a nuisance.

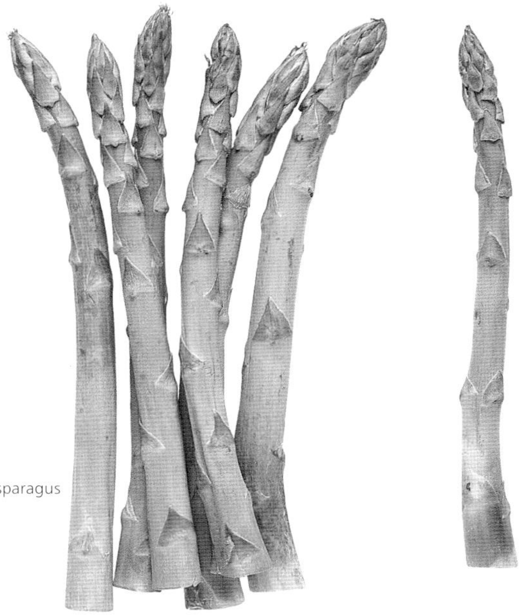

asparagus

Celery

Apium graveolens

Celery is an important vegetable for the kitchen as it is used, at least in part, in many dishes, including basic recipes such as stocks. Its culinary importance is not reflected in the garden, however. At one time no vegetable garden was complete without celery, but it is seen less often today, which may be partly because it is slightly difficult to grow and partly because it needs a constantly moist soil to do well. Whatever the reason, it is a shame it is not more widely grown, because if you do grow it you will find that you are constantly using it and, as always, will find the flavour so much better than shop-bought stalks.

ABOVE **Green varieties of celery, such as the one shown here, do not need blanching.**

Celery grows wild throughout Europe and Asia, and it is rather surprising to learn that it has entered cultivation only in relatively recent times. Celery was first cultivated in Italy as recently as the 16th century but it did not arrive in Britain until the end of the 17th century.

It is the blanched leaf stalks of celery that are eaten. These can be eaten green but taste sweeter if the light has been excluded, causing the stalks to turn white. This always used to be done by heaping earth up round them, but more often these days the stems are wrapped in cardboard or felt. This type of celery is often referred to as trench celery. Breeding has produced celery with self-blanching stems, although not everybody feels that these are wholly successful and that the old-style blanched stalks taste better. There are also forms with green, pink or red stems. There is a form of celery, known as green or American celery, which does not require blanching.

As well as the stems, some people like to eat the heart, the solid part of the plant, where the stems join the root. Some recipes also call for the leaves to be included, particularly when the celery is a flavouring agent rather than a vegetable in its own right. It can be cooked or eaten raw.

Cultivation

There are two ways of growing celery, depending on what type is being grown. To grow traditional trench celery, in the preceding autumn or winter dig out a trench 45cm/18in wide and 30cm/12in deep and put in an 8cm/3in layer of rotted manure. Backfill the trench, leaving it about 10cm/4in deep. Sow the seeds under glass in modules in early spring and place them in moderate heat of 10–16°C/50–61°F. Do not check the plants by subjecting them to a sudden change of temperature or by allowing them to dry out. Once the frosts are over, harden off the plants and plant them out in the trench at 30cm/12in intervals. When the plants reach about 30cm/12in, tie the stems loosely together just below the leaves and draw up earth over part of the stems. Repeat the process three weeks later, pulling up more soil, and again three weeks after this, until the soil is up to the lower leaves. Alternatively,

BLANCHING CELERY

1 Blanching celery stems will make them taste sweeter. When the stems reach a height of about 30cm/12in, tie them loosely together just below the leaves.

2 A collar of cardboard or waterproof paper is tied around the stems of celery. The stems eventually blanch because of the lack of light.

3 Soil can be used to hold the collar in place. Although soil can also be earthed up around the stems to blanch them, a collar will stop soil from getting into the crown.

ABOVE **The celery planted here with some cabbages is one of the self-blanching varieties now available – 'Golden Self-blanching'.**

plant on flat ground and wrap cardboard or waterproof paper round the stems when they are 30cm/12in long. When the stems grow taller, wrap a second collar round them. Keep the celery well watered and do not allow the soil to dry out.

Self-blanching celery is started in the same way from seed and then planted out in blocks rather than rows, setting the plants at intervals of 23cm/9in in all directions. The dense foliage helps to blanch the stems. Place straw around the outside of the block to help keep out the light. Green celery can be grown in the same way, although there is no need for the straw.

HARVESTING

Harvest the celery by digging beneath it with a fork and levering it out of the soil. Replace any soil around the next plant if it falls away.

Harvesting

Trench celery can be lifted in autumn by digging it up with a fork. Replace soil around the next plant if it falls away. Continue to dig as required. The flavour is improved by the first frosts, but cover the plants with straw in severe weather so that penetrating frosts do not reach the stems. Self-blanching celery can also be harvested as required from the autumn onwards, but it should be lifted by the time of the first winter frosts.

Storage

Leave trench varieties where they are growing until required. In colder areas, before the weather becomes severe, lift and store in a frost-free place, where they should stay fresh for several weeks. Celery can be frozen, but it becomes mushy when it is defrosted, so it can only be used as flavouring or in cooked dishes.

Pests and diseases

Slugs are one of the worst enemies of celery, and it is important to cull them regularly by your preferred method. Other problems can include celery fly and carrot fly.

Diseases include celery heart rot and celery leaf spot. Boron deficiency, which causes the stems to crack, may also be a problem.

Cultivation

Trench
Sowing time early to mid-spring
Planting date early summer
Planting distance 30cm/12in
Distance between sown rows 60cm/24in
Harvesting autumn onwards

Self-blanching
Sowing time early to mid-spring
Planting date early summer
Planting distance in blocks 23cm/9in
Harvesting autumn

Varieties

Trench
'Giant Pink'
'Giant Red'
'Giant White'
'Hopkins Fenlander'
'Martine'
'New White Dwarf'

Self-blanching
'Celebrity'
'Golden Self-blanching'
'Ivory Tower'
'Lathom's Self-blanching'
'Victoria'

Green
'Greensnap'
'Imperial'
'Tall Utah'

trench celery

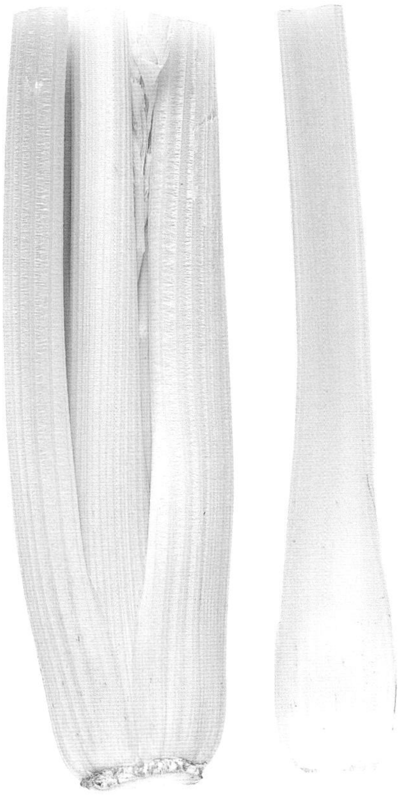

Celeriac (Celery Root)

Apium graveolens var. *rapaceum*

Although it is often thought of as a root crop, celeriac (celery root) is considered in this section partly because it fits more neatly beside celery and partly because it is not, in fact, the root but the swollen stem that forms the vegetable. Like cultivated celery, celeriac is derived from the wild celery which is a native plant found in Europe and the Middle East. It was a much later development than celery and is said to have been introduced to Britain from Alexandria in the early 18th century.

Celeriac (celery root) is the swollen area of the plant where the leaf stalks join the root. This produces a hard, round vegetable, often with knobbles and leaf scars over its dirty-looking surface. Although it looks far from appetizing, it is a useful vegetable. It is most frequently used as a flavouring, making an excellent winter substitute for celery, but it is also used as a vegetable in its own right, either cooked or grated raw in a salad.

Celeriac (celery root) is easier to grow than celery because it does not need blanching and is less prone to pests and diseases. However, like celery, it does need a moist soil in order to keep it growing.

Celeriac (celery root) should be given as long a growing season as possible or it will not develop into a large enough size that is worth harvesting and eating. This means that you will have to start off the celeriac plants early under glass.

EARTHING (HILLING) UP

Earth (hill) up the lower half of the celeriac (celery root) bulb in order to keep it white.

Cultivation

Celeriac (celery root) likes an open, sunny position, but it will tolerate a little light shade. The soil must be rich in organic material, not only to provide nutrients but also to help retain moisture around the roots.

BELOW **A row of celeriac (celery root), showing perfect spacing between the plants, and leaves trimmed from the tops of the bulbs.**

Sow celeriac (celery root) under glass in modules or fibre pots in late winter or early spring. Place them in a propagator at about 15°C/59°F. Maintain an even temperature and keep them watered so that growth is not checked. Towards the end of spring, when the plants are about 8cm/3in tall, harden them off and plant out at 30cm/12in intervals in rows set 30cm/12in apart. Plant them so that the base of the stem is level with the surface of the soil. Remember to keep them watered so that growth is not checked.

Cut off any side shoots that appear and towards late summer remove a few of the lower leaves and earth up around the swollen stem so that it stays white. In cold areas cover the plants with straw to protect from severe frosts.

ABOVE **Remove a few of the lower leaves from the bulb to let the light onto the top. This should be done in late summer.**

Harvesting

Dig celeriac (celery root) as needed from autumn onwards. They should be left to develop until they are as large as possible, although they are edible from about 8cm/3in across.

Storage

Unless the weather is particularly severe, celeriac (celery root) can be left in the ground until it is required. A covering of straw will help protect it if necessary. In colder areas it can be lifted, cleaned and placed in trays filled with just-moist sand or peat (peat moss) and kept in a frost-free place.

Pests and diseases

On the whole, celeriac (celery root) is relatively trouble free, although slugs can be a problem with young plants. Carrot fly and celery fly may also cause problems.

WATERING

The growth of celeriac (celery root) must not be checked; it must be watered during dry spells.

Cultivation

Sowing time late winter to mid-spring
Planting time late spring to early summer
Planting distance 30cm/12in
Distance between sown rows 30cm/12in
Harvesting autumn onwards

Varieties

'Alabaster'	'Marble Ball'
'Balder'	'Monarch'
'Brilliant'	'Snow White'
'Giant Prague'	'Tellus'

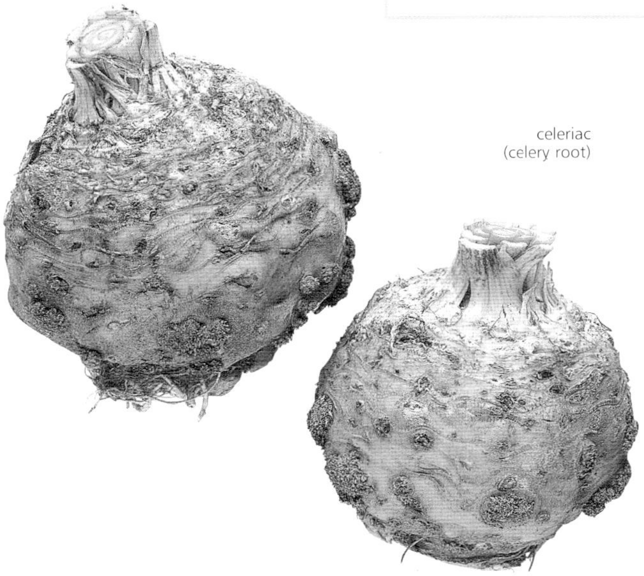

celeriac (celery root)

Globe Artichokes

Cynara cardunculus Scolymus Group

Globe artichokes were not much grown by the old country gardeners, who tended to concentrate on staple foods rather than "fancy ones". The artichoke was regarded as belonging on the tables of the rich. Today, however, although many people still grow their own vegetables, they are not dependent on doing so and can, therefore, afford to include a few delicacies that are not absolutely necessary to everyday life. Once you have grown and tasted globe artichokes, however, you may join the growing ranks of gardeners who consider them an essential part of their diet.

Unlike most vegetables, the part of globe artichokes that is eaten is the flower-head or, rather, the flower-bud before the flower begins to open. The whole head is boiled or steamed and then various parts consumed. First, the scale-like bracts are removed and the soft fleshy part at the base of each is eaten. As these are removed, the hairy tuft of the flower, the "choke", is revealed. This is usually removed and discarded and then the base of the flower, or the heart, is scooped out and eaten. It can then be served with lots of butter, which, needless to say, gets everywhere.

Globe artichokes were grown by the Ancient Greeks and the Romans, before spreading to the rest of Europe. They are handsome plants, looking a bit like the giant thistle, to which they are related. They are usually grown in the vegetable garden because you need several plants to give a constant supply throughout the summer, but if you decide to have only a couple of plants you could easily grow them in the flower border to save space. They have attractive silvery foliage, and if you leave a few flowers they develop large purple heads, which will usually be covered in bees.

Globe artichokes are usually grown from offsets rather than from seed, which is likely to produce variable results. If you have difficulty in getting offsets, you could initially grow them from seed and select the best plants, then continue to propagate these by division. This can be done by cutting off the young, outer growth from the old plant with a sharp knife in spring. Each shoot should be growing strongly and have some roots attached. Plant out immediately. Divisions can also be taken in autumn, when the offset can be potted up and over-wintered in a greenhouse or cold frame.

BELOW **Harvesting an artichoke by cutting the stem just below the head.**

Cultivation

Globe artichokes need an open, sunny situation. Because they will be in the ground for several years, the soil must be thoroughly prepared. Remove all perennial weeds and incorporate plenty of organic material. In spring plant the offsets at 75cm/30in

CUTTING BACK

Cut down all stems to ground level when the plant dies back in the autumn. Replace plants after three or, at most, four years.

COVERING WITH STRAW

Cover the plant with straw during autumn in colder areas.

ABOVE **A bed of globe artichokes with heads that are nearly ready for cutting.**

intervals in rows set 90cm/3ft apart. Trim off about a third of each leaf to reduce water loss while the plant is getting established. Water and keep watered in dry periods.

Seed can be sown in spring about 2.5cm/1in deep in rows 30cm/12in apart. Thin to 15cm/6in apart. Transplant the following spring. In autumn cut down the main stems and draw up soil around the crown. Cover with straw in very cold areas. Replace plants after three or, at most, four years, and aim to replant a third of your plants every year.

Cultivation

Seed
Sowing time spring
Sowing depth 2.5cm/1in
Distance between sown rows 30cm/12in
Thinning distance 15cm/6in
Transplanting following spring
Offsets
Planting time spring
Planting distance 75cm/30in
Distance between rows 90cm/3ft
Harvesting summer of second year onwards

Harvesting

Harvest from the second year onwards. Take the flower-heads before they open and while they are still green, cutting about 2.5cm/1in below the head with a sharp knife or secateurs (pruners).

Storage

Globe artichokes should be eaten straight from the plant. They can be frozen but remove the stem and choke first.

Varieties

'Green Globe'
'Purple Globe'
'Vert de Laon'
'Violetta di Chioggia'

Pests and diseases

On the whole globe artichokes are not troubled by many problems. Blackfly can be a nuisance in bad seasons.

globe artichokes

Rhubarb

Rheum × hybridum

Gardening has many contradictions and rhubarb is one of them. It is a vegetable, but it is mainly used as a fruit – that is, it is eaten with sugar as a dessert. Tomatoes, on the other hand, are, strictly speaking, fruit but are used as a vegetable. Does it matter? These are problems only when you start classifying plants or writing books; in the garden and kitchen it doesn't matter at all.

Cultivation

Seed
Sowing time spring
Sowing depth 2.5cm/1in
Distance between sown rows 30cm/12in
Thinning distance 23cm/9in
Transplanting following winter
Division
Planting time winter or (if potted) spring
Planting distance 90cm/3ft
Distance between rows 90cm/3ft
Harvesting summer of second year onwards

Originally rhubarb was grown as a medicinal plant (the root was powdered and used as a laxative), and it was only much later that it was used as a vegetable. It was used in medicine nearly 5,000 years ago in Ancient China, but it was only in the 18th century that it was realized that it also made a good vegetable. Forcing to obtain an early crop was not discovered (accidentally, as all good discoveries seem to be) until early in the following century, less than 200 years ago.

Only the young stalks are eaten, and these must be cooked. The leaves are poisonous, so do not be tempted to experiment with them in an attempt to invent new dishes. The crop is normally harvested from spring to early summer, but it is possible to "force" it, by covering the dormant crown with a box, bucket or, if you can afford it, a decorative terracotta rhubarb forcer. This produces a crop of sweet-tasting stems, several weeks earlier than if the plant is left in the open.

Rhubarb is an easy crop to grow and, once planted, it is not at all demanding. It can be left where it is for 20 years or more, although some gardeners prefer to replace their plants every five years or so in order to keep them vigorous. Rhubarb does take up quite a bit of space, but a couple of plants will keep a small family well supplied. The space may be considered well used because rhubarb plants are also quite decorative, with their huge green leaves and attractive red stems. In summer they throw up large flowering stems, covered with masses of creamy flowers, which can be spectacular.

LEFT **A decorative terracotta rhubarb forcer for producing sweet early rhubarb. Alternatively, a box or bucket can be used.**

Cultivation

Rhubarb must have a sunny position, away from shade. The soil should be rich in organic material but it should also be reasonably free draining. Because the site will be in use over a long period of time, take care in its preparation, removing all perennial weeds and digging deeply to incorporate as much well-rotted manure as possible. In the past new plants were bare rooted and were planted in winter, while they were dormant. This is also a good time to divide an existing plant to start a new one: dig up the old plant and remove an outer section that includes at least one bud. Plants that are purchased in pots can be planted in spring or even summer if they are kept well-watered. They should be spaced 90cm/3ft apart.

Rhubarb can also be grown from seed, but this method takes longer and the quality of the plant cannot be guaranteed in the same way as buying a named cultivar. However, the seed can be sown in 2.5cm/1in drills and thinned to 23cm/9in once they have germinated. Plant out in their final position, in the same way as for dormant crowns, during the following winter. Water well in dry weather. Apply a mulch of well-rotted, seed-free manure in autumn and again in spring.

To force a rhubarb plant, cover it with a large upturned bucket or other similar container in midwinter. Do not force the same plant for two years running or it will be weakened.

HARVESTING

Harvest by pulling on the sticks of rhubarb so that they come out of their "socket". Cut off the leaves and discard on the compost heap.

Harvesting

Rhubarb is harvested from spring to early summer unless it has been forced, when it can be pulled a few weeks earlier. It is harvested by pulling each stem vertically from close to the base – it will come out of its "socket". Cut off the leaves and discard on the compost heap.

Storage

Rhubarb is best cooked straight from the garden. Otherwise it can be stored by freezing or bottling.

Pests and diseases

There are a few pests and diseases that trouble rhubarb, but you will be unfortunate if you come across them.

Varieties

'Appleton's Forcing'
'Canada Red'
'Champagne'
'Early Victoria'
'Glaskin's Perpetual'
'Hawkes Champagne'
'Macdonald'
'The Sutton'
'Timperley Early'
'Victoria'

ABOVE **A bed of healthy looking rhubarb is an attractive sight. Remember that rhubarb leaves are poisonous and cannot be eaten.**

rhubarb

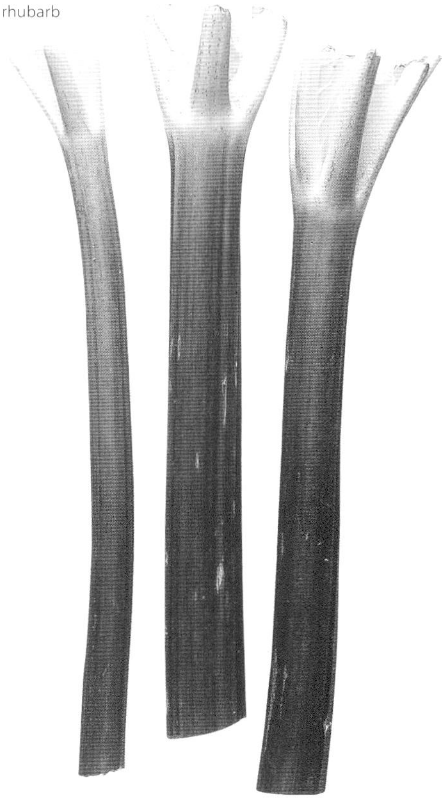

Seakale

Crambe maritima

Although seakale is one of the least popular of vegetables, it is not only delicious but is very easy to grow. Perhaps we are all too used to looking abroad for delicacies, which now come with startling ease from all corners of the globe to even the humblest of greengrocers. Seakale has been in cultivation from at least the beginning of the 18th century, but the wild plant was harvested long before that. It is, in fact, native to Britain, where it grows on shingle shores around the coast. Don't rush off and start picking it, however, because, like many leaf and stem plants, it needs blanching before the taste is palatable (also, of course, you should never pick wild plants). The blanched stems are harvested in spring and then cooked and eaten, like asparagus, with lots of butter or with olive oil. The flowering shoots can also be eaten while they are still in bud, much in the manner of broccoli.

Seakale is usually grown from "thongs" or root cuttings, although it can also be grown from seed. There are only a few named varieties – it is a vegetable that varies little from its wild ancestor. Because it is sometimes difficult to obtain plants, it may be easier to grow from seed, discarding any inferior plants and propagating the better forms. 'Lilywhite' is about the only named cultivar, but it is doubtful if all the plants sold under that name are, in fact, true to the original of that name.

Although primarily grown for its blanched stems, seakale is a very attractive plant and is well worth growing in a decorative kitchen garden for its curly, glaucous, purple leaves and the dense mass of honey-scented, white flowers, which appear in early summer. Anyone creating a potager purely for its decorative effect should consider seakale a prime candidate, as should anyone who wants to grow vegetables in the flower border.

Cultivation

Seakale needs an open, sunny position. The soil must be free-draining – sandy or gravelly soil is ideal – and if your soil is very heavy, it may be necessary to create a raised bed. Incorporate manure during the autumn digging. Plants can be grown from bought plants, from root cuttings or "thongs" or from seed. Bought plants should be planted out in spring at 45cm/18in apart in rows the same distance apart.

Take root cuttings or thongs from existing plants in autumn. Cut a few side roots that are about 1cm/½in thick into 15cm/6in lengths. Tie these in a bundle and put them vertically (make certain the top of the root is at the top) in the garden in well-drained soil or in a large pot filled with free-draining compost (soil mix). The top of the roots should be about 5cm/2in below the surface. Towards the end of next spring, once shoots have appeared from the bundle, separate them and plant them out at the same intervals as for bought plants. Alternatively, dig up the plants in autumn and place them in boxes of compost with the buds at the surface. Place in a dark place with the temperature about 10°C/50°F.

Seed should be sown in spring in drills 4cm/1½in deep. Soak the seed in water overnight before sowing. Thin seedlings to 23cm/9in. Transplant the resulting seedlings to their final position the following spring.

LEFT **A bed of seakale that will be blanched next winter. To blanch, cover the stems with an upturned bucket or special terracotta pot.**

Cultivation

Seed
Sowing time spring
Sowing depth 4cm/1½in
Distance between sown rows 30cm/12in
Thinning distance 23cm/9in
Transplanting the following spring

Plants
Planting time spring
Planting distance 45cm/18in
Distance between rows 45cm/18in
Harvesting summer of second year onwards

Thongs
Cuttings struck autumn
Transplanting late spring
Planting distance 45cm/18in
Distance between rows 45cm/18in
Harvesting summer of second year onwards

The stems of seakale can be blanched by covering the plants in late winter or early spring with a special terracotta pot or an upturned bucket. Terracotta pots have the advantage of looking more decorative. It is important that no light enters, or the stems will turn green and taste bitter.

Harvesting

Plants and thongs can be harvested in the second year; those grown from seed in the third year. Harvest when the blanched stems are long enough and remove the covers once harvesting is complete. Discard the plants after harvesting (but remember to take root cuttings when you lift the plants in order to provide the crop for next year).

Storage

Eat seakale straight from the garden.

Pests and diseases

On the whole, seakale is trouble free. The worst pests are slugs and caterpillars, especially those belonging to the cabbage white butterfly.

Varieties

Usually listed simply as seakale, except for 'Lilywhite'.

seakale

ABOVE **Some blanched seakale after the terracotta pot or upturned bucket has been removed. The seakale is now ready for harvesting.**

LEFT **This is a blanched seakale plant that has been exposed to the light once more to grow away again.**

Florence Fennel

Foeniculum vulgare var. dulce

With a name like Florence fennel it does not take much imagination to guess that the fennel we grow today originated in Italy, during Roman times. Italy is, in fact, still the centre of cultivation because it is very widely used in Italian cooking. Although it was introduced to Britain in the 18th century it has never been widely grown until recently, because the popularity of Italian dishes has encouraged more gardeners than ever to grow it.

Fennel is a versatile plant. As a vegetable it is grown for the bulbous swelling at the base of the leaf stalks, but other parts of the plant can also be eaten. The leaves are used as a herb, for both flavouring and garnish, and the seeds are used for their aniseed flavour. Fennel also makes a superb foliage plant and is often grown just for its decorative, finely cut foliage, which has a light, airy quality about it. The main vegetable forms have bright green foliage, but some perennial forms grown in the flower garden have very attractive bronze leaves. In the first year it grows to about 75cm/30in, but it gets much taller before it flowers in the following year.

It is, however, the bulbous part for which the plant is mainly grown. This consists of the overlapping swollen bases of the leaves, and it is either cooked or eaten raw in salads as a crisp, aniseed-flavoured alternative to celery.

BELOW **A bed of Florence fennel, showing the bulbs and the decorative foliage.**

Cultivation

Sowing time early to midsummer
Sowing depth 1cm/½in
Distance between sown rows 45cm/18in
Thinning distance 23cm/9in
Harvesting autumn

The secret of growing fennel is to make certain that it is kept moist and grows fast. If there are any checks, especially through drought, the plants will quickly run to seed before the bulb is formed.

Cultivation

Fennel needs an open, sunny position and, because of its height, one that is sheltered from the wind. It prefers light, well-drained soil, and if your soil is heavy, a raised bed might be better. The soil should be well manured to help make sure that it does not dry out. Do not be in too much of a hurry to sow, because plants from seed sown in spring are likely to bolt. Early to midsummer is the

HARVESTING

These bulbs are nearly ready for harvesting. They can be pulled directly from the ground or cut just below the bulb so that the root produces more foliage.

best time. Sow the seed in drills 1cm/½in deep and 45cm/18in apart. Seed can also be sown in modules under glass, but the transplanting may cause the plants to check and bolt, so it is preferable as well as less time-consuming to sow in situ. Thin the resulting seedlings to intervals of 23cm/9in. Keep the bed well watered, especially during dry periods. When the bulbs begin to swell, draw some soil up round them to at least half their height. As they continue to swell, draw up more soil to blanch the bulbs, which makes them taste sweeter.

Harvesting

Florence fennel is ready to harvest when the bulb is about the size of a tennis ball, which is about two or three weeks after earthing (hilling) up. It can either be pulled from the ground and then the root and leaf stems cut off, or cut from the root while still in the ground. This has the advantage that the root will sprout again and produce new feathery foliage that can be used for flavouring or decoration. If seed is required, the plants will have to be left in the ground for a second year, during which they will flower and set seed. This can be collected on a dry day and dried thoroughly in a warm place before being stored in an airtight jar.

Storage

Fennel is best eaten when it is fresh, straight from the garden. It will then keep for a few days if it is stored in a refrigerator but not for any longer.

ABOVE **This row of healthy looking Florence fennel contains a variety called 'Dover'.**

Pests and diseases

Fennel is blessed as being one of the vegetables that rarely suffers from any problems with pests and diseases. Bad weather is likely to cause more of a problem.

Varieties	
'Argo'	'Perfection'
'Cantino'	'Sirio'
'Dover'	'Sweet Florence' ('Di Firenze')
'Fino'	'Tardo'
'Herald'	

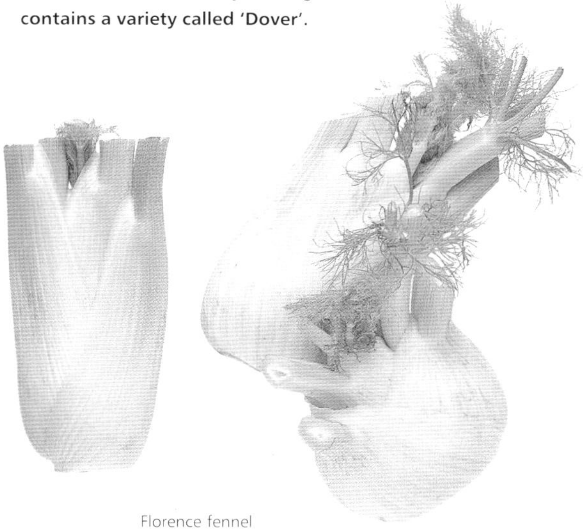

Florence fennel

FRUITING VEGETABLES

Aubergines (Eggplants)

Solanum melongena

Surprisingly the aubergine (eggplant) is related to the potato although so different. Now popular vegetables in the shops, aubergines have never really been widely grown in the garden and the young plants especially need shelter and warmth. Things are changing, however, and more gardeners are attempting to grow these attractive fruits.

The aubergine (eggplant) is a tropical plant, coming mainly from India where it was grown over 2,000 years ago. Introduced into southern Europe, in particular Spain, in the 16th century by the Arabs, it subsequently became popular throughout the countries bordering the Mediterranean, especially Greece.

The plants grow to about 45cm/18in tall, although they will be taller under glass, and they have soft, felted leaves. Some forms retain prickly fruit stems, but this characteristic has been bred out of some of the more modern cultivars. The fruits that we usually see in shops are long and a deep, shiny purple, sometimes almost black, but those that are grown from seed can be a variety of colours. The alternative name, eggplant, derives from those forms that produce round, white, egg-shaped fruit – there is even a variety called 'Easter Egg'. Other varieties bear fruits that are striped in white and purple or white and mauve. The shapes of the fruits also vary considerably, from almost round to long and thin, and these look like a cross between a bean and a chilli pepper (to which they are, in fact, related). The variation is such that the aubergine has become something of a cult with a number of growers in much the same way that pumpkins and squashes are with others. It is easy to see why.

The aubergine (eggplant) can be cooked as a vegetable by itself or it can be combined with other ingredients in more complicated dishes. Increasing interest in Mediterranean cooking has also stimulated interest in growing these plants, and there is now good reason to grow them as a vegetable rather than just as a curiosity.

Because of its tropical origins, aubergine (eggplant) is best grown under glass unless a favoured sunny spot can be found. This is, perhaps, one reason why it has not hitherto been popular, as most greenhouses are taken up with tomatoes and cucumbers.

PLANTING IN CONTAINERS

Aubergines (eggplants) can be planted in pots or window boxes and moved outside when the weather is warmer.

ABOVE **This swelling fruit shows the glorious purple colour of the most common aubergines (egglants).**

Cultivation

Aubergines (eggplants) need a warm, sunny position, which is usually best provided in a greenhouse. Even where they can be grown outside, they need to be started off inside. Soak the seeds in water overnight before sowing, then sow in spring in modules or individual pots. The seeds will germinate in a temperature of 21–25°C/70–77°F. If seed is sown in trays, prick out the seedlings as soon as they are large enough to handle. Once they are big enough they can be planted out into growing bags (two to a bag) or into large pots in the greenhouse. If the temperature does not drop below 15°C/59°F, after hardening off they can be planted outside or moved in the pots to a sheltered position outside. The best results, however, are usually obtained by growing under glass.

Use canes or strings to support the growing plants once they get above 45–60cm/18–24in. Pinch out the tips of the plants when they reach about 38cm/15in high to encourage the formation of fruit. Keep the plants well watered, and feed once every ten days with a high-potash liquid feed once the fruit has started to develop.

Harvesting

The fruits can be picked as soon as they are large enough, which should be from mid-summer onwards in a greenhouse, but from

ABOVE **In warm areas, aubergines (eggplants) can be planted directly in the soil in the open garden.**

autumn outside. Cut each one with a piece of stalk on it, and remember that those that have lost their shine taste bitter and are not worth eating.

Storage

Aubergines (eggplants) are best eaten fresh from the plant, straight from the garden, although they can be kept for up to two weeks before use in the kitchen.

Cultivation

Sowing time spring
Sowing in modules or pots
Planting time inside mid-spring
Planting time outside early summer
Planting distance 50cm/20in
Distance between sown rows 50cm/20in
Harvesting midsummer onwards

Pests and diseases

The pests that are most likely to cause trouble are the normal greenhouse ones, such as aphids, red spider mite and whitefly. Dampen the floor of the house and spray the plants with water to maintain humid conditions to discourage red spider mite.

Varieties

'Black Beauty'	'Easter Egg'
'Black Bell'	'Long Purple'
'Black Enorma'	'Moneymaker'
'Black Prince'	'Short Tom'
'Bonica'	'Slice Rite'

aubergines

Peppers

Capsicum species

*Increasing interest in Mediterranean cooking has been accompanied by an increase in the popularity of peppers, of which the main type are the sweet peppers or bell peppers (*Capsicum annuum *Grossum Group). These are the large green, red and yellow fruits we see in supermarkets – the green peppers are, in fact, the unripe versions of the red and yellow fruit. They can be used raw or cooked, usually with all the seeds removed. The plants are bushy in habit, growing up to 75cm/30in in good conditions.*

Cultivation

Sowing time spring
Sowing in modules or pots
Planting time inside mid-spring
Planting time outside early summer
Planting distance 50cm/20in
Distance between sown rows 50cm/20in
Harvesting midsummer onwards

The chillies (*Capsicum annuum* Longum Group) are also a fairly recent crop for most gardeners, again stimulated by changes in eating habits, although they were probably the first types to be grown in Europe. The fruits, usually red in colour, are long and pointed. They are hot to the taste, becoming hotter as the fruit matures. It is the seed and the pith that are the main hot ingredients, and if these are removed, the fruit can be made milder. Chillies are often dried.

Finally, there are the hot or cayenne peppers or tabasco, which belong to a different species, *Capsicum frutescens*. These are smaller than chilli peppers and are generally even hotter. The narrow fruits, which can be yellow, orange or red in colour, are often used dried. They are the most difficult and less usual of the peppers to grow.

Peppers originated in Mexico and Central America, and they were thus a relatively late introduction to Europe – sometime late in the 15th or early 16th century. They have, however, been cultivated in their native lands for at least 7,000 years and perhaps much longer. Once in Europe, they were adopted far more readily in the Mediterranean countries, where they are still used more than in northern Europe.

Peppers can be grown outside in warmer districts, but generally they do best under glass. If they are grown outside, the best method is to grow them in containers or growing bags, in a warm, sheltered position, against a south-facing wall. In warmer areas they can be grown in a border.

Cultivation

Seed should be sown in spring in a propagator, set at about 18°C/65°F. They can be sown in modules, individual pots or trays. If trays are used, prick out the resulting seedlings as soon as they are large enough to handle. As soon as they are big enough they can be transferred to growing bags (two or three to a bag) or into large pots. The advantage of pots is that they can easily be moved outside if the weather is warm enough. Pinch out the tops of the young plants when they get to 15–20cm/6–8in to make them bush out. If the bushes get above 45–50cm/18–20in they may need to be supported with canes or strings. If they are grown in an outside bed, plant them out in early summer when the temperature has warmed up and set them at 50cm/20in intervals in a fertile, but free-draining soil. Keep the peppers well watered and feed every ten days with a high-potash liquid feed once the fruits start to swell.

Harvesting

Start picking in mid- to late summer when the fruits are large enough – for peppers this is usually when they are about the size of a tennis ball. They can be harvested when they are green or have changed to

LEFT **Green peppers are the unripe fruit, yellow peppers are the first stage in the ripening process, and red peppers are the final stage.**

their final red or yellow coloration. Some cultivars are best picked green. The hot or cayenne peppers should be fully ripe and coloured before they are picked. Cut the fruit so that about 2.5cm/1in of stalk is left.

Storage

Sweet peppers are best eaten straight from the plant, but they can be kept for up to two weeks before being used. Other types of pepper can be dried.

Pests and diseases

The pests that are most likely to cause trouble are the usual greenhouse ones such as aphids, red spider mite and whitefly. Dampen the floor of the house and spray the plants with water to maintain humid conditions to discourage red spider mite. Both inside and outside the greenhouse, however, the major problem is likely to be aphids on the young shoots.

ABOVE **Not all peppers are the evenly shaped fruit that we find in our supermarkets.**

Varieties

Sweet peppers	Chilli peppers
'Ace'	Sometime listed simply as chillies.
'Antaro'	'Apache"
'Ariane'	'De Fresno Chilli Grande'
'Bell Boy'	'Hot Gold Spike'
'Bendigo'	'Hot Mexican'
'California Wonder'	'Red Chilli'
'Canape'	'Serrano Chilli'
'Clio'	**Cayenne peppers**
'Delphin'	Often listed simply as cayenne.
'Gypsy'	'Cayenne Large Red'
'Hungarian Wax'	'Cayenne Long Slim'
'Luteus'	'Red Cherry Small'
'Marconi'	'Super Cayenne'
'New Ace'	'Tabasco'
'Redskin'	
'Sweet Spanish Mixed'	
'Yellow Lantern'	

Sweet Corn (Corn)

Zea mays

*Sweet corn, maize or corn-on-the-cob (*Zea mays*) is a cereal. It is a rather dramatic plant, growing up to 1.5m/5ft or more. The airy spikes of male flowers decorate the top of the plant, and the cobs, with their female flowers, form where the broad strap-like leaves join the main stem. They have an ornamental quality that makes them worth growing in the decorative kitchen garden.*

ABOVE **The dying tassel of a female flower hangs from the developing cob. This is an indication that the cob is ready for harvesting. Twist the cobs so that they snap off from the stem.**

Although maize has a long history, going back to prehistoric times, it is a relatively recent introduction to Europe. This is because it comes from Mexico and it was only after the Spanish Conquest in the early 16th century that it was brought to the Old World. In Europe the main varieties are yellow or yellow and white, but in the Americas, where it has had such a long tradition, there are many more varieties, often with quite deeply coloured seeds, including black.

Because of its size, sweet corn (corn) takes up a lot of space in the garden, but the superior taste of fresh sweet corn, compared with corn bought in the shops, which may be days old, makes it worth trying to find the space, even if it is only for a few plants. Sweet corn needs to be grown in a block rather than in rows, which increases the chances of pollen falling from the higher male flowers onto the female ones below. This may be inconvenient in terms of the shape of your vegetable garden, but it is worth making the effort to find room.

Sweet corn (corn) needs as long a growing season as possible, but it is, unfortunately, frost tender, so the plants have to be started off under glass and transferred to open ground only when there is no further danger of frost. Seed can be sown directly into the soil, but this may not give a long enough season in some regions. Seed often carries a powdery fungicide to stop it from rotting in wet soils.

Cultivation

Sweet corn (corn) needs a warm, sunny position, sheltered from strong winds. The soil should be free draining and well prepared with rotted organic material. Sow the seeds in individual pots under glass in mid-spring, and germinate under gentle heat of 13–15°C/55–59°F. Harden off the plants before planting out in early summer or whenever there is no likelihood of frost. Plant in a block and set 30cm/12in apart.

Seed sown outside should be sown in late spring and protected by cloches. Sow two seeds together at 30cm/12in intervals in a block rather than a row. After germination remove the weaker seedling.

Once established, growing plants should have earth drawn up around the stems for about 15cm/6in or more to support them against wind in exposed areas. Avoid deep hoeing – this can disturb the shallow roots.

LEFT **These young sweet corn (corn) plants have been grown from seed under glass and then planted out in a block.**

Cultivation

Sowing time inside mid-spring
Sowing time outside early summer
Sowing inside in modules or pots
Planting-out time early summer
Planting and sowing distance 30cm/12in
Distance between sown rows 30cm/12in
Harvesting autumn

Varieties

'Butterscotch'	'Morning Sun'
'Dawn'	'Northern Belle'
'Dynasty'	'Pilot'
'Earliking'	'Sundance'
'Fiesta'	'Sunrise'
'Honeycomb'	'Sugar Boy'
'Kelvedon Glory'	'Sweet 77'
'Miracle'	'Yukon'

LEFT **These maturing sweet corn (corn) plants clearly show the spiky male flowers which are situated higher up than the female flowers.**

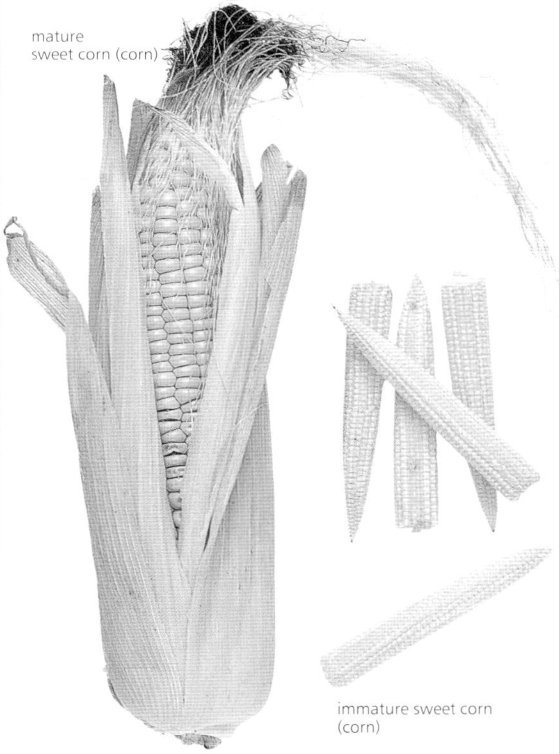

Harvesting

Harvest sweet corn (corn) when the tassels on the cobs begin to turn brown. Twist the cobs so that they snap off from the stem.

Storage

Sweet corn (corn) is best when cooked and eaten straight from the plant, although the cobs will keep a few days after they have been harvested. Cobs can also be frozen and then kept for winter use.

Pests and diseases

The main problem with sweet corn (corn) comes from mice and birds, which steal the seed. Frit fly and corn smut are the only other likely troubles, but fortunately they are not common.

Tomatoes

Lycopersicon esculentum

Tomatoes are probably the most widely grown of all vegetables. Even people without a garden often manage to grow a plant or two on a balcony or patio. One reason for this is that tomatoes are relatively easy to grow, but another must surely be that supermarket-bought tomatoes bear little resemblance to what a gardener knows as a tomato – there is very little relationship between the two flavours. Another reason may well be the sheer range of tomatoes that you can now grow. They come in all manner of tastes, sizes and colours, and even some of the old-fashioned varieties that have the best flavours are becoming more readily available. The largest, such as the beefsteak tomatoes, can weigh up to 450g/1lb each, while the smallest are not much more than the size of grapes.

ABOVE **Cordon tomatoes should be well supported. These special spirals support the plant without the necessity of tying them.**

Tomatoes can either be grown on cordons (upright plants) or as bushes. It is well worth not only growing your own particular favourite varieties each year, but also experimenting with at least one new one. This may well result in a glut of tomatoes, but they are wonderful things to give away.

Tomatoes are a very close relation to the potato. (If you want to try your skill at grafting, graft a young tomato plant onto one of the stems of a potato plant; it is actually possible to get potatoes underground and tomatoes above.) Like the potato, the tomato comes from South America, where it had probably been grown for centuries before it was bought to Europe in the 16th century. Because they belong to the family Solanaceae, of which deadly nightshade is also a member, they were at first treated with suspicion in Europe and used as ornamental plants. However, once they were accepted, it was the Mediterranean countries that used them most often in their cuisine. They do, of course, make very decorative plants, with their red, yellow or green fruits, and they are a valuable addition to potagers and other ornamental gardens.

Tomatoes are used widely both in raw and cooked dishes. They can even be used in their unripened state, so that any that have not ripened by the time the frosts arrive can still be used.

Tomatoes are half-hardy and can be grown under glass or outside. Earlier and later crops, as well as heavier ones, are obtained under glass, but outside crops often taste better, particularly if the summer has been hot and the fruit has ripened well.

Cultivation

If you are growing under glass, sow the seed in mid-spring in a very gentle heat or an unheated greenhouse. An earlier start can be made in a heated greenhouse to obtain earlier crops. As soon as they are big enough to handle, prick out the seedlings into individual pots. When the plants are large enough, transfer them to growing bags, large pots or a greenhouse border.

LEFT **A bed of tomato plants with good exposure to the sun for ripening.**

USING GROWING BAGS

Tomatoes can be grown in bags of compost (soil mix).

PINCHING OUT SIDE SHOOTS

The side shoots on cordon varieties should be pinched or cut out.

HARVESTING

Harvest tomatoes when they are ripe, which will usually be when they turn red. Leave the stalk on.

RIPENING TOMATOES

At the end of the season, dig up any remaining plants and hang them upside down under protection to ripen.

(The soil will need changing, preferably every year, if tomatoes are planted directly into a border.) Arrange some form of support, such as strings or canes, for the tomatoes to be tied to as they grow. Remove any side shoots as they appear. Keep well watered and feed every ten days with a high-potash liquid fertilizer once the fruits begin to swell. Pinch out the top of the plant when it reaches the glass.

For cordons grown outdoors, the same procedure as above is followed, except that the plants are hardened off before being planted out, which should not be until after the last of the frosts. They should be in an open, sunny position and a fertile soil. Bush forms are treated in the same way, except that there is no need to remove the side shoots. They will also benefit from a straw mulch to keep the fruit off the soil. The end of the season usually comes before all the fruit has ripened. Either use them in recipes that call for unripe tomatoes or dig up the whole cordon or bush and hang it upside down in a greenhouse or frost-free shed so that the last ones ripen. Alternatively, cut down the plant from its support, lay it on a bed of straw and cover with a cloche.

Harvesting

Pick the tomatoes as they ripen, which will usually be when they turn red. At this stage they should come away, bringing a short piece of stem, simply by twisting them.

Storage

Tomatoes are best eaten straight from the plants, although they will keep for a few days. They can be frozen, but then used only in cooked dishes as they lose their firmness.

Pests and diseases

Tomatoes are cursed with a number of pests and diseases. Fortunately, they are generally not troublesome enough to deter those who grow them. Pests include aphids, potato cyst eelworm, whitefly and red spider mite. Diseases include tomato blight, grey mould, potato mosaic virus, greenback, tomato leaf mould and scald. Many problems can be avoided by good ventilation. Cracked fruit is often caused by uneven watering.

Cultivation

Indoors
Sowing time early to mid-spring
Sowing inside in modules or pots
Planting time mid- to late spring
Planting and sowing distance 45cm/18in
Harvesting summer onwards

Outdoors
Sowing time inside mid-spring
Planting-out time early summer
Planting distance (cordon) 45cm/18in
Planting distance (bush) 60cm/24in
Distance between sown rows 75cm/30in
Harvesting late summer onwards

Varieties

Inside
'Aromata'
'Big Boy'
'Buffalo'
'Dombito'
'Eurocross'
'Grenadier'
'Libra'
'Nimbus'
'Shirley'
'Super Sweet'

Inside or outside (cordon)
'Ailsa Craig'
'Alicante'
'Gardener's Delight'
'Golden Sunrise'
'Harbinger'
'Mirabelle'
'Moneymaker'
'Sungold'
'Tigarella'

Outside (cordon)
'Marmande'
'Outdoor Girl'

Outside (bush)
'Golden Sunrise'
'Ida Gold'
'Incas'
'Marmande Super'
'Red Alert'
'The Amateur'
'Tornado'
'Totem'
'Tumbler'

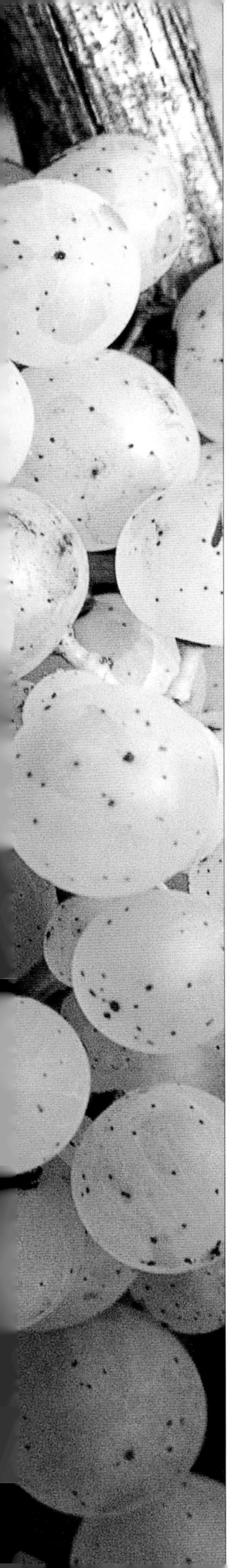

growing fruit

Fruit can be one of the most enjoyable crops that comes from the kitchen garden, and yet it is probably the most neglected area of gardening. It is difficult to know why this should be the case. In the past, it may have been that fruit was considered to take up too much space, but the modern cultivars now available even make it possible to grow apple trees in containers on a balcony.

One possible reason for people's reluctance to grow fruit is that it can take time to see results. An apple tree may take several years before it produces fruit in any quantity. However, the wait is usually worth it because fresh fruit straight from the plant is one of the great joys of life. Another reason could be that many gardeners are put off by what they see as the complicated art of pruning. But most people perform tasks that are far more complicated than this, and soon pruning becomes second nature.

One point to bear in mind if you are considering planting fruit trees or bushes is that they can be very decorative, especially trained as fans or espaliers, for example. Full-sized fruit trees also have their advantages – they are wonderful for sitting under on hot summer days.

Growing Fruit Trees and Bushes

Fruit tends to be the poor relation in the garden, possibly because it can take up large amounts of space. However, fresh fruit is even more delightful than fresh vegetables and it need not take up as much space as you might think.

ABOVE **Strawberries can be grown in containers. If these are kept under glass, as here, then an early crop can be obtained.**

Where to grow your fruit

The traditional place to grow fruit is in a fruit garden, a separate area of the garden that is devoted to fruit. This has one especial advantage in that it can be completely protected in a fruit cage. Scattering the fruit over the whole garden means that individual plants have to be protected, which can be rather tedious.

Apart from the protection they require, however, there is no reason for keeping the fruit together. In a decorative kitchen garden, fruit can be mixed in with the vegetables, trees and standard bushes providing visual height in individual beds. Many fruit trees can also be grown along walls or fences, and they can be used as dividers or screens between various parts of the garden. If you have a small garden and want a shady tree to sit under, why not plant an apple tree rather than a species that is solely ornamental?

Choosing fruit

As long as it will grow in your garden, there is nothing to prevent you choosing whatever fruit you want. There is a slight complication in that some tree fruits need pollinators to make sure that the fruit is set, and this means that if you want a particular apple you may have to have another apple to act as a pollinator. This may not be necessary if your neighbour has a compatible tree.

Ground preparation

Most fruit trees and bushes are likely to remain in the ground for a long time and so it is important that the soil is thoroughly prepared. It is particularly important that all perennial weeds are removed. If any small piece is left in the ground it is bound to regrow and is likely to be difficult to extract from around the roots of the tree or bush without digging them up.

Another reason for preparing the ground thoroughly is to make sure that there is plenty of organic material tucked right down among the roots of the plants. This will help keep the soil moist as well as giving a continuous supply of nutrients until the plants are established. Once the tree and shrubs are planted, any organic material will have to be applied to the soil's surface and taken down by the worms. Double dig the soil if possible, incorporating as much well-rotted organic material as you can spare. Take this opportunity to make sure that all perennial weeds are removed. If the ground is heavy and it is

PLANTING A FRUIT TREE OR BUSH

When planting a fruit tree or bush, always ensure that it is planted at the same depth as it was in its container or in its nursery bed.

TYING IN A NEWLY PLANTED TREE

Using tree ties, ensure that a newly planted tree is firmly anchored to a stake. Attach the tie approximately 30cm/12in above the ground.

ABOVE **Even apple trees can be grown in containers. However, it is essential to water them every day, and at least twice on hot dry days.**

likely to be difficult to remove the weeds, spraying some time before digging may be the only answer to cleaning the soil.

Planting

As long as the weather is neither too wet nor too cold the best time to plant fruit trees and bushes is between late autumn and mid-spring. If bare-rooted plants are delivered when it is impossible to plant, heel them into a spare piece of the vegetable garden until they can be planted in their permanent position. Container-grown plants can be planted at other times of the year, but they need more attention to make sure that they survive.

Fruit trees and bushes should be planted to the same depth as they were in their pots or nursery bed when you purchased them. If a tree needs staking, place the stake in the ground before planting. Water the plants in thoroughly and keep them watered in dry weather until they are firmly established. Apply a mulch around the base of the plant in order to help preserve moisture as well as to keep the weeds down. Remove any weeds that do appear.

Try to keep a record of what you have planted. Fruit trees and bushes often outlive any label that comes with them, and it is often annoying when asked for the variety of an apple or raspberry, for example, when you cannot remember. A notebook with details of the variety, where you purchased the plant as well as the date on which you planted it, will be of future interest.

TOP-DRESSING FRUIT BUSHES

In the autumn, and again in the spring, top-dress fruit bushes with a layer of well-rotted organic material such as farmyard manure.

MULCHING STRAWBERRIES

Strawberries can be grown through a black polythene (plastic) mulch. This not only protects the fruit from mud-splashes, but also reduces the need for weeding and watering.

Supporting Fruit Trees and Shrubs

Once they are established, some fruit shrubs and most trees are free-standing, but most benefit from, and some require, permanent support. If this is provided adequately and properly from the start, these supports should last many years.

ABOVE **This apple tree is being supported by wires in a very decorative manner.**

Wall and fence fruit

Several types of trees and shrubs can be trained flat against walls or fences. The effects created can be decorative. These plants will need some means of holding them against the wall, and this usually takes the form of wires. To make sure that the framework lasts as long as possible use a galvanized wire, which will not corrode. The wire is held in place by vine eyes, of which there are several types available. Some are flat, metal spikes, which are hammered into the brickwork, while others are screw eyes, which are screwed into wall plugs that have been inserted into holes in the brick or stonework of the wall. They can be screwed directly into wooden fences. The eyes are placed 60–90cm/ 2–3ft apart and a wire led through the hole in each one. The wire is secured at the end eyes by pulling it back and twisting it around itself or by using a tensioning screw that can be tightened to tension the wire. The wires should be parallel to each other and 30–45cm/12–18in apart.

Free-standing wirework

Berried fruit – like raspberries, blackberries and the various hybrid berries – and grapes need a permanent framework. They are grown in the open, and it is necessary to build a structure that will carry the supporting wires. The end posts are the most important part of the structure because they take a strain in one direction only, and if they are not secured properly they can be pulled from the ground. Each post should be treated with a preservative to prolong its life. The end posts should be sunk into the ground by at least 60cm/ 24in and braced with another post set at an angle. Intermediate posts, every 2m/6ft or so, are set to a similar depth but do not need bracing. Galvanized wire is stretched along the length of the row, at 30cm/12in intervals, the first wire being 60cm/24in from the ground. These wires should be as taut as possible. They can be fixed with staples, or holes can be drilled in the posts and eye-bolts inserted, which can be used to tension the wire by tightening the nut on the outside of the end posts.

Individual support

Trees need individual support when they are first planted. In exposed positions some shrub fruit, especially standards, will also benefit from being supported.

SUPPORTING A TREE AGAINST A WALL

1 To support trees against walls, use wires held by vine eyes. Depending on the type of vine eye, either knock them into the wall or drill and plug before screwing them in.

2 Pass galvanized wire through the holes in the eyes and fasten to the end ones, keeping the wire as tight as possible.

The stake should be inserted before the tree is planted so that there is no chance of damaging the roots. Although the stake should be knocked well into the ground, there need only be about 45cm/18in above ground. Current practice is to support trees low down, at about 30cm/12in above the ground, so that the lower part of the tree and, more importantly, the rootball, are held in place, while the top is allowed to move freely, gaining strength as it does so.

Tie the tree to the stake, using a proper tree tie that will provide good support, but at the same time not cut into or chafe the trunk of the tree. It is important that you check at least twice a year that the tie is not too tight and cutting into the growing trunk. Adjust the tie if necessary.

If the tree is already in position, place the stake at an angle to the trunk so that it enters the ground some way from its base in order to avoid damaging the tree's roots. Alternatively, insert two posts, each some distance from, and on either side of, the trunk. Fix a crossbar between these two posts, and then tie the tree to this.

BELOW **The branches of small apple trees can be trained to spread by tying them down with string tied to the trunk.**

STAKING FRUIT

1 Knock a stout post well into the ground at the end of the row. An alternative is to dig a hole and insert the post before refilling and ramming down the earth.

2 Knock another post at a 45° angle to the vertical to act as a support to the upright post. Nail it firmly so that the upright post is rigid and will not be pulled by tight wires.

3 Fasten the wires around one end post and pull tight along the row stapling it to each post. Keep the wire as taut as possible. If necessary, use eye-bolts on the end posts to tension the wire.

4 Fasten the canes – in this case raspberry canes – to the wire with string or plant ties. Space the canes out evenly along the wire so that the maximum amount of light reaches the leaves.

Pruning Fruit Trees and Bushes

Pruning is a subject that terrifies many gardeners. Indeed, many gardeners fail to prune at all, to the detriment of the tree or the bush and to their subsequent crops. Like so many other things connected with gardening it is largely a question of experience. Once you have practised it a couple of times, you will be able to do it without any trouble at all.

Basic pruning cuts

Although trees and shrubs need different methods of pruning and training, the pruning cuts are the same in all instances. Always cut a stem just above a bud and make sure that the cut is angled away from the bud.

Branches that are large enough to be cut with a saw are usually cut across the branch at right angles. If the branch is thick and heavy and likely to break, thereby splitting the wood before the cut is complete, the sawing is done in three separate stages. The first cut is made on the underside of the branch, 5cm/2in from the final cutting position. The second cut is made slightly further out along the branch, this time from above, by sawing down until the branch splits along to the first cut and is then severed. The final cut can be made straight through from the top because there is now no weight to cause splitting.

Shapes

There are so many different ways of pruning and training fruit trees and bushes that it is impossible to explain every case here. Detailed pruning advice is given for individual fruits in the Directory of Fruit section

Rootstocks

The rootstock on which a fruit tree grows affects the size and rate of growth of the tree. It is important that you get the right stock for the type of tree you want to grow. Always check with the supplier that the tree or bush is suitable for your needs.

ABOVE **A standard apple tree is a particularly good shape for a traditional garden. It also provides shade in the summer.**

Fruit Tree and Bush Shapes

Standard trees are full-sized trees with a natural shape. These need space as they can grow large, but they create good shade for sitting under.

Half-standard trees are similar to standard trees, but, as the name implies, they are smaller.

Bush trees are much smaller than standards but are still quite large for a small garden. The trees are quite short but bushy with an open centre.

Spindle-bush trees are short – to 2.1m/7ft high – and cone shaped, with a central leader and side branches that are tied down to make them spread.

Dwarf pyramid trees are short growing and pruned into a pyramid shape. In general, more branches are retained than in the similarly shaped spindle-bush trees.

Fan trees or bushes are trained so that the branches are in a two-dimensional fan, radiating from the top of a short trunk. They are grown against a wall, a fence or post-and-wire supports.

Espalier trees or bushes are trained flat against a wall, a fence or post-and-wire supports. They have a main trunk and parallel branches coming from it at right angles.

Cordon trees or bushes consist of a single main stem. They are usually trained at 45° to the ground, but they can be also be vertical.

Double cordon trees or bushes are similar to ordinary cordons, except two shoots are trained vertically, forming a U-shape.

Triple cordons are similar to ordinary cordons, except three stems are trained vertically.

Standard bushes are grafted onto a single tall stem to give it a "lollipop" appearance.

ABOVE **Pears are the perfect fruit to grow in all manner of decorative shapes. Here, the pear is being trained into a crown shape.**

TOP LEFT **An espaliered pear tree on wire supports. Many other fruit trees can be trained in the same decorative way.**

OPPOSITE PAGE, TOP **This pear tree has been beautifully trained into a fan. The fan is supported on wires, but it could also be grown against a wall.**

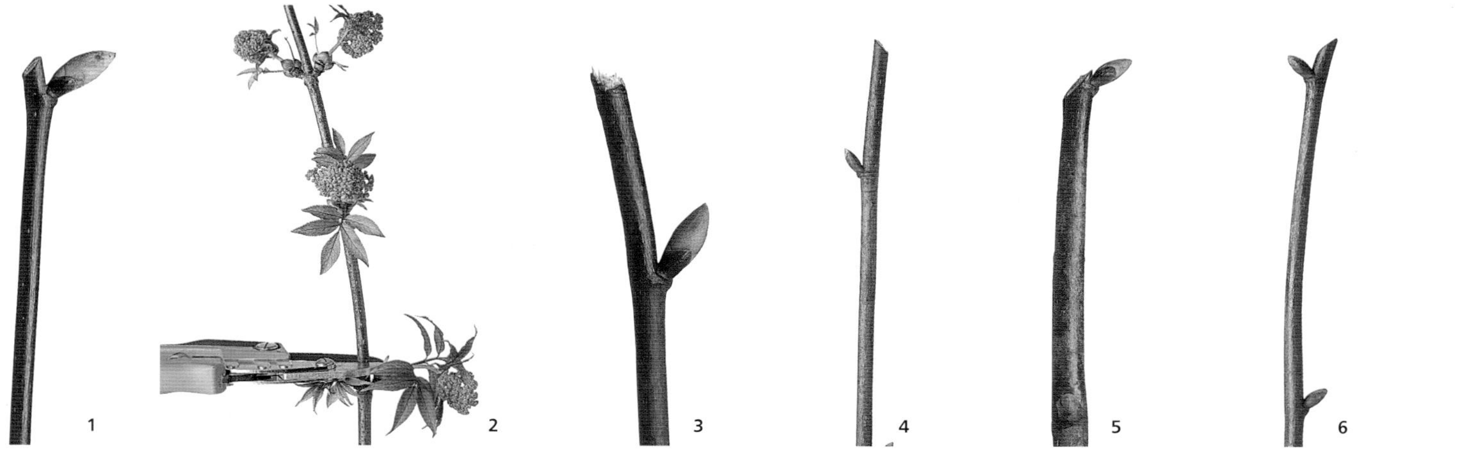

Good and Bad Pruning Cuts

1 A good pruning cut is made just above a strong bud, about 3mm/⅛in above the bud. It should be a slanting cut, with the higher end above the bud. The bud should generally be outward bound from the plant rather than inward; the latter will throw its shoot into the plant, crossing and rubbing against others, which should be avoided. This is an easy technique and you can practise it on any stem.

2 If the stem has buds or leaves opposite each other, make the cut horizontal, about 3mm/⅛in above the buds.

3 Always use a sharp pair of secateurs (pruners). Blunt ones will produce a ragged or bruised cut, which is likely to introduce disease into the plant.

4 Do not cut too far above a bud. The piece of stem above the bud is likely to die back and the stem may well die back even further, causing the loss of the whole stem.

5 Do not cut too close to the bud otherwise the bud might be damaged by the secateurs (pruners) or disease might enter. Too close a cut is likely to cause the stem to die back to the next bud.

6 It is bad practice to slope the cut towards the bud as this makes the stem above the bud too long, which is likely to cause dieback. It also sheds rain on to the bud, which may cause problems.

Protecting Fruit

Gardeners are not the only animals to like fruit. Many others, birds in particular, do so as well, and the only way to make sure that there is enough left for the gardener to enjoy is to protect the fruit bushes and trees in some way. The only practical way to do this is to put some form of physical barrier between the predators and the fruit.

ABOVE **A tunnel of wire netting can be used to protect low-growing strawberries. The netting can be in short sections for easy removal and storage.**

Fruit cages

There is no doubt that the easiest way to protect fruit is with a complete cage. The advantage of this is that it covers the area completely and that the gardener can walk around within it, maintaining the bushes or harvesting the fruit. When individual protection is provided, each cover has to be removed in turn, which can be tiresome, especially if netting snags on branches.

The only problem with caging on a large scale is that it can be expensive. If you have every intention of leaving the fruit cage where it is, it might be more economical in the long term to build a cage with long-lasting materials. Use thick posts and make the covering from galvanized wire netting, which, although more expensive than plastic, will outlive many replacements of its plastic equivalent.

Ready-made fruit cages are expensive but they still probably work out cheaper than making one of your own, unless, of course, you have access to free materials, such as posts. Fruit cages are supplied in kit form and are easy to erect; they can usually be ordered to whatever size you require. Make sure that there are no gaps in the netting and that it is well pegged down or buried at the base because birds have a knack of finding the smallest hole to squeeze through.

A homemade fruit cage is time-consuming to construct, but you can make it fit any shape and cover any area you want. Metal posts, such as scaffolding poles, will last for ever but most gardeners find that wooden poles are more practical. They should be sturdy and treated at their base with preservative. Each should be let into the ground by about 60cm/24in for security, because the netting will act as a sail, putting great pressure on the posts in strong winds.
The covering can be plastic netting, but galvanized wire netting will last longer and be less likely to tear accidentally. Some gardeners like to remove the top covering to allow birds in to eat pests when the fruit is not actually ripening, and if you want to do this, use wire sides and a plastic netting for the top. Another reason for being able to remove the top covering in winter, especially if it is plastic, is that a heavy fall of snow can

LEFT **A fruit cage is expensive but it is the only really effective way of protecting fruit from birds.**

ABOVE **Strawberries can be protected against frost with cloches.**

LEFT **Fruit trees and bushes trained against a wall or fence can be protected with a home-made frame, as seen here. A similar frame can be covered with polythene (plastic) to protect the blossom from frosts.**

stretch and break it. The tops of the poles are best covered with a smooth rounded object – the bottom of a plastic drinks bottle is ideal – and although it may look ugly, it will prevent the plastic netting from being chaffed and worn as the wind moves it against the posts.

Make a door wide enough to get a wheelbarrow through and make certain that it fits well, or birds will get in.

Low-level protection

It is easier to provide protection for individual crops when low-level protection is required because less material is needed. The simplest method is to bend some wire-netting into an inverted U-shape and peg it to the ground with wires. This works well for strawberries. Alternatively, put short stakes in the ground at intervals all round and in the middle of the crop and drape plastic netting over this.

Draped netting

There is no satisfactory way of protecting taller, free-growing subjects, such as fruit bushes or trees. Draping them with netting is the only possible method, but gaps are usually left and the netting snags on twigs and shoots

If a fruit is growing against a wall or fence, then the netting can be held away from the plant by building a simple frame, and this can also be covered with polythene (plastic) in the spring in order to protect the blossom against frost.

Non-netting protection

Netting is the only satisfactory way to protect fruit crops in the garden. Commercial methods, such as bangers, are impracticable in a domestic garden. Humming wires have a limited success but do not really work. Covering the bushes with threads may keep the birds off but they make harvesting awkward and they are difficult to remove for pruning.

The traditional scarecrow makes a good feature in the garden, but it has no success in deterring birds and animals. Plastic birds of prey or owls at strategic points often work well for a while, but birds soon get used to them.

Propagation

While most gardeners do not have much space to increase their stock, and many do not need to replace their tree fruit, they need to know how to propagate soft fruits, so that they can be replaced from time to time. The techniques involved are all fairly simple to master.

ABOVE **This strawberry plant is producing plenty of runners, which root to produce a number of different plants.**

Hardwood cuttings

Currants, gooseberries, blueberries and grape vines are usually increased by taking hardwood cuttings. This process does not need any propagators or other equipment other than a pair of secateurs (pruners) or a sharp knife.

The best time for taking hardwood cuttings is autumn, preferably early autumn. Select a few shoots that have grown during the previous year and are now firm and well-ripened. They should be straight and about 30cm/12in long.

Choose a sheltered site, away from drying winds and hot sun. Make a narrow trench by inserting a spade into the soil and pushing it to one side to open up a narrow V-shaped slit. If the soil is heavy, trickle some clean sharp sand into the bottom of the slit and insert the cuttings. Place them about 15cm/6in apart, planting them so that about half of the cutting is below ground. Place the spade into the ground about 10cm/4in away from the initial slit and lever it so that the slit closes up, firmly holding the cuttings. Firm down the soil gently with your feet.

By the next autumn the cuttings should have rooted. They can be dug up and transplanted to their final positions or moved to a nursery bed for another year.

Layering

Blackberries and hybrid berries are best increased by the simple process of layering, as are strawberries, although the latter are usually obliging enough to do it themselves, leaving the gardener to transplant the new plants.

At some time during the growing season choose a healthy blackberry cane that is long enough to touch the ground. At the point where the tip makes contact with the soil, dig a hole about 10cm/4in deep. Place the tip in it and bury it by replacing the soil. If it is in an exposed position and it is possible that the cane will be blown or knocked out of the ground, you can secure it with a peg, although this is not normally necessary. By late autumn the tip will have rooted. Cut the new plant from its parent shoot, about 30cm/12in from the ground. Dig up the young plant and transplant it to its fruiting position.

If you want to grow a few new plants in pots, perhaps for selling, the young plant can be transplanted directly into a pot. However, it is possible to cut out this stage by burying the tip of the parent cane into a pot of potting compost (soil mix) instead of a hole in the ground; it will root just as easily. The pot can be let into the ground, which will prevent it from being knocked over and it will not dry out as quickly as it would if left standing on the ground.

Strawberries can be treated in a similar way. After fruiting they send out runners, which will drop roots at intervals along their length to produce new plants. To make sure that they root, you can peg them down or cover a short length of runner with soil, but

LAYERING

1 Blackberries, hybrid berries and strawberries can all be increased by layering. Choose a healthy shoot, dig a hole near the tip and then bury it.

2 After a short period the tip will have produced roots. It can then be cut from the parent plant and replanted where required.

3 If you would like to have potted specimens, then bury a flowerpot in the ground, fill it with compost (soil mix) and bury the tip in this.

this is usually unnecessary as the plant will root itself quite naturally. Again, the runners can be pegged into pots of compost (soil mix) if you want ready-potted plants.

Division

Raspberries are usually increased by division. It is a simple matter to lift some of the suckers that emerge a little way from the parent plant. In the autumn dig up a healthy, strong-growing sucker and cut through the root that is still attached to the main clump. Replant this in its fruiting position. It is advisable never to divide diseased plants for replanting. If you are in any doubt, it is always better to start from scratch, using certified disease-free stock that has been sold by a reputable nursery.

Methods of Propagation

Division Blackberries, hybrid berries, raspberries and strawberries

Layering Blackberries, hybrid berries and strawberries

Hardwood Cuttings Blackcurrants, gooseberries, grapes, red currants and white currants

Semi-ripe Cuttings Blueberries

Grafting Tree fruits

TAKING HARDWOOD CUTTTINGS

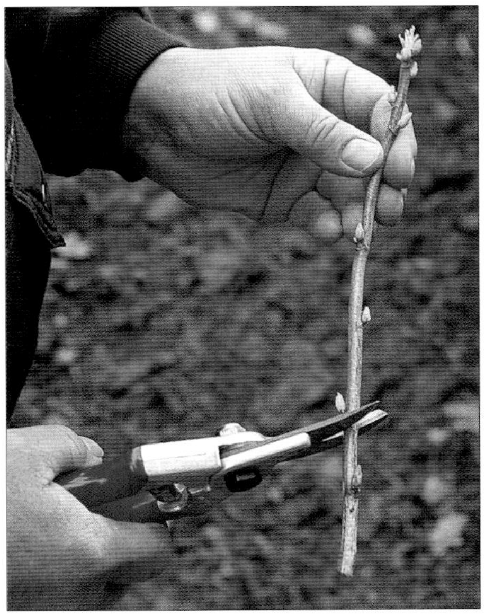

1 Take the hardwood cuttings in the autumn, with each cutting measuring approximately 30cm/12in in length. Cut the cutting off just below a bud.

2 Dig a slit trench by pushing a spade into the ground and levering it backwards and forwards. If the ground is heavier, open the slit a bit more and part fill it with some clean sharp sand.

3 Place the cuttings vertically in the trench at about 15cm (6in) intervals.

4 Dig the spade in a short distance from the trench and lever it so that the slit closes up.

5 Firm down the soil around the cuttings with your foot and generally tidy up the surface of the soil with a rake.

Harvesting and Storing Fruit

The best fruit is always the crop you pick and pop straight into your mouth. Given kind weather and a certain amount of skill on the gardener's part, however, there should be sufficient fruit not only to supply the kitchen but also to store for later use.

Harvesting

Fruit should be properly ripe before it is harvested for immediate use. There is little point in picking it early and leaving it to ripen – it will always ripen better on the stem. Fruit for storing should be mature and ripe – but do not pick at the very peak of ripeness, aim for just a little before. This is a matter of judgement and will come with experience. The time to pick is when the fruit comes away easily in the hand. Apples, for example, will come free with a little twist of the wrist, while raspberries will come away when twisted with the fingers.

With the exception of cane fruit, such as raspberries and blackberries, most fruit is picked with the stalks left on. Normally fruit is picked individually, but the various types of currant and grapes are usually picked in bunches. Pick fruit during dry weather and be careful not to bruise or otherwise damage it.

Storing

On the whole, the only types of fruit that can be satisfactorily stored without some method of preservation are apples, pears and quinces, and it is worth remembering that some varieties of fruit store better than others. 'Cox's Orange Pippin' apples, for example, can be kept until spring, but 'Beauty of Bath' apples have to be eaten right away, because they last not much longer than a week. As a general rule, early maturing apples do not store, but later ones do.

ABOVE **Apples are removed with a twist of the wrist. All fruits, other than cane fruit such as raspberries and blackberries, are picked with the stalks left on.**

Keep only fruit that is in perfect condition and throw out any that are marked or beginning to rot. Place the apples or pears in trays separated with paper so that they do not touch each other. Place the trays in a cool, dark place. Check periodically and throw out any fruit that is beginning to rot. Some apples will shrivel in storage and it is better to wrap these individually in greaseproof paper or to place several in a polythene (plastic) bag that has a few small holes in it.

ABOVE AND LEFT **Soft fruit, such as strawberries, raspberries and gooseberries should be carefully picked between thumb and finger. The fruit may then be placed in small individual containers so that they are not squashed or bruised.**

Storing Fruit

Apples, pears and quinces

Store in a cool place for up to 12 months, depending on the variety.

All other fruit

Eat immediately or freeze. Alternatively, preserve fruit by bottling or making into jam. Fruit can be kept for up to 12 months, depending on the method of preservation that has been used.

RIGHT **A filbert tree (*Corylus maxima*) is a rare but welcome sight in the garden. The variety shown here is 'Purpurea'.**

Do not place quinces close to apples and pears because the strong aroma will taint the other fruit. Store quinces in open trays.

Freezing

It is possible to freeze most fruit. However, although the taste will remain, many will lose their "solid" appearance when thawed and are, therefore, better used for cooking than for eating raw. Soft fruits are the easiest to freeze, but it is also possible to freeze apples, although it is best to cut them up or even cook and purée them before freezing.

Again, only choose sound fruit. Place the fruit on trays so that they are not touching each other and then put them in the freezer. Once frozen, they can be put into a bag. The fruit can be put straight into a bag before freezing, but they are likely to stick together and so the whole batch will have to be used at once. If you have no room for trays, split the fruit up into small usable quantities and place each batch of fruit in an individual bag.

Preserving

Freezing is a modern method of preserving fruit, but there are also a number of traditional ways. Some fruits, such as apples and pears, can be dried while others, such as plums and gooseberries, can be bottled. Another way is to turn the fruit into chutneys or jams. All these methods are dealt with in good cookery books.

ABOVE **Apples, pears and quinces can be stored in trays in a cool place. It is best if they are laid on paper so that the individual fruits do not touch. The length of storage time depends on the variety.**

ABOVE **With the exception of apples, pears and quinces, most fruit cannot be kept for any length of time without some form of preserving. The simplest method of preserving fruit is to freeze it.**

Preserving and Bottling Fruit

Fresh fruit can be preserved in a variety of ways, giving you delicious, and often economical, jams, jellies, preserves and chutneys the whole year through. Making jams and jellies is a perfect way to deal with a glut of fruit and they have an intensity of flavour rare in commercial varieties.

ABOVE **Poached spiced plums with lemons are preserved in brandy.**

Fruit preserves

Jams contain whole fruits or pieces of fruit, while jellies are made from the strained liquid produced during the initial cooking of the fruit. Windfall and end-of-season fruit makes good chutney, but always choose good-quality, unbruised fruit for bottling. As a rule, when bottling fruit, the syrup should just cover the surface.

Home-made candied fruit, so much better than purchased mixed peel, is best made when tbe new season's citrus fruit is available. Pickles, chutneys and relishes are piquant and easy to make. Always use stainless steel or enamelled pans that will not react with the vinegar or the acid in the fruit. Don't forget to make extra quantities, as jams and preserves make excellent and much appreciated gifts.

Choosing containers

Glass jars and bottles are a popular choice for all kinds of preserves because they are durable and versatile, enhancing the appearance of their contents. Modern recycled glass has many of the qualities of antique glass, such as colourings, and is inexpensive. Earthenware jars and pots are also good choices for chutneys and home-made mustards. Specially made preserving jars are best for bottled fruit and vegetables and can be reused. You should always use fresh seals.

ABOVE **Make sure you always use sterilized, heatproof jars and fresh seals when preserving and bottling fruit. Labels should indicate the date the fruit is bottled.**

Sterilizing

To ensure that harmful bacteria are eliminated, it is essential to sterilize bottles and jars and their lids, if they have them. This can be done in many ways. To sterilize in the oven, stand the containers on a baking sheet lined with newspaper or on a wooden board and rest their lids on them, but do not seal. Make sure they do not touch. Place them in a cold oven and then turn it on to 110°C/225°F/Gas ¼ and leave the containers for 30 minutes. This method has the advantage of ensuring the containers are warm when they are filled with hot jam, syrup or chutney; otherwise they would crack. If you are not going to use them immediately, cover with a clean cloth and make sure they are warmed again before being filled.

An alternative method is to put the containers and their lids in a dishwasher and run it on its hottest setting, including the drying cycle, but without adding any detergent. This, too, ensures the containers are warm when they are filled.

It is also necessary to sterilize a jelly bag before use. Set the bag over a large bowl and pour boiling water through it. Discard the water and replace the bowl with a clean one.

Seals and labels

The type and effectiveness of the seal required depends on the kind of preserve and the process used. Jams and jellies can be covered with a disc of greaseproof (waxed) paper and the top covered with paper or Cellophane held in place with an elastic band. Bottled fruit and vegetables must be sealed with new rubber seals and the lids clipped in place. Chutneys and pickles should be sealed with vinegar-proof lids that will not corrode.

Ideally, all preserves should be labelled with a description of the contents and the date they were made. Self-adhesive labels may be attached to the surface of the container or wooden or metal labels may be tied around the neck.

Setting point

To test jams and jellies for the setting point, spoon a small quantity on to a chilled saucer. Chill for 3 minutes, then push the jam with your finger. If wrinkles form on the surface, the jam is ready. Alternatively, you could use a sugar thermometer clipped to the side of the pan, but not touching the base. When the temperature reaches 105°C/220°F, the jam is ready.

Most jams will benefit if left to stand for about 15 minutes before being ladled into jars. This ensures that the pieces of fruit are evenly distributed. A jam funnel is useful for preventing hot spillages; it can also be used when filling jars with chutney.

ABOVE **You can create your own recipes by mixing herbs and vegetables for pickles and chutneys, or fruit and spices for delicious jams and jellies.**

ABOVE **Choose firm, ripe and unbruised fruit for bottling and preserving.**

Drying fruit

Suitable fruits are usually high in acid and include apples, pears, stone (pit) fruits, figs and dates, lychees, grapes and bananas. Commercial dehydrators are available but to benefit you would have to produce large amounts of fruit. You can dry fruit in a low oven.

Make sure the fruit is firm and just ripe. Prepare the fruit by peeling, coring and slicing apples; core and halve pears; halve and stone peaches or similar fruits. Leave smaller fruits, such as berries, whole. Lay the fruit on clean, wooden slatted trays, cut side-up. Dry in an oven preheated to the lowest possible temperature. Do not exceed a temperature of 120–40°F (49–60°C) as the fruit may become too tough. Cool completely before storing in a glass or plastic container.

Preserving in alcohol

All fruits can be preserved in alcohol. In the 18th century, seafarers discovered that their cargoes of exotic fruits could be preserved in barrels of rum. Dark rum is still a classic preserving spirit, but brandy and other spirits can also be used. The ideal container is a purpose-made *rumtopf*, but a wide-mouthed preserving jar will do.

Start with summer fruits, then add other fruits as they come into season. Wash and dry the fruit to prepare it. Place it in a bowl and cover with an equal weight of sugar. Leave for approximately one hour. Tip the fruit mixture into a *rumtopf* or preserving jar. Pour in just enough rum or similar spirit to completely cover the fruit. Cover the jar with clear film and store in a cool, dark place.

Leave for approximately one month before using the fruit, but note that soft fruit can lose its texture if stored for too long.

directory

of fruit

There is a surprisingly large range of fruit available to the gardener, both in the types and in their varieties. The improvement in the rootstocks of many tree fruits means that even fruit that once needed a large garden can be grown in a relatively small plot. A local fruit expert will be able to advise on which stock is best suited to your particular soil and climate. The biggest problem when growing fruit is deciding from this great wealth which ones you are going to grow. The following directory should help you make your choice.

Strawberries

Fragaria × ananassa

Strawberries are one of the best loved fruits. No matter how readily they are available in the supermarkets, there is nothing quite like wandering into the garden and picking a few to eat there and then. The taste is always better, especially if the fruit is still warm from the sun.

ABOVE **After fruiting, the strawberry plant sends out a series of runners that root along their length to produce new plants.**

It is now possible to pick strawberries from early summer right through to the first frosts and even beyond, if protection is provided. Strawberries are categorized by their time of fruiting and are known as "early", "mid-season" and "late", which continue to fruit well into autumn. There are also perpetual strawberries, which produce fruit in summer, have a break and then start again in autumn. If you have space it is a good idea to plan your strawberry bed so that you have as long a productive season as possible. There are also alpine strawberries, which produce very small fruits over a long period. All strawberry plants should come from certified stock to ensure against virus diseases.

Strawberries are not very difficult to grow. If grown in beds they take up quite a bit of space, but they can also be grown in pots or in towers – a series of containers one on top of the other. They can be grown in a greenhouse, which produces earlier and later crops, but the flavour is not as good as that of crops grown outdoors.

The plants will remain productive for only about three years, and it is important to have a rolling programme to renew a third of the plants each year. Unfortunately, they really need to be planted in fresh ground, so it is not simply a question of taking out one row and replacing it with another; the new plants should ideally go elsewhere in the garden. Alternatively you can create a completely new bed in the third year, and abandon the old one immediately after the fruit has been produced.

CARE AFTER FRUITING

After the strawberries have produced their fruit, cut off all the leaves and burn or destroy them, along with the straw mulch. This helps prevent the spread of diseases.

Cultivation

Strawberries need an open, sunny site. The soil should be fertile and well drained. The plants should be set out in late summer or early autumn, at intervals of 38cm/15in, with each row 75cm/30in apart. As the plants come into fruit the following year, place clean straw under the leaves and fruiting stems to keep the fruit off the ground. Polythene (plastic) or felt mats will serve the same purpose. Deep water during dry periods.

Pruning and training

Strawberries are not pruned or trained as such, but after fruiting it is normal practice to cut off all the old leaves and burn or destroy these, together with the straw mulch, to remove any pests and diseases. Remove any runners as they are formed unless you want keep a few new plants.

Harvesting

Pick the fruit as it ripens. Pick with a short piece of stalk attached.

Storage

The fruit is best eaten straight from the plants, although it can also be frozen or bottled. Unfortunately, frozen strawberries go mushy when they defrost.

Pests and diseases

Birds and slugs are two of the worst problems. Birds can be kept at bay if the plants are netted while they are in fruit. Viruses and grey mould can also be problems. Burn or destroy any plant with viral disease.

RUNNERS

The strawberry runners have produced a perfect new plant through layering. The layered plants can be dug up once they have rooted and used to start a new bed.

ABOVE **On this plant a succession of stages can be seen, from flowers to ripe fruit. Fruit picked straight from the plant tastes best.**

PROTECTING THE FRUIT

Place a layer of straw under the leaves of the strawberry plants in order to prevent the developing fruit from getting muddy or covered with dirt.

Varieties

Early
'Cambridge Early Pine'
'Cambridge Prizewinner'
'Cambridge Vigour'
'Honeoye'
'Maxim'

Mid-season
'Cambridge Favourite'
'Cambridge Sentry'
'Grandee'
'Hapil'
'Jamil'
'Redgauntlet'
'Tamella'
'Tenira'

Late
'Cambridge Late Pine'
'Domanil'
'Fenland Wonder'
'Merton Dawn'
'Montrose'
'Saladin'
'Le Sans Rivale'
'Symphony'
'Troubadour'

Perpetual (remontant)
'Calypso'
'Mara des Bois'
'Rabunda'
'Red Rich'
'St Claude'

Alpine
'Alexandria'
'Baron Solemacher'
'Delicious'
'Yellow Wonder'

strawberries

Raspberries

Rubus idaeus

ABOVE **Ripening and immature fruit on a raspberry cane. Ripe raspberries can be obtained over a very long period if the varieties are chosen carefully.**

Raspberries are an appealing fruit, although they are often overshadowed by strawberries, which come into season at the same time. They are a good fruit for eating straight from the plant or for freezing and for making into jams and preserves. Raspberries can be used in a wide range of cakes and desserts as well as sauces for both sweet and savoury dishes.

It is possible to provide a good "taste" of raspberries by growing a group of just a few canes, but it is more usual to grow the canes in a row. This may take up quite a large amount of space, but it can be used as a hedge or screen, so fulfilling a double function. The canes are tied into wires that are supported on posts, which adds to the initial cost, but once the framework has been erected it will last for a long time, as will the raspberries.

As with strawberries, new varieties of raspberry have been developed so that it is possible to have a supply of fruit from early summer right through to the first frosts, which in a mild year can mean early winter. Rather than having three separate rows, which would take up a great deal of space, it is possible to divide a single row into three or even four separate sections for early, mid-season, late and autumn fruit.

Cultivation

Like most fruit, raspberries like an open situation with plenty of air circulating among them, but, unlike most other fruit, they will tolerate a little partial shade. The soil should be fertile and moisture retentive, but it should not be waterlogged. Permanent supports in the form of posts and wires should be erected. The wires should be 75cm/30in, 1.1m/3ft 6in and 1.5m/5ft from the ground. Allow 1.5m/5ft between rows. Plant the canes at intervals of 38–45cm/15–18in, spreading out their roots, during late autumn or early winter. Remove any suckers that appear out of the row, and use them as new stock if required. Mulch with garden compost or manure every spring.

Pruning and training

Each autumn remove all the old fruiting canes by cutting them off at the base. Tie in the new canes to the wires. In late winter cut off the tip of each cane to a bud about 15cm/6in above the top wire. If you grow autumn-fruiting varieties, cut *all* canes to the ground in late winter.

Harvesting

Pick as the fruit becomes ripe, squeezing gently with the fingers so that the fruit slides off its "plug".

LEFT **If this crop of ripening raspberries is left uncovered in this way, there will be few to eat because the birds will strip them away.**

ABOVE **This double row of raspberries is supported by wires that are secured on a well-constructed wooden framework.**

ABOVE LEFT **These raspberry canes are tied into wire supports by twisting a continuous piece of string around the wire in order to trap the canes.**

Storage

The fruit is best eaten straight from the plant. However, it can be stored by freezing, bottling or turning into jam or other preserves. Frozen fruit becomes mushy and loses its shape and firmness, although it is still useful as fillings and sauces. You can overcome the storage problem by selecting and growing a range of varieties. This means you will have a continuous supply of fresh fruit from early summer right through to the first frost.

Pests and diseases

Birds are a nuisance unless the raspberry canes are netted or protected in a fruit cage. Raspberry beetle – the grub is found in the fruit – is often a nuisance. Spray with derris as soon as the first fruits begin to ripen, and then make a second application two weeks later. Grey mould can cause the fruit to rot and there is also the possibility of some virus diseases. Infected canes should be removed and either burned or destroyed.

Varieties

Early
'Delight'
'Glen Clova'
'Glen Coe'
'Glen Moy'
'Malling Exploit'
'Malling Promise'
'Sumner'

Mid-season
'Glen Lyon'
'Glen Prosen'
'Julia'
'Malling Jewel'
'Malling Orion'

Late
'Augusta'
'Leo'
'Malling Admiral'
'Malling Joy'

Autumn
'Autumn Bliss'
'Fallgold'
'Heritage'
'Norfolk Giant'
'September'

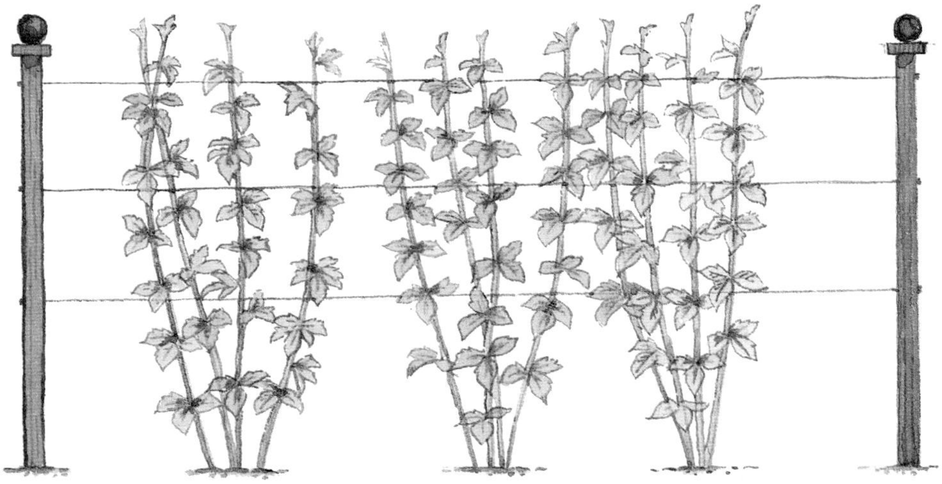

Growing raspberries on posts and wires It is essential that raspberries have a strong supporting system of posts and wires. The plants are set at 38–45cm/15–18in intervals. Each year, new raspberry canes are thrown up. When fruiting has finished on the old canes, these are cut out and the new canes are tied to the wires in their place. This sequence is followed every year. Raspberry plants put out suckers which can become established in the gangways between the rows. These should be dug up as soon as they appear.

raspberries

Blackberries and Hybrid Berries

Rubus fruticosus

Although blackberries that are picked in the wild have a great deal to offer, there are advantages to be gained from growing cultivated forms. The first is that they are conveniently at hand. Second, the fruit is usually much larger and often sweeter. Then there is the fact that you can get thornless varieties, which makes picking much easier. A disadvantage, however, is that you do need quite a bit of space to grow them successfully, although they do not need to be a free-standing crop. They can, for example, be grown along a boundary fence, which may well be a good use of space as well as acting as a deterrent to intruders.

ABOVE **Blackberries fruit over a long season, as is shown by a sprig of ripe and immature blackberries.**

RIGHT **This vigorous stand of blackberries shows the prodigious nature of many of these plants.**

Cultivated blackberries are derived from their wild relatives; the hybrid berries are crosses between various *Rubus* species, often involving blackberries and raspberries in their parentage. Each of these berries, including loganberries, boysenberries and tayberries, has a distinctive flavour and is grown in the same manner as blackberries.

They come into fruit from late summer onwards and are, therefore, available later than most other soft fruit, which is another advantage. Like most fruit, blackberries and hybrid berries are best eaten straight from the garden, but they can also be used in a wide range of dessert dishes and sauces.

Blackberries are usually grown on post and wire supports, the wires being placed at 38cm/15in intervals up to about 1.8m/6ft. The thornless varieties are not as vigorous and take up less space. In a really large garden, blackberries could be left to grow free, like their wild cousins, but this is not recommended because cultivated varieties are often much more vigorous than wild forms.

Cultivation

Blackberries prefer a sunny spot, but will grow in a modicum of partial shade. The soil should be well prepared, with plenty of added humus. Plant the canes in late winter or early spring, placing them 3.5–4.5m/12–15ft apart (thornless varieties can be closer together), and immediately shorten them to a bud about 23–30cm/9–12in above ground. Do not plant deeply; the soil should only just cover the roots, which should be spread out in the planting hole. Mulch with manure in the spring and water in dry weather. They can be increased by bending down a vigorous shoot and planting its tip to form a layer. A new plant will quickly form and can be severed from the parent.

Pruning and training

In autumn cut out all the old fruiting stems and tie in the new growth. There are several methods of training blackberries and hybrid berries. One is to tie in all of one year's growth to one side, several canes to each wire, and the new growth to the other side. Another is to tie the fruiting growth along the wires, allowing the new growth to grow up the middle. A more formal and higher yielding method is to create a fan, with the shoots tied in a radiating pattern from the base, again leaving the centre free for new growth.

Harvesting

Pick as fruit becomes ripe, without any stalks.

Storage

Fresh blackberries last a day or so but can be frozen, bottled or used in preserves.

Pests and diseases

Blackberries are prone to the same problems as raspberries.

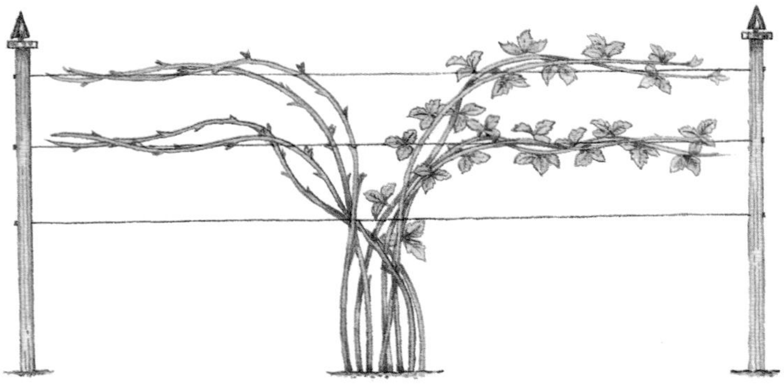

Alternate bay One way to train blackberries is to tie all the new growth to one side of the wirework. After fruiting, remove the previous year's growth from the other side and then use this for the next year's new growth. Repeat each year.

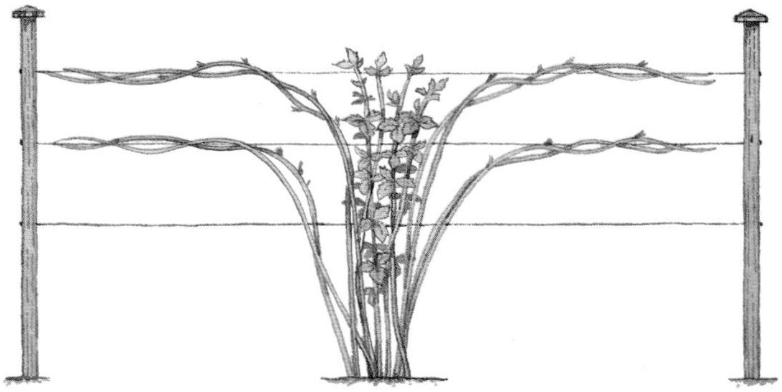

Rope training A second way to train blackberries is to temporarily tie in all new growth vertically to the wirework and along the top wire. The current fruiting canes are tied in groups horizontally. These are removed after fruiting and the new growth tied into their place.

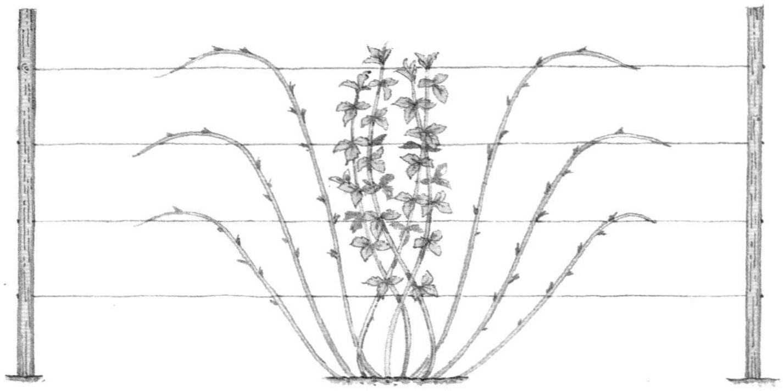

Fan training The new canes are temporarily tied vertically and along the top wire, while the fruiting canes are tied in singly along the wires. Any excess canes are removed. After fruiting, these canes are taken out and the new growth tied into their place.

Varieties

Blackberries
'Ashton Cross'
'Bedford Giant' – early
'Himalayan Giant'
'John Innes'
'Loch Ness'
'Merton Early'
'Merton Thornless'
'Oregon Thornless'
'Smoothstem'
'Thornfree'

Hybrid berries
Boysenberry
Loganberry
Marionberry
Sunberry
Tayberry
Tummelberry
Vietchberry
Worcesterberry

Red and White Currants

Ribes rubrum

The only difference between red and white currants is the colour of the fruit. Both types of currant have a very distinctive, slightly tart flavour, but, unlike many other types of fruit, they have a comparatively short season, around midsummer. Red currants in particular are very attractive, and the bushes can be trained into standards, cordons or fans and used as a decorative feature.

As well as being used as fruit in their own right, both are widely used as decoration on cakes and in a wide range of desserts and savoury dishes.

Cultivation

Both red and white currants prefer a sunny site and a rich, moisture-retentive soil. Plant between autumn and early spring at intervals of 1.2–1.5m/4–5ft. Cordons can be 30cm/12in apart and fans can be 1.8m/6ft apart. Mulch in spring with well-rotted organic material. Propagate from hardwood cuttings taken in early autumn.

Pruning and training

Initially, prune back all main stems to four buds. After that, prune in spring and summer, reducing the growth on the new leader by about half and that on laterals to about 8cm/3in in spring and to four or five leaves in summer. Once the bushes are established, cut back all side shoots to one bud and take the tip out of the main stems. Let new shoots from the base replace older wood. If you are growing them as cordons, in early spring remove a third of the new growth on the leader and cut back laterals to three buds. In summer cut back all laterals to five leaves.

Harvesting and storage

Pick when the currants are ripe, taking the whole cluster of fruit. They can be frozen or turned into preserves – but remove the stalks first.

Pests and diseases

Birds, which will attack both buds and fruit, are likely to be the biggest problem. Aphids and black currant gall mites may also be troublesome. Grey mould may be a problem and coral spot can affect the branches.

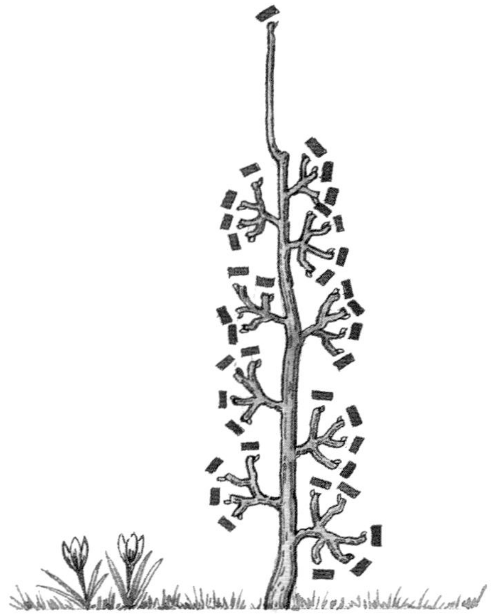

Pruning a red or white currant cordon On planting, cut back the leader by half of its new growth and cut back the side shoots to one bud. Thereafter, cut back the side shoots every summer to five leaves and, in winter, further reduce these to one bud.

Pruning a red or white currant bush After planting, cut back each shoot by about half. Subsequent pruning involves ensuring that the plant becomes an open bush. Cut back all new growth on the main shoots and reduce the new growth on all side shoots to one bud.

BELOW **These cordons of red and white currants have been tied to vertical canes which are, in turn, tied to horizontal wires.**

Varieties

Red currants	White currants
'Jonkheer van Tets'	'Versailles Blanche'
'Junifer'	'White Dutch'
'Laxton's Number 1'	'White Grape'
'Red Lake'	'White Pearl'
'Redstart'	
'Rondom'	
'Rovada'	

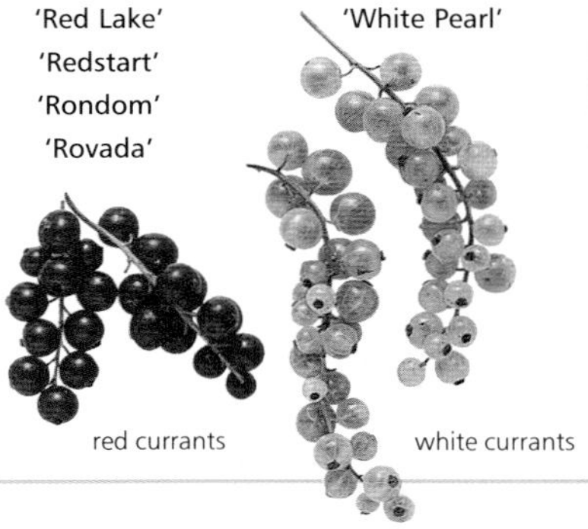

Blackcurrants

Ribes nigrum

Not only do blackcurrants have a unique flavour, but they are much valued for their high vitamin C content. They are used widely in desserts as well as jams and drinks. Blackcurrants, like red and white currants, tend to have a relatively short season compared with other soft fruit, but although related to red currants it is important to realize that they are pruned in a different way. Because the fruit is produced on the previous season's growth, it is important that this is not removed. Unlike red currants, blackcurrants can only be grown on bushes.

Varieties

'Baldwin'
'Ben Connan'
'Ben Lomond'
'Ben More'
'Ben Sarek'
'Boskoop Giant'
'Malling Jet'
'Mendip Cross'
'Wellington XXX'

blackcurrants

They are long-lived plants, lasting up to 15 years or more. Joostberries, a cross between blackcurrants and gooseberries, are grown in the same way.

Cultivation

Blackcurrants prefer a sunny site, although they will tolerate a little light shade. The soil should be well prepared and have plenty of well-rotted humus added to it. Plant between autumn and early spring, setting the plants at intervals of 1.5m/5ft. Mulch in spring with a layer of organic material. Water during dry spells but not when the fruit starts to ripen or it may split. Propagate from hardwood cuttings taken in autumn.

Pruning and training

After planting, reduce all shoots to one bud above the ground. The following winter remove any weak wood. After that remove any weak wood and up to a third of the older wood so that new growth is produced. Never reduce the lengths of the shoots.

Harvesting and storage

Pick the fruit as it ripens, retaining the stalks. Store by freezing or preserving, removing all stalks first.

Pests and diseases

Birds are likely to be the biggest problem. Aphids, big bud mite and gall mites may also be troublesome. Leaf spot and powdery mildew can also be a problem.

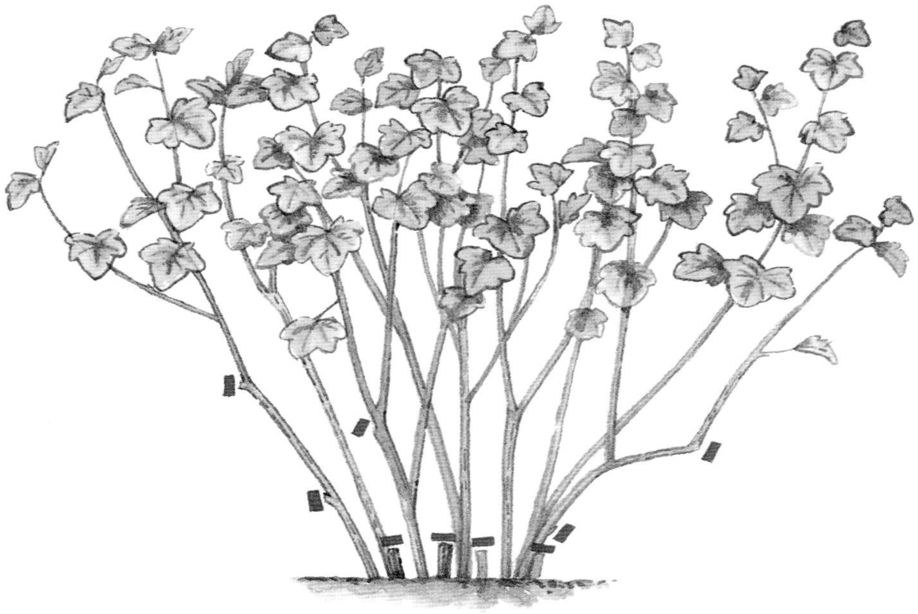

Pruning a blackcurrant bush After planting, cut blackcurrant bushes back to a single bud above the ground. The following winter, remove any weak or misplaced growth. Subsequent pruning should take place after fruiting and consists of cutting out up to a third of two-year-old or older wood in order to stimulate new growth. Also remove any weak or misplaced stems.

RIGHT **Blackcurrants and red currants are usually picked in bunches, complete with their stalks. They can be collected in a trug for convenience.**

Gooseberries

Ribes uva-crispa

Because most people think that gooseberries need cooking and so do not fit into the world of convenience foods, they are not, perhaps, as popular as they were in the past. This is a pity, partly because gooseberries have a very distinctive flavour, suitable for a range of dishes and sauces, but also because gooseberries can be eaten raw – there are some delicious dessert varieties. Unfortunately, these rarely find their way into shops, and so it is only gardeners who are likely to appreciate them – an excellent reason for growing your own.

Pruning a gooseberry The basic aim when pruning gooseberries is to create an open framework. Establish a framework, first of all, by removing the basal shoots and cutting back the main shoots by about half in their first and second years. After this, cut back the new growth on the leaders in winter by about half and reduce the side shoots from these to two buds. Remove any damaged wood and any branches that cross or rub. Remove suckers and basal growth. In summer, prune the side shoots back to five leaves, but leave the main stems uncut.

Gooseberries are easy plants to grow, the only drawback being the thorns, which can be very sharp, but well-trained bushes and the use of cordons make it easier to get at the fruit without being torn to pieces. Typical gooseberries are green, but there are also red and yellow varieties.

Cultivation

Gooseberries require an open, sunny position, although they will take some light shade. The soil should contain plenty of well-rotted organic material. Plant the bushes at any time between autumn and early spring when the weather and soil are favourable. They should be set 1.5m/5ft apart. Mulch in spring with a good layer of manure. Avoid hoeing because the roots are only just below the surface and can be damaged. New plants can be propagated by hardwood cuttings taken in autumn.

Pruning and training

Gooseberries can be grown as bushes, cordons or standards. They are treated in the same way as red currants. Keep the centre of the bush open so that plenty of air can circulate as well as making it easier to get at the fruit.

Harvesting and storage

Start harvesting before the fruit is quite ripe. Such fruit can be cooked or frozen. Wait until fruit is fully ripe if it is for eating raw. Continue picking as the fruit ripens. Pick with a stalk, although this must be removed before storing. Store by freezing, bottling or by making jam or other preserves.

Pests and diseases

One the whole, gooseberries are not prone to a great many pests and diseases. The main problem is powdery mildew, and one way to prevent this is to ensure that plenty of air can circulate around and through the bushes. Birds can also be a nuisance in spring when they strip off buds.

Varieties

'Broom Girl'	'Lancashire Lad'
'Careless'	'Leveller'
'Early Sulphur'	'Whinham's Industry'
'Greenfinch'	'White Lion'
'Invicta'	'Whitesmith'
'Jubilee'	'Yellow Champagne'

gooseberries

LEFT **Gooseberries can be grown as single cordons. This is achieved by tying them into canes which are supported by horizontal wires.**

Blueberries

Vaccinium corymbosum

The high-bush blueberry is becoming more popular in the garden. The rich, fruity flavour that is a characteristic of the berries has made it popular as a fruit to be eaten straight from the bush and for inclusion in an ever-increasing number of desserts and other dishes. Its disadvantage as a garden fruit, at least for some people, is that it must have acid conditions. In chalky or limestone (alkaline) regions bushes could be grown in large containers away from the normal garden soil, but this could become quite a chore, no matter how tasty the resulting berries.

The bushes and berries are decorative and are a useful addition in the potager or ornamental border.

Cultivation

Choose a sunny site, although a little light, partial shade will be tolerated. The soil must be acidic. Add ericaceous compost (soil mix) if your garden soil is just on the borderline. Set out the plants at any time the weather and soil conditions allow between autumn and early spring. Plant them as free-standing bushes, 1.5m/5ft apart. Mulch with manure, but only if it has not been "sweetened" with chalk or limestone. An ericaceous compost can be used or marginally acid soil. Do not allow the soil to become dry, watering regularly as necessary. Propagate from soft-wood cuttings taken in midsummer.

Pruning and training

Because the fruit appears on the second- or third-year wood, do not prune until cropping starts. After that, cut out any dead or weak wood and then remove up to a third of the oldest wood to promote new growth. Prune in winter or early spring.

Harvesting and storage

Pick as the fruit ripens and store, if necessary, by freezing or bottling.

Pests and diseases

Blueberries are remarkably trouble free. The worst problem will be birds, which will steal the fruit, but netting will solve this.

ABOVE **This healthy looking cluster of ripening blueberries clearly shows the distinctive powdery bloom of the fruit which most gardeners try to retain when picking.**

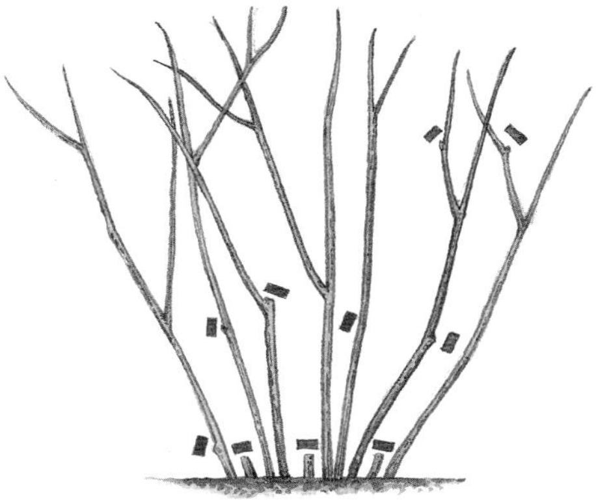

Pruning an established blueberry bush Blueberries fruit on older wood, so no pruning is needed for several years. Thereafter, cut out any weak or misplaced shoots as well as the old wood that has ceased fruiting in order to stimulate new growth.

BELOW **A vigorous blueberry bush, such as this, with plenty of ripening fruit, must be protected to stop birds from stripping away the fruit before it ripens.**

Varieties

- 'Berkeley'
- 'Bluecrop'
- 'Bluejay'
- 'Bluetta'
- 'Duke'
- 'Goldtraube'
- 'Herbert'
- 'Patriot'
- 'Spartan'

blueberries

Apples

Malus domestica

Apples are a staple fruit, grown in many countries around the world, but although there are, literally, thousands of varieties, the number available in shops can be limited. Unlike many other fruits, in which the taste is only marginally different from one variety to another, apples exhibit a great range of flavours and textures. Some are suitable for cooking, others are dessert (eating) apples, and others combine these qualities.

To help you choose among the vast range of apple varieties, visit one of the open days held by specialist apple nurseries and collectors. It is usually possible to taste several different varieties of ripe fruit and see the trees themselves, which you can often buy or order.

One aspect of apple growing that may restrict your choice is pollination. Most apples need another variety to pollinate them, and because the flowering time varies from variety to variety it is essential to choose two that flower during the same period.

Another question that will have to be addressed is what type of plant do you want. The old standard trees look best and produce a heavy crop, but they are usually too large for today's smaller garden, and ladders are needed for pruning and harvesting. Cordons take up the least space, but the crop is small. On the other hand, cordons allow you to have several different varieties in a small space. There are, however, all kinds of shapes and sizes between the two extremes, some of them very decorative. Always check the rootstock of the plants you buy to see how vigorous and large the tree will be ultimately.

Cultivation

Apple trees will be in position for years, so prepare the soil well, adding plenty of organic material. An open, sunny position is best. Plant young trees at any time of year between late autumn and early spring, as long as weather and soil conditions are favourable. The planting distances vary considerably depending on the type and size of tree. Cordons, for example, may be only 75cm/30in apart, whereas the full standards can be 10m/ 30ft or more apart, so check first with your supplier. Stake young trees, especially in a windy position. Newly planted trees should not be allowed to dry out. Mulch around the tree every spring with organic material. If necessary protect the blossom from late frosts with fleece.

BELOW **These pole apples have been grown as vertical cordons. The bottoms of the trunks have been protected against attacks by rabbits.**

Rootstocks

The rootstock on an apple tree affects the size and rate of growth of the tree.

M27 an extreme dwarfing stock (bush, dwarf pyramid, cordon)
M9 dwarfing stock (bush, dwarf pyramid, cordon)
M26 semi-dwarfing stock (bush, dwarf pyramid, cordon)
MM106 semi-dwarfing stock (bush, spindle bush, cordon, fan espalier)
M7 semi-dwarfing stock (bush, spindle bush, cordon, fan espalier)
M4 semi-vigorous stock (bush, spindle bush)
MM4 vigorous stock (standard)
M2 vigorous stock
MM111 vigorous stock (half-standard, standard, large bush, large fans, large espaliers)
M25 vigorous stock (standard)
MM109 vigorous stock
M1 vigorous stock

Thin the apples in early and midsummer if there are too many of them – a good guide is to ensure that individual fruits should not touch each other. If branches begin to sag under the weight of fruit, the fruit may need thinning or the branches may need to be supported.

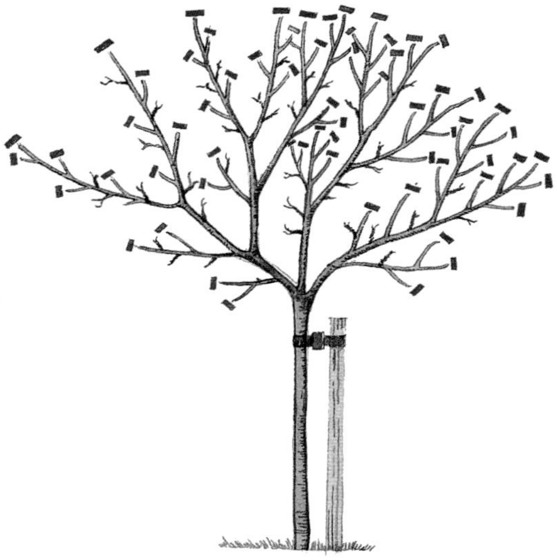

Spur pruning an apple bush tree After planting, cut back the leader to about 75cm/30in above the ground. Leave any side shoots that appear just below this cut and remove any others lower down. The following year, reduce all new growth by about half. This will form the basic framework. Subsequent pruning is restricted to reducing the length of new growth by about a third and removing overcrowded growth.

ABOVE **Apples are not only delicious when they are picked straight from the tree, but they also retain their qualities when stored. This crop of ripening apples will make for a successful harvest.**

LEFT **Training cordon apples against a fence in this way is a suitable method of growing fruit if you only have a small garden.**

Pruning and training

Pruning is not difficult once you have done it the first time. Apple trees fall into two groups, depending on where the fruit is borne. On tip bearers the fruit develops near the tip of the shoots, so it is, obviously, important that you cut back shoots in spring. Trees in the other group produce fruit on spurs, which are found on older wood. Most training and pruning involves cutting out dead or weak wood and maintaining the shape and open nature of the tree. Larger trees are pruned in winter only, but those with a more controlled shape need to be pruned in both winter and summer.

Harvesting and storing

Apples should be picked when ripe, which is usually when the fruit comes away easily with a quick twist of the wrist. Some apples store better than others; in general, early apples do not store as well as later ones. If possible, store in a dark, dry, cool place, and ensure the fruits do not touch. Only store sound fruit. Freezing is appropriate for apples that have already been cooked and puréed.

Pests and diseases

A wide range of pests and diseases can affect the trees and fruit. Birds, wasps and codling moths are three of the most important pests. Canker is one of the worst diseases.

Varieties

Dessert (eating)
'Blenheim Orange'
'Cox's Orange Pippin'
'Discovery'
'Egremont Russet'
'George Cave'
'Idared'
'James Grieve'
'Jonathan'
'Laxton's Fortune'
'Laxton's Superb'
'Lord Lambourne'
'Millers Seedling'
'Ribston Pippin'
'Starking'
'Sturmer Pippin'
'Worcester Pearmain'

Cooking
'Bramley's Seedling'
'Grenadier'
'Howgate Wonder'
'Lord Darby'
'Newton Wonder'

Planting and pruning an apple cordon Cordons are planted as feather maidens at 45° to the wirework. All side shoots are cut back to three buds on planting. Subsequent summer pruning (above right) consists of cutting back any new side shoots to three leaves and new growth on existing side shoots to one leaf. Winter pruning consists of thinning out any of the older spurs if they have become congested.

Pears

Pyrus communis

In the past, pears were, like apples, widely grown, partly for eating and cooking, and partly for turning into perry, a drink akin to cider. Pears for cooking and perry did not have to be the luscious juicy ones that are wanted for eating, and so many people have inherited trees in their gardens that bear pears that are as hard as bullets. This, unfortunately, has put them off growing pears altogether, which is a shame, because ripe eating pears, picked straight from tree can be mouth-watering.

Pears can be grown as standard or dwarf trees as well as in the form of cordons, espaliers and fans. For the smaller garden, cordons are ideal as they make it possible to have several different varieties in a relatively small area. This means that you do not have a glut of one variety but can spread the harvest over a longer period. Pears need warmth to grow well, which is one reason that they are frequently grown against a wall. The warmth is needed not only during the spring at blossom time – they flower early and are particularly susceptible to frosts – but also during summer and autumn so that the fruit can ripen properly. In cold years, when the pears remain hard, they can still be cooked, often by poaching, to make them soft and edible.

Pear trees are vigorous and are, therefore, often unsuitable for small gardens and for some of the smaller forms in which the trees are grown. It is more usual to grow a pear tree that has been grafted onto a quince rootstock to curb its vigour. This means that any suckers appearing below the graft should be removed.

As with apples, pears must be grown near a different variety so that the blossom can be pollinated. Unless there happens to be a compatible tree in a neighbouring garden, you will have to plant at least two trees. Unfortunately, you cannot use any variety – the trees must be compatible. Consult your supplier about suitable pairs.

LEFT **These pears have been grown in a cordon against trellis, a method suitable for small gardens.**

Cultivation

Pear trees must have a sheltered, warm site and fertile, free-draining, but moisture-retentive, soil. Add plenty of organic material while preparing the ground. Set out new plants at any time between late autumn and spring with favourable weather and soil conditions. Planting distances vary according to the type of plant. Bush trees can be up to 4.5m/15ft apart, dwarf pyramids 1.5m/5ft apart, cordons 75cm/30in apart, and espaliers and fans 4.5m/15ft apart. Stake free-standing trees to prevent wind-rock. Mulch with manure in the spring. Thoroughly water during dry spells. If the crop is heavy, thin out young fruit in early to midsummer so that they do not touch.

Pruning and training

Most varieties of pears are spur-bearers, which means that they produce fruit on spurs that grow on two-year-old or older wood. The leader's new growth can, therefore, be safely cut back in winter by about a third of its length, and laterals can be pruned to three or four buds. Spurs are readily produced and should be thinned once the tree is established. Before starting to prune and shape a tree, always remove any dead, dying or weak growth and then work with what is left.

ABOVE **Conference pears have a distinctive elongated shape. These healthy specimens are ripe for picking and enjoying.**

Harvesting and storage

The picking time for pears is crucial. The fruit should be just ripe; any that is left on the tree beyond this stage will soon become overripe. Pick as soon as the fruit comes away readily to a twisting motion of the hand. Early varieties can be picked just before they ripen, but mid-season and late varieties should be left until they are ripe. Pears can be stored in slatted trays in a cool room. Only store sound fruit and position them so that they do not touch each other.

Rootstocks

As with apples, the rootstock on which a pear tree grows affects the size and rate of growth of the tree.

Quince C moderately dwarfing stock (bush, cordon, dwarf pyramid, espalier, fan)

Quince A semi-vigorous stock (bush, cordon, dwarf pyramid, espalier, fan)

Pear vigorous stock (standards, half-standards)

RIGHT **A pear tree trained in the shape of a cone.**

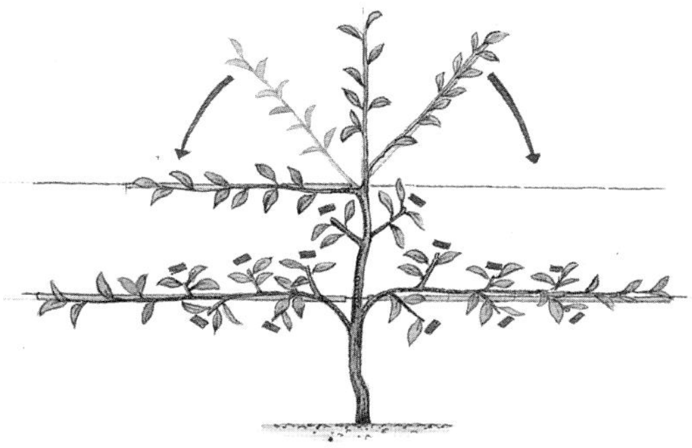

Pruning an espaliered pear After planting, cut back to two buds above the bottom wire. In the first summer, tie the central growth to a vertical cane and the next two shoots to canes at 45°. Cut back all other shoots to two leaves. In autumn, lower the two side shoots to the horizontal and tie the cane to the bottom wire. In winter, cut back the leader to two buds above the second wire and repeat the above until the espalier covers all the wires. When established, cut back all new shoots to three leaves each summer.

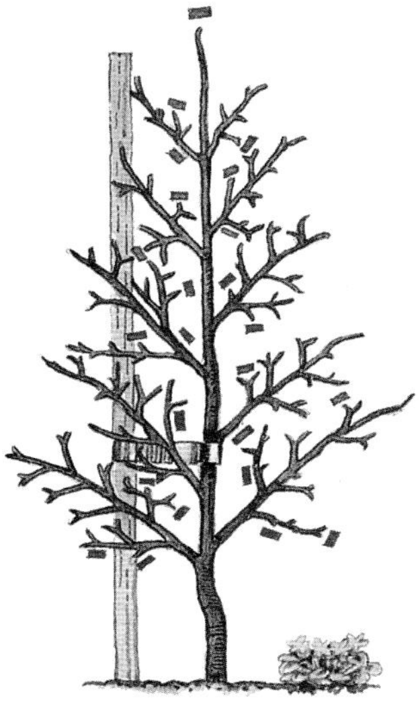

Pruning a dwarf pyramid pear After planting, cut back the leader by about a third. Cut side shoots back to about 15cm/6in. In the first summer, cut back the new growth on the main side shoots to about five leaves and on the secondary shoots to three leaves. Thereafter, cut back new growth on the main stems to five leaves and reduce other new growth to one leaf. During the winter, thin out any congested spurs.

Pests and diseases

Pears are prone to a number of problems, including aphids, codling moth and pear midge. Diseases include fireblight, canker, scab and brown rot. Fireblight will probably mean the removal of the entire tree; it must then be burned or destroyed. For other pests and diseases, check on the latest controls with your local nursery or garden centre.

Varieties

'Beth'
'Beurré Hardy'
'Black Worcester'
'Concorde'
'Conference'
'Doyenné du Comice'
'Durondeau'
'Glou Morceau'
'Jargonelle'
'Joséphine de Malines'
'Louise Bonne of Jersey'
'Merton Pride'
'Onward'
'Williams' Bon Chrétien'

pears

Cherries

Prunus species

Although cherries are a really delicious fruit, they are not widely grown in gardens. One reason for this is that until relatively recently cherries could be grown only on large trees. This was a problem in small gardens as well as creating a problem in trying to prevent birds from stealing the whole crop since it is virtually impossible to net a large tree. Now that dwarfing stock are available, much smaller trees can be grown and it is worth finding the space to grow them.

There are two types of cherry: sweet cherries (*Prunus avium*) and sour or acid cherries (*P. cerasus*). Sweet cherries are perfect for eating, while the sour varieties, typified by "Morello" cherries, are cooked or bottled. Most people prefer sweet cherries, but the sour forms are easier to grow in a small garden. This is because they are less vigorous, and when they are on "Colt" dwarfing stock they do not make very large trees. They are also self-fertile, so one tree is sufficient.

If you do not have room for a big tree, sweet cherries are best trained as fans on a warm wall, where their size can be controlled and they can be easily covered against marauding birds. Improvements are being made in the development of dwarfing stock for cherries, and it may soon be possible to grow them as small trees, smaller than the current 4m/13ft. Sweet cherries generally need two varieties in order for pollination to be effective, except for 'Stella', Sunburst' and a few other self-fertile varieties.

Cultivation

Cherries need a warm, sunny position – a south-facing wall is ideal. The soil should be well-drained so that it is not waterlogged but it must be sufficiently moist to provide the precise conditions that cherries like. Plant full-sized trees 9m/30ft apart. Smaller trees and fan-trained cherries can be 4.5–5.5m/15–18ft apart. Stake young trees firmly so that the lower part of the trunk and the rootball are not rocked by the wind. If possible, mulch with manure or other organic material to help retain moisture. Water cherries in dry spells but keep the level of moisture even, because a sudden glut of water during a dry spell is likely to crack the fruit, which ruins it. There is no need to thin cherries.

ABOVE **The delicate blossom that appears in early spring is an attractive feature of cherry trees and a welcome bonus.**

Pruning and training

Sweet cherry trees need little pruning, apart from removing dead or damaged growth, unless they are trained as fans, when new growth is cut back to five leaves every summer. In early spring remove all new side growth. Sour cherries grow

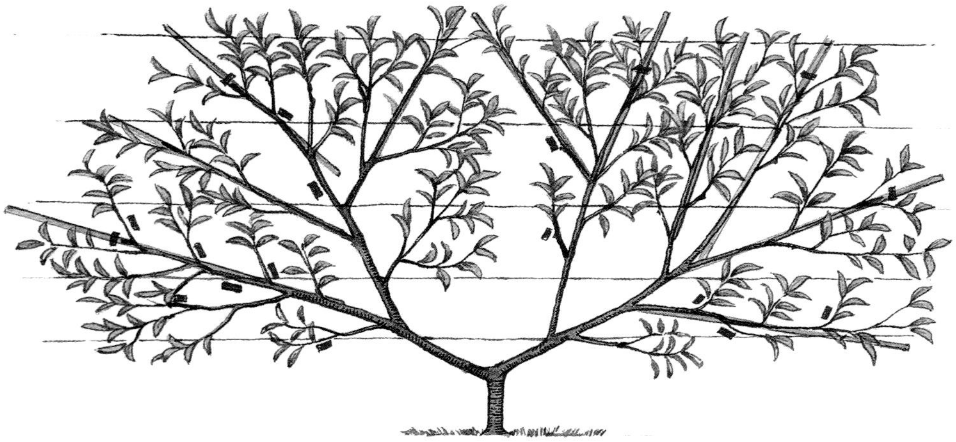

Sour cherry fan Once established, there are two purposes to pruning a cherry fan: to keep the fan shape and to ensure that there is a constant supply of new wood. To keep the shape completely, remove any shoots that are pointing in the wrong direction. For renewal, cut back in summer all shoots that have fruited, preferably as far back as the next new shoot. Tie these new shoots to the cane and wire framework.

Sour cherry bush or tree Once established, bush and full-sized sour cherry trees need little pruning other than to remove a third of the old fruiting wood, cutting back to a new growth. Also remove any crossing branches.

ABOVE **This fan-trained cherry has been netted to protect it against marauding birds. Here, it is trained against wires, but it could also be trained against a wall or fence.**

on year-old wood, and so some of the older wood is removed each year so that new growth is produced. After picking the fruit in summer, cut back existing, one-year-old shoots on which the fruit was borne to the first new growth. In early summer reduce the number of new side shoots to about one every 8cm/3in. Remove all shoots that face towards or away from the wall. Remove any "water" shoots that appear from the bottom of the tree. Bush and full-size trees need little pruning.

Harvesting and storage

Pick sweet cherries as they become ripe. If you have a lot of cherries to pick, early in the morning is the best time because the leaves are crisp and stand up, revealing the fruit. Later in the day, especially if it is hot, the leaves tend to be limp and hang over the fruit, hiding it. Pick the fruit with the stalks on. The stalks of sour cherries should be cut rather than pulled to avoid tearing, which would allow disease to enter. Cherries can be frozen or bottled. They should be stoned (pitted) first.

Pests and diseases

Birds are the worst problem – given the chance, they will eat every cherry long before the gardener can get to them. Aphids can also be a problem. Canker, silver leaf and brown rot are the most likely diseases.

Varieties

Sweet
'Colney'
'Early Rivers'
'Governor Wood'
'Greenstem Black'
'Kent Biggarreau'
'Merton Bigarreau'
'Merton Favourite'
'Merton Glory'
'Napoleon Bigarreau'
'Noir de Guben'
'Stella'
'Sunburst'
'Waterloo'

Sour or acid
'Kentish Red'
'May Duke'
'Montmorency'
'Morello'
'Nabella'
'Reine Hortense'
'The Flemish'

sweet cherries

Plums

Prunus domestica

Plums are one of the great unexplored parts of the fruit world. In the past there were many different varieties, all with different flavours and textures, but now all knowledge of such fruit seems to have been lost. At most, one or two varieties surface occasionally in shops, but few people seem to know of the treasury of delights that could be available. Fortunately, many of the old varieties are available from specialist nurseries, and anyone who takes the trouble to search them out is really in for a treat.

ABOVE **A cluster of plums that would have benefited from thinning out – they are growing too close together and could have filled out more.**

The name "plum" actually encompasses a great diversity of fruit, including damsons, bullaces and the gages. Plums come in all shapes and sizes as well as a range of colours, from red to black and from yellow to green. The flesh, too, varies from red to yellow. As with the other main tree fruits, distinctive cultivars have been developed for dessert (eating uncooked) purposes and for cooking. The former are succulent and mouthwatering; the latter are firmer and less sweet.

In general, plums like a sunny situation, but there are plums for all sorts of climates and you may well find that some are better suited to local conditions than others. Check to see what varieties are still grown in your neighbourhood area and what may have been grown in the past when they were more widely grown.

Plums are mainly grown as trees, varying from full-sized standards to spindle bushes and pyramids. They can also be trained as fans. Unfortunately, they cannot be grown as cordons. Plums trees are not usually large and can be accommodated, even in small gardens.

Damsons were traditionally grown as hedgerow trees and can be planted in a hedge, saving a lot of space and yet producing a good crop of fruit. Plums vary in fertility, some being self-fertile, but they all do better for having a pollinator in the area.

Pruning a plum fan in spring and summer The main aim when pruning a plum fan is to maintain the fan shape. In spring, cut out any new side shoots that are pointing to or away from the wall. If necessary, reduce the number of new shoots to about one every 15cm/6in. In summer, cut back all new shoots to about six leaves, leaving any that are needed to fill in gaps in the main framework. In autumn, after cropping, further cut back the shoots to three leaves.

Cultivation

Plums must have a sunny position; in cooler areas, a position against a wall will be ideal. They flower early and so should not be planted in frost pockets, where the blossom will be lost. The soil should be

Rootstocks

The rootstock on which a plum tree grows affects the size and rate of growth.

Pixy dwarfing stock (bush, pyramid)
Damas C moderately vigorous stock
St Julien A semi-vigorous stock (bush, fan, pyramid)
Brompton A vigorous stock (half-standards, standards)
Myrobalan B vigorous stock (half-standards, standards)

Varieties

Dessert	'Merton Gem'
'Ariel'	'Oullin's Gage'
'Cambridge Gage'	'Victoria'
'Coe's Golden Drop'	**Cooking**
'Early Laxton	'Belle de Louvain'
'Greengage'	'Czar'
'Jefferson'	'Early Rivers'
'Kirke's Blue'	'Laxton's Cropper'
'Marjorie's Seedling'	'Pershore Yellow'

fertile and moisture retentive, although they will tolerate drier soil than many other tree fruits. Plant the trees at any time between autumn and early spring, as long as weather and soil conditions allow. Planting distance will vary from 3m/10ft to 7.5m/25ft, depending on the size of tree. Fan-trained trees will need to be 3–4.5m/10–15ft apart. Smaller trees and fan-trained varieties should be covered if frost threatens while they are in blossom. Mulch in early spring with a good layer of organic material. If the crop is heavy, thin the fruit as soon as the stones begin to form. Thin so that they are 5–8cm/ 2–3in apart.

Pruning and training

Any pruning should be carried out in summer to reduce the chances of the tree being infected with silver leaf. Once the initial shape has been determined, larger trees do not need any pruning apart from the removal of dead or damaged wood. On fans, remove all new shoots that face towards or away from the wall. Shorten any retained new growth to six leaves.

Harvesting and storage

Pick the plums as they ripen. For cooking and preserving pick a little earlier, just before the fruit is ripe. Keep the stalk on the fruit as you pick them. They can be frozen or bottled for storage, but it is best to remove the stones first.

ABOVE **Ripening damsons are suitable for cooking once they have coloured. Eat fresh when fully ripe.**

Pests and diseases

Wasps and birds can cause problems as can larger animals such as rabbits and hares. Other insect pests include aphids and winter moths. The main diseases are silver leaf, canker and brown rot. Trees that are affected with silver leaf and canker should be burnt or destroyed at once.

Peaches and Nectarines

Prunus persica and *P. p.* var. *nectarina*

Peaches and nectarines are closely related, the main difference between the two is that peaches have a downy skin, while nectarines are smooth skinned. They are treated similarly in the garden, although nectarines do better in warmer conditions and are less hardy.

Both fruits can be grown as free-standing trees, but in cooler climates both are better grown as fans against a warm, south-facing wall or even a solid fence.

Cultivation

Peaches and nectarines need a warm, sunny site. The soil should be free draining, but it is also important that it is moisture retentive, so plenty of organic material should be added to the soil. Plant the trees or fans in autumn or early winter, with both at a distance of 4.5m/15ft. Trees should be staked to avoid wind-rock. Mulch in the spring with a good layer of manure or garden compost. If frosts are forecast when they are in blossom, cover the plants with fleece or polythene (plastic) frames. Water during dry periods.

It may be necessary to assist pollination by hand pollinating. Use a soft brush to transfer pollen from the anthers of one flower to the stigmas of another. The flowers should be fully open and the weather dry and warm. With a good fruit set it will be necessary to thin them, removing the excess fruits so that they are 15cm/6in apart.

Pruning and training

Mature trees do not require much pruning apart from the removal of dead or damaged wood and the cutting out of some of the older wood to promote new, vigorous growth. Remove all the shoots that face towards or away from the wall. Initially, thin other shoots to intervals of about 15cm/6in, tying them to the wires and removing the tips if they are longer than about 45cm/18in. Once the plant is established, allow a new bud to form at the base of each lateral in spring, but remove all other buds.

After fruiting, remove the fruiting wood and tie in the new lateral to replace it. Remove the tip if it is too long.

Harvesting and storing

Pick the fruit as it ripens. They are best eaten straight from the tree but can be kept for a few days in a cool place. They can be stored for longer periods by freezing or bottling.

Varieties

Peaches
'Amsden June'
'Bellegarde'
'Duke of York'
'Dymond'
'Peregrine'
'Rochester'
'Red Haven'
'Royal George'

Nectarines
'Independence'
'John Rivers'
'Lord Napier'
'Pineapple'

Pests and diseases

Birds and aphids can be a common problem with peaches and nectarines as can earwigs and red spider mites. Diseases include peach leaf curl, powdery mildew and canker.

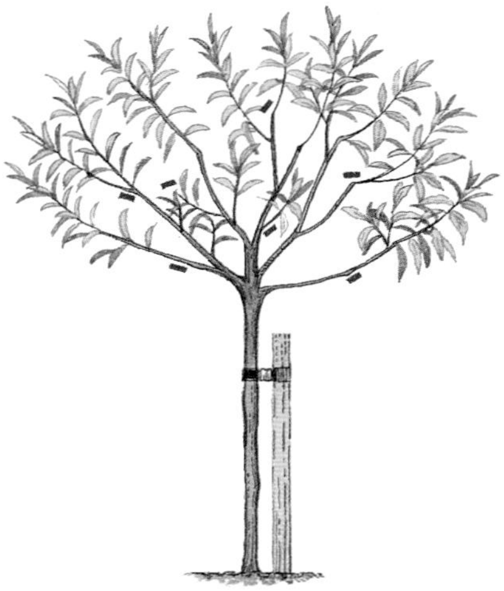

Peach bush tree Not a great deal of pruning is required for a peach bush tree. In spring, cut back some of the older barren wood as far as a replacement new shoot. Also remove any awkwardly placed branches and keep the bush open and airy. Avoid making large cuts, as this is likely to allow canker to infect the tree.

LEFT **Fan-trained peaches such as this healthy specimen provide a decorative feature for a wall.**

Rootstocks

The rootstock will affect the size and rate of growth of the tree.

St Julien A semi-vigorous stock (bush, fan)
Brompton A vigorous stock (bush)

Apricots

Prunus armeniaca

Apricots are not grown as frequently as most other fruit, partly because they are not very easy to grow and partly because, with limited space, most gardeners prefer to grow the more luscious peaches. Home-grown apricots may well be a revelation, however, because they taste much better than shop-bought fruit ever does.

One of the problems with apricots is that they flower very early and are susceptible to frosts. They are, therefore, suitable only for warm areas. Their need for warmth means that they are best grown as fans against a south-facing wall, which will help to protect them from the cold. They are self-fertile, so there is no need for different varieties and only one tree need be grown if space is limited.

Cultivation

A warm, sunny, frost-free site is required to grow apricots successfully. The soil should be free draining but moisture retentive. You will have to incorporate plenty of organic material before planting. Plant in autumn or early winter, placing fans about 4.5m/15ft apart. The blossom will need to be protected if there is the possibility of frost. Mulch the ground with a good layer of manure and keep the ground watered during dry spells. If there is a potentially heavy crop, thin out the fruits to about 8cm/3in apart.

Apricot fan Once the fan has been established, the object of most subsequent pruning is to maintain the shape. Cut out any shoots that are pointing in the wrong direction, especially those that point towards or away from the wall. Thin new shoots, leaving one every 15cm/6in. Prune the remaining shoots to five leaves in the spring and then again, after fruiting, back to three leaves.

Varieties

'Alfred'	'Luizet'
'Bergeron'	'Moorpark'
'Breda'	'New Large Early'
'Early Moorpark'	'Polonais'
'Hemskerk'	

apricots

Pruning and training

On mature fans pinch out the laterals in summer to about 8cm/3in. Remove any laterals that face towards or away from the wall. Later, in summer, remove any more laterals that have developed. Apart from that, little pruning is required because most apricot fruit is borne on old wood. Every few years, remove some of the older wood and allow new laterals to develop in order to replace it.

Harvesting and storage

Pick the fruit once it has fully ripened and can be removed easily from the stalk. Apricots do not store well, although they can be frozen or dried.

Pests and diseases

Protect fruit from birds by netting. Aphids may also be a problem. The most likely diseases are silver leaf, canker, brown rot and die back.

LEFT **An elegant fan-trained apricot spread out across a large wall. The canes, supported by wires, help to maintain the fan shape.**

Rootstocks

The rootstock will affect the size and rate of growth of the tree.

St Julien A semi-vigorous stock (bush, fan)

Brompton A vigorous stock (bush)

Grapes

Vitis vinifera

Grapes have long been appreciated, not only as fresh fruit, but also for making wine. Varieties of white or black grapes are specially selected for their purpose, and growing grapes for wine-making in particular is a very specialized business. Soil and weather conditions as well as choice of variety or varieties can make all the difference. If there ever was a case for checking what other gardeners in your area are doing, this is it.

Grapes need a great deal of sun, and in cooler areas it is easier to grow them under glass, especially if they are for eating. Outside they can be grown in the open if they are trained onto wires, but they may well do better if they are grown against a warm, south-facing wall. From a decorative point of view they make excellent climbers to cover a pergola or arbour, when they provide a dappled shade that is perfect for sitting under. However, with vines climbing over such large structures it is not easy to protect the ripening fruit from the birds.

Patience is required because it will be at least three years before grapes in any quantity are produced, but once they are established the vines may live up to 50 years, so investment in thorough initial work will be well repaid.

There are several methods of training grapevines. They can be grown against a wall as single, double or multiple cordons; in the open on wirework the double guyot is a good method. Although pruning and training are not complicated, the formative work takes place over several seasons and it is worth consulting specialist publications to check on the best methods and techniques.

Cultivation

Grapes must have a warm, sunny situation. The soil must be very free draining, and if your soil is heavy it will need a lot of work before it can be used. South-facing hillsides, with a gravelly, lightish soil are perfect. Plant the new vines in spring at intervals of 1.5m/5ft. Apply a mulch of manure in spring. Water during dry spells.

Dessert grapes need to be thinned to produce large grapes. Bunches should be thinned to 30cm/12in intervals and then the grapes themselves thinned to allow them to swell and the air to circulate. Use long-pointed scissors for the thinning. Net to prevent fruit loss to birds.

Varieties

Outdoor

'Brant' black, wine
'Chardonnay' white, wine
'Chasselas' ('Royal Muscadine') white, dessert
'Léon Millot' black, wine
'Madeleine Angevine' pale green, dual-purpose
'Madeleine Silvaner' white, wine
'Müller-Thurgau' white, wine
'Noir Hatif de Marseilles' black, wine
'Perlette' black, dual-purpose
'Pirovano 14' red-black, wine
'Précoce de Malingre' white, wine
'Riesling' white, wine
'Siegerrebe' golden, dual-purpose
'Triomphe d'Alsace' black, wine

Greenhouse

'Alicante' black, dessert
'Buckland Sweetwater' white, dessert
'Foster's Seedling' white, dessert
'Gros Maroc' black, dessert
'Reine Olga' red-black, dessert
'Schiava Grossa' ('Black Hamburgh') black, dessert
'Seyval Blanc' white, wine

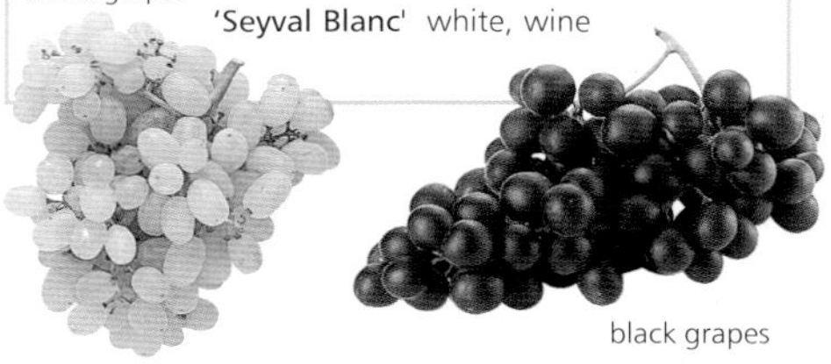

Pruning and training

Whether they are grown under glass or outside, against a wall or as free-standing plants, vines need wire supports. Immediately after planting reduce the leader to 45cm/18in. From this the various basic shapes will be grown. Specialist books should be consulted for formative and established training and pruning methods for vines grown under glass. The guyot system of training and pruning may be used for outdoor vines, the double guyot system is illustrated opposite.

Harvesting and storing

Pick the grapes when they are ripe by cutting the entire bunch from the vine. It is usual practice to cut a little of the

LEFT **These bunches of wine grapes are growing on vines that are supported on wirework.**

RIGHT **Small quantities of grapes can be grown over trellis and archways as long as they have a warm, sunny situation. Grown in this way, they provide a highly decorative feature which is ideal for a small garden.**

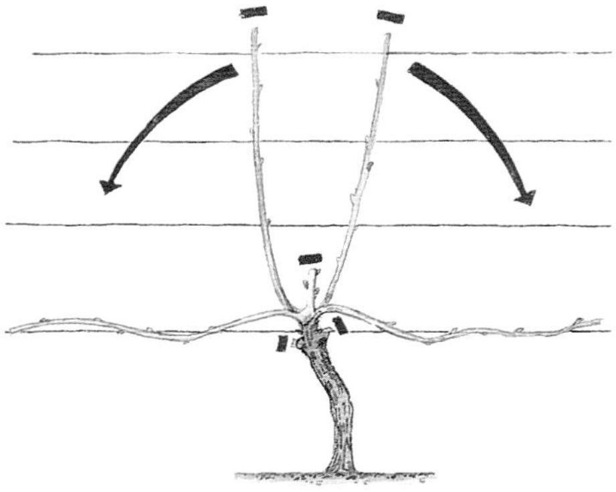

Established double guyot, winter pruning Each year remove the horizontal branches that carry fruiting stems, leaving three vertical central shoots. Pull two of these down on each side of the central shoot, so they are horizontal, and tie in place on the wire. The third shoot should be cut back to leave three strong buds which will form the three verticals for the following year.

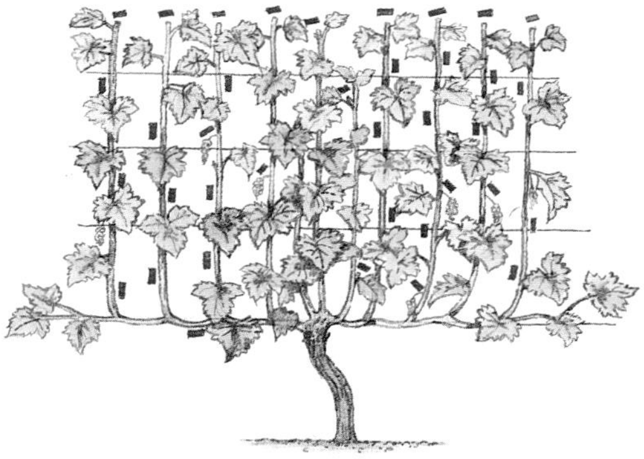

Established double guyot, summer pruning In the summer, train the new shoots from these buds vertically, removing any side shoots that develop on them to one leaf. Allow the vertical fruiting shoots to grow on the horizontal branches, removing any side shoots that appear. Cut back above the top wire to three leaves. After fruiting, completely remove the horizontal branches and train the remaining three central shoots as described above.

woody vine stems on each side of the bunch in order to form a useful "handle". A mature vine should provide about 7kg/15lb of grapes. It is advisable to store the grapes in a container with a soft lining so that the delicate fruits are not bruised or damaged. Grapes are best eaten straight away, but they can be kept for a couple of weeks if a longer handle is cut and placed in a tall container of water so that the fruit hangs down outside the container.

Pests and diseases

Wasps and birds are two common nuisances, but scale insects, mealy bugs and red spider mite can also be a problem. Grey mould and powdery mildew are among the diseases.

Melons

Cucumis melo

It is debatable whether melons should be regarded as a fruit, which they strictly are, or as a vegetable together with marrows (zucchini) and cucumbers, to which they are closely related. However, since they are grown to be eaten as fruit, they have been treated separately from their relatives.

ABOVE **These melons have been grown vertically under glass. The plants are supported on a wire frame and the ripening fruit is held in a net.**

Melons are tropical fruit and therefore need plenty of warmth, both during germination and for their subsequent growth. In temperate climates, therefore, they are really suited only to greenhouse culture, unless they can be grown in a particularly warm position. It is possible to grow them in cold frames in the same way as in a greenhouse, except that they are grown horizontally over framework (or even on the ground) rather than vertically up canes and wires.

There are several types of melon. The cantaloupes are often considered the sweetest and best flavoured, but the honeydew, or winter, melons are popular with some growers because they can be kept for up to a month after harvesting.

Cultivation

Seed is sown in individual pots in a propagator at about 18°C/64°F. When the plants are large enough to handle, plant them in the greenhouse border or into containers, such as growing bags. Grow them as single cordons, when they should be 38cm/15in apart, or as double cordons, when they should be 60cm/24in apart. The temperature in the greenhouse should be 30°C/86°F during the day, dropping to 24°C/75°F at night. A framework of canes and wires or plastic netting should be erected to provide support. Pinch out the top of single cordons when the plant reaches 1.8m/6ft. Pinch out the leader for a double cordon low down and allow two shoots to develop. As the fruit develops support each in a net.

Harvesting and storage

Harvest melons when the fruit is ripe. A good indication of this is that the stems will start to crack and the fruit has a sweet smell. All types of melon can be stored for a few days, but honeydew melons can be kept for up to a month.

Pests and diseases

Aphids, whitefly, red spider mite and powdery mildew are likely to be the worst problems.

Varieties	
'Alaska'	'No Name'
'Amber Nectar'	'Ogen'
'Blenheim Orange'	'Ring Leader'
'Charentais'	'Romeo'
'Classic'	'Superlative'
'Galia'	'Sweet Dream'
'Hero of Lockinge'	'Sweetheart'
'Honeydew'	'Sweet 'n' Early'
	'Venus'

LEFT **Melons can be grown horizontally in a cold frame. The fruit can be kept clear of the soil by resting it on straw or saucers.**

Cobnuts and Filberts

Corylus avellana and *C. maxima*

Cobnuts or hazelnuts are not very large nuts, but they are sweet, tasty and easy to crack. The trees are easy to grow and have the advantage of producing catkins or tassels of male flowers from midwinter to early spring. The female flowers are inconspicuous red tufts. Fortunately, both types are wind pollinated, which compensates for the lack of pollinating insects so early in the year. There are several self-fertile varieties, so it is not necessary to grow more than one if you are short on space. They are perfect for providing shade in which to sit plants as well as to grow shade-loving plants. They are really a large bush, rather than a tree, growing to no more than about 4m/13ft high, which makes them suitable for a small garden, unlike many of the other nut trees.

ABOVE **The bracts and shells will eventually go brown as the nuts ripen on this typical cluster of cobnuts.**

The main visual difference between cobnuts and filberts is that the husk surrounding the shell does not completely cover the cobnut – you can still see the tip of the nut – whereas on the filbert the husk completely encloses it. The trees produce better crops if they are pruned and maintained, but they can be planted in a wilder part of the garden and left to their own devices if you prefer.

Cultivation

Unlike most fruit, cobnuts like a partially shaded spot that is sheltered from strong winds. The soil should be free draining but moisture retentive, and it should not be too rich. Plant the young bushes in autumn or early winter at distances of about 4.5m/15ft. Mulch with manure to help retain moisture around the roots.

Pruning and training

Both can be grown in two main ways. They are either grown as a tree with a short "trunk" about 45cm/18in high with up to a dozen branches or as a stool, in which all the main stems come directly from the ground, more in the manner of a bush. Whichever way you choose, train the plants to be open centred. Heavier crops can be obtained by "brutting" which opens up the bush so more female flowers can form. This involves the curious practice of part-breaking some of the outer side shoots and letting them hang down.

Harvesting and storage

Pick the fruit as the husks are beginning to turn yellow. The nuts are borne after three to four years. They can be eaten fresh or dried and then stored until you need them.

Pests and diseases

These plants have few problems with the exception of squirrels that steal the nuts.

BELOW **A hazel bush can be used for decorative as well as nut-producing purposes. For larger crops, the bushes should be trained.**

Varieties

Cobnuts	Filberts
'Cosford Cob'	'Butler'
'Fuscorubra'	'Ennis'
'Pearson's Prolific'	'Gunslehert'
'Webb's Prize Cob'	'Kentish Cob'
	'Red Filbert'
	'White Filbert'

cobnuts

growing herbs

Herbs have been an important part of gardening for generations. Indeed, some of the first gardens were herb gardens. However, our perception of herbs has changed over the centuries. Gone are the times when it was essential to grow your own headache remedies and now few people grow medicinal herbs for their own use.

On the other hand, culinary herbs are still widely grown. There are two possible approaches to growing culinary herbs: one is simply to grow those that you actually cook with and the other is to make a comprehensive collection so that you can make a feature of the herb garden. For either type of garden, there is a tremendous range of herbs from which to choose.

Herbs can be grown in a variety of ways. For many people, the traditional herb garden remains the only way to grow them and with care it can become an attractive part of the whole garden. Herbs can also be grown in the vegetable garden or mixed with flowers in the ornamental garden. Another alternative is to grow your herbs in containers which is often the ideal solution for many gardeners because they can be sited near the kitchen for convenience.

Choosing Herbs

When working out planting schemes it pays to think about the colour and texture of the herbs you choose and to group them for best effect. They will flourish and make a better show, too, if given the right conditions – damp or dry, sun or shade. One of the many advantages of a herb garden is that it has quite a long season of interest – often provided by the colour of the leaves (many of which are evergreen). Foliage colours available include silver, or silvery-blue, bronze, purple and gold as well as all the greens.

Above *Rue and curry plant in flower.*

Silver

Artemisia abrotanum – Southernwood. Greeny-grey, feathery leaves.
Artemisia absinthium – Wormwood. Silvery-grey, finely indented leaves.
Artemisia ludoviciana 'Silver Queen' – Western mugwort. Fine, silvery lanceolate leaves.
Artemisia pontica – Roman wormwood. Silver, upright, foliage spikes.
Dianthus spp. – Pinks. Foliage colouring varies, most are blue-grey.
Eucalyptus globulus – Eucalyptus. Silvery-blue, smooth oval leaves, round when immature.
Helichrysum italicum – Curry plant. Silver, spiky leaf clusters.
Lavandula dentata var. *candicans* – Lavender. Woolly, finely toothed silvery-grey leaves.
Marrubium vulgare – Horehound. Greeny-grey, rounded, textured leaves.
Ruta graveolens 'Jackman's Blue' – Rue. Steely-blue, strikingly indented foliage.
Salvia officinalis – Sage. Greeny-grey, oval, rough-textured leaves.
Santolina chamaecyparissus – Cotton lavender. A good strong silver, finely indented foliage.
Thymus vulgaris 'Silver Posie' and *T.* x *citriodorus* 'Silver Queen' – Best of the silver thymes, with delicate variegations.

Bronze and Purple

Ajuga reptans 'Burgundy Glow' – Bronze bugle. Glossy, bronze foliage.

Above Thymus x citriodorus *'Silver Queen'.*

Above *Feathery, bronze fennel.*

Atriplex hortensis 'Rubra' – Red orache. Purple-red, smooth, pointed leaves.
Foeniculum vulgare 'Purpureum' – Bronze fennel. Golden-bronze foliage.
Ocimum basilicum 'Dark Opal' – Purple basil. Glossy, purple leaves.
Ocimum basilicum 'Purple Ruffles' – Purple basil with purple, frilly leaves.
Salvia officinalis Purpurascens Group – Purple sage. Purple-green leaves.
Sambucus nigra 'Guincho Purple' – Purple-bronze elder with indented foliage.

Gold

Many of these are variegated, but the predominant effect is gold.

Above Origanum vulgare *'Aureum'.*

Buxus sempervirens 'Latifolia Maculata' – Golden box. Small golden leaves.
Laurus nobilis 'Aurea' – Golden bay. Smooth, oval golden leaves.
Melissa officinalis 'All Gold' – Golden lemon balm. Bright golden-yellow leaves, splashed with green.
Melissa officinalis 'Aurea' – Variegated lemon balm with gold and green leaves.
Mentha x *gracilis* 'Variegata' – Gingermint. Boldly-patterned gold-and-green-striped leaves.
Origanum vulgare 'Aureum' – Golden marjoram. Yellow-gold, oval leaves.
Salvia officinalis 'Icterina' – Golden sage. Gold and grey-green variegation.
Thymus spp. – Thymes. Several of these have strong gold foliage. Among the best are *Thymus.* x *citriodorus* 'Archer's Gold', *T.* x *citriodorus* 'Aureus', *T.* 'Nitidus' and olive-green and gold *T.* 'Doone Valley'.

Above Mentha suaveolens *'Variegata'.*

Variegated

Agave americana 'Variegata' – Agave. Yellow margins to spiky, blue-grey leaves.
Ajuga reptans 'Multicolor' – Bugle. Green, pink and cream variegated foliage.
Armoracia rusticana 'Variegata' – Variegated horseradish. A cultivar with striking, creamy-white stripes on green.
Mentha suaveolens 'Variegata' – Pineapple mint. Creamy-white margins to leaves.
Pelargonium crispum 'Variegatum' – Scented geranium. Crinkly, golden-edged leaves.
Pelargonium 'Lady Plymouth' – Scented geranium. Light-green leaves with creamy margins.
Ruta graveolens 'Variegata' – Variegated rue. Foliage dappled green and cream.
Salvia officinalis 'Tricolor' – Tricolor sage. Striking variegations of pink, greeny-grey and cream.

Above Ruta graveolens *'Variegata'.*

Herbs with Colourful Flowers

Many herbs have colourful flowers which transform the garden when they are in bloom. Even those that do not have large flowers like their cultivated cousins, such as *Hypericum perforatum*, put on a good show in a mass planting.

Above *Red and white valerian with catmint.*

Ajuga reptans – Bugle. Blue flower spikes.
Alchemilla mollis – Lady's mantle. Frothy, greeny-yellow flowers.
Borago officinalis – Borage. Tiny, star-shaped flowers provide a mist of blue when planted en masse.
Calendula officinalis – Pot marigold. Brilliant, orange-yellow blooms.
Dianthus spp. – Pinks. Deep reds and pinks.
Helichrysum italicum – Curry plant. Bright-yellow button flowers.
Hypericum perforatum – St John's wort. Bright-yellow star-shaped flowers.
Hyssopus officinalis – Hyssop. Deep-blue flower spikes.
Inula helenium – Elecampane. Yellow, daisy-like flowers.
Lavandula spp. – Lavender. A range of misty-blues, mauves and purples.
Monarda didyma – Bergamot. There are many cultivars which come in a range of pink, red, purple and white.

Above *Sunflowers and nasturtiums.*

Nepeta x *faassenii* – Catmint. Mauve-blue flowers, spectacular in a mass planting.
Origanum onites, Origanum vulgare – Pot marjoram and oregano. Clusters of purple-red flowers.
Rosa spp. – Rose. Old-fashioned varieties have pink, red and white blooms.
Salvia officinalis – Sage. Massed purple-blue flower spikes.
Santolina chamaecyparissus – Cotton lavender. Bright yellow button flowers.
Thymus spp. – Many of the thymes have mauve to pinkish-red flowers.
Tropaeolum majus – Nasturtium. A range of bright yellows and oranges and a long-flowering season.

Above *Old-fashioned pinks (*Dianthus *spp.).*

Above *A variety of white-flowering herbs.*

Above *Bronze fennel and rosemary standing tall over a bed of low-growing herbs.*

Herbs with White Flowers

A garden of white-flowering herbs has a restful quality, especially if combined with silver-leafed plants and white and green variegated foliage. Many herbs have white flowers, others, such as borage, lavender and sage, have white-flowering forms. This is a selection:

Achillea millefolium – Yarrow. Small creamy-white umbels.
Allium tuberosum – Garlic chives. White star-shaped flowers.
Borago officinalis 'Alba' – A white-flowering borage.
Chamaemelum nobile – Chamomile. White daisy-like flowers.
Digitalis purpurea f. *albiflora* – White foxglove. Creamy-white spires.
Galium odoratum – Sweet woodruff. Small white stars.
Lilium candidum – Inimitable pure-white lilies.
Myrrhis odorata – Sweet cicely. Large white umbels.
Thymus serpyllum var. *albus* – A creeping, white-flowering thyme.
Valeriana officinalis – Valerian. Effective in a mass planting.

Right *Tall herbs – elecampane, fennel and a white-flowering goat's rue at the back of a border.*

Tall Herbs

When it comes to planning beds and borders it helps to know the eventual height and spread of plants. The ultimate size of individual herbs is indicated in this book, but the selection below are a reminder of "what not to put at the front". They are also useful for adding height to a scheme.

Angelica archangelica – Angelica. A classic for adding architectural impact.
Cynara cardunculus Scolymus Group – Globe artichoke. Earns a place in any scheme for the decorative value of its striking, purple heads.
Foeniculum vulgare – Fennel. A graceful feathery plant, which needs plenty of room.
Levisticum officinale – Lovage. Large clumps of glossy, green leaves need space to spread sideways and upwards.
Onopordum acanthium – Scotch thistle. The patterned leaves are relatively low-growing, but the flower stalks rise to a height of 2 m (6 ft 6 in).

Climbers

Another way to add the dimension of height to an otherwise flat design is by training creeping plants over arbours, archways, obelisks and twiggy tepees. Herbal creepers to choose from include:

Humulus lupulus – Hops. There are both green and golden-leaved varieties.
Jasminum officinale – Jasmine. This has star-shaped, perfumed white flowers in midsummer.
Lonicera periclymenum – Wild honeysuckle with creamy flowers, borne throughout summer. There are also many cultivars to choose from.
Rosa spp. *R. eglanteria* – Eglantine rose. Has very short-lived flowers. An old-fashioned climber, such as Mme Alfred Carrière, might be more rewarding. *R. gallica* 'Complicata' reaches 2 m (6 ft 6 in) and may be used as a pillar rose.

Top Humulus lupulus *'Aureus'.*

Above *A bay tree with climbing roses.*

Above *Creeping thymes make effective and appealing ground cover.*

Ground-cover Herbs

For the front of a border, to fill an awkward corner, or as paths and lawns, ground-cover plants are invaluable.

Arctostaphylos uva-ursi – Bearberry. A mat-forming evergreen shrublet.
Chamaemelum nobile 'Treneague' – Non-flowering lawn chamomile. A non-flowering cultivar.
Juniperus communis 'Prostrata' – Juniper. Forms a dense, neat carpet, which no weed can penetrate.
Symphytum ibericum – Dwarf comfrey. A fast-spreading plant. Also comes in a gold and green variegated form.
Thymus serpyllum – There are many creeping thymes, ideal for paths, lawns and ground cover.
Vinca minor – Periwinkle. The dark-green leaves form dense, weed-defying cover. Cheerful blue flowers in spring.

Dry or Damp Soil?

It is usually easier to fit the plant to the right environment, rather than the other way about. Changing the soil and microclimate to accommodate a plant's particular preference can often be difficult and costly. The good news is that herbs are relatively easy-going plants and will often adapt to and grow well in conditions they would not choose in the wild. But to make things easier, it usually pays to give them what they want.

Dry, or certainly well-drained, soil suits the majority of plants, especially the shrubby herbs such as rosemary and thyme.

Damp-lovers to watch for include angelica, the *Mentha* genus and *Monarda didyma*. The mints and angelica will also grow happily in shade or semi-shade.

Herb Containers

Growing herbs in containers has many advantages. Where space is limited there is always room for a few pots, even in the smallest of gardens. Sited near the house, they provide the added convenience of being handy for harvesting – important for culinary herbs. As part of a garden scheme, containers can be placed in a bed to fill a temporary bare patch, used as focal points or arranged symmetrically to link different elements of a design.

Their mobility is a definite plus. Of course it must be borne in mind that very large pots, or those made of stone, will be too heavy to move. But, unlike static planting in a bed, small and medium pots, or those made of a lighter material, can be moved around to make a change. This is also useful for plants past their best, which need a less prominent position in which to recuperate. Tender and half-hardy herbs in containers can be moved under cover for winter protection.

Above *Comfrey has deep roots and needs a tall container (left back). Marjoram (centre) and thyme thrive in smaller pots.*

Planting

Growing a single species in a container gives plants room to develop and to provide plenty of leafy growth. For larger specimens, such as bay, sage and lemon verbena, it is essential that they do not have to share a pot if they are to be left undisturbed for several years. The pot should be large enough to allow roots to spread. Mixed herb pots make very attractive features and are a good way of growing a variety of plants in a small space, but plants are inevitably cramped; roots become congested and annual replanting is usually necessary for a mixed planting.

Above *Large pots planted with angelica add impact to a parterre.*

Good drainage is one of the keys to success. Before you start, check that there is a large hole in the base of the pot, or several holes in the case of plastic pots and troughs. Put in a layer of crocks (broken terracotta pots), then cover with a layer of sand or grit (gravel) before filling with potting compost (soil mix).

Most herbs flourish in a free-draining environment and, as a general rule, a 3:1 mixture of soilless compost (planting mix) and loam-based compost (soil mix) gives the best results. For shrubby herbs, such as bay, sage and rosemary, and for scented pelargoniums, add a few handfuls of grit (gravel) to the mix to improve drainage. Do not be tempted to use garden soil; it will not provide enough nutrients and might harbour weeds and pests.

Maintenance

Extra fertilizer must be added after about four weeks, with subsequent weekly feeds throughout the growing season. An organic plant food based on seaweed extract is preferable, but slow-release fertilizer granules save time as they are added when potting up.

Pot-grown plants need frequent watering during the growing season. As a general rule, it is better to let them almost dry out and then give them a good soaking, rather than to keep dribbling in small amounts of water. Water-retaining gel mixed into the growing medium at the time of planting makes watering less of a chore. During the winter months pot-grown perennials should be given the minimum amount of water possible.

Plants that are kept in the same container for several years should have the top layer of compost, about 5 cm (2 in), scraped off and replaced with fresh every year. They will need re-potting in a container one or two sizes larger as roots become congested – try not to leave it until the plant is obviously suffering, with roots bursting out of the pot, yellowing leaves and poor, straggly growth.

Above *Herbs growing in separate pots with* Lavandula stoechas *at rear right.*

Planting a pot of mixed culinary herbs

1 Mix slow-release fertilizer and water-retaining gel, following instructions, into a potting medium made up of 3:1 parts of soilless compost (planting mix) and loam-based compost (soil mix).

2 Put a layer of crocks (broken terra-cotta pots) in the bottom of the pot.

3 Fill to the first hole with the potting medium, settling it evenly.

4 Tap a plant out of its pot and feed it gently through the hole, working from the inside outwards.

5 Cover the roots with more compost and firm it down before adding a further layer of plants.

6 Put in more plants until all the holes are filled and finish with one or two plants on top. Water in thoroughly.

YOU WILL NEED

Slow-release fertilizer; water-retaining gel; soilless compost; loam-based compost; trowel; terracotta pot; crocks (broken terracotta pots); a selection of culinary herbs

Right *Marjoram (top), alpine strawberry, thymes and parsley go well together in a pot of herbs for culinary use.*

Potting Composts

Potting composts (soil mixes) come in two main types: based on sterilized loam, and the soilless composts (planting mixes), based on peat or peat substitutes such as coir. Soilless composts are lighter and easier to handle, but they do not retain nutrients as long as the loam-based ones. They provide a more moist environment, but, if left unwatered, they also dry out more quickly, and are difficult to remoisten. Both types of potting compost are available containing nutrients in a range of proportions: "seed and cuttings" formula contains the least and a "potting" formula the most, with "all-purpose" in between.

Indoor Herb Gardening

Some herbs adapt well to being grown as houseplants. In regions with cold winters which suffer frosts, it is one way of cultivating tender herbs successfully. A conservatory gives scope for keeping a wider range, but is by no means essential. Give indoor plants as much natural light as possible and regular liquid feeds in summer, and do not overwater, especially in winter.

Vigorous and colourful, easy-to-grow scented pelargoniums are a rewarding group to grow this way as they come in such a variety of scents and leaf forms. Don't be afraid to prune them hard if they become straggly and never keep them too damp. Tender pineapple sage (*Salvia elegans*) does well indoors and produces scarlet flowers in late autumn or winter just when colour is welcome. It needs a big pot and more water than most. *Aloe vera* adapts well to an indoor regime, requiring the minimum of attention. A gritty, free-draining compost (soil mix) suits it best and infrequent but thorough watering. Myrtles do not always survive frosts and are another good choice. The dwarf *Myrtus communis* 'Tarentina', having a compact and tidy habit of growth, is eminently suitable, and *Myrtus communis* 'Variegata', being even less hardy, is well worth growing inside.

Herbs on the Windowsill

A supply of indoor culinary herbs is a great convenience. It is possible to grow them on the kitchen windowsill as long as you take into account the stress this puts on the plants. If you put a young plant into a small pot and then keep cutting off its leaves, it will be hard pressed to survive. At the same time, it is being kept short of air, the atmosphere may be too hot and steamy and changes of temperature extreme. From the point of view of flavour, there is little sun to bring out the essential oils.

The best way to counteract these problems is to alternate pots kept on the windowsill with another set left standing outside. Keep the different herbs in individual pots and group them together. They grow better in close proximity to one another because transpiration from the massed leaves increases the overall humidity.

Standing the pots on a gravel tray, or in a container with a layer of gravel on the base, keeps them cool and helps to retain moisture, without the plants becoming waterlogged.

Above *Herbs grouped together on the windowsill are handy for cooking.*

Far left *Scented pelargoniums and lemon verbena grow well as houseplants.*

Left *Culinary herbs in separate pots, standing in an outer container of gravel.*

Herbs in the Greenhouse

It is perfectly possible to grow many herbs without any form of winter protection or artificial heat. But in colder regions a small, frost-free greenhouse is a great help in extending both the season of growth and the range of plants it is possible to grow.

It is often easier to raise plants from seed sown in trays. Under controlled conditions, the success rate is usually higher. With a greenhouse you can start sowing much earlier than if you had to wait for the right outdoor conditions. But remember that young plants, grown on from seedlings, must be acclimatized gradually to being outside, before they are finally planted in the garden. Do this by standing them outside in the daytime for a short period, or transferring them to a cold frame.

Parsley is a good candidate for sowing under glass. Although it is reasonably hardy, it needs heat to germinate (about 18°C, 65°F), which is why it takes so long to emerge when planted straight into the garden early in the year before the soil has warmed up. Germination will be much quicker and more reliable if the seeds are started in trays in the greenhouse, with a view to transplanting outside once grown.

Basil is almost impossible to raise from seed in temperate regions without the benefit of glass. But it is not difficult to get good results if you follow a few guidelines:

- Do not start too early in the year; allow spring to get well under way first, when it will be easier to supply a temperature of 15–18°C (60–65°F).
- Scatter seeds as sparsely as possible, so that little thinning-out is required later and root disturbance minimized.
- Provide the seedlings with adequate ventilation and do not overwater to reduce risk of "damping-off" disease.
- Grow plants on in a large container, rather than planting them directly into the soil. They can then be kept outside or moved into a greenhouse, according to current weather conditions.

Above Capsicum frutescens *'Gipsy', in flower, in a greenhouse.*

Summer Herbs

Unless the summer is exceptionally cool and wet, sweet basil (*Ocimum basilicum*) will usually grow well in a pot outside, but the purple-leafed kinds seldom reach their full potential unless kept under glass.

Chilli peppers (*Capsicum* spp.) also need to be grown in the greenhouse in cooler climates if they are to produce mature, ripe fruits. In parts of the United States chilli peppers can be grown outside. Other herbs to try are the popular Japanese salad plants known as shiso (*Perilla frutescens* and *P. frutescens* 'Crispa') and the culinary flavouring plant, lemon grass, much used in Thai cookery (*Cymbopogon citratus*).

Adequate shading and copious watering are necessary for plants grown under glass in the summer.

Winter Protection

For container-grown plants that are not fully frost-hardy, such as bay, lemon verbena and myrtle, as well as more tender subjects such as scented pelargoniums, a cold greenhouse, provided it is frost-free, gives enough protection to keep them alive through the winter. In the summer months they can stand outside in the garden, as long as they are moved under cover before the first winter frosts.

Many of these plants will lose their leaves, even if they remain evergreen in warm climates. Once they have been moved into the greenhouse in the autumn, cut them back or trim lightly, according to individual requirements. Over the succeeding winter months give them a minimal amount of water and no fertilizer to ensure dormancy.

Planning Your Planting

Many of the most familiar herbs are Mediterranean in origin and grow best where there is plenty of sun. Bear this in mind when deciding on the location for your herb garden. Choose an area that has the sun for most of the day and where there is little dense or permanent shade. Take the time to watch the movement of the sun, so that you know exactly where shadows fall. This will help with planning the planting, allocating the right areas for herbs needing sun, shade or semi-shade and deciding where to site features such as a sundial, arbour, fountain or a seat. If you are at the survey stage in winter when the trees have no leaves, don't forget to take into account the deep shade cast by summer foliage.

Shelter is also important. Chilly winds, particularly in winter, can be devastating to many shrubby herbs such as thyme and rosemary. You may be able to make good use of an existing boundary wall to act as a windbreak. Consider putting in hedges, trelliswork or wicker fences to provide a sheltered, secluded environment, but remember that they will cause some shade and loss of light to plants. It may be better to install them on one or two sides only, according to prevailing wind direction, leaving other sides open or with low balustrade fencing.

If productivity is the main objective it is best not to overdo the number of low hedges, central features and dividing pathways, all of which will diminish the amount of space available for cultivation. Nevertheless, the plot can still achieve considerable charm if the production is arranged in an orderly fashion and by building in a feature or two that will add overall interest.

Top *A carefully planned bed, with silvery spokes of* Santolina chamaecyparissus *in a wheel of block planting.*

Right *Herbs flourish in a garden sheltered by a high brick wall.*

Soil and Site Preparation

Time spent preparing the site by improving the soil and eliminating weeds will be repaid many times over. This is not as daunting as it might seem. Improving the texture of the soil (though not weed elimination) applies only to the planting areas and does not have to be carried out where paths and hard surface areas are to be laid.

A light, free-draining soil is best for most herbs. It warms up quickly in spring and does not become as cold and waterlogged as heavy soil in winter. But if it is too porous, moisture and nutrients will be quickly leached away, resulting in a soil so poor and dry that few plants will flourish. Forking in organic matter – garden compost or leaf mould – will ensure better results. On heavy soil, if areas are inclined to become water-logged it is worth digging out trenches and filling them with rubble to form land drains. Chalk and sand both drain rapidly whilst clay retains moisture. The ideal is a crumbly loam which retains the right degree of water and nutrients.

Many herbs, including lavender, do not grow well in a heavy clay soil. One way to overcome the problem is to put

Above *A raised bed provides good drainage.*

in raised beds filled with loamy topsoil. But if you intend to plant straight into existing ground, once again it will be necessary to incorporate organic matter.

For a very heavy soil, the addition of plenty of coarse grit helps to open up the texture further. Double digging, though hard work, is the way to do this most effectively. Take out a trench to the depth of two spades at one end of the plot, turning it straight into a wheelbarrow and removing it to the other end of the area to be treated. Add a layer of grit and compost to the first trench, covering it with soil from the next section. Continue in this pattern until the whole area has been dug over and organic matter incorporated. When the last trench is reached fill this with the soil from the first trench. After digging, tread down the soil lightly to ensure that no air pockets remain and that the soil does not subsequently settle unevenly. Rake over in several different directions until the surface is level and leave it for a week or so before planting.

Beware of overmanuring ground where herbs are to grow. The object of digging in bulky organic matter is to improve texture and drainage. For the majority of herbs, heavy feeding with rich farmyard manure or artificial fertilizers encourages soft growth, reduces aroma, and lays the plants open to attack by pests and diseases.

Another factor to consider is the alkaline or acid content of the soil, measured by the pH factor. A figure of seven is taken as neutral – anything higher is alkaline, anything lower is on the acid side. An inexpensive soil-testing kit will tell you what you have. Herbs are a disparate group, but as a rule most will grow in a neutral soil.

Above *Double digging eliminates weeds and improves soil texture.*

Above *Forking out weeds.*

Above *Removing all trace of roots helps keep the soil clear for longer.*

Weeding

Eliminating perennial weeds as thoroughly as possible before putting in plants pays great dividends. Another advantage of double digging is that you can take out deep roots and every speck of greenery you see as you go along. Fork out all weeds as painstakingly as possible. For stubborn or dense weed growth, cover the area for a full season with a layer of thick black polythene (plastic). Once this is removed, all but the most persistent weeds will be obliterated.

If you would rather get started on the planting immediately, put down a layer of black polythene (plastic), cut with holes for planting pockets, making sure these are completely weed free. Then put in the plants and cover the surface of the polythene with a mulch of gravel or bark chippings.

Laying Out a Garden

The first thing to do is to make a plan to fit your plot and requirements. You can take it from an existing design in a book, but you will need to tailor it to fit your own site. Check that you have the space to carry out your chosen scheme, that it will complement its surroundings and not be too cramped. Then measure the site and note the position of any existing walls, trees or other features that are to be kept.

Decide on a scale and draw up the plan on graph paper, but remember that it is all too easy to put in too much, too close together. It may look good on paper but will not work in reality. Keep checking as you go along that the layout you have drawn is feasible on site. The simpler it is and the fewer fussy elements you include, the more impact the finished garden is likely to have.

Marking Out a Garden

Once you have worked out the design and chosen the site, it is time to lay it out on your plot and put in hard surfaces.

Take your paper plan on to the chosen area and mark the key points on the ground with stakes. Designate the boundaries and outline the beds and paths with string and pegs, measuring carefully and ensuring that right angles are accurate with a builder's square. A length of garden hose is useful for marking out curves. At this stage it is possible to check that the proportions are right, that the whole scheme is well balanced and that other parts of the garden do not intrude or clash with the general concept. An upstairs window is often the best place to get a good overall view. Now is the time to change anything that does not look right – it will be difficult and costly to alter later on. It is best to decide on the order of work before you start:

- Changes of levels or major earthworks, including digging out ponds, need to be done first.
- Construction work, paths, terraces, hard surface areas, herb wheels and raised beds come next.
- Boundaries need to be clearly marked before you start, and, if putting in a wall, you may want to do this first, as well as putting in fence posts. But for ease of access and wheelbarrow movement it usually pays to leave fences till after the hard construction is done. Hedges, too, should be put in at a later stage with the bulk of the planting.
- Features such as pergolas, arbours and fountains may be put in at the same time, or after the hard-surface construction.
- Preparation of the soil in the beds should be done a few days in advance of planting if possible.
- Planting the herbs is practically the last stage.
- Finishing touches include adding container plants to the scheme and movable features such as sundials.

Above *Contrasting coloured stones, in this cobbled surface, pick out a star motif and decorative border.*

Putting in Paths and Hard Surface Areas

All paths and hard surface areas require a firm, level base. This can be done by marking a series of pegs with a line 5 cm (2 in) from the top. Hammer the pegs into the ground across the area to be levelled, tapping them in until the tops are flush with each other (using a spirit level to check). Then level and firm down the soil to the mark on the pegs.

Above *Drawing out the design on paper helps to achieve a successful result.*

Above *A random pattern of paving stones.*

Above *Bricks provide a colourful surface.*

Gravel is a relatively inexpensive, quickly laid surface. It comes in a range of colours and in two main types: crushed stone from quarries and pea shingle (pea stone) from gravel pits. It should be laid on a level, well-compacted base of soil covered with a layer of dry concrete, eight parts ballast (gravel) mixed with one part cement, which has been left to dry off for several days. Hessian mesh (burlap), laid over the path before the gravel is spread, prevents weeds.

Stone slabs are a good surface for a terrace or large paved area. They are also useful for using as stepping stones in a wide border and for a mixed surface path of gravel and paving slabs. Bed them into mortar on a hardcore base (stones and broken bricks), as for the brick path, below.

Cobblestones are an attractive finish for a small scale area. They can be used to fill in round shrubs and trees or to lay in conjunction with other hard-surface materials. Pack them together as closely as possible, set in a bed of mortar on a hardcore base.

Bricks must be hard, impermeable and resistant to frost. Reclaimed bricks, from specialist merchants, have the best mellow colour. They must be laid on a firm, hardcore surface or they will expand and lift with the moisture in the soil and form an uneven path. For a path with less heavy wear a sand base without hardcore is sufficient.

Laying a brick path

This construction will be suitable for main paths in a herb garden and should withstand average domestic use and weather conditions.

YOU WILL NEED

Timber boarding; wooden pegs; mallet; spirit level; hardcore (stones and broken bricks); ballast; cement; rake; hard, impermeable bricks (about 24 for an area 60 cm (2 ft) wide by 1 m (3 ft) long); sand, a large broom

1 Dig out soil for the path to a depth of one brick plus 10 cm (4 in) for the base. Tread it down till level. Put in an edging of timber boards, held in place with hammered-in pegs, with their upper edges at the level of the finished path. Spread a 7.5 cm (3 in) layer of hardcore, rolling it in until firmly compacted.

2 Cover the hardcore base with a dry mix of eight parts ballast to one part cement, approximately 2.5 cm (1 in) thick, lightly tamp it with the head of the rake to fill in any gaps in the hardcore, and then rake to a loose, level surface.

3 Lay the bricks into the ballast and cement base, arranging them in a staggered pattern so that you don't have a line of joints. Tap each one down with a mallet, butting it as close to its neighbour as possible; check with a spirit level that the path is even in all directions as you go.

4 When all the bricks are in place, spread more ballast and cement over the surface, brushing it repeatedly into the joints to fill them, before cleaning off the surplus. Moisture from the soil will set the cement, but a light spray of water may be applied to hasten the process.

5 Before the cement hardens, ease sand from the joints to create pockets for prostrate herbs, then fill in with a little topsoil and sow seeds or plant divisions from established plants.

Planting the Garden

Once you have a stock of established perennials you will be able to increase them by propagation, and many annuals and biennials will conveniently seed themselves. But you are sure to need to buy some plants in order to get your herb garden started.

Buying Plants

Specialist herb nurseries should have many of the more unusual varieties, but many garden centres now offer a reasonable selection. As you will require several of each species for a good show, the initial outlay could be considerable, so make sure you buy only strong, healthy specimens and follow these tips to get the most for your money:

- Check that a plant has not been too recently potted and whether it lacks a strong root system, or conversely that it has not been too long in the pot and the roots have become congested. Make sure there are no weeds, algae or moss.
- Examine the plant carefully for pests – red spider mite and whitefly may not be obvious at first glance.
- Don't buy anything with discoloured , wilting or blotched leaves – it could be diseased.
- Never assume that a stunted, straggly and overgrown or poor and sickly specimen will improve once planted out. It won't.
- Resist the temptation to buy annuals potted up singly. Many do not transplant well and seed quickly in hot, dry weather – these include coriander (cilantro), chervil, dill and borage. Grow them yourself from seed. Once established they often self-seed.
- Look for annual flowering herbs, such as pot marigolds and nasturtiums, sold as bedding plants in trays, rather than in single pots – or grow them yourself from seed.
- It will probably be necessary to thin seedlings to give them room to develop; and keep them well weeded to prevent competition for moisture and nutrients.

Planting the Design

If you have drawn in the herbs on your plan, this can be very useful as a guideline. A pre-designed scheme helps to group plants effectively for colour, texture, height and so on. However, it is not always easy to visualize on paper how it will look on the ground. Standing the plants in their pots on the soil, and shifting them around as necessary, helps with spacing and final decisions on position which often leads to a happier end result. It cannot be stressed enough that plants always look best in groups, rather than being scattered about singly. A whole bed of purple sage makes a much more dramatic statement than one little clump lost in a mass of competing colour. A broad sweep of catmint or borage is a sight to savour.

The same principle applies to climbers grown over an arched walkway. With several different plants the result can be very haphazard. One variety will have impact.

Above *One healthy and one poor container-grown vervain plant.*

Top *A well-stocked herb garden.*

Invasive Herbs

Be careful where you put invasive plants. Comfrey, horseradish, sweet cicely and other herbs with strong tap roots can be very difficult to eradicate if you later want to change the planting scheme.

Some herbs, particularly those with creeping roots, encroach on their neighbours. Mint is a well-known culprit; soapwort and tansy can also prove overpowering. It is best to confine them with divisions in the bed: bricks or tiles buried in the soil work very well for shallow-rooting invasive herbs.

Another way to curtail them is to grow them in a large container buried in the soil – but make sure it has adequate drainage holes, or the base removed, if the plants are not to become choked.

Planting a herb garden

1 *When you have put in all the hard surfaces in your garden and prepared the soil as necessary (see Soil and site preparation) it is time to plant up the scheme. Fork in a little organic fertilizer first, to give your herbs a good start, but avoid heavy manure.*

2 *Always water plants well in their pots first, as plants never take up moisture as well after planting if put in dry. Add water until it trickles out of the base of the pot – this is important for trees, shrubs and larger specimens, which may look damp on top but are dry at the rootball.*

3 *Mark your planting positions with sand. Tap each herb out of its pot, make a hole with a trowel, and put in the plant, firming the soil lightly around it afterwards. Water in well. Under very dry conditions it helps if you fill the planting hole with water first.*

4 *Keep the area free of weeds so that the newly set out herbs do not have to compete for moisture and nutrients.*

YOU WILL NEED

Garden fork; organic fertilizer; a selection of herbs; watering can; trowel; sand

Right *Recently planted aromatic herbs, set out in a knot pattern, surround a dwarf standard tree.*

Propagation

Propagating your own herbs is a rewarding occupation and the best way to replace plants and to stock your garden economically. The basic techniques are not difficult, but, as herbs are such a disparate range of plants, their requirements and the degree of difficulty in raising them varies. Some are much easier to propagate than others. Many respond better to one method than another so check for the optimum propagation method for each plant.

Raising from Seed

Many herbs are easy to grow from seed. Spring is generally the best time for sowing, but do not start too early: seeds sown when air and soil temperatures are warmer and light levels higher will grow into stronger plants. Some seeds are sown in autumn, as indicated here.

Annuals: All annuals – plants whose life cycle is completed in one year – can be grown from seed sown in spring. Hardy annuals, such as chervil (*Anthriscus cerefolium*), coriander (cilantro) (*Coriandrum sativum*) and pot marigold (*Calendula officinalis*) may also be sown in autumn to give them an early start the following spring. Half-hardy annuals, such as nasturtiums (*Tropaeolum* spp.), should not be sown until late spring or early summer in areas where there is frost. Basil (*Ocimum basilicum*) is tender and should be sown in seed trays under glass in late spring to early summer.

Biennials: These are planted in the late summer or early autumn of one year, to flower the following year – though some of them go into a third year, their life cycle is over once they have flowered. Although parsley is a biennial, it is worth sowing seed every year because the stems coarsen and it does not produce such good leaf in its second year. Biennials include angelica (*Angelica archangelica*), caraway (*Carum carvi*), clary sage (*Salvia sclarea*) and evening primrose (*Oenothera biennis*).

Perennials: These live for a number of years and many perennial herbs can be successfully raised from seed. But not all of them produce seed, such as French tarragon (*Artemisia dracunculus*) and the non-flowering golden sage (*Salvia officinalis* 'Icterina'). Many hybrids and cultivars do not come "true" from seed, which means they may vary considerably from the parent plant. This includes all the mints, most lavenders and ornamental thymes. These must be vegetatively propagated.

Vernalization: A few herb seeds need to be subjected to a period of intense cold before they will germinate. In the wild, this ensures their survival where winters are cold. To reproduce these conditions artificially, in a process known as "vernalization" or "stratification", put the seeds in a polythene (plastic) bag of moist sand and leave in a refrigerator or freezer for 4–6 weeks before sowing.

This is necessary for: aconitum or monkshood (*Aconitum napellus*), arnica (*Arnica montana*), agrimony (*Agrimonia eupatoria*), juniper (*Juniperus communis*), hawthorn (*Crataegus laevigata*), *Primula* spp., *Rosa* spp., sweet cicely (*Myrrhis odorata*), sweet woodruff (*Galium odoratum*) and sweet violet (*Viola odorata*).

Scarification: Some hard-coated seeds, such as those of legumes, which include broom, clovers and vetches, will germinate more readily if first rubbed with fine sandpaper. This breaks up the outer coating and allows moisture to penetrate, which all seeds require before they will germinate.

Left *Careful labelling prevents misidentification when new seedlings emerge.*

Sowing in seed trays

The success rate for seeds sown in trays under controlled conditions is higher than for seeds sown outdoors. It is the best method for very fine seeds, such as parsley, and essential for raising tender plants, such as basil. It is also a good way to give many plants an earlier start.

YOU WILL NEED

Cellular seed tray; soilless seed and cuttings compost (soil mix); watering can; herb seeds; garden sieve; label; polythene (plastic) dome or plastic bag; 7.5 cm (3 in) pots

1 *Fill a seed tray with soilless growing medium. A tray divided into cells makes it easier to sow thinly and to pot up seedlings with minimum root disturbance. Water first, then scatter two or three seeds in each compartment.*

2 *Cover the tray with a layer of sieved compost (soil mix). Never bury seeds too deeply, especially small ones such as parsley. Water again and don't forget to label the tray (tiny seedlings look similar).*

3 *Put a polythene (plastic) dome over the tray, or enclose it in a plastic bag, to retain moisture. Put the tray on a windowsill or in the greenhouse until the seedlings emerge.*

4 *When the seedlings come through remove the cover and put the tray in a light place out of direct sunlight. Keep moist, but never waterlogged.*

5 *As soon as the seedlings are large enough to handle, pot them up in 7.5 cm (3 in) pots filled with fresh potting compost (soil mix). When strong and bushy they can be planted out.*

Sowing Outdoors

Many seeds can be sown outdoors directly into the soil where they are to grow, or in nursery beds for later transplantation. It is also the sensible way to raise herbs that do not respond well to being transplanted. These include coriander (cilantro), chervil and dill. It is as well to remember that there is a higher failure rate for seeds sown outdoors, rather than in a tray in the greenhouse, due to unexpected adverse weather conditions or the unwanted attention of birds or rodents. On the other hand it saves time and energy in pricking out, potting up and hardening off, and plants raised this way are often sturdier. For a good chance of success with outdoor seeds:

- It is best not to start too early in spring, if still cold. But to speed things up cover the area with cloches for a week or two in advance of sowing to warm up the soil.
- First weed the area thoroughly and rake it to a fine texture and level surface.
- Next make a shallow depression with a stake, or rake handle, in the soil and sprinkle in seeds as thinly as possible. Larger seeds, like nasturtiums or coriander (cilantro) can be placed individually rather than scattered.
- Cover seeds with a thin layer of soil, patting it down lightly, but beware of burying them too deeply.
- Don't forget to mark the area planted clearly. Sowing in straight lines, as appropriate for producing some culinary herbs, makes it easier to distinguish seedlings from weeds.
- Water well after planting and keep the area moist until the seedlings appear.

Above Calendula officinalis *grown from seed.*

Germination Requirements

For seeds to germinate successfully they require:

Moisture: The surface of the growing medium in seed trays must not be allowed to dry out, and outdoor seeds need frequent watering in dry spells.

Warmth: Most seeds need some degree of warmth to germinate, though temperature requirements can vary considerably. Most plants native to northern Europe and North America germinate at 10–13°C (50–55°F); plants from tropical and southern latitudes 15–21°C (60–70°F). Those herbs with special requirements include: lavender, exceptionally low at 4–10°C (40–50°F), parsley, 18–21°C (65–70°F), and rosemary, especially high at 27–32°C (80–90°F).

Light: Seeds should not be sown too deeply, in order that light may penetrate the soil and waken the seed into growth. This is particularly important for fine seeds – larger ones can be buried a little deeper. Light is crucial for thyme (*Thymus vulgaris*), winter savory (*Satureja montana*), poppies (*Papaver* spp.) and also sweet marjoram (*Origanum majorana*).

Air: A peat-based (or peat-substitute) growing medium is best for seeds, as the open texture allows air to circulate and oxygen to reach the developing plant. This is why breaking up the soil to a fine tilth is necessary for outdoor sowing and why seeds fail in compacted, waterlogged soil.

Vegetative Propagation

Many perennial herbs are best propagated vegetatively, rather than by seed. This includes those that do not flower and set seed.

Above *Mint (in pot) grown from cuttings.*

Taking cuttings from the stems during the growing season is an effective method for many. Softwood cuttings are taken from soft, new growth in spring through to midsummer. They root quickly with warmth and humidity. Suitable for: *Origanum* spp., *Pelargonium* spp., *Santolina* spp., *Tanacetum* spp., *Mentha* spp. and *Salvia elegans*.

Semi-ripe cuttings are taken from harder, half-ripened wood in mid to late summer and can be taken from many shrubby herbs, including *Buxus* spp., *Citrus* spp., *Helichrysum italicum*, *Rosmarinus officinalis, Thymus* spp., *Lavandula* spp. and *Myrtus* spp. Some plants, including *Salvia elegans* and *Artemisia abrotanum*, root from stem cuttings taken at any time during the growing season.

Hardwood cuttings are taken from mature wood in mid to late autumn. They are slow to root (up to 12 months), and are usually kept in a cold frame over winter. This is suitable for trees, shrubs and roses.

Stem cuttings

Many herbs, such as rosemary and southernwood, are best propagated from cuttings. It is also the only way to perpetuate a special flower colour, such as pink-flowered hyssop, or a leaf variation, such as variegated rue. Stem cuttings are all taken in the same way. Do not cram in too many cuttings or put one in the middle of the pot.

YOU WILL NEED

Plants; sharp knife or secateurs (pruners); polythene bag; hormone rooting powder; 15 cm (6 in) pot; cuttings compost (growing medium); dibber (dibble), pencil or stick; plastic dome or bag

1 *Collect only a small amount of material at a time and be sure to keep in the shade in a polythene bag, to minimize water loss. Choose sturdy, non-flowering stems, with lots of leaves. Cut a section about 10 cm (4 in) just below a leaf joint and remove all but the top two or three leaves. These are necessary to supply the plant with nutrients as the root system develops.*

2 *Dip the cuttings into hormone rooting powder, tapping off any excess, and insert them into holes made with a dibber (dibble) round the edge of a pot filled with moist cuttings compost (growing medium). Water lightly and cover with a plastic dome or polythene bag held over a wire frame and sealed at the bottom – this is to maintain maximum humidity.*

3 *Once the cuttings have rooted – 2–4 weeks for softwood cuttings, 4–6 weeks for semi-ripe cuttings – repot into new compost and harden them off gradually before planting out.*

Root cuttings

A method of increasing herbs with creeping roots, such as mint (*Mentha* spp.), soapwort (*Saponaria officinalis*), bergamot (*Monarda didyma*) and herbs with taproots such as horseradish (*Armoracia rusticana*).

YOU WILL NEED

Garden fork; mint, or other suitable plant; secateurs (pruners); seed tray; cuttings or all-purpose compost (growing medium); watering can

1 *Lift a root of mint and cut it into 4 cm ($1\frac{1}{2}$ in) pieces. Try to cut at a point where there is a small bud from which a new plant can grow.*

2 *Fill a seed tray with cuttings compost. Lay the pieces of root on the surface, press them in and cover with a further layer of compost. Water and leave in a shady place. There is no need to cover the tray or enclose it in polythene, but do keep it moist.*

3 *Once there are plenty of leaves showing through, divide the new plants and grow them on in bigger pots or plant them out in the open ground.*

Division of roots

Herbs with fibrous or fleshy taproots are very easy to propagate by division. These include: chives (*Allium schoenoprasum*), oregano (*Origanum* spp.), lemon balm (*Melissa officinalis*), lovage (*Levisticum officinale*) and comfrey (*Symphytum* spp).

1 *Dig up a clump of chives. Divide it into several new pieces, pulling it apart with your hands or the aid of a small fork if necessary.*

2 *Cut off some of the top growth. Replant in open ground or firm each new piece into a pot filled with all-purpose compost.*

3 *Keep the new plants well watered. They will soon grow strongly to provide plenty of fresh leaf.*

Layering

A useful method of propagation for shrubby herbs such as bay, rosemary and sage. It works by inducing a side stem to develop new roots while still attached to the parent plant. Mound layering is particularly suitable for thymes, which become straggly after a few years. Pile gritty loam in a mound over the lower, leafless stems, leaving the crown of the plant showing. This stimulates new roots to develop at the base, when they can be separated and then planted in a different position.

1 *Trim the lower leaves from a side stem, attached to the shrub. Bend it over and bed into soil beside the plant.*

2 *Fasten it down with a staple or peg. Water in and leave for several months until roots have formed. Divide the new plant from the parent and replant it.*

Maintenance

Herbs are easy-going plants. Most are not difficult to grow, coming up year after year, or self-seeding exuberantly; but a herb garden, like any other garden, needs regular care and maintenance to keep it looking at its best. Keeping paths and gravel areas free of weeds makes all the difference to the overall appearance, especially in formal gardens, which depend on symmetry and orderliness for effect. If you don't like using weedkiller, there is nothing for it but to hoe out offenders as soon as you see them. Try not to let weeds seed or else the problem will be compounded.

Mulching is a good way to keep beds and borders weed-free. Use well-rotted garden compost, mushroom compost, leaf mould or bark chippings and pile it on thickly round plants. Weeds that come up through the mulch will be weak and easy to pull out. Gravel is also a suitable mulch and weed suppressant for thymes and many shrubby herbs. Grass clippings are useful for mulching round fruit bushes and the base of trees – they can be used fresh, added in a thick layer and allowed to rot down. For weeds with persistent roots, spreading heavy-duty black polythene (plastic) over the area for a full season helps to eradicate them by depriving the seedlings of light and air.

Deciding which plants are undesirable is not always straightforward, as plenty of herbs are wild plants and often described as "weeds". You may decide to keep some self-sown plants, either leaving them in situ or transplanting to a more convenient spot, and this can add to the interest of the garden. The main thing is to be in control and not to let unwanted plants take over and dominate the scheme.

Above *A meticulously maintained garden.*

Clipping

In a formal scheme keeping plants clipped is all-important. Some will need cutting only twice a year, but others may require more frequent light trims to keep them in shape.

Many herbs grow prolifically, if left to themselves, and need frequent cutting back if the garden is not to become untidy and overgrown. Pruned plants can often be harvested for culinary or household use and any spares should be added to the compost heap. Spring is a good time to do some initial tidying and trimming, but many plants will need further cutting back during the summer months or in autumn.

Watering

It should not be necessary to give extra water to fully grown herbs planted out in the garden, except under severe drought conditions. Many of the shrubby herbs of Mediterranean origin are resistant to a shortage of water – rosemary flourishes in the driest of summers. But moisture-lovers, such as angelica, bergamot and mint, may need some help at these times. And of course it is essential in dry spells to water newly-planted young herbs until they are well-established.

Mulching often helps to conserve moisture, but if it is to be effective for this purpose it must be added early in the season before the soil dries out.

The main task is to water container-grown herbs throughout the growing season. In their dormant period, during winter, they should be kept barely moist, or root rot may ensue.

Feeding

Although it is important to keep the soil "in good heart" with the addition of garden compost, heavy manuring and fertilizing with high-nitrogen inorganic products is to be avoided. It results in soft, sappy growth which is susceptible to blackfly infestation and will not withstand the stress of droughts or extreme cold. Worst of all the herbs will lack fragrance and aroma.

A slow-release organic fertilizer, such as blood, fish and bone, forked into the soil, helps to get new plants off to a good start. And any fruit and vegetables in the herb garden will require extra nourishment in the form of liquid seaweed or a comfrey fertilizer. Container-grown plants benefit from regular liquid feeds throughout the growing season, especially older plants that have been in the same pot for some time.

Above *A standard bay in a tub needs regular clipping with secateurs (pruners) and feeding.*

Opposite *A rotting compost heap.*

Comfrey Fertilizer

Comfrey is invaluable as a herb garden fertilizer, containing all the nutrients necessary for healthy plant growth in digestible form. It has a high potash content and is also a source of nitrogen, phosphorus and many other elements. Use it in the following ways:

• As a mulch by spreading freshly cut comfrey leaves round plants (blackcurrants and other fruit bushes benefit particularly). Topping the comfrey with a layer of lawn mowings adds bulk and speeds decay.

• Add comfrey leaves to the compost heap in thin layers – it doesn't add to the humus content, but works as an "activator", encouraging the breakdown of other plant material. Be careful to avoid adding roots and flowering stems, which will regenerate and form unwanted plants.

• As a liquid fertilizer, by filling a bucket to the halfway mark with comfrey leaves, fill it with water and cover with a lid – to exclude insects. Leave for 4–5 weeks, then strain off the liquid (which will be very smelly) and use it undiluted as an organic fertilizer for container plants, tomatoes and general garden use.

• A more concentrated version may be made by standing a bucket with a hole in the bottom over another container, filling the bucket with comfrey leaves and pressing them down with a weighted board. The bucket should then be covered with a lid and the leaves left to rot down for several weeks, until a black, tarry liquid seeps out. This should be diluted in water before use.

Above *A variety of garden clippings and fresh vegetable material is added to the heap, for a good supply of garden compost.*

Making a Compost Heap

A good supply of garden compost is always needed in the herb garden for improving the structure and fertility of the soil and as a mulch material.

Containers: There are many types of manufactured compost bins available in plastic, wood and other materials, suitable for gardens of varying sizes, but you can easily make your own. Build the heap straight on to the earth, with a surround of wire mesh, or timber boards to contain it. If using boards, leave airspaces between them.

Materials: Any plant material is suitable, such as, leaves, flowers, lawn clippings, straw, vegetable peelings. Woody stems should be included only if they have been mechanically shredded. Do not add difficult-to-eradicate perennial weeds, especially with their roots or main flowering stems attached. Annual weeds are best avoided if there is any chance of their seeding.

Construction: Build up the heap in layers, alternating lawn clippings with leaves and open-textured material – a variety of materials leads to a better texture. Add an activator every two or three layers – a sprinkling of chicken manure, seaweed meal, blood, fish, and bone, or comfrey leaves.

Processing: Covering up the heap with polythene (plastic), or a manufactured lid helps conserve moisture, so that the heap rots more rapidly. It is not usually necessary to "turn" the heap if it has been well constructed, but it does help to break up material added in clumps, such as lawn mowings. It will take 3–6 months to achieve a dark colour and moist crumbly texture.

Management: Have at least two heaps simultaneously at different stages of decay – one being for current use and one under construction. Dig out the compost from the bottom so that the old material is used first.

Topiary and Training

Shrubs and trees clipped into geometric shapes have been a garden feature since Roman times. They introduce an appearance of order and formality to the herb garden and provide a contrast for the exuberant growth of many of the other plants. Grown in a pot as a standard, one plant alone makes an interesting focal point, and several placed at strategic intervals lend unity to a scheme. Standards may also be planted in the soil of a parterre (rather than being container-grown) to add height and punctuate the design. Lower-growing herbs clipped into mounds as path edgings or to infill beds emphasize the structure of the design.

Above *Mounds of clipped box .*

Herbs for Topiary

Shrubs or trees with small leaves and a tight habit of growth make ideal subjects for topiary work.

Buxus sempervirens – Box, easy to shape, is the favourite for taller standard trees, cones, spirals and pyramids. Also comes in gold- and silver-leafed varieties.

Buxus sempervirens 'Suffruticosa' – Dwarf box is best for miniature standards and small globes.

Juniperus communis – Juniper, for tall cones and pyramids. Prune in autumn and winter to prevent bleeding of sap.

Above *An imposing display of topiary.*

J. c. 'Compressa' – A dwarf form of juniper that is suitable for lower topiary shapes.

Laurus nobilis – Bay, traditional herb-garden centrepiece as a "lollipop" or standard "mophead".

Myrtus communis – Myrtle responds well to clipping for all topiary shapes. Trim after flowering and give winter protection as it is not fully hardy.

M. c. subsp. *tarentina* – A dwarf form of myrtle ideal for compact globes and low mounds.

Rosmarinus officinalis – Rosemary, for training over wire shapes and clipping into formal hedges.

Ruta graveolens – Rue, effective clipped into mounds.

Santolina chamaecyparissus – Cotton lavender, much used in knot-garden work, also good for clipping into mounds and edges.

Satureja montana – Winter savory responds well to being clipped into low mounds or trained over a frame.

Taxus baccata – Yew, a traditional topiary tree and a favourite for hedging.

Teucrium chamaedrys – Wall germander, for knot gardens and central mounds.

Cones, Pyramids and Spheres

These are relatively simple to achieve as they require no complicated training and pruning, though it helps to have a good "eye"for the job and to stand back frequently, as you clip, to assess progress. Box is the most rewarding to work with as it produces a clean outline and is easy to shape. For a cone, start with a bushy young plant and clip it roughly to shape by eye in its first year. Feed and water it well so that it puts on new growth. In the second year, trim it into a more pronounced cone, using a tripod of canes, encircled with wires as a guide. Keep the shape by trimming twice a year in late spring and early autumn.

Above *Training rosemary over a frame.*

Wire-framed Globes

Plants with flexible stems can be trained to grow over a balloon-shaped wire frame. This works well for rosemary, curry plant (*Helichrysum italicum*), ivies, scented-leaf pelargoniums and climbers such as jasmine. Start with a young plant which has developed a reasonable length of stem. Repot it, cut out any middle growth and push the spiked end of the wire frame into the growing medium. Then tie the stems to the wire frame with twine, avoiding tight knots, which will damage the plant and impede its growth. Clip straggly stems to shape two or three times a year during the growing season.

Standards

Free-form standards: Lemon verbena (*Aloysia triphylla*) can be grown as a free-flowing standard, in contrast to formally clipped box and bay. It is more appropriate in an informal scheme where height and a structural element are required.

Select a young plant with a strong central leader. Remove any competing leaders and strong side stems, leaving higher shoots and some lower laterals to provide food, but shortening the lower laterals by half. Stake the stem to keep it straight. As the plant grows, the shortened laterals can be removed to leave a bare stem. As top laterals develop, pinch out the tips to encourage bushiness. When the plant has reached the desired height and developed a thick head of foliage, pinch out the leading shoot.

Rose standards: Old-fashioned roses trained as weeping standards make a romantic focal point in any scheme and lend colour and contrast to the strict pattern of a potager. Train them over a plastic-covered metal frame shaped like an umbrella for a more formal effect.

Aftercare

Topiary trees in containers all need regular watering and feeding throughout the whole summer to keep them healthy and growing actively. The roots of pot-grown plants are more vulnerable in cold weather than those grown in the soil, so wrap them in hessian (burlap) during frosty spells if they are hardy plants and if less than hardy move them to the protection of a cold greenhouse. Myrtle, bay, rosemary and lemon verbena are all best kept under cover during the winter months.

A mophead bay with a twisted stem

This shows how to make a standard bay with a twisted stem. For a version with a straight stem, simply cut off all side growth to leave one strong central leader, instead of three. Feed regularly throughout the growing season. Replace the top 5 cm (2 in) with fresh compost (soil mix) annually.

YOU WILL NEED

Large pot; multipurpose compost (soil mix); coarse grit (gravel); fertilizer granules; watering can; bay tree; secateurs (pruners); ratchet secateurs or pruning saw

1 *Fill a pot with free-draining, multi-purpose growing compost (soil mix), and add a few handfuls of grit (gravel) and a handful of slow release fertilizer.*

2 *Repot a sturdy bay tree with plenty of straight, flexible growth. Clip off side growth to leave three straight stems.*

3 *Using ratchet secateurs or a pruning saw remove lower shoots up to about two-thirds of the overall height.*

4 *Bend over the stems, twisting them carefully, to form a plait.*

5 *Clip the crown to your preferred shape during subsequent years with secateurs (pruners).*

Harvesting Herbs

Harvesting the herbs you have grown is a continuous process rather than a one-off annual event. Once established, most will grow strongly enough to allow plenty of repeat picking, which in itself encourages new growth in healthy, well-cared-for plants. It makes sense not to denude small, immature plants before they have much foliage, but many annuals and herbaceous perennials, such as lovage (*Levisticum officinale*), will produce a second crop once they have flowered, if they are cut back almost to the ground. When cutting perennial, shrubby herbs think of it as pruning and aim to improve the overall shape of the plant.

The optimum time for harvesting plant material to preserve it for later use depends on the growth pattern of the individual herb and the part of it that is required – leaf, flower, seed or root. Usually it will be during the growing season, but a few herbs, such as thyme, rosemary and sage, may be lightly picked when dormant, although they will not have such a full flavour. Whether harvesting herbs to dry for culinary use, cosmetics and pot-pourri or for home remedies, the following guidelines will ensure good results:

- Choose a fine, sunny day for picking, so that the essential oil content, which gives the plant its flavour and scent, is at its best. Wait until any dew or residual raindrops have evaporated – herbs tend to go mouldy before the drying process is complete if picked when wet – but try to finish in the morning before volatile oils have been drawn to the surface by the heat and dissipated.
- Use only sharp scissors or secateurs (pruners) so as not to damage the plant and limit further cropping. Make sure that your equipment is clean and that sticky blades do not pass pest or disease problems from one plant to another.
- Pick only prime material from plants that are at their peak – avoid anything damaged, discoloured, diseased or spent with age.
- Pick herbs in small quantities, only as much as you can deal with at one time. Herbs should not be left in heaps, waiting to be processed, as even quite a small pile encourages heat and deterioration sets in. The idea is to preserve the plant before the active constituents start to break down and lose viability.
- Flowers and foliage must be wiped clean and be insect free before they are processed: they can be lightly sponged and patted dry with a paper towel, but do not try to wash them as this will impede drying.

Above *Cutting a head of angelica to collect the seeds.*

Left *A freshly-gathered harvest of garden herbs, ready to be preserved and stored in containers for future use.*

Leaves: Most should be picked before they come into flower, when leaf flavour and texture are at their best. Pick small-leafed plants on the stem for stripping later – larger leaves may be picked individually. Shrubby perennials which last through the winter should not be cut severely late in the season, as this will weaken them and leave them vulnerable to frost damage.

Flowers: These should be cut soon after they have opened when they are at their best, and not left to drop their petals, when colour and scent will be minimal. Pick single blooms or flower heads as appropriate and strip off petals or florets when spreading them to dry. Lavender should be picked with a long stem, and flowers such as borage, where only the tiny blue "star" is required, need careful individual collection.

Seeds: The pods or seed heads must be picked as soon as they are ripe, when they are no longer green, but before they fall. This means watching them carefully, as they can ripen and disperse very quickly.

Roots and rhizomes: These are usually collected during their dormant period in autumn or winter. When digging them up, try to leave some portion of the root so that the plant can regenerate. With some herbs, such as horseradish, this is not difficult, as it will regrow vigorously from the tiniest portion of root. Wash roots and rhizomes thoroughly with plenty of cold water and cut into pieces before processing.

Bulbs: These include garlic and onions. Dig them up in late summer to early autumn.

Bark: Bark should not be stripped from very young trees. They must never be ring-barked (stripped of bark all round the circumference of the trunk), nor should too much be taken in one year as this could kill the tree. Tools should be clean and sharp, and the lowest cut made at 1 m (3 ft) above ground level. Endangered or protected species should not be harvested at all.

Wild plants: Wild plants should be picked with the utmost caution, both for safety reasons and for the sake of the environment. Many wild plants are protected by law (check if this applies), and should not be touched – in any case none should be uprooted or overpicked, especially if less than common. Any that grow near crops should be treated with suspicion, as they may contain pesticide residues, and of course you must be confident of correct identification. If you are not sure, leave them alone.

Right *Fresh sage leaves tied up in small bunches for drying.*

Harvesting marjoram

1 *Cut bunches of healthy material at mid-morning on a dry day.*

2 *Strip off the lower leaves, which may otherwise become damaged.*

3 *Twist an elastic (rubber) band around the stems to hold them tightly together.*

4 *Gather as many bunches as you need, then the bunches can be hung in a dry, well-ventilated place where they are protected from light.*

Drying

Successful drying depends on removing the moisture in the fresh material without sacrificing the volatile oil content. The process has to be completed quickly so that oils are not lost through a natural process of decay, but not so quickly that they are destroyed by heat. The key to success is the right temperature and low humidity.

An average temperature for commercially dried herbs is 38°C (99°F), but this would be difficult to provide at home without special equipment. Between 20–32°C (68–90°F) works well and can be found in an airing cupboard, or a cupboard near a hot-water heater. A spare room, with an electric heater (not directed straight at petals or loose material), could also be used.

The place chosen should be dry and well ventilated (garages are not really suitable, but a clean shed may be ideal) and, for better colour preservation, dark. Sun drying is a traditional method in climates where air temperatures are high and humidity low, but it does lead to colour loss and there is also a greater risk of contamination than in an indoor, controlled environment.

Oven drying is generally too fierce for flowers and foliage, even at its lowest setting, but it is suitable for roots. Microwaving is not ideal as it is necessary to include a small container of water to prevent arcing, and this makes for humidity, which is counterproductive.

Green Herbs

Small-leaved green herbs may be dried on the stem and larger leaves dried individually. Spread them on slatted trays, or on fine netting stretched over a frame so that air can circulate beneath, and put them in a warm, dark place with some ventilation.

Leave the herbs until they are crackly-dry to the touch. The length of time will depend on the thickness and moisture content of the leaf, the level of heat provided and humidity in the air. The process takes from 3–4 days to a week at the most. Once dried, strip leaves off the stems, or crumble larger ones into small pieces ready to store. Wearing cotton gloves makes the job easier on the hands.

Herbs may also be tied in bunches with raffia or string and hung up in a clean, airy place to dry.

Above *Herbs drying in a dark, clean and well-ventilated shed.*

Above *Lavender, tied in bunches for drying, is well spaced to allow air to circulate.*

Above *Drying lavender commercially on a custom-built, movable frame.*

Flowers

Twist off heads of large blooms, such as roses, and spread out the petals on paper on slatted trays. Put in a warm place and leave them until papery dry.

Pot marigold (*Calendula officinalis*) flowers are easier to dry whole, then twist off the petals afterwards if required.

Lavender is best hung up in bunches, tied loosely with string or raffia, and with the heads in paper bags to exclude dust and catch petals that may fall as they dry.

Once the flowers are dried, they may be left whole, according to their intended use, or stripped from the stems in the same way as green herbs.

Chive flowers, or rosebuds that are required for decorative purposes, will keep a good shape if dried upright, with stems pushed through wire cake trays.

Specially treated dry sand or silica gel may also be used for drying flowers, resulting in a good colour and perfect shape. Place a flower on a thin layer of sand, sift more sand gently over it until covered and leave for three weeks in a warm, dry place. Uncover carefully.

Seeds

A good way to dry seeds is to pick the seed heads with stems attached. Tie them in bunches, insert the heads into paper bags and hang them up in a warm, airy place. When completely dry, clean off the pods or husks before storing in clearly marked envelopes. Seeds should not be stored in polythene (plastic), which encourages moisture.

Roots

Roots require a higher temperature than flowers and leaves for successful drying from 50–60°C (120–140°F). An oven, at a very low setting, with the door left open is suitable. Make sure the roots are scrubbed clean, then cut them in pieces and spread on baking trays. Put them in a cool oven and turn at intervals to ensure even heat. Leave until brittle, but test frequently as they should not become shrivelled and overbrown – length of time depends on the size and moisture content of root pieces.

Storing

Dried herbs and flowers deteriorate quickly, losing aroma and colour, if left exposed to light and air. Always store them in the dark and keep in a dry place. Flowers and foliage required for pot-pourri can be kept in paper bags, airtight tins or glass jars.

Above *Dried bay leaves in a jar.*

Right *Pot-pourri ingredients, stored in glass, are best kept in a dark cupboard.*

Above *Dried herbs retain colour and flavour stored in opaque containers.*

Preserving

Preserving the flavour and perfume of herbs in vegetable oils or in vinegar is easy to do and these have many uses in culinary and cosmetic recipes or in home remedies. A mixed-herb oil, or one with a single flavour, such as basil, adds interest to salad dressings, stir-fries, pizza and pasta dishes, grilled or barbecued meat, fish or vegetables. Rosemary oil is the ideal ingredient for bath lotions and beauty treatments and oil infused with garlic makes an effective liniment for relieving aches and pains.

Above *Finish off oil bottles by neatly winding cotton string around waxed paper and then tying it securely with a reef knot.*

Tips for success:

- Use a good-quality, mild-flavoured oil, such as sunflower or safflower, so that the taste of the oil doesn't compete with the flavour of the herbs. Extra-virgin olive oil, which has a strong flavour of its own, is not suitable.
- Always cover herbs completely with oil during the infusing process. Any bits left sticking out will start to deteriorate and affect the quality of the oil.
- It is important to remove the plant material before storage. If left it will start to decay and the oil will become cloudy and sour.

To make herb oil

1 *Put a good handful of herbs or flower heads into a clean glass jar – either a single herb, such as marjoram used here, or a mixture, such as oregano, rosemary and thyme – and crush them lightly to release the essential oils.*

2 *Pour in a mild vegetable oil until the herbs (or flowers) are completely covered, otherwise any that are not covered will go mouldy. Cover the jar and stand it in a warm place – a sunny windowsill is fine.*

3 *After about a week, strain off the herbs, replace with fresh ones and leave to infuse for a further week. This process can be repeated until the flavour is strong enough.*

4 *Remove the herbs and pour the oil into a clean, sterilized bottle with an airtight lid. The oil will keep for a few weeks if extra flowers have been added, or 6 months without extra flowers.*

YOU WILL NEED

A handful of fresh herbs or about 12 flower-heads; 400 ml/¾pt light vegetable oil; jar with top; filter

Herb Vinegars

Herb vinegar is made in the same way as a herb oil. A great variety of flavouring materials can be used: fresh or dried leaves, spices, chillies, garlic, fruit or flower petals. Tarragon vinegar is a classic for salad dressing. Fruit and flower flavours, such as raspberry, blackberry, lavender or rose petal, add sharpness to sweet dishes and are useful as home remedies. Raspberry vinegar helps to ease a sore throat, and lavender, applied as a compress, may relieve a headache.

Some herb vinegars can be used as antiseptics for cleaning surfaces or as poultices; some can be dabbed on the skin to counteract a range of conditions; others can be taken internally as a tonic or prophylactic.

An excellent ingredient for home-made cosmetics is cider vinegar; it restores the acid mantle of the skin and is a traditional ingredient in skin lotions and hair rinses. Use it to make a mint-and-marigold or rose petal vinegar, which is then diluted – two or three tablespoons in a basin of water – to splash over the face as a general toner.

To make herb vinegar: Fill a clean jar to about one-third with herb leaves, spices, fruit or flowers of your choice, top up with cider vinegar and leave to infuse for two or three weeks. It is not usually necessary to use more than one batch of herbs or other flavouring ingredient to obtain a strong enough flavour, as it is for oil.

Vinegar is a better preservative than oil, so it is possible to leave in some of the herb used, such as a sprig of tarragon, for decorative effect, but always replace the infused material with a fresh piece. Dried material can be left in vinegar indefinitely. Coloured peppercorns, rosemary, chillies and dried bay leaves look most attractive when left in a spiced vinegar.

Above *Fresh herbs add a spicy, aromatic flavour to vinegar. Clockwise from front, rosemary, sage and marjoram.*

Right *Tarragon (left) and a mixed herb vinegar with bay leaves.*

Preserving in Sugar

Sugar makes an excellent preservative and was a traditional method of retaining the properties of herbs and flowers. Old herbal manuscripts are full of recipes for herbal syrups and conserves made with sugar, or more often, honey.

Above *Sugar, flavoured with lavender flowers, is ideal for baking.*

Lavender sugar: This is a delicious way to impart a subtle fragrance to cakes, biscuits, meringues and other sweet dishes, without the coarse texture of the whole petals. To make lavender sugar, bruise dried lavender flowers, stripped from the stem, and add them to caster (superfine) or icing (confectioner's) sugar before storing in an airtight jar until required. Sieve out the flowers before use. Ten to 15 heads of lavender will be enough to lend fragrance to 450g (1 lb) of sugar.

Crystallized petals: Many edible flowers may be used for this purpose. To make the petals: Check the petals are dry, clean and insect-free. Spread them on a greaseproof-paper covered baking tray. Then paint them, using a fine artist's brush, with a thin coat of lightly whipped egg white (just broken up, rather than frothy), and sprinkle thickly with caster (superfine) sugar. Put in the bottom of a very low oven with the door left open, until completely dry and brittle, but not brown.

Top *Crystallized violas make delicate decorations for cakes and sweets.*

Above *Lavender honey is easy to make and has a subtly distinctive flavour.*

Herb honey: The finest honeys are those which are made by bees collecting from a single flower source such as lime blossom or thyme. Both honey from the hive and many herbs, such as rosemary and garlic, have antiseptic properties. In combination they are helpful for soothing sore throats and cold or flu symptoms, taken in teaspoonfuls. They can also be used as a sweetener for herb teas.

To make herb honey: Put a small handful of herbs, such as rosemary, thyme or lavender flowers, into a saucepan. Bruise with a wooden spoon, add the contents of a 225 g (8 oz) jar of honey and heat gently until melted but not boiling. Leave to infuse for about one hour before straining the mixture. Discard the herbs and pour the honey into a jar with an airtight lid for storage.

Freezing Herbs

A convenient way to preserve fresh herbs for later use is to freeze them in ice cubes for adding to soups, stews and other cooked dishes. Simply chop them finely, put into ice-cube trays and top up with water before freezing. Whole mint leaves or borage flowers may be frozen in the same way for floating in drinks.

Culinary herbs, stripped from the stems but not chopped, can be frozen packed in polythene (plastic) bags, or cartons, for short periods of time. They will not, of course, have the texture of fresh leaves once thawed. This is a useful method of preserving herbs that do not keep a good aroma when dried, such as basil, parsley, chives and mint.

Tinctures

Many herbs may be preserved in alcohol for medicinal use. They are best made as a cold infusion using dried herbs and alcohol with little flavour of its own, such as vodka. This makes a potent preparation, as the essential oils and active constituents of many herbs are soluble in alcohol. It should be taken in small doses of drops, or teaspoons, and, it is strongly suggested, as directed by a qualified practitioner.

To make a tincture: Put dried herbs in a jar and top up with a mixture of one part of water to two parts of vodka. As a general guideline, 15 g ($^1/_2$oz) of dried herbs to 300 ml ($^1/_2$ pint/$^2/_3$ cup) of alcohol and water mixed are standard quantities. Seal the jar and leave in a warm, dark place for one week, after which time the active constituents will have been extracted and the herbs will start to deteriorate. Strain out the herbs and rebottle.

Making herb ice cubes

1 *Pick some mint leaves, selecting small undamaged ones, and strip them from the stem.*

2 *Put a single leaf into each compartment of an ice-cube tray, top up with water and freeze.*

Left *From left to right: lavender, violet leaf and juniper tinctures.*

Above *Edible flowers and herb leaves make unusual ice-cubes for floating in drinks.*

Herbal Essential Oils

What are essential oils? The essential, or volatile, oil in a plant gives it its scent. Despite the name, essential oils are not oily – a drop applied to paper does not usually leave any mark. They are volatile liquids, which evaporate at normal air temperatures and are secreted from minute glands and hairs in the leaves, stems, flowers, seeds, fruit, roots or bark of plants and trees.

Some plants, such as roses, contain their essential oil mainly in the flowers; others, such as lemon balm (*Melissa officinalis*) mainly in the leaves. The orange tree (*Citrus aurantium*) contains three differently-named essential oils, in the flowers (neroli), the leaves (petitgrain) and the rind of the fruit (orange oil).

The organic chemical structure of plant essential oils is extremely complex. Analysis by gas liquid chromatography (GLC) reveals that peppermint oil, whose 50 per cent menthol content provides its minty smell, has 98 other constituents. Flower essential oils have as many as several hundred components. For this reason it is impossible to chemically reproduce an exact copy of a naturally occurring essential oil in the laboratory.

Above *The leaves of* Melissa officinalis *are distilled to produce a cheering, tonic essential oil.*

Above right *Essential oils have long been valued for their therapeutic properties.*

Production

Essential oils are soluble in fats, vegetable and mineral oils and in alcohol. For the most part they do not dissolve in water, though some of their constituents may do so. The main fragrance molecules of roses and orange flowers, for example, are soluble in water. Steam distillation is the most frequent method of extraction, and volatile solvents and alcohol are sometimes used in the process. A few fragile flower fragrances are still obtained by the centuries-old method of macerating the petals in trays of fat, and volatile oil from orange rind is extracted by expression: that is by pressing it out, nowadays by machine, but formerly pressed by hand. Quality is affected by varying soils, climates and harvesting conditions. Some oils may have been diluted or adulterated. It is not easy to tell, so look for a reliable source.

Using Essential Oils

Plant essential oils and extracts are widely used in the pharmaceutical, cosmetic and food industries. In the home they are used therapeutically in aromatherapy and herbal medicine, by taking them internally, by inhaling them in vaporizers and in fragrance products such as pot-pourri, by massaging them into the skin, by applying them in compresses, or by putting them in the bath. They are sometimes used in a domestic context to flavour food, but only in very small quantities, the whole plant being safer and usually more satisfactory for culinary use.

The important thing to remember is that, as extracts of the active principles of plants, essential oils are concentrated substances and should be taken internally only in controlled, drop-sized doses. When applied externally they must be diluted in a carrier oil.

Essential Oils in History

Essential oils take their name from the *quinta essentia*, or quintessence, a term coined by a Swiss physician Paracelsus, 1493–1541. He took the medieval theory of alchemy, which sought to isolate the *prima materia*, or elemental matter, of a substance, and applied it specifically to plants. His goal was to divide the "essential matter" of a plant from its "non-essential" components.

In ancient times, extracting plant fragrance by macerating it in oil or fat was common, and a technique of destructive distillation, such as that which produces oil of turpentine, was also known. At the beginning of the 11th century, steam distillation as a means of making plant-scented waters was discovered, usually credited to the physician, Avicenna, 980–1037, author of the *Canon of Medicine*. Arnald de Villanova, d. 1311, a Spanish doctor, further popularized the use of distilled herb waters for medicinal purposes.

Distillation was seen at the time as a means of refining plant material to its purest form, through fire, and alcohol was widely used in the process as producing the best results. But it was not until the mid-16th century that the nature of essential oils was understood and the process of separating them from the distillate put into practice.

By the beginning of the 17th century plant essential oils were available from professional pharmacies, as well as being produced on a domestic scale in the stillrooms of grand houses. Many herbals and old recipe books contained detailed instructions.

Inhaling Essential Oils

Breathing in the fragrance of essential oils has an immediate effect on mood and can be immensely therapeutic. An essential oil burner or vaporizer is one of the best ways to do this. You could also put a few drops of oil on a handkerchief to tuck under a pillow, or mix some into a pot-pourri of flowers and herbs.

To lift depression, anxiety and nervous tension try essential oil of frankincense, jasmine, neroli, rose or sandalwood. Sedative oils for insomnia include chamomile, juniper, lavender and marjoram. For stress and shock there is cedarwood, melissa or peppermint, and for mental fatigue and lethargy use basil, black pepper, cardamom or pine.

Bath Oils

Adding essential oil in drops to the bath water is another way to benefit from the fragrance. To make a bath oil for dry skins, mix about 20 drops of essential oil into a 10 ml (2 tsp) bottle of almond or sunflower oil which has first been infused with fresh flowers or herbs, such as chamomile or lavender.

A lavender bath is deeply relaxing, mildly antiseptic and helps to heal tiny cuts and scratches, bites or swellings. It is also soothing when you have a cold.

Right *A bath oil including essential oil of chamomile is soothing to sensitive skins.*

Below *Lavender, mixed with a light oil for massage, releases an aroma which will help ease stress headaches and promote calm and restful sleep. It also helps muscular aches and pains. To release the scent, warm the oil slightly before you begin.*

Insect Repellent Oils

Essential oil of lavender makes an effective insect repellent. Good quality and pure lavender and tea-tree oils are two of the few oils that may be applied directly to the skin. But if you are not sure of its provenance, or are likely to suffer from allergies, dilute it in a carrier (such as sunflower) oil first. Candles scented with citronella or eucalyptus help deter midges and flying insects.

directory of herbs

Each entry in this herb directory gives a brief history of the herb, its description, habitat, growth and cultivation, any related species and the principal uses. The medicinal uses described here are for general interest only and should not be taken as practical recommendations. All herbs can be toxic if taken to excess, especially in the form of essential oils. Some may cause adverse reactions in certain people. Consult a qualified practitioner before using herbs medicinally.

PINACEAE

Abies alba

Silver fir

History and traditions The silver fir was the source of "Strasbourg Turpentine", as described by the French doctor and botanist Pierre Belon in *De Arboribus coniferis*, 1553, and listed in the London *Pharmacopoeia* until 1788. Its manufacture is covered in the famous work on distillation techniques, *Liber De Arte Distillandi* by the Strasbourg physician Hieronymus Braunschweig, 1450–1534. Turpentine is now more usually made from a selection of several different species of pine, but both *Abies alba* and *A. balsamea* still have a place in many herbal medicines and modern pharmaceutical preparations.
Description It grows from 25–45 m (80–150 ft) and has glossy, dark-green needles, silver underneath. It is monoecious – that is, the small male cones and much larger female cones, which are reddish-brown when ripe and up to 15 cm (6 in) long, are produced on the same tree.
Related species *A. balsamea* has smooth grey bark, studded with resin blisters, and is strongly scented with balsam.
Habitat/distribution Native to mountainous regions of central and southern Europe, also found in North and Central America.
Growth Prefers moist but well-drained, slightly acid soil and does not flourish in polluted air. It may be propagated from seed, sown in late autumn or winter, with a period of stratification to aid germination.
Parts used *A. alba,* leaves, resin tapped from mature trees. *A. balsamea,* leaves, oleo-resin collected from blisters on the trunk. Essential oil from resin of both species.

USES Medicinal *A. alba* and *A. balsamea* have aromatic, antiseptic properties, stimulate circulation and increase blood flow and are expectorant and diuretic in action. They are common ingredients of proprietary remedies for coughs and colds, bath preparations, liniments and rubs for rheumatism and neuralgia. Oleo-resin from *A. balsamea* is used in North American traditional medicine for chest infections, cuts, burns, skin eruptions and venereal disease.
Cosmetic The essential oil is an ingredient of cosmetics, perfumes and soaps.

Above *Leaves of a silver fir.*

CAUTION Silver fir is an irritant, which can cause skin reaction in sensitive subjects.

LEGUMINOSAE/MIMOSACEAE

Acacia senegal

Gum Arabic

History and traditions The ancient Egyptians imported what appears to be acacia gum, and it was referred to in the writings of the Greek physician, Theophrastus, in the 4th century BC. Gum Arabic is mentioned in many old herbals as an ingredient of pomanders and medicines.
Description *A. senegal*, which produces gum Arabic, reaches 6 m (19 ft) tall, has grey bark, pale-green pinnate leaves and small pale-yellow balls of flowers. There are over 1,000 species in the *Acacia* genus, often called wattles, many of which produce gums for commerce. *A. nilotica* (above) is the source of an inferior gum Arabic.
Habitat/distribution The genus is found in dry areas in tropical to warm-temperate zones of Africa, Asia, Australia, Central and South America.
Growth *A. senegal* is tender, requiring a minimum temperature about 15°C/60°F. It needs a slightly acid, well-drained soil and full sun and is propagated by seed, germinated at 21°C/70°F.
Parts used Resin of *A. senegal* (it dissolves in water to form a mucilage which makes a bonding agent).

USES Medicinal Gum Arabic is a demulcent, soothes inflamed tissues and is used in pastilles, lotions and pharmaceutical preparations.
Culinary Although it has no place in the domestic kitchen it is used in the food industry in a wide range of products, including confectionery and chewing gum.

CAUTION There are statutory restrictions on cultivation of wattles in some places.

COMPOSITAE/ASTERACEAE

Achillea millefolium

Yarrow

History and traditions The generic name honours the legendary Achilles, whose soldiers are said to have staunched their wounds with this plant in the Trojan War, and it has a long tradition as a wound herb. *Millefolium* refers to the many segments of the finely divided leaves. This herb has attracted a wealth of folklore over the centuries, as its many common names reveal.

Description A pungent perennial with flat, creamy-white to pinkish flower heads rising on tough stalks 15–30 cm (6–12 in) above a mat of greyish-green, finely-divided leaves. With its creeping roots and efficient self-seeding it is extremely invasive.

Related species There are many ornamental cultivars of *A. millefolium* including 'Moonshine', with light yellow flowers and the rich crimson 'Fire King'. *A. ageratum* (formerly *A. decolorans*), English mace, is a little-known culinary herb with a mildly spicy flavour, used to flavour chicken dishes, soups, stews and sauces.

Habitat/distribution Widespread in temperate zones, found in grasslands, waste ground and by roadsides. Native of Europe and western Asia, naturalized in North America, Australia and New Zealand.

Growth Propagated by division of roots. The wild species is invasive and when grown as a garden plant it is advisable to keep it in a container or to restrict the roots by surrounding with tiles pushed into the soil.

Yarrow folklore

As "devil's nettle" or "devil's plaything", yarrow was supposed to be dedicated to Satan and widely used in charms and spells. It had a place in Druid ceremonies and was made into herbal amulets or strewn on the threshold of houses against witches and evil forces. A bunch hung on the door, and tied to the baby's cradle for good measure on Midsummer's Eve, was supposed to ensure an illness-free year ahead.

Several claims are made for yarrow's supernatural powers in the 15th-century "Book of Secrets", attributed to Albertus Magnus. If put to the nose it will protect "from all feare and fatansye or vysion" and rather more wildly, if the juice is smeared on the hands, when plunged into water they will act as magnets for fish.

Yarrow features in many traditional rhymes connected with finding true love:

Yarrow, yarrow, long and narrow,
Tell unto me by tomorrow,
Who my husband is to be.

Another rhyme, variously attributed to the county of Suffolk, in England and to eastern Europe (with slightly different words), refers to yarrow's propensity to cause a nosebleed (one of its common names):

Green 'arrow, green 'arrow, you bears a white blow,
If my love loves me my nose will bleed now.

And if eaten at the wedding feast, it was claimed that bride and groom would remain in love for seven years.

As well as its role as a wound herb, reflected in the names soldier's woundwort, herb militaris and carpenter's weed, it was credited with both stopping a nosebleed or bringing one on (a supposed way of relieving migraine), as occasion demanded. It has a pungent smell and, as "old man's pepper", was made into snuff.

Parts used The whole plant, fresh or dried.

USES Medicinal The essential oil contains azulene, which has anti-inflammatory properties. It increases perspiration and is taken internally, as a tea, for colds and feverish conditions; applied externally for wounds, ulcers and nosebleeds. It is also thought to lower blood pressure and to relieve indigestion.

Cosmetic A weak infusion of the flowering tops in distilled water makes a cleanser or refreshing toner for oily skins.

Other names Soldier's woundwort, herb militaris, carpenter's weed, old man's pepper, nose bleed, devil's nettle, milfoil and also thousand leaf.

Above right *The finely divided leaves of* Achillea millefolium, *also known as thousand leaf.*

Right Achillea ageratum, *English mace.*

CAUTION Large doses can cause headaches. Allergic rashes and skin sensitivity to sunlight may result from prolonged use.

RANUNCULACEAE

Aconitum napellus

Aconite

History and traditions The generic name is from the Greek for a dart (*akontion*) in recognition of its one time use as an arrow poison, but the species name, *napellus*, meaning "little turnip", is supposedly for the shape of the roots, and gives no hint of the deadly nature of this plant. The popular name, monkshood, describes the curious shape of the flowers, while the common name for *A. lycoctonum,* wolf's bane, is a reference to its ability to despatch this once much-feared animal by sprinkling the juice over raw meat as bait. Stories of the dangers of aconite abound in herbals through the ages, such as Gerard's account of the "ignorant persons" of Antwerp who were taken with "most cruel symptoms and so died" when served the leaves in a salad as a "lamentable experiment".

Description The helmet-shaped inky-blue flowers give this hardy herbaceous perennial a slightly sinister appearance appropriate to its properties. It has tuberous roots and delphinium-like foliage from which the flowering stems rise to a height of 1.5 m (5 ft).

Related species There are about 100 species, all of which are highly poisonous. *A. lycoctonum* has yellow, sometimes purple, flowers and *A. carmichaelii,* syn. *A. fischeri*, is sometimes used in Chinese medicine as a painkiller.

Habitat/distribution Widespread in Europe and in northern temperate regions, in damp woodlands, meadows and mountainous areas.

Growth Plant in moist, fertile soil and part-shade. Propagation is by division of roots in the autumn for flowering in the second year. Seeds sown in spring will not flower for 2–3 years.

Parts used Dried root tubers.

Other name Monkshood.

USES Medicinal The alkaloid, aconite, gives it toxicity. As a strong sedative and painkiller, it should be used only by qualified practitioners. A very small dose causes numbness of lips, tongue and extremities and can lead to vomiting, coma and death.

CAUTION The whole plant is highly toxic and if ingested can kill. Contact with skin may cause allergic reactions – always handle with gloves. Subject to legal restrictions in some countries.

ACORACEAE

Acorus calamus

Calamus

History and traditions The first specimens to reach Europe were imported from Asia by the botanical garden in Vienna in the 16th century. Calamus, which means "reed" in Greek, then became popular as a scented strewing herb. Cardinal Wolsey used it extensively for this purpose in Hampton Court Palace. This was yet another example of his extravagance in the eyes of his contemporaries, due to its comparative rarity – at the time calamus was grown only on the Norfolk Broads some distance away. It was also one of the ingredients in Moses's instructions to make "an ointment compound after the art of the apothecary" as a holy anointing oil (Exodus 30:25).

Description A pleasantly aromatic perennial with a thick much-branched rhizome, it has similar-shaped leaves to the irises, although is not botanically related to them. The flower head is a spadix, emerging from the side of the leaf, but it is not usually fertile in Europe and cool northern climates, owing to lack of appropriate insects for pollination.

Related species *A. gramineus*, native to the Far East, is a miniature species, used in Chinese

medicine. Its compact size makes it suitable for growing in ornamental ponds.

Habitat/distribution *A. calamus* (above) is indigenous to central Asia and eastern Europe, and is now widespread in marshy areas and by shallow waterways of northern temperate zones.

Growth Vigorous and easy to propagate, it must have moist soil and plenty of water. Grows best by water margins. Propagate in spring or autumn by cutting rhizomes in small pieces, each with 2–3 buds, and planting in muddy ground.

Parts used Rhizomes, essential oil.

USES Medicinal Calamus can be taken internally, as an infusion for digestive problems and to dispel intestinal worms. It is slightly sedative to the central nervous system and is traditionally used in Ayurvedic medicine following strokes, and also for bronchial complaints. Externally it is used as an alcohol rub for aching muscles.

Aromatic The essential oil, separated by steam distillation, is a perfumery ingredient. Herbalists of old called it "*calamus aromaticus*", and the ground root was added to pot-pourris, scented sachets, tooth and hair powders.

Household In Asia it is sometimes used as an insecticide powder to deter ants.

Other names Sweet flag, sweet rush and myrtle grass.

CAUTION Excessive dose causes vomiting.

UMBELLIFERAE/APIACEAE

Aegopodium podagraria

Ground elder

History and traditions The specific name comes from the Latin word for gout, *podagra*, and it was grown in monastery gardens in medieval times as a cure for that disease. The name bishops' weed could be a reference to a one-time episcopal tendency to gout, due to high living and a rich diet of meat and alcohol, or to the plant's prevalence around ecclesiastical sites. It is dedicated to St Gerard, the patron saint of gout sufferers.

Description A herbaceous perennial with a creeping root system, it spreads rapidly, smothering other plants and self-seeds. Umbels of white flowers rise on long stems to 90 cm (36 in) above the leaves, 30 cm (12 in), in summer.

Related species *A. podagraria* 'Variegatum' is a variegated cultivar with cream patterning at the leaf margins. It is not as invasive as the common variety and makes a pretty border, especially when grown with white lilies or tulips.

Habitat/distribution Native to Europe, naturalized in North America; found in woodlands and wasteground.

Growth Ground elder is a rampant weed that grows in any soil and is almost impossible to eradicate once established. This plant is definitely not suitable for cultivation as it will take over.

Parts used Leaves, stems.

USES Medicinal An anti-inflammatory herb with mildly sedative properties, it has a long tradition as a treatment for gout, sciatica and rheumatism. It can be taken internally as an infusion, and is applied externally for stings and burns.

Culinary Though fairly unpleasant tasting, the young leaves and shoots can be added to salads, or cooked like spinach.

Other names Goutweed, bishops' weed and herb Gerard.

Above Aegopodium podagraria *'Variegatum' (Variegated ground elder) in the foreground with white, lily-flowered tulips.*

HIPPOCASTANACEAE

Aesculus hippocastanum

Horse chestnut

History and traditions This spectacular tree was introduced to western Europe in the mid-16th century, when it was grown in Vienna from seeds brought from Istanbul by the botanist Clusius (Charles de L'Ecluse), although it does not seem to have been widely used for medicinal purposes until the late 19th century. The origins of the name are confused, but are all tied to the use of this tree as animal fodder. *Hippocastanum* is the Latin for "horse chestnut", which the Romans supposedly fed to their livestock.

Description A stately, deciduous tree, 30–40 m (98–130 ft) in height, it has palmate leaves, sticky resinous buds and candelabras of white or pink-tinged flowers in spring. The spiny, globular, green fruit contains glossy reddish-brown seeds (conkers, also chestnuts).

Habitat/distribution Occurs in eastern Europe, eastern Asia and North America, introduced to Britain and western Europe.

Growth Propagate by seeds, sown in autumn. Often self-seeds and grows rapidly in any soil.

Parts used Bark, seeds.

USES Medicinal Contains coumarin glycosides and saponins (of which aescin is the most important) giving it astringent, anti-inflammatory properties. It strengthens arteries and veins and is used against heart attacks, strokes, thrombosis, varicose veins and haemorrhoids. The active principles are extracted for use in pharmaceutical preparations.

CAUTION The whole fruit is mildly toxic and should never be eaten. Only for use by qualified practitioners.

LABIATAE/LAMIACEAE

Agastache foeniculum

Anise hyssop

History and traditions A traditional medicinal herb of Native Americans, it became popular with colonists as a bee plant for the distinctive aniseed flavour it gave to honey.

Description A hardy, short-lived perennial with soft, ovate leaves, strongly scented with aniseed. Bold purple flower spikes last all summer. Clumps are 60–90 cm (24–36 in) in height.

Related species *A. rugosa*, known as Korean mint, or wrinkled giant hyssop, is also a hardy perennial, 1 m (3 ft) high, with pointed, mint-smelling leaves and mauve flower spikes.

Habitat/distribution *A. foeniculum* is native to North and Central America, and *A. rugosa* comes from eastern Asia.

Growth Grows best in rich moist soil in full sun. Although reasonably hardy, *A. foeniculum* will not stand prolonged frost or temperatures below -6°C (20°F). Propagate by division or softwood cuttings in spring.

Parts used Leaves, flowers – fresh or dried.

USES Medicinal The leaves have antibacterial properties and are taken as an infusion to alleviate coughs and colds, or as a digestive.

Culinary The leaves of both *A. foeniculum* and *A. rugosa* make refreshing tea with a minty flavour. They can be floated in soft drinks and fruit cups to add piquancy or snipped into salads. The flowers make a pretty garnish. The dried or fresh leaves may be added to cooked meat dishes and go well with pork.

RUTACEAE

Agathosma betulina

Buchu

History and traditions A prized medicinal plant of the indigenous people of South Africa, its virtues were discovered by colonists of the Cape who introduced it to Europe at the end of the 18th century. In the 1820s the dried leaves were exported in some quantity to Britain and thence to America, to be included in proprietary medicines and used to flavour cordials. John Lindley in his *Flora Medica*, 1838, records that several species of *Agathosma*, collected as 'bucku', were "found to be an excellent aromatic stomachic and very efficacious as a diuretic. The infusion is much praised as a remedy in chronic inflammations of the bladder and urethra and in chronic rheumatism." All of these uses remain valid in herbal medicine today.

Description A tender, evergreen shrub, 1–2 m (3–6 ft) in height, it has glossy, yellowish-green leaves, which are leathery in texture and studded with oil glands which smell of blackcurrants. White flowers appear in spring. A member of the rue family, it is highly aromatic, scenting the air wherever it grows in quantity.

Related species Several species are used, all indiscriminately termed buchu, or "buka", meaning powder in the local language. *A. betulina* is held to be the most effective for medicinal purposes, *A. crenulata,* oval buchu, has ovate leaves and *A. serratifolia*, long buchu, serrated, lance-shaped foliage. These plants were once classified as "barosma" and the term "barosma powder" for buchu is still sometimes used.

Habitat/distribution Dry hillsides of Cape Province, South Africa.

Growth Grown as a conservatory plant in temperate zones, a minimum temperature of 5°C (41°F) is required. Pot in ericaceous (lime-free) compost. It must not be overwatered, which can lead to rot, and should be cut back hard in spring to keep it in shape and control size. Grown outside in warm, frost-free regions, it needs well-drained, acid soil and full sun.

Parts used Leaves, which are harvested when the plant is in flower, and dried.

USES Medicinal The volatile oil contains up to 40% diosphenol, a strong antiseptic. Used internally for urinary infections, especially cystitis, coughs and colds, rheumatism, arthritis and digestive disorders. Applied externally for bruises and sprains.

Culinary Gives a blackcurrant taste to soft drinks and cordials and is used to flavour a local liquor "buchu brandy".

Household Made into a powder to deter ants and other insects.

Other name Round buchu.

AGAVACEAE

Agave americana

Agave

History and traditions Agave comes from the Greek for admirable. It gained the name "century plant" from the mistaken belief that it flowers only after a hundred years – but most bloom after ten years.
Description A tender succulent whose rosettes of spiky grey-green leaves are 1–2 m high (3–6 ft) with a spread of 2–3 m (6–10 ft). The tall bell-shaped flower spikes, resembling small trees, rise to 8 m (26 ft). Agaves should not be confused with aloes, and are not botanically related.
Related species *A. americana* 'Variegata' is a cultivar with yellow margins to the leaves.
Habitat/distribution Originally from tropical zones of the Americas, especially Mexico, this plant is now naturalized in southern Europe, India, and Central and South Africa.
Growth Needs well-drained soil, full sun and a minimum temperature of 5°C (41°F). Propagate by offsets. In cool climates it can be grown as a conservatory plant but takes up a lot of space.
Parts used Leaves, roots, sap.

USES Medicinal The sap has anti-inflammatory properties, and is applied externally for burns, bites and stings, by breaking open a leaf.
General The root has cleansing properties and is used for washing clothes and in commercial soap production. Fibres are woven into rope. The powdered leaf makes snuff and the whole plant is much employed as a stock-proof fence.

CAUTION Can provoke an allergic reaction when used medicinally.

ROSACEAE

Agrimonia eupatoria

Agrimony

History and traditions The species name is from Mithradates Eupator, King of Pontus, who died in 64 BC. He practised magic, was a great believer in herbal potions and was thought to have rendered himself immune to injury by saturating his body with lethal poisons. The Anglo-Saxons also attributed magical powers to agrimony, including it in charms and dubious preparations of blood and pounded frogs. A sprig under the pillow supposedly brought oblivion, until removed. It was also credited with healing wounds, internal haemorrhages, snake bites, charming away warts and mending bad backs. Retaining its reputation through the centuries, it became the principal ingredient of *eau d'arquebusade*, a lotion for treating the wounds inflicted by the arquebus, a 16th-century firearm and forerunner of the musket. It was an essential ingredient of a springtime drink, still taken by country folk into the early years of this century as a "blood purifier".
Description A perennial with compound pointed leaves, covered in soft hairs. In summer and autumn it has small yellow flower spikes with a hint of an apricot scent. It grows to a height of 30–60 cm (1–2 ft).
Habitat/distribution Found on waste grounds and roadsides throughout Europe, Asia and North America.
Growth A wild plant which tolerates poor, dry soil, it can be propagated by seed sown in spring or by root division in autumn.

Above *Agrimony in flower.*

Parts used Dried flowering plant.

USES Medicinal Has anti-inflammatory, anti-bacterial and astringent properties and is taken internally for sore throats, catarrh, diarrhoea, cystitis and urinary infections. Applied externally as a lotion for wounds.
Household Yields a yellow dye.
Other names Church steeples, sticklewort and cockleburr.

Above Aguja reptans *'Atropurpurea'.*

Below Aguja reptans *'Multicolor'.*

LABIATAE/LAMIACEAE

Ajuga reptans

Bugle

History and traditions The apothecaries knew it as "bugula" and along with self-heal, *Prunella vulgaris,* it was valued for many centuries as a wound herb. Culpeper thought highly of it: "if the virtues of it make you fall in love with it (as they will if you be wise) keep a syrup of it to take inwardly, and an ointment and plaster of it to use outwardly, always by you". He recommended it for all kinds of sores, gangrene and fistulas. Gerard, who found many specimens growing "in a moist ground upon Black heath, near London", backs him up, expressing the view that it is common knowledge in France "how he needs neither physician nor surgeon that hath Bugle and Sanicle".

Description A hardy perennial, 10–30 cm (4–12 in) high, growing on a creeping rootstock, it has attractive blue flower spikes in spring or early summer, growing from rosettes of basal leaves. White or pink-flowered mutants occasionally occur.

Related species Cultivars with richly coloured foliage make rewarding subjects for the herb garden. *A. r.* 'Atropurpurea' has purple-bronze leaves, *A. r.* 'Multicolor' has colourful variegated foliage of, pink, crimson and cream with a hint of green, and *A. r.* 'Variegata' has greyish-green leaves with creamy margins.

Habitat/distribution In damp ground in woodlands and meadows. Native to Europe and introduced elsewhere, it is also found in northern Africa and parts of the Middle East.

Growth Ajugas make excellent ground cover and are easy to propagate by separating and replanting the leafy runners at any time of the year, but preferably in spring or autumn when sufficient moisture can be provided. They do need a moist soil to flourish well and sun or partial shade.

Parts used Whole plant.

USES Medicinal Its reputation, sadly, has not stood the test of time and bugle is no longer widely used in herbal medicine today. But it is said to be mildly astringent and is sometimes still recommended, in the form of a lotion or ointment, for treating cuts and bruises.

Other names Carpenter's herb and sicklewort.

ROSACEAE

Alchemilla vulgaris

Lady's mantle

History and traditions This herb was unknown to the writers of the ancient classical world, but was a popular "magic" plant in northern Europe from earliest times, rising to prominence during the Middle Ages for its connections with alchemy. It was also sometimes associated with the Virgin Mary and dubbed Our Lady's mantle, subsequently shortened to lady's mantle, the scalloped leaves supposedly resembling a sculptured cloak. It was traditionally prescribed for infertility and "women's troubles" and was said to regulate the menstrual cycle and ease menopausal symptoms – as it still is prescribed by herbalists today.

Description A perennial 40–50 cm (16–20 in), it has hairy, branched stems and deeply lobed leaves (seven or nine lobes) with serrated edges and a froth of yellowish-green flowers in late spring and throughout summer.

Related species *A. alpina*, another medicinal species, is lower-growing, 10–20 cm (4–8 in) with star-shaped leaves. *A. mollis,* from the Carpathian mountains and known as "the garden variety", is the most attractive of the three with paler green, scalloped leaves and a more luxurious show of greeny-yellow flowers. It is widely grown in herb gardens, but has less medicinal value.

Habitat/distribution Found in mountainous areas, meadows, pasture lands and on rock ledges in Europe and throughout northern temperate regions.

Growth Grows in any soil in sun or partial shade. Self-seeds prolifically but germination of seed sown artificially is erratic. The easiest way to propagate is by division in spring or autumn. Species planted together hybridize readily.

Parts used Leaves.

USES Medicinal Has astringent and anti-inflammatory properties, controls bleeding and is taken as an infusion for menstrual and menopausal problems. Applied externally for vaginal itching, as a mouthwash or lotion for sores and skin irritation.

Culinary The leaves are edible and sometimes shredded and added to salads, but their slightly bitter, undistinguished taste hardly warrants this treatment.

Other names Lion's foot, bear's foot and leontopodium (in French, it is called Pied-de-Lion and in German, Frauenmantle).

Above Alchemilla mollis *has a froth of greeny-yellow flowers throughout summer.*

Right *The concave shape of* Alchemilla vulgaris *and* A. mollis *leaves forms a dip where drops of moisture collect.*

The alchemy connection

The magic of lady's mantle lies in its ability to hold moisture drops, often dew, trapped in the central dips of the leaves and by their waxy surface. Dew was a much-prized ingredient in the recipes of the alchemists of old and here was an accessible source. So the herb was named "Alchemilla" – the little alchemist.

In its narrowest and best-known sense, the primary concern of alchemy was the transformation of base metal into gold, but its wider significance is that it marked the beginnings of systematic chemistry. With origins in ancient Egypt, the science of alchemy passed to the Greeks of Alexandria, to the Arabs and then to the West. Leading alchemists of the 13th century were Albertus Magnus, Roger Bacon and Arnold de Villeneuve, who wrote widely on the subject. Although they believed in the"philosopher's stone" (the instrument capable of transmuting metals into gold), they were also pre-occupied with the discovery of a divine water, or elixir of life, capable of healing all maladies – with the purest dew as a necessary component.

In the 16th century, the Swiss physician, Paracelsus, took up some of the tenets of alchemy, including the concept of the "prima materia" and the "quinta essentia", the primary essence of a substance, but gave it a new direction. The chief objective was the making of medicines, not gold, dependent on a study of the properties of plants and their effects on the body.

LILIACEAE/ALOEACEAE

Aloe vera syn. *A. barbadensis*

Aloe vera

History and traditions The medicinal value of this plant was recognized by the Egyptians and used as an embalming ingredient. One story goes that Aristotle tried to persuade Alexander the Great to conquer the Indian Ocean island of Socotra (near the Gulf of Aden), for its aloes, being the only known place where they grew at the time. The plant was introduced to Europe in the 10th century and became established over the centuries as an important ingredient in proprietary medicines.

Description A tender succulent, 60–40 cm (2–3 ft) tall, with clusters of elongated, very fleshy, greeny-grey leaves, spiked at the edges, and tubular yellow flowers.

Related species Of the 300 species of aloes only a few have medicinal properties, including *A. perryi* and the South African, *A. ferox,* which has red spikes at the leaf edges. But *A. vera* is the most potent.

Habitat/distribution Origins are uncertain, but it is widespread in tropical and subtropical regions in dry, sunny areas.

Growth It needs a well-drained soil, full sun and a minimum temperature of 5°C (41°F). In cold climates it can be successfully grown as a conservatory or house plant. Pot up in gritty compost (soil mix), do not overwater, and allow to dry out completely between waterings.

Parts used Leaves, sap. The leaves are cut and the sap is used fresh, preserved and bottled or dried to a brown crystalline solid for use in creams, lotions and medicinal preparations.

USES Medicinal It is the mix of constituents in this plant that gives it exceptional healing properties. It contains anti-inflammatory and antimicrobial agents; long-chain polysaccharides which boost the immune system; minerals; antioxidant vitamins C, E, B^{12} and beta-carotene and lignin, a woody substance which aids penetration of the skin and tissues. *A. vera* gel from the leaf is applied externally to promote healing of wounds, burns, sunburn, eczema and skin irritations. It is taken internally for digestive tract problems and there is also some evidence that it may help conditions where the immune system is not functioning well. It has laxative properties and "bitter aloes" is the name for the strong, purgative medicine that is made from the leaves.

Cosmetic It is an ingredient of many commercial cosmetic products.

Other names Aloes, Barbados aloe, Cape aloe and Curacao aloe.

CAUTION Should not be taken internally by pregnant women. Subject to legal restrictions in some countries. Not to be taken in large doses.

VERBENACEAE

Aloysia triphylla syn. *Aloysia citriodora*

Lemon verbena

History and traditions This lemon-scented shrub from South America was introduced to Europe in the 1790s. It is said to be named after Maria Louisa, wife of Carlos IV of Spain, Aloysia being a corruption of Louisa. The Victorians took to it for its long-lasting lemon fragrance, calling it "the lemon plant", and dried it for use in scented sachets.

Description Frost- to half-hardy deciduous shrub with rough-textured, strongly lemon-scented, spear-shaped leaves, dotted on the underside with oil glands. Racemes of tiny mauve-white flowers appear in late summer. In warm climates, where no frost occurs, it grows to 4.5 m (15 ft), but in cooler regions it is unlikely to grow to more than 1.5 m (5 ft). It is closely related to the *Lippia* genus, with which it was once classified.

Habitat/distribution Native to Chile and Argentina, it is widely grown in tropical and subtropical zones of the world, in Australia, New Zealand and temperate regions of Europe.

Growth It will usually survive a minimum temperature of -5°C (23°F), provided it is grown in a sheltered, south-facing site in well-drained soil. It will not tolerate prolonged cold and frost, especially if grown in a heavy soil. May be grown as a pot plant if given winter protection.

Right *Lemon verbena in flower – it keeps its scent well when dried.*

New leaves do not appear until late spring or early summer. Cut back hard in spring, when it will regenerate from old wood. It is propagated from cuttings, taken in late summer, but needs heat to produce roots and during development of the seedlings.

Parts used Leaves, essential oil.

USES Culinary The leaves (fresh or dry) make a refreshing tea. If used with great discretion, as the taste is strong, they can be included in savoury stuffings and sauces, or used to flavour cakes and ice cream.

Aromatic The benefit of this herb is that the leaves retain their lemon scent, when dried, for several years. They help to deter insects and are ideal for sachets and making pot-pourri. The essential oil was widely used in perfumery, but has been discovered to sensitize the skin to sunlight.

Lemon verbena pot-pourri

dried peel of 1 lemon
2 cups dried lemon verbena leaves
1 cup dried chamomile flowers
15 cm/6 in cinnamon stick, crushed
1 cup dried pot marigold petals
1 tsp orris root powder
2–3 drops essential oil of lemon verbena (optional)

To dry the lemon peel, scrape it off the fruit with a vegetable peeler, spread on paper and put in a warm place (such as an airing cupboard) for about two weeks, until crisp.

Mix the ingredients together. Seal in a tin and put in a warm place for 2–3 weeks, shaking occasionally. Put in a bowl to scent the room, covering when not in use to retain the scent, or in drawstring sachets to hang in a wardrobe.

Lemon verbena essential oil will give the pot-pourri a stronger fragrance. It is also useful for adding zest to the mixture at a later date, as it will lose strength when constantly exposed to light and air.

ZINGIBERACEAE

Alpinia officinarum

Galangal

History and traditions Very similar to ginger, this plant has a long history as a spice and medicinal plant and has been used in Ayurvedic and Chinese medicine since ancient times. 'Galangal' comes from the Arabic word *Khalanjan*, which could in turn be derived from a Chinese word meaning "mild ginger". Known in Europe since the 9th century, it was probably introduced by Arab or Greek physicians.

Description A tropical evergreen with tall clumps of ovate to lanceolate leaves growing from ginger-scented rhizomes to a height of 1.2 m (4 ft). Flowers are pale green and white. *A. officinarum*, lesser galangal, is the more important species for both medicinal and culinary purposes.

Related species *A. galanga*, greater galangal, is a larger plant, growing to 2 m (6 ft), and has a less marked ginger aroma.

Habitat/distribution Found in tropical rainforest and grassland areas of southeast Asia and Australia.

Growth It can be grown only in climates with high humidity and minimum temperatures of 15–18°C (59–64°F). Needs well-drained soil and partial shade. Propagated by division of the rhizomes when new shoots appear.

Parts used Rhizome, oil.

USES Medicinal A good digestive, it also has antibacterial and antifungal properties, is used for feverish illnesses and fungal infections. *A. galanga* is considered less effective medicinally.

Culinary Both species are used as a ginger-like flavouring in Thai and southeast Asian cookery.

MALVACEAE

Althaea officinalis

Marshmallow

History and traditions The generic name comes from the Greek, *altho*, meaning "tc cure". The family name, Malvaceae, is also of Greek derivation, from *malake*, meaning soft, both indicating the emollient, healing properties of this plant, which have long been recognized. Pliny remarked: "Whosoever shall take a spoonful of Mallows shall that day be free from all diseases that may come to him." Early recorded uses include poultices to reduce inflammation and spongy lozenges to soothe coughs and sore throats – from which the modern confectionery is descended, though it no longer contains any of the herb. Marshmallow root was eaten as a vegetable by the Romans and in many Middle Eastern and European countries was a standby in times of famine when food was scarce. In more recent times it was a springtime country tradition to eat the young shoots, or make them into a syrup, to "purify the blood".

Description A hardy perennial with soft, downy leaves and pale pink flowers in summer, it reaches 1–1.2 m (3–4 ft) in height. It has large, fleshy taproots.

Habitat/distribution Found in salt marshes, near sea coasts and in moist inland areas, throughout Europe, in temperate regions of Asia, North America and Australia.

Growth Prefers moist to wet soil and a sunny situation. Propagated by division in autumn or by seed sown in late summer, though germination is often erratic.

Parts used Leaves, roots, flowers.

USES Medicinal The whole herb contains a sweet mucilage that is soothing and softening. Relieves inflamed gums and mouth, gastric ulcers, bronchial infections and coughs. Applied externally for ulcers, boils, inflammation of the skin and insect bites.

Culinary At one time the young roots and leaves were boiled, then fried with onions as a spring vegetable, or added to salads – but neither is very palatable.

Althea officinalis

Below left and right Alcea rosea, *the garden hollyhock, has racemes of single blooms in pink, purple and white. There are also many cultivars with double flowers.*

Related species

MALVACEAE

Alcea rosea formerly *Althaea rosea*

Hollyhock

This spectacular biennial, which first came to Europe from China in the 16th century, is closely related to *Althaea officinalis* and used to be classified in the same genus. It too has soothing properties and the flowers were once used to make cough syrups and to treat chest complaints, but the medicinal properties of its less showy relative are now considered superior. It is still worth its place in the herb garden for its old-fashioned grace and large colourful blooms (pink, purple, yellow or white) on towering spikes. It is easy to grow in well-drained soil and a sunny position from seeds sown *in situ* in spring or late summer.

ANACARDIACEAE

Anacardium occidentale

Cashew nut

History and traditions A native of South and Central America and the Caribbean islands, this well-known nut tree was introduced to India from Brazil by Portuguese colonists in the 16th century, who originally planted it to prevent soil erosion on hillsides in Goa.

Description An evergreen tree, reaching 12 m (40 ft), it has dark-green, rounded, oval leaves. Panicles of pinkish-green flowers are followed by the fleshy fruit, known as the cashew apple, each of which has a kidney-shaped nut suspended from its base, containing a white seed.

Habitat/distribution Naturalized and cultivated in tropical zones worldwide.

Growth Tender trees which need well-drained, sandy soil, periodic high rainfall and a minimum temperature of 18°C (64°F).

Parts used Leaves, bark, fruits, seeds.

USES Medicinal Bark and leaves are used in treating malaria, especially in parts of Africa. Oil from the nut shell has been applied externally for ringworm and ulcers and to remove corns and warts – but its caustic action makes this a hazardous treatment.

Culinary The nut, or kernel, is rich in minerals and is a high-protein food. Juice from the fruit is made into soft drinks and distilled to produce spirits.

Other The outer shell of the nut produces a thick, tarry black oil used in engineering, and as a timber preservative to protect against insects.

CAUTION Oil from the cashew nut shell is an irritant and can cause painful skin blistering.

UMBELLIFERAE/APIACEAE

Anethum graveolens

Dill

History and traditions An ancient herb known in biblical times and described both by Pliny, AD 23–79, and by the Greek physician Dioscorides, AD 40–90, in *De Materia Medica*. It appears in the 10th-century writings of Alfric, Archbishop of Canterbury, and was a favourite herb in Anglo-Saxon charms against witchcraft, at which time it was also burned "to disperse thunder clouds and sulphurous air". The common name is likely to have come from the Saxon word *dillan*, to lull, for its ability to soothe colicky babies and for the ancient Greek tradition of covering the head with dill leaves to induce sleep. The culinary connection with cucumber goes back a long way. Charles I's cook, Joseph Cooper, records a recipe for pickling cucumbers in dill in his book of 1640. It has a long tradition of use in India and Eastern countries as a medicinal and culinary herb.

Description An aromatic annual, 1 m (3 ft) tall, with a single stem and feathery leaves. It has terminal umbels of tiny yellow flowers in midsummer and elliptic, flattened fruits. Resembles fennel, but is shorter and has a subtler, less strongly aniseed flavour.

Anethum graveolens *has a long history as a culinary herb.*

Related species Indian dill is known as sowa. It is usually classified as *A. sowa,* but this is either a subspecies of *A. graveolens* or very closely related.

Habitat/distribution Originated in southern Europe and Asia, now widely grown in herb gardens worldwide.

Growth Plant dill in well-drained but nutrient-rich soil, in full sun. Requires adequate moisture as it bolts (runs quickly to seed) in poor, dry soil. Best propagated from seed sown in spring, straight into the ground where it is to grow, as it does not take well to being transplanted. Should not be grown near fennel as the two plants crosspollinate.

Parts used Leaves, seeds.

USES Medicinal A cooling, soothing herb which aids digestion, prevents constipation and is an ingredient of "gripe water" given to babies for indigestion. In Indian herbal medicine dill and fenugreek seeds are included in preparations for diarrhoea and dysentery. Poultices of the leaves are applied to boils and to reduce swelling and joint pains. Seeds are chewed to cure bad breath.

Culinary Leaves and seeds add a caraway-like flavour to fish, seafood and egg dishes and go well with bland-tasting vegetables, especially cucumber and potatoes. Widely used in Scandinavian cuisine. In Indian cookery, it is added to curries, rice dishes, soups, pickles and chutneys.

UMBELLIFERAE/APIACEAE

Angelica archangelica

Angelica

History and traditions According to legend, this herb took its name from the angel who revealed its virtues to a monk during a plague epidemic. It was widely thought to give protection from infection and, during the Great Plague of 1664–5, people were recommended to "bite and chaw" on its roots. It is also variously connected with the archangel Gabriel who is said to have appeared to the Virgin Mary at the Annunciation, celebrated at the end of March, and the archangel Michael, whose feast day is in May. In all northern European folklore it has an ancient reputation for its powers against witchcraft and evil spirits. In Lapland poets wore crowns of angelica, supposedly to gain inspiration from its scent. John Parkinson in his *Theatre of Plants*, 1640, wrote of it: "The whole plante, both leafe, roote and seede, is of an excellent comfortable scent, savour and taste."
Description Angelica is a statuesque biennial, though it often lives for three years. The whole plant is subtly aromatic. Standing 1.2 m–2.4 m (4–8 ft) high, it has hollow stems, large, deeply divided pale-green leaves and globular umbels of green flowers in early summer, followed by flat, oval seeds.

Related species *A. atropurpurea*, American angelica, has red stems. *A. sylvestris* is the wild European angelica.
Habitat/distribution Native to Europe and parts of Asia. Introduced in other parts of the world.
Growth Prefers a rich, damp soil but tolerates most conditions, provided it is not too dry. Plant in sun or partial shade. Self-seeds freely. Propagate by seed sown in autumn, in situ or in pots; seed remains viable for 6–12 months.
Parts used Leaves, stems, roots, seeds.

USES Medicinal Has anti-inflammatory properties, lowers fevers and acts as an expectorant. Infusions of the root are used to aid digestive disorders and bowel complaints. A poultice of the leaves has been known to soothe sunburn, but should be used with caution.
Culinary In Europe young stems are candied, cooked with rhubarb, tart fruits and berries to reduce acidity. It can be added to jams or marmalade (ginger and angelica make a good combination), seeds are added to biscuits (cookies). Seeds and roots are constituents of Benedictine, Chartreuse and other liqueurs.
Aromatic Leaves and seeds are dried and added to pot-pourri.

CAUTION Furocoumarin content increases skin photosensitivity and may cause skin irritation in susceptible people.

Far left Angelica atropurpurea *is a North American species.*
Left *A seed head of angelica.*

Culinary angelica

Angelica and rhubarb

Angelica has a pleasantly aromatic, slightly sweet taste, which enhances the flavour of rhubarb and reduces its acidity, so that less sugar is necessary. Only the very young leaf stems should be used, as older ones are coarse and stringy. Allow two or three 15 cm (6 in) pieces for each 450 g (1 lb) of rhubarb sticks. Cut them into small pieces and add to your favourite rhubarb pie or crumble recipe. Angelica is also excellent puréed with rhubarb to make a mousse or fool.

Candied angelica

Old recipe books contain instructions for candying leaves and roots, as well as stems of angelica. "Boil the stalks of Angelica in water till they are tender; then peel them and cover with other warm water. Let them stand over a gentle fire till they become very green; then lay them on a cloth to dry; take their weight in fine sugar with a little Rose-water and boil it to a Candy height. Then put in your Angelica and boil them up quick; then take them out and dry them for use."

UMBELLIFERAE/APIACEAE

Anthriscus cerefolium

Chervil

History and traditions The Romans were very fond of chervil and it is listed in 15th-century manuscripts as an essential kitchen herb. Confusion sometimes arises, however, as at that time both *A. cerefolium* and sweet cicely, *Myrrhis odorata*, were known as "chervil", sometimes distinguished as "sweet chervil" and "common chervil". John Parkinson, who wrote during the 17th-century in England, indicates: "Common chervil is much used of the French and Dutch people to bee boiled or stewed in a pipkin either by itself or with other herbs, whereof they make a Loblolly and so eate it. Sweete chervil gathered while it is young and put among other herbs for a sallet addeth a marvellous good relish to all the reste."

Description A hardy annual, 30–60 cm (1–2 ft) high, with bright green, finely divided feathery leaves and flat umbels of small white flowers in early summer.

Habitat/distribution Native to the Middle East and southern Russia. Widely cultivated elsewhere in warm and temperate climates.

Growth Chervil prefers light, moist soil and a sunny situation. Propagate from seed sown successionally for a continuous supply. It does not transplant well and runs to seed quickly, but can be sown where it is to grow, or cropped straight from the seed tray.

Parts used Leaves, preferably fresh, cut just before flowering.

USES Medicinal Although it has mild digestive properties, and is sometimes taken as a tea for this purpose, its chief use is culinary.

Culinary The delicate taste, which is more distinctive than parsley, complements most dishes. It brings out the flavour of other herbs and is an essential ingredient, along with parsley, tarragon and chives, of the classic French combination, *fines herbes*. It is best used raw or in a very short cooking process, if the subtle flavour is to be retained.

Chervil's light aniseed flavour makes it a culinary herb of distinction.

ROSACEAE

Aphanes arvensis

Parsley piert

History and traditions The common name comes from this herb's vague resemblance to parsley and from the French name for it, *perce-pierre*, meaning to pierce or break a stone. Breakstone is an alternative country name in English also and refers to its traditional use in treating kidney stones. Culpeper lists as its chief use that "it provokes urine, and breaks the stone", and it is still used for the treatment of kidney stones in herbal medicine today.

Description A prostrate annual with small fan-shaped leaves and inconspicuous green flowers in summer.

Habitat/distribution Found in dry places and wastelands, it is native to Britain and widely distributed throughout the world.

Growth As a wild plant, it grows best in well-drained soil, in sun or partial shade, and tolerates gravelly, stony soils. Propagated by seed sown in spring.

Parts used Leaves.

USES Medicinal A diuretic which also soothes irritated and inflamed tissues. It is used for painful urination and in the treatment of kidney and bladder stones.

Culinary It was a popular salad herb during the 16th century, but the taste is uninteresting and it is seldom eaten today.

UMBELLIFERAE/APIACEAE

Apium graveolens

Wild celery

History and traditions Remains of this plant were found in Egyptian tombs, including that of Tutankhamun, *c.* 14th century BC. Although rather bitter in flavour, it was the only celery known until the 17th century, when the cultivated variety we enjoy today, *A. g. var. dulce,* was developed in Italy.
Description An aromatic biennial with a bulbous, fleshy root. Grooved stems grow from 30–90 cm (1–3 ft) high in the second year. It has pointed, divided leaves (similar in shape to cultivated celery) and umbels of sparse, greenish-white flowers in late summer, followed by small, ridged seeds.
Habitat/distribution Found in marshy, often salty ground in Europe, Asia, northern Africa, North and South America.
Growth It prefers rich, damp soil, sun or partial shade and tolerates saline conditions. Does best in a sheltered position, and bears flowers for seed production in warm climates. Propagated by seed sown in spring, but needs a minimum temperature of 13–16°C (55–61°F) to germinate.
Parts used Roots, stems, leaves, seeds.

USES Medicinal It has digestive, anti-inflammatory properties and is also a diuretic. Used in the treatment of arthritis and rheumatism and in Ayurvedic medicine as a nerve tonic.
Culinary The plant is seldom eaten today, and is toxic in large quantities. Seeds may be used for flavouring in small amounts.

COMPOSITAE/ASTERACEAE

Arctium lappa

Greater burdock

History and traditions This plant comes into the thistle group of the extended Compositae/ Asteraceae family. Its names relate to the clinging nature of the burs which follow the flowers. *Arctium* comes from *arktos*, Greek for a bear (supposed to indicate the plant's roughness), and *lappa* from a word meaning to seize, though some authorities also connect the species name with the Celtic word for hand, *llap*. The English common name is a little more obvious in derivation, "bur" referring to the prickles and "dock" to the shape of the large leaves. Culpeper lists its popular names as "Personata", "Happy-Major" and "Clot-bur", adding that it is too well known to describe, "even by the little boys, who pull off the burs to throw at one another".
Description A biennial, or short-lived perennial, which grows to 1.5 m (5 ft) tall. It has long, ovate leaves covered in down and thick, hairy stems. Purple thistle-like flowers appear in mid to late summer, followed by fruits (seed heads) made up of hooked spines or burs.
Related species *A. minus,* lesser burdock, has similar properties. *A. lappa* 'Gobo' is a culinary cultivar grown in Japan.
Habitat/distribution Greater burdock is native to temperate regions of Asia and widely distributed throughout Europe and North America, found on roadsides, waste ground and in nitrogen-rich soil.
Growth It is usually collected from the wild, but a cultivated species is grown in Japan. Prefers a moist soil, sun or partial shade and it self-seeds quite freely.
Parts used Roots, stems, seeds, leaves (rarely).

Arctium lappa

USES Medicinal It has antibacterial and fungicidal properties and is used as a decoction or poultice for inflamed skin, sores, boils and disorders such as eczema and psoriasis. It is also taken for gastric ulcers and said to increase resistance to infection. Used in traditional Chinese medicine.
Culinary It is cultivated in Japan for the roots, which are eaten as a vegetable. The stalks, before flowering, can be chopped and added to salads, or cooked as a celery-like vegetable. In the past, they were sometimes candied, in the same way as angelica.
Cosmetic An infusion of the leaves, or decoction of the roots, makes a tonic skin freshener or hair rinse for dandruff.
Other names Lappa and beggar's buttons.

Right *Close up of leaf.*

ERICACEAE

Arctostaphylos uva-ursi

Bearberry

History and traditions The generic name from the Greek, *arcton staphyle*, and the specific, *uva-ursi*, from the Latin, both mean "bear's grapes", perhaps because bears enjoyed the fruit, or perhaps because the sour taste of this plant was only thought fit for consumption by bears. It is listed in 13th-century herbal manuscripts and was described in detail by the 16th-century Dutch botanist Clusius (Charles de L'Ecluse). In the 17th century John Josslyn discovered this herb growing in North America, where many of the Native American tribes made use of its medicinal properties and added it to smoking mixtures. He found it to be highly effective against scurvy. It was considered medicinally important in 18th-century Europe, and remained so into the 20th century, appearing in the British *Pharmacopoeia*.

Description A creeping, evergreen shrub, growing to 15 cm (6 in), with dark-green, leathery, small, oval leaves. Terminal clusters of tiny, white or pink, bell-shaped flowers appear in summer, followed by red fruit.

Habitat/distribution Found in rocky moorland and woodland, in northern Europe, Scandinavia and Russia, northern Asia, Japan, North America and cool, northern hemisphere regions.

Growth Needs moist, sandy or peaty soil. Ericaceous compost (soil mix) must be used if container-grown and for propagating, which can be done from seed, by layering in spring or from cuttings, taken with a heel, in summer.

Parts used Leaves – usually dried. For commercial use they are collected from the wild, mostly in Scandinavia and Russia, field cultivation having proved too costly.

USES Culinary Although the berries are edible, they taste extremely sharp, and are more suitable as "grouse feed", (a use given in one herbal). The leaves were at one time a popular tea in Russia.

Medicinal Constituents include arbutin and methylarbutin, which have been established as effectively antibacterial, especially against urinary infections, such as cystitis.

General The leaves have a high tannin content and have been used in the past in leather tanning and to produce a dark-grey dye.

Other names Mountain box and uva-ursi.

CAUTION Bearberry should not be taken by women during pregnancy, by children, or where kidneys are diseased.

PALMAE/ARECACEAE

Areca catechu

Betel nut

History and traditions The Chinese discovered the medicinal properties of this tree by 140 BC, when they brought it back from their conquests of the Malayan archipelago. It is the main ingredient of paan or "betel nut", a mixture of areca nut, lime and spices, wrapped in betel leaf, *Piper betle*, and it is widely chewed throughout the Middle East and Asia. It induces mild euphoria and is supposed to increase sexual virility.

Description A tall palm, reaching 20 m (65 ft) in height, with numerous feathery leaflets making up its 2 m (6 ft) long leaves. The pale yellow flowers appear when the tree is about 6–8 years old, followed by bunches of up to 100 round, orange fruits.

Habitat/distribution A native of Malaysia, and found throughout India, the Far East and eastern Africa, usually on coastal sites. Introduced in American tropical zones.

Parts used Fruit, rind, seeds.

USES Medicinal Stimulates the flow of saliva, and accelerates heart and perspiration rates. Chewed to sweeten breath, strengthen gums, improve digestion, and suppress intestinal worms – but permanently stains teeth red. Research is being carried out in America on this tree as a source of a potential anticancer drug. However, excessive chewing can lead to cancer of the mouth.

CAUTION Toxic in large doses, excess causes vomiting and stupor. Legal restrictions are in force in some countries.

CRUCIFERAE/BRASSICACEAE

Armoracia rusticana

Horseradish

History and traditions Horseradish was valued in the Middle Ages for the medicinal properties of both leaves and root. The great English botanist and herbalist William Turner, writing in 1548, referred to it as 'Red Cole', and it was not commonly called horseradish until so named in Gerard's Herbal of 1597, (England). At that time it was used in Germany and Scandinavia to make the hot and spicy condiment we know today, but this did not become popular in Britain until well into the 17th century. John Parkinson, in 1640, describes its use as a sauce in Germany, adding, "and in our own land also", but he considered it "too strong for tender and gentle stomaches". In 1657, William Coles reiterated that it was the practice in Germany for "the root, sliced thin and mixed with vinegar (to be) eaten as a sauce with meat".

Description A perennial, with a deep, fleshy taproot and large bright-green, oblong to ovate leaves, with serrated margins, sprouting from the base to a height of 60 cm (2 ft). Racemes of tiny, white flowers on drooping stems, up to 1.2 m (4 ft) long, appear in summer.

Habitat/distribution In the wild it is found in dampish soils in Europe and western Asia. Now naturalized in many parts of the world.

Growth In theory it prefers a moist soil, but in practice flourishes in most conditions. It can be propagated by seed in spring, or by root cuttings in spring or autumn. It grows vigorously and, once established, is nearly impossible to eradicate as it regenerates from the tiniest scrap of root left in the soil.

Parts used Leaves, roots.

USES Medicinal The root may be taken in the form of a syrup for bronchial infections, catarrh and coughs and as a general tonic for debility. The sliced root is applied externally to boils, or in a poultice to relieve rheumatic pains (but see CAUTION below).

Culinary The young, fresh leaves have a milder flavour than the pungent root and can be added to salads or chopped into smoked-fish pâtés. The fresh root is shredded to make a strong-flavoured, creamy-textured sauce, traditionally served with beef, but also excellent as an accompaniment to cold, especially smoked, meat and fish, hard-boiled eggs and stuffed aubergines (eggplant). For a milder flavour, grated apple, sprinkled with lemon juice and vinegar, can be mixed with horseradish.

To make horseradish sauce

2–3 pieces of fresh horseradish root
2 tbs cider vinegar
115 g/4oz fromage frais
salt, pepper and a pinch of sugar
2 tsp fresh, chopped dill

Scrub the horseradish root, grate it finely, and cover with the vinegar. Or, for a smoother texture, mix the horseradish and vinegar in an electric blender till pulped. Mix in the fromage frais, season with salt, pepper, sugar and chopped dill.

CAUTION May provoke allergic reactions. Large internal doses may cause vomiting. Should not be taken if suffering from stomach ulcers or thyroid problems.

Above *Digging up roots of established plants to make horseradish sauce.*

Above *Leaving some behind will ensure an ongoing supply of material.*

Above *Home-grown horseradish roots make a pungent sauce.*

Above *Flowers of* Arnica montana.

Right *Golden arnica flowers and pink* Mimulus lewisii *cover a hillside in bloom in Glacier National Park, United States.*

COMPOSITAE/ASTERACEAE

Arnica montana

Arnica

History and traditions Pier Andrea Mattioli, a household name in herbs in the 16th century, and physician at the Court of the Holy Roman Emperor Ferdinand I, in Prague, rated arnica highly. It became fashionable when he wrote about it in his standard work, *Commentarii*, a version of which appeared in Venice in 1544. It was widely used in the folk medicine of other European countries, principally Germany and Austria, where it has remained an important medicinal herb to this day. Arnica was used by Native Americans to treat muscular injury and back pain.

Description An alpine perennial with a creeping rootstock, it has a basal rosette of small, ovate, downy leaves and flowering stems growing to 30–60 cm (1–2 ft). The daisy-like flowers are golden yellow and borne in midsummer.

Related species *A. fulgens* is a North American species said to be even more medically powerful.

Habitat/distribution Found in mountainous regions of central and northern Europe and North America. *A. montana* is becoming rare in the wild and is protected in many countries.

Growth It prefers a sandy soil, enriched with humus, and a sunny position. As an alpine plant it needs a cool climate, and does not thrive in wet, waterlogged soil – grow arnica in containers or raised beds if necessary.

Parts used Flowers – dried, for use in pharmaceutical preparations.

USES Medicinal Recent research has established both the therapeutic value of this herb and its toxicity. It has a stimulating effect on the heart muscle and the circulatory system, but effects are rapid and correct doses crucial, with a high risk of overdose. It has antiseptic, anti-inflammatory properties when applied externally and is available as a pharmaceutical ointment for bruises. It is also used in homeopathy, for a range of conditions, including sprains, aching muscles, sore throats and sea sickness. In Germany it is widely available; in Britain it is legal only for external use and in the United States it is considered unsafe.

Other names Leopard's bane, mountain arnica, mountain daisy and mountain tobacco.

CAUTION Highly toxic and should not be taken internally, except in homeopathic remedies when the dosage is very small. It may cause dermatitis when used externally – do not apply to broken skin. Legally restricted in some countries. Use with advice from qualified medical practitioners.

COMPOSITAE/ASTERACEAE

Artemisia

This genus of some 300 species, containing many garden ornamentals, supplies four of the best-known herbs. These include one of the most popular culinary herbs, tarragon, which is the exception of the four in character and uses.

Artemisia abrotanum
Southernwood

History and traditions A native of southern Europe, southernwood was introduced to Britain in about 1548, where the popular name, southernwood, directly described its origins as a woody plant from the south. It soon became established as a cottage garden favourite, attracting new names and associations. Lad's love and old man came about because smearing its ashes in an ointment base was supposed to make pimply youths sprout virile beards and bring new growth to bald heads. Other authorities claim that boys in love wore it in their hats, or gave sprigs as love tokens to the objects of their affections. The French name "*garde-robe*" refers to the habit of including this herb in sachets to protect clothes from insect infestation. It was also thought to protect from infection and was included in nosegays carried for the purpose.

Description A shrubby semi-evergreen (it loses foliage in winter in cold climates and as the plants age), it grows to 1 m (3 ft) tall and has feathery, grey-green leaves with a clean, lemony scent. It seldom flowers in northern c imates, but in warmer southern regions small yellow flowers appear in summer.

Habitat/distribution Southernwood is native to southern Europe and parts of Asia, introduced and widespread in temperate zones and naturalized in North America.

Growth Prefers a light soil, full sun and tolerates drought. It is easy to propagate from softwood cuttings throughout summer, or heeled cuttings from old wood in autumn. Needs clipping back hard in late spring to prevent straggly, woody growth. Plants are best replaced after 6–8 years.

Parts used Leaves.

USES Medicinal Southernwood tea is said to stimulate the appetite and digestion. It is also prescribed for menstrual problems. At one time it was given to children to rid them of their threadworms.

Culinary Although there is some evidence of its use in southern European cookery, it s really far too bitter for the purpose.

Aromatic Its insect repellent properties and pleasant smell when dried make it a first choice herb for sachets to keep moths and insects at bay, or to include in pot-pourri.

Other names Lad's love and old man.

Artemisia abrotanum *is easy to propagate from cuttings.*

CAUTION Taken internally, southernwood stimulates the uterus and should never be given to pregnant women.

Artemisia absinthium
Wormwood

History and traditions Known since antiquity, this bitter herb was highly valued medicinally, with a reputation for overcoming bodily weakness. As a 15th-century manuscript declares: "Water of wormwood is gode – Grete Lords among the Saracens usen to drinke hitt." And Sir John Hill, in his *Virtues of British Herbs* (1772), alleging that the Germans have a tendency to overeat, says this is made possible by a habit of washing down each mouthful with a decoction of wormwood.

Description A perennial subshrub, 1 m (3 ft) in height, leaves are silvery-grey, downy and finely divided. Flowers are yellowish-green, tiny and ball-shaped, borne on bracts in late summer.

Habitat/distribution Found wild in temperate regions of Europe, North and South America, Asia and South Africa. Widely introduced as a garden plant.

Parts used Leaves, flowering tops.

USES Medicinal Has anti-inflammatory properties, expels intestinal worms and stimulates the uterus. Sometimes recommended for digestive problems, poor appetite and general debility, but there are more modern and safer ways to deal with these conditions.

Aromatic Strongly insect-repellent, it is dried for inclusion in sachets against moths, fleas and other insects, or made into tinctures and infusions to deter them.

CAUTION As a medicinal preparation, should not be given to children or pregnant women. Taken habitually, or in excess, can cause vomiting, convulsions and delirium.

Artemisia dracunculus
French tarragon

History and traditions The species' name, *dracunculus*, is from the Latin meaning "a little dragon" after its supposed ability to cure the bites of serpents and mad dogs. A native of southern Europe, it was first introduced to the royal gardens of Britain in Tudor times. John Evelyn in his *Acetaria*, 1699, recommended it as "highly cordial and friendly to the head, heart, and liver" and advised that it "must never be excluded from sallets".
Description A perennial 1 m (3 ft) high, with branched erect stems, and slim, pointed leaves. Flowers are inconspicuous and greyish-green but appear only on some plants grown in warm climates – it does not flower at all in cool northern climates. Not to be confused with the subspecies, known as Russian tarragon, a larger, more vigorous plant, with coarser leaves and practically no discernible aroma.
Habitat/distribution A native of southern Europe and Asia, widely distributed in temperate zones worldwide.
Growth It prefers a fairly moist, but well-drained soil and full sun. Tarragon needs protection in winter in colder climates, especially in areas where frost is prolonged or where the ground becomes waterlogged. Propagate by division of roots in spring or autumn. It cannot be propagated from seed.
Parts used Fresh or dried leaf.

French tarragon is a superbly flavoured culinary herb.

USES Culinary One of the top culinary herbs for distinction of flavour, it is used in salads, savoury pâté, cooked meat, fish and egg dishes. Well known for its affinity with chicken, it also enhances the flavour of root vegetables such as carrots and parsnips. Vinegar flavoured with tarragon is a classic condiment and it is a main ingredient of sauces and stuffings.

Artemisia vulgaris
Mugwort

History and traditions Ascribed magical properties by cultures in Europe, China and Asia, this plant has accumulated many legends and superstitions. It was one of the nine herbs in the Anglo-Saxon charm against flying venom and evil spirits, when it was held to be "Mighty against loathed ones / That through the land rove" (Anglo-Saxon Ms, Harleian Collection). Roman soldiers are said to have put it in their shoes to prevent aching feet on long marches, a claim updated by William Coles in The Art of Simpling, 1656, with his assertion, "If a Footman take mugwort and put it into his shoes in the morning, he may goe forty miles before Noon and not be weary." In Europe it is connected with St John the Baptist.
Description A tall straggly perennial, 1–1.5 m (3–5 ft) in height. The leaves are grey-green with white undersides and slightly downy. Panicles of inconspicuous grey-green flowers appear in the summer.
Habitat/distribution A wild plant growing in a variety of soils, in wastelands, hedgerows, field margins, by streams and rivers in Europe, Asia and North America.
Parts used Leaves.

USES Medicinal As with some of the other artemisias, it is said to have digestive properties, stimulate appetite and act as a nerve tonic. It is a diuretic and used in regulating menstruation. Used in Chinese medicine for rheumatism.
Culinary At one time it was included in stuffings and sauces for meat and poultry such as duck and goose – but the slightly bitter, unpalatable taste makes it hardly recommendable.
Aromatic Has insect-repellent properties.

LEGUMINOSAE/PAPILIONACEAE

Aspalathus linearis

Rooibos

History and traditions A traditional tea plant of native South Africans of the Cape, it was adopted by European travellers and colonists in the late 18th century. Today, it is steadily gaining in popularity, due to for its soothing, medicinal properties and because it makes a pleasant-tasting tea with a similar flavour to ordinary, Asian tea.

Description A small shrub up to 2 m (6 ft) in height, with bright-green, thin, linear leaves bearing short, leafy shoots in their axils. Small yellow pea flowers are followed by long pods. The leaves turn a reddish-brown during processing, which gives the tea its name.

Habitat/distribution Native to dry, mountainous areas of Cape Province, South Africa.

Growth A frost-hardy bush – it cannot tolerate temperatures below –5°C (23°F), or prolonged severe weather. Requires dry, sandy soil and full sun. Propagated by seed sown in spring. Pinch out shoots, as it grows, to encourage bushiness. Commercially cultivated in South Africa.

Parts used Leaves and shoots – sun-dried and fermented to make tea.

USES Medicinal High in vitamin C and mineral salts, it is taken internally for digestive disorders and to relieve allergies and eczema, and applied externally for skin irritations.

Culinary It has a refreshing flavour, is low in tannins and makes a caffeine-free substitute for Asian tea. It is sometimes used as a flavouring herb in sauces and soft drinks and as an ingredient of a local alcoholic liquor.

Other name Red bush tea.

CHENOPODIACEAE

Atriplex hortensis

Orache

History and traditions This herb was eaten as a spinach-like vegetable by Native American tribes, and was introduced to Britain in 1548. Sixteenth-century herbalists considered it to be effective against gout when applied as a poultice with honey, vinegar and salt. John Evelyn in his *Acetaria*, 1719, refers to its "cooling properties" and recommends it as a salad herb or vegetable, advising that, like lettuce, it should be boiled in its own moisture. Culpeper agreed that it could be eaten as a salad but thought its real virtue lay in the seeds, which he claimed made an effective laxative in the form of an alcohol tincture.

Above *Atriplex hortensis var. 'Rubra', red orache, makes a spectacular plant in the border, and the leaves add colour to salads.*

Description An upright annual, growing to 1.2 m (4 ft), it has spear-shaped green to purple leaves, slightly downy when young, and a mass of yellow-green, sorrel-like flowers, borne on tall spikes, in summer.

Related species *A. hortensis* var. 'Rubra', or red orache (above) is a more attractive cultivar, with purple-red foliage and flowers, followed by spectacular seed heads sought after by flower arrangers.

Habitat/distribution Occurs in Asia, North America and Europe, often in coastal areas. It is widely cultivated in temperate and warm regions worldwide.

Growth Flourishes in any soil – tolerates dry conditions but growth is more luxuriant in moister, more fertile soil. Prefers an open, sunny position. Propagated by seed sown *in situ* in spring. Self-seeds prolifically.

Parts used Leaves.

USES Culinary Leaves of red orache add colour and interest to salads, but, despite some recommendations, neither red nor green orache makes very succulent spinach substitute when cooked as a vegetable.

Other name Mountain spinach.

Left *Leaves of Atriplex hortensis var. 'Rubra'.*

SOLANACEAE

Atropa belladonna

Deadly nightshade

History and traditions In 16th-century Venice this plant was known as *herba belladonna*, and was used by women who sought to beautify themselves to dilate the pupils of their eyes. Its potential to cause fatalities was well understood at the time, the apothecaries' name for it being *solatrum mortale,* which translates as "deadly nightshade". Writing at the end of the 16th century, Gerard pontificates on its dangers, advising that a plant "so furious and deadly" should be banished from "your gardens".

Description A bushy perennial, 1–1.5 m (3–5 ft) tall, it has ovate, dull-green leaves, bearing single, purple-brown, bell-shaped flowers in the axils in summer, followed by shiny black berries.

Related species Not to be confused with the *Solanum* genus, many of which are also poisonous and include other nightshades – as well as potatoes, aubergines (eggplants) and climbers.

Habitat/distribution Native to Europe and Asia, introduced and naturalized elsewhere.

Growth Grown as a commercial crop (for the pharmaceutical industry) in well-drained, moist soil and full sun – warm, dry conditions increase the alkaloid content.

Parts used Whole plant – dried and processed.

USES Medicinal It contains the alkaloid, atropine, which dilates the pupils of the eye and gives the plant its toxic, sedative properties. A constituent of pharmaceutical drugs, used as premedication before surgery and in eyedrops for ophthalmic treatment.

CAUTION A highly poisonous herb. Subject to legal restrictions in most countries. For use when prescribed by qualified medical practitioners only.

MELIACEAE

Azadirachta indica

Neem tree

History and traditions A common tree of southern Asia, it has played an important role in Ayurvedic medicine, and in agriculture and domestic life as an insect repellent since earliest times. The first part of the botanical name is from a Persian word meaning "noble tree", reflecting its many useful properties, which remain valid to this day. The Neem Foundation, Bombay, dedicated to its study, was established in 1993 and the tree's potential as a source of a low-cost, environmentally-friendly pesticide for field crops in developing countries is currently being investigated.

Description A large, evergreen tree, 12–15 m (40–50 ft) tall, it has dense pinnate leaves. Clusters of small white flowers appear in spring to be followed by long greeny-yellow fruits each containing a seed. The wood secretes resin, and *margosa* or *neem* oil is made from the seeds.

Habitat/distribution Occurs in India, Sri Lanka, Myanmar, southeast Asia and tropical regions of Australia and Africa. Widely planted as shade trees to line the roads.

Growth It will not grow in temperatures below 15°C (59°F). It requires sun and tolerates poor, dry soil.

Parts used Leaves, bark, seeds, oil, resin.

USES Medicinal Neem has anti-inflammatory and insecticidal properties, reduces fever, and acts as a tonic and detoxicant, increasing vitality. It is used in the treatment of malaria and has been found to have some effect against leprosy. Also used externally for skin disorders and irritations, especially boils and ulcers, and in eye and ear complaints. Twigs can be used to clean teeth, prevent breath odour and protect from infection.

Cosmetic Reputed to prevent hair loss if a decoction of the leaves is applied as a rinse. The oil is used in hair and skin lotions, toothpaste and soap.

General Makes an effective mosquito and insect repellent, and insecticide for crops. In its countries of origin the dried leaves are used to protect stored clothes or books from insect damage. Although it has been found to be safe and efficient as a sheep dip, this use has not been developed commercially.

Other name Margosa.

Above *Neem leaves have excellent insecticidal properties.*

BERBERIDACEAE

Berberis vulgaris

Barberry

History and traditions Barberry has been grown since medieval times for medicinal and culinary use and as a dye plant, producing a yellow colour. It was said to be excellent for "hot agues" and all manner of burnings and scaldings. It had a reputation for blighting wheat, now justified, as it is a known host of the disease, wheat rust.

Description A shrub which grows to 2 m (6 ft), with sharp spines on the stems and small oval leaves. Clusters of yellow flowers in late spring are followed by the shiny red fruits (berries).

Habitat/distribution Found in hedges and woodland in Europe, also in Asia, the Americas and northern Africa.

Growth A wild plant, it grows on any soil in sun or partial shade. It is propagated by layering or by taking cuttings in early autumn and can also be grown from seed sown in spring or autumn.

Parts used Leaves, bark, roots, fruit.

USES Medicinal It contains an anti-bacterial alkaloid, berberine, and is used in the treatment of tropical diseases, including dysentery and malaria. It has also been found to contain anti-cancer compounds and is included in chemotherapy drugs. Used in Ayurvedic medicine for liver complaints and as an anti-inflammatory.

Culinary The berries are very bitter, but high in vitamin C. At one time they were made into jams, jellies, preserves and tarts.

CAUTION Restrictions on the cultivation of barberry exist in some countries.

BORAGINACEAE

Borago officinalis

Borage

History and traditions There are various historical references to the ability of this herb to bring comfort and cheer. Gerard mentions references to it in this context by Pliny and Dioscorides, along with the Latin tag: "*Ego Borago, gaudia semper ago*", which he translates as "I, Borage, bring alwaies courage". He goes on to advise adding the flowers to salads to "exhilerate and make the mind glad", the leaves to wine to "drive away all sadnesse, dulnesse and melancholy", making a syrup of the flowers to calm a "phrenticke or lunaticke person" or, for even greater force and effect, candying them with sugar. According to John Parkinson, their attractive colour and form made the flowers a favourite motif in women's needlework.

Description A short-lived hardy annual, 60–90 cm (2–3 ft) high, with a sprawling habit of growth, hollow, hairy stems, downy leaves and blue (sometimes pink) star-shaped flowers with black centres. It is very attractive to bees.

Related species *B. officinalis* 'Alba' is a white-flowered variety.

Habitat/distribution Native to the Mediterranean region from Spain to Turkey. Now naturalized in most of Europe and in many other parts of the world.

Growth Grows in any soil, even if poor and dry, but it makes a lusher, healthier plant, less prone to mildew, given better soil and more moisture. Prefers a sunny position. It is easy to propagate from seed sown in spring or autumn, and despite common advice to the contrary, the seedlings may be successfully transplanted when young, if they are well watered until established. It also self-seeds.

Parts used Leaves, flowers, oil from the seeds.

USES Medicinal A cooling, anti-inflammatory herb with diuretic properties. It is also said to be mildly antidepressant. Used externally to soothe inflamed skin and in mouthwashes and gargles. The seeds contain gamma-linolenic acid, and oil extracted from them is used as an alternative to evening primrose oil for hormonal problems and skin complaints. Borage is grown as a commercial crop for its oil, which is used in pharmaceutical drugs and cosmetic products.

Culinary The leaves have a faint flavour of cucumbers and are added to soft drinks and wine cups. The flowers make a pretty garnish for salads, and are candied or dried as decorations for sweet dishes and cakes.

CAUTION Borage may cause allergic reactions in some people. The leaves, but not the oil, have been found to contain very small amounts of an alkaloid that may cause liver disease. The plant, but not oil extracted from the seeds, is legally restricted in some countries. Use with advice from qualified medical practitioners.

Top left *Borage is grown as a commercial crop for the pharmaceutical and cosmetic industries.*

Top Borago officinalis *'Alba'.*

Above *Borage flowers make a pretty garnish for salads.*

BURSERACEAE

Boswellia sacra syn. *B. carteri*

Frankincense

History and traditions Since ancient times, frankincense has been an ingredient of incense, used in the religious ceremonies of the Egyptians, Babylonians, Assyrians, Hebrews, Greeks and Romans, and is still used in religious ritual to this day. It was highly valued by early civilizations as an item of trade, considered as precious as gold, and was one of the gifts said to have been given to Jesus Christ at his birth by the wise men from the east (Matt. 2:11). It is also thought to have been used by Cleopatra as a cosmetic for smoothing skin. In charred form it made *kohl*, the black eyeliner worn by eastern women. Ancient medicinal uses include Pliny's claim that it provided an antidote to hemlock poisoning and Avicenna's recommendations that it should be prescribed for tumours, ulcers, vomiting, dysentery and fevers. There is also some evidence that at one time it was used in China for leprosy.
Description A small deciduous tree, 2–5 m (6–16 ft) in height, with papery bark, pinnate leaves and racemes of small greenish-white flowers. The gum is secreted in the wood.
Related species Several species of *Boswellia* produce frankincense – formerly it was mostly derived from *B. sacra* and *B. papyrifera*. Today, *B. carteri* and *B. frereana* are usual sources. *B. serrata* (from India) is grown for timber.
Habitat/distribution *B. sacra* comes from Somalia and southern Arabia, *B. papyrifera* from Nigeria and Ethiopia, *B. carteri* and *B. frereana* from Somalia across to eastern Africa, found in desert scrubland. Many *Boswellia* species are threatened with extinction in the wild, due to over-exploitation and over-grazing.
Growth Grows wild, in shallow, rocky soil.
Parts used Gum resin – obtained by incising the trunk to produce a milky sap, which hardens into yellowish globules. Available in the form of grains or powder.

USES Medicinal The resin has antiseptic properties and has many uses in both Chinese and Ayurvedic medicine. The essential oil is used in aromatherapy to counteract anxiety (often by heating the essential oil in a vaporizer).
Aromatic Its chief use is as an ingredient of incenses and fragrant preparations. Also added to commercial cosmetics and is a constituent of an antiwrinkle face cream.
Other name Olibanum.

CRUCIFERAE/BRASSICACEAE

Brassica nigra

Mustard

History and traditions Mustard has a long history both as a medicinal and as a flavouring herb. The ancient Greeks thought highly of it and Hippocrates recommended that it be taken internally, or as a poultice, for a variety of ailments. It probably came to Britain with the Romans, who mixed the seeds with wine as a condiment and ate the leaves as a vegetable. Gerard describes pounding the seeds with vinegar to make an "excellent sauce" for serving with meat as a digestive and appetite stimulant.
Description An erect annual, 1–1.2 m (3–4 ft) high, with narrow, lobed leaves and racemes of bright yellow flowers, followed by pods containing reddish-brown seeds.
Related species *B. juncea,* or brown mustard, being easier to harvest mechanically, though less pungent, has largely replaced the medicinal *B. nigra.* White mustard (*Synapsis alba,* syn. *Brassica alba)* is also grown for commercial production. It is used to make American mustard and is the species that was sown with cress as a salad.
Growth Requires rich, well-dressed soil and full sun and is propagated by seed sown in spring.
Parts used Leaves, seeds – seedpods are picked before they are fully ripe and dried.

USES Medicinal Mustard has warming and antibiotic properties and is applied externally in poultices, baths or footbaths for rheumatism, aching muscles and chilblains. A mustard foot-bath is a traditional British remedy for colds.
Culinary The ground seeds, mixed into a paste, make the familiar "hot-flavoured" condiment to serve with a range of dishes. The whole seeds are added to curries, soups, stews, pickles and sauces. Young leaves are eaten with cress, or added to salads.

BUXACEAE

Buxus sempervirens

Box

History and traditions The gardens of ancient Rome featured formally clipped box hedges and topiary, a fashion which was enthusiastically revived in Renaissance Europe, when knot gardens and elaborate parterres dominated garden design. Box foliage has been used to decorate the house for American Thanksgiving and at Christmas time in Europe, when it was made into "kissing boughs" or "Advent crowns" (depending on inclination and piety) – sprigs were tied on to frames and decorated with ribbons, candles and shiny red apples. Sometimes known as "boxwood" for its hard, durable wood, traditionally used to make engraving blocks, wooden tools, musical instruments and fine furniture.

Description Common box is an evergreen shrub, or small tree, growing to about 4.5 m (14 ft), with glossy green, ovate leaves and a strange, rather acrid scent.

Related species There are over 70 species, ranging from tender to hardy. *B. sempervirens* 'Suffruticosa' is a dwarf form – for edging and low hedges: *B. sempervirens* 'Elegantissima' is slow-growing with variegated cream and silver-green foliage; *B. sempervirens* 'Latifolia Maculata' has gold leaves; and *B. microphylla* makes low-growing mounds of dark green.

Habitat/distribution Occurs in Europe, Asia, Africa, North and Central America.

Growth Requires well-drained, but not poor, soil, sun or shade. Although hardy, *B. sempervirens* does not thrive in very cold winters and new growth is damaged by frosts – clip after frosts to avoid encouraging vulnerable new shoots. Propagated by semi-ripe cuttings, in late summer.

Parts used Leaves, bark, wood.

USES Medicinal Said to be effective against malaria, but contains toxic alkaloids, and is little used in herbal medicine today. It is currently being researched for its potential as treatments for cancer, HIV and AIDS.

CAUTION Poisonous, can be fatal if taken internally. May cause skin irritations.

Above Buxus sempervirens, *common box.*

Below left to right *Clipped dwarf box,* Buxus sempervirens *'Suffruticosa', the variagated leaves of* B. sempervirens *'Elegantissima' and the compact and very hardy* B. microphylla *var.* Koreana.

LABIATAE/LAMIACEAE

Calamintha nepeta

Calamint

History and traditions Now regarded as an ornamental, calamint was once an important medicinal herb, considered to be effective for "hysterical complaints" and "afflictions of the brain", as well as for a range of ailments from leprosy to indigestion. It had a reputation for hindering conception and as an abortifacient.

Description A small, bushy perennial, 30–60 cm (1–2 ft) high, it has small, ovate leaves and a mass of tubular pinky-mauve flowers in summer.

Related species The medicinal calamint of the apothecaries was *C. officinalis,* now classified as *C. sylvatica*, but *C. nepeta* seems to have been used interchangeably. *C. grandiflora* has larger flowers and *C. grandiflora* 'Variegata' is a cultivar with cream and green variegated foliage.

Habitat/distribution Native to Europe, found in grassland, woodland and chalky uplands of central Asia and northern temperate zones.

Growth Prefers well-drained, not-too-rich soil and a sunny position. The easiest method of propagation is by division in spring.

Parts used Leaves or flowering tops.

USES Medicinal It is taken as a tonic, or for indigestion, in the form of an infusion.

Culinary The young leaves and flowers, fresh or dried, may be infused to make a lightly mint-scented tea or added to salads.

CAUTION It is not advisable for pregnant women, as one of its constituents is pulegone (also found in pennyroyal, *Mentha pulegium),* which stimulates the uterus.

COMPOSITAE/ASTERACEAE

Calendula officinalis

Pot marigold

History and traditions This cheerful, familiar flower was valued for its medicinal, culinary and cosmetic properties in early civilizations of both east and west. Calendula is the diminutive of the Latin *calendulae* and thus "a little calendar or little clock" (*Oxford English Dictionary).* This ties in neatly with its habit of closing its petals when there is no sun as described by Shakespeare in *A Winter's Tale*:

The Marigold that goes to bed wi' the sun
And with him rises weeping.

In medieval England the usual name was simply "golds" – Chaucer refers to a garland of "yellow golds" as an emblem for jealousy and it was only later dubbed "marigold" in honour of the Virgin Mary. Its brightness inspired claims of exceptional virtues from an ability to draw "wicked humours" out of the head (*Macer's Herbal,* 15th century), which makes some sense of a fantastical tale in the *Book of Secrets of Albertus Magnus,* 1560, of how an amulet of marigold petals, a bay leaf and a wolf's tooth will ensure that only words of peace will be spoken to the wearer. In Tudor times the petals were dried in huge quantities and sold in grocers' shops to flavour winter stews. They were made into conserves and syrups and also added to salads.

Description A low-growing annual – to 50 cm (20 in) – with hairy, slightly sticky leaves and large orange-yellow daisy-like flowers throughout summer into early autumn.

Related species There are a number of hybrids and ornamental cultivars that do not necessarily have the same medicinal value, but may be used for culinary and cosmetic purposes and to add to pot-pourri. The *Tagetes* genus of marigolds are not related. Many are toxic and should not be used for the same purposes as *Calendula.*

Growth Easy to grow in any soil. Propagate from seed sown in autumn or spring. Regular dead-heading ensures a good supply of blooms over a long period. Self-seeds prolifically.

Parts used Flowers – petals can be used fresh or dried.

USES Medicinal Pot marigold or calendula has anti-inflammatory, antiseptic properties and is also antibacterial and antifungal. It makes an excellent ointment for soothing irritated, chapped skin, eczema, insect bites and sunburn. It may also be made into an infused oil, for the same purpose, by steeping petals in warm vegetable oil.

Culinary Once known as "poor man's saffron", the fresh or dried petals add rich colour to rice dishes and salads and may be sprinkled over sweet dishes or baked in buns and biscuits.

Cosmetic Petals are added to face and hand creams, or made into an infusion as a lotion for spotty or oily skins.

Aromatic Whole dried flowers, or petals lend colour to a fragrant pot-pourri.

CAUTION Not to be confused with inedible marigold (tagetes).

Pot marigold skin salve

300 ml/½ pint/1 ¼ cups boiling water
15 g/½ oz dried pot marigold petals or 30 g/1 oz fresh petals
60 ml/4 tbs emulsifying ointment
15 ml/1 tbs glycerine
4 drops tincture of benzoin
4–5 drops infused calendula oil (optional)

First make a strong marigold infusion by pouring the boiling water over the marigold petals in a jug or bowl. Cover and leave until cool before straining.

Put the emulsifying ointment and glycerine in a bowl set over a pan of gently simmering water and stir until melted – which will take about 10 minutes.

Remove from the heat and mix in 150 ml/¼ pint/ ⅔ cup of the marigold infusion, with the tincture of benzoin and calendula oil. Stir the mixture until it has cooled and reached a consistency similar to double (heavy) cream. Pour into a small jar before it sets.

• Emulsifying ointment, tincture of benzoin and calendula oil are available from specialist herbal suppliers.

CANNABACEAE

Cannabis sativa

Cannabis

History and traditions Cannabis has a long history as a medicinal plant, being mentioned in ancient Chinese and Indian texts dating from the 10th century BC. Herodotus reports that the Scythians (nomadic people of Iranian origin, living between the 7th and 2nd centuries BC) "crept into their huts and threw the seeds onto hot stones". Pliny thought very highly of this plant's medicinal values. Hildegarde of Bingen, AD 1150, refers to it as a relief for headaches and it is mentioned in all the great Renaissance herbals – though its narcotic effects were well understood and it was known as "The Leaf of Delusion". As hemp, it has been grown for its fibre since ancient times, and it provided rope for the hangman in 16th-century Britain (old names are "gallowgrass" and "neckeweed". The word "assassin" comes from the Arabic for hashish-taker.

Description An annual which grows to 5 m (16 ft) in height, on erect stems with narrow, toothed leaves and panicles of inconspicuous green flowers.

Habitat/distribution Cannabis is native to northern India, southern Siberia, western and central Asia; it can be grown throughout temperate and tropical regions.

Parts used Leaves, flowering tops – processed in various forms, under various names, such as "marijuana", "pot", "dagga", "kif", "ganja", "charas" or "churras", and "bhang".

USES Medicinal Cannabis is widely used as an illegal narcotic drug. It can be addictive, and is weakening and harmful in excess, but there is some evidence of its therapeutic value for diseases such as cancer, multiple sclerosis, cerebral palsy and glaucoma.

General Rope is made from the fibre. Seeds are the source of hempseed oil used in varnishes, foods and cosmetics. Hemp *per se* does not contain appreciable amounts of THC and is a legal crop in some places – as a weed it grows with abandon and great success in Iowa.

Other name Hemp.

CAUTION It is illegal in most countries.

CRUCIFERAE/BRASSICACEAE

Capsella bursa-pastoris

Shepherd's purse

History and traditions Most of its names in English, Latin and other European languages refer to the resemblance of the seeds to purses or little pouches. It is of ancient origin, seeds were found at Catal Huyuk, a site dating from 5950 BC, and in the stomach of Tollund Man. Following a visit to America, John Josselyn listed it in his herbal, 1672, as one of the plants unknown to the New World before the Pilgrims went there. Despite being a common weed, it has proved a valid medicinal plant in this century; extracts were used during World War I to treat wounds.

Description An annual, or more usually biennial, plant with a flower stem rising to 50 cm (20 in) from a basal rosette of oval, dentate leaves. It has tiny white flowers, followed by triangular seedpods.

Habitat/distribution Grows worldwide in temperate zones in fields and waysides on gravelly, sandy and nitrogen-rich soils.

Growth A wild plant, it tolerates poor soil. It can be propagated from seed. Self-seeds freely.

Parts used Leaves – fresh, or dried for use in infusions and extracts.

USES Medicinal Contains a glycoside, diosmin, which has blood-clotting effects and is reputed to stop internal haemorrhages and reduce heavy menstruation when taken as an infusion of the dried leaf. Also taken for cystitis and applied externally for eczema and skin complaints.

Culinary The leaves are rich in vitamins A, B and C and, although not very tasty, make a healthy addition to salads.

SOLANACEAE

Capsicum

History and traditions Capsicums were first brought to Europe and the West from Mexico following Columbus's voyage of 1492, when the doctor who accompanied him noted their uses by the Native Americans as pain relievers, toothache remedies and for flavouring food. The Portuguese were responsible for their spread to India and Africa.

Habitat/distribution They are now grown in tropical and subtropical regions worldwide, and under glass in temperate zones. They can be grown outside in many areas of North America and in the southern states are a major commercial crop.

Description *Capsicum annuum* var. *annuum* are annuals, sometimes short-lived perennials, and most grow into small bushy plants 60–90 cm (2–3 ft) high; a few may reach 1.5 m (5 ft). They have glossy lance-shaped to ovate leaves and small white flowers followed by conical, or spherical, green, ripening to red, fruits.

Species Most cultivated peppers are of the species *C. annuum* var. *annuum*. There are over 1,000 cultivars grown across the world, with fruit in a wide range of shapes, sizes and degrees of pungency, divided into five main groups:

1. **Cerasiforme Group (cherry peppers)** – with small, very pungent fruits.
2. **Conoides Group (cone peppers)** – with erect, conical fruits.
3. **Fasciculatum Group (red cone peppers)** – slender, red, very pungent fruits.
4. **Grossum Group (bell peppers, sweet peppers, pimento)** – these have large, sweet, bell-shaped fruit, green, then ripening to red or yellow. Rich in vitamin C, they lack the medicinal properties of the hot, pungent peppers.
5. **Longum Group (cayenne peppers, chilli peppers)** – fruits are usually drooping, very pungent and the source of chilli powder, cayenne pepper and hot paprika. *C. frutescens* is a name often used for varieties of *C. annuum* whose fruits are used in Tabasco sauce.

Growth Frost-tender plants, which must be grown under glass in cool temperate climates. Plant in loam-based (John Innes) growing medium (soil mix), water freely, feed with a liquid fertilizer once a week and mist flowers with water daily to ensure that fruit sets. Propagation is from seed, at a temperature of 21°C (70°F) in early spring. Outside, they are grown in well-drained, nutrient-rich soil.

Parts used Fruits – are eaten ripe or unripe; or dried (ripe only) for powders.

USES Medicinal It is the bitter alkaloid, capsaicin, which gives peppers their hot taste and has been established by modern research as an effective painkiller – it works by depleting the nerve cells of the chemical neurotransmitter which sends pain messages to the brain. Peppers are antibacterial and also contain vitamins A, C, and mineral salts. Pungent varieties increase blood flow, encourage sweating, stimulate the appetite and help digestion. In tropical countries they are useful food preservatives and help prevent gastric upsets. Taken internally or used as gargles (infusions of the powder) for colds, fevers and sore throats; applied externally (in massage oil or compresses) for rheumatism, arthritis, aching joints and muscles. A pharmaceutical analgesic cream, with capsaicin as active ingredient, has recently been developed for reducing rheumatic pain.

Culinary Sweet red or green peppers make delicious cooked vegetables or raw salad ingredients. Hot chilli peppers are added to pickles and chutneys; dried to make cayenne pepper, chilli powder or paprika (from milder-tasting fruits); added to dishes in Indian, Mexican, Thai and other worldwide cuisines.

Other names Peppers and chilli peppers.

Top centre Capsicum frutescens, *a hot chilli pepper.*

Top right Capsicum annuum *var.* annuum, *Grossum Group, a sweet, bell pepper.*

CAUTION Hot chilli peppers may cause inflammation and irritation to skin and eyes, so wear gloves when handling them. If taken internally to excess, they may cause digestive disorders.

CARICACEAE

Carica papaya

Papaya

History and traditions Originally from South and Central America and the West Indies, this tree with its fragrant, fleshy fruit was unknown in Europe before the end of the 17th century. The Spanish took it to Manila and, with the expansion of trade and travel at the beginning of the 18th century, it made its way to Asia and Africa and is now grown in tropical countries around the globe.

Description A small, evergreen tree, up to 6 m (20 ft) in height with deeply cut, palmate leaves, forming an umbrella-shaped crown. The large, ovoid fruits have dark-green, leathery skin, ripening to yellow, containing sweet orange-yellow flesh and numerous tiny black seeds surrounding a central cavity.

Habitat/distribution Native to South and Central America, occurs widely in tropical zones.

Growth A tender, tropical plant it will not grow in temperatures below 13°C (55°F). Requires rich, moist soil, and a sunny, humid climate.

Parts used Fruit, seeds, leaves – fresh. Sap, known as "papain", is extracted from the unripe fruits by scarification, and produced in dried or liquid form.

USES Medicinal The fruit is one of the best natural digestives, containing enzymes similar to pepsin. Juice is applied externally to destroy warts and for skin eruptions and irritations. Seeds and papain are used in preparations to expel intestinal worms.

Culinary Fruit is high in vitamin C and minerals, and is eaten fresh, canned or made into ice creams, desserts and soft drinks. Papain is used commercially as a meat tenderizer, and, on a domestic level, the inside of the skin of the fruit and leaves are wrapped round meat for the same purpose. Seeds have a pungent flavour and are sometimes eaten, or used as food flavouring, in countries where it is grown.

Cosmetic Juice smooths skin, removes freckles and reduces sun damage. Papain is included in commercial cosmetic products.

General Papain is used as an insecticide against termites, as an ingredient of chewing gum, to reduce cloudiness in beer and to make woollen and silk fabrics shrinkproof.

Above *Papaya leaves leaves are used to tenderize meat.*

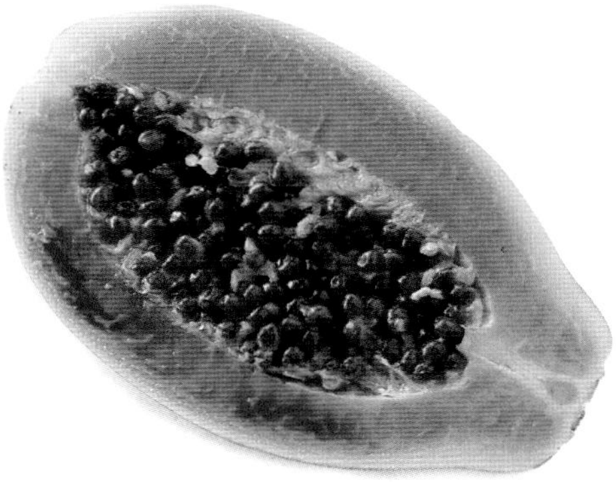

Papaya fruit has excellent digestive properties.

COMPOSITAE/ASTERACEAE

Carlina acaulis

Carline thistle

History and traditions In medieval times this thistle was thought to be an antidote to poison and the root was sometimes chewed to relieve toothache. It is said to be named after the Emperor Charlemagne following a dream that it would cure the plague.

Description A low-growing, short-lived perennial, 5–10 cm (2–4 in) high, with a deep tap root, it has basal rosettes of spiny leaves and large stemless flowers with silvery-white bracts surrounding a brown disc-shaped centre.

Habitat/distribution Native to Europe and Asia, it is found in fields, grasslands and waste ground on poor dry soils in sunny positions.

Growth It grows best in a poor, dry soil. If kept too wet it will rot, and if the soil is too rich it becomes lax, overgrown and loses its neat, stemless habit. Propagated from seed sown in autumn and overwintered in a cold frame.

Parts used Roots – dried for use in decoctions, liquid extracts and tinctures.

USES Medicinal It has antibacterial and diuretic properties. A decoction of the roots is used externally as a gargle for sore throats, for skin complaints and to clean wounds. It is taken internally for urine retention.

Culinary Claims have been made for the flower centres as substitute artichoke hearts.

CAUTION Large doses taken internally are purgative and emetic.

COMPOSITAE/ASTERACEAE

Carthamus tinctorius

Safflower

History and traditions Cultivated in Egypt, China and India since ancient times, safflower was a valued dye plant – producing several colours, including a pink dye, used for the original "red tape" of Indian bureaucracy. It was introduced to Europe from the Middle East during the mid-16th century, for its medicinal properties, and is now cultivated for the oil extracted from the seeds.

Description A hardy annual, growing to 1 m (3 ft) high, with finely toothed, long, ovate leaves and shaggy, thistle-like, yellow flower heads set in spiny bracts.

Habitat/distribution Native to Asia and Mediterranean regions, widely cultivated for its seeds in many countries, including Asia, India, Africa and Australia.

Growth Grows in any light, well-drained soil and tolerates dry conditions. Propagated by seed, sown in spring.

Parts used Flowers, seeds, oil.

USES Medicinal Tea, infused from fresh or dry flowers, is taken to induce perspiration and reduce fevers and is mildly laxative. Infusions are also applied externally for bruises, skin irritations and inflammations.

Culinary Oil extracted from the seeds is low in cholesterol and has a delicate flavour. The flower petals, which are slightly bitter, have been used as a substitute for saffron in colouring food.

Household Flowers produce a yellow dye with water and red dye with alcohol. They are dr ed for adding to pot-pourri and as "everlasting" flowers for dried arrangements.

UMBELLIFERAE/APIACEAE

Carum carvi

Caraway

History and traditions Caraway seeds have been found during archaeological excavations at Neolithic sites in Europe and the plant was well known to the Egyptians, Greeks and Romans. The seeds were a popular culinary flavouring in Tudor England, cooked with fruit and baked in bread and cakes. They were made into sugared "comfits", and frequently served as a side dish with baked apples, as in Shakespeare's *Henry IV* when Falstaff is invited to take "a pippin [apple] and a dish of carraways". This custom is said to have continued into the early 20th century at formal dinners of London livery companies. There is also an old superstition that caraway has retentive powers, and, if sprinkled about, is capable of preventing people and personal belongings from straying.

Description A biennial 45–60 cm (18 in–2 ft) tall, it has feathery leaves, with umbels of white flowers appearing in its second year, followed by ridged fruits (popularly known as seeds).

Habitat/distribution Native to Asia and central Europe in meadowlands and waste grounds. Introduced and cultivated elsewhere.

Growth Prefers well-drained soil and a sunny position. Propagated from seed sown in spring, preferably *in situ* as it does not transplant well.

Above *Young, tender caraway leaves add flavour to salads.*

Parts used Leaves, seeds, essential oil from the seeds.

USES Medicinal The seeds are taken as an infusion or decoction for digestive disorders and to relieve flatulence. Seeds may be chewed as breath sweeteners.

Culinary Seeds are used to flavour cakes, biscuits, bread, cheese, stewed fruit, baked apples, cabbage and meat dishes. Also as a pickling spice and to flavour the liqueur, Kümmel. Young leaves make a garnish and are added to salads.

Aromatic Essential oil (containing over 50% carvone, which gives it its aromatic scent) is used as a flavouring in the food industry and in perfumes and cosmetics.

FAGACEAE

Castanea sativa

Sweet chestnut

History and traditions Sweet chestnut trees were grown in ancient Greece and Rome. The Greek physician, Theophrastus, wrote of their medicinal virtues and the Romans enjoyed eating them. They were probably introduced to Britain by the Romans and there are records of chestnuts grown in the Forest of Dean being paid as tithes, during the reign of Henry II, 1154–1189. Writing in the mid-17th century Culpeper considered the "inner skin" of the chestnut would "stop any flux whatsoever" and that the ground, dried leaves made into an electuary with honey made "an admirable remedy for the cough and spitting of blood". Their culinary diversity was praised by the 17th-century diarist and gourmet, John Evelyn, as "delicacies for princes and a lusty and masculine food for rusticks", while he regretted that all too often they were mere animal fodder.
Description A deciduous tree, growing to 15 m (50 ft) with dark grey, furrowed bark, and narrow, glossy, serrated-edged leaves. The small white flowers, appearing in spring, are followed by clusters of prickly green spherical fruits, containing 1–3 edible brown nuts. Trees grown in cool, northerly regions do not produce the same quality of large, succulent fruits as those grown in warmer, Mediterranean climates.
Habitat/distribution Occurs in woodlands of southern Europe, Asia, North America and northern Africa.

Growth Grows best in well-drained loam in sun or partial shade. Propagated by seed sown in autumn.
Parts used Leaves, seeds (nuts).

USES Medicinal Infusions of the leaves are taken for coughs and colds and used as a gargle for sore throats. Also said to be helpful for rheumatism.
Culinary Chestnuts are equally suited to savoury and sweet dishes. They are the classic stuffing ingredient for turkey, other poultry and game, make excellent soups, pâtés, and accompaniments to vegetable and meat dishes. Sweetened purée forms the basis of desserts, especially in France, where chestnuts are also crystallized as "marrons glacés".
Other name Spanish chestnut.

Sweet chestnuts.

Left *Spiky fruits contain the edible nuts.*

BERBERIDACEAE

Caulophyllum thalictroides

Blue cohosh

History and traditions A herb used in the traditional medicine of the Native Americans to facilitate childbirth. Its value being appreciated by the wider population, it was listed at the end of the 19th century as an official medicinal herb in the United States pharmacopoeia. The name "cohosh" is from a local tribal language.
Description A perennial which grows on a rhizomatous rootstock. The palmate leaves develop with, or just after, the yellow-brown flowers. Fruits split open to reveal spherical seeds, which turn from green to deep blue as they ripen.
Habitat/distribution Occurs in moist woodlands in North America.
Growth Requires moist, rich soil, in partial or deep shade. Divide plants in spring. Propagation from seed is slow and germination may often be erratic.
Parts used Rhizomes and roots are dried for inclusion in powders, liquid extracts and other medicinal preparations.

USES Medicinal A herb which stimulates the uterus and is taken internally, as a decoction or infusion to facilitate contractions during labour and for other conditions connected with childbirth. It also has anti-inflammatory and diuretic properties and is used to treat inflammation of the pelvis and endometriosis.
Other names Squaw root and papoose root.

CAUTION Not to be used without the advice of a qualified medical practitioner.

LABIATAE/LAMIACEAE

Cedronella canariensis syn *C. triphylla*

Balm of Gilead

History and traditions This upstart from the Canary Islands is something of a fraud, sniffily dismissed by Mrs Grieve as being "called Balm of Gilead for no better reason than that its leaves are fragrant". But it has largely taken over from ancient, more worthy contenders for the name, because it has a similar musky, balsam scent, though not, apparently, any worthwhile medicinal uses. The original Balm of Gilead is usually taken to be *Commiphora opobalsamum,* a now rare and protected desert shrub, once greatly valued for its balsam-scented resin. Another source of Balm of Gilead is the balsam poplar, *Populus balsamifera.*

Description A half-hardy shrubby perennial, up to 1 m (3 ft) in height, it has lightly serrated, trifoliate leaves and pink flower clusters, made up of tubular, two-lipped florets.

Habitat/distribution A native of the Canary Islands, where it is found on sunny, rocky slopes. Introduced elsewhere.

Growth Requires well-drained soil and full sun. It does not withstand frost and although it may be grown outside in a sheltered position, in cool climates it needs winter protection. Propagation is easiest from softwood cuttings taken in late spring. Germination from seed is erratic and requires heat.

Parts used Leaves, flowers.

USES Culinary Fresh or dry leaves may be infused to make an invigorating tea.

Aromatic Leaves and flowers are dried for adding to pot-pourri.

PINACEAE

Cedrus libani

Cedar of Lebanon

History and traditions The ancient Egyptians used oil of cedar for embalming and in their religious rituals. These beautiful, wide-spreading trees, with their head-clearing pine scent, were much prized in biblical times and celebrated in the Song of Solomon ("His countenance is as Lebanon, excellent as the cedars"). And in the Canticles, that evocative Hebrew love poem, also attributed to Solomon, the beloved is compared to many plant fragrances, and told, "The smell of thy garments is like the smell of Lebanon." King Solomon is also alleged to have denuded Lebanon of its cedars to build his massive temple.

Description A tall, 30–40 m (100–130 ft) coniferous tree, with a dark-brown or grey, deeply ridged trunk and wide branches bearing whorls of needle-like leaves. It carries both male and female cones, the latter being the larger. They are green at first, turning brown as they ripen over a two-year period, when they break up to release the seeds. Cedars often reach a great age, living for several hundred years.

Related species There are only four species of conifers which are true cedars, all rich in aromatic essential oil. As well as *C. libani,* there is *C. atlantica* (Atlas cedar) and *C. brevifolia* (Cyprus cedar), both classified by some authorities as subspecies of *C. libani,* and *C. deodara,* the Indian cedar.

Habitat/distribution Native to forests of the Mediterranean region from Lebanon to Turkey (*C. libani),* the Atlas Mountains in North Africa (*C. atlantica),* Cyprus (*C. brevifolia)* and the western Himalayas (*C. deodara).*

Growth Fully hardy trees, they grow in any well-drained soil and a sunny position.

Parts used Wood, essential oil.

USES Medicinal The essential oil has antiseptic, fungicide and insect-repellent properties. It is used as a steam inhalation for bronchial and respiratory complaints, to soothe skin irritations, for alopecia, dandruff and other scalp problems. It also has a calming effect for states of anxiety.

Aromatic The oil is added to perfumery, soaps and cosmetics. The wood is used to make furniture and storage chests which, due to its aromatic properties, helps to deter moths and insects.

BOMBACACEAE

Ceiba pentandra

Cotton tree

History and traditions The Ceiba is the national tree of Guatemala and was held sacred by the ancient Mayans of Central America. They believed it grew through the centre of the universe, with its roots in the nine levels of the underworld, its trunk in the thirteen levels of the upperworld and its branches in heaven. The myth still prevails in the area, that this graceful tree is the home of the temptress, Ixtobai, recognizable by her backward-facing feet, who lures unfaithful husbands to disappear with her into the underworld through the trunk.
Description A deciduous, or semi-evergreen, tree growing to 40 m (130 ft) with wide-spreading branches and palmate leaves. The flowers are followed by large pods, containing seeds protected by white, fluffy, silky-textured padding, collected to make kapok.
Habitat/distribution Occurs in rainforests and other damp, wooded areas in tropical North, South and Central America, Africa and Asia.
Growth Requires a temperature of 15°C (59°F). Grown in fertile, moist, but well-drained soil and full sun. Usually propagated by cuttings.
Parts used Leaves, bark, seeds, seed-pod fibre.

USES Medicinal The bark and leaves are made into decoctions, taken internally, for bronchial and respiratory infections, or applied externally in the form of baths. The leaves are boiled in sugar to make cough syrup and applied as a compress for headaches, fevers and sprains.
Culinary The seeds are toxic, but an edible, non-toxic oil is extracted from them which is used locally for cooking.

COMPOSITAE/ASTERACEAE

Centaurea cyanus

Cornflower

History and traditions These pretty blue flowers were once a common sight in cornfields, as their name suggests, but have largely been ousted by the techniques of modern agriculture. In his *Herbal* of 1597, Gerard reports that the Italian name for the cornflower is a reference to blunting sickles, "because it hindereth and annoyeth the reapers, dulling and turning the edges of their sickles" and he includes "hurt-sickle" among its English names of blew-bottle, blew-blow and corne-floure. Although Culpeper found many uses for these flowers, Gerard's view was that there is "no use of them in physic", although they are recommended by some for inflammation of the eye.
Description An annual which grows from 20–80 cm (8–32 in) tall, with grey-green lanceolate leaves and bright-blue shaggy flower heads. Cultivated kinds also have pink, purple or white flowers.
Related species *C. montana* is a perennial species, found mainly in mountainous areas of Europe. The wild plant, *C. scabiosa,* is often called knapweed.
Habitat/distribution Native to Europe and the Mediterranean region, naturalized in North America, also found in Asia and Australia. Becoming less common in the wild, widely cultivated and grown in gardens.

Above *Cornflowers, once a common weed, are frequently cultivated in gardens for their striking colour and form.*

Growth A hardy annual, it is easy to grow from seed sown in spring *in situ*, as it resents being transplanted. May be given an early start by sowing in autumn or very early spring, in plugs, or biodegradable pots, to minimize root disturbance. Plant in well-drained soil and a sunny position.
Parts used Flowers.

USES Medicinal Traditionally used in the past to make eyewashes for tired or strained eyes, but seems to have little place in herbal medicine as practised today.
Aromatic Flowers are dried for pot-pourris.
Other names Bluebottle and batchelor's button.

COMPOSITAE/ASTERACEAE

Chamaemelum nobile

Chamomile

History and traditions "Thys herbe was consecrated by the wyse men of Egypt unto the Sonne and was rekened to be the only remedy for all agues", says William Turner in his *Newe Herball,* 1551, in reference to the veneration of chamomile by the ancient Egyptians. The Greeks called it "earth apple", from which its generic name is derived (*kamai*, meaning "on the ground" and *melon*, apple), and in modern Spanish chamomile is called *"manzanilla"*, meaning "little apple". It does indeed have an apple-like fragrance, especially noticeable after rain or when the plant is lightly crushed. To the Anglo-Saxons it was *"maythen"* and was one of the sacred herbs of Woden, featuring in the Nine Herbs Lay, a charm against the effects of "flying venom" and "loathed things that over land rove", from the *Lacnunga* in the Harleian manuscript collection, British Museum. Over the centuries chamomile has been celebrated for its soothing properties and its fragrance heads the list in an antistress prescription from *Ram's Little Dodoen,* 1606: "To comfort the braine smel to camomill, eate sage … wash measurably, sleep reasonably, delight to heare melody and singing".

Description An evergreen perennial with finely divided, feathery leaves growing to 15 cm (6 in). The white daisy-like flowers, with yellow disc centres, are borne singly on long stems rising to 30 cm (1 ft).

Related species *C. nobile* 'Flore Pleno' is a cultivar with creamy-coloured double flowers. The whole plant is more compact than the species, about 10 cm (4 in) tall, including flower stems, and makes a good edging plant. *C. nobile* 'Treneague' is a non-flowering cultivar which forms a dense carpet useful for lawns and seats and grows to about 6 cm ($2^1/2$ in).

Habitat/distribution Indigenous to Europe, it is widely grown in North America and many other countries. It is found in the wild on sandy soils in grasslands and waste ground.

Growth Prefers light, sandy soil and a sunny position. It is possible to propagate *C. nobile* from seed sown in spring, but the easier and more usual method is by division of runners or "offsets". *C. n.* 'Flore Pleno' and *C. n.* 'Treneague' must be vegetatively propagated.

Parts used Flowers, essential oil.

USES Medicinal Chamomile has an antiseptic, anti-inflammatory action and is soothing and sedative. It is taken as a tea for nausea and indigestion and to help promote sound sleep, and may also be helpful in relieving painful menstruation. It is made into ointments or lotions for skin irritations and insect bites. The true essential oil is very expensive and contains azulene, which gives it a deep-blue colour. It is frequently used for skin complaints and eczema (diluted in witch hazel or a pure, mild vegetable oil) and as a steam inhalation for asthma, sinusitis or catarrh.

Cosmetic An infusion of the flowers makes a rinse to give a shine to fair hair, or a skin freshener for sensitive skins. Essential oil or infusions are added to face or hand creams and fresh flowers floated in hot water make a deep-cleansing facial steam treatment.

Aromatic The dried flowers are added to sleep pillows and sachets or put into pot-pourri.

Other name Roman chamomile.

Chamaemelum nobile *'Flore Pleno'.*

Top *The double flowers of the dwarf edging plant* C. nobile 'Flore Pleno'.

CAUTION Despite being such a benevolent herb (when recommended doses and guidelines are followed), if taken internally to excess it may cause vomiting and vertigo. The plant may cause contact dermatitis.

Related species

COMPOSITAE/ASTERACEAE

Matricaria recutita

Wild chamomile

History and traditions The name *matricaria* comes from its early gynaecological uses in herbal medicine.

Description *M. recutita* syn. *M. chamomilla* is a tall hardy annual which grows to 60 cm (2 ft). Although from a different genus (due to botanical differences), flowers, feathery foliage and scent are similar in appearance to that of *Chamaemelum nobile*. Not to be confused with the scentless mayweeds, or false chamomiles *Matricaria inodora* and *Tripleurospermum maritimum*, or the almost scentless corn chamomile (*Anthemis arvensis*).

Habitat/distribution Occurs all over Europe, Western Asia and India.

Growth Propagated from seed, sown *in situ* in early spring, it grows easily in any dry, light soil.

Parts used Flowers – they have similar properties to those of *Chamaemelum nobile*.

USES As for *C. nobile*.

Other names German chamomile and scented mayweed.

Matricaria chamomilla

To make oyle of chamomile

Take oyle a pint and halfe, and three ounces of camomile flowers dryed one day after they be gathered. Then put the oyle and the flowers in a glasse and stop the mouth close and set it into the sun by the space of forty days.

The Good Housewife's Handbook, 1588

A chamomile lawn

Chamomile has been popular since medieval times for scented lawns, paths or places to sit, all of which still make delightful features in the herb garden.

A chamomile lawn

The main problem is that it requires regular hand weeding to keep it looking good and does not take heavy wear. The trick is to think small – grow it as a scaled-down version of a lawn, plant it round a fountain or sundial, or as a mini-lawn between paving stones.

- Use rooted cuttings or offsets of non-flowering *Chamaemelum nobile* 'Treneague', edged (or for a "flowery-mead" effect, interspersed) with *C. n.* 'Flore Pleno'.
- Choose an area with light, preferably sandy soil, prepare it well, eliminating weeds and removing stones. Rake in a little peat to hold water and help the plants settle in quickly.
- Set plants 10 cm (4 in) apart, water them in and keep lightly moist until established.
- To maintain the lawn, weed regularly and fill in any gaps that appear with new plants.

Above *A lawn of* C.n. *'Treneague'.*

Above *A brick-built chamomile seat.*

A chamomile seat

These are always attractive and have the added advantage that the area of chamomile is small enough to make maintenance simple. It is also a good way to grow chamomile in a garden with heavy or clay soil, as the seat forms a raised bed to provide a free-draining environment.

- The base of the seat may be constructed with brick, stone or timber, filled with rubble and a good layer of topsoil for planting.
- It is best to keep to *C. n.* 'Treneague' only for this, as flowers sticking out of a bench spoil the effect. Plant as for the lawn.
- If back and arm rests are required, they could be of the same material as the base. Clipped box also looks very effective.

CHENOPODIACEAE

Chenopodium ambrosioides

American wormseed

History and traditions American wormseed was introduced to Europe in the 17th century from Mexico, where it was taken as a tea and used in traditional medicine.

Description An annual, 60 cm–1.2 m (2–4 ft) high, it has longer, more lanceolate leaves than those of *C. bonus-henricus* and a strong acrid scent. The tiny, green flowers are followed by small nutlike, one-seeded fruits.

Habitat/distribution Native to tropical Central America, naturalized throughout much of North America and grown in other countries also.

Growth Frost-hardy (to -5°C/23°F), American wormseed grows in any well-drained soil. Propagated by seed sown in spring; in warm climates it often self-seeds freely.

Parts used Flowering stems, essential oil.

USES Medicinal Its chief use has always been to expel intestinal worms. It has also been recommended for nervous disorders, asthma and problems with menstruation. The volatile oil of chenopodium is a powerful insecticide as well as a vermifuge, but should never be administered in this concentrated form as it is highly toxic.

Other name Mexican tea.

CAUTION Poisonous in large doses, it should be taken only under medical supervision and is legally restricted in some countries.

CHENOPODIACEAE

Chenopodium bonus-henricus

Good King Henry

History and traditions According to the 16th-century physician and botanist, Rembert Dodoens, of the Netherlands, this plant was dubbed *bonus henricus,* "good Henry", to distinguish it from a poisonous plant *malus henricus,* "bad Henry". There is some uncertainty as to who "Henry" was, but one source claims it is a generic term for mischievous elves. "King" appears to have been spin-doctored into the English popular name to give this rather unattractive plant a spurious connection with King Henry VIII, "Good King Hal". The Latin name *Chenopodium* is derived from the Greek for "goose foot", an eloquent reference to the shape of the leaves.

Description A perennial which grows 60 cm (2 ft) tall and spreads indefinitely, it has fleshy, downy stems, dark-green, arrow-shaped leaves and greenish-yellow spikes of sorrel-like flowers in early summer.

Related species *Chenopodium album*, White Goosefoot – also known as allgood and fat hen (because it does a good job of fattening poultry) – as well as pigweed, mutton tops and lamb's quarters. It has long been a staple food of both animals and people. The Iron Age Dane, Tollund Man, made a last meal of it before he was hanged, seeds being found in his stomach.

Habitat/distribution Native to Europe but found worldwide on waste ground and previously cultivated land.

Growth This is an invasive plant which needs no cultivation and thrives in any soil. Said to be of "superior quality" if grown in rich soil, but little difference in taste or texture will be noticed. Tough taproots can make it difficult to eradicate if no longer wanted. Easily propagated from seed, or division, in spring.

Parts used Leaves, stems.

USES Medicinal Once made into ointments and poultices for skin complaints (an old name was "smearwort") but has no known medicinal value currently, apart from being mildly laxative.

Culinary Extravagant claims have been made for this plant as being a spinach-like vegetable (leaves) and asparagus substitute (young stems). Although edible if picked when young and tender, the leaves develop a fibrous texture with age which makes them less palatable. John Evelyn (*Acetaria* 1719) was right when in reference to one of its names, "blite", from the Greek for insipid, he commented that "it is well-named, being insipid enough". It is rich in vitamins C, B^1, iron and calcium – so it may be a case of "eating up your greens" for the sake of your health.

Other names Goosefoot, allgood, fat hen, English mercury and Lincolnshire asparagus.

The leaves of Chenopodium bonus-henricus *were thought to resemble goose feet.*

COMPOSITAE/ASTERACEAE

Cichorium intybus

Chicory

History and traditions This herb was cultivated in Egypt over 2,000 years ago, and known to the ancient Greeks and Romans, who used it as a salad ingredient and vegetable. Its use as a coffee substitute is thought to date from 1806 when Napoleon's Continental blockade prevented imports of coffee. It was widely used for the same purpose during the World Wars.

Description A tall, hardy perennial, growing to 1.5 m (5 ft). It has a deep taproot and thick stem which exudes a milky sap when cut. It has toothed, oval to lanceolate leaves and pale blue flowers appear in summer.

Habitat/distribution Native of the Mediterranean region, western Asia and North Africa, introduced and established worldwide.

Growth For best results grow in rich, but well-drained soil. Propagate from seed sown in spring. Sometimes self-seeds, especially on dry soils.

Parts used Leaves, roots.

USES Medicinal A bitter tonic herb, the dried, crushed root is made into infusions or decoctions for digestive upsets and to improve appetite. It is also a mild stimulant and laxative.

Culinary There are various cultivars whose leaves are added to salads, including red, broad-leafed radicchio types. Blanched heads, or chicons, eaten in salads and cooked as vegetables, are produced by lifting the roots, packing them in boxes in a growing medium, cutting off the leaves and keeping them in complete darkness until white, elongated shoots have sprouted.

RANUNCULACEAE

Cimicifuga racemosa

Black cohosh

History and traditions The root of this herb was used in the traditional medicine of Native Americans for female complaints and it was supposed to be an antidote to poison and to rattlesnake venom. Hence two of its popular names, "squaw root" (which it shares with blue cohosh) and "black snakeroot", after the colour of the rhizome and to differentiate it from another plant known as "snakeroot" (*Aristolochia serpentaria*). The generic name comes from the Latin *cimex*, a bug, and *fugere*, to run, in reference to its insect-repellent properties.

Description A tall, clump-forming, aromatic perennial, with a rather unpleasant smell. But it makes an attractive plant for the border with spires of creamy-white, bottle-brush flowers, rising to 1.5 m (5 ft) above the three-lobed basal leaves (40 cm (16 in) high).

Habitat/distribution Native to North America, it is grown in northern temperate regions and occurs in moist grassland or woodland.

Growth Fully hardy, it requires moist, fertile soil with plenty of humus and partial shade. It can be propagated by division of roots or by seed, sown in pots in autumn for overwintering in a cold frame for germination the following spring.

Parts used Rhizomes – dried for use in decoctions, tinctures and extracts.

USES Medicinal For arthritis, rheumatism and menstrual and menopausal problems.

CAUTION Large doses may cause abortion. Legal restrictions apply in some countries.

RUBIACEAE

Cinchona officinalis

Cinchona

History and traditions Said to be named after the Countess of Chinchon, wife of the Viceroy of Peru, after she had been cured of a fever (probably malaria)with a cinchona bark medicine in about 1638.

Description Cinchona species are tender, evergreen trees varying in height, according to species and habitat, from 10–25 m (30–80 ft). The oval leaves are often red-veined and small, crimson flowers are borne in panicles.

Related species There are several species of *Cinchona* of medicinal value, all closely related, including *C. calisaya* and *C. pubescens.*

Habitat/distribution Native to mountainous regions of South America, widely introduced and cultivated in tropical regions worldwide.

Growth In the wild, trees occur in dense, wet forest. Commercial plantations provide well-drained, moist soil and high humidity. Propagated by cuttings.

Parts used Bark – dried and powdered or as a liquid extract.

USES Medicinal Cinchona bark contains the antimalarial alkaloid, quinine, as well as quinidine, which slows the heart rate. It was the major treatment for malaria from the mid-17th century until recently, now largely replaced for this purpose by synthetic drugs. It is still an ingredient of many pharmaceutical preparations for colds and influenza, and of tonic water.

CAUTION Excess doses cause convulsions and may lead to deafness and blindness.

LAURACEAE

Cinnamomum zeylanicum

Cinnamon

History and traditions An important aromatic spice since biblical times, cinnamon was an ingredient of the holy ointment made by Moses. It is also cited as amongst the costly merchandise and luxury items available in Babylon, when the fall of that misguided city is predicted in the biblical book, Revelation. The Portuguese occupied Sri Lanka for its cinnamon in 1536. By the 18th century, cinnamon had become such a valuable commodity in Europe, that the Dutch took control of the island and set up a trading monopoly in the spice.

Description A medium-sized evergreen tree, it grows to about 9 m (30 ft) and has brown, papery bark and ovate, leathery green leaves. Creamy-white flowers are borne in short panicles, followed by olive-shaped dark-blue fruits.

Habitat/distribution Native to forest areas of Sri Lanka, southern India and Malaysia and widely cultivated in India, the Seychelles, Brazil, the Caribbean and tropical zones.

Growth Cinnamon grows in sandy soils, and needs plenty of rain, sun and a minimum temperature of 15°C (59°F). Young trees are cut to within 30 cm (1 ft) of the ground, stumps covered in mulch to encourage sprouting for re-harvesting within 2–3 years. It is also propagated by seed.

Parts used Inner bark of young stems – dried and wrapped round thin rods to form quills. Essential oil.

USES Medicinal It has digestive properties, dispels nausea, and is taken for colds, sore throats and rheumatic conditions. The essential oil is antibacterial and antifungal, helps deaden the nerve where there is toothache and is added to steam inhalations for colds and upper respiratory tract infections.

Culinary A popular spice for savoury and sweet dishes. It adds flavour to curries, baked goods, stews and meat dishes, savoury and sweet rice and is a traditional ingredient of Christmas puddings, mince pies, mulled wine and hot spiced drinks.

Aromatic Ingredient of pot-pourri (powdered or whole pieces) and clove-and-orange pomanders. The essential oil is used in perfumery.

Cinnamon sticks are formed from the rolled bark.

CISTACEAE

Cistus ladanifer

Cistus

History and traditions In his *Relation d'un voyage du Levant,* 1717, French botanist, Pitton de Tournefort, gives an eloquent description of collecting ladanum, a fragrant resin exuded by several species of cistus, by means of dragging a leather-thonged rake (a *ladisteron)* across the plants. He also refers to a method in use since Dioscorides' day, of combing it from the beards of goats allowed to browse on the sticky foliage. It has a perfume reminiscent of ambergris and was one of the main ingredients in the solid, resin-based pomanders popular in the Middle Ages for repelling infection.

Description A hardy evergreen shrub, growing to 2 m (6 ft), with lanceolate, sticky, dark-green leaves. The papery, saucer-shaped white flowers bloom for only one day.

Related species *C. creticus* syn. *C. incanus* subsp. *creticus*, the Cretan rock rose, and also a source of ladanum, is a more compact shrub, growing to 1 m (3 ft) with purplish-pink flowers and yellow stamens.

Habitat/distribution Found in Crete, southern Europe, Turkey, northern Africa and the Canary Islands, on dry, stony soils and sunny hillsides. Introduced and widely grown elsewhere.

Growth Prefers a light, well-drained soil and sheltered site in full sun. It is propagated from seed, sown in containers, in late summer or from softwood cuttings in early summer.

Parts used Dried leaves, oleo-resin – collected from young stems and leaves.

USES Aromatic Used as a fixative in perfumery, and in pot-pourri and home fragrance products.

RUTACEAE

Citrus

History and traditions The citrus species were unknown to Greek and Roman writers, but they have been cultivated for so long that their origins are hazy. Both oranges and lemons are probably natives of northern India, certainly China, and are thought to have been brought to the West by Arab traders via North Africa, Arabia and Syria, thence to Spain and Sicily. *C. limon,* found in the valleys of Kumaon and Sikkim, in the foothills of the Himalayas, has the Hindustani name *limu* or *nimbu*, which was taken into Arabic as *limun. C. aurantium,* the bitter Seville orange, is the species mentioned in a medicinal context by the Arabian physician, Avicenna, 980–1037, practising at Salerno, and was the orange tree planted in Rome by St Dominic in AD 1200. These must also have been the oranges which Edward I's Queen, Eleanor of Castille, is purported to have bought from a Spanish ship which called at Portsmouth in 1290 – sweet oranges were not known in the West before the mid-15th century, introduced from the East by the Portuguese. The custom of wearing orange blossom at weddings is said to have originated with the Saracens, who considered it an emblem of fecundity, and the practice was introduced to Europe by returning Crusaders. Essential oil distilled from the flowers of the bitter orange was said to have an "exquisite fragrance" by the Italian Giambattista Porta in his herbal of 1588. It became known as "oil of Neroli" from 1680, because it was favoured by the wife of the Count of Neroli for perfuming gloves.

Habitat/distribution Originated in Asia, cultivated in the Mediterranean region, in southern parts of North America and other countries.

Growth Orange and lemon trees are tender, and must be protected from frost, but they prefer cool rather than hot conditions. If grown in northern climates, with cold, frosty winters, they should be kept outside in summer and in a temperate conservatory or greenhouse in winter. They need a well-drained, not too acid compost – the correct pH value is crucial, 6–6.5 for lemons and 6.5–7 for oranges. *C. aurantium* and *C. limon* may be grown from seed, or from semi-ripe cuttings – but cultivars do not come true from seed.

Citrus limon

Lemon

Description A small evergreen tree, 2–6 m (6–19 ft) tall, with light-green, oval leaves and thorny stems. Clusters of white flowers, opening from pink-tinted buds, are followed by ovoid, bitter-tasting yellow fruits.

Parts used Fruits, essential oil, expressed from the peel.

USES Medicinal Rich in vitamin C and once used by British seamen to prevent scurvy (limes were also used). Lemons have anti-inflammatory properties and are used in home remedies for colds, frequently in conjunction with honey, which is antiseptic. Applied externally for insect bites and skin irritations.

Culinary The juice and rind are widely used as a flavouring in cooking, and in soft drinks, sauces, pickles, preserves and marinades.

Aromatic The peel is dried for pot-pourri and home fragrance preparations. The oil is used commercially in perfumery, and to scent soaps and household cleaning products.

Citrus aurantium

Bitter orange

Description An evergreen tree, growing to 8 m (26 ft) high, with shiny, ovate leaves and fragrant white flowers, followed by bitter, orange fruits.

Parts used Leaves, fruits, flowers. Essential oil of neroli, distilled from flowers; essential oil of petitgrain, distilled from leaves and twigs; distilled orange-flower water; oil of orange, expressed from the rind.

USES Medicinal Rich in vitamins A, B and C, and has energizing tonic properties. Infusions of leaves and flowers are used for digestive disorders. The essential oil of neroli is an antidepressant and calming. It may also be helpful for insomnia.

Culinary The fruits are used to make Seville orange marmalade and a bitter sauce to complement fatty poultry such as duck and goose. Orange-flower water has a delicate fragrance, ideal for flavouring sweet dishes. Oil of orange is a flavouring in commercial food products.

Aromatic Essential oils of neroli and petitgrain are used in perfumery.

Cosmetic Orange rind pounded, mixed with rainwater and applied as a poultice is a traditional Indian remedy for acne. Oil of neroli is soothing for dry, sensitive skins as an ingredient of creams and lotions. Also used in many citrus-based cleaning products.

Other name Seville orange.

Left Citrus limon *'Jambhiri'*.

ASTERACEAE

Cnicus benedictus syn. *Carduus benedictus*

Holy thistle

History and traditions It is known as Holy or Blessed Thistle for much the same reasons as the Carline Thistle (*Carlina acaulis*) is named after Charlemagne – it was all down to visions of this plant as a cure for plague. Considering that it does have antiseptic and antibiotic properties, this may not be as far-fetched as it sounds. One writer of a dissertation on treating plague with this thistle said, "I counsell all that have gardens to nourish it, that they may have it always to their own use, and the use of their neighbours that lacke it."

Description The only plant in the *Cnicus* genus, sometimes classified as *Carduus benedictus*. It is an annual with hairy, branched stems, spiny grey-green leaves and solitary yellow flowers set in prickly bracts.

Habitat/distribution A Mediterranean native, it is widely naturalized throughout Europe and North America.

Growth A wild plant, it grows in any ordinary soil, is easily propagated by seed, and self-seeds. Cultivated commercially in Europe for the pharmaceutical industry.

Parts used Whole plant – leaves and flower tops.

USES Medicinal A very bitter herb with antiseptic, antibiotic properties. Taken in the form of an infusion as a tonic and to stimulate the appetite. It was traditionally used for fevers and is said to be helpful for nursing mothers to improve the supply of milk.

Culinary All parts of the plant are edible and have been eaten cooked or in salads.

BURSERACEAE

Commiphora myrrha syn. *C. molmol*

Myrrh

History and traditions Myrrh has long been valued for its medicinal properties and as an ingredient of incense, perfumes and ointments. A symbol of suffering, myrrh was used in embalming from the Egyptian period, and the name comes from an ancient Hebrew and Arabic word, *mur*, meaning bitter. It was one of the gifts of the wise men to Jesus Christ at his birth and was used, along with aloes and spices, to embalm his body following his crucifixion.

Description A small tree or shrub, growing to about 3 m (10 ft) tall, with spiny branches and sparse trifoliate leaves, made up of small oval leaflets. The gum exudes from the bark naturally, and after incisions have been made, when it flows out as a pale-yellow liquid and quickly hardens to a reddish-brown resin.

Habitat/distribution Native to Arabia, Somalia and Ethiopia, where it grows in desert scrub.

Growth Grows wild.

Parts used Oleo-gum resin – known as *bdellium*.

USES Medicinal Myrrh has antiseptic, anti-inflammatory properties and encourages healing when applied to wounds, ulcers, boils and bleeding gums. Sometimes added to tooth powders. A preparation is made from the bark for treating skin diseases. In parts of Africa some species are chewed as a source of moisture and used for cleaning teeth.

Aromatic An ingredient of incense. It has fixative properties when used in perfumery, and is added to pot-pourri, in granule or powdered form, to "fix" the scent.

UMBELLIFERAE/APIACEAE

Conium maculatum

Hemlock

History and traditions Poisoning by hemlock was the official method of state execution in ancient Athens. The philosopher Socrates was its best-known victim. It was also used as a medicinal herb in the classical world, mainly for external application. Dioscorides and Pliny, echoed by Avicenna, recommended it for the treatment of skin diseases and cancerous tumours. It appeared in Anglo-Saxon herbals and an old English myth associated the splotches on the stems with the mark of Cain.

Description A tall, unpleasant-smelling biennial, 1.5–2.4 m (5–8 ft) in height, with purplish-red speckles towards the base of the stems, finely divided, feathery leaves and large umbels of white flowers in midsummer.

Habitat/distribution Indigenous to Europe and parts of Asia, widely distributed in temperate parts of the world and found in damp, weedy places, waste grounds and waysides.

Growth A wild plant in Australia and other countries, cultivation is legally restricted.

Parts used Leaves, seeds.

USES Medicinal Hemlock contains the highly toxic alkaloid, coniine, in all parts, but especially in the seeds. At one time it was used as a sedative and powerful pain-reliever – but its toxicity made this a risky business and it is seldom used in herbal medicine today.

CAUTION All parts of the plant are highly poisonous, and may also cause skin irritations on contact.

LILIACEAE/CONVALLARIACEAE

Convallaria majalis

Lily-of-the-valley

History and traditions This pretty cottage-garden plant was known to the Anglo-Saxons for its medicinal properties and appeared in early manuscript herbals, including one attributed to Apuleius, AD 400 (written in Latin). Many of the 16th- and 17th-century herbalists, from Dodoens to Culpeper, took the line that a distillation of the flowers in wine was good for strengthening the memory and comforting the heart. The specific name is a reference to the month of May, when the flowers bloom – or to Maia, Roman goddess of fertility, if you prefer.
Description A hardy perennial with ribbed ovate to lance-shaped leaves and racemes of fragrant white flowers, hanging like little bells, followed by fruits which are round, red berries.
Habitat/distribution Native to Europe, Asia and North America and found in woodlands and alpine meadows.
Growth Prefers humus-rich, moist soil and partial shade. Propagation is easiest by division of the rhizomes in autumn – keep well watered until established and apply a leaf-mould mulch.
Parts used Leaves, flowers.

USES Medicinal It contains glycosides similar to those of foxgloves (*Digitalis* spp.), which affect the action of the heart. It is considered safer than *Digitalis* by some herbal experts and as having less of a cumulative effect.

CAUTION A poisonous plant which should not be eaten. It should be stressed that it is for use by qualified practitioners only.

UMBELLIFERAE/APIACEAE

Coriandrum sativum

Coriander

History and traditions Seeds of this herb were found in Tutankhamun's tomb of 1325 BC. It was known to the Greeks and Romans and features in many medieval herbals – though the authorities were not always in agreement as to its properties. Galen said it was "warm", Dioscorides and Avicenna took it to be "cold". The *Herbarius Latinus,* printed in Mainz in 1484 by Peter Schoeffer, has much to say on the subject. There are recommendations for mixing the juice with houseleek (*Sempervivum tectorum)* and warm vinegar to put on abscesses, for taking it with vinegar soon after dining heavily to "prohibit vapours from rising to the head", and for mixing it with violets for a hangover. If smelled, sniffed or blown up the nostrils, it is claimed, it will restrain a nosebleed, and is effective against St Anthony's fire (erysipelas) and "in tremors of the heart when its powder is given with borage water". William Turner took the strange line that "Coriander taken out of season doth trouble a man's wit with great jeopardy of madness" (*A Newe Herbal,* 1551). From Tudor times until the beginning of this century coriander seeds coated in sugar (comfits) were a popular sweet.
Description An annual 30–60 cm (1–2 ft) tall, with pungent finely divided leaves – the basal ones are pinnatifid and wider than the upper ones, which are linear and feathery. Small umbels of white to mauvish flowers are followed by ridged, spherical, pale-brown fruits (seeds). There are related species and numerous cultivars, some developed for leaf quality, others for their seeds. A variety with smaller seeds is grown in temperate zones, and one with larger seeds in warmer climates.
Habitat/distribution Originating in northern Africa and the Mediterranean region, it is widely grown in southwest Asia, North and South America and in temperate regions.
Growth A hardy annual, it is propagated from seed sown in spring, preferably *in situ* as it does not transplant well. It succeeds best grown in a well-drained, fertile soil, with ample water in the early stages followed by warmth and sunshine. Young plants quickly run to seed if attempts are made to transplant them in hot, dry spells.
Parts used Leaves, fruits (seeds), essential oil.

Above *The lower leaves are used in cookery.*

USES Medicinal The leaves and seeds have digestive properties and stimulate appetite. The essential oil has fungicidal, antibacterial properties. In traditional Indian medicine decoctions of the seeds were taken as a small-pox preventive. They are still considered helpful in lowering blood cholesterol levels.
Culinary The leaves have a stronger, spicier taste than the seeds, which are milder and sweeter. Both are used in curries, pickles and chutneys and in Middle Eastern, Indian, south-east Asian and South American cuisines. Leaves are added to salads, seeds used in sweet dishes, breads, cakes and to flavour liqueurs.
Aromatic The crushed seeds are added to scented sachets and pot-pourri. The essential oil has fixative properties.
Commercial The essential oil is used in the pharmaceutical, cosmetic and food industries.
Other name Cilantro.

ROSACEAE

Crataegus laevigata

Hawthorn

History and traditions Many superstitions surround this tree, often known as "may", or "mayblossom", for its time of flowering, associations with May Day celebrations and the return of summer. (It usually flowers later than 1 May owing to the revision of the British calendar in 1752.) It was considered an omen of both ill and good fortune – unlucky to bring into the house, yet tied outside as a protection from witches, storms and lightning or to stop milk going sour. The strange perfume, with its overtones of decay, contributed to its reputation as an emblem of death and the plague.

Description A deciduous shrub or small tree, growing to 8 m (26 ft), with thorny branches and small dark-green, lobed, ovate leaves. It is densely covered with clusters of white scented flowers with red anthers in spring, followed by red globe-shaped fruit in autumn.

Related species *C. monogyna* is very similar and hybridizes with *C. laevigata.* There are also many ornamental cultivars, some with pink or red flowers, but they lack therapeutic properties.

Habitat/distribution Native to Europe, northern Africa and western Asia, introduced in temperate regions elsewhere. Occurs in hedges and woodland.

Growth A traditional hedging plant, which grows in any soil in sun or partial shade. Propagated from seed, sown in early spring – stratification is necessary for germination.

Parts used Flowers, leaves, fruits.

USES Medicinal An important medicinal herb in Europe, it acts on the circulatory system, strengthens the heart, regulates its rhythm and lowers blood pressure. It is said to be gradual in effect and well tolerated by the body.

Culinary Leaves, sometimes berries, were once eaten in sandwiches by country people (especially children), and young shoots cooked in savoury, suet puddings. The fresh flowers add an interesting scented flavour to syllabubs and creamy desserts.

Other names May, Mayblossom, quickset and quickthorn.

IRIDACEAE

Crocus sativus

Saffron crocus

History and traditions The Greeks called it *krokos,* the Romans *korkum,* and its common name is derived from the Arabic for yellow, *zafran*. In the classical world saffron was appreciated for its scent, flavour, medicinal properties and above all as a luminous yellow dye. In Greece it was a royal colour and in eastern cultures, too, it was reserved for dyeing the clothing of those of high rank or caste. Originating in Persia it spread to northern India and the Mediterranean by the 10th century. Its popularity in Europe followed the Crusades and it became a valuable trading commodity. So valuable indeed that adulteration was always a temptation – but penalties were high. Regular saffron inspections were held in Nuremberg in the 15th century and records reveal that at least one man was burned in the market place and three others buried alive for tampering with their saffron. Gerard certainly thought highly of its powers: "For those at death's doore," he wrote, "and almost past breathing, saffron bringeth breath again" (*The Herball,* 1597).

Description A perennial, it has linear leaves, growing from the rounded corm. Fragrant, lilac flowers, with deeper purple veins and yellow anthers, appear in autumn. The saffron spice is produced from the three-branched red style.

Habitat/distribution Occurs in southern Europe, northern Africa, the Middle East and India, with major centres of commercial cultivation in Spain and Kashmir, northern India.

Growth Needs well-drained soil, sun and warm summers in order to flower. Plants are sterile and can be propagated only by offsets.

Parts used Flower pistils – dried. It takes over 4,000 flowers to produce 25g (1 oz) of dried saffron. Cheap or powdered product is often adulterated – the genuine herb is always expensive and should be a dark reddish-yellow in colour.

USES Medicinal Saffron is known to have digestive properties and improves circulation and helps to reduce high blood pressure – its high consumption in Spain has been put forward as an explanation for the low incidence of cardiovascular disease there. It is also the richest known source of Vitamin B^2. Externally it is applied as a paste for inflamed skin and sores.
Culinary It is widely used as a flavouring and colourant in Middle Eastern and northern Indian cookery, in rice dishes, such as the classic Spanish paella, and fish soups including bouillabaisse from France. It is also used in sweets and cakes – especially in eastern cuisine, and the traditional saffron cakes and loaves of Cornwall in England.

Top Saffron crocus *corms.*

Above *The dried threads have medicinal and culinary uses.*

UMBELLIFERAE/APIACEAE

Cuminum cyminum

Cumin

History and traditions Cumin was grown in Arabia, India and China from earliest times. There are descriptions of how it was cultivated in the Bible (Isaiah 28:25–27) and the practice of paying it in tithes (a church tax) is referred to in the New Testament. It is mentioned by the Greek physicians, Hippocrates and Dioscorides, and Pliny reports that the ground seed was taken with bread and water or wine as a remedy for "squeamishness". Cumin's strong taste made it a very a very popular spice in Britain and Europe during the Middle Ages.
Description A half-hardy annual with finely divided, feathery leaves and umbels of very small white flowers. The fruits (seeds) are yellowish-brown and ovoid in shape with a distinctive, warm and spicy lingering aroma. The plant is a little like caraway (*Carum carvi*) in appearance, and occasionally confused with it, but quite different in taste.
Habitat/distribution Indigenous to Egypt and the Mediterranean, it is widely grown in tropical and subtropical regions, including northern Africa, India and North and South America.
Growth Grow in a well-drained to sandy soil. Propagated from seed and should be sown under glass in cool temperate regions and transplanted after all frosts. Although it may flower, it is unlikely that fruits will ripen in cool climates.

Parts used Seeds, essential oil.

USES Medicinal Decoctions or infusions of the seeds are taken for digestive disorders, diarrhoea, colds and feverish illnesses. In Ayurvedic medicine it is also used to treat piles and renal colic. The essential oil has antiseptic and antibacterial properties and is applied externally (diluted) for boils and insect bites.
Culinary Widely used in Indian and Middle Eastern cookery to flavour curries, soups, meat and vegetable dishes, bread, biscuits and cheese; and as an ingredient of spice mixtures, pickles and chutneys. There are several species of cumin which produce seeds of varying colour and strength of flavour.

White cumin seeds.

Black cumin seeds.

ZINGIBERACEAE

Curcuma longa syn. *domestica*

Turmeric

History and traditions Turmeric is an ancient herb of India – mentioned in Sanskrit writings and used in Ayurvedic and Unani traditional medicine. A native of southeast Asia, it spread across the Pacific, taken by the Polynesians as far as Hawaii and Easter Island. Used as a dye and food flavouring in the manner of saffron (though it does not have the same subtlety of colour or flavour), the generic name is from the word used in ancient Rome for saffron, *korkum*.
Description A perennial, up to 1.2 m (4 ft) tall, it has shiny, lanceolate leaves and dense spikes of pale-yellow flowers, enclosed in a sheathing petiole. From the same family as ginger, turmeric grows on a tuberous rhizome.
Growth A tender, tropical plant, it requires well-drained but moist soil, a humid atmosphere and minimum temperatures of 15–18°C (59–64°F). It is propagated by division of the rhizomes.
Parts used Rhizomes – boiled, skinned, dried and ground into bright-yellow powder.

USES Medicinal Turmeric has antiseptic properties and is applied, in the form of a paste made with water, to boils, cuts and wounds. It is taken internally, as an infusion in milk or water, for intestinal disorders and diarrhoea, for colds, coughs and sore throats. Rich in iron, it is helpful in counteracting anaemia.
Culinary An ingredient of Worcestershire sauce and curry powder, adding colour and a musky flavour to meat, vegetable and savoury dishes.
Cosmetic It makes an excellent skin softener and facial conditioner.

GRAMINEAE/POACEAE

Cymbopogon citratus

Lemon grass

History and traditions Lemon grass did not come to the attention of the West as a medicinal or culinary plant until the modern era. It is now extensively cultivated, in various tropical countries, mainly for distillation of the essential oil, which is used in commercial products. It has also risen in popularity as a culinary herb.
Description A tall, clump-forming perennial, growing to 1.5 m (5 ft) in height, it has linear, grasslike leaves, strongly scented with lemon.
Habitat/distribution Indigenous to southern India and Sri Lanka, found wild and cultivated in tropical and subtropical zones of Asia, Africa, North and South America.
Growth A tender plant, which is grown in fertile, well-drained soil, but needs plenty of moisture and minimum temperatures of 7–10°C (45–50°F). In cool temperate climates it must be grown as a conservatory or warm greenhouse plant, and moved outside in the summer.
Parts used Leaves, young stems, essential oil.

USES Medicinal The essential oil has antiseptic properties and is used externally for rheumatic aches and pains, ringworm and scabies. Internally (in doses of a few drops) it is sometimes taken for indigestion and gastric upsets.
Culinary The young white stem and leaf base are chopped and used in stir-fry dishes and in Thai, Malaysian and southeast Asian cookery. Leaves may also be infused to make tea.
Aromatic The essential oil is used in home fragrance preparations, in commercial perfumery, soaps and cosmetics and as a flavouring in the food and liquor industries.

Above Cymbopogon nardus, *Citronelle Grami*

or medicinal purposes.

LEGUMINOSAE/PAPILIONACEAE

Cytisus scoparius

Broom

History and traditions Known in medieval times as *planta genista,* common broom gave its name to the Plantagenet royal line. It was the adopted emblem of the father of King Henry II of England, Count Geoffrey of Anjou, who wore a sprig in his helmet when going into battle. Broom is mentioned in Anglo-Saxon writings and the earliest printed herbals make much of its medicinal powers. Pickled broom-buds were a popular ingredient of Tudor salads.
Description An upright, deciduous shrub, growing to 1.5 m (5 ft), it has arching, twiggy branches, small trifoliate leaves and is covered in a mass of bright-yellow pea flowers in spring.
Related species There are many hybrids and cultivars that are not suitable for medicinal use.
Habitat/distribution A native of Europe and western Asia, found in heathlands, woods and scrublands. Introduced elsewhere.
Growth Grows in any well-drained soil in a sunny position. Propagation is by seed or semi-ripe cuttings, but seedlings do not transplant as well as established container-grown plants.
Parts used Leaves, flowers.

USES Medicinal A narcotic herb containing alkaloids similar to those in poisonous strychnine, which affect respiration and heart action.

CAUTION The whole plant is toxic and if eaten leads to respiratory failure. Subject to legal restrictions in some countries. For use by qualified practitioners only. Under statutory control as a weed in Australia.

SOLANACEAE

Datura stramonium

Datura

History and traditions A native of North and South America, this plant was brought to Europe by the Spaniards in the 16th century. It was named "devil's apple" after European settlers in America discovered its narcotic effects, and "Jimson Weed" after Jamestown, Virginia, where they first found it growing. Also indigenous to India, datura appears in ancient Hindu literature of the Vedic period, when its intoxicant and healing powers were well understood and the seeds were smoked as a treatment for asthma.
Description A tall, bushy annual, 2 m (6 ft) tall, it has strong-smelling, triangular, lobed leaves and large white, or violet-tinged, trumpet-shaped flowers.
Habitat/distribution Indigenous to the Americas and temperate, hilly regions of India, now widely grown in other countries.
Growth A half-hardy annual, it does not tolerate frost. Grows in any light soil and is propagated by seed sown in spring.
Parts used Leaves, flowers, seeds.

USES Medicinal Of the same family as *Atropa belladonna,* it contains similar poisonous alkaloids, including atropine. It has been found useful in mitigating the symptoms of Parkinson's disease and for treating asthma.

CAUTION All parts of the plant are highly poisonous. Subject to legal restrictions in some countries. For use by qualified practitioners only.

CARYOPHYLLACEAE

Diant*hus*

History and traditions Pinks are of ancient origin; one species is thought to be represented in the murals at Knossos in Crete and there are records that *D. caryophyllus* were cultivated by the Moors in Valencia in 1460. The Elizabethan name for the pink was gillyflower (or "gillofloure"). This included wild and alpine species and the much-prized clove gillyflower, which seems to have covered any clove-scented pinks. By the 17th century there were many cultivated garden varieties, as featured by Parkinson in his *Paradisi,* 1629, with delightful names like 'Master Tuggie's Princesse', 'Fair Maid of Kent' and 'Lusty Gallant'. Some were known as sops-in-wine after the practice of soaking them in wine to flavour it. Herbals and stillroom books are full of recipes for making

Top Dianthus *'Pink Jewel'.*

Above *An old-fashioned pink* D. *'Mrs Sinkins'.*

syrups and conserves of gillyflowers, pickled and candied gillyflowers and wine. According to Gerard, a conserve of clove gillyflowers and sugar "is exceedingly cordiall, and wonderfully above measure doth comfort the heart, being eaten now and then" (*The Herball,* 1597).

Description The leaves of all *Dianthus* are linear, lance-shaped and blue-grey or grey-green in colour, with a waxy texture. The flowers are pink, white or purple (some bicoloured) with short tubular bases and flat heads with double or single layers of petals, some with toothed or fringed margins. Old-fashioned varieties often have fragrant, clove-scented blooms but only one flowering period in early summer. (Modern varieties repeat-flower.) Garden pinks are 25–45 cm (10–18 in) high, and alpine species a more compact 8–10 cm (3–4 in) high. All are fully hardy.

Habitat/distribution Found in mountains and meadows of Europe, Asia and South Africa.

Species There are about 300 species, with over 30,000 hybrids and cultivars recorded. Pinks traditionally grown in the herb garden include ***D. deltoides*** (Maiden Pink) with cerise, single flowers with toothed petals (to 20 cm (8 in) high) or the more compact ***D. gratianopolitanus*** **syn.** ***D. caesius,*** which has very fragrant single pink flowers (to 15cm (6 in) high) or any of the fragrant old-fashioned pinks such as ***D.*** **'Mrs Sinkins'**, with its highly scented double white flowers and fringed petals. There are also numerous modern pinks, with an old-fashioned look, to choose from, such as ***D.*** **'Gran's Favourite'** or the laced ***D.*** **'London Delight'**.

Growth Pinks need a very well-drained neutral to alkaline soil and full sun. In gardens with heavy, clay soils, they can be grown in raised beds to provide sharp drainage. Easily propagated from cuttings of non-flowering shoots in summer or by division in spring or autumn.

Parts used Flowers – fresh or dried.

USES Medicinal At one time thought to have tonic properties, but they are little used today for medicinal purposes.

Culinary Fresh flowers may be added to salads, floated in drinks or crystallized for garnishing cakes and desserts. Before culinary use remove the bitter petal base.

Aromatic Flowers are dried for inclusion in potpourri and scented sachets. Flowers should be cut when just fully out, the heads twisted off the stems and dried whole.

Gillyflower vinegar

"Gilliflowers infused in Vinegar and set in the Sun for certaine dayes, as we do for Rose Vinegar do make a very pleasant and comfortable vinegar, good to be used in time of contagious sickness, and very profitable at all times for such as have feeble spirits."

John Evelyn, *Acetaria*, 1719.

Other names Pinks, gillyflower, clove gillyflower and sops-in-wine.

Top left D. gratianopolitanus, *known as the Cheddar pink.*

Top centre D. deltoides, *often called the maiden pink.*

Above *A pink-flowering cultivar of* D. *'Mrs Sinkins'.*

Below *Garden pinks, raised from several wild species of dianthus, are a mainstay of the traditional garden. They thrive on an alkaline soil and dislike damp conditions.*

RUTACEAE

Dictamnus albus

Dittany

History and traditions It is called "burning bush" because the whole plant is rich in volatile oil, which can allegedly be set alight as it evaporates, leaving the foliage intact and undamaged. It has a similar lemony, balsamic scent to that of *Origanum dictamnus*, or dittany of Crete, and both plants are probably named after Mount Dicte in Crete. According to Mrs Grieve (*A Modern Herbal,* 1931), *Dictamnus albus* was an ingredient of a number of exotic pharmaceutical preparations available in the early decades of the 20th century, including "Solomon's Opiate", "Guttète Powder", "Balm of Fioraventi" and "Hyacinth Mixture".
Description A clump-forming, aromatic perennial, 40–90 cm (16–36 in) tall, with pinnate leaves, made up of lance-shaped leaflets, and tall racemes of white flowers.
Related species *D. albus* var. *purpureus* has pale-pink flowers, striped with darker pink, and is more commonly grown in gardens than the species, but shares its characteristics.
Habitat/distribution Found from central and southern Europe across to China and Korea in dry grasslands and woodlands.
Growth Dittany grows in any well-drained to dry soil in full sun or partial shade. Propagated by seed sown in late summer, in containers and over-wintered in a cold frame. It does not transplant well and is not easy to establish from division.
Parts used Root – dried and powdered.

USES Medicinal It was once prescribed for nervous complaints and feverish illnesses, but does not seem to be widely used in Western herbal medicine today. The root bark of a similar species is used in Chinese medicine for its cooling, antibacterial properties.
Horticultural The chief use of this herb today is as an aromatic ornamental in the border or herb garden.
Other name Burning bush.

Above Dictamnus albus *var.* purpureus.

SCROPHULARIACEAE

Digitalis purpurea

Foxglove

History and traditions The foxglove was given its Latin name by the German botanist, Leonard Fuchs, in 1542 (it does not appear in any classical texts). He called it *digitalis,* for its supposed resemblance to fingers (*digit* = finger), and the common name in German, as in several other European languages, is connected with thimbles. Various ingenious explanations have been put forward for what it has to do with foxes: that they wore the flowers on their feet to muffle their tread when on night-time prowls; that it is really from "folksglove" for the "fairy folk"; or from an Anglo-Saxon word "*foxes-glew*" meaning fox-music, for its resemblance to an ancient musical instrument – you can take your pick. Once used in folk medicine for a variety of disorders (despite occasional fatalities), it was its effectiveness as a diuretic against dropsy which led to the discovery of its action on the heart by a Dr Withering, who published his findings in 1785.
Description A biennial or short-lived perennial, reaching 2 m (6 ft) in height. The plant has a rosette of large, downy leaves and spectacular one-sided flower spikes of purple or pink

tubular flowers, with crimson on the inside.
Related species *D. purpurea* f. *albiflora* is a white-flowering form and *D. lanata* has fawn-coloured flowers with purplish-brown veins. Both *D. purpurea* and *D. lanata* contain the active principles, though *D. lanata* is most commonly grown in Europe for the pharmaceutical industry.
Habitat/distribution Occurs throughout Europe, northern Africa and western Asia, mostly on acid soil in grassland and woodland.
Growth Although it will grow in most conditions, it prefers moist, well-drained soil in partial shade, with a mulch of leaf mould. Propagate from seed sown in autumn and over-winter in a cold frame. Self-seeds.
Parts used Leaves – from which the active principles digitoxin and digoxin are extracted.

USES Medicinal The foxglove contains glycosides which affect the heartbeat and is used in orthodox medicine as a heart stimulant. It should never be used for home treatments.

CAUTION Foxgloves are poisonous and should not be eaten or used in any way for self-medication. A prescription drug only. Legal restrictions apply.

COMPOSITAE/ASTERACEAE

Echinacea purpurea

Purple coneflower

History and traditions Coneflowers were used by Native Americans as wound-herbs, to treat snakebite and as a general cure-all. The early settlers took to them as home remedies for coughs, colds and a variety of infections. In recent years their medicinal properties have been established by modern research.
Description A tall, hardy perennial, 1.2 m (4 ft) high, with a rhizomatous rootstock and ovate-lanceolate leaves. The purplish-pink daisy-like flowers have raised conical centres, made up of prickly brown scales, reminiscent of hedgehogs (*Echinacea* is from the Greek word for hedgehog). There are also white-flowered cultivars.
Related species *E. angustifolia* and *E. pallida* are species with similar properties, which were also used by the Native Americans.
Habitat/distribution Native to Central and eastern North America, found in dry prairies and open woodlands. Introduced and grown in other temperate regions of the world.
Growth It prefers well-drained, humus-rich soil and a sunny position or partial shade. Cut back the stems as the flowers fade to encourage a second blooming. Propagate by seed sown in spring, under glass at a temperature of 13°C (55°F), or by division of roots in late spring or autumn.
Parts used Roots, rhizomes – dried, powdered or made into capsules.

USES Medicinal Recent research has shown that echinacea has a beneficial effect on the immune system and stimulates the production of white blood cells – and has been used in treating AIDS. It has antiviral, antifungal and antibacterial properties and is taken internally in the form of capsules or tinctures, for respiratory tract infections, kidney infections, skin diseases, boils, abscesses and slow-healing wounds. A decoction of the roots is applied externally as a wash for infected wounds and skin complaints.

Echinacea purpurea *boosts the immune system.*

BORAGINACEAE

Echium vulgare

Viper's bugloss

History and traditions Early herbalists thought that the stems, speckled with pustules, looked like snakeskin, the fruits like snakes' heads and the flower stamens like snakes' tongues. So, in line with the medieval Doctrine of Signatures (whereby the appearance of a plant indicates what it can cure) *E. vulgare* was considered an antidote to the bite of an adder and by extension to anything else that was poisonous. In the words of William Coles, "a most singular remedy against poyson and the sting of scorpions" (*The Art of Simpling*). It was also widely dispensed against "swooning, sadness and melancholy" (Parkinson). A native of Europe, this attractive but invasive plant spread around the world, and became known as a tiresome weed in many countries, notably Australia and North America – where it is known as "blue devil".

Description A bushy, bristly biennial, 60–90 cm (2–3 ft) tall, with narrow lance-shaped leaves, spotted, hairy stems and dense spires of bell-shaped, violet-blue flowers in summer, opening from pinkish buds.

Habitat/distribution Native to Europe and Asia, it occurs on poor, stony soils and semi-dry grassland. Introduced to, and widespread in, many countries worldwide.

Growth Grows in any well-drained soil, in full sun. Propagated from seed sown in spring or early autumn.

Parts used Leaves, flowers and seeds (formerly).

USES Medicinal Once widely respected as an antidote to poison, its medicinal properties are now doubtful.

Horticultural Traditionally grown in herb gardens for its historical associations.

Other names Blue weed and blue devil.

The stems of Echium vulgare *were thought to resemble snakeskin.*

CAUTION May cause stomach upsets if ingested and irritate skin on contact. For use by qualified practitioners only.

ZINGIBERACEAE

Elettaria cardamomum

Cardamom

History and traditions This pungent spice was known to the Greeks and Romans and mentioned by Theophrastus, Dioscorides and other classical writers. It features in Chinese medical texts, dating from AD 270, and has long been used in Ayurvedic medicine as a treatment for impotency. Cardamom is a traditional ingredient of eastern aphrodisiacs and mentioned in this context in the *Arabian Nights* stories. *Elettaria* is taken from an Indian name for this plant, *elaichi*.

Description A large perennial, 2–2.4 m (6–8 ft) tall, with a clump of long lanceolate leaves, growing from a fleshy rhizome. Flowers arise from the base of the plant, followed by pale-green capsules, which dry to a pale yellow, containing many small, pungent black seeds.

Related species There are various species, including black cardamom, a taller plant with large, dark-brown seed capsules, containing small black seeds with a strong eucalyptus aroma.

Habitat/distribution Native to southern India and Sri Lanka, it is also grown in Thailand, Central and tropical South America.

Above *Green cardamom seed pods.*

Growth It needs a minimum temperature of 18°C (64°F), well-drained, rich soil, partial shade, plenty of rain and high humidity. Propagated by seed or division of the rhizomes.
Parts used Seeds, essential oil.

USES Medicinal A warm, stimulating herb, it acts as a tonic and has antidepressant properties. It is also used as a digestive, and an infusion of the seeds is said to relieve hiccups. Seeds are chewed to freshen the breath.
Culinary A major curry spice, the seeds are also used to flavour hot wine punches, sweet, milky rice puddings and egg custard.
Aromatic The pleasant-smelling essential oil is used in perfumery and pharmaceutical products.

Above *Black cardamom.*

EQUISETACEAE

Equisetum arvense

Horsetail

History and traditions The Latin generic name comes from *equus*, a horse, and *seta*, a bristle. In former times this strange-looking, bottle-brush plant was used to clean pewter vessels and scour wooden kitchen utensils – the stems contain silica, which has a polishing action, as well as being a healing agent. In northern counties of England until the 19th century horsetail was commonly employed by milkmaids for cleaning out their pails. The Swedish botanist, Carl Linnaeus, claims that in his country it was eaten by both cattle and reindeer, though inclined to provoke diarrhoea. There are no records as to whether poor Romans, who were reputed to have eaten it (as an ubiquitous asparagus substitute), were similarly affected. Rich Romans, presumably, did not have to put it to the test. Culpeper lists many medicinal uses for horsetail, and declares that "it solders together the tops of green wounds and cures all ruptures in children".
Description A relic from prehistory, closely related to the vegetation which decayed to form modern coal seams, it is a perennial, which grows on a creeping rhizome to about 50 cm (20 in) in height. Brown stems, topped by cones, release spores and then wither, the method of reproduction of this plant being very similar to that of ferns. The mass of branched green stems, with black-toothed sheaths, are sterile.
Habitat/distribution Occurs throughout Europe from the arctic region to the south, also in Asia and China, and is found in moist waste ground. In some countries, where it has been introduced, it is regarded as a pernicious weed.
Growth A hardy plant, it grows in most conditions, although it prefers moist soil and sun or partial shade. It is propagated by division, but is invasive – and it would be wise to take this into account before introducing it into the garden.
Parts used Stems – fresh or dried.

USES Medicinal It has astringent, diuretic properties and is said to be helpful for prostate problems, cystitis and urinary infections, but it can be an irritant and self-medication is not advised. It is also said to be beneficial, when applied externally, for haemorrhages and ruptured ligaments.
Other names Bottle-brush and paddock pipes.

CRUCIFERAE/BRASSICACEAE

Eruca vesicaria subsp. *sativa*

Rocket (Arugula)

History and traditions Rocket (arugula) has been a salad herb since Roman times. Its strong, mustard-like taste is indicated by the generic Latin name, which comes from *urere,* to burn. Various claims were made for it in the past as a painkiller. William Turner said the seed was effective "against the bitings of the shrew-mouse and other venemous beasts". Gerard made the claim that "whosoever taketh the seed of Rocket before he be whipt, shall be so hardened that he shall easily endure the paines" (*The Herball*, 1597). Culpeper declared it to be "celebrated against diseases of the lungs" and that "the juice is excellent in asthmas … as also against inveterate coughs". But none of this has stood the test of time and salad rocket (arugula) is no longer used medicinally.
Description A frost-hardy annual, 60–100 cm (2–3 ft) tall, with dentate, deeply divided leaves. Small, four-petalled, white flowers, streaked at the centre of each petal with violet, appear in late winter to early summer. Originally a wild plant, rocket (arugula) has been cultivated for so long that it is now classified as a subspecies.
Habitat/distribution Native to the Mediterranean and Asia, introduced and widely grown elsewhere.
Growth Propagate from seed, sown successionally, *in situ*, from late winter to early summer. When grown on poor, dry soil, with plenty of sun, it has a more pungent taste than if grown on moist soil in cooler conditions.
Parts used Leaves.

USES Culinary A pungent herb that lends interest to lettuce and other bland-tasting leaves as a salad ingredient.
Other name Salad rocket.

Peppery rocket (arugula) leaves add interest to salads.

PAPAVERACEAE

Eschscholzia californica

Californian poppy

History and traditions This bright-yellow poppy is the state flower of California. It has similar properties to those of the opium poppy – but milder – and was used by Native Americans as a gentle narcotic and pain reliever, especially against toothache.
Description A hardy annual up to 60 cm (2 ft) tall, with finely divided, feathery leaves. A mass of shallow-cupped flowers in orange, yellow, red and occasionally white appear in early summer, followed by long curved seedpods. There is also a wide range of cultivars.
Habitat/distribution Native to western North America, introduced and widely grown in many other countries.
Growth Grow this plant in well-drained to poor soil and full sun, for the best-quality flowers. Propagated by seed sown *in situ* in spring or autumn. Sow successionally for a continuous show of flowers.
Parts used Whole plant – dried as an ingredient for infusions and tinctures.

USES Medicinal The Californian poppy is a sedative herb that relieves pain and it is taken internally as an infusion, for anxiety, nervous tension and insomnia. It also has diuretic properties and promotes perspiration.

MYRTACEAE

Eucalyptus spp.

Gum tree

History and traditions Eucalyptus trees are native to Australia and were used by the Aborigines in their traditional medicine. They have been widely adopted by other countries, including Africa, the Americas, India and southern Europe, as timber and shade trees, for planting in marshy ground to dry out malaria-inducing swamps, and for their volatile (essential) oil content. Commercial production of eucalyptus essential oils began in Australia in the second half of the 19th century, coinciding with their introduction to the West by a German botanist and director of the Melbourne Botanical Gardens.

Description Large, fast-growing evergreen trees which grow to considerable heights in warm climates, averaging 70 m (230 ft), with varying estimates for the record, dating from 1872 between 97 m (318 ft) and 132.5 m (434 ft). Many have distinctive, rounded juvenile foliage, adult leaves of *E. globulus* and *E. gunnii* are lanceolate, blue-grey and studded with oil-bearing glands. Clusters of fluffy cream-coloured flowers appear in summer, followed by globe-shaped fruits.

Species There are over 500 species and all contain antiseptic essential oils, though constituents and properties vary. *E. globulus* (blue gum) has been most widely cultivated around the world and has attractive, juvenile leaves much sought after in floristry. *E. gunnii* is one of the hardiest and most suited to growing in cool temperate regions.

Habitat/distribution: Native to Australia, *E. globulus* is found in moist valleys of New South Wales and Tasmania, *E. gunnii* in Tasmania. All are native to Australia and have been introduced elsewhere.

Growth *Eucalyptus* spp. vary from tender to fully hardy – but none will stand prolonged low temperatures, especially when immature. *E. globulus* is half-hardy, -5°C (23°F), and *E. gunnii* is frost-hardy, -15°C (5°F). Grow in well-drained soil and full sun. Propagate from seed, sow under cover in spring or autumn.

Parts used Leaves, essential oil.

USES Medicinal Eucalyptus has decongestant, expectorant properties and helps to lower fever. The essential oil is highly antiseptic. Leaf or oil is used in steam inhalations and vapour rubs to ease the symptoms of colds, catarrh, sinusitis and respiratory-tract infections. Essential oil is used in massage oils and compresses for inflammations, rheumatism and painful joints.

Above left *Eucalyptus trees are rich in volatile oils.*

Above *Immature foliage of* Eucalyptus gunnii, *syn.* E. divaricata, *Tasmanian Blue Gum.*

Lavender and eucalyptus vapour rub

50 g/2 oz petroleum jelly
15 ml/1 tbs dried lavender
6 drops eucalyptus essential oil

Melt the petroleum jelly in a bowl over a pan of simmering water. Stir in the lavender and heat for 30 minutes.

Strain the liquid jelly through muslin, leave to cool slightly, then add the eucalyptus oil. Pour into a clean jar and leave to set.

- Use as a soothing decongestant rub for throat, chest and back.

COMPOSITAE/ASTERACEAE

Eupatorium

Eupatorium cannabinum
Hemp agrimony

History and traditions The Latin specific name and common name are taken from the words *cannabis* and *hemp*, because of a similarity in the shape of the leaves. Hemp being used for rope fibre, by extension *E. cannabinum* gained the name "holy rope" – a plant with beneficent characteristics was often arbitrarily associated with holiness. But it was never in fact a source of rope and shares none of the properties of *Cannabis sativa*. It has a history of medicinal use as a diuretic, purgative, cure for dropsy, general spring tonic and antiscorbutic. Seventeenth-century herbalists also recommended it for healing "fomenting ulcers" and "putrid sores".
Description A woody-based, hardy perennial, up to 1.2 m (4 ft) tall, leaves are opposite and mostly subdivided into 3–5 leaflets. A froth of pinky-white flowers, borne in corymbs, appear in mid-summer – giving rise to another of the herb's country names, "raspberries and cream".
Habitat/distribution Indigenous to Europe, found in damp, rich soils, marshy places and fens.
Growth Grow in moist soil, in full sun or partial shade. Propagate by division in spring or sow seed in containers in spring.
Parts used The whole plant – the flowering tops are dried for use in infusions, extracts and other preparations.

USES Medicinal It has long been known for its diuretic properties, as a tonic for debility and a treatment for influenza-like illnesses, but the wider medicinal action of this herb is complex, even contradictory. Recent research suggests that it contains compounds that are capable of stimulating the immune system and combating tumours, but it also contains alkaloids that are potentially dangerous to the liver and in large enough doses could cause liver damage. Externally, it is applied, as in previous times, to ulcers and sores.
Other names Holy rope, St John's herb and ague weed.

Boneset in flower.

Eupatorium perfoliatum
Boneset

History and traditions Boneset was an important herb in the traditional medicine of native Americans, used for fevers, digestive disorders, rheumatism and as a powerful emetic and laxative. It also had magical protective properties assigned to it – infusions were sprinkled to keep evil spirits away. The name has nothing to do with its ability to mend bone fractures, but refers to its efficacy in treating "break bone fever", a virulent flu-like illness, from which the early settlers suffered. It was listed in Dr Griffith's *Universal Formulary*, 1859, to be administered in combination with sage and cascarilla bark "for a hectic fever".
Description A tall, hardy perennial, growing to 1.5 m (5 ft), with lanceolate, rough-textured leaves surrounding the stems (perfoliate), and large clusters of white flowers in late summer.
Habitat/distribution A native of North America in open, marshy regions – introduced in other countries.
Growth Grow in moist soil in full sun or partial shade. Propagate by seed sown in containers in spring or by division in spring or autumn.
Parts used Whole plant – dried for use in infusions, extracts and tinctures.

USES Medicinal A herb which lowers fevers and relieves congestion, it is taken internally for colds, influenza and bronchitis. It is also thought to stimulate the immune system, as is *E. cannabinum*.
Other names Feverwort, ague weed, thoroughwort, Indian sage, sweating plant.

Eupatorium purpureum
Joe Pye weed

History and traditions Joe Pye is said to have been a traditional healer from New England, with a reputation for successful cures, who swore by *E. purpureum,* using it in his remedies. The name gravel root pertains to the herb's ability to clear urinary stones, for which it is still used today, and Queen of the meadows is because the massed plants, when in flower, are a truly splendid sight.
Description A handsome hardy perennial which grows to at least 2.1 m (7 ft) tall, with purplish stems, whorls of slender, finely toothed, ovate leaves and dense, domed corymbs of purple-pink flowers in late summer to autumn. (It makes a magnificent plant for the border and is often sold as an ornamental.)
Habitat/distribution A North American native, found in woodland and grassland on moist or dry soils.
Growth Grows best in moist, well-drained soil in partial shade or sun. Propagated by seed sown in containers in spring, or by division when dormant.
Parts used Rhizomes, roots – dried for use in decoctions and tinctures.

USES Medicinal It has a restorative, cleansing action, mainly used in modern herbal medicine for kidney and urinary disorders, including stone, cystitis and prostate problems. Also used for painful menstruation, rheumatism and gout.
Other name Gravel root.

SCROPHULARIACEAE
Euphrasia officinalis
Eyebright

History and traditions The botanical name of this plant comes from the Greek for gladness, presumably for the cheer experienced when an eye problem is resolved. It was unknown to the classical writers and first introduced as an "eye" herb by Hildegard of Bingen, in her *Physica,* compiled *c.* 1150. In the 16th century, Fuchs and Dodoens also promoted it as a specific for eye complaints. The Doctrine of Signatures had a considerable bearing on the matter, as the markings on the little white flower were supposed to resemble a bloodshot eye.
Description An annual semi-parasitic herb, 5–30 cm (2–12 in) in height, it attaches itself to the roots and stems of grasses, absorbing mineral substances from them. Leaves are rounded, toothed and small – 1 cm (1/2 in) long – and the tiny white flowers are double-lipped with yellow throats and dark-purple veins.
Habitat/distribution Native to northern Europe, found also in Siberia and the Himalayas in meadowland and pastures on poor soil.
Growth A wild plant that is difficult to cultivate because of its semi-parasitic habit. If propagation is to be attempted, seeds should be sown near to potential host grasses.
Parts used Whole plant – dried for use in infusions and herbal preparations.

USES Medicinal A herb which reduces inflammation and is said to be helpful, taken as an infusion, for hayfever, allergic rhinitis, catarrh and sinusitis. For external use it is made into washes for sore, itchy eyes and conjunctivitis, or for skin irritations and eczema.

UMBELLIFERAE/APIACEAE
Ferula asa-foetida
Asafoetida

History and traditions The specific name refers to the strong, fetid smell of the gum resin obtained from the roots of this plant. It was valued throughout the Middle Ages as a prophylactic against plague and disease, and a piece was sometimes hung around the neck for this purpose. Asafoetida is still popular in India today as a flavouring and condiment and for its medicinal properties.
Description A herbaceous perennial, growing to 2.3 m (7 ft), it has a thick, fleshy taproot, finely divided, feathery leaves and yellow flower umbels in summer – and looks like giant fennel.
Habitat/distribution Occurs in western Asia from Iran to Afghanistan and Kashmir, on rocky hillsides and open ground.
Growth It is frost-hardy, withstanding temperatures to -5°C (23°F) and should be grown in well-drained, reasonably rich soil. Propagated by seed sown in autumn as soon as it is ripe.
Parts used Gum resin – produced from the base of the stems and root crown when the plant is cut down, drying as reddish tears. Sold whole, in powdered form, or as a tincture.

USES Medicinal It has a long tradition of use in Ayurvedic medicine for many complaints, including digestive disorders, respiratory diseases, impotence, painful menstruation, and problems following childbirth, and is said to counteract the effects of opium.
Culinary Despite its strong, sulphurous aroma, when added in small quantities, this herb enhances the flavour of curries and spicy food. The green parts are used as a vegetable.

MORACEAE

Ficus carica

Fig

History and traditions Figs originally came from Caria, a region of modern Turkey, which is the source of the species name. They were widely cultivated in ancient Greece and Rome and there are many references to them in classical writings from Homer to Theophrastus, Dioscorides and Pliny. Greek athletes ate figs to improve their strength and performance and the Romans fed them to their slaves (presumably for similar reasons). In Roman mythology the fig was dedicated to Bacchus and renowned as the tree which gave shelter to the wolf who suckled Romulus and Remus. Figs have been grown in the rest of Europe since they were popularized by the Emperor Charlemagne in the 9th century.
Description A deciduous tree, growing to 10 m (33 ft) with deeply lobed, palmate leaves. The flowers are completely concealed within fleshy receptacles and are followed by small green, pear-shaped fruits, ripening to dark purple, when the flesh surrounding the seeds becomes sweet and juicy.
Habitat/distribution Native to Turkey and southwest Asia, naturalized throughout the Mediterranean region and grown in many warm temperate zones worldwide.
Growth Although fig trees will withstand temperatures to -5°C (23°F), they need some protection from prolonged frost and cold. Warm, sunny summers are necessary to produce good fruit. Grow in well-drained, rich soil in a sunny position, and provide a sheltered place in cool areas. Propagated from semi-ripe cuttings in summer.
Parts used Fruits – fresh or dried.

USES Medicinal Well known for their laxative properties – syrup of figs is a traditional remedy for constipation – they are also highly nutritious, containing vitamins A, C and minerals, including calcium, phosphorus and iron, and are considered restorative and strengthening to the system. The milky juice, or sap, from green figs helps to soften corns and calluses on the skin.
Culinary The fruits are delicious raw, or as a cooked ingredient of sweet pies, pastries, desserts and conserves. Dried figs are stewed, or eaten as they are.

Related species

MORACEAE

Ficus religiosa

Peepal

Ficus religiosa is a large, spreading tree with distinctive, broad oval leaves, each tapering to a point. It was while meditating beneath a peepal tree that the Buddha achieved enlightenment, and it is revered by both Hindus and Buddhists. In Ayurvedic medicine it is used to treat various diseases, including dysentery and skin disorders.

ROSACEAE

Filipendula ulmaria

Meadowsweet

History and traditions The Dutch named this herb *"reinette"* (little queen) and it is known in several European languages as queen of the meadows. It features in the poetry of Ben Jonson as "meadow's queen" and John Clare celebrates its beauty in his poem "To Summer". It is said to have been Queen Elizabeth I's favourite strewing herb.
Description A herbaceous perennial, on a stout rootstock, 1–1.2 m (3–4 ft) tall, with irregularly pinnate, inversely lance-shaped leaves and dense corymbs of fluffy, creamy flowers in summer. Leaves have a more pleasant, aromatic scent than the sickly, hawthorn-like smell of the flowers.
Habitat/distribution Native to Europe and Asia, introduced and naturalized in North America. Widely grown in northern temperate regions, in marshlands and meadows, by ponds and streams.
Growth Grow in moist to boggy soil, or by a pond margin, in sun or partial shade – dislikes acid soil. Propagated by seed sown in spring or in autumn and overwintered in a cold frame, or by division in autumn or spring.
Parts used Leaves, flowers – fresh or dried.

USES Medicinal A traditional remedy, taken as an infusion, for heartburn, excess acidity and gastric ulcers. Also said to be helpful for rheumatism, arthritis and urinary infections.
Culinary The leaves may be used to flavour soups and stews.
Aromatic Leaves and flowers, dried, are added to pot-pourri – the scent of the flowers improves with keeping.

UMBELLIFERAE/APIACEAE

Foeniculum vulgare

Fennel

History and traditions The Romans enjoyed fennel both as a culinary plant, eating the stems as a vegetable, and for its medicinal properties – Pliny listed it as a remedy for no fewer than 22 complaints. It appears in early Anglo-Saxon texts and European records of the 10th century and was associated with magic and spells, being hung up at doors on Midsummer's Eve to deter witches. It was also used as a slimming aid and to deaden the pangs of hunger. William Coles wrote that it was "much used in drinks and broths for those that are grown fat, to abate their unwieldiness and cause them to grow more gaunt and lank" (*Nature's Paradise,* 1650). A use which is still valid today, it may be relevant that the chemical structure of fennel bears certain similarities to that of amphetamines.

Description A graceful aromatic perennial, up to 2 m (6 ft) tall, with erect, hollow stems and mid-green, feathery foliage – the leaves are pinnate, with threadlike leaflets. Umbels of yellow flowers are borne in summer, followed by ovoid, ridged, yellow-green seeds. The whole plant is strongly scented with aniseed.

Related species *F. v.* 'Purpureum' has bronze foliage and makes an attractive ornamental. *F. v.* var. *dulce* (Florence fennel, sweet fennel, finocchio) is cultivated for its bulbous, white stem bases.

Habitat/distribution Native to Asia and the Mediterranean, and occurs in much of Europe on wasteland, on dry sunny sites and in coastal areas. Widely naturalized in other countries.

Growth Grow *F. vulgare* and *F. v.* 'Purpureum' in well-drained to sandy soil in a sunny position. Does not always survive severely cold or wet winters, especially if grown on heavy soil. *F. v.* var. *dulce* needs a richer but well-drained soil, and plenty of water to produce the requisite swollen stems, which are blanched by earthing up around them. Propagation is from seed sown in spring.

Parts used Leaves, stems, roots, seeds, essential oil.

USES Medicinal An infusion of the seeds soothes the digestive system, and is said to increase the production of breast milk in nursing mothers as well as being settling for the baby. Also used as a mouthwash for gum disorders and a gargle for sore throats.

Culinary Leaves and seeds go well with fish, especially oily fish, such as mackerel. Seeds lend savour to stir-fry and rice dishes. The bulbous stems of Florence fennel are eaten raw in salads or cooked as a vegetable.

Aromatic The essential oil is used in perfumery, to scent soaps and household products, and as a flavouring in the food industry.

CAUTION Not suitable for pregnant women as in large doses fennel is a uterine stimulant.

Above F. v. *var* dulce, *florence fennel.*

Above centre *Fennel foliage.*

Fennel tea

Drinking fennel tea can have a good effect when on a slimming regime. Try taking a cup before meals to reduce appetite, or at any time instead of tea or coffee laced with milk and sugar.

250 ml/½ pt/1 cup of boiling water
1 tsp of fennel seeds
½ thin slice of fresh orange/or fresh shredded rind

Put the fennel seeds in a cup or pot, crush them lightly and pour over the boiling water. Cover and leave to infuse for 5 minutes.

Strain before pouring and add a slice of orange, or shred of curled orange rind, for extra flavour.

Wild strawberry leaves are included in blended herbal teas.

ROSACEAE

Fragaria vesca

Wild strawberry

History and traditions The large garden strawberry was not developed until the end of the 18th century by cross-breeding with American species. Until then, wild strawberries were the only kind known, although they were cultivated – when "by diligence of the gardener" the fruits were "as big as the berries of the Bramble in the hedge", as Thomas Hill puts it in *The Gardener's Labyrinth*,1590. Hill recommended eating them with cream and sugar, or, preferably in his view, with sugar and wine. Old stillroom books give recipes for strawberry teas and cordials, and for beauty aids, such as a face wash of strawberries, tansy and new milk. Culpeper had great faith in the powers of this plant to counteract all manner of disorders from cooling the liver, blood and spleen, refreshing and comforting fainting spirits and quenching thirst, to washing foul ulcers, fastening loose teeth and healing spongy gums.
Description A low-growing perennial, 25 cm (10 in) tall, which spreads by sending out rooting runners. It has shiny, trifoliate leaves, made up of ovate, toothed leaflets, and small white, yellow-centred flowers, followed by red ovoid fruits with tiny yellow seeds embedded in the surface.

Related species Alpine strawberries are cultivars of the species, *F. vesca,* and have smaller, but more distinctively aromatic fruits.
Habitat/distribution Found in Europe, Asia and North America, in grassland and woodland. Widely grown in temperate and subtropical regions.
Growth Grow in fertile, well-drained soil (on the alkaline side), in sun or partial shade. Propagate by separating and replanting runners – or by seed sown in containers at a temperature of 13–18°C (55–64°F).
Parts used Leaves, roots, fruits.

USES Medicinal Infusions or decoctions of the leaves and root are traditionally recommended for gout, are also taken for digestive disorders and used as a mouthwash to freshen breath. (Leaves of large, garden varieties do not have medicinal properties.) Leaves are diuretic, fruits mildly laxative. Preparations made with the fruits can be applied externally for skin inflammations, irritations and sunburn.
Culinary Rich in vitamin C, fruits are eaten fresh or made into desserts, conserves and juices. Dried leaves are included in blended herbal teas to improve taste and aroma.
Cosmetic The wild strawberry fruits have a cleansing, astringent action on the skin and are often added to face masks, skin toners and cleansing lotions.

Strawberry cleansing milk

A soothing lotion suitable for oily, spotty or blemished skins.

225 g/8 oz fresh, ripe strawberries
150 ml/¼ pt/⅔ cup milk

Mash the strawberries to a pulp and mix with the milk – or blend the ingredients in a blender. Pour into a clean bottle and keep in the refrigerator. Apply to the face on pads of cotton wool (cotton balls). (Lotion does not keep and should be used within two days.)

PAPAVERACEAE

Fumaria officinalis

Fumitory

History and traditions Shakespeare had no high opinion of this plant, referring to it twice as "rank fumitory" – it was one of the "idle weeds" with which King Lear crowned himself when mad, and a plant which grew in "fallow leas", left uncultivated because of war (*Henry V*). *Fumaria* is from the Latin for smoke, *fumus*. Various explanations have been put forward for its application to this plant – from the leaves having a "smoky appearance" to smoke from the plant when burnt, dispatching evil spirits; or the view, attributed to Pliny, that putting the juice in the eyes makes the tears run to such an extent that it's like being blinded by smoke.
Description An annual herb, 15–30 cm (6–12 in) tall, with trailing stems, small, finely divided grey-green leaves and racemes of tubular, pink flowers, in midsummer to autumn.
Habitat/distribution A European native, also found in western Asia and naturalized in North America, occurs on weedy ground, in fields and gardens (once a common cornfield weed).
Growth A wild plant, it will grow in any light soil, in sun or shade. Propagated from seed sown in spring, it also self-seeds readily.
Parts used Whole plant; cut in flower and dried.

USES Medicinal Contains small amounts of similar alkaloids to those found in poppies. Formerly used internally for digestive complaints and externally for eczema, skin disorders and conjunctivitis, but is little used today.

CAUTION Mildly toxic – not for self-medication.

LEGUMINOSAE/PAPILIONACEAE

Galega officinalis

Goat's rue

History and traditions The generic Latin name is said to come from the Greek for milk, *ghala*. The reputation of this herb for increasing the milk supply of cattle and other animals who eat it was established at the end of the 19th century by studies carried out in France. It was, at one time, thought to be helpful in cases of plague and was a favourite choice for fevers. Culpeper advised that "a bath made of it is very refreshing to the feet of persons tired of over-walking". The common name "goat's rue" is possibly because the crushed leaves have a rank smell.
Description A bushy, hardy perennial, up to 1.5 m (5 ft) tall, with lax stems, pinnately divided leaves and racemes of mauve, white or bicoloured flowers borne throughout the summer – it makes an attractive plant for the border or herb garden.
Related species *G. offinalis* 'Alba' is a white-flowering cultivar.
Habitat/distribution Native to Europe and western Asia, introduced in other countries, found in moist meadows and pasturelands.
Growth Goat's rue will grow in most soils, but prefers moist conditions, thrives and spreads rapidly in rich, fertile soil. Plant in full sun or partial shade. Propagated from seed sown in spring (soaking seeds overnight, or scarifying them, encourages germination).
Parts used Flowering tops – dried.

USES Medicinal An infusion of the herb is supposed to improve lactation for humans, just as eating the plant does for animals. It also has digestive properties and is said to lower blood-sugar levels, making it helpful for late-onset diabetes.
General High in nitrogen, it makes a useful "green manure" when ploughed into the soil.
Other name French lilac.

Below *Galega officinalis 'Alba'*.

RUBIACEAE

Galium

Galium odoratum syn. *Asperula odorata*

Sweet woodruff

History and traditions A strewing herb since medieval times, it is one of many species containing compounds which release coumarin, with its characteristic scent of new-mown hay, as the plant dries. Thomas Tusser called it "sweet grass" and recommended it for making a water to improve the complexion as well as for strewing. Gerard recommended it as a kind of air conditioning: "The flowers are of a very sweet smell as is the rest of the herb, which, being made up into garlands or bundles, and hanged up in houses in the heat of summer, doth very well attemper the air, cool and make fresh the place" *(The Herball,* 1597). The dried leaves were put into sachet mixtures to deter moths, used to stuff pillows and mattresses and placed between the pages of books.
Description A spreading perennial, growing on a creeping rhizome, about 40 cm (16 in) tall, it has four-angled stems, whorls of rough-textured, lanceolate leaves and a mass of tubular, star-shaped, scented, white flowers in summer.
Habitat/distribution Native to Europe and Asia, also found in northern Africa and naturalized in North America. Found on loamy, nutrient-rich soils in mixed woodland.
Growth Grow in humus-rich soil in partial shade. Propagation is easiest by division of runners in spring or autumn. Can also be grown from seed, sown as soon as ripe in late summer.
Parts used Whole plant – cut when in flower and dried.

USES Medicinal Coumarin gives it sedative properties and infusions are taken for nervous irritability and insomnia. Modern research has found that two of its coumarin molecules join to produce dicoumarol, which prevents blood-clotting and strengthens capillaries, and it is taken internally for varicose veins and thrombophlebitis. It is a diuretic and said to improve liver function and have a tonic effect on the system.
Aromatic The coumarin smell intensifies and improves with keeping, so the dried herb is added to pot-pourri or sachets for the linen cupboard – it helps repel insects.

Galium verum

Ladies' bedstraw

This member of the *galium* species has the characteristic four-angled stems and whorls of clinging, bristled leaves, but the flowers are bright-yellow and smell of honey. It too emits the sweet, coumarin scent when dry and was much used in the past as a mattress stuffing – hence its popular name. Dioscorides wrote about it as a "milk" plant and it was used in his time and for centuries afterwards as an agent for curdling cheese and colouring it yellow – it does in fact contain a rennin enzyme.

Galium aparine

Goosegrass

This familiar, creeping, clinging plant may look like a tiresome weed (and all too often behave like one) but is not without its uses. It is a traditional springtime tonic in central Europe, taken as an infusion of the fresh green parts, or as a pulped juice, and is said to help eliminate toxins from the system. Some herbalists recommend it for debilitating conditions such as myalgic encephalomyelitis (ME) and glandular fever. It may also be eaten, as a lightly cooked vegetable, as they do in China apparently, and the seeds have even been recommended as a coffee substitute. Gerard's comment was "Women do usually make pottage of cleavers ... to cause banknesse and keepe them from fatnes."
Other name Cleavers.

Above *Ladies' bedstraw.*

ERICACEAE

Gaultheria procumbens

Wintergreen

History and traditions This shrub is the source of the original wintergreen, later extracted from a species of birch, *Betula lenta,* and nowadays mostly produced synthetically. It was used as a tea and medicinally by Canadian Indians for aching muscles and joints. Its Latin name comes from Dr Jean-Francois Gaulthier, who worked in Quebec in the mid-1700s. The leaves were officially in the United States *Pharmacopoeia* until towards the end of the 19th century and wintergreen oil is still listed.
Description A prostrate shrub, 15 cm (6 in) high, it has dark-green, glossy, oval leaves and clusters of small, white, drooping, bell-shaped flowers in summer, followed by scarlet berries.
Habitat/distribution A North American native, found in woodlands and mountainous areas.
Growth Grow in a moist soil, on the acid side of neutral, in partial shade. Dividing the rooted suckers is the easiest way to propagate this plant. Semi-ripe cuttings can be taken in summer, or seeds can be sown in containers and overwintered in a cold frame.
Parts used Leaves, essential oil – obtained by distillation of the leaves.

USES Medicinal The leaves contain methyl salicylate, an anti-inflammatory with similar properties to aspirin. The essential oil has antiseptic properties and is used for massaging aches and pains, for rheumatism and arthritis. Infusions of the leaves are used as gargles.

CAUTION The oil is toxic in excess.

GENTIANACEAE

Gentiana lutea

Yellow gentian

History and traditions Gentians are said to be named after a King Gentius of Illyria (an ancient country of the East Adriatic), who was credited by Pliny and Dioscorides as having been the first to recognize its medicinal properties. In the Middle Ages it was popular as a counter-poison and the German physician and botanist Hieronymus Bock in his *Neue Kraüter Buch*, 1539, refers to the use of the roots in dilating wounds. Nicholas Culpeper, inventive as ever, recommends it as a healing decoction for cows unlucky enough to be bitten on the udder by venomous beasts. It is not certain which species were used in former times, but *G. lutea* has proved to be the most important from a medicinal point of view. In former times gentian wine was taken as an aperitif.
Description A hardy herbaceous perennial, it grows on a thick taproot, to a height of 1–2 m (3–6 ft). Erect stems have fleshy, ribbed leaves in pairs, joined at the base, and bright-yellow flowers, with short, tubular petals, borne in clusters in the leaf axils. It usually flowers about three years after planting.
Habitat/distribution Native to Europe and western Asia. Found in mountainous pastures and woodlands.
Growth Grow in well-drained, humus-rich soil, in sun or partial shade, and keep fairly moist – heavy, waterlogged soil is likely to induce root rot. Propagated by division or offshoots in spring, or by seed sown in autumn.
Parts used Roots, rhizomes – dried for use in decoctions, tinctures and other preparations.

USES Medicinal The most bitter of herbs, yellow gentian has been used in tonic medicines for centuries. It is said to be anti-inflammatory and to reduce fevers and is taken internally for digestive complaints and loss of appetite. Said to stimulate production of blood corpuscles and to reduce anaemia.
General An ingredient of commercially produced tonics and bitter aperitifs.

CAUTION It should not be used without advice from a qualified practitioner, as it could have adverse effects on some gastric disorders. Not to be taken by anyone with high blood pressure, nor by pregnant women.

GERANIACEAE

Geranium maculatum

Cranesbill

History and traditions The common name refers to the beak-like shape of the fruit, and the generic name is from the Greek word for a crane, a stork-like bird with a long bill. The leaves become distinctively speckled as they age, and the specific name *maculatum* means spotted. Traditionally used in the folk medicine of Native Americans, it was at one time listed in the United States *Pharmacopoeia*.

Description A hardy, clump-forming perennial, it grows to 75 cm (30 in) and has deeply divided palmate leaves. Large, round, purple-pink flowers appear in the axils in late spring to early summer, followed by the beak-shaped fruits.

Geranium sanguineum, *(Bloody Cranesbill)*

Related species *G. robertianum* (herb Robert) is a common wild plant, growing to 50 cm (20 in), with a creeping decumbent habit and soft, downy, reddish stems. Leaves have three pinnately-lobed leaflets and small five-petalled, rose-pink flowers, striped in white. It gives off an unpleasant smell when crushed. It was formerly associated with magic and widely used in folk medicine for inflammations of the skin and mouth and for diarrhoea.

Habitat/distribution *G. maculatum,* native to North America, and found in a variety of habitats. Widely grown in temperate regions elsewhere. *G. robertianum* is native to Europe, North America, Asia and northern Africa in poor, dry soils.

Growth *G. maculatum* prefers moist soil and a sunny position or partial shade. Most easily propagated by division in early spring or late winter, seeds may be sown in spring or autumn. *G. robertianum* is a wild plant and grows best in poor, dry soil.

Parts used *G. maculatum* – whole plant, roots – dried for use in infusions, powders, tinctures and other preparations.

USES Medicinal *G. maculatum* is an astringent herb, which is said to control bleeding and discharges. It was formerly used in the treatment of diarrhoea, dysentery and cholera. Externally it is applied to wounds and used as a gargle for sore throats and mouth ulcers.

Other names American cranesbill and spotted cranesbill.

Above Geranium robertianum.

ROSACEAE

Geum urbanum

Wood avens

History and traditions The medieval name was *herba benedicta*, or the blessed herb, for its supposed ability to repel evil spirits – and the second part of one of its common names, herb bennet, is a contraction of *benedicta*. The three-part leaf and the five petals of the flower supposedly represented the Holy Trinity and five wounds of Christ, and it appears as a carved decoration in 13th-century churches. As a medicinal herb there were rules laid down as to the time and season for digging up the root for maximum efficacy and it was included in cordials to be taken as a plague preventative.

Description A rather undistinguished, hardy perennial plant, growing from 20–60 cm (8–24 in), with downy stems, three-lobed leaves and tiny, yellow, five-petalled flowers in summer, followed by fruits with brown, hooked bristles.

Habitat/distribution Native to Europe and found in wasteland, hedgerows and woodlands on moist, high-nitrogen soils.

Growth A wild plant, it grows best on rich, moist soils and self-seeds freely.

Parts used Whole plant, roots – the flowering tops are dried for use in infusions, roots used fresh or dried in decoctions.

USES Medicinal An antiseptic, anti-inflammatory herb with tonic properties, taken internally for digestive upsets, applied externally to wounds, or used as a gargle for sore gums and mouth inflammations.

Culinary The roots were formerly used for their supposed clove-flavouring in soups and ale.

Other name Herb bennet.

ROSACEAE

Gillenia trifoliata

Indian physic

History and traditions A medicinal plant of Native Americans with emetic, purgative properties. Also known as "bowman's root", for its wound-healing effects, and "American ipecacuanha". The early colonists adopted it and it was formerly listed in the United States *Pharmacopoeia*.

Description A graceful hardy perennial, growing to 1 m (3 ft), with red-tinged, wiry stems, bronze-green, three-palmate leaves and irregularly star-shaped flowers, with narrow white petals and red-tinted calyces.

Habitat/distribution Native to eastern North America, found in moist woodlands, introduced and widely grown as a garden plant in Europe and temperate regions.

Growth Grow in humus-rich, moist soil in partial shade. Propagated by division in spring or autumn, or by seed sown in autumn in containers and overwintered in a cold frame.

Parts used Root bark – dried for use in decoctions and powders.

USES Medicinal It is used as a purgative and expectorant.

Right Gillenia trifoliata.

GINKGOACEAE

Ginkgo biloba

Ginkgo

History and traditions Identical in appearance to tree fossils 200 million years old, ginkgo has always been a sacred tree in China – it was grown for centuries in temples, some specimens reaching a great age, with circumferences up to 9 m (29 ft). It has been cultivated in Europe since the early 18th century with seeds brought from China or Japan. The seeds have long been used in traditional Chinese medicine, and modern research has discovered constituents in the leaves of potential therapeutic importance, unknown in any other plant species.

Description There is only one species in the genus. A deciduous tree growing to 40 m (130 ft), it has lobed, fan-shaped leaves (similar in appearance to maidenhair fern foliage, but larger), which turn yellow in autumn. Flowering takes place after 20 years, with male and female flowers and fruits borne on separate trees. Male trees have an earlier leaf-fall and less spreading form; female fruits have a rancid smell when fallen. Ginkgo is a very robust tree and suffers from few pests, tolerates pollution well and a salty atmosphere.

Habitat/distribution Originating in China and Japan, it is no longer found in the wild, but is cultivated as specimen and shade trees, and now widely grown in other countries.

Growth Fully hardy, it does best in well-drained but fertile soil and a sunny position. Propagated from seed sown in containers in autumn or from cuttings taken in summer. It should not be pruned as this leads to die-back.

Parts used Leaves – picked in autumn and dried. Seeds – used in decoctions.

USES Medicinal The leaves have recently been discovered to contain compounds called ginkgolides, which promote blood flow, inhibit allergic reactions and have been found helpful for Parkinson's disease. The seeds have anti-fungal and antibacterial properties, and are used in Chinese medicine for asthma and coughs.

Culinary Ginkgo nuts (the female fruits with the outer unpleasant layer removed) are roasted and sometimes served with bird's-nest soup in Chinese cuisine.

General Seeds produce oil, which may cause dermatitis in sensitive people, and leaves contain insecticidal compounds.

LEGUMINOSAE/PAPILIONACEAE

Glycyrrhiza glabra

Liquorice

History and traditions Liquorice has been valued for thousands of years for the sweetness of its root (it contains glycosides, including glycyrrhizin, that are 50 times sweeter than sugar) and for its medicinal powers. The generic name is from the Greek *glykys* (sweet) and *rhiza* (a root). This became corrupted to "*gliquiricia*" and thence to "liquorice". The Egyptians put it into funeral jars and some was found in the burial chamber of Tutankhamun. The Chinese believed it was rejuvenating and gave them long life and strength. Roman legionaries chewed it on the battlefield – a habit taken up by Napoleon, who believed it had a calming effect on the nerves. It did not reach Europe until the 15th century, when it soon became established as a remedy for many ailments, including coughs, chest infections and digestive disorders. In 1760 a Pontefract apothecary, George Dunhill, thought of adding sugar and flour to the liquorice essence to produce the well-known confectionery. Liquorice confectionery is still made from the plant and it is an ingredient of many pharmaceutical products with principal centres of commercial cultivation in Russia, Spain and the Middle East.

The dried roots are used in medicinal preparations and to make confectionery.

Description A hardy perennial, growing up to 1.2 m (4 ft), the leaves are pinnate, divided into 9–17 oval leaflets; the violet, pealike flowers are borne in short racemes, followed by long seed pods.

Related species *G. lepidota* is a North American wild species of liquorice, used by Indian tribes to ease childbirth.

Habitat/distribution Originally from the Middle East, Asia and China, it is now cultivated in temperate regions worldwide, including parts of Australia, North and South America.

Growth It requires a deep, rich, moisture-retentive soil and a sunny position. Propagated by division of roots in autumn or spring. Germination from seed is slow. To encourage strong root growth, remove flower heads.

Parts used Roots – lifted in autumn, when plant is 3–4 years old, and dried for use in decoctions, liquid extracts and powders. Roots are boiled to extract the essence used in confectionery.

USES Medicinal An important herb in Ayurvedic medicine for stomach disorders, sore throats, respiratory infections and as first aid for snake or scorpion bites. In Chinese herbal medicine, it is used for sore throats and food poisoning. It has soothing anti-inflammatory properties and is added to proprietary cough mixtures, lozenges and laxatives. Liquorice root should not be used for self-medication.

General As well as being used in confectionery production, liquorice is used to flavour beers and tobacco, and is employed in the manufacture of shoe polish, plastics and fibreboard.

CAUTION For use by qualified practitioners only. May increase fluid retention, blood pressure and blood potassium levels. It should not be given to pregnant women, or anyone with high blood pressure, kidney disease or on digitalis drugs.

HAMAMELIDACEAE

Hamamelis virginiana

Witch hazel

History and traditions Native American tribes used decoctions of the bark to reduce swellings and bruises. Colonists took note and it was listed in the United States *Pharmacopoeia* from 1860 onwards. It was also thought to have supernatural properties and the forked branches were used as divining rods in the search for water and gold.

Description A deciduous tree or shrub, up to 5 m (16 ft) in height, it has smooth brown bark and obovate leaves. Clusters of fragrant, yellow flowers appear in late autumn to early winter.

Habitat/distribution Native to North America, now widely cultivated in other countries as a garden ornamental.

Growth A hardy shrub, it requires moderately fertile, moist but well-drained soil and a sunny or partially shady position. Propagation is from seed sown in containers in autumn.

Parts used Twigs – cut after flowering, to make the distilled extract. Bark – used in tinctures and extracts. Leaves – dried for use in powders, liquid extracts, ointments.

USES Medicinal Distilled witch hazel is available for external use on bruises and sprains. The tincture is much stronger and should be used only under the guidance of a qualified practitioner. Witch hazel extract is a constituent of proprietary haemorrhoid ointments and other pharmaceutical preparations.

COMPOSITAE/ASTERACEAE

Helianthus annuus

Sunflower

History and traditions The sunflower originated in the Americas, probably Mexico. There is evidence that before 1000 BC it was grown there, for its seeds. It was among the many plants introduced to Europe from the New World in the 16th century, but did not become a major food plant and source of oil until large-scale cultivation began in Russia two centuries later (by the 1970s it was second only to soya bean as an oil crop). At some point it gained a reputation for being antimalarial and was used in Russian folk medicine for reducing fevers. The common name is a translation of the generic term, which is taken from the Greek for sun, *helios,* and flower, *anthos* – both for its sunlike appearance and because it turns its head to follow the sun's direct rays.

Description A tall, impressive annual, up to 3 m (10 ft) in height, with erect stems and oval, hairy leaves. The showy daisy-shaped flower heads, up to 30 cm (1 ft) across, have bright yellow ray florets, and brown disc florets at the centre, followed by the striped black and white seeds, about 1,000 per head.

Habitat/distribution Native to Central, North and South America, introduced and widely grown in Europe and other countries in open sunny sites.

Growth A hardy annual which tolerates most soils, as long as reasonably well-drained. Propagate by seed sown in spring.

Parts used Whole plant – cut when flowering begins for use in extracts and tinctures. Seeds are collected when ripe in autumn, and used fresh or pressed to produce a fatty oil.

USES Medicinal Sunflower seeds and oil are a good source of vitamin E, which has anti-oxidant properties, and are high in poly-unsaturates, especially linoleic acid, needed for the maintenance of cell membranes – they also help lower blood cholesterol levels. Formerly, preparations made from the seeds were used for treating coughs and bronchial infections, applied externally to bruises and for easing rheumatic pains.

Culinary Seeds are eaten fresh or roasted in salads, bread and bakery products. Oil is used for cooking and in salad dressings. Also a constituent of margarine.

Above Helianthus annuus *'Velvet Queen' is an attractive cultivar.*

COMPOSITAE/ASTERACEAE

Helichrysum italicum syn.
H. angustifolium

Curry plant

History and traditions A native of southern Europe, it seems to have crept into modern herb gardens, where it is now firmly established, because of the popular name, curry plant, relating to its strong smell. But it is not a culinary plant and has nothing to do with curry – or curry leaves (see *Murraya koenigii*). It is one of the "everlasting" flowers (most of which have a papery texture and retain form and colour when dried). It justifies its position as a herb because it is included in pot-pourri and has insect-repellent properties.

Description An evergreen subshrub, 60 cm (2 ft) in height, it has linear, silver-grey leaves and clusters of yellow button-shaped flowers in summer.

Habitat/distribution Native to the Mediterranean and grown throughout Europe, other species occur in Africa and Asia.

Growth Although frost hardy, it does not tolerate prolonged cold, wet winters. Grow in light, well-drained soil in full sun. Propagated by semi-ripe or heel cuttings in summer.

Parts used Leaves, flowers.

USES Aromatic Dried flowers and foliage may be added to pot-pourri and insect-repellent sachet mixtures. The essential oil is said to be antiviral, but it is not confirmed.

CANNABACEAE

Humulus lupulus

Hops

History and traditions The hop plant was described by Pliny, who named it "*lupus salictarius*", or "willow wolf", for its habit of twining round willow stems and strangling them "as a wolf does a lamb". The Romans ate the young shoots as vegetables, as did country folk in Britain into the 20th century. Its major importance was that it changed the character of beer, acting as an efficient preservative (it has bacteriostatic properties) and giving it a bitter flavour. It was first used for this in Flanders in the 14th century, but there was great opposition to it in Britain, where it was thought to "spoil" the traditional ales, so it was not in general use there before the 17th century. Even then John Evelyn wrote, "Hops transmuted our wholesome ale into beer. This one ingredient ... preserves the drink indeed, but repays the pleasure in tormenting diseases and a shorter life" (*Pomona*, 1670). But it did become established as a medicinal plant and Culpeper's view was that a "decoction of the tops cleanses the blood, cures the venereal disease, and all kinds of scabs, itch, and other breakings out of the body; as also tetters, ringworms, spreading sores, the morphew, and all discolourings of the skin".

Description A hardy, twining, herbaceous climber, it has clinging hairy stems and 3–7 lobed palmate leaves. Male and female flowers are borne on different plants – the male ones are in small inconspicuous clusters, the female in conelike, pale-green inflorescences, which are the hops used in beer making.

Related species *H. lupulus* 'Aureus' has golden-green foliage and it makes an attractive and vigorous ornamental climber for the herb garden.

Habitat/distribution Its country of origin is not certain, but it is found in Europe, western Asia and North America and widely distributed in northern temperate zones. Naturalized in woodland and hedgerows.

Growth Prefers moist, fertile, well-drained soil and a sunny position or partial shade, but is a vigorous plant that grows under most conditions. Propagated by softwood cuttings in spring.

Parts used Female flowers (strobiles) – dried; oil distilled from flowers; fresh young shoots.

USES Medicinal Has sedative and antibacterial properties and is taken internally in infusions or tinctures for insomnia, nervous tension and anxiety; applied externally for skin complaints.

Culinary Young shoots can be cooked and eaten like asparagus.

Aromatic Dried flowers are added to sleep pillows, distilled oil used in perfumes. Active principles are thought to help prevent ageing of skin and brittleness of hair. Flowers or essential oil are included in rejuvenating baths and hair treatments.

General Flowers (hops) used to flavour beers and ales, distilled oil and extracts used in the food industry.

Above Humulus lupulus *'Aureus', golden hops.*

RANUNCULACEAE

Hydrastis canadensis

Golden seal

History and traditions This was once a very common herb in North America, its orange root being variously used to make a yellow dye, in medicinal remedies for digestive problems, bruises and swellings and also as an insect repellent. Early settlers were impressed by its properties and it was listed in the United States *Pharmacopoeia* from 1831 to 1936. Its continued popularity has led to overexploitation: it is now rare in the wild, from which all trade supplies come (cultivation is difficult).

Description A hardy perennial, 20–30 cm (8–12 in) in height, it has a thick, knotted, yellow rhizome, palmate, deeply lobed leaves, and single greenish-white flowers, with no petals, in late spring to early summer. Fruits are red and raspberry-like, but inedible.

Habitat/distribution Native to north-eastern North America, found in damp forests.

Growth It requires moist, humus-rich soil and a shady position. Propagation is by seed sown in autumn, though germination is slow and erratic, or by division in early spring or late autumn. Plants do not establish easily.

Parts used Rhizome – dried for use in tinctures, decoctions and pharmaceutical preparations.

USES Medicinal It has anti-inflammatory properties, helps to check bleeding, is also antibacterial, decongestant and mildly laxative. Popular in North America for boosting the immune system, taken as a tea in combination with other herbs, such as *Echinacea purpurea*.

CAUTION Poisonous in large doses. Not to be given to pregnant women or anyone with high blood pressure.

SOLANACEAE

Hyoscyamus niger

Henbane

History and traditions This is a poisonous herb with a long history. It appears in the works of Dioscorides, Pliny and other classical writers as a sleep-inducing and pain-relieving drug and is mentioned in Anglo-Saxon herbals under the name of "Henbell". In Greek mythology the dead, consigned to the underworld kingdom of Hades, were crowned with wreaths of henbane. Its narcotic properties, inducing giddiness and stupor, made it a sought-after herb for witches' brews and sorcerers' spells. It is thought to have provided the "leprous distillment" poured into the ear of Hamlet's father as he lay sleeping. Seventeenth-century herbals recognized its deadly nature, recommending it for external use only, and dental practitioners of the time burned seeds of henbane in chafing dishes to produce analgesic fumes as they treated their patients.

Description An annual or biennial, growing to 60–90 cm (2–3 ft), it has a rank, unpleasant smell and coarsely toothed, grey-green, sticky leaves. Bell-shaped, creamy-yellow flowers, veined with purple, grow from the leaf axils and appear throughout the summer, followed by fruit capsules containing many seeds.

Habitat/distribution Probably originated in the Mediterranean region, now widely distributed in Europe and Asia, found in sandy waste ground and coastal sites.

Growth Grow in poor, stony or sandy soils. Propagated from seed sown *in situ* in spring, often self-seeds.

Parts used Leaves, flowering tops – dried for use by the pharmaceutical industry.

USES Medicinal It contains toxic alkaloids hyoscyamine, hyoscine and atropine (as in *Atropa bella-donna*) which affect the central nervous system. These constituents are included in some pharmaceutical drugs for asthma and nervous disorders. Also for muscle spasms and tremors as suffered in senility and diseases associated with old age.

Other name Hogbean.

CAUTION All parts are highly poisonous. Henbane is for use by qualified practitioners only and should never be used for self medication. Legally restricted in some countries.

GUTTIFERAE/CLUSIACEAE

Hypericum perforatum

St John's wort

History and traditions This is a herb that has attracted a wealth of folklore over the centuries and been ascribed many magical and mystical properties. It is named after St John the Baptist, the red pigment, hypericin, which exudes from the crushed flowers signifying his blood. It is in full flower on St John's Day, 24 June, which also coincides with northern hemisphere midsummer rituals, and it was ascribed the power to drive away ghosts and witches and protect from thunderbolts and lightning. Many superstitions surrounded it, including gathering it on St John's Eve with the dew still on it in order to find a husband, or as a childless wife, gathering it naked to ensure a speedy conception. Despite all this, it has been discovered recently to be an effective antidepressant, without the side effects of conventional drugs. In Germany it has a medical licence and has been widely prescribed for depressive states, outselling Prozac eight times over. But as with many beneficial plants, there are contra-indications which should be taken into account (see CAUTION).

Description It is a hardy perennial, about 30–60 cm (1–2 ft) in height, the stems are erect, woody at the base, with small linear-oval leaves, dotted with glands, which can be seen as little pinpricks when held up to the light. The flowers have five petals, edged with glands.
Habitat/distribution A native of Europe and temperate Asia, found in woodlands, and in hedgerows on semi-dry soils. Naturalized in America and Australia.
Growth Grow in well-drained, dryish soil in full sun or partial shade. Propagation by division is the easiest method; it can also be grown from seed sown in spring or autumn, and spreads rapidly once established.
Parts used Flowering tops – fresh or dried for use in infusions, creams, oils, and as liquid extracts for use in pharmaceutical preparations.

USES Medicinal It is said to have calming properties. Infusions are taken for anxiety and nervous tension. It also has antiseptic and anti-inflammatory properties and promotes healing; creams and infused oils are applied to burns, muscular pain, neuralgia and sciatica. Prescribed in Germany as an antidepressant (Jarsin), a lower-dose product is available in Britain (Kira).

Above *The flowers of* Hypericum perforatum *contain the active principle hypericin.*

St John's wort oil

To make an infused massage oil:

25 g/1 oz fresh flowering tops of St John's wort
600 ml/1 pint/2 ½ cups sunflower oil

Put the flowering tops into a bowl and crush them lightly. Pour in the oil. Stand the bowl over a pan of barely simmering water and heat very gently for about 1 hour.

Strain off the herb by pouring it through muslin or a jelly bag (cheesecloth) fixed over a jug, then transfer to a clean, airtight bottle.

CAUTION Harmful if eaten, and poisonous to livestock – this herb is statutorily controlled in some countries (including Australia). It is also a skin allergen in sunlight.

Above left *Hyssop flowers add colour to the garden in mid to late summer.*

Above *The leaves have a pungent flavour and were popular in culinary dishes during the Elizabethan era.*

LABIATAE/LAMIACEAE

Hyssopus officinalis

Hyssop

History and traditions The name is an ancient one – it is virtually the same in all European languages and comes from the Greek, *hyssopos.* In Hebrew it is *ezob,* meaning a "holy herb", though it is not certain whether the hyssop we know is the plant referred to in the Bible. Hippocrates and Dioscorides rated it highly as a medicinal herb, recommending it for respiratory disorders – as it is still used in herbal medicine today. Its strong, aromatic smell meant it was suitable for strewing in rooms in the house – and is included for this purpose in Thomas Tusser's list (*Five Hundred Points of Good Husbandry,* 1580). It frequently featured in designs for knot gardens of the 17th century, was a popular culinary herb used in "pottages" (soups) and salads, and was taken as a tea, or made into syrups and cordials for coughs and colds. It was one of the original ingredients of the liqueur, Chartreuse.

Description Classed as a semi-evergreen, because it loses some foliage in winter, mainly if weather is severe. It is a bushy perennial, about 60–90 cm (2–3 ft) high. The stems are woody at the base with small, dark-green, linear leaves and dense spikes of deep-blue flowers in late summer, which are very attractive to bees. There are also forms with pink and white flowers.

Habitat/distribution Native to the Mediterranean region and western Asia, found on dry, rocky soils. Introduced and widely grown throughout Europe and North America.

Growth Grow in well-drained to dry soil in a sunny position. Propagated by seed sown in spring, or by cuttings taken in summer. Prune back hard in spring to prevent it becoming straggly (it will regenerate from the old wood).

Parts used Leaves, flowers – fresh or dried.

USES Medicinal Hyssop has expectorant properties, promotes sweating and is anti-catarrhal and antibacterial. Infusions are taken for coughs, colds and chest infections.

Culinary The leaves have a strong, slightly bitter flavour and may be added to soups and cooked meat and vegetable dishes with discretion. The attractive blue flowers make a pretty garnish for salads.

Old recipes for hyssop

- A Water to Cause an Excellent Colour and Complexion
  Drink six spoonfuls of the juice of Hyssop in warm Ale in a Morning and fasting.
  From *The Receipt Book of John Nott,* cook to the Duke of Bolton, 1723.

- To Make Syrup of Hysop for Colds
  Take an handful of Hysop, of Figs, Raysins, Dates, of each an ounce, French Barley one ounce, boyl therein three pintes of fair water to a quart, strain it and clarifie it with two Whites of Eggs, then put in two pound of fine Sugar and boyl it to a Syrup.
  The Queen's Closet Opened, W. M., cook to Queen Henrietta Maria, 1655.

COMPOSITAE/ASTERACEAE

Inula helenium

Elecampane

History and traditions It is said to be named after Helen of Troy, who was gathering this herb when abducted by Paris, or, according to another version, it grew from her tears on the same occasion. In any case it is an ancient herb, well known to the Greeks and Romans, who ate it as a bitter vegetable and digestive after a heavy meal. They also appreciated its medicinal properties – Galen recommended it for sciatica and Pliny thought that the root "being chewed fasting, doth fasten teeth". It appears frequently in Anglo-Saxon medical texts and in the writings of the Welsh physicians of Myddfai of the 13th century. It remained popular in folk medicine as a cough and asthma remedy over the centuries, and was grown in cottage gardens. The roots were often candied and old herbals contain many recipes for conserves, cough remedies and tonics made of this plant. John Lindley in his *Flora Medica*, 1838, remarks, "The plant is generally kept in rustic gardens, on account of many traditional virtues."

Description A hardy perennial, with tall, erect, softly hairy stems, to 2 m (6 ft) in height, it has ovate, pointed leaves, toothed at the edges, and terminal yellow flower heads, shaped like shaggy daisies, in late summer.

Habitat/distribution Native to southern Europe and western Asia, naturalized in North America, introduced elsewhere in warm and temperate zones. Found on damp soils, near ruins, in woodland and field edges.

Conserve of elecampane root

Cleanse and scrape the root. Cut them into thin round slices, letting them soke in water over the hot embers for a long space, and boil them till all the liquor be wasted. Beat them in a stone mortar, very fine. Boyle the whole with a like weighte of honey or sugar two or three times over.

All other roots may in like manner be candied and made into Conserve, but far pleasanter in the eating if to the confection a quantity of cinnamon be added. Candy the roots in October.

From *The Gardener's Labyrinth*, by Thomas Hill, 1577.

Growth Grow in rich, moist soil in a sunny position. Propagated by division of roots in spring or autumn, or by seed, which may be slow to germinate.

Parts used Roots, flowers – fresh or dried.

USES Medicinal The constituents of this herb include up to 40 per cent insulin and it is sometimes recommended as a sweetener for diabetics. But its chief use in herbal medicine is for coughs, hay fever, asthma, catarrh and respiratory infections, taken as infusions or decoctions (these must be filtered to exclude irritant fibres). Elecampane is also said to have a beneficial effect on the digestion when taken internally. Applied externally it is said to relieve many skin inflammations and irritations and has sometimes been recommended as an embrocation, or rub, for the relief of sciatica and neuralgia.

IRIDACEAE

Iris germanica var. *florentina*

Orris

History and traditions Orris, taken directly from the Greek *iris*, is the name for the powdered rhizome of the Florentine iris, which has been valued since ancient Egyptian times for its faint violet scent and fixative properties in perfumery and pot-pourri. During the 18th century it was incorporated in many cosmetic powders for wigs, hair and teeth. This variety of iris has been associated with Florence, in Italy, since the 13th century, when it was first cultivated there on a large scale, and can still be seen on the city's coat of arms.

Description A hardy perennial, growing on a stout rhizome, 60–90 cm (2–3 ft) tall, with narrow, sword-shaped leaves. Flowers are white, with outer petals mauve-tinged and yellow-bearded, or occasionally pure white.

Habitat/distribution Native to southern Europe, naturalized in central Europe, the Middle East and northern India, introduced elsewhere. Found in sunny, stony, hilly locations.

Growth Grow in well-drained soil in full sun. Propagated by division of rhizomes and offsets in late summer to early autumn.

Parts used Rhizomes – dried and powdered.

USES Aromatic An indispensable ingredient for making pot-pourri and scented sachet mixtures. It enhances the scent of the other ingredients and gives the whole preparation a more lasting quality. Also used in commercial pot-pourri products and perfumery.

Cosmetic Occasionally seen as an ingredient of home-made toothpowders. A constituent of commercial dental preparations and scented dusting powders.

Other name Florentine iris.

Above *The rhizome of the Florentine iris is dried to make orris root powder.*

CAUTION All parts of the plant are harmful if eaten – the powdered root causes vomiting. May cause skin irritations.

CRUCIFERAE/BRASSICACEAE

Isatis tinctoria

Woad

History and traditions Woad was the source of the blue body paint of the ancient Britons, described by Pliny and other Roman writers. Although largely replaced by indigo, from the subtropical *indigofera* species, in the 1630s and then by synthetics at the end of the 19th century, a factory producing dye from woad existed in England until the 1930s.

Description A hardy biennial (or short-lived perennial if flower heads are cut before seeding), it grows on a taproot, from 50 cm –1.2 m (20 in–4 ft) tall. In the first year it produces a rosette of ovate leaves, from which branching stems with lanceolate leaves topped by racemes of yellow flowers grow in summer, followed by pendulous black seeds.

Habitat/distribution Indigenous to Europe and western Asia, introduced elsewhere. Found on chalky (alkaline) soils in sunny, open sites.

Growth Grow in humus-rich, moist but well-drained soil, in full sun. Propagated by seed sown in containers in spring, maintaining a temperature of 13–18°C (55–64°F) or in autumn for overwintering in a cold frame. Does not flourish in the same ground for more than a few years.

Parts used Leaves – dried, fermented and also powdered for use as a dye. Leaves and roots – dried for Chinese herbal preparations.

USES Medicinal Traditionally a wound-healing herb, as well as a dye, it has long been used in Chinese herbal medicine and recently discovered to have antiviral properties.

General The leaves yield a very fast blue dye.

JUGLANDACEAE

Juglans regia

Walnut

History and traditions The walnut tree has been valued since ancient Greek times for its medicinal properties and many uses. It was known to the Romans as a fertility symbol and Pliny was the first to give directions for making it into a dye for restoring grey hair to brown – a use which lasted into the 20th century.
Description A variable deciduous tree, growing to about 30m (99ft), it has pinnate leaves, with 7–9 ovate leaflets. Male catkins and female flowers are followed by dark green fruits, each containing a wrinkled brown nut.
Habitat/distribution Native to south eastern Europe, Asia, China and the Himalayas, widely introduced elsewhere.
Growth Walnut trees require deep, rich soil and a sunny position.
Parts used Leaves, bark, fruit, oil.

USES Medicinal Infusions of the leaves are taken internally as a digestive tonic and applied externally for cuts, grazes and skin disorders, such as eczema. Decoctions of the inner bark are used for constipation and of the outer nut rind for diarrhoea.
Culinary The nuts are included in many dishes. Oil from the seeds is popular for salads, especially in France.
Cosmetic An infusion of the nut rind is said to make a hair restorer.

CUPRESSACEAE

Juniperus communis

Juniper

History and traditions From biblical times juniper has symbolized protection, and there are many references to people using it for shelter. "Elijah went a day's journey into the wilderness and came and sat down under a juniper tree" (I Kings 19:4). In medieval Europe a fire of juniper wood was burned to discourage evil spirits and protect from plague – and it was thought that felling a tree would bring a death in the family within a year. Its medicinal properties were recorded by the ancient Greek and Roman physicians. Culpeper recommended it, among many other uses, as "a counter-poison, resister of the pestilence and excellent against the biting of venomous beasts". It is famous as a flavouring ingredient of gin – the English word being an abbreviation of "Holland's Geneva" as gin was first known, from the Dutch word for juniper, *jenever.*
Description A hardy, coniferous, evergreen shrub or small tree, 2–4 m (6–13 ft) tall, of upright or prostrate form with needle-like leaves. The small, spherical fruits, borne on the female plants, are green at first, and take two years to ripen to blue-black.
Related species Various junipers were used medicinally by Native Americans, including *J. virginiana*, which produces the extremely toxic red cedar oil. *J. sabina* has poisonous berries and should not be confused with those of *J. communis.*
Habitat/distribution Widely distributed in the northern hemisphere of Europe, Asia and North America on heaths, moors and mountain slopes. Those grown in warmer regions, with longer, sunnier summers, such as the Mediterranean, have sweeter more aromatic berries.

Above *Unripened juniper berries.*

Growth Tolerant of most soils. For berry production grow female plants in a sunny position. Propagated by heel cuttings in late summer, or by seed sown in containers under cover in spring or autumn.
Parts used Fruits – collected from wild plants by beating them from the bushes on to ground-sheets, for use fresh, dried or for distillation of the volatile oil.

USES Medicinal The berries have antiseptic, anti-inflammatory and digestive properties and are thought to be helpful for rheumatism, gout, arthritis and colic.
Culinary Juniper is added to pickles, chutneys, sauces, marinades, meat and game dishes, pâtés and sauerkraut.
General Used to flavour gin. Oil is used in cosmetics and perfumery.

CAUTION The berries are not given to patients with kidney disease, or to pregnant women, as they are a uterine stimulant.

LAURACEAE

Laurus nobilis

Bay

History and traditions This is the plant from which the victor's crown of laurels was made – the Latin name is from *laurus* (praise) and *nobilis* (renowned or noble). It was dedicated to Apollo, Greek god of music, healing, light and truth, and many superstitions arose as to its powers. In the writings of Theophrastus there is a reference to the custom of keeping a bay leaf in the mouth to prevent misfortune and by Roman times it had gained a reputation for preventing lightning strikes – the emperor Tiberius always wore a laurel wreath on his head during thunderstorms as a precaution. Bay trees were also thought to purify the air where they grew. During a plague epidemic, the Roman emperor Claudius moved his court to Laurentium, named after the bay trees that grew there, because of the protection they would provide. Introduced to Britain from the Mediterranean, the sweet bay tree brought its reputation with it. Writing in the 17th century, Culpeper said of it, "Neither witch nor devil, thunder nor lightning will hurt a man where a bay tree is." A wreath of bay leaves was the traditional garnish for the boar's head, centrepiece of the Yuletide feast.

Description An evergreen shrub, or small tree, 3–15 m (10–50 ft) tall, it has aromatic dark-green, glossy ovate leaves. Clusters of small creamy-yellow flowers, opening from tight round buds, appear in spring, followed by purple-black berries.

Related species *L. n.* 'Aurea' is an attractive cultivar with golden-yellow foliage.

Habitat/distribution Native to southern Europe, the Mediterranean and North Africa, introduced and widely grown in other warm temperate regions.

Growth Grow in fertile, reasonably moist but well-drained soil in a sheltered, sunny position. Although frost-hardy, it needs winter protection when immature; and foliage is sometimes damaged by severe frosts and cold winds. Propagated by semi-ripe cuttings in summer.

Parts used Leaves – fresh or dried. Essential oil.

USES Medicinal Bay is not widely used in modern herbal medicine. But studies carried out in the late 1980s on the ability of herbs to inhibit bacterial growth showed bay to be one of the most effective.

Culinary A first-rate culinary herb, a bay leaf is always included in a *bouquet garni,* and adds flavour to marinades, casseroles, stews, soups and dishes requiring a long cooking time. Also used to flavour sweet sauces and as a garnish for citrus sorbets.

Above *Bay leaves for culinary use have a more agreeable, less bitter flavour when dried.*

Below *A standard bay tree in a pot.*

Decorative bay

The Romans embellished their houses with branches of bay for the festival of Saturnalia, celebrated between 17–23 December, to coincide with the winter solstice. With Christianity, bay became a symbol of eternal life, as did other evergreens, and was once widely used as a decoration for homes and churches during the Christmas season.
The aromatic, dark-green leaves make it ideal for festive decorations today:

- Bay leaves make an impressive and welcoming wreath for the front door. Push them into a base of floral foam, in a circular holder, and decorate with sprays of golden cupressus, fir cones, shiny red apples and ribbon.
- A glass bowl filled with floating candles surrounded by bay leaves makes a spectacular, fragrant table-centre.
- A mophead bay (tree-form standard), studded with baubles, makes an attractive alternative to a fir Christmas tree.

LABIATAE/LAMIACEAE

Lavandula

History and traditions The Romans are said to have scented their bathwater with lavender (the Latin name is from *lavare,* to wash) and its inimitable fragrance has ensured its lasting popularity. But its medicinal and insecticidal properties were recognized early and have been largely vindicated since. In 1387 at the court of Charles VI of France all the cushions were stuffed with lavender both for its pleasant scent and to deter insects. It was an essential ingredient of "Four Thieves' Vinegar", which is supposed to have given immunity to those who robbed the bodies of plague victims, and William Turner had the idea "that the flowers of Lavender quilted in a cap and dayly worne are good for all diseases of the head that come of a cold cause and that they comfort the braine very well" (*A New Herball,* 1551). In the early years of this century, René Gattefosse, one of the founders of aromatherapy, discovered the powers of lavender when his badly burned hand was healed after it had been immersed in neat essential oil of lavender. And since then, modern scientific research has established the antiseptic, antibacterial properties of this herb.

Description and species Lavender has been cultivated for so long that accurate identification is not always easy, and most of those grown in gardens are hybrids or cultivars. There are three important groups of lavenders (but this by no means provides a definitive list or complete explanation of lavender nomenclature):

1. ***L. angustifolia*** **(common lavender, English lavender)** – Has small purple flowers, grows to 60–90 cm (2–3 ft), and is said to be effective for medicinal purposes. It has many attractive cultivars, which may not have the same degree of medicinal qualities, but are probably more suitable for fragrant, culinary and decorative purposes. These include ***L. a.*** **'Hidcote'** – with a neat, erect habit and strongly scented, deep violet flowers, 30–60 cm (1–2 ft). ***L. a.*** **'Munstead'** is more compact, 30–45 cm (12–18 in), with paler, purple flowers. ***L. a.*** **'Alba Nana'** is a dwarf, white-flowered cultivar, 15–30 cm (6–12 in). There are also some pink-flowered cultivars, such as ***L. a.*** **'Rosea'**.
2. ***L.*** **x** ***intermedia*** are hybrids of ***L. angustifolia*** and ***L. latifolia*** and include ***L.*** **x** ***intermedia*** **'Grappenhall'**, which has long spikes of lavender-blue flowers, and ***L.*** **x** ***intermedia*** **'Twickel Purple'**, with shorter, bushier flowers.
3. ***L. stoechas*** **(French or Spanish Lavender)** – This is a species that is also considered to have medicinal value – and was probably the type of lavender known to the Greeks and Romans. It has short, fat spikes of dark-purple flowers, topped by butterfly wing bracts, and grows from 30–90 cm (1–3 ft).

Habitat/distribution Lavender is native to the Mediterranean and Middle East, introduced and widely grown elsewhere.

Growth Requires a very well-drained soil and plenty of sun. Lavenders hybridize easily; most do not come true from seed and they are best propagated from heel cuttings taken in mid- to late summer. *L. angustifolia* and cultivars are hardy, so are *L.* x *intermedia* and cultivars. *L. stoechas* is frost-hardy. (Some other species of lavender are tender or half-hardy).

Parts used Flowers – fresh or dried, and the essential oil.

USES Medicinal Infusions of the flowers may be applied as a compress to ease headaches, and are sometimes taken internally (made weak) for anxiety and nervous exhaustion. As an embrocation an external stimulant and antiseptic.

Above left Lavandula angustifolia *'Hidcote'*.

Above right Lavandula angustifolia *'Munstead'*.

Lavandula stoechas

Essential oil (diluted in a carrier oil) is applied to sunburn, burns and scalds, or used as a massage oil for tension headaches, migraine and muscular aches and pains. Inhaling the fragrance of flowers or oil can be very calming, anti-depressive and may help relieve insomnia. The oil is applied to prevent and relieve insect bites and discourages head lice when applied to the comb.

Culinary Flowers are used to flavour sugar for making cakes, biscuits, meringues, ice-creams and desserts. They can be added to vinegar, marmalade or jam, or cooked (tied in a muslin bag) with blackcurrants or soft fruit mixtures.

Cosmetic Infusions of fresh flowers make a fragrant hair rinse, or they can be tied in bags to scent bathwater. Drops of essential oil are also added to baths or included in home-made beauty preparations. Lavender oil is widely used in commercial perfumery.

Aromatic Flowers are dried for pot-pourri and scented sachets.

Top left Lavandula x intermedia *'Twickle Purple'.*

Top right Lavandula stoechas *subsp.* pedunculata *with purple sage in the background.*

Centre right Lavandula angustifolia *'Rosea'.*

Above *Dried lavender is a traditional filling for scented sachets.*

Lavender sachets

The flowers have been used for centuries to scent clothes and deter moths and insects.

- **To make them from your own lavender:**
  First dry the flowers by cutting them, with long stalks, as soon as they are fully open, on a dry day. Tie with raffia or string, in small bunches and hang up in a warm, dry place, with the heads suspended in paper bags – to keep off dust and catch petals as they fall. When fully dry – this will take about a week, depending on humidity and air temperature – rub the petals off the heads.
- **To make the sachets:**
  Cut circles of muslin, or any fine see-through fabric, put a small handful of dried lavender in the centre, gather up to form a bundle and fasten at the neck with an elastic band. Finish with a ribbon.

LABIATAE/LAMIACEAE

Leonurus cardiaca

Motherwort

History and traditions In ancient Greece, this herb was first given to pregnant women to calm their anxieties, which is the origin of its common name. The generic name, *Leonurus,* refers to the plant's supposed resemblance to a lion's tail, but the specific name, *cardiaca,* comes directly from the Greek word for heart because of its widespread use in former times for treating heart palpitations and afflictions. *Macer's Herbal*, 1530 goes further, giving it supernatural powers against wicked spirits.

Description A tall, hardy, strong-smelling perennial, growing to 1.2 m (4 ft), it has square, hollow stems, with deeply lobed, prominently veined leaves, set opposite each other. The mauve-pink, double-lipped flowers appear in the upper leaf axils throughout summer. Widely grown in herb gardens for its attractive foliage.

Habitat/distribution Indigenous to Europe and western Asia. Introduced elsewhere. Found on roadsides and waste grounds on light, calcareous soils.

Growth Grow in moist but well-drained soil in a sunny position. Propagated by seed sown in spring, or by division in spring or autumn.

Parts used Flowering tops – dried for use in infusions, liquid extracts and tinctures.

USES Medicinal Research has shown that this herb does have a beneficial and calming effect on the heart, and is mildly sedative. It also has antibacterial and antifungal properties – but despite its original usage, origins and name, it is not to be given to pregnant women in modern herbal medicine.

UMBELLIFERAE/APIACEAE

Levisticum officinale

Lovage

History and traditions Lovage has been cultivated since the time of Pliny as a seasoning and digestive herb, but has somehow failed to capture popular imagination, and has attracted neither stories nor superstitions. The Greeks and Romans chewed the seed to aid digestion, a practice followed by Benedictine monks of the Middle Ages, and Parkinson refers to its "hot, sharpe, biting taste" and culinary usage: "The Germans and other Nations in times past used both the roote and seede instead of Pepper to season their meates and brothes and found them as comfortable and warming" (*Paradisi,* 1629). An earlier writer mentions lovage as a bath herb for its aromatic scent: "This herbe for hys sweete savoure is used in bathe" (*The Gardener's Labyrinth,* 1577). Its former medicinal uses, referred to by many herbalists, included "expelling stone of the kidneys and bladder". All of which remains broadly valid today, though the leaves are used in preference to seeds and roots for culinary purposes.

Description A hardy herbaceous perennial, growing on deep fleshy roots to 2 m (6 ft) in height, it has glossy, deeply divided leaves with a spicy, celery-like scent, and umbels of undistinguished, dull-yellow flowers in summer, followed by small seeds.

Habitat/distribution Lovage probably originated in Europe, but has long been widely cultivated throughout the world. Rarely found in the wild, except as a garden escape.

Growth A vigorous, spreading plant, it will grow in most soils (except heavy clay), but thrives best in well-manured, moist but well-drained soil, in sun or partial shade. Propagated from seed sown in spring or by division of the roots in spring or autumn.

Parts used Leaves – fresh or dried for culinary use and infusions; stems – fresh; roots, seeds – dried for use in decoctions and other medicinal preparations; essential oil – distilled from leaves and roots.

USES Medicinal It is taken internally for digestive disorders, colic and flatulence, also for cystitis and kidney stones. Lovage tea was formerly taken for rheumatism.

Culinary Leaves are used to flavour soups, stews, meat, fish or vegetable dishes; young shoots and stems are eaten as a vegetable (like braised celery) and may be candied like angelica; seeds are added to biscuits and bread. Lovage cordial used to be a popular drink.

Aromatic Essential oil is used in perfumery, and as a flavouring in the food and drink industry.

LILIACEAE

Lilium candidum

Madonna lily

History and traditions *L. candidum* appears in Cretan frescoes dating to 3000 BC and has been cultivated since at least 1500BC for its scent and its medicinal properties. The flawless white flowers ensured its place as a symbol of purity and its association with the Virgin Mary and it is frequently featured in religious paintings. Shakespeare makes endless references to the whiteness of the "unsullied lily", the "sweetest and the fairest", and Gerard records that the white lily was known as "Juno's Rose" because it grew from her milk, which had fallen to the ground (*The Herball,* 1597). He also writes of using the bulbs of the white lily, mixed with honey, to heal wounds, but makes it clear that a variety of lilies were used for medicinal purposes. He ascribes many virtues to the "red lily", including its ability to remove facial wrinkles, and reveals that Pliny recommended it as a corn remover. *L. candidum* is little used in modern herbalism, but the flowers are cultivated commercially in some countries for their perfumed essence, and it remains a traditional herb garden ornamental.

Description A perennial, growing from a scaly bulb to 1–1.5 m (3–5 ft) in height, it has stiff, erect stems with small, lance-shaped leaves and racemes of 5–20 fragrant, trumpet-shaped, white flowers, tinged inside with yellow, and with bright-yellow anthers. It is the only lily to have overwintering basal leaves.

Habitat/distribution A Mediterranean native, widely cultivated in other countries.

Growth Can be difficult to grow and requires conditions that suit it exactly before it will flourish. All lilies dislike heavy, clay soils.

Parts used Roots, flowers – juice is used fresh in ointments and herbal preparations.

Above *The flawless white blooms of* Lilium candidum *were considered a symbol of purity and innocence from earliest times and were closely associated with the Madonna.*

USES Medicinal It has soothing, healing properties and is used externally (but only rarely) for burns, skin inflammations and disorders.

Growing Madonna lilies

Lilium candidum is one of the oldest flowering plants in cultivation and the flowers are strongly fragrant. These beautiful white lilies can be unpredictable to grow, but the following guidelines will help to ensure success:

- Plant bulbs immediately they arrive. If there is a delay, keep it as short as possible, and meanwhile store bulbs in peat in a dark place – if exposed to light, they soften and deteriorate quickly.
- Good drainage is essential. Prepare soil thoroughly. Dig out to two spades' depth, put in a layer of coarse gravel, then replace the top soil, mixing it with sand and leaf mould. Alternatively, plant in containers, putting in a layer of coarse gravel, topped by a gritty, open compost (soil mix).
- Plant in early autumn (preferably at the beginning of September, no later than October, in the northern hemisphere).
- Bulbs should be only just covered – unlike other lilies, which require deeper planting.
- Once planted and established, do not disturb – Madonna lilies resent being moved.

LINACEAE

Linum usitatissimum

Flax

History and traditions Flax has been an important economic crop since 5000 BC, valued for its fibre in making linen and for its oil-producing seeds. The Bible has many references to linen woven from flax, and both seeds and cloth have been found in Egyptian tombs. In medieval Europe it was promoted by the Emperor Charlemagne for the health-giving properties of the seeds and there are detailed descriptions in old herbals of the process of turning flax stems into fibre for making clothing, sheets, sails, fishing nets, thread, rope, sacks, bags and purses. Many superstitions have arisen, especially concerning its cultivation: sitting on the seed bag three times and facing east before planting, ringing church bells on Ascension Day and jumping over midsummer fires were all thought to ensure a good crop – and of course the seeds provided protection from witchcraft. It has also been a valued medicinal herb since Hippocrates recommended it for colds and is still used in herbal medicine.

Description A hardy, slender annual, about 90 cm–1.2 m (3–4 ft) in height. It has narrow, lanceolate, greeny-grey leaves and simple, five-petalled, pale-blue flowers borne in summer, followed by spherical seed capsules, rich in oil.

Related species *L. usitatissimum* is thought to be a cultivar of *L. bienne* in the distant past. Tall cultivars have been developed for textiles, and shorter ones for the production of seeds for linseed oil. *L. perenne,* grown in Europe and North America, is a perennial species. *L. catharticum* (purging flax) is a white-flowered annual with oval leaves; used homeopathically to treat bronchitis and piles.

Habitat/distribution Probably of Middle Eastern origin, it is widely distributed in temperate and subtropical regions of the world and found as a cultivated escape on sunny waste ground and waysides.

Growth Grow in dry, sandy soil in full sun. Propagated from seed sown *in situ* – does not respond well to transplantation. Sow in late spring or early summer.

Parts used Whole plant – used fresh in infusions, cut after flowering for fibre; seeds – collected when ripe – dried for use whole, in infusions and other preparations, or extracted for linseed oil.

USES Medicinal Seeds are used as laxatives, in infusions and macerations for coughs, sore throats and gastric disorders, in poultices for boils and abscesses. Linseed oil contains linolenic essential fatty acids, necessary for many bodily functions, as well as vitamins A, B, D, E, minerals and amino acids. It is said to be helpful for many disorders, including rheumatoid arthritis, menstrual problems and skin complaints.

General Stem varieties are soaked ('retted') in water to release fibres for making linen cloth. Linseed oil from seed varieties is one of the most important commercial drying oils, used in paints, varnishes and putty.

Other name Linseed.

CAUTION Contains traces of prussic acid, but this plant is not thought to be harmful unless taken in very large doses. Some *Linum* species have been suspected of poisoning stock in Australia. Artists' linseed oil should not be taken medicinally.

CAMPANULACEAE

Lobelia inflata

Indian tobacco

History and traditions This North American plant gained its common name from the local tradition of smoking it to relieve chest infections and asthma. It was enthusiastically adopted by early settlers as a cure-all for a wide variety of complaints and promoted in the early 19th century by the herbalist Samuel Thomson, who was charged with murder after one of his patients died from its effects. The generic name *Lobelia* (there are over 350 species) is named after the Flemish botanist Matthias de L'Obel (1538–1616). The specific name is a reference to the inflation of the seed capsule as it ripens.

Description A hardy annual, 20–60 cm (8–24 in), it has hairy stems and ovate leaves, toothed at the edges. Inconspicuous flowers borne in terminal racemes are pale violet, tinged with pink, followed by two-celled, oval capsules.

Habitat/distribution Native to North America.

Growth Grow in rich, moist soil in full sun or partial shade. Propagated by seed.

Parts used Whole plant – cut when flowering.

USES Medicinal It contains alkaloids that increase the rate of respiration and induce vomiting. It is also an expectorant and emetic. In small doses it dilates the bronchioles and is used for conditions such as bronchitis, asthma and pleurisy, but is for use by qualified practitioners only. Used in proprietary cough medicines.

CAUTION Poisonous and can cause fatalities.

CAPRIFOLIACEAE

Lonicera

History and traditions Various species of honeysuckle have been used since ancient Greek times for their medicinal properties. Dioscorides is quoted by Gerard as recommending the seeds for "removing weariness" and "helping the shortness and difficulty of breathing" and a syrup of the flowers for diseases of lung and spleen. Little used medicinally today, honeysuckle keeps its place in the herb garden as a fragrant climber, memorably described by Shakespeare as the "lush woodbine" and "sweet honeysuckle" which "over-canopied" Titania's bower (*A Midsummer Night's Dream*). The name honeysuckle comes from the old practice of sucking the sweet nectar from the flowers.

Description and species The two species that were most often recommended for medicinal purposes are ***L. periclymenum*** **(woodbine, wild or common honeysuckle)** – Has whorls of very fragrant, creamy-white to yellow, tubular two-lipped flowers, followed by red berries. ***L. caprifolium*** **(Italian, Dutch or perfoliate honeysuckle)** – Has upper leaves surrounding the stem and creamy-white to pink flowers. Both are fully hardy, *L. periclymenum* grows to 7 m (23 ft), *L. caprifolium* to 6 m (19 ft). ***L. japonica*** **(Japanese honeysuckle)** – Often has violet-tinged white flowers, which are followed by black berries.

Habitat/distribution Widely distributed in the northern hemisphere, in woodlands, hedgerows and rocky hillsides.

Growth Grow in fertile, well-drained soil in full sun or partial shade. Propagated by seed sown in late summer to autumn in containers and overwintered in a cold frame, or by semi-ripe cuttings taken in summer. Prune out straggly or overgrown branches.

Parts used Flowering stems.

USES Medicinal *L. caprifolium* and *L. periclymenum* were formerly used for their expectorant, laxative properties. *L. japonica* (*jin yin hua*) is used in traditional Chinese medicine for clearing toxins from the system.

CAUTION Honeysuckle berries are poisonous.

Top right *A cultivar of* Lonicera periclymenum.

Above *Honeysuckle flowers contain sweet-tasting nectar.*

LABIATAE/LAMIACEAE

Lycopus europaeus

Gipsyweed

History and traditions This herb is said to have gained its name because gipsies used it to stain their skins darker. It was also effective in dyeing fabrics and at one time was a valuable medicinal plant.

Description A perennial, mint-like herb, but with no aroma, it grows on a creeping rootstock to about 60cm (2ft) in height. It has single stems with opposite, deeply-toothed, pointed leaves and whorls of small, pale-mauve flowers in the leaf axils in late summer.

Related species *L. virginicus* (Virginia bugle weed) also known sometimes as gipsyweed is native to North America. It is a very similar plant to *L. europaeus* and shares the same properties.

Habitat/distribution *L. europaeus* is a native of Europe and western Asia.

Parts used Whole flowering plant – it can be used fresh or dried.

USES Medicinal Gipsyweed is reputed to have sedative properties. It was used in the past for the control of internal haemorrhages, including excessive menstrual bleeding; and it was also thought to be effective for other conditions such as an overactive thyroid.

General It produces a black or dark-grey dye on woollen and linen fabrics.

LYTHRACEAE

Lythrum salicaria

Purple loosestrife

History and traditions The name loosestrife is connected to this herb's old reputation for soothing ill-behaved animals. Gerard, in his *Herball* of 1597, writes of it "appeasing the strife and unruliness which falleth out among oxen at the plough, if it is put about their yokes". As it was also supposed to drive away flies and gnats, perhaps this was the reason for its calming influence. The generic name is from the Greek, *luthron*, meaning blood, a reference to the colour of the flowers, and it was considered by herbalists of old to be effective against internal haemorrhages, excessive menstruation and nosebleeds. John Lindley, in *Flora Medica*, 1838, refers to it as "an astringent, which has been recommended in inveterate cases of diarrhoea," and it was often used in his day to treat outbreaks of cholera.

Description Purple loosestrife is a perennial which grows on a creeping rhizome with erect stems reaching 60cm–1.5 m (2–5 ft) in height. It has long, lanceolate leaves and crimson-purple flowers borne on whorled spikes in mid to late summer.

Habitat/distribution A European native, it occurs widely in Asia, northern Africa, Australia and North America. It is usually found in wet and marshy places.

Growth It grows best in moist to wet soil in sun or partial shade and is propagated by seed or division in autumn or spring. It often self-seeds and spreads rapidly. It is classed as a noxious weed in some countries and imports of the plants and seeds are forbidden.

Parts used The whole flowering plant – it is used fresh or dried in infusions, decoctions and ointments.

USES Medicinal It has been found in modern research to have antibacterial properties and is still recommended by modern herbalists for diarrhoea and dysentery as well as for haemorrhages and excessive menstrual flow. It is said to be soothing, when applied externally, to sores, ulcers, skin irritations and eczema.

Lythrum salicaria

MALVACEAE

Malva sylvestris

Mallow

History and traditions The common mallow was cultivated by the Romans as a medicinal and culinary herb, the leaves being cooked as a vegetable and seeds added to salads and sauces. By the 16th century it had gained a reputation as a cure-all, commended for its gentle purgative action, a process that was thought to rid the body of disease. But its culinary uses remained paramount, and herbals and household books of the period are full of recipes for cooking the leaves with butter and vinegar, making "suckets" (candy) of the stalks, and, even more imaginatively, cutting and rolling them into balls and passing them off as green peas (*Receipt Book of John Nott,* 1723). The generic name, *Malva,* meaning soft, refers to the downy leaves and soothing properties of the plant.

Description A perennial, growing from 45–90 cm (18 in–3 ft), it has much-branched erect or trailing stems, with 5–7-lobed leaves, and pink, five-petalled flowers, streaked with darker veins, borne throughout summer.

Related species *M. moschata* (musk mallow) grows to 90 cm (3 ft) and has purple-spotted stems, heart-shaped basal leaves and narrowly divided upper leaves, both scented faintly with musk. Solitary pale pink flowers are borne in the leaf axils. It is weaker in effect than *M. sylvestris,* but with the same uses. The closely related plant *Althaea officinalis* (marsh mallow) is considered more medicinally effective than either of the *Malva.*

Above *A flower of the musk mallow,* Malva moschata.

Habitat/distribution Native to Europe, western Asia and North America. Found at field edges, embankments and on waste ground, in porous soils and sunny situations.

Growth Grow in well-drained to dry soil, in a sunny position. Propagated by seed sown in the spring or by division of the roots in late autumn or early spring.

Parts used Leaves, flowers – used fresh or dried. Fruits (seed capsules) – picked unripe and used fresh.

USES Medicinal Mallow contains a high proportion of an emollient mucilage, reduces inflammation and calms irritated tissues. Infusions are taken internally for coughs, sore throats and bronchitis. The leaves are applied externally as a poultice for skin complaints, eczema and insect bites. It is also an expectorant herb and large doses can have a laxative effect.

Culinary Young leaves and shoots contain vitamins A, B^1, B^2 and C and can be eaten raw in salads or cooked as vegetables. Unripe fruits are sometimes added to salads.

Other name Common mallow.

Malva moschata *f.* alba

SOLANACEAE

Mandragora officinarum

Mandrake

History and traditions Mandrake has attracted more stories and superstitions than almost any other herb – perhaps because of its hallucinogenic properties, coupled with its strange appearance and forked roots, fancifully thought to resemble the human form. Closely related to *Atropa belladonna* and *Hyoscyamus niger* (henbane), it contains the toxic alkaloids atropine and hyoscyamine and has been used since the ancient Greek and Roman period as a powerful sedative, when it was first found to deaden the pain of surgery. An early introduction to Britain, it features in many Anglo-Saxon medicinal texts and was mentioned by Turner in 1551 for its anaesthetic properties. Just holding the fruit (mandrake apple) in the hand was said to be a cure for insomnia. At the end of the 19th century it became an official homeopathic preparation but is rarely used today and retains its place as a "herb" because of its historical interest.

Description A low growing perennial, 15 cm (6 in) in height, it has a basal rosette of broad, oval, veined and rough-textured leaves, with wavy margins, which start erect and spread flat as they grow. Clusters of bell-shaped, greenish-white flowers, flushed with purple, arise from the base and are followed by large, spherical green fruits ripening to yellow.

Habitat/distribution Originated in the Himalayas and southeast Mediterranean, introduced into western Europe, Britain and other countries. Found on sunny sites, in poor, sandy soil.

Above *Mandrake fruits, sometimes known as the devil's apples.*

Growth Although hardy to -10°C (14°F), mandrake needs protection from prolonged cold and wet weather in winter. Grow it in a sheltered, sunny spot such as at the base of a wall, or in a rockery, in well-drained, reasonably fertile soil. It resents disturbance once properly established and is propagated by seed in autumn, root cuttings in winter.

Parts used Roots.

USES Medicinal Formerly used as a sedative and painkiller.

Other name Devil's apples.

CAUTION A dangerously poisonous plant, which should not be used internally or externally. Can be fatal. Subject to legal restrictions in some countries.

Mandrake myths

One of the most popular superstitions about mandrake was that its unearthly shrieks, when pulled up, sent people mad if it did not kill them. As Shakespeare records: "And shrieks like mandrakes torn out of the earth/That living mortals hearing them run mad" (*Romeo and Juliet*) or "Would curses kill as doth the mandrakes groan" (*Henry VI*, Part 2).

An ingenious way to avoid death on digging up the plant was to tie it to a hungry dog, with a dish of meat just out of reach, so that he would die instead as he pulled the root from the ground. Once dug up it could be handled with impunity.

The fancied resemblance of the roots to people meant they were sought after as amulets to protect from witchcraft and bring prosperity. This led to a lucrative scam (scathingly described by Turner in his *New Herbal*, 1551) of false mandrake manikins being sculpted out of bryony roots and sold to the gullible at high prices. The sensible Gerard, too, dismissed the mandrake myths with these words: "There have been many ridiculous tales brought up of this plant, whether of old wives or runnegate surgeons, or phisick mongers, I know not, all which dreames and old wives tales you shall from henceforth cast out your bookes of memorie" (*The Herball,* 1597).

LABIATAE/LAMIACEAE

Marrubium vulgare

Horehound

History and traditions This herb has been known since Egyptian times, and is thought to be one of the bitter herbs which the Jews consumed at the Feast of the Passover. The generic name *Marrubium* comes from the Hebrew word *marrob* – a bitter juice. Its reputation as a remedy for coughs and colds goes back to at least Pliny's time. Several 16th-century herbalists, including Gerard, use almost the same words to recommend a syrup of the fresh leaves in sugar as a "most singular remedie against the cough and wheezing of the lungs." Horehound candy was still being made to the old recipes well into the 20th century.

Description A hardy perennial growing to 60 cm (2 ft), with erect, branched stems and greeny-grey, soft, downy, ovate leaves, bluntly toothed, arranged opposite. Whorls of small, white, tubular flowers appear in the leaf axils in summer.

Related species *Ballota nigra,* although from a different genus, is known as black horehound, and was once used for similar purposes. However, it has an unpleasant smell and is considered less effective and has been superseded by *M. vulgare*.

Habitat/distribution Native to Europe, northern Africa and Asia, introduced elsewhere. Found on dry grassland, pastures and field edges.

Growth Grows in any soil and prefers a sunny situation. Propagated from seed sown in spring, but can be slow to germinate, or by division of roots in spring. (It is under statutory control as a weed in Australia and New Zealand.)

Parts used Flowering stems – fresh or dried.

USES Medicinal Taken as an infusion for coughs, colds and chest infections. Combined with hyssop, sage or thyme to make a gargle for sore throats. Made into cough candy.

Above Marrubium vulgare, *or white horehound.*

Top right and right Ballota nigra, *or black horehound, is considered inferior as a medicinal plant.*

Horehound recipes

• **Horehound and ginger tea – for a cold**

15 g/½ oz fresh horehound leaves
1 tsp powdered ginger
600 ml/1 pint/ 2 ½ cups boiling water
honey to taste

Put the roughly chopped leaves into a pot or jug with the ginger, pour in the boiling water, cover and leave to infuse for 5–7 minutes. Strain off the leaves and sweeten with honey to taste before drinking.

• **A Recipe for horehound candy from *The Family Herbal* (1810)**

Boil some horehound till the juice is extracted. Boil up some sugar to a feather height, add your juice to the sugar, and let it boil till it is again the same height. Stir it till it begins to grow thick, then pour it on to a dish and dust it with sugar and when fairly cool cut into squares. Excellent sweetmeat for colds and coughs.

MYRTACEAE

Melaleuca alternifolia

Tea-tree

History and traditions Tea-tree was named by Captain Cook's crew when, following local custom, they drank it as a tea substitute. The Australian Aborigines used it medicinally and in World War II tea tree oil, distilled from *M. alternifolia,* was used in Australia as a powerful germicide. It has since gained ground in herbal medicine for its remarkable healing properties.
Description Melaleucas are half-hardy to tender evergreen trees, 15–40 m (50–130 ft), with thin, peeling, corky bark, narrow, pointed, leathery leaves and bottle-brush-shaped flowers.
Related species Several species of melaleuca are used medicinally. *M. leucadendron* produces distilled cajuput oil, which has similar uses to eucalyptus oil. *M. viridiflora* is the source of niaouli oil used in perfumery.
Habitat/distribution Native to Australia and Malaysia, introduced in other tropical regions. Often found in swampy areas.
Growth *M. alternifolia* is half-hardy, *M. leucadendron* is tender. Grow in moisture-retentive to wet soil, in full sun. They must be grown as conservatory plants in cool, temperate regions. Propagated by seed or by semi-ripe cuttings.
Parts used Essential oil.

USES Medicinal Strongly antiseptic, antibacterial and antifungal, tea-tree oil is used diluted in a carrier oil and applied externally for healing cuts, burns, stings, insect bites, acne, and athlete's foot. It is also said to be effective against warts, verrucas and head lice eggs when used undiluted.
General A constituent of many pharmaceutical and cosmetic industry products.

LEGUMINOSAE/PAPILIONACEAE

Melilotus officinalis

Melilot

History and traditions Once popular as a strewing herb for the haylike scent it develops when drying, due to the coumarin content, the name of the genus means "honey-lotus" for the sweet smell of its nectar and it is very attractive to bees. It was used in the Greek physician Galen's time, AD 130–201, as an ingredient of ointments for reducing swellings, tumours and inflammations, and appears in later European herbals for similar purposes. Culpeper adds that "the head often washed with the distilled water of the herb and flowers is good for those who swoon, also to strengthen the memory".
Description An erect, straggly biennial, 60 cm–1.2 m (2–4 ft) high, it has ridged, branched stems with trifoliate leaves and narrow ovate leaflets. The yellow, honey-scented flowers are borne in slender axillary racemes, from midsummer to autumn.
Habitat/distribution Native to Europe and Asia, naturalized in North America. Found in dry, chalky embankments, wastelands and roadsides.
Growth Grow in well-drained to dry soil, in a sunny situation. Propagated by seed sown in spring or autumn.
Parts used: Flowering stems – dried for use in herbal preparations.

Melilotus officinalis

USES Medicinal An aromatic herb with sedative, anti-inflammatory properties, it was formerly taken as an infusion or tincture for insomnia, tension headaches and painful menstruation, and applied externally to wounds and skin inflammations. It also has a reputation for helping to prevent thrombosis and has been used for bronchial complaints and catarrh.
Aromatic It has insect-repellent properties and the dried herb is sometimes included in scented sachets for the wardrobe.
Other names Yellow melilot and yellow sweet clover.

CAUTION Dicoumarol, a powerful anticlotting factor, is sometimes produced if fermentation takes place during the drying process; it is poisonous in excess and harmful to sheep and cattle.

LABIATAE/LAMIACEAE

Melissa officinalis

Lemon balm

History and traditions Lemon balm has been cultivated as a bee plant for over 2000 years, bunches being put into empty hives to attract swarms. It is thought that that the leaves contain the same terpenoids as found in glands of honey bees. The Arab physicians of the 1st and 2nd centuries are credited with introducing it as an antidepressant medicinal herb. John Parkinson wrote that "the herb without question is an excellent help to comfort the heart" (*Paradisi*, 1629) and many of the old herbalists refer to it as driving away "all melancholy and sadnesse". It has been taken as a calming tea, for its gently sedative effects ever since. Unsubstantiated stories of regular drinkers of balm tea living into their hundreds have been perpetuated by modern herbal writers.

Description A vigorous, bushy perennial, 30–80 cm (12–32 in) in height, it has strongly lemon-scented, rough-textured, ovate, toothed leaves. Inconspicuous clusters of pale-yellow flowers appear in the leaf axils in late summer.

Related species *M. officinalis* 'Aurea' is a cultivar with bright gold and green variegated leaves. It is inclined to revert as the plant matures, so cut back after flowering to encourage new variegated growth. *M. officinalis* 'All Gold' has bright-yellow foliage, but should be planted in partial shade, as it is inclined to scorch in a position where it receives full sun.

Habitat/distribution Native to southern and central Europe, introduced and widely distributed in northern temperate zones. Often found as a garden escape.

Growth Grows in any soil in sun or partial shade. Spreads and self-seeds freely. The easiest method of propagation is by division in spring. The species can be grown from seed, but cultivars must be vegetatively propagated.

Parts used Leaves – best used fresh, as scent and therapeutic properties are lost when dried and stored; essential oil – distilled from leaves.

USES Medicinal Lemon balm has sedative, relaxing, digestive properties and infusions are taken internally for nervous anxiety, depression, tension headaches and indigestion. It also has insect-repellent properties, is antiviral and antibacterial and is applied externally, in infusions, poultices or ointments, for sores, skin irritations, insect bites and stings. The essential oil is used in aromatherapy for anxiety states.

Culinary Fresh leaves add lemon flavour to salads, soups, sauces, stuffings, poultry game and fish dishes, desserts, cordials, liqueurs and wine cups.

Above centre Melissa officinalis *'All Gold'*.

Above Melissa officinalis *'Aurea'*.

Recipes for lemon balm

- **Chicken lemon balm**
  Use handfuls of the fresh leaves to stuff the body cavity of a chicken, and sit it on a further bed of leaves before roasting it, to keep flesh moist and impart a subtle lemon flavour.
- **Orange and lemon balm salad**
  Snip fresh lemon balm over peeled, thinly sliced oranges, sprinkled with a mixture of fresh orange and lemon juice, sweetened with honey.
- **Carmelite cordial**
  Lemon balm was one of the chief ingredients of Carmelite water, which also included lemon peel, nutmeg and angelica root – said to be the favourite tipple of the Holy Roman Emperor, Charles V (1500–1558).

LABIATAE/LAMIACEAE

Mentha

History and traditions The Romans made great use of mint for its clean, fresh scent, putting it in their bathwater and making it into perfumes. The poet Ovid describes scouring the boards with "green mint" before setting out food for the gods, and Pliny has been attributed with the view that the smell of mint stirs up the taste buds "to a greedy desire of meat". This conflicts with a modern study, carried out in the United States in 1994, which found that the smell of mint helped alleviate hunger pangs of subjects on diets. The Romans introduced spearmint to Britain, where it soon became established and is mentioned in medieval texts and plant lists. In the late 16th century, Gerard talks of its popularity as a strewing herb "in chambers and places of recreation". It is now one of the most popular herbs worldwide.

Habitat/distribution Mints are widely distributed in Europe, Asia and Africa, introduced and naturalized elsewhere, often found in damp or wet soils. Cultivated as a crop in many countries including Europe, North America, the Middle East and Asia.

Species There are 25 species of mint in all, but they are often variable and individual plants can be difficult to identify because mints hybridize readily both in the wild and under cultivation. The following hardy perennials are top favourites for the herb garden. Most are vigorous, the variegated ones less so, and spread rapidly on creeping rootstocks.

M. x *gracilis* 'Variegata' (gingermint) – Has gold and green variegated, smooth, ovate leaves, scented with a hint of ginger, and grows 30 cm–1 m (1–3 ft) tall. Tiny, pale lilac flowers are borne in whorls in the leaf axils in mid- to late summer.

M. x *piperita* (peppermint) – Has dark-green (often tinged with purple) lanceolate to ovate, toothed leaves and whorls of pale pink flowers in summer. It grows to 30–90 cm (1–3 ft) tall. Peppermint is a variable hybrid of *M. spicata* and *M. aquatica*, sometimes assigned two different forms as black peppermint, *M.* x *piperita* f. *rubescens,* and white peppermint, *M.* x *piperita* f. *pallescens.* It is rich in menthol, which gives it the characteristic cooling, slightly numbing, peppermint taste, but is too dominant for general cookery and is used to flavour sweet foods.

M. x *piperita citrata* (eau-de-Cologne mint) (Bergamot, Lemon or Orange Mint) – A cultivar with large, toothed, ovate leaves, 30–90 cm (1–3 ft) tall. The scent is reminiscent of lavender water with citrus overtones.

M. pulegium (pennyroyal) – There are creeping (to 10 cm/4 in) and upright (to 40 cm/16 in) varieties. Both have small, elliptic to ovate, usually smooth-edged leaves, and prolific, distinctive whorls of mauve flowers in the leaf axils. The high concentration of pulegone gives it a pleasantly antiseptic smell, but it is toxic in very large doses and abortifacient.

*Mentha requienii (*Corsican mint) – A creeping, mat-forming mint, 2.5–10 cm (1–4 in), with very small, smooth and shiny, rounded leaves and tiny, mauve flowers in summer. It makes a good ground cover herb for a damp, shady situation.

M. spicata (spearmint) – This has bright-green, wrinkled, finely toothed leaves, with a fresh, uncomplicated, not too overpowering mint scent. White or pale-mauve flowers are borne in terminal spikes in mid- to late summer. A popular culinary mint, used since the time of the Romans; 30–90 cm (1–3 ft) tall.

M. suaveolens 'Variegata' (variegated applemint also known as pineapple mint) – This has soft, downy, cream and white variegated leaves and a sweet, apple scent. 30–90 cm (1–3 ft) tall. Pineapple mint makes a very attractive ornamental and container plant.

M x *villosa* f. *alopecuroides* (Bowles' Mint) – Formerly known as *M. rotundifolia* var. 'Bowles', it is in fact a variety of a sterile hybrid between *M. spicata* and *M. suaveolens*. The rounded, ovate, toothed leaves are greyish-green; soft and downy, lilac-pink flowers are borne in terminal, branched spikes. It is popular for culinary use, the clean mint flavour has overtones of apple.

Growth Mints grow best in rich, damp soil and partial shade. Most do not come true from seed or are sterile hybrids. They are easily propagated by division or by taking root cuttings from early spring, throughout the growing season.

Parts used Peppermint, spearmint – leaves, essential oil; pennyroyal, gingermint, Bowles' mint, eau-de-Cologne mint – leaves.

USES Medicinal Peppermint can be taken as a tea for colds and to aid digestion. The essential oil has decongestant, antiseptic, mildly anaesthetic effects and is used externally, often as an inhalant to relieve colds, chest infections, catarrh and asthma. It also has insect-repellent properties. Excess use may cause allergic reactions. Pennyroyal is taken internally as an infusion for indigestion and colic. Stimulates the uterus and is not given to pregnant women. Toxic in large doses. An insect-repellent plant, used to deter ants when planted in the garden. Spearmint can be taken as a tea for digestive disorders; it is less pungent than peppermint and a non-irritant.

Culinary Spearmint and Bowles' mint are used in sauces, mint jelly, to flavour yoghurt as a savoury dip or side dish, in salads, rice dishes, meat, fish or vegetable dishes, as a garnish, to flavour herb teas and drinks. Peppermint is used to flavour sweets and chocolates, icings, cakes, desserts, ice creams, cordials and as a tea. Gingermint leaves may be floated in fruit cups and summer drinks. Pennyroyal is traditionally used to flavour black pudding (an old name is pudding grass).

Aromatic Any of the fragrant mints, dried or as essential oils, may be added to pot-pourri, fresh leaves or essential oils are added to baths, cosmetics and fragrant household preparations.

General Essential oils are used in food, pharmaceutical and cosmetic industries.

Top, from left to right Mentha x gracilis *(gingermint);* M. x piperita *f.* rubescens *(black peppermint)*; M. x piperita *f.* citrata *(eau-de-Cologne mint);* M. pulegium *(pennyroyal);* M. requienii *(Corsican mint);* M. spicata *(spearmint).*

Above right M. suaveolens *'Variegata' (variegated applemint).*

Above Mentha suaveolens, *or apple mint.*

LABIATAE/LAMIACEAE

Monarda didyma

Bergamot

History and traditions The Monarda or horse-mint genus is named after Nicholas Monardes, author of *Joyfull Newes Out of the Newe Found Worlde,* 1577. Native Americans used several monarda species medicinally. *M. didyma* became known as "Oswego tea" after the Oswego river, near Lake Ontario, where it was found growing by European settlers and its refreshing taste made it a good tea substitute. The scent of both flowers and leaves is similar to the Bergamot orange, which is how it gained its popular name.
Description An aromatic, hardy perennial, 40–90 cm. (16 in–3 ft) in height, it has soft, downy, greyish-green, ovate leaves, with serrated edges, and red or mauve flowers in solitary terminal whorls in late summer.
Related species: *M. fistulosa* (wild bergamot) is closely related and has purple flowers – also called "Oswego tea". There are many attractive hybrids including 'Cambridge Scarlet' (above) and 'Croftway Pink'.
Habitat/distribution Native of eastern North America, found in damp woodlands, introduced and widely grown elsewhere.
Growth Grow in humus-rich, damp soil. Prefers partial shade, but tolerates full sun if kept moist. Prone to mildew in dry conditions. Propagated by division or by seed sown in spring.
Parts used Leaves, flowers – fresh or dried.

USES Medicinal Taken as a digestive tea.
Culinary Fresh leaves are added to wine cups, fruit drinks and to oriental tea to give it an "Earl Grey" flavour.
Aromatic Flowers are dried for pot-pourri.

RUTACEAE

Murraya koenigii

Curry leaves

History and traditions The Indian name for the leaves of this shrub is "curry patta" and they have long been used in southern India and Sri Lanka in local dishes as well as for their medicinal properties. Curry leaves are not widely used in the West because much of the flavour is lost on drying – but they are imported fresh by wholesalers for use in the food industry.
Description An aromatic, more or less deciduous shrub, growing to 6 m (20 ft) in height, it has bright-green pinnate leaves, with smooth, ovate leaflets. Clusters of small white flowers are followed by edible berries, which turn from green to purple as they ripen.
Habitat/distribution Native to southern India and Sri Lanka, introduced and grown in all tropical zones, found in rich soils.
Growth A tender, tropical shrub, it is grown in humus-rich, moist but well-drained soil in sun or partial shade. Propagated by seed or cuttings.
Parts used Leaves – picked and used fresh; seeds; essential oil – distilled from leaves.

USES Medicinal Contains alkaloids with anti-fungal activity. The juice of the leaves contains vitamin C and minerals, including calcium, phosphorus and iron and is used as a herbal tonic for digestive disorders. Eating the fresh leaves is reputed by some to help prevent the onset of diabetes and to encourage weight loss. Juice of the crushed berries, mixed with lime juice, is applied to insect bites and stings.
Culinary Used in Indian cookery to flavour a variety of dishes, including curries and chutneys.
General Essential oil used in the soap industry.

MYRICACEAE

Myrica gale

Bog myrtle

History and traditions This was once an indispensable plant in much of northern Europe for its many household uses. It was used as a hops substitute to flavour beer and improve its foaming; the fruits were boiled to produce wax for making candles; it made a yellow dye; and its insect-repellent properties meant it was often put into mattress stuffings, which gave it the former name "flea wood".
Description Hardy, deciduous shrub, growing to 1.5 m (5 ft), it has narrow, bright-green, oval to lanceolate leaves and yellowish-green flowers, borne in dense catkins in late spring to early summer, followed by flattened yellow-brown fruits.
Habitat/distribution Native to North America, northwest Europe and northeast Siberia, found in wet heathlands.
Growth Prefers a damp, acid soil (tolerates boggy conditions) and partial shade, but can be grown in full sun. Propagated by separating suckers, by cuttings, or by seed sown in spring or autumn.
Parts used Leaves – dried.

USES Aromatic Strongly insecticidal. Dried leaves can be added to insect-repellent mixtures and sachets.
Other name Sweet gale.

MYRISTICACEAE

Myristica fragrans

Nutmeg/Mace

History and traditions Nutmeg and mace are different parts of the same fruit of the nutmeg tree. The scent of the nutmeg has variously been compared with myrrh and musk. The common name comes from "nut" and the Latin, *muscus,* or old French, *mugue,* meaning musk. Nutmegs were probably introduced to Europe in about the 6th century by Arab or Indian traders, who brought them to the Mediterranean from the Far East. The Portuguese set up a trade monopoly in this valuable spice at the beginning of the 16th century after taking possession of the Moluccan islands where the trees grew. This was taken over by the Dutch, who limited cultivation of nutmeg to the Moluccas and continued the monopoly into the 19th century. Today nutmeg is widely grown in tropical regions, with Indonesia and the West Indies as leading world producers. It has been used over the centuries as a medicinal tonic and culinary spice, its hallucinogenic properties have long been recognized and it acquired a reputation as an effective aphrodisiac.

Description An evergreen dioecious tree, usually 9–12 m (29–39 ft) but occasionally up to 15–20 m (49–65 ft) tall, with glossy, pointed oval leaves and inconspicuous pale yellow flowers, male in clusters with numerous fused stamens, the female solitary or in groups. Brownish-yellow globular fruits each containing an ovoid brown seed (nutmeg), surrounded by a shredded crimson aril (mace), do not appear before the tree is 9–10 years old.
Habitat Indigenous to Molucca (Maluku) and Banda islands, now widely grown in Indonesia, Sri Lanka, India, the West Indies, Brazil and elsewhere in tropical zones, frequently on volcanic soils in areas of high humidity.
Growth A tender, tropical tree, grown in sandy, humus-rich soil. Prefers shade or partial shade. Propagated by seed or cuttings. May be grown as a conservatory or hothouse plant in temperate regions, with a minimum temperature of 18°C (64°F) and a humid atmosphere.
Parts used Seed (nutmeg), aril (mace) – dried and used whole or powdered; volatile oil distilled from fruits; fatty oil compressed from mace (nutmeg butter, mace oil).

USES Medicinal Nutmeg is taken internally, in small doses, for digestive disorders, nausea and insomnia. Applied externally for toothache and rheumatic aches and pains.

CAUTION Nutmeg should always be used sparingly. It contains a toxic compound, myristicin, whose chemical structure has similarities with mescaline, and can cause hallucinations and convulsions even in moderate doses.

Above *The outer shell splits to reveal the nutmeg seed, enclosed in a red aril.*

Above left *Whole nutmeg fruits on the tree.*

Culinary Both nutmeg and mace are ground or grated and used in a wide range of sweet and savoury dishes, but mace is less pungent. Added to soups, sauces, milk and cheese dishes, meat and vegetable dishes, biscuits, fruit cakes, puddings and drinks.
General Volatile oil and fatty oil (nutmeg butter) are used in the pharmaceutical and perfumery industries.

Top *Nutmegs with outer covering of mace (dried aril).*

Centre *Ground nutmeg.*

Right *Dried nutmeg seeds.*

UMBELLIFERAE/APIACEAE

Myrrhis odorata

Sweet cicely

History and traditions The Latin name refers to the sweet aniseed smell of this herb, said to resemble myrrh – *Myrrhis* comes from the Greek word for fragrance. It is probable that the "wild chervil", or "sweet chervil", referred to in old herbals is the same plant. *The Leech Book of Bald, c.* AD 950, gives a salve of wild chervil for the treatment of tumours. It was used as a medieval strewing herb, and the roots and leaves were cooked as a pot-herb. Recent scientific research has found that compounds isolated from *M. odorata* are related in chemical structure to podophyllotoxin, the highly poisonous active ingredient of *Podophyllum peltatum* (American may-apple). However, this does not mean that *M. odorata* as a whole plant, or the isolated compounds, have the same high level of toxicity as *Podophyllum peltatum*, and it is not thought to be harmful as a culinary herb.

Description A vigorous, hardy, herbaceous perennial, with a strong taproot, grows 90 cm–1.2 m (3–4 ft) tall, with hollow stems and soft, downy fernlike leaves. Compound umbels of white flowers appear in late spring, followed by large, distinctively beaked and ridged brown fruit. The whole plant is pleasantly scented.

Habitat/distribution Native to Europe, introduced and naturalized in other temperate regions, found in hedgerows and field edges often in shady positions.

Growth Grows under any conditions, in sun or shade, but said to prefer moist, humus-rich soil. An invasive plant which self-seeds and spreads rapidly and is virtually impossible to eradicate once established. Propagated by seed, after vernalization, or by division of roots in spring.

Parts used Leaves – fresh.

Myrrhis odorata

USES Culinary Traditionally used as a sweetening agent and flavouring for stewed soft fruits and rhubarb. Leaves also make a pretty garnish for sweet and savoury dishes.

MYRTACEAE

Myrtus communis

Myrtle

History and traditions This sweet-smelling shrub from the Mediterranean was dedicated to Venus, goddess of love. Myrtle has long been associated with weddings and included in bridal bouquets. After the ceremony, sprigs were often planted as cuttings in the garden of the marital home or beside the front door, to ensure peace and love within, which happy states would be lost if the plants died or were dug up.

Description An evergreen shrub, to 3 m (10 ft) tall, with glossy ovate to lanceolate leaves, dotted with oil glands. Fragrant white five-petalled flowers, which appear in early summer, are followed by blue-black berries.

Related species *M. communis* subsp. *tarentina* is a compact variant, 90 cm–1.5 m (3–5 ft) tall.

Habitat/description Native to the Mediterranean region and western Asia, introduced and widely grown elsewhere.

Growth Frost-hardy, but does not tolerate prolonged cold spells and waterlogged soils. Propagated by semi-ripe cuttings in late summer.

Parts used Leaves – fresh for culinary use, dried for infusions; fruits – fresh or dried; volatile oil.

USES Medicinal Myrtle has antiseptic, decongestant properties and it is taken internally, in infusions, for colds, chest infections, sinusitis and for urinary infections.

Culinary The leaves and fruits are used in Middle Eastern cookery with lamb and game.

General The essential oil is used in perfumery, cosmetic and soap industries.

VALERIANACEAE

Nardostachys grandiflora

Spikenard

History and traditions This plant was an ingredient of the expensive perfumed unguents of the Romans and ancient Eastern nations, prized for the durability of its scent. It was the "very costly" ointment of spikenard with which Mary wiped the feet of Jesus (John 12:3–5). The Indian name *jatamansi* refers to the bearded appearance of the fibrous rhizomes, or "spikes", which were supposed to resemble ears of corn.
Description An erect perennial, 25–30 cm (10–12 in) in height, with a fibrous rootstock, crowned by nearly basal lanceolate leaves and from which stems bearing pale-pink flowers in terminal clusters arise.
Habitat/distribution Native to the Himalayas from Kumaon to Sikkim and Bhutan, at altitudes of 3,000–5,000 m (9,800–16,400 ft), where the atmosphere is cool and moist, on poor, stony soil and rocky ledges.
Growth Fully hardy; grow in gritty, well-drained, poorish soil, in a rockery or similar situation, but provide midday or partial shade and plenty of moisture to keep roots cool.
Parts used Roots – dried for use in decoctions; volatile oil distilled from roots.

USES Medicinal: An important herb in Ayurvedic medicine for over 3,000 years, the root has antiseptic, bitter tonic properties and is soothing to the nervous system. It is used for insomnia and as a gentle tranquillizer, for menopausal problems, respiratory disorders and in the treatment of intestinal worms.

Above Nepeta x faassenii.

LABIATAE/LAMIACEAE

Nepeta cataria

Catmint

History and traditions This herb often proves irresistible to cats. It is mildly hallucinogenic, which could be the attraction, but another theory is that the plant has overtones of tomcats' urine and is associated with courtship behaviour. It is also said to be hated by rats. Chewing the root is reputed to make humans aggressive, and one old British story recalls that a reluctant hangman used it to give him courage to carry out his duties. There are references to its medicinal properties in old herbals, it was occasionally used for flavouring, and found its way into herbal tobaccos, but it does not seem to be widely used today, except perhaps to make toys for cats.
Description A hardy perennial, 30–90 cm (1–3 ft) tall, it has coarse-textured, ovate, grey-green leaves, with serrated edges. Pale-mauve flowers in terminal or axillary whorls are borne from midsummer to autumn. The whole plant has a strong, antiseptic, mintlike odour, similar to pennyroyal.
Related species The hybrid *N.* x *faassenii*, commonly known as *N. mussinii*, is a more attractive plant, frequently grown in herb gardens for its prolific, soft-blue flowers, which bloom over a long period. It has no medicinal virtues – but cats have been observed rolling in it.
Habitat/distribution Occurs in Europe, Asia and Africa, introduced and naturalized in North America and temperate zones. Found in moist, calcareous soils, on roadsides, in hedgerows and field edges.
Growth Catmint prefers moist soil and a sunny position. Propagated by root division in spring or autumn or by cuttings in summer.
Parts used Leaves and flowering stems – dried or fresh.

USES Medicinal Catmint lowers fever, increases perspiration and is mildly sedative. It is sometimes taken as an infusion for feverish colds, influenza, nervous tension, anxiety and gastric upsets, or applied externally to cuts and bruises.
Culinary It makes a stimulating, minty tea.
Household The dried herb is used to stuff toys for cats.
Other names Catnip and catnep.

Nepeta cataria *'Citriodora', a lemon-scented cultivar.*

Nepeta cataria

LABIATAE/LAMIACEAE

Ocimum basilicum

Basil

History and traditions A native of India, basil first came to Europe in the 16th century. In India, where it is known as *tulsi,* it is sacred to the god Vishnu, thought to protect from misfortune and is planted in temple gardens and offered at Hindu shrines. A basil leaf was traditionally placed on the chest of a corpse, after the head had been washed in basil water, and in other Eastern cultures it became a funeral herb, planted or scattered on graves. But basil has a mass of conflicting associations. As Culpeper remarked, "This is the herb which all authors are together by the ears about and rail at one another (like lawyers)" (*The English Physician*, 1653). The Greeks and Romans thought it represented hate and misfortune, and that shouting abuse at it encouraged it to grow. In some later European cultures it represented sympathy and the acceptance of love. In Crete, it stood for love washed with tears, taking a middle line. There was no agreement on its properties either, in former times. Some said it was poisonous, others that it was health-inducing. In 16th-century Britain it was appreciated for its scent. Thomas Tusser listed it as a strewing herb and John Parkinson wrote, "The ordinary Basil is in a manner wholly spent to make sweete or washing waters among other sweete herbs, yet sometimes it is put into nosegays" (*Paradisi,* 1629). Today it is among the most popular and widely grown of culinary herbs.

Description A much-branched half-hardy annual, to 20–60 cm (8–24 in) tall, with soft, ovate, bright-green leaves and whorls of small white flowers, borne in terminal racemes in mid to late summer.

Related species Basils are extremely variable. Even within the same species, the pungency and flavour vary considerably, according to the composition of their volatile oils, which depends on soil, climate and growing conditions. They also hybridize easily under cultivation and many that are sold commercially are not recognized as distinct varieties or cultivars by botanists. *O. b.* **'Dark Opal'** is a reliable cultivar with purple leaves and bright cerise-pink flowers. *O. b.* **'Purple Ruffles'** has large crinkled, purplish leaves with curly edges and makes a vigorous bush. *O. b.* var. *crispum* **(curly basil)** has coarse, curled, dark-green leaves, and is sometimes known as "Neapolitana". *O. b.* **'Genovese'** has soft but broader leaves than the species, is strongly aromatic, and frequently offered as a culinary variety – popular in pesto sauce. ***O. b.*** **var.** ***minimum*** **(bush basil, Greek basil)** is very compact and bushy, growing 15–30 cm (6–12 in) tall, and has small, but pungent leaves and tiny white flowers. ***O. sanctum*** **(holy basil, tulsi)** is a shrubby perennial, 45–60 cm (18–24 in), with green, slightly hairy, ovate leaves and thin white to pale-mauve flower spikes. Other cultivars with interesting flavours include ***O. b. 'Thai'***, often used in oriental cuisines; and ***O. b. 'Cinnamon'***, which is from Mexico, about 30–60cm (12–24in) high, with pink flowers and a distinctive cinnamon scent.

Habitat/distribution Native to India and the Middle East, naturalized in parts of Africa and other tropical and subtropical regions, introduced and widely grown elsewhere.

Growth Basil requires well-drained, moist, medium-rich soil and full sun. It is propagated from seed, which must be sown after any danger of frost in cool regions. In cold, wet, northern summers it may need to be grown on under glass, but flourishes as a container plant and should be kept outside in hot, dry spells to develop the best flavour.

Parts used Leaves – fresh, essential oil.

Top, from left to right Ocimum basilicum; O.b. *'Dark Opal'*; O.b. *'Purple Ruffles'*; O.b. *'Cinnamon'*; O.b. *'Green Ruffles'*; O.b. *'Thai'*.

Right Ocimum basilicum *var.* minimum.

Below right Ocimum sanctum.

USES Medicinal Has antidepressant, antiseptic, soothing properties. The fresh leaves are rubbed on insect bites and stings to relieve itching, made into cough syrups with honey and taken as an infusion for colds. The leaves or essential oil are used in steam inhalations as a decongestant for colds; diluted essential oil makes an insect repellent or massage oil for depression and anxiety.

Culinary The leaves do not retain their flavour well when dried and are better used fresh in a wide range of Mediterranean dishes. They have an affinity with tomatoes and aubergines (eggplant), and add a distinctive fragrance to ratatouille, pasta sauces, pesto sauce and pizza toppings. Fresh basil should be added towards the end of the cooking process so that its fragrance is not lost. Basil is a good choice for planting in a kitchen herb garden.

Aromatic The essential oil is used in aromatherapy and as a perfumery ingredient.

Other name Sweet basil.

Pesto sauce

The traditional way of making this sauce was to pound the ingredients with a pestle and mortar – the name is from the Italian *pestare* (to pound or crush), but it is much easier to make in a food processor or blender.

Serves 4
50 g/2 oz fresh basil leaves
25 g/1 oz fresh parsley
2–3 cloves of garlic
8 tbs extra virgin olive oil
25g/1 oz grated Parmesan cheese
salt and freshly ground black pepper, to taste

Put all the ingredients, except the cheese and seasoning, into a liquidizer (food processor or blender) and blend until smooth. Pour the mixture into a bowl, stir in the grated Parmesan and season to taste with salt and pepper. Keep refrigerated for up to a couple of weeks.

CAUTION Essential oil should not be used during pregnancy.

ONAGRACEAE

Oenothera biennis

Evening primrose

History and traditions An American native, the evening primrose was introduced to Europe in 1619, when seeds were brought to the Padua Botanic Garden in Italy. Although it had some place in the folk medicine of Native Americans, in Europe it was used more as a culinary than a medicinal herb – leaves were put into salads and roots cooked as vegetables. It came to prominence after modern research in the 1980s established that oil from the seeds contains GLA, or gamma-linolenic acid, an unsaturated fatty acid which assists the production of prostaglandins, hormone-like substances, which act as chemical messengers and regulate hormonal systems. It is not related to the primrose, but takes its name because it opens in the evening.

Description An erect biennial, up to 1.5 m (5 ft) tall, with a thick, yellowish taproot and a rosette of basal leaves from which the flowering stems arise. These have alternate, lanceolate to ovate leaves, and are topped by bright, yellow flowers, which open at night to release their fragrance and are pollinated by moths. Downy pods follow, containing tiny seeds.

Habitat/distribution Originated in North America, introduced and naturalized throughout Europe and in temperate zones. Found on poor, sandy soils, waste ground and embankments, as a garden escape.

Growth Grow in open, sandy soil in a warm sunny position. This plant self-seeds freely once established. Propagated from seed sown in autumn or spring.

Parts used Seeds – pressed to produce oil.

USES Medicinal The oil is thought to benefit the immune system and regulate hormones. It is taken internally for premenstrual tension, menopausal problems, allergies, skin complaints, such as eczema and acne, and to counteract the effects of excess alcohol. It may also be helpful for high blood pressure, arthritis and multiple sclerosis.

Cosmetic The fresh flowers are often made into face masks to improve skin tone. The oil is an ingredient in commercial cosmetics and pharmaceutical products.

OLEACEAE

Olea europaea

Olive

History and traditions There is evidence that the olive tree has been cultivated north of the Dead Sea since 3700–3600 BC. Known to the Egyptians, it was always prized for the quality of the oil from the fruits. The Romans called the tree *"olea"*, from *oleum,* meaning oil, the Greek word being *elaio*. The olive branch has been a symbol of peace and reconciliation since the biblical story of the dove returning with a sprig of olive in its beak to Noah's Ark after the flood had subsided.

Description An evergreen tree, 9–12 m (29–40 ft) tall, it has pale-grey bark and pendulous branches, with smooth, leathery, grey-green, lanceolate to oblong leaves. Creamy-white flowers are borne in short panicles in summer, followed by green, ripening to dark-purple fruits, known as drupes.

Habitat/distribution Native to the Mediterranean region, introduced in warm temperate regions of Africa and Asia.

Growth Requires well-drained to dry soil and full sun. Although frost-hardy, it can be grown outside successfully only in Mediterranean climates. Propagated by seed sown in autumn or by semi-ripe cuttings in summer.

Parts used Leaves – dried for use in infusions and other herbal preparations; fruits – harvested in autumn and winter, by beating them from

the trees on to groundsheets; oil – pressed from the fruit. Extra-virgin, cold-pressed oil, extracted without heat or chemical solvents, has the best flavour and properties.

USES Medicinal The oil is monounsaturated and its consumption is thought to help lower cholesterol levels and blood pressure, reducing risk of circulatory diseases. Leaves are antiseptic and astringent, taken internally in infusions for nervous tension and high blood pressure and applied externally to cuts and abrasions. The oil is thought to be helpful when taken internally for constipation and peptic ulcers.
Culinary The fruits of the olive tree are eaten as appetizers, made into *tapenade* spread, added to salads, sauces, bread, pizzas, pasta and many other dishes. The oil is used in salad dressings, sauces, mayonnaise and as a general cooking oil.

Top *The olive tree is slow growing and often attains a great age, revealed by the girth of the trunk.*

Above *An olive grove in Extremadura, Spain.*

ASTERACEAE/COMPOSITAE

Onopordum acanthium

Scotch thistle

History and traditions This is thought to be the thistle that is the national emblem of Scotland, dating from the time of James III of Scotland (d. 1488). It is also the emblem of the ancient, knightly Order of the Thistle, inaugurated by James V of Scotland, 1513–1542. Some bizarre claims were made for the properties of this plant. Pliny recommended it for baldness and Dioscorides as "a remedy for those that have their bodies drawne backwards".
Description A hardy biennial, growing on a strong taproot, the spiny, toothed, dark-green leaves have a striking cobweb-effect pattern of white veins, with purple thistle-head flowers rising on long stems to 1.5 m (5 ft).
Habitat/distribution Occurs in the Mediterranean, Europe and Asia, introduced and naturalized in other countries.
Growth Grows in most conditions, but flourishes in reasonably fertile, well-drained soil and a sunny position. Propagated by seed sown in autumn or spring.
Parts used Leaves, stems, flowers.

USES Medicinal Scotch thistle is rarely used medicinally currently.
Culinary The whole plant is edible if not very palatable. Young stems can be boiled as a vegetable; flower receptacles are said to be substitutes for artichoke hearts.
Horticultural It is widely grown as a herb garden ornamental.
Other names Cotton thistle and woolly thistle.

LABIATAE/LAMIACEAE

Origanum

Above *Origanum onites, or pot marjoram, surrounded by Golden marjoram.*

Origanum vulgare, popularly known as oregano, adds flavour to Mediterranean cookery.

History and traditions *Origanum* means "joy of the mountains" from the Greek *oros,* a mountain, and *ganos,* brightness or joy. According to legend, Aphrodite, Greek goddess of love, found this herb in the depths of the ocean and took it to the top of a mountain where it would be close to the sun's rays. Ever since it has been associated with the return of sunshine and warmth, with love and the banishing of sorrow. It found a place at both weddings and funerals, being used to crown newly married couples and to provide comfort to mourners. The tradition arose that planting origanum on a grave ensured a happy afterlife for the deceased and Gerard recommends it for those "given to over much sighing" (*The Herball,* 1597). It is one of the most versatile herbs, variable in form, and valued through the centuries for its fragrant, medicinal and culinary properties alike.

Species and nomenclature There is often confusion about the difference between oregano and marjoram. Marjoram is the common English name for the *Origanum* species, but *O. vulgare*, or 'wild marjoram', is widely known as 'oregano' and *O. onites* is sometimes called 'Greek oregano'. To complicate matters further, there are many hybrids among cultivated marjorams, which are difficult to identify and variously named.

Origanum majorana

Sweet marjoram

Description A half-hardy perennial, often grown as an annual, 60 cm (2 ft) tall, with elliptic pale greyish-green leaves, arranged opposite. The small, white, sometimes pinkish, flowers grow in distinctive knotlike clusters, surrounding the stems, giving it the once popular name "knotted marjoram".

Habitat/distribution *O. majorana* originated in the Mediterranean and Turkey and is widely naturalized in northern Africa, western Asia, parts of India and introduced to many places elsewhere. Found on dryish but often nutrient-rich soils in sunny positions.

Growth Requires well-drained, but not too dry, fertile soil and full sun. Propagated by seed sown in spring, after danger of frost in cool temperate regions.

Parts used Leaves, flowering stems – fresh or dry; essential oil distilled from leaves.

USES Medicinal A warming, relaxing herb with antiseptic properties, taken internally as an infusion for nervous anxiety, insomnia, tension headaches, colds and bronchial complaints, digestive complaints and painful menstruation. Dilute oil is applied externally for muscular aches and pains, sprains and stiff joints.

Culinary It is said to have the most delicate flavour of the marjorams and is widely used in Italian, Greek and Mediterranean cookery, especially in pasta sauces, pizza toppings, tomato sauces, vegetable dishes, and to flavour bread, oil and vinegar.

Aromatic Dried flowering stems add fragrance to pot-pourri. Essential oil is used in food and cosmetic industries.

Origanum onites
Pot marjoram

Description A hardy to frost-hardy perennial, 60 cm (2 ft) tall, with hairy stems, and ovate-elliptic, bright-green, downy leaves. White or purple flowers are borne in dense clusters in mid to late summer.
Habitat/distribution Native to the Mediterranean and the Middle East, introduced and widely grown in other countries. Grows on light, well-drained soils and open hillsides.
Growth Grow in well-drained soil in a sunny position. Propagated by division or by cuttings taken in summer.
Parts used Leaves, flowers – fresh or dried.

USES Culinary The flavour is less delicate than *O. majorana,* and not as pungent and aromatic as most *O. vulgare*, but it makes an acceptable alternative for similar culinary uses.
Aromatic Dried leaves and flowers are added to pot-pourri.

Origanum onites

Origanum vulgare
Oregano

Description A variable, bushy, hardy perennial, to 60 cm (2 ft), with aromatic, ovate, dark-green leaves and panicles of pink to purple tubular flowers in summer. It usually has a higher proportion of thymol than *O. majorana,* giving it a more thyme-like scent. The composition of the essential oils and flavour of the plant varies according to soil, sun and general growing conditions. Oregano grown in cooler, wetter regions does not have the same intensity of flavour as that grown in a Mediterranean climate.
Related species There are many attractive, ornamental cultivars of *O. vulgare,* which are not suitable for culinary and medicinal use but are frequently grown in herb gardens, including *O. v.* 'Aureum', a golden marjoram, and *O. v.* 'Polyphant', a variegated marjoram.
Habitat/distribution Native to the Mediterranean, found in dry soils on sunny, open hillsides. Introduced and widely grown in other countries.
Growth Requires well-drained soil and a sunny position. *O. vulgare* is best propagated by division or by cuttings taken in summer – the cultivars must be vegetatively propagated.
Parts used Leaves, flowers – fresh or dried; essential oil distilled from the leaves.

Top Origanum vulgare *'Polyphant' is a variagated cultivar with white flowers.*

Below Origanum vulgare *'Aureum', or golden marjoram, an attractive ornamental.*

USES Medicinal Similar uses to *O. majorana*.
Culinary: Similar uses to *O. majorana*.
Other name Wild marjoram.

CAUTION Marjorams are not given to pregnant women in medicinal doses or in the form of essential oil, as they are uterine stimulants.

ARALIACEA

Panax ginseng

Ginseng

History and traditions Used as a tonic and "vital essence" in Chinese medicine for thousands of years. It was so highly prized for its medicinal properties that emperors set up monopolies and wars were fought over the rights to harvest ginseng. First introduced to Europe as early as the 9th century, it did not catch on until the 1950s when scientific studies discovered that its active principles have a "normalizing" effect on various bodily functions. The name *panax* comes from *pan,* all, and *akos*, a remedy. The Chinese name, from which the word ginseng is adapted, means man root, or like a man. *Panax ginseng* is probably extinct in the wild, but various *Panax* species are cultivated in Asia, China, Russia, Japan, the United States and Britain.

Description A hardy perennial, 70–80 cm (28–31 in) tall, it usually has a forked root, erect stems, with fleshy scales at the base and whorls of palmate leaves, with finely serrated leaflets. Insignificant greenish-yellow flowers are followed by bright red berries.

Related species There are several species of ginseng with similar medicinal properties, and as the plants look very alike they are often confused. These include *P. japonicus*, which grows wild in wooded areas of central Japan; *P. quinquefolius* (American ginseng); *Eleutherococcus senticosus* (Siberian ginseng), which has almost identical properties to the Panax species, but is stronger and considered very beneficial. *P. pseudoginseng* refers to several sub-species found in Asia, from the Himalayas to China.

Habitat/distribution The *Panax* species are native to China, Korea and Japan. Found in damp, cool, woodlands. *Eleutherococcus senticosus* is from Siberia.

Growth For successful cultivation well-drained, sandy loam, with added leaf-mould, is essential. Propagation is from seed, but germination is often erratic.

Parts used Roots – processed from 6–7-year-old plants for use in tablets, extracts, tea and medicinal preparations.

USES Medicinal Ginseng is said to stimulate the nervous and immune systems, improve and regulate hormonal secretion, increase general stamina and strength, lower blood-sugar and blood cholesterol levels. Modern research has not managed to isolate an active principle in this herb which relates to any one of the specific claims made for it. However, it has been found that the combined action of its many constituents has a general tonic effect on the whole body.

Top left Panax ginseng *roots.*

Top right Panax japonicus.

Centre right Eleutherococcus senticosus – *the berries are borne in single clusters at the ends of the stems.*

Right Panax quinquefolius.

CAUTION Should only be taken under qualified medical supervision for short periods. Excess or regular intake may cause headaches, giddiness, nausea, double vision, raised blood pressure and other side effects.

PAPAVERACEAE

Papaver somniferum

Opium poppy

History and traditions Opium, made by lancing the green seed capsule to extract the milky latex, has been used for medicinal purposes since earliest times and the Greek authorities, Theophrastus and Dioscorides, wrote of it in this context. It was probably introduced to Europe by early Arabian physicians, and a cough syrup made from the opium poppy, widely recommended by the Arabian, Mesue, in the 11th century, was adopted as a standard for many centuries following. But as a highly addictive, powerful narcotic, opium caused as many problems as it solved. Opium poppies are now cultivated on a large scale as the source of powerful pain-killing drugs, including morphine and codeine (two of the most important of its 25 alkaloids), as well as to produce the illegal drug, heroin (diamorphine). The flowers are frequently grown in herb gardens as ornamentals.

Description A hardy annual, up to 1.5 m (5 ft) tall, it has oblong, deeply lobed, blue-green leaves. Large, lilac, pink or white flowers, with papery petals, borne in early summer, are followed by blue-green seed pods.

Habitat/distribution Native to south-east Europe, the Middle East and Asia. Introduced elsewhere. Grows on shallow, chalky (alkaline) soils in sunny positions.

Growth Prefers well-drained soil and full sun. Propagated by seed sown in spring, often self-seeds once established.

Parts used Fruits, seeds.

USES Medicinal Proprietary drugs and pharmaceutical products are made from the fruits. Not for home remedies or self-treatment.

Culinary The seeds do not contain any of the alkaloids found in the capsules. They are dried for use whole or ground in breads, biscuits, bakery products and as a garnish. Commercially produced seed is from a subspecies of *P. somniferum*, developed for its seed production.

CAUTION Legal restrictions apply to this plant and its products in most countries.

PASSIFLORACEAE

Passiflora incarnata

Passion flower

History and traditions A plant of tropical and subtropical regions of the Americas, it was imaginatively dubbed "Calvary Lesson" by Roman Catholic missionaries in South America, taking the intricate form of its flower to represent Christ's crucifixion. The three styles are for the nails used on the cross; the five anthers for the five wounds; the corona is the crown of thorns; and the ten sepals are for ten of the twelve apostles – leaving out Peter and Judas Iscariot, who betrayed him. The lobed leaves and tendrils symbolize the hands and scourges of Christ's tormentors.

Description A hardy perennial, climbing plant on a woody stem, to 8 m (26 ft), it clings to its support with axillary tendrils and has deeply lobed leaves and attractive creamy-white to lavender flowers, with purple calyces.

Habitat/distribution Native to tropical regions of North and South America, occurs in Asia and Australia, introduced and grown elsewhere.

Growth Requires well-drained, sandy soil and a sunny position. Propagation is easiest from semi-ripe cuttings taken in summer. Seed requires heat to germinate and can be slow and erratic to grow.

Parts used The whole plant – cut when fruiting and dried for use in infusions and medicinal preparations.

USES Medicinal Has sedative, pain-relieving properties and is taken for nervous conditions and insomnia.

GERANIACEAE

Pelargonium

History and traditions Most scented pelargoniums, often familiarly known as "geraniums", come from South Africa and were introduced to Europe some time in the 17th century. The scented-leafed varieties were very popular in Britain with the Victorians, who grew them as house plants, and in France distilled oil from the "rose-scented" group became an important perfume ingredient in the mid-19th century.

Description and species There are numerous hybrids and cultivars with differing foliage, habits of growth and types of fragrance. It is the leaves that are scented. The flowers, appearing in summer, are virtually unperfumed, smaller and more insignificant than those of regal and zonal pelargoniums, grown as colourful bedding plants. These are some of the most popular scented-leafed pelargoniums:

***P.* 'Graveolens'** – An upright shrubby plant, it grows 60–90 cm (2–3 ft) tall, and has deeply cut, triangular, rough-textured, bright-green leaves and small pink flowers. It grows vigorously and is slightly hardier than most of the others. This is the original "rose geranium" though the scent is much harsher and more spicy than a true rose fragrance, with strong overtones of lemon.

P. odoratissimum – A low-growing, species 30 cm (1 ft) – with a trailing habit and little white flowers borne on long stems. The soft, rounded, bright-green leaves are wavy at the edges and apple-scented.

P. crispum – Has a neat, upright habit, and grows 60–70 cm (24–28 in) tall. It has pink flowers and clear green, three-lobed, crinkly leaves, which are coarse to the touch and pungently lemon-scented.

***P. crispum* 'Variegatum'** – Is an attractive variegated cultivar, with crisply curled leaves, edged with creamy yellow and the same, strong lemon scent as the species.

P. tomentosum – Is a lovely trailing, or prostrate species, 90 cm–1.2 m (3–4 ft), which makes a good container plant, if grown on a stand and allowed to drape downward. It has small white flowers and soft, downy, grey-green leaves with a strong peppermint fragrance.

***P.* 'Fragrans'** – A small, upright subshrub, 45 cm (18 in) tall, it has clusters of small, greyish-green, rounded leaves, with finely cut, crinkled edges and a smooth, silky texture.

The flowers are white and the foliage pleasantly pine-scented with overtones of nutmeg.

P. 'Lady Plymouth' – An attractive hybrid, 60 cm–1.5 m (2–5 ft) tall, it has triangular, deeply lobed, crisp-textured leaves, with a cream and green variegation, little pink flowers and a citrus fragrance with a hint of rose.

Habitat/distribution Most pelargoniums are natives of South Africa; a few come from tropical Africa, the eastern Mediterranean, the Middle East, India, western Asia and Australia. Cultivated in France, northern Africa and Réunion for essential-oil production.

Growth All are tender and must be grown as conservatory plants in cool, temperate regions, though they are best kept outside in the summer months. A few (including *P.* 'Graveolens' and *P.* 'Fragrans') may survive a mild winter in a cold greenhouse. They make good container plants and should be given a gritty, loam-based compost. Cut back in autumn and prune lightly in spring to maintain a neat, bushy habit. Pelargoniums grown outside need free-draining soil and a sunny position. They are easily propagated by softwood cuttings taken in summer.

Parts used Leaves, essential oil – distilled from the leaves.

USES Culinary The pungency of the leaves makes them suitable as flavouring agents, to be removed after cooking rather than being eaten themselves. Leaves of *P.* 'Graveolens' and *P. odoratissimum* are best for flavouring ice creams and cakes (put 2–3 leaves in the base of the cake tin before baking) and fruit punches.

Aromatic Dried leaves and essential oil are added to pot-pourri and their strong scents make them effective in insect repellent or anti-moth sachets. "Geranium oil" is used as a commercial flavouring and perfume ingredient and used in aromatherapy.

Other name Scented pelargonium.

Opposite page, far left and top right Pelargonium *'Graveolens'*; **below right** Pelargonium odoratissimum.

This page, clockwise from top to bottom Pelargonium tomentosum; Pelargonium *'Fragrans'*; Pelargonium *'Lady Plymouth'* Pelargonium crispum.

LABIATAE/LAMIACEAE

Perilla frutescens

Perilla

History and traditions In China, perilla has been a medicinal herb for centuries and it has long been cultivated in the East, from India to Japan, as a culinary herb and for its many economic uses. The leaves produce a sweet volatile oil, the seeds a pressed oil, which is used in similar ways to linseed oil. It has recently become increasingly popular in the West for its culinary uses and as an ornamental garden plant.
Description A half-hardy annual with broadly ovate, deeply-veined leaves, reddish stems and small spikes of white flowers in summer. There are both green and purple-leaved forms.
Related species *P. frutescens* 'Crispa' (pictured below) is a variety with curly-edged leaves.
Habitat/distribution Occurs from the Himalayas to East Asia, naturalized in parts of Europe and North America.
Growth Grows best in deep, rich, moist but well-drained soil, in sun or partial shade. Propagated by seed sown in spring, after frosts in cool temperate regions. Pinch out tips to encourage and maintain bushy plants.
Parts used Leaves – fresh for culinary use, dried for medicinal infusions and decoctions; seeds – dried for decoctions; volatile oil – from leaves; pressed oil – from seeds.

USES Medicinal Used in Chinese herbal medicine for colds and chest infections, nausea, stomach upsets and allergic reactions.
Culinary Leaves and seeds are a popular ingredient in Japanese cookery and add colour and an unusual spicy flavour to salads, seafood and stir-fry dishes.
General Volatile oil is added to commercial food, confectionery and dental products; oil from seeds is used to waterproof paper for umbrellas, in paints and printing inks.
Other names Beefsteak plant and shiso.

Above P. frutescens *'Crispa'*.

UMBELLIFERAE/APIACEAE

Petroselinum crispum

Parsley

History and traditions Petroselinum comes from the Greek name given to it by Dioscorides, *petros selinon*. In the Middle Ages this became corrupted to *petrocilium*, ending up in the anglicized version, by a process of "Chinese whispers" as parsley. The Greeks associated it with death and funerals and according to Homer fed it to their chariot horses, but it was the Romans who took to it as a major culinary herb. Pliny complained that every sauce and salad contained it, and it has remained ubiquitous as a sauce, salad and garnishing herb to this day. Parsley has attracted a mass of silly superstitions. Transplanting it, giving it away, picking it when in love and so on, all foretold disaster. Some said it flourished only where the "mistress is master", others that it would grow only for the wicked, or, conversely, for the honest. Its slowness to germinate when soil is cold led to tales that it had gone seven times to the devil and back, and should be sown on Good Friday to outwit him. *A Grete Herball,* 1539, has some ingenious ideas on how to ensure it is well "crisped" or curly: "Before the sowing of them, stuffe a tennis ball with the seedes and beat the same well against the ground, whereby the seedes may be a little bruised. Or when the

parcelye is well come up, go over the bed with a waighty roller whereby it may so presse the leaves down."

Description A frost-hardy biennial, growing on a short, stout taproot to 30–60 cm (1–2 ft), it has triangular, three-pinnate leaves, curled at the margin. Yellow-green flowers are borne in umbels in its second year.

Related species *Petroselinum crispum* 'Italian', also known as French or flat-leaved parsley, is a larger, hardier plant, growing to 80–90 cm (32 in–3 ft) and has smooth, uncurled three-pinnate leaves. *P. c.* var. *tuberosum,* Hamburg parsley, has small, flat leaves, with a celery-like flavour and is grown for its large roots, which are eaten as a vegetable.

Habitat/distribution The genus is native to the Mediterranean region of Europe, found in fields and on rocky slopes. *P. crispum* has been developed under cultivation and is widely grown as a crop in many countries.

Growth Parsley requires rich, moist but well-drained soil and a sunny position, or partial shade. As leaves coarsen in the second, flowering, year, it is often grown as an annual and is propagated by seed, sown in spring. If sown *in situ* before soil has warmed up, germination may be slow or erratic. For best results, sow in containers, maintaining a temperature of 18–21°C (64–70°F) until seedlings appear. The young plants can then be hardened off to grow outside at lower temperatures.

Parts used Leaves, stems – best fresh or frozen for culinary use as flavour is lost with drying; roots – of 'Hamburg' variety; essential oil – distilled from leaves and seeds.

Flat-leaved parsley.

Above left *Hamburg parsley.*

Above *'Italian' or flat-leaved parsley.*

USES Medicinal Parsley is rich in vitamin A and C, and acts as an antioxidant. It also contains a flavonoid, apigenin, which is an anti-allergen. Although used in herbal medicine for a variety of complaints, including menstrual problems, kidney stones, urinary infections, rheumatism and arthritis, it is not for self-treatment. Tea can be made from leaves or roots used to treat jaundice and coughs.

Culinary The leaves of this extremely popular herb are added to salads, sauces, salad dressings, savoury butter, stuffings, snipped into meat, fish and vegetable dishes and used as a garnish. The stalks, which have a stronger flavour than the leaves, are essential to a *bouquet garni* for flavouring casseroles and cooked dishes. The roots of *P. tuberosum* are cooked as a vegetable. The essential oil is used in commercial food products.

CAUTION Although parsley is perfectly safe, used whole in culinary dishes, it is toxic in excess, particularly in the form of essential oil. *Petroselinum*, especially the flat-leaved varieties, should not be confused with *Aethusa cynapium*, fool's parsley, a highly poisonous wild plant.

MONIMIACEAE

Peumus boldus

Boldo

History and traditions The medicinal properties of this small, shrubby tree from Chile were first investigated in Europe by a French doctor in 1869. It was discovered to be effective in stimulating the liver and expelling intestinal worms. In its country of origin it was formerly taken as a tonic tea and digestive, prescribed as a substitute for quinine and made into a powder to take as snuff.
Description An aromatic, dioecious, evergreen tree growing to 6–7 m (19–23 ft), it is the sole species of its genus. It has light to grey-green, leathery leaves, rich in a balsamic volatile oil. Greenish male and female flowers appear in late summer, borne on separate trees.
Habitat/distribution It is native to Chile, introduced elsewhere. Occurs on sunny slopes of the Andes mountains.
Growth It is frost-hardy, and grows best in sandy, acid soil in a sunny position. Propagated by semi-ripe cuttings in summer, may also be grown from seed sown in spring.
Parts used Leaves – dried for use in infusions and other medicinal preparations; bark – dried for extracts.

USES Medicinal It has mainly been used for liver complaints, urinary infections and to expel intestinal worms. Extracts are included in commercial and pharmaceutical products.

PHYTOLACCACEAE

Phytolacca americana

Pokeweed

History and traditions A poisonous plant, once used by Native Americans as a purgative and powerful treatment for various complaints. They knew it as *pocan*, which is where the name pokeweed comes from. It was adopted by European settlers as a treatment for venereal disease, and for its painkilling and anti-inflammatory properties. In modern times, its complex chemical structure has attracted much scientific interest. It contains compounds that affect cell division and it is currently being investigated as a potential source of drugs to combat AIDS-related diseases and cancers.
Description A large, frost-hardy perennial, 90 cm–1.5 m (3–5 ft) tall, with smooth, hollow, purplish stems and ovate to lanceolate leaves. It has racemes of white, sometimes pink-tinged flowers in late summer, followed by large drooping spikes of purple-black berries, which provide a dye to colour ink.
Habitat/distribution A North American native, it has been introduced elsewhere and widely grown in the Mediterranean region of Europe. Occurs in rich soils at field edges.
Growth Grow in rich, moist soil. Propagated by seed sown in spring or autumn or by division.
Parts used Roots and fruits (berries) – collected in autumn and dried for use in decoctions, tinctures and other medicinal preparations.

USES Medicinal Pokeweed has anti-inflammatory, antibacterial, antiviral, antifungal properties and is destructive to many parasitic disease-causing organisms. It is also capable of stimulating the immune and lymphatic systems. Used for many disorders, including autoimmune diseases, skin diseases, bronchitis and arthritis, but is for qualified practitioners only. Despite its toxicity, the leaves of this plant are sometimes boiled as a vegetable, the water being discarded.

CAUTION The whole plant is toxic if eaten, especially roots and berries.

PIPERACEAE

Piper nigrum

Black pepper

History and traditions Black pepper has been a valuable trading commodity since Alaric I, King of the Visigoths, demanded 3,000 lb of it as a ransom during his siege of Rome between 410–408 BC. Its high price during the Middle Ages was a major incentive for the Portuguese to find a sea route to India, where it came from, although the price fell following the discovery of a passage round the Cape of Good Hope in 1498. As cultivation was extended into Malaysia, the Portuguese retained a lucrative trading monopoly in pepper into the 18th century, and much of the wealth of Venice and Genoa depended on its trade. In Britain it was heavily taxed from the 17th to the 19th centuries. Pepper's virtues as a digestive were early recognized in the West and it has a long tradition of medicinal use in Ayurvedic and Chinese systems of healing.
Description A perennial climber, growing to 6 m (20 ft), with a strong, woody stem and ovate, prominently-veined, dark-green leaves. It has drooping spikes of inconspicuous white flowers, followed by long clusters of spherical green fruits or berries, which redden as they mature. Black pepper is produced from whole fruits, picked and dried just as they start to go red; white pepper is from ripe fruits, with the outer layer removed, and green pepper is from unripe fruits, pickled to prevent it turning dark.
Habitat/distribution Native to southern India and Sri Lanka, introduced and cultivated in Indonesia, Malaysia, Brazil and many tropical regions. In the wild it grows in humus-rich, moist soil. It is cultivated by training it up trees or horizontally along frames.
Growth Pepper requires deep, rich, manured soil, plenty of water, a humid atmosphere and a shady position. It is sometimes grown as a pot plant in temperate climates.
Parts used Fruits (peppercorns).

USES Medicinal A pungent, stimulating digestive, which relieves flatulence. It is used in Ayurvedic medicine for coughs and colds and as a nerve tonic. It also has a reputation as an aphrodisiac.
Culinary Its chief use is as a condiment and flavouring in a wide range of dishes in the cookery of most countries. It is currently the most widely consumed spice in the world.

Mixed peppercorns.

PLANTAGINACEAE

Plantago major

Plantain

History and traditions The Saxons called it "*waybroad*", because it was so often found by the wayside. And the story goes that this plant was once a beautiful young girl, who was changed into plantain for refusing to leave the roadway where she expected her lover to appear. As a medicinal herb it was highly rated by Pliny, who attributed to it the ability to fuse together pieces of flesh cooking in a pot, and to cure the madness of dogs – or their bites. It was often recommended as an antidote to poison and in the US it was held to be a remedy for rattle-snake bite by native tribes.
Description A small, undistinguished perennial, 40 cm (16 in) high, it has a basal rosette of ovate leaves and cylindrical spikes of inconspicuous brownish-green flowers.
Habitat/distribution Native to Europe and introduced in other temperate zones worldwide. Occurs widely in cultivated land, garden paths and lawns, fields, wastelands and roadsides.
Growth Said to prefer moist soil, but tolerates any conditions in sun or shade. Self-seeds freely.
Parts used Leaves – fresh or dried.

USES Medicinal Plantain was thought to promote healing and to have antibacterial properties. Mainly used as a poultice or in ointments to be applied externally to wounds, sores, ulcers, bites and stings.

BERBERIDACEAE

Podophyllum peltatum

American mandrake

History and traditions A poisonous herb, *Podophyllum peltatum* was formerly used by Native Americans as a powerful purgative medicine, vermifuge and wart remover. They also made it into an insecticide for potato crops and reputedly took it to commit suicide. It was introduced to Western medicine in the 1780s by a German doctor involved in the American War of Independence and by 1820 was listed in the United States *Pharmacopoeia*. It is called may apple for the juicy fruits, which were sometimes eaten, despite their relative toxicity. The generic name comes from the Greek for *podos*, a foot, and *phyllon*, a leaf, for its supposed resemblance to a bird's webbed foot. The specific term, *peltatum*, means shield-shaped. Despite being called mandrake it is not related to *Mandragora*. In recent years, the active ingredient, podophyllotoxin, has been isolated for use in anti-cancer drugs.

Description A hardy perennial with a creeping rhizome, and usually unbranched stems, it is 30–45 cm (12–18 in) tall. The large leaves are deeply divided into 4–7 wedge-shaped segments, lobed at the tops. Small, drooping white flowers, with yellow centres, are followed by fleshy, lemon-shaped fruits. The whole plant has an unpleasant smell.

Related species *P. hexandrum* (Indian podophyllum) which grows in the Himalayas, has red fruits and is more poisonous, with a higher concentration of podophyllotoxin.

Habitat *P. peltatum* is native to North America, found in damp woods and meadows.

Growth Grow in humus-rich, moist soil in dappled shade. Propagated by division of runners.

Parts used Rhizomes – extracted for commercial drugs.

USES Medicinal It is a component of pharmaceutical drugs for treating certain cancers.

Other name May apple.

CAUTION Although once used in herbal treatments, it is very poisonous and should never be used for self-medication. Subject to legal restrictions in most countries.

POLEMONIACEAE

Polemonium caeruleum

Jacob's ladder

History and traditions This is an ornamental plant, which retains its place in the herb garden through its ancient traditions and associations. Known to the Greeks, it was mentioned by Dioscorides, used for treating dysentery and thought to be effective against the bites of venomous beasts. It was still listed in various European pharmacopoeias into the 19th century. The whole flowering plant and roots were used and it was recommended for venereal disease and the bites of rabid dogs, but it is no longer considered to be of medicinal value. The name Jacob's ladder comes from the ladder-like arrangement of the leaves, and someone thought of associating it with the ladder to heaven of Jacob's dream in the biblical story (Genesis 28:12), with the sky represented by the blue flowers.

Description A hardy, clump-forming perennial, 30–90 cm (1–3 ft) tall, it grows on a creeping rootstock, with pinnate leaves divided into lance-shaped leaflets. The lavender-blue, bell-shaped flowers are borne on erect stems in drooping panicles.

Habitat/distribution Occurs widely in northern and central Europe, North America, and Asia in damp areas and shady woodlands.

Growth Requires rich, moisture-retentive soil and a shady or partially shady position. Propagated by seed sown in spring or by division in autumn.

USES Medicinal Rarely used today.

POLYGONACEAE

Polygonum bistorta

Bistort

History and traditions The generic name comes from the Greek *poly*, many, and *gonu*, knee, for the knotted shape of the stems, not unlike little joints, of many polygonum species. Bistort was not known as a medicinal plant until the 16th century, but soon gained a reputation as a wound-healing herb. It was cited in *The Universal Herbal*,1832, as a treatment for "intermittent fever", and considered helpful for diabetes into the early 20th century.

Description A hardy perennial with a stout, twisted rhizome, it has a clump of broad, ovate basal leaves, from which the pale-pink, cylindrical flower spikes arise on erect "jointed" stems to about 50 cm (20 in).

Habitat/distribution Occurs throughout Europe and Asia, frequently found near streams and waterways in damp meadows, mixed woodlands and on high slopes.

Growth Grows best in rich, moist soil, in sun or partial shade. Easily propagated by division, it is an invasive plant, but can make useful ground cover in damp areas.

Parts used Rhizomes – dried for powders, extracts, decoctions and other medicinal preparations.

USES Medicinal Said to reduce inflammation and promote healing, it is used as a gargle for gum disease, mouth ulcers and sore throats, applied externally to haemorrhoids, cuts and wounds and taken internally for diarrhoea.

PORTULACACEAE

Portulaca oleracea

Purslane

History and traditions A herb of ancient origin, purslane was known to the Egyptians, and grown in India and China for thousands of years. The Romans ate it as a vegetable and it was cultivated in Europe from at least the beginning of the 16th century, though not introduced to Britain until 1582. An important remedy for scurvy, it was one of the herbs that the early settlers thought indispensable and took with them to North America. Although it had some medicinal applications in former times, especially in China, it has always been chiefly valued for its culinary uses. It is still appreciated in France and commercially cultivated there for this purpose.

Description A half-hardy annual, with pink, prostrate, much-branched stems and rounded, fleshy, bright-green leaves, it grows to about 30 cm (12 in). It has very small, yellow flowers in late summer which soon fade to reveal the seed capsules with opening lids and filled with numerous black seeds.

Related species There is a golden-leafed variety, *P. oleracea* var. *aurea*, and the widely cultivated *P. oleracea* var. *sativa*.

Habitat/distribution Native to southern Europe, Asia and China, introduced elsewhere. Occurs on dry, sandy soils in sunny sites.

Growth Grow in light, well-drained soil, but provide plenty of water for good leaf development. Propagated from seed, sown after danger of frosts in cool temperate regions.

Parts used Leaves – fresh, picked before flowering for culinary use, fresh or dried for medicinal use.

USES Medicinal Recent scientific studies have found that *P. oleracea* contains omega-3 fatty acids, thought to be helpful in preventing heart disease and strengthening the immune system. The leaves are also a good source of Vitamin C and contain calcium, iron, carotene, thiamine, riboflavin and niacin. Purslane is also a diuretic and mildly laxative.

Culinary In 18th-century Britain it was a popular salad herb and is still eaten in the Middle East and India as a cooked vegetable and in salads. In France it is used in sorrel soup, helping to reduce the acidity of the sorrel.

Sorrel and purslane soup

Serves 4–6

1 tbs olive oil
1 medium onion, chopped
2 cloves garlic, crushed
225 g/8 oz sorrel leaves
50 g/2 oz purslane leaves
225 g/8 oz potatoes, peeled and diced
1.2 litres/2 pints/5 cups water
salt, pepper and a dash of grated nutmeg

Heat the oil in a large pan, add the onion and garlic and cook gently for 5 minutes, until soft but not browned.

Add the sorrel, purslane and potato and stir over a low heat for a further 2–3 minutes. Season with salt, pepper and a little grated nutmeg, pour in the water, bring to the boil then simmer for about 15 minutes until the potatoes are tender.

Cool slightly, then liquidize the soup in a blender or food processor, and reheat before serving.

PRIMULACEAE

Primula veris

Cowslip

History and traditions Cowslips were sometimes known as "keyflowers", suggested by the shape of the flower clusters, which look like a little bunch of keys. In Norse mythology they were dedicated to Freya, giving access to her palace, but in the Christian era became "St Peter's Keys" or the "Keys to Heaven". The generic name, *Primula*, comes from *primus*, first, in recognition that they are among the earliest flowers of spring. At one time, when they were plentiful, they were gathered in vast quantities to make spring tonics and the gently soporific, pale-yellow cowslip wine. Many medicinal uses were assigned to the flowers and distilled cowslip water was said to be good for the memory. The cosmetic applications were mentioned reprovingly by William Turner: "Some women we find, sprinkle ye floures of cowslip with whyte wine and after still it and wash their faces with that water to drive wrinkles away and to make them fayre in the eyes of the worlde rather than in the eyes of God, Whom they are not afrayd to offend" (*The New Herball*, 1551).

Description A perennial on a short rhizome with dense fibrous roots and a rosette of broadly ovate, rough-textured leaves. Flower stems rise above the basal leaves, 15–20 cm (6–8 in), and are topped by terminal umbels of fragrant, golden-yellow flowers, with tubular calyces.

Habitat/distribution Native to Europe and parts of Asia, introduced and sometimes naturalized elsewhere, found in meadows and pasture lands. A once common plant, it is now rare in the wild and a protected species in many European countries.

Growth Prefers deep, humus-rich, moist soil and partial shade. Propagated by seed sown in late summer in containers, left outside through the winter as a period of stratification, when they are exposed to frost, is necessary for germination. Easily propagated by division in autumn.

Parts used Flowers – fresh (but must not be picked from the wild, as they are quite rare).

USES Medicinal Cowslips have sedative, expectorant properties and contain salicylates (as in aspirin). They are taken as a tea for insomnia, anxiety, respiratory tract infections and rheumatic disorders.

Culinary Flowers may be added to salads.

CAUTION Should not be taken during pregnancy or if sensitive to aspirin. May cause allergic skin irritations.

PRIMULACEAE

Primula vulgaris

Primrose

History and traditions The medicinal properties of the primrose, *P. vulgaris*, are similar to those of the cowslip (*P. veris*) and have been listed in old herbals, since Pliny's time, for similar complaints. The primrose was made into salves and ointments and considered an important remedy for paralysis, rheumatic pain and gout. Its value as a sedative was well known and Gerard remarks that primrose tea, drunk in the month of May, "is famous for curing the phrensie". It was popular in cookery, and recipe books include instructions for making soup, pies, and a pudding based on rice, almonds, honey, saffron and ground primrose petals.

Description A low-growing perennial, to 15 cm (6 in), with a rosette of deeply veined, softly hairy, broad ovate leaves and clusters of saucer-shaped, pale-yellow, slightly fragrant flowers in early spring.

Habitat/distribution A European native, also found in northern Asia, introduced elsewhere, found on rich, damp soils in shady woodlands and hedgerows. Once common, now becoming rare in the wild, and a protected species in many countries.

Growth See *P. veris*.

Parts used Flowers (must not be picked from the wild, as they are becoming very rare).

USES Medicinal Primroses are taken as a tea to calm anxiety. It has similar properties to cowslips.

Culinary Flowers are added to salads and desserts or candied to decorate cakes.

LABIATAE/LAMIACEAE

Prunella vulgaris

Selfheal

History and traditions A herb with an ancient history in Chinese herbalism, but apparently unknown to the ancient Greeks and Romans. *Prunella vulgaris* has featured in Chinese medical texts since the end of the previous millennium, where it is said to be mainly associated with "liver energy" disorders. In Europe its common names, "self-heal", "all-heal" and "hook-heal", all indicate its former use as a wound herb and activator of the body's defences, as explained by Culpeper: "Self-heal, whereby when you're hurt you heal yourself." It was held to be "a special remedy for inward and outward wounds" (Culpeper, *The English Physician*, 1653) and commonly taken to have the same virtues as *Ajuga reptans* (bugle). It was taken to North America by settlers, where it soon became established and known as "heart of the earth" and "blue curls". However, unlike *Ajuga* it still has a limited place in modern herbal medicine.

Description An aromatic perennial on a creeping rootstock, it is 50 cm (20 in) in height. Leaves are linear to ovate, and compact spikes of violet, two-lipped florets are borne in the leaf axils in midsummer to mid-autumn.

Habitat/distribution Native to Europe, northern Africa and Asia, naturalized in North America, found on sunny banks, in dry grassland and open woodland.

Growth Grow in light soil in sun or dappled shade; tolerates most conditions. Propagated by seed sown in spring or by division in spring. It is inclined to be invasive.

Parts used Flowering stems – dried for use in infusions and medicinal preparations.

USES Medicinal It has antibacterial properties and is used externally to soothe burns, skin inflammations, bites and bruises, sore throats and inflamed gums.

BORAGINACEAE

Pulmonaria officinalis

Lungwort

History and traditions Both the Latin and common names of this herb point to its principal former use in treating lung complaints. The spotted leaves were thought to resemble lungs and it is often cited as an example of the application of the Doctrine of Signatures, an influential Renaissance philosophy, which held that the medicinal uses of plants were indicated by their correspondence in appearance to the part of the human body affected. It is often grown in herb gardens for its historical associations and attractive foliage and habit.

Description A hardy perennial, growing to 30 cm (12 in), it has hairy stems and dark green leaves, blotched with creamy-white spots. The tubular flowers, borne in spring, are pink at first, then turn blue.

Habitat/distribution Occurs in Europe, parts of Asia and North America, in woodlands.

Growth Grows best in humus-rich, moist soil and a shady position. Propagated by division, in late spring after flowering, or in autumn. Although it self-seeds in the garden, collected seed seldom germinates satisfactorily.

Parts used Leaves – dried for use in infusions and extracts.

USES Medicinal The herb contains a soothing mucilage and has expectorant properties. It is still sometimes used for bronchial infections and coughs, but it is now thought that it may mirror some of the toxicity discovered in *Symphytum*, to which it is closely related.

FAGACEAE

Quercus robur

Oak

History and traditions Few plants have been invested with as much magic, mystery and symbolic importance in Britain and much of Europe as the common oak. It was used in Druid ceremonies and thought to protect from lightning strikes – especially if planted near buildings to attract lightning away from them. Carrying an acorn was said to preserve youth, and dew gathered from beneath an oak was a potent ingredient in beauty lotions. They are exceptionally long-lived trees, and individual oaks were attributed characters of their own, complete with their own canon of folklore. They were also greatly valued for the durability of the wood, used in furniture, buildings and ships. The medicinal properties of the bark were well recognized by herbalists in former times. Culpeper lists many uses for it, declaring that it will "assuage inflammation and stop all manner of fluxes in man or woman".

Description A large, monoecious, deciduous tree, growing up to 25 m (82 ft) in height. It has wide spreading branches, rugged grey-brown bark and small dark-green ovate leaves, with deep rounded lobes. Male flowers are thin catkins; female flowers are borne in spikes in the leaf axils and followed by ovoid fruit, in little "cups" (acorns).

Related species The North American *Q. alba*, the white oak, also has a history of medicinal use, and was said to be effective against gangrene.

Habitat/distribution Native to Europe, occurs widely in the northern hemisphere in forests, open woodland and parkland, often found on clay soils.

Growth Grow in deep, fertile soil. May be propagated from seed, sown in containers in autumn. Very slow-growing.

Parts used Bark – stripped from mature trees and dried for use in decoctions and extracts.

USES Medicinal The oak has astringent, anti-inflammatory, antiseptic properties and is said to control bleeding. Applied externally to cuts, abrasions, ulcers, skin irritations, varicose veins and haemorrhoids. Sometimes recommended to be taken internally for haemorrhage, diarrhoea and gastric upsets. It was formerly used as a substitute for cinchona bark.

Other names Common oak and English oak.

Top *An English oak,* Quercus robur, *growing in a park in Germany.*

Above *An oak tree in springtime growth.*

Left *The lobed dark-green leaves of the oak tree feature in decorative carvings through the centuries, as family emblems.*

Opposite *A sheltered wood full of oak trees.*

ROSACEAE

Rosa

History and traditions Roses have been cultivated for thousands of years and were once valued as much for their medicinal and culinary qualities as for their fragrance. Asian species of roses were used in ancient Chinese medicine and roses of Persian origin by the Greeks and Romans. The Greek poet Anacreon referred to their therapeutic value when he wrote, "The rose distils a healing balm, the beating pulse of pain to calm." And, in AD 77 the Roman writer Pliny listed over 30 disorders as responding to treatment with preparations of rose. Medieval herbals contain many entries on the healing and restorative power of the rose, and in *The English Physician,* 1653, Culpeper gives pages of rose remedies for inflammation of the liver, venereal disease, sores in the mouth and throat, aching joints, "slippery bowels" and a host of other complaints. Red rose petals were listed in the British *Pharmacopoeia* as ingredients for pharmaceutical preparations until the 1930s. Their medicinal, culinary and fragrant uses are celebrated in all the old herbals and stillroom books with a huge range of recipes for ointments, lozenges, syrups, vinegars, conserves, cakes, candies and wafers. There are instructions for making rose-water, rose oil and cosmetic lotions. Sir Hugh Platt, in *Delights for Ladies,* 1594, has at least three lengthy entries on different methods of drying rose "leaves" (petals) to best effect.

Description and species

R. canina **(Dog rose)** – This is the wild rose of English hedgerows, known as the dog rose for its supposed ability, according to Pliny, to cure the bites of mad dogs. Its succulent, but acidic, red hips were made into tarts in the 17th century, and came to be greatly valued in the 20th century for their high vitamin C content. It is a hardy, deciduous climber, 3 m x 3 m (10 ft x 10 ft), with prickly stems and single flat, white, or pink-tinged flowers, followed by scarlet, ovoid hips.

R. eglanteria **(Sweet briar**, or **Eglantine)** – A vigorous semi-climber, 2.5 m x 2.5 m (8 ft x 8 ft), it has lovely apple-scented foliage and numerous single pink flowers, followed by rounded ovoid red hips. This is the rose which appears in the works of Chaucer and is described by Shakespeare as adorning Titania's bower:

With sweet musk roses and with eglantine
There sleeps Titania, sometime of the night
Lull'd in these flowers with dances and delight.

R. gallica var. ***officinalis*** **(Apothecary's rose)** – Probably the oldest of garden roses, it was widely grown in medieval times for its medicinal properties (though *R. damascena*, the damask rose, said to have been brought to Europe by the Crusaders in the 11th century, was almost as popular). A hardy deciduous, bushy shrub, 1.2 m x 1.2 m (4 ft x 4 ft), it has large, very fragrant, semi-double, bright-pink blooms and distinctive golden stamens.

R. gallica versicolor, also known as Rosa Mundi, after the 'Fair Rosamund', mistress of King Henry IV of England, (1367–1413). A sport from *R. g. officinalis*, it has crimson-pink petals, splashed with cream.

Growth Fertile, moist soil and a sunny position are best for producing thriving rose plants with large flowers. However, *R. eglanteria* does quite well on a poor, dry soil. The most suitable method of propagation is by hardwood cuttings in the autumn.

Parts used Flowers of *R. gallica*, hips of *R. canina*, essential oil, distilled rosewater from various rose species.

USES Medicinal Rose essential oil is used in aromatherapy for depression and nervous anxiety. In its purest form it is said to be the least toxic of the essential oils, safe to use undiluted. But many are adulterated, synthetic or semi-synthetic, and of no therapeutic value. Both hips and flowers are still sometimes recommended by herbalists to be taken internally in various preparations for colds, bronchial infections and gastric upsets and applied externally for sores and skin irritations. Rose hips are used nutritionally for their vitamin C content.

Culinary Hips are used for making vinegar, syrups, preserves and wines. Flower petals are added to salads and desserts, crystallized, made into jellies, jams and conserves. Distilled rosewater is used to flavour confectionery and desserts, especially in Middle Eastern dishes.

Aromatic Dried petals and essential oil are added to pot-pourri, other fragrant articles for the home and beauty preparations, such as hand lotions and masks. Rosebuds and whole flowers are dried for decorative use. Dry roses in a warm, dry room but not in direct sunlight, which will bleach the petals.

Opposite page, clockwise from lower left Rosa eglanteria; Rosa canina; *and the superb double cultivar* Rosa *'Charles de Mills'.*

This page, clockwise from top left Rosa gallica *'Versicolor'; the nutritious hips of* Rosa canina; *a single flower of* Rosa gallica *var.* officinalis – *the famed Apothecary's rose; and the massed blooms of the Apothecary's rose on a bush.*

Rose-petal skin freshener

40 g/1½ oz fresh rose petals (any fragrant red rose petals are suitable)
600 ml/1 pint/2½ cups boiling distilled water
15 ml/1 tbs cider vinegar

Put the rose petals in a bowl, pour over the boiling water and add the vinegar. Cover and leave to stand for 2 hours, then strain into a clean bottle.

Apply to the face with cotton wool (cotton ball) to tone the skin. Keep chilled or in a refrigerator and use up within 2–3 days.

LABIATAE/LAMIACEAE

Rosmarinus officinalis

Rosemary

History and traditions Rosemary was well known in ancient Greece and Rome and the Latin generic name, *Rosmarinus*, means "dew of the sea", from its coastal habitat and the appearance of its flowers. It gained an early reputation for improving memory and uplifting the spirits, which is referred to in many herbals. *Bancke's Herbal*, 1525, includes a long list of remedies, practical suggestions and superstitions regarding rosemary, including putting it under the bed to "be delivered of all evill dreames", boiling it in wine as a cosmetic face wash, binding it round the legs against gout, and drinking it in wine for a cough or for lost appetite. It was also a major ingredient of Hungary Water, said to be invented by a hermit for Queen Elizabeth of Hungary, who was cured of paralysis after rubbing it on daily. A symbol of remembrance, it found a place at weddings, funerals and in Christmas decorations, when it was often gilded. In Spanish folklore rosemary is believed to give protection from the evil eye and to have sheltered the Virgin Mary, during the flight into Egypt, when the once white flowers took on the celestial blue of her cloak.

Description A variable evergreen shrub, to 2 m (6 ft), it has woody branches and strongly aromatic, needle-like foliage. A dense covering of small, tubular, two-lipped flowers, usually pale blue (but there are dark-blue and occasionally pink variants) appear in spring.

Habitat/distribution Native to the Mediterranean coast, found on sunny hillsides and in open situations. It is introduced and widely grown elsewhere.

Growth Thrives on sharply drained, stony soils and requires little moisture. Although *R. officinalis* is frost-hardy (not all species are), it needs a sunny, sheltered position and protection in cold winters and periods of prolonged frost. Easily propagated from semi-ripe cuttings taken in summer. It becomes straggly unless pruned hard in summer, after flowering, but must not be cut back to old wood.

Parts used The leaves and flowering tops are used fresh or dried for cookery and in medicinal preparations; essential oil distilled from leaves.

USES Medicinal A restorative, tonic herb, with antiseptic and antibacterial properties. It is taken internally as an infusion for colds, influenza, fatigue and headaches, or as a tincture for depression and nervous tension; and applied externally in massage oil for rheumatic and muscular pain. The essential oil is added to bath water for aching joints and tiredness.

Above left *Flowers of* Rosmarinus officinalis.

Above Rosmarinus officinalis *'Miss Jessopp's Upright'*.

Culinary A classic flavouring for roasted or broiled lamb, stews and casseroles, and added to marinades, vinegar, oil and dressings. Used sparingly, it adds spice and interest to cakes, biscuits, sorbets and baked or stewed apples.

Cosmetic Infusions are used as rinses for dry hair and dandruff and added to bath lotions and beauty preparations. Essential oil is used in perfumery and cosmetic industries.

Aromatic Dried leaves add fragrance to pot-pourri and insect-repellent sachets.

CAUTION Not suitable to be taken internally in medicinal doses when pregnant, especially in the form of essential oil, as excess may cause abortion. Safe for normal culinary use.

Rumex scutatus, *French sorrel.*

POLYGONACEAE

Rumex acetosa

Sorrel

History and traditions Various species of sorrel were used medicinally from at least the 14th century, but it was always chiefly valued as a culinary herb, especially in France and Belgium, where it was even potted as a preserve for winter use. Recipe books of the 17th and 18th centuries reveal that sorrel was not just made into soup, but frequently served with eggs, put into a sweet tart with orange flowers and cinnamon, as well as being cooked as a spinach-like vegetable. John Evelyn considered that it should never be left out of a salad, lending it sharpness, as a useful substitute for lemons and oranges when they were scarce. He also wrote that it "sharpens appetite ... cools the liver and strengthens the heart" (*Acetaria*, 1719). Culpeper recommended it for many medicinal purposes, including the breaking of plague sores and boils.

Description A hardy perennial, growing up to 1.2 m (4 ft), with large, pale-green, oblong to lanceolate leaves, and large terminal spikes of small disc-shaped reddish-brown flowers on long stalks.

Related species *R. scutatus*, Buckler-leaved, or French Sorrel, is a lower-growing plant, with shield-shaped leaves and less acidity, and is favoured for culinary uses in France.

Habitat/distribution Occurs in Europe and North Asia in grasslands and is frequently found on nitrogen-rich soils.

Growth Grows best and runs to seed less quickly in rich, moist soil, in a sunny or partially shady position. Propagated by seed sown in spring or by division in spring or autumn.

Parts used Leaves – when fresh and young.

USES Culinary Sorrel adds a pleasant, lemony flavour to soups, sauces, salads, egg and cheese dishes. But it is acidic and not recommended for rheumatism and arthritis sufferers. The leaves have the best flavour and texture in spring, before they become coarse and fibrous.

Above left Rumex acetosa – *the leaves are high in vitamin C.*

Above *Sorrel in flower.*

CAUTION Sorrel contains oxalates, also found in spinach and rhubarb, which are toxic in excess.

Above Ruta graveolens *'Variegata'.*

Left Ruta graveolens *in flower.*

RUTACEAE

Ruta graveolens

Rue

History and traditions Rue has a long tradition as an antidote to poison and defence against disease. The Greek physician Galen (*c.* AD 130–201) took rue and coriander (cilantro), mixed with oil and salt, as a protection against infection, and Dioscorides (*c.* AD 40–90) recommended it against every kind of venom. Most 17th-century herbalists continued the anti-venom theme, as illustrated by William Coles: "The weasell when she is to encounter the serpent arms herselfe with eating of rue" (*The Art of Simpling*, 1656). Rue was an ingredient of the celebrated anti-plague concoction, Four Thieves Vinegar, and always included in the judge's posy, placed in the courtroom to protect him from diseased prisoners and the dreaded jail-fever. The name "herb of grace" is said by some to originate from the practice of sprinkling holy water with a sprig of rue at Sunday mass. Its potent smell and protective attributes ensured its place as a powerful anti-witchcraft and spells herb. Although it is an attractive plant and widely grown in herb gardens, it has few herbal uses today. Far from being a protective, it is now recognized as a toxic irritant.

Description An evergreen, or semi-evergreen, shrubby perennial to 60 cm (2 ft), it has deeply divided blue-green leaves, with rounded spatulate leaf segments and a mass of small yellow, four-petalled flowers in midsummer.

Related species *R. graveolens* 'Jackman's Blue' is a widely grown cultivar with steel-blue foliage. There is also a variegated cultivar with cream and grey-green leaves.

Habitat/distribution Native to southern Europe on dry rocky soils, introduced and often naturalized throughout Europe, North America and Australia.

Growth Prefers light, well-drained soil and, although reasonably hardy, requires a sunny, sheltered position in cooler regions. Variegated cultivars are slightly less hardy. Propagated from seed (not cultivars) sown in spring, or from cuttings taken in spring (always wear gloves to handle). Prune in spring, or just after flowering in summer, to maintain a neat shape, but do not cut into old woody stems. It should not be planted at the front of a border where it can be brushed against.

Parts used Leaves.

USES Medicinal Although recommended by some herbalists for various complaints, including painful menstruation, it is a dangerous, toxic herb and there are safer alternative remedies for such conditions.

Aromatic It has insect-repellent properties and leaves may be dried for adding to pot-pourri.

CAUTION Rue is a skin irritant, especially when handled in full sun, and causes severe blistering. Gloves should be worn when handling. Toxic if taken internally in excess, it affects the central nervous system and may be fatal. It is also an abortifacient.

SALICACEAE

Salix alba

Willow

History and traditions The willow contains salicylic acid and is the origin of aspirin (acetylsalicylic acid), which was synthesized from it as early as 1853. The bark had been used in Europe for centuries to reduce pain and fever, and in Native American traditional medicine several willow species were used for the same purposes. Willow branches were popular church decorations in Britain and used as substitute palms (which were not readily available) on Palm Sunday. In Russia, the week leading up to Easter was often called "willow week". The tree was always an emblem of sadness (it was a willow beneath which the "children of Israel" sat down and wept) and garlands of it were worn by the forsaken in love.

Description A spreading, fast-growing deciduous tree, up to 25 m (82 ft), it has greyish, fissured bark, arching branches and silvery-green, slender lanceolate leaves. Stalkless, yellow male and female catkins are borne in spring.

Related species There are several species of willow with medicinal properties in this large genus, including the North American *S. myrsinifolia* or black willow.

Habitat/distribution *S. alba* occurs widely in Europe and Asia, most often near rivers, streams and waterways.

Growth Requires damp soil and even does well on heavy clay, but dislikes chalk. Propagated by greenwood cuttings in spring, or by hardwood cuttings in winter.

Parts used Bark – collected from 2–3-year-old trees and dried for use in decoctions and other preparations; leaves – are also occasionally used in infusions.

USES Medicinal The salicylic compounds it contains give willow fever-reducing, analgesic, anti-rheumatic properties. Although it has been completely replaced by synthetics in pharmaceutical preparations it is still sometimes used in herbal medicine for fevers and neuralgia (taken internally), in baths for rheumatic pain and in ointments and compresses for cuts, burns and skin complaints.

Above right Salix alba *(white willow).*

Right Salix alba *subsp.* vitellina *(golden willow), coppiced to maintain its ornamental stems.*

LABIATAE/LAMIACEAE

Salvia

Salvia officinalis
Sage

History and traditions The Latin name comes from *salvere*, to save or heal, and this herb has always been connected with good health and a long life – even immortality. An old Arabian proverb asks, "How can a man die who has sage in his garden?" and John Evelyn wrote, "Tis a plant, indeed, with so many and wonderful properties as that the assiduous use of it is said to render men immortal", (*Acetaria*, 1719). And Sir John Hill in *The Virtues of British Herbs,* 1772, has many anecdotes of people living to improbable ages through regular intake of sage. It is another plant, like rosemary, which is said to thrive where the woman rules the household: "If the sage tree thrives and grows/The master's not master and he knows."

Description An evergreen, highly aromatic, shrubby perennial, growing to 60 cm (2 ft), it has downy, rough-textured, grey-green, ovate leaves and spikes of tubular, violet-blue flowers in early summer. *S. officinalis* is one of the few hardy plants in this huge genus of around 900 species worldwide.

Related species ***S. o.*** **'Icterina' (golden sage)** – Has gold and green variegated leaves. It seldom flowers in cool climates, but in warmer regions sometimes has pale mauve blooms. Although it may be used as a culinary herb it does not have such a good flavour as the species, or as the purple sages. But it does add colour when used in salads. It is reliably variegated, not as prone to revert as many and makes an attractive contrasting foliage plant for the border. ***S. o.*** **Purpurascens Group (purple sage, or red sage)** – Has striking purple, grey and green foliage. Some of its variants produce blue flower spikes. It has a strong flavour, is often used as a culinary herb and widely cultivated for its ornamental value. ***S. elegans*** **(pineapple sage)** – This is a half-hardy perennial with green, soft, ovate leaves, scented with pineapple, and scarlet, tubular flowers in winter.

Habitat/distribution Sage is native to southern Europe, found on dry, sunny slopes, introduced in cool temperate regions.

Growth Grow in light, well-drained soil in full sun. Although *S. officinalis* is hardy, it does not always withstand prolonged cold below -10°C (14°F), especially in wet conditions. The cultivars are slightly less hardy than the species. *S. officinalis* may be propagated from seed; cultivars must be propagated from cuttings or by layering. Prune sage in the spring to keep it

Salvia officinalis *Purpurascens Group.*

Above Salvia elegans *in flower.*

in good shape, or just after flowering, but do not cut into old wood. After a few years, sages can become straggly and need to be replaced. Pineapple sage must be protected from frost and kept under cover during the winter. Grow in moist soil and if container-grown keep the compost (soil mix) damp. It is very easy to propagate from softwood cuttings taken throughout the summer.

Parts used Leaves – fresh or dried, essential oil.

USES Medicinal An astringent, antiseptic, antibacterial herb, infusions of the leaves are used as a gargle or mouthwash for sore throats, mouth ulcers, gum disease, laryngitis and tonsillitis. Infusions are taken internally as tonics, to aid digestion and for menopausal problems and applied externally as compresses to help heal wounds.

Culinary Leaves are used to flavour Mediterranean dishes, cheese, sausages, goose, pork and other fatty meat. In Italy it is added to liver dishes. It is also made into stuffings, a classic combination is sage and onion. Leaves of pineapple sage may be floated in drinks.

Aromatic/cosmetic An infusion of the leaves makes a rinse for dark hair and to treat dandruff. The essential oil is used in the perfume and cosmetic industries.

Above Salvia officinalis *in flower.*

Opposite page, bottom left Salvia officinalis; **top left** *A flowering form of* S. o. *Purpurascens Group;* **top right** S. elegans *in leaf;*

This page, top left S. o. *'Icterina';* **top right** S. o. *'Tricolor'.*

CAUTION Sage, especially the essential oil, is toxic in excess doses, and should not be taken medicinally over long periods, by pregnant women or by epileptics (the thujone content may trigger fits). It is quite safe used in small amounts in cookery.

Salvia sclarea

Clary sage

History and traditions The specific name, *sclarea*, comes from *clarus*, meaning clear, and is also the origin of the common name clary, a corruption of "clear eye" which refers to an old use, mentioned in many herbals, of clary sage as a lotion for inflammations of the eye. It has long been a flavouring for alcoholic drinks – as it remains to this day – and clary wine is said to have been a 16th-century aphrodisiac. In the 19th century it was sometimes used as a hops substitute, to make beer more heady and intoxicating. In conjunction with elderflowers, it provided German wine producers with a way of adding a muscatel flavour to Rhenish wine.

Description A biennial, up to 1.2 m (4 ft) tall, it has a large basal clump of broadly ovate grey-green leaves, and in its second year a tall, branched, flower spike of silvery, lilac-blue and pink two-lipped florets. The whole plant has an unpleasantly overpowering scent, but it is showy and decorative in the border.

Habitat/distribution Native to southern Europe, found on dry, sandy soils.

Growth Grow in free-draining, but reasonably moist and fertile soil. Propagated by seed sown in spring or autumn. Often self-seeds.

Parts used Leaves – fresh or dried, essential oil.

USES Medicinal Infusions of the leaves are used as lotions for cuts and abrasions, and as a gargle for mouth ulcers. Sometimes recommended to be taken internally in small doses for promoting appetite.

Aromatic Essential oil is used to flavour vermouth and liqueurs, and widely used in commercial soaps, scents and eau-de-Cologne.

CAPRIFOLIACEAE

Sambucus nigra

Elder

History and traditions The elder has been associated since earliest times with myth and magic, witchcraft and spells. At the same time it was always valued for its many practical uses, medicinal, household, culinary and cosmetic. In Norse mythology, hauntings, deaths and harmed babies were the result of upsetting the Elder-Mother and guardian spirit, by not obtaining her permission before cutting down a tree to make furniture or cradles. Christian legends, referred to in English literature from the 14th-century *Piers the Plowman*, by William Langland, to Spenser and Shakespeare, included the story that Judas hanged himself on an elder tree, and that it was the wood used to make the cross of Calvary. From this it became a symbol of sorrow and death and was planted in graveyards. The idea that elders provided protection from witchcraft and evil spirits has ancient roots, and it is cited in Coles's *The Art of Simpling,* 1656, as being planted near cottages and fixed to doors and windows on the last day of April for this purpose. Some years earlier, in 1644, *The Anatomie of the Elder* was published, which celebrated its medicinal properties and asserted its capability of curing all known ills. Old herbals are full of culinary recipes, too, for the flowers, shoots, buds and berries, and the distilled water was said to ensure a fair complexion. The timber was valued for making fences, skewers, pegs and small household articles and the easily removable core of soft pith made elder prime material for pop-guns (as referred to by Culpeper), penny whistles and musical pipes, a use it has been put to since classical times. The generic name, *Sambucus*, is from the Greek for a musical instrument.

Description A small deciduous tree, up to 10 m (33 ft) tall, it has dull-green, pinnate leaves, divided into five elliptic leaflets. Flat umbels of creamy, musk-scented flowers in early summer are followed by pendulous clusters of spherical black fruits on red stalks in early autumn.

Related species There are a few ornamental cultivars which make attractive subjects for the garden but have no medicinal or culinary value.

Habitat/distribution Native to Europe, western Asia and northern Africa. Occurs widely in temperate and subtropical regions in hedgerows, woodlands and roadsides.

Growth Prefers moist but well-drained, humus-rich soil in sun or partial shade. Propagation by suckers or semi-ripe cuttings in summer are the easiest methods. The species, but not cultivars, can also be grown from seed. Elders often self-seed prolifically.

Parts used Leaves – fresh; flowers – fresh or dried; fruits – fresh.

USES Medicinal Has anticatarrhal and anti-inflammatory properties. Infusions of the flowers are taken for colds, sinusitis, influenza and feverish illnesses, and are said to be soothing for hayfever. The fruits (berries) are made into syrups, or "elderberry rob", also for colds.

Culinary Fresh flower heads in batter make elderflower fritters; fresh or dried flowers give a muscatel flavour to gooseberries and stewed fruits, and are added to desserts and sorbets. Flowers and berries are used to make vinegars, cordials and wines.

Cosmetic Fresh or dried flowers are used in skin toners, face creams and other home-made beauty preparations.

General The leaves have insecticidal properties and are boiled in water to make sprays against aphids and garden pests.

Elderflower

An old recipe

To take away the freckles in the face Wash your face, in the wane of the Moone, with a sponge, morning and evening, with the distilled water of Elder-leaves, letting the same dry into the skinne. Your water must be distilled in May. This from a Traveller, who hath cured himselfe thereby.

Delights for Ladies, 1659

Elderflower skin freshener

An infusion of elderflowers makes a soothing and refreshing lotion for sensitive or sunburned skin.

Pour 600ml/1 pint/2½ cups boiling distilled water over 25 g/1 oz dried elderflowers in a jug. Leave to cool, strain off the flowers and apply to the skin on cotton wool (cotton balls).

Keep the lotion cool and refrigerated and use within 2–3 days.

CAUTION Leaves contain toxic cyanogenic glycosides and should not be eaten. Berries are harmful if eaten raw.

Top left Sambucus nigra *in flower.*

Left *Elderberries.*

ROSACEAE

Sanguisorba minor

Salad burnet

History and traditions This is a traditional herb-garden plant recommended by Francis Bacon in his essay on the ideal garden (1625), to be planted in "alleys", or walks, along with thyme and water mints, for the pleasant perfume when crushed. The common name is a reference to the fact that this herb often lasted through the winter, providing welcome edible greenery when little else was available. It was also added to wine cups or ale for the cooling effect of the leaves. The generic name, *Sanguisorba*, comes from the Latin for *sanguis*, blood, and *sorbere*, to absorb, as it was formerly used medicinally as a wound herb interchangeably with *S. officinalis*, greater burnet.

Description A clump-forming perennial, 15–40 cm (6–16 in) in height, it has pinnate leaves with numerous pairs of oval, serrated-edged leaflets and long stalks topped by rounded crimson flower heads.

Habitat/distribution It is native to Europe and Asia, naturalized in North America. It is found on chalky soils in grassy meadows and roadsides.

Growth Thrives on chalk (alkaline). Requires reasonably rich, moist soil for good leaf production and a sunny or partially shady position. Propagated by seed sown in spring. Cut it back as soon as the flower buds appear in order to ensure a continuous supply of leaves.

Parts used Leaves – fresh.

USES Culinary The leaves have a mild, cucumber flavour, make a pleasant addition to salads and are floated in drinks or wine punch.

COMPOSITAE/ASTERACEAE

Santolina chamaecyparissus

Cotton lavender

History and traditions Cotton lavender is a native of southern Europe and was well known to the ancient Greeks and Romans and has long been valued as a vermifuge and for its insect-repellent properties. Culpeper recommended it also against poisonous bites and skin irritations (*The English Physician*, 1653). The neat, silvery foliage responds well to close clipping and it was introduced to Britain and northern Europe in the 16th century as hedging for knot gardens.

Description A small highly aromatic shrub, growing to about 60 cm (2 ft), it has silvery-grey, finely divided, woolly foliage and bright yellow, globular button-shaped flowers.

Related species *S. rosmarinifolia* subsp. *rosmarinifolia* syn. *S. viridis* has bright green foliage and makes an interesting contrast in knot-garden work.

Habitat/distribution Cotton lavender is native to the Mediterranean region, introduced and widely cultivated worldwide. Found in fields and wastelands on calcareous soil.

Growth Grow in light, sandy soil and a sunny position. Tolerates drought. Propagated by semiripe cuttings in summer. Prune hard in spring to maintain a neat, clipped shape. It will regenerate if cut back to old wood.

Parts used Leaves – dried.

USES Medicinal Formerly used to expel intestinal worms. It is said to have anti-inflammatory properties and is sometimes made into an infusion as a lotion for skin irritations and insect bites, but in general it is little used in herbal medicine today.

Aromatic Dried leaves are added to pot-pourri and insect-repellent sachets.

Other name Lavender cotton in the United States.

Below Santolina chamaecyparissus.

Bottom Santolina rosmarinifolia *subsp.* rosmarinifolia *syn.* S. viridis.

CARYOPHYLLACEAE

Saponaria officinalis

Soapwort

History and traditions Soapwort is indigenous to Europe and the Middle East and has been used there for its cleansing properties for many centuries. Some authorities claim that it was even known to the Assyrians around the 8th century BC. The name *Saponaria* comes from *sapo*, the Latin for soap, and, because of the high saponin content, soapwort roots produce a foamy lather when mixed with water. In Syria it was used for washing woollens, in Switzerland for washing sheep before shearing, and the medieval fullers, who "finished" cloth, used soapwort in the process. The common name, bouncing Bet, is a reference to the activity of plump washerwomen. It had its medicinal uses too. A decoction of the roots was formerly used for a variety of ailments from rheumatism to syphilis. Soapwort has been used until very recently by museums and by the National Trust in Britain, as it was found to be more suitable for cleaning delicate old tapestries and fabrics than most modern detergents.

Description A spreading, hardy perennial, on a creeping rhizomatous rootstock, 60–90 cm (2–3 ft) tall, it has bright-green, fleshy, ovate to elliptical leaves, and clusters of pale-pink flowers in mid- to late summer.

Habitat/distribution Native to Europe, the Middle East and western Asia, naturalized in North America and widely grown in temperate regions. Found near streams and in wastelands, often as an escape from gardens.

Growth Prefers moist, loamy soil, but tolerates most conditions and can become invasive. The easiest method of propagation is by division of the runners in spring. It can also be grown successfully from seed.

Parts used Roots, leafy stems – fresh or dried.

USES Medicinal It is seldom used in herbal medicine today.

Cosmetic An infusion or decoction of the roots and leafy stems makes shampoo – the addition of eau-de-cologne improves the slightly unpleasant smell.

Household Used for cleaning delicate fabrics.

Other name Bouncing Bet.

Above left Saponaria officinalis.

Above right *A decoction of the whole plant makes a gentle shampoo.*

Soapwort shampoo

If you are used to a detergent-based shampoo you will find this does not lather in the same way, although it will froth up if you whisk it. The gentle cleansing properties of soapwort shampoo are very beneficial if you suffer from an itchy scalp or dandruff.

25 g/1 oz fresh soapwort root, leaves and stem or 15 g/½ oz dried soapwort root
750 ml/1¼ pints/3 cups water
lavender water or eau-de-Cologne

Break up the soapwort stems, roughly chop the root and put the whole lot into a pan with the water. Bring to the boil and simmer for 20 minutes.

Strain off the herbs and add a dash of lavender water or eau-de-Cologne, as soapwort has a slightly unpleasant scent.

Use like an ordinary shampoo, rubbing well into the scalp and rinsing.

CAUTION Soapwort should not be taken internally as it can be upsetting to the digestive system and is capable of destroying red blood cells if taken in large quantities.

LABIATAE/LAMIACEAE

Satureja

Satureja hortensis
Summer savory

History and traditions Both summer and winter savory are Mediterranean herbs that were appreciated by the Romans and commonly used in their cuisine. The poet Virgil, 70–19 BC, celebrated them as being among the most fragrant of plants suitable for growing near beehives. Shakespeare too, writes of the scent of savory and it is included in Perdita's herbal gift to Polixenes in *The Winter's Tale*. The savories were among the herbs listed by John Josselyn which were taken to North America by early settlers to remind them of their English gardens. Culpeper promotes both herbs to ease a range of ailments, including asthma, and for expelling "tough phlegm from the chest", with summer savory especially suitable for drying to make conserves and syrups. It has been established by modern scientific studies (carried out in the 1980s) that the savories do have strong antibacterial properties. However, the subtle, spicy flavour (like marjoram, with a hint of thyme) ensures that both summer and winter savory remain first and foremost culinary herbs.

Description A small, bushy, hardy annual, to 38 cm (15 in) high, it has woody, much-branched stems and small, leathery, dark-green, linear-lanceolate leaves. Tiny white or pale-lilac flowers appear in summer.

Habitat/distribution Mediterranean in origin, introduced and widely grown in warm and temperate regions elsewhere. Occurs on chalky soils (alkaline) and rocky hillsides.

Growth Grow in well-drained soil in full sun. Propagated from seed sown in containers, or *in situ,* in early spring. It may help reduce the incidence of blackfly when grown near beans.

Parts used Leaves, flowering tops – used fresh or dried.

USES Medicinal Has antiseptic, antibacterial properties and is said to improve digestion.

Culinary Summer savory has an affinity with beans and adds a spicy flavour to dried herb mixtures, stuffings, pulses, pâtés and meat dishes. Extracts and essential oil are used in commercial products in the food industry.

CAUTION The savories stimulate the uterus and are not to be given to pregnant women in medicinal doses.

Below *The leaves have a mildly spicy flavour.*

Satureja montana
Winter savory

Description A clump-forming, hardy perennial, to 38 cm (15 in) tall, it is semi-evergreen (does not keep all its leaves in cool temperate regions through the winter, especially if frosts are prolonged). It has dark-green, linear-lanceolate, pointed leaves and dense whorls of small white flowers in summer. It has a stronger, coarser fragrance than summer savory, due to the higher proportion of thymol it contains.

Growth Grow in well-drained soil, in full sun. Propagated by seed, by division in spring, or by cuttings in summer. Prune lightly in early summer, after flowering, to maintain a neat shape.

USES It has the same uses as summer savory, but to most tastes has a less refined flavour for culinary purposes.

Satureja montana

SCROPHULARIACEAE

Scrophularia nodosa

Figwort

History and traditions This herb was used in the past to treat scrofula or "the king's evil", a disease which affected the lymph glands in the neck. It conformed to the Doctrine of Signatures theory because the knots on the rhizome were thought to resemble swollen glands. Culpeper, writing in 1653, called it "Throatwort", adding that "it taketh away all redness, spots and freckles in the face, as also the scurf and any foul deformity therein".

Description A strong-smelling perennial on a stout, knotted rhizome, 40–80 cm (16–32 in) in height, it has ovate to lanceolate leaves and terminal spikes of small, dull-pink flowers.

Habitat/distribution Native to Europe and temperate parts of Asia, naturalized in North America. Found in woods and hedgerows.

Growth Grow in very damp soil, in sun or partial shade. Propagated by division in spring, or by seed sown in spring or autumn.

Parts used Rhizomes – dried for use in decoctions and other medicinal preparations; leaves and flowering stems – fresh or dried.

USES Medicinal This has cleansing properties. Infusions of the leaves are taken internally or applied externally in washes or compresses for skin disorders and inflammations. Decoctions of the root are taken internally for throat infections, swollen glands and feverish illnesses.

CAUTION This herb has a stimulating effect on the heart and is not given to patients with heart diseases.

CRASSULACEAE

Sempervivum tectorum

Houseleek

History and traditions In the folklore of most European countries, houseleek is dedicated to Jupiter or Thor and was deemed to provide protection from lightning. It has been planted on thatched roofs or in the crevices of roof tiles ever since the Emperor Charlemagne, 747–814 AD, decreed to this effect. The second part of the common name, houseleek, is from the Anglo-Saxon word for plant, *leac*. Its Latin name refers to its ability to withstand any conditions, and comes from *semper*, always, and *vivum*, living or alive. The specific name *tectorum* is a reference to its roof habitat. This herb has been used since the time of Dioscorides and Pliny as a soothing agent for skin complaints. And Culpeper, writing in the 17th century, suggests a first-aid measure, which is equally valid today: "the leaves being gently rubbed on any place stung with nettles or bees, doth quickly take away the pain".

Description A mat-forming hardy succulent, it has blue-green, rounded leaves with pointed spiny tips, arranged in rosettes. Erect, hairy stems, to a height of 30 cm (12 in), bear pinkish-red star-shaped flowers in summer.

Habitat/distribution Native to southern Europe and western Asia, found on rocky slopes and in mountainous areas. Introduced and widely grown elsewhere.

Growth Thrives in gritty or stony, sharply drained soil and withstands drought. The easiest method of propagation is by separating and replanting offsets in spring.

Parts used Leaves – fresh.

USES Medicinal The leaves are made into infusions, compresses, lotions and ointments, or cut open to release the sap and applied directly to insect bites and stings, sunburn, skin irritations, warts and corns.

Above *A cultivar of* Sempervivum tectorum *with red suffused leaves.*

Below *Break open leaves to release the sap.*

COMPOSITAE/ASTERACEAE

Silybum marianum

Milk thistle

History and traditions It is called milk thistle for its milky-white veins, from which it earned its reputation, under the Doctrine of Signatures, as improving the milk supply of nursing mothers. The Latin specific name, *marianum*, associates it with the Virgin Mary, from the tradition that her milk once fell upon its leaves, and the genus name is a corruption of *silybon*, which was Dioscorides' term for this herb. Milk thistles were formerly frequently cultivated as a vegetable and it was decreed by Thomas Tryon (*The Good Housewife*, 1692) that "they are very wholesome and exceed all other greens in taste".

Description A tall annual or biennial, up to 1.2 m (4 ft) in height, it has large, deeply lobed, spiny leaves with white veins and purple thistle flowers in summer.

Habitat/distribution Native to Europe, introduced elsewhere and naturalized in North America and other countries. Found on dry, stony soils, in fields and roadsides.

Growth Grows in any well-drained soil in a sunny position. Propagation is by seed, sown in spring or autumn, and it self-seeds prolifically.

Parts used Leaves and flowering stems – dried for use in infusions or for extractions of the active principle silymarin.

USES Medicinal Taken as an infusion to stimulate appetite and for digestive disorders. Contains compounds, known as silymarin, which are said to be effective as an antidote to toxic substances that cause liver damage.

Other name Marian thistle.

SIMMONDSIACIAE

Simmondsia chinensis

Jojoba

History and traditions The oil from the seeds of this herb was used by Native Americans as a cosmetic and for softening garments made from animal skins. In the 1970s jojoba was discovered to be a valuable replacement for sperm whale oil and large commercial plantations have since been established in Arizona and across wide areas of semi-arid grassland in the United States.

Description A dioecious shrub, up to 2 m (6 ft) in height, with leathery, ovate leaves, it is the only species in the genus. Pale-yellow male flowers appear in axillary clusters, the greenish female flowers are usually solitary and followed by ovoid seed capsules.

Habitat/distribution It is native to south-western North America and Mexico, and is widely grown as a crop in the United States and the Middle East.

Growth Tolerant of drought, it thrives in dry, gravelly soil. A half-hardy plant, it is propagated by seed sown in spring, or by heel cuttings taken in autumn.

Parts used Oil – expressed straight from the ripe seeds.

USES Medicinal Jojoba oil has exceptionally soothing and softening properties and is used in pharmaceutical ointments for dry skins, psoriasis and eczema.

Cosmetic It is also an important ingredient of moisturisers, body lotions and sunscreens.

General The oil is used as an engine lubricant. The shrubs are planted to prevent further encroachment of total desert in arid areas.

APIACEAE

Smyrnium olusatrum

Alexanders

History and traditions Alexanders was valued chiefly as a culinary herb from the days of the ancient Greeks until well into the 19th century. It is high in vitamin C and at one time was recognised as a useful antiscorbutic. It was also thought to have some medicinal properties, chiefly as a diuretic and stomachic. It was taken for asthma and to help menstrual flow, but it is no longer used in herbal medicine.

Description A large perennial, it grows up to 1.5 m (5 ft) tall, with thick ridged stems, dark-green. shiny leaves and domed umbels of greenish-yellow flowers, followed by black seeds. It is sometimes confused with angelica, of which it is taken to be a wild species.

Habitat/distribution Native to Europe and the Mediterranean, frequently found on coastal sites.

Growth It grows best in sandy, but moist and reasonably fertile soil, and is propagated by seed sown in spring.

Parts used Leaves, young stems, flower buds, seeds, roots.

USES Culinary The whole plant is edible. Leaves and young stems may be used like celery, the roots cooked as parsnips, the flower buds added to salads and the seeds lightly crushed or ground as a seasoning.

Other name Black lovage.

COMPOSITAE/ASTERACEAE

Solidago virgaurea

Golden rod

History and traditions Most of the nearly 100 species of *Solidago* came from North America, where a number of them were used in the traditional Native American medicine for healing wounds, sores, insect bites and stings. In the 17th century the dried herb was imported and sold on the London market for high prices as an exotic cure-all, until one day someone noticed golden rod growing wild on Hampstead Heath in London and the bottom dropped out of the market. As Thomas Fuller put it in his *History of the Worthies of England,* 1662, "When golden rod was brought at great expense from foreign countries, it was highly valued; but it was no sooner discovered to be a native plant, than it was discarded." However, by the19th century it was firmly established as a popular ornamental in Britain, causing William Cobbett to complain in *The American Gardener,* 1816, "A yellow flower called the 'Plain-weed', which is the torment of the neighbouring farmer, has been above all the plants in this world, chosen as the most conspicuous ornament of the front of the King of England's grandest palace, that of Hampton Court."

Description A vigorous hardy perennial, growing to 1 m (3 ft) in height. It has branched stems, lanceolate, finely toothed leaves and terminal panicles of golden-yellow flowers in late summer. It is an invasive plant and spreads very rapidly.

Related species *S. canadensis*, native to Canada and North America, is a taller plant, growing to 1.5 m (5 ft), often seen in gardens, and also has medicinal properties. Most garden varieties of golden rod are hybrids.

Habitat/distribution *S. virgaurea* is the only native European species, and is found in woodland and grassland on acid and calcareous (alkaline) soils. Many closely-related species are native to North America.

Growth Prefers not too rich soil and an open, sunny position. Propagated by seed sown in spring, or by division in spring and autumn.

Parts used Leaves, flowering tops – dried for use in infusions, powders, ointments and other medicinal preparations.

USES Medicinal Golden rod has antifungal, anti-inflammatory and antiseptic properties. It is applied externally in lotions, ointments and poultices to help heal wounds, skin irritations, bites, stings and ulcers. Infusions are taken internally for urinary infections and chronic skin problems and to make gargles for sore throats.

Above left *A garden hybrid of* Solidago canadensis *and* S. virgaurea *in flower, and in bud (*above*).*

Golden rod superstitions

- Where golden rod grows, secret treasure is buried.
- When it springs up near the door of a house, it brings good fortune.

LABIATAE/LAMIACEAE

Stachys officinalis

Betony

History and traditions Betony was highly prized as a medicinal herb in Roman times, when Antonius Musa, physician to the Emperor Augustus, wrote a treatise on its virtues, assigning 47 remedies to it. It was of great importance to the Anglo-Saxons for its magical as well as its medicinal properties and is mentioned in the 10th-century manuscript herbal, the *Lacnunga*. It was made into amulets to be worn against evil spirits, planted in churchyards and held to be capable of driving away despair. *The Herbal of Apuleius* (*c.* AD 400) describes betony as "good for a man's soul or his body". Betony was much valued throughout Europe, and inspired the Italian proverb "sell your coat and buy betony". It was always associated with treatments for maladies of the head and said to be a certain cure for headaches – a use that it retains today in modern herbal practice. The name betony derives from *vettonica*, as the Romans knew it, which became *betonica* (as it was until recently classified). *Stachys* is from the Greek for a spike or ear of corn and refers to the shape of the flower cluster.

Description A mat-forming, hairy, hardy perennial, it has a basal rosette of wrinkled, ovate leaves with dentate margins. Flower stems rise to 60 cm (2 ft) with smaller opposite leaves and dense, terminal spikes of magenta-pink two-lipped flowers borne in summer.

Above S. byzantina *syn* S. lanata.

Related species *S. byzantina* syn. *S. lanata* is popularly known as "lambs' ears", "lambs' lugs", "lambs' tails" or "lambs' tongues" for its white, woolly foliage. It forms a mat of whitish-green, soft, downy, wrinkled leaves with short mauve flower spikes to 45 cm (18 in) tall. Although it has no medicinal or culinary properties it is grown as a herb garden ornamental.
Habitat/distribution Native to Europe, grows on sandy loam in open woods and grassland.
Growth Grow in ordinary, dry soil in sun or partial shade. Propagated by seed sown in spring or by division during dormancy.
Parts used Leaves, flowering stems – fresh or dried for infusions, ointments and lotions.

USES Medicinal Infusions are taken for headaches, especially if associated with anxiety and nervous tension, often combined with *Hypericum perforatum* and *Lavandula*. Made into lotions or ointments (often in combination with other herbs) for applying to cuts, abrasions and bruises.

Conserve of betony
(after the Italian way)

Betony new and tender one pound, the best sugar three pound, beat them very small in a stone mortar, let the sugar be boyled with two quarts of betony water to the consistency of a syrup, then mix them together by little and little over a small Fire, and so make it into a Conserve and keep it in Glasses [bottles].

The Queen's Closet Opened by W. M., cook to Queen Henrietta Maria, 1655.

CARYOPHYLLACEAE

Stellaria media

Chickweed

History and traditions The common name, chickweed, and the popular names in several other European languages refer to this herb's former usefulness as bird feed. It provided a source of fresh greens and seeds during the winter when other foods were scarce. For the same reason it was much valued as a culinary herb in broths and salads. Although it does not seem to have made its mark in the classical world, it appears in herbals from medieval times usually as an ingredient in a mixed green ointment based on lard, for rubbing on sores and swellings. The Latin name of the genus is from *stella*, a star, for the shape of the flowers.
Description A spreading, mat-forming annual, the much-branched stems grow up to 40 cm (16 in) long, but most are decumbent and creep along the ground. It has small ovate leaves and tiny, white, star-shaped flowers. It propagates quickly, reappearing throughout the year, and is often seen in the winter months.
Habitat/distribution Chickweed is native to Europe but naturalized in many countries throughout the world. Found on moist cultivated land and field edges.
Growth Grows in any reasonably moist soil in sun or partial shade. Self-seeds.
Parts used Leaves – fresh.

USES Medicinal It is rich in mineral salts, including calcium and potassium, and has anti-rheumatic properties when taken internally as a juice or infusion. Applied as a poultice or ointment for eczema, skin irritations and other skin complaints.
Culinary A pleasantly neutral-tasting herb for inclusion in salads or for cooking as a vegetable. It combines well with parsley to make a dip.

Chickweed and parsley dip

25 g/1 oz fresh chickweed
25 g/1 oz flat-leaved parsley
225 g/8 oz fromage frais
1 tbs mayonnaise
Salt and freshly ground black pepper, to taste

Rinse and pick over the chickweed, and chop it finely with the parsley. Put this into a bowl with the other ingredients and mix well together.

Serve as a dip with raw vegetables, such as carrots, celery, cucumber and peppers.

BORAGINACEAE

Symphytum officinale

Comfrey

History and traditions Comfrey has been known since at least the Middle Ages as a healing agent for fractures. The generic name, *Symphytum*, is from the Greek, *sympho*, "growing together", and *phyton*, a plant. The common English name, comfrey, is derived from the medieval Latin, *confervia*, meaning to heal or "boil together". Gerard wrote that "a salve concocted from the fresh herb will certainly tend to promote the healing of bruised and broken parts" (*The Herball*, 1597), and he and other herbalists of his time advised taking it internally for "inward hurts" as well. The modern history of this herb is a chequered one. In about 1910 it was established that it contained allantoin, a cell-proliferant substance, which promotes healing of bone and bodily tissues. By the 1960s Russian comfrey, *S.* x *uplandicum*, was being promoted as a herbal wonder cure. But scientific studies of the late 1970s and 1980s, mostly carried out in Australia and Japan, revealed that comfrey also contains pyrrolizidine alkaloids (levels are higher in the roots than the leaves), shown to cause liver damage and tumours in laboratory animals when extracts were injected in large quantities. This has led to a ban on comfrey in many countries, including Australia, New Zealand, Canada and the United States.

Description A vigorous perennial, growing on thick taproots, 60 cm–1.2 m (2–4 ft) in height, it has oval, lanceolate leaves, with a rough, hairy texture. Pinkish-purple to violet, tubular flowers are borne in drooping clusters in early to midsummer.

Related species *S.* x *uplandicum* (Russian comfrey) is a larger – to 2 m (6 ft) – and more vigorous hybrid.

Habitat/distribution Native to Europe and the Mediterranean, and also from Siberia to Asia, introduced and naturalized elsewhere. Found in damp meadows, near rivers and streams.

Growth Although it favours damp soil in the wild, comfrey is a vigorous plant, which flourishes under any conditions and grows happily when planted in dry soil, in sun or partial shade. It is easily propagated by division of roots in spring, but is invasive and almost impossible to eradicate once established.

Parts used Leaves – fresh.

USES Medicinal The leaves are made into poultices, compresses and ointments and applied externally to bruises, varicose veins, inflamed muscles and tendons. While external use of the whole leaf is considered safe, it is inadvisable to take comfrey internally.

Horticultural The leaves are high in potash and make a good garden fertilizer, mulch and compost activator.

Other name Knitbone.

Top, from left to right *The flowers of* Symphytum officinale *are usually pink or blue, but there are forms with white or yellow flowers too.*

Below Symphytum x uplandicum *(Russian comfrey).*

CAUTION Comfrey is subject to legal restrictions in some countries.

MYRTACEAE

Syzygium aromaticum

Clove tree

History and traditions The medicinal use of cloves is first mentioned in ancient Chinese texts, and it was a custom during the Han dynasty (266 BC–AD 220) to keep a clove in the mouth when addressing the emperor. Cloves originally came from the Molucca Islands, a group of islands in Indonesia, and were brought to the Mediterranean by Persian and Arab traders. They are mentioned in the writings of Pliny under the name *caryophyllon*, and were widely used in Europe by the 4th century, when their strong fragrance made them popular as ingredients of pomanders and as prevention against plague and infection. During the 17th century there was rivalry between the Dutch and the Portuguese over establishing a trading monopoly in this valuable spice. But by 1770 the French were growing their own crops in Mauritius and they were subsequently cultivated in Guiana, Brazil, the West Indies and Zanzibar. The name cloves comes from the French word for nail, *clou*, which they are supposed to resemble.

Description An evergreen tree, 20 m (65 ft) in height, it has soft, grey bark and dark-green, ovate leaves, with a shiny, leathery texture. At the beginning of the rainy season fragrant, green buds (cloves) appear at the ends of the branches. They gradually turn red and, if left unpicked, develop into pink or crimson flowers.

Habitat/distribution Native to the Moluccas, introduced and cultivated in other tropical zones.

Growth Tender, tropical trees, grown in fertile soil and requiring high humidity and minimum temperatures of 15–18°C (59–64°F). Propagated by seed or cuttings. The cloves (the unopened flower buds) are harvested when the tree is 6–8 years old. The crop can be sporadic: one year heavy and the next light. Cloves are usually hand picked to avoid damage to the branches which would jeopardize subsequent crops.

Parts used Unripe flower buds – sun-dried; essential oil.

USES Medicinal Cloves have digestive properties, help relieve nausea, control vomiting and prevent intestinal worms and parasites. Oil of cloves is still used as a dental antiseptic and analgesic. A cotton bud soaked in oil of cloves and applied directly to the tooth will ease toothache.

Culinary Widely used as a spice in whole or ground form to add flavour to curries, pickles, preserves, chutneys and meat dishes – especially baked ham. It is also used in baked apples and apple pie, desserts and cakes, and for making mulled wine.

Aromatic Added whole or ground to pot-pourri and used to make pomanders. Essential oil is used in perfumery, and added to tooth-pastes, mouthwashes and gargles.

Whole cloves.

Ground cloves.

COMPOSITAE/ASTERACEAE

Tanacetum

Tanacetum balsamita
Alecost

History and traditions Alecost came to Europe from the Middle East during the 16th century and soon became popular for its pleasant balsam fragrance. As Culpeper wrote a century later, "This is so frequently known to be an inhabitant in almost every garden, that I suppose it is needless to write a description thereof." As its common name suggests, it was used to flavour ale, the second syllable "cost" is from a Greek word, *kostos*, meaning fragrant or spicy. In the 17th century it was taken to America by settlers, where it became known as Bible-leaf from the custom of using it as a Bible bookmark and sniffing its revivifying scent during long sermons. As a medicinal herb it was frequently recommended for disorders of the stomach and head and Culpeper gives instructions for making it into a salve with olive oil, thickened with wax, rosin and turpentine. But it is now little used as a medicinal herb.
Description A hardy perennial, up to 1 m (3 ft) tall, it has a creeping rhizome and oval, silvery-green, soft-textured leaves, with a minty-balsamic fragrance. Small, daisy-like flowers are borne in mid- to late summer. Formerly classified in the *Chrysanthemum* genus.
Habitat/distribution Native to western Asia, naturalized in Europe and North America.
Growth Prefers a moisture-retentive but well-drained soil and a sunny position. Most easily propagated by division or cuttings in spring, but can also be grown from seed.
Parts used Leaves – fresh or dried.

USES Medicinal An infusion of the leaves helps reduce the pain of insect bites and stings, and a fresh leaf may be applied directly to the spot as "first aid".
Culinary Fresh leaves may be added to fruit cups and drinks; fresh or dried leaves make an aromatic tea.
Aromatic The dried leaves are added to pot-pourri and make fragrant bookmarks.
Other names Costmary and Bible-leaf.

The fresh leaves of Tanacetum balsamita *have a pleasant minty fragrance.*

Tanacetum parthenium
Feverfew

History and traditions The medicinal properties of feverfew have long been recognized. The Greek philosopher, Plutarch, writing in 1st-century Athens, says that the plant was named *parthenium* after treatment with feverfew saved the life of a workman who fell from the Parthenon. The common name comes from the Latin *febris*, fever, and *fugure*, to chase away. In the centuries that followed, herbalists recommended this herb, usually in a mixture of honey or sweet wine to disguise its bitterness, for a range of ills. *Bancke's Herbal,* 1525, advocates it for stomach disorders, toothache and insect bites, Culpeper recommends it for women's troubles and as an antidote to a liberal intake of opium (*The English Physician*, 1653). But others evidently recognized its value for the relief of headaches and migraine. Gerard wrote, "it is very good for them that are giddie in the head, or which have the turning called Vertigo, that is, swimming and turning in the head" (*The Herball*, 1597). And Sir John Hill, in his *Family Herbal*, 1772, states clearly, "in the worst headaches, this herb exceeds whatever else is known." Feverfew came to prominence in modern times after a Welsh doctor's wife found relief in 1974 from both chronic migraine and rheumatism by

eating feverfew leaves. Since then this herb has undergone much scientific study and has been found to be a relatively effective and safe remedy for these complaints.
Description A bushy, hardy perennial, to 1 m (3 ft), with bright-green, pungently aromatic, pinnately-lobed leaves and a mass of white daisy-like flowers, with yellow centres, in early to midsummer.
Related species There are a number of cultivars, including some with golden foliage (as above), or double flowers, which make attractive ornamentals, but do not have the same medicinal properties.
Habitat/distribution It is native to southern Europe, widely introduced elsewhere. Found on dry, stony soils.
Growth Grows in any poor, free-draining soil and tolerates drought. Propagate by seed sown in spring, or by cuttings or division in spring. Self-seeds prolifically.
Parts used Leaves, flowering tops – for eating fresh, or dried for use in tablets and pharmaceutical products.

USES Medicinal Feverfew lowers fever and dilates blood vessels. Fresh leaves are sometimes eaten (usually sweetened with honey, as they are very bitter) to reduce the effects of migraine headaches. It is also taken in tablet form for migraine, rheumatism and menstrual problems.

Above *Golden feverfew does not have the medicinal properties of the species.*

CAUTION Feverfew may cause dermatitis or mouth ulcers if consumed to excess.

Above Tanacetum vulgare.

Tanacetum vulgare

Tansy

History and traditions Tansy is one of the essential strewing herbs, listed by Thomas Tusser in *One Hundred Points of Good Husbandry,* 1577, doubtless chosen for its insect-repellent properties. Despite the bitter flavour, there is plenty of evidence that it was widely used for culinary purposes in the past, with many recipes appearing in old household books. It was a popular ingredient of cakes and puddings, made with eggs and cream, traditionally served on Easter Day. William Coles, in *The Art of Simpling,* 1656, refers to the effect of tansy on the constitution after a Lenten diet of salt-fish. Tansy was also a popular substitute for mint in a sauce to accompany lamb. One authority refers to its cosmetic application. "I have heard that if maids will take wild Tansy and lay it to soake in Buttermilk for the space of nine days and wash their faces therewith, it will make them look very faire" (Jerome Braunschwyke, *The Virtuose Boke of Distyllacion*, 1527).
Description A spreading rhizomatous perennial, to 1.2 m (4 ft) in height, it has dark-green, feathery, pinnately-divided leaves, which are pungently aromatic, and terminal clusters of button-like bright yellow flowers in summer.
Related species *T. vulgare* var. *crispum* is a more compact plant, with attractive, curly, fern-like leaves.
Growth Grows well in dry, stony soil and prefers a sunny position. Propagated by seed, division or cuttings in spring.
Parts used Leaves.

USES Medicinal This herb is said to have been used in enemas for expelling intestinal worms, but is seldom used in herbal medicine today.
Culinary Despite the wealth of recipes in old books, tansy is not recommended as a pudding ingredient as it has an unpleasantly bitter taste, although the leaves used to be added to lamb dishes and spring puddings.
Horticultural Tansy is supposed to be an insect repellent and ward off aphids in companion planting.

CAUTION It is unsafe to take internally as a medicinal herb. The volatile oil is extremely toxic and should be avoided.

COMPOSITAE/ASTERACEAE

Taraxacum officinale

Dandelion

History and traditions Although known much earlier in Chinese medicine, the dandelion was first recognized in Europe in the 10th or 11th century, through the influence of the Arabian physicians, then prominent as medical authorities. The name, dandelion, comes from the French *dents de lion*, lion's tooth.
Description A perennial which grows on a stout taproot to 30 cm (1 ft) long, it has a basal rosette of leaves and yellow, solitary flowers followed by spherical, fluffy seed heads.
Habitat/distribution Native to Europe and Asia, and occurs widely in temperate regions of the world, often found on nitrogen-rich soils.
Growth Grows in profusion in the wild and self-seeds. Cultivated dandelions are grown in moist, fertile soil. Propagated from seed.
Parts used Leaves, flowers – fresh for culinary use, fresh or dried for medicinal preparations; roots – dried.

USES Medicinal An effective diuretic, it is taken internally for urinary infections and diseases of the liver and gall bladder. Considered beneficial for rheumatic complaints and gout. Also said to improve appetite and digestion. Of great benefit nutritionally, high in vitamins A and C and a rich source of iron, magnesium, potassium and calcium.
Culinary Young leaves of dandelions are added to salads, often blanched first to reduce bitterness, or cooked, like spinach, as a vegetable. Flowers are made into wine. The roasted root makes a palatable, soothing, caffeine-free substitute for coffee.

TAXACEAE

Taxus baccata

Yew

History and traditions Yews were sacred to the Druids and used in their ceremonies. They have also been grown in churchyards from the beginning of the Christian era. As evergreens and exceptionally long-lived trees (1,000–2,000 years), they were a life symbol and often used to decorate the church or to scatter in graves. *Taxus* is from the Greek word *taxon*, a bow, and the flexible, close-grained wood was the traditional material for longbows. Yew is from the Anglo-Saxon name for the tree. There are rare references to its former medicinal uses, in treating snakebite and rabies for example, but its poisonous nature was always recognized and it was known to kill cattle at a stroke. It has sometimes been used in homeopathy. In recent times yews have come to prominence as a source of taxol, used in the treatment of ovarian cancer.
Description *T. baccata* is a spreading, evergreen tree, growing to about 15 m (50 ft), with a rounded crown and reddish-brown scaly bark. The leaves are dark-green, flattened needles, arranged alternately. It is a dioecious tree, and the male flowers are small globular cones, which release clouds of pollen in very early spring; the female flower is a small green bud, followed by the fruit, a highly poisonous seed, partially enclosed in a fleshy, red, non-poisonous aril.
Related species *T. brevifolia*, the Pacific yew, has the highest taxol content, mostly in the bark, and is the main source of the drug. But six trees are needed to make one dose and wild stocks have been grossly over-exploited. *T. baccata*, the common yew, contains less significant levels of taxol-yielding compounds, found in the leaves, but is now used in taxol synthesis.

Above Taxus brevifolia.

Top Taxus baccata *'Fruco-luteo', a cultivar with yellow fruits.*

Left Taxus baccata *'Fastigiata', the Irish yew.*

Habitat/distribution *T. baccata* is native to Europe, Asia and northern Africa and *T. brevifolia* is found in north-western North America to the south-west of Canada.
Growth Yews will grow in any soil, including chalk. Propagated by seed, sown in early spring, or by cuttings in September. *T. baccata* responds well to close clipping and is frequently used as a hedge, or in topiary work.
Parts used Leaves, bark – for extraction of taxol.

USES Medicinal Extracts of yew are used in drugs for treatment of cancers, mainly ovarian, breast and lung.

CAUTION All parts of yew are poisonous and it should never be used for self-medication.

LABIATAE/LAMIACEAE

Teucrium chamaedrys

Wall germander

History and traditions *T. chamaedrys* is said to be named after Teucer, son of Scamander, King of Troy, who, according to Greek mythology, was the first to recognize the medicinal properties of this herb. It is mentioned in the works of Dioscorides and developed a reputation over the centuries for being an effective treatment for gout. It was also taken in powdered form for catarrh and as a herbal snuff. Germander comes from the Latin form, *gamandrea*, of the Greek *khamaidrys*, and means "ground-oak", from *khamai*, on the ground, and *drus*, oak, a reference to the shape of the leaves.
Description A shrubby, evergreen perennial, 10–30 cm (4–12 in) in height, it has creeping roots and dark-green, glossy foliage, shaped like miniature oak leaves. Tubular, rose-purple flowers are borne in dense terminal spikes.
Habitat/distribution It is native to Europe and western Asia, widely introduced elsewhere and found in rocky areas, on old walls and in dry woodlands.
Growth Flourishes in light, dry, stony soils. Easily propagated by semi-ripe cuttings taken in early summer. Although the branches are erect to start with, it is inclined to sprawl, especially if allowed to flower. Clip hard in late spring or early autumn to maintain a neat shape.
Parts used Leaves, flowering stems.

USES Medicinal Although it is said to have some medicinal uses and digestive properties, it may cause liver damage and is best avoided.

LABIATAE/LAMIACEAE

Teucrium scorodonia

Wood sage

History and traditions A bitter-tasting herb, wood sage is one of the many plants said to have been used at one time for flavouring beer before hops became common for this purpose. One old story tells that hinds, wounded in the chase, sought it out for its healing properties. In past times it was used, like *Teucrium chamaedrys*, to treat gout and rheumatism and as a poultice or lotion for "moist ulcers and sores" (Culpeper). Its specific name, *scorodonia*, is from a Greek word for garlic, and if the leaves are crushed, it is possible with a little imagination, to detect a faint garlic odour.
Description: A hardy perennial, 30–60 cm (1–2 ft) tall, it has ovate to heart-shaped, pale-green, soft-textured leaves and inconspicuous greenish-yellow flowers in summer. *T. scorodonia* 'Crispum' has attractive, curly-edged foliage.
Habitat/distribution Native to Europe, naturalized in many northern temperate regions. Found in dry, shady woodland areas.
Growth It will grow in most conditions, but prefers a light, gravelly soil and partial shade.
Parts used Leaves (formerly).

USES Its herbal uses are now obsolete, but it makes an attractive traditional herb-garden plant – especially the curly-leaved form.

LABIATAE/LAMIACEAE

Thymus

History and traditions To the Greeks, thyme was an emblem of courage, to the Romans a remedy for melancholy, and appreciated by both for its scent. To tell someone they smelled of thyme was a compliment in ancient Greece, and Gerard refers to a description by the 3rd-century Roman writer, Aelianus, of the houses of a newly taken city being strewn with roses and thyme to sweeten them. *Thymus* is the original Greek name, used by Dioscorides. The scent of thyme is irresistible to bees, and the finest-flavoured honey comes from its nectar. The image of bees hovering over thyme was a frequent embroidery motif in former times. Its medicinal virtues were well known to the 16th- and 17th-century herbalists. Gerard recommended it to treat "the bitings of any venomous beast, either taken in drinke, or outwardly applied" and for Culpeper it was "a noble strengthener of the lungs". In modern times its antiseptic, antibacterial credentials have been fully established.

Description and species There are some 350 species of thyme, many hybrids and cultivars. The classification of them is complex and there are many synonyms and invalid names. For medicinal purposes, *T. vulgaris* and *T. serpyllum* are the main ones. For cookery, *T. vulgaris* and *T.* x *citriodorus* have the best flavour, though most of the others may also be used.

T. serpyllum (wild thyme) – Also sometimes called the "mother of thyme" and "creeping thyme", has a prostrate habit, growing to about 7.5 cm (3 in), and has tiny, ovate leaves and clusters of mauve to pink flowers in early summer, but is very variable in form. It is found throughout Europe and Asia on well-drained, stony or sandy soils and on sunny slopes.

T. vulgaris (common thyme) – Is a variable sub-shrub, 30–45 cm (12–18 in) tall, with gnarled, woody stems, dark-green to grey-green leaves and white, sometimes mauve, flowers. Native to southern Europe and the Mediterranean region, introduced elsewhere.

T. x *citriodorus* (lemon thyme) – A variable hybrid, 25–30 cm (10–12 in) tall, with bright-green, ovate to lanceolate, lemon-scented leaves and pale-mauve flowers in early summer. Cultivated worldwide.

T. x *citriodorus 'Aureus'* (golden lemon thyme) – Is a cultivar with golden foliage, which may be used interchangeably with *T.* x *citriodorus*.

Of the many ornamental thymes, these are some of the most attractive:

T. serpyllum, 'Pink Chintz' – Is a creeping thyme with grey-green woolly foliage and striking, bright-pink flowers. First selected as a cultivar, at the Royal Horticultural Society gardens at Wisley in 1939.

T. serpyllum var. *coccineus* – Is a favourite prostrate variety for the depth of colour of its crimson-pink flowers and the attractive form of dark-green foliage.

Above far left Thymus vulgaris *in flower with* T. x citriodorus; **above left** Thymus serpyllum.

Above Thymus serpyllum *'Pink Chintz'*.

Below Thymus serpyllum *var.* coccineus.

T. vulgaris, 'Silver Posie', and *T.* x *citriodorus,* 'Silver Queen' – Are grown for their variegated silver foliage, useful for giving contrast to an ornamental scheme.

T. pseudolanuginosus (woolly thyme) – Is a prostrate form with grey-green woolly leaves and pale-pink flowers.

Thyme and the ageing process

Research carried out by Dr Stanley Deans at the Scottish Agricultural College, Ayr, during the 1990s, in conjunction with Semmelweiss Medical University in Budapest, has found that laboratory animals fed with thyme oil aged much slower than animals that did not receive it. Thyme oil apparently delayed the onset of age-related conditions such as deterioration of the retina, loss of brain function and wasted muscles.

A key factor was the high level of antioxidants present in thyme oil, which helped prevent a decline in PUFAs (polyunsaturated fatty acids), important components of every living cell which help keep cell membranes fluid and strong.

Above Thymus x citriodorus *'Silver Queen'*.

Right A decorative thyme pot.

Below left Thymus pulegioides *'Broad-leafed thyme'*; **below right** Thymus pseudolanuginosus.

Growth All thymes require very free-draining, gritty soil and a sunny position. Though the ones mentioned are hardy to at least -10°C (14°F), in cool temperate climates they may need some protection in winter, as they are vulnerable to cold winds, especially if soil becomes too wet. Propagated by layering in spring, or by cuttings in summer. *T. vulgaris* and *T. serpyllum* can be propagated by seed sown in spring.
Parts used Leaves – fresh or dry for culinary use; leaves, flowering tops – fresh or dried for infusions and medicinal preparations; essential oil – distilled from leaves and flowering tops.

USES Medicinal A strongly antiseptic, antibacterial and antifungal herb. Infusions are taken for coughs, colds, chest infections and digestive upsets. Made into syrups for coughs, and gargles for sore throats. The essential oil is diluted in a vegetable oil (such as sunflower) as a rub for chest infections, or as a massage oil for rheumatic pain and aching joints.
Culinary Widely used as a culinary flavouring in marinades, meat, soups, stews and casseroles.

CAUTION Avoid medicinal doses of thyme, and especially of thyme oil during pregnancy, as it is a uterine stimulant.

TILIACEAE

Tilia cordata

Lime

History and traditions Linden tea, made from the flowers of *T. cordata*, has always been popular in Europe, especially in France, where it is called "tilleul" – as a soothing drink and for its medicinal properties. An infusion of the leaves as a complexion wash is an old prescription for a "fair" skin. The tree has been valued over the centuries for its many economic uses. The white, close-grained wood was used to make household articles, piano keys and carvings (notably by Grinling Gibbons, 1648–1721, at Windsor Castle and Chatsworth House, England). The inner bark produced fibre for matting and baskets; the sap provided a sweetener and the foliage animal fodder.
Description A hardy, deciduous tree, to 25 m (82 ft) in height, with a large rounded crown, it has smooth, silver-grey bark and heart-shaped leaves, dark green above and greyish below. The five-petalled, fluffy, pale-yellow flowers have a honey scent and appear in clusters in midsummer, followed by globe-shaped fruits.
Related species *T. cordata* is the small-leaved lime. Flowers of *T. platyphyllos*, the large-leaved lime, and of hybrids, such as *T.* x *europaea*, are also collected for tea. *T. tomentosa* (silver lime) and *T. americana* (American lime) do not have the same concentrations of active principles.
Habitat/distribution *T. cordata* occurs in Europe and western Asia.
Growth Prefers moist, well-drained soil in full sun or partial shade. Propagated from seed, which needs a long period of stratification (at least three months) to germinate.
Parts used Flowers – collected when they first open and dried for teas.

USES Medicinal A soothing herb, which increases perspiration and is said to help lower blood pressure, the flowers are taken as an infusion, often sweetened with honey and flavoured with lemon, for colds, catarrh and feverish illnesses, for anxiety and as a digestive.
Other name Linden.

Above *The flowers of* Tilia cordata, *the small-leaved lime, are collected for tea.*

LEGUMINOSAE/PAPILIONACEAE

Trifolium pratense

Red clover

History and traditions Red clover has been an important agricultural and animal fodder crop since ancient times. But it was seldom used medicinally until its early introduction to the United States, where the Native Americans of the Unami and Ani-Stotini tribes discovered its therapeutic properties. They used it to treat cancerous tumours and skin complaints, took it during pregnancy and childbirth and as a general purification for bodily systems. As a result it was adopted by early settlers and found its way into British herbal medicine sometime during the 19th century.
Description A short-lived perennial, it is decumbent to erect, 20–60 cm (8 in–2 ft) in height. The leaves are trifoliate and the flowers rose-purple to white.
Habitat/distribution It is native to Europe, found across Asia to Afghanistan, and naturalized in North America and Australia, growing both wild and as a field crop.
Growth It requires moist, well-drained soil and is propagated from seed.
Parts used Flowering tops.

USES Medicinal Red clover blossoms are taken internally for skin complaints such as eczema and psoriasis, and applied externally for ulcers, sores and burns. Infusions were at one time thought to be helpful for bronchial complaints and the herb is also said to be effective in balancing blood sugar levels.

Red clover

LEGUMINOSAE/PAPILIONACEAE

Trigonella foenum-graecum

Fenugreek

History and traditions A herb with an ancient history, fenugreek has been cultivated since the time of the Assyrians and its seeds were found in Tutankhamun's tomb, *c.*1325 BC. In Europe it was one of the many herbs promoted by the Emperor Charlemagne, *c.* AD 742–814, and the seeds were sold for medicinal uses by the 16th- and 17th-century druggists and apothecaries. In Chinese medicine they have a history as a tonic and in Ayurvedic medicine are renowned for their exceptional ability to cleanse the system of impurities. They also have a reputation as an aphrodisiac. *Trigonella*, meaning triangle, refers to the leaf shape and the specific name, *foenum-graecum*, translates as "Greek hay", a reference to its long use as horse fodder. In recent times it has aroused interest for components of the seeds: the alkaloid, trigonelline, for its anti-cancer potential and a steroidal saponin diosgenin for its contraceptive effects.
Description A hardy annual, 60 cm (2 ft) tall, it has an erect, branched stem and trifoliate leaves. Pale-yellow pea-flowers appear in the upper leaf axils in summer followed by the fruit, a curved pod with a pointed "beak", containing up to 20 light-brown, aromatic seeds.
Habitat/distribution Native to southern Europe and Asia, widely cultivated in the Middle East, India and northern Africa.
Growth Grow fenugreek in well-drained, fertile soil in a sunny position. Propagated by seed, sown in spring.
Parts used Leaves – fresh for culinary use; seeds – dried for cookery or for making infusions, decoctions, powders or extracts.

USES Medicinal The seeds are rich in a softening mucilage and are used in compresses or ointments to ease swellings, inflammations, ulcers and boils. They are taken in infusions to reduce fevers, have digestive properties and are said to rid the body of toxins, dispelling bad breath and body odour. Fenugreek is also thought to control blood sugar levels in cases of diabetes.
Culinary Leaves, which have a high vitamin, mineral and iron content, are cooked as vegetables, mainly in India. Seeds are sprouted as salad vegetables, and used as a flavouring and condiment in northern African, Ethiopian, Middle Eastern, Egyptian and Indian cookery.

Fresh fenugreek leaves.

LILIACEAE/TRILLIACEAE

Trillium erectum

Bethroot

History and traditions Bethroot – the name is a corruption of birthroot – was traditionally used by Native Americans to control bleeding after childbirth and for soothing the sore nipples of nursing mothers. It was taken up by the Shaker community for the same purposes, for easing excessive menstruation and for haemorrhages in general. Sniffing the unpleasant smell of the flowers, which has been likened to rotting meat, was said to stop a nosebleed. The generic name comes from the triple arrangement of all its parts.
Description A variable perennial, 25–38 cm (10–15 in) tall, it has broadly rhomboid three-sectioned leaves and solitary three-petalled flowers, ranging from crimson-purple to white.
Habitat/distribution Native to north-eastern North America and the Himalayan region of Asia and found in damp, shady woodland.
Growth Trilliums require moist, humus-rich soil and partial shade. Propagation by division in the dormant period is the easiest method, as growing from seed is slow and erratic.
Parts used Rhizomes – dried for use in decoctions and extracts.

USES Medicinal An antiseptic, astringent herb, it is said to be helpful to the female reproductive system and to control bleeding. Poultices are applied for skin diseases and the roots were at one time boiled in milk to be taken for diarrhoea and dysentery.

TROPAEOLACEAE

Tropaeolum majus

Nasturtium

History and traditions The garden nasturtium comes from South America. It was introduced to Spain, from Peru, in the 16th century and originally known as *Nasturtium indicum*, or Indian cress, for the spicy flavour of its leaves. Leaves and flowers were popular 17th-century salad ingredients. As nasturtiums are high in vitamin C, they were useful for preventing scurvy. The generic name *Tropaeolum* comes from *tropalon*, the Greek word for a trophy, as the round leaves were thought to resemble the trophy-bearing shields of the classical world.

Description In South America it is a perennial, but in Europe and cool temperate regions it is a half-hardy annual. It has trailing stems, to about 3 m (10 ft), and circular leaves with a radiating pattern of veins. The yellow or orange flowers grow on stalks arising singly from the leaf axils, and have prominently spurred calyces. They are followed by the globular fruits. There are many low-growing and climbing cultivars.

Habitat/distribution Native to South America, now widely grown throughout the world.

Growth Grow in relatively poor soil for the best production of flowers, but supply plenty of moisture. Easily propagated from seed sown in containers, or *in situ*, in spring.

Parts used Leaves, flowers, seeds – used fresh.

USES Medicinal The seeds have antiseptic, antibacterial properties and are taken in infusions for urinary and upper respiratory tract infections.

Culinary The leaves are added to salads for their peppery taste and the flowers for their colour. Flowers are also used as a flavouring for vinegar. Seeds, when still green, are pickled as a substitute for capers.

Other name Indian cress.

Above *The flowers and leaves make colourful and nutritious additions to a summer salad.*

Tropaeolum majus

An old recipe for pickled nasturtium seeds

Gather your little knobs quickly after your blossoms are off; put them in cold water and salt for three days, shifting them once a day; then make a pickle (but do not boil it at all) of some white wine, shallot, horse-radish, pepper, salt, cloves, and mace whole and nutmeg quartered; then put in your seeds and stop them close; they are to be eaten as capers.
The Complete Housewife, 1736.

A simple modern version of pickled nasturtium seeds

Collect the nasturtium seeds while they are still green, until you have about 50 g/2 oz. Stir 25 g (1 oz) salt into 300 ml /$^1/_2$ pint/1 $^1/_4$ cup water, add the nasturtium seeds and leave for 24 hours. Then strain them and rinse well in fresh water. Put the seeds into a jar with a muslin bag filled with mixed pickling spice, top up with malt vinegar and seal with an airtight lid. Leave for 3–4 weeks before eating.

COMPOSITAE/ASTERACEAE

Tussilago farfara

Coltsfoot

History and traditions Known since the days of Dioscorides and Pliny as a herb to relieve coughs, often taken in the form of a smoking mixture, it is still a basic ingredient of herbal tobaccos. The generic name comes from *tussis*, a cough (from which we get the word tussive), and *agere*, to take away. In the Middle Ages it was sometimes known as *Filius ante patrem* (son before father), because the flowers appear before the leaves. Although still used in herbal medicine for cough remedies, recent tests have revealed that it contains low quantities of pyrrolizidine alkaloids, which are carcinogenic in high doses. (Also found in *Symphytum officinale* – comfrey).

Description A small perennial, on a creeping rhizome, 15–20 cm (6–8 in) in height. The bright-yellow, dandelion-like flowers, borne singly, appear before the rosette of toothed heart-shaped leaves.

Habitat/distribution Native to Europe, western Asia and northern Africa, introduced elsewhere including North America. Found on roadsides, wastelands, fields and hedgerows, in moist, loamy soil.

Growth It is an invasive plant that needs no cultivation. Propagated from seed or by division.

Parts used Leaves, flowers – fresh or dried.

USES Medicinal Coltsfoot is said to have tonic effects and contain mucilage, which is soothing to the mucous membranes. It is still recommended by herbalists to be taken in infusions for coughs and applied externally as a wash or compress, or as fresh leaves mixed in a paste of honey, for sores, ulcers, skin inflammation and insect bites.

Culinary Traditionally, leaves were added to springtime salads and soups.

Above *The leaves of* Tussilago farfara *appear after the flowers have faded.*

Tussilago farfara

ULMACEAE

Ulmus rubra

Slippery elm

History and traditions The common name is taken from the slippery texture of the inner bark when moistened. It was a traditional medicine of Native Americans, used mainly for gastric problems and healing wounds, and was taken up by early settlers, who made the powdered bark into a nutritious gruel for invalids with weak digestions.

Description A deciduous tree 15–20 m (50–65 ft) in height, it has dark-brown, rough bark and obovate, toothed, deeply-veined leaves. Inconspicuous clusters of red-stamened flowers are followed by reddish-brown, winged fruits.

Habitat/distribution Native to eastern and central North America and eastern Canada. It is found in moist woodlands.

Growth This tree grows well in poorish soil and is propagated by seed or cuttings. It is liable to Dutch elm disease.

Parts used Inner bark – dried and ground into powder. (Bark should not be stripped from wild trees, which are becoming rare, only from those cultivated for the purpose.)

USES Medicinal Rich in mucilage, slippery elm powder is taken for stomach and bowel disorders, gastric ulcers, cystitis and urinary complaints. It is soothing to sore throats and applied in poultices for skin inflammations, boils, abscesses and ulcers and to encourage the healing of wounds.

Other name Red elm.

CAUTION Subject to legal restrictions in some countries, especially as whole bark.

Urtica dioica

URTICACEAE

Urtica dioica

Stinging nettle

History and traditions The common stinging nettle may be an unpopular weed, but over the centuries it has been put to many practical uses, remaining an important nutritious and medicinal herb. It was named *Urtica* by Pliny, from *urere*, to burn. Roman legionaries are said to have flailed themselves with nettles against the bone-chilling cold of a northern British winter. They even brought their own seeds, in case no plants grew locally. Whipping with nettles later became an established cure for rheumatism. The nettle was a common source of fibre (similar to that of flax and hemp) in many northern European nations. One of Hans Andersen's fairy-tales tells of the Princess who wove nettle coats for swans. Above all, in former times, it made a valuable springtime pot-herb, tonic and anti-scorbutic after the deprivations of winter and was made into all manner of soups, puddings and porridges, as well as nettle beer.
Description A tough, spreading perennial, the erect stems grow to 1.5 m (5 ft) tall, on creeping roots. The stems and ovate, toothed, dull-green leaves are covered in stinging hairs. Inconspicuous greenish-yellow flowers (male and female on separate plants) appear in mid to late summer.
Related species *U. urens* is a small, annual nettle, found in cool, northern temperate regions. *U. pilulifera* (Roman nettle) originates in southern Europe.
Habitat/distribution Found in waste ground, grassland, field edges, gardens, near human habitation or ruins, in nitrogen-rich soil.
Growth Cultivation is usually unnecessary for domestic use as nettles are plentiful in wild and semi-wild areas and can be invasive in the garden. Grown as a crop they require moist, nitrogen-rich soil. Cut back before flowering to ensure a second crop of young leaves.
Parts used Leafy stems – cut in spring, before flowering, fresh for cookery, fresh or dried for infusions, extracts, lotions and ointments. Roots – fresh or dried for decoctions for hair use.

USES Medicinal Constituents include histamine and formic acid, which causes the sting, vitamins A, B, C, iron and other minerals. The high vitamin C content ensures proper absorption of iron and the juice is taken for anaemia. Its diuretic properties help rid the body of uric acid and it is taken as an infusion for rheumatism, arthritis and gout, or applied as a compress to ease pain. It also stimulates the circulation and is said to lower blood pressure. Decoctions of the root and leaves are applied for dry scalp, dandruff and are said to help prevent baldness.
Culinary Only fresh young leaves should be used, cooked as a spinach-like vegetable or made into soup. Leaves should not be eaten raw as they are highly irritant in this state.

VALERIANACEAE

Valeriana officinalis

Valerian

History and traditions This is thought to be the same plant known to the medical authorities of ancient Greece, Dioscorides and Galen, as *phu*, for the offensive odour of its roots, and recommended by them for its diuretic properties. The name *Valeriana* dates from about the 10th century and is said to be from the Latin *valere*, to be in good health. It was promoted by the Arabian physicians of this era, appears in Anglo-Saxon leech-books of the 11th century and became known in medieval Europe as "All-Heal" for its supposed therapeutic powers. Despite the early Greek name, the smell of the root was not unpleasant to everybody: it was appreciated as a perfume in the 16th century and Turner's *Herbal*, 1568, describes laying the aromatic dried roots among linen. In fact it has a musky scent, similar to *Nardostachys*

Above *Flowers of* Centranthus ruber.

jatamansi (once classified as a valerian), and the essential oil is a perfumery ingredient to this day. It is also attractive to cats and rats.
Description A tall, hardy perennial, growing to 1.5 m (5 ft), it has grooved stems and pinnate leaves with lanceolate, toothed leaflets. The white, sometimes pinkish, flowers are borne in terminal clusters in summer. *V. officinalis* should not be confused with red valerian, *Centranthus ruber*, which has no medicinal value, but is grown as a herb garden ornamental.
Habitat/distribution Native to Europe and western Asia, introduced to many temperate regions and naturalized in North America. Found in damp meadows and ditches, often near streams.
Growth Grow in damp, fertile soil in a sunny position. Propagated by seed sown in spring, or by division in spring or autumn. It is inclined to be invasive.
Parts used Roots – dried for use in decoctions, medicinal preparations and extracts; essential oil – distilled from roots.

USES Medicinal It has sedative properties and is taken as a tea for insomnia, nervous tension, anxiety, headaches and indigestion. Also said to lower blood pressure.
Aromatic The essential oil is used in perfumery, and extracts as a flavouring in the food industry.

CAUTION Excess doses are harmful and may cause headaches or a racing heart. It can be addictive and should not be taken for long periods. It should not be taken by anyone with liver disease.

SCROPHULARIACEAE

Verbascum thapsus

Mullein

History and traditions "Candlewick plant" and "hag's taper" are two of the many country names for this plant and refer to its former use, when dried, as a lamp wick or taper. The tall flower spires also look like giant candles, as described by Henry Lyte: "the whole toppe, with its pleasant yellow floures sheweth like to a wax candle or taper cunningly wrought" (*The Niewe Herball*, 1578). As a medicinal herb, it was taken for colds, in the form of "mullein tea", as indeed it still is, and was sometimes smoked as a tobacco for coughs and asthma (which must have made things worse). It also made a yellow hair dye. Throughout Europe and Asia mullein had an ancient reputation as a magic plant, capable of driving away evil spirits.
Description A tall, hardy biennial, growing to 2 m (6 ft), it has a basal rosette of soft, downy, blue-grey leaves, broadly ovate in shape, in the first year. Yellow flowers are borne on tall spikes in the second year.
Habitat/distribution Native to Europe, Asia and northern Africa, found on shallow, stony soils in grassland and wasteland.
Growth Thrives in dry, stony or gravelly soil and a sunny position. Propagated by seed sown in autumn. Often self-seeds.
Parts used Leaves – dried for use in infusions and liquid extracts; flowers – fresh or dried for infusions. Preparations must be carefully strained to eliminate irritating fine particles.
USES Medicinal It has antiseptic properties and is rich in soothing mucilage. Its main use is for coughs, colds, influenza and respiratory infections, when it is taken as an infusion. It is also sometimes recommended for colic, digestive upsets, nervous tension and insomnia. An infused oil, made of the flowers, has been applied to sores and chapped skin.
Other name Aaron's rod.

Above *The tall flower spikes of* Verbascum thapsus *appear in the second year.*

VERBENACEAE

Verbena officinalis

Vervain

History and traditions This unspectacular plant has a long history as a magical herb of exceptional powers and features widely in the folklore of Celtic and northern European cultures. It was venerated by the Romans, who scattered it on their temple altars and whose soldiers carried sprigs to protect them. A story began that it grew at the site of Christ's crucifixion and was used to staunch his wounds on the cross. It was called *herba sacra*, a holy herb, when used in religious ceremonies, and *herba veneris* for its supposed aphrodisiac powers. In Anglo-Saxon and medieval times it was worn as an amulet to protect against plague, snakebites and evil in general. And, with so much going for it, by the 16th century it became an "official" herb of the apothecaries, used for at least 30 complaints. Although it had largely fallen from favour by the early 19th century, it does have a place in herbal medicine today and in traditional Chinese medicine.

Related species Many of the ornamental verbenas grown in gardens come from Brazil and South America. Others with medicinal properties include a West Indian species and *V. hastata*, with blue flowers, which is indigenous to eastern North America.

Description A hardy, rather straggly perennial, with an erect, branched stem, it has ovate, deeply lobed, sometimes pinnate, leaves, which are dull green and slightly hairy. Small, pale-lilac flowers are sparsely arranged in terminal spikes.

Habitat/distribution Native to Europe, western Asia and northern Africa, found in waste places and roadsides, usually in a sheltered, sunny position.

Growth Grow in well-drained but moist soil in full sun. Propagated by seed sown in spring.

Parts used Leaves, flowering stems – dried for use in infusions, ointments, liquid extracts and other medicinal preparations.

USES Medicinal Vervain has mildly sedative and hypnotic properties and is taken in infusions for nervous exhaustion, anxiety, insomnia, tension headaches and migraine. Also for disorders associated with the stomach, kidneys, liver and gall bladder. Externally it is used in compresses and lotions for skin complaints and as a gargle for sore gums and mouth ulcers.

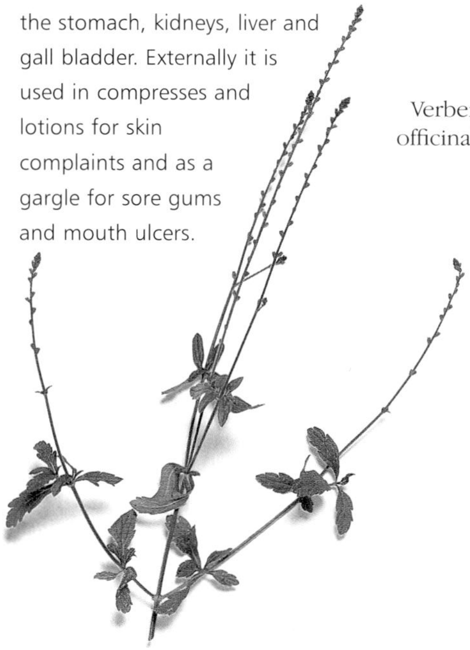

Verbena officinalis

GRAMINEAE/POACEAE

Vetiveria zizanioides

Vetiver

History and traditions A large coarse grass with many economic uses in the East, it was at one time planted on Sri Lankan tea estates to control erosion. An Indian name for it is *khus-khus*, and it has been used since the time of the Moghul Emperors to make scented screens, popularly known as "*khus-khus* tatties" which were sprinkled with water to keep buildings cool before the days of air conditioning, and which deterred insects as well. It is now widely cultivated for the volatile oil contained in its roots, especially in Réunion, which produces more than 35 tons annually.

Description A clump-forming grass, which grows to about 1.5 m (5 ft), with aromatic, rhizomatous roots, it has linear spears of leaves and brownish flowers produced on long stalks.

Habitat/distribution Grows wild in tropical Asia, eastern Africa and Central America and is widely cultivated there as well; also in Java, Réunion, the Seychelles, New Guinea and Brazil.

Growth A tender, tropical plant. Propagated by division or layering.

Parts used Roots – distilled for essential oil.

USES Aromatic The essential oil has a woody, musky odour, is strongly insect-repellent and antiseptic, and has sedative properties. It is used as a fixative for perfumes and as an ingredient of soaps and cosmetics.

Above left Vinca major *is often used as a climber, scrambling through shrubs and hedges. It retains its glossy green leaves throughout the winter and produces bright blue flowers in early spring.*

Above Vinca major *'Variegata' looks good against dark hedges.*

APOCYNACEAE

Vinca major

Greater periwinkle

History and traditions The periwinkle is mentioned by Pliny and was woven into garlands in ancient Greece and Rome to decorate rooms, or to wear at celebratory banquets. An old name for it is "sorcerer's violet" and it has a long tradition in early herbal literature as an anti-witchcraft herb. *Macer's Herbal*, dating from the 11th century, writes of its power against "wykked spirits", and the *Herbal of Apuleius* (1481 – translated from a manuscript of *c.* AD 400) recommends it "against devil sickness and demoniacal possession". The always imaginative *Boke of Secrets of Albertus Magnus,* 14th century, tells of a recipe for wrapping it in earthworms, reducing it to a powder and mixing it with houseleek, to be eaten with a meal for inducing love between man and wife. In European cultures it has variously been seen as a flower of death, of immortality and of friendship. The generic term *Vinca* is from the Latin, *vincire*, to bind, a reference to the plant's twining stems. The name periwinkle is derived from the full Latin version of the name, *pervinca.*

Description A trailing evergreen perennial, to 45 cm (18 in), it has prostrate stems, which root at the nodes, and glossy, ovate, dark-green leaves. Five-petalled, violet-blue flowers appear in the axils of the upper leaves in summer.

Related species *V. minor* is quite similar in appearance, but lower-growing and with smaller flowers; it also has similar medicinal properties. The Madagascan periwinkle, *Catharanthus roseus*, formerly *Vinca rosea*, contains the toxic alkaloids vincristine and vinblastine. These are isolated to make drugs used in the treatment of certain cancers.

Habitat/distribution Periwinkle is native to Europe, found on loamy calcareous (alkaline) soils, often in woodland.

Growth Tolerates dry conditions, but prefers moist soil and shade or partial shade. It is propagated by division throughout the dormant period. Periwinkle makes useful ground cover, but can be invasive. Cut back hard in autumn to restrict its spread.

Parts used Leaves, flowering stems – processed for extraction of alkaloids.

USES Medicinal Both *V. major* and *V. minor* contain the alkaloid vincamine, which dilates blood vessels and reduces blood pressure, and is used in pharmaceutical preparations for cardiovascular disorders.

CAUTION All parts of the plant are poisonous if eaten. Self-treatment is not advised.

VIOLACEAE

Viola odorata

Sweet violet

History and traditions Violets were greatly esteemed in the classical world and are mentioned by Theophrastus (400 BC) as well as appearing in the works of Horace, Pliny and Juvenal. The Greek word for violet is *io* and in Greek mythology Io, daughter of the King of Argos, was ravished by Zeus and then turned into a heifer so that his wife Hera wouldn't find him out. But at least he had the decency to provide sweet-scented flowers (later named after her) for Io in heifer-form to eat. Violet was the favourite perfume of Josephine and the flowers became the emblem of the Bonapartes after Napoleon became sentimentally attached to them. Despite its elusive scent, the violet has long been an emblem of constancy. Many medicinal uses are listed in old herbals and syrup of violets was a gentle laxative, still in use at the beginning of the 20th century. Household recipe books from the 16th to the 19th centuries give many examples of violet flower syrups, honey, conserve, cakes and vinegar. John Evelyn suggests eating the leaves and this is his recipe: "Violet Leaves, at the entrance of spring fried brownish and eaten with Orange or Lemon Juice and Sugar is one of the most agreeable of all the herbaceous dishes" (*Acetaria*, 1719).

Description A low-growing, hardy perennial, 15 cm (6 in) tall, with a short rhizome and creeping stolons that root at the tips. The toothed, heart-shaped leaves form a basal rosette from which the solitary, drooping, purple or white flowers arise on long stalks, in spring.

Related species *V. tricolor*, heartsease, or wild pansy, is a hardy annual or perennial, which has branched stems and alternately arranged, lobed or toothed, ovate to lanceolate leaves. The flowers, like small pansies, are in combinations of yellow, white, purple or mauve borne on leafless stems sprouting from the leaf axils. Medicinal uses are similar to those of *V. odorata*. Strong doses may cause vomiting and allergic skin reactions. The common dog violet and wood violets are unscented and have no herbal value.

Habitat/distribution Native to Europe, Asia and northern Africa, introduced elsewhere. Found on damp soils in shady woodland.

Growth Grow in humus-rich, moist but well-drained soil, in sun or partial shade. The easiest method of propagation is by division in autumn. Also grown from seed sown in spring or autumn.

Parts used Flowers – fresh for culinary use; leaves, flowers, rhizomes – fresh or dried for use in infusions and medicinal preparations; essential oil – extracted from flowers.

USES Medicinal A healing, anti-inflammatory herb with expectorant, diuretic properties, it is taken internally as a tea for coughs, colds and rheumatism. Applied externally in compresses and lotions for skin complaints, swellings and ulcers and in gargles for mouth and throat infections. The essential oil is used in aromatherapy. *V. tricolor* is known to be a heart tonic, used to treat high blood pressure, colds and indigestion.

Culinary The flowers are candied, made into jellies, jams, conserves and vinegars, or added fresh to salads and desserts.

Aromatic The essential oil is used in perfumery.

Top Viola tricolor *(heartsease or wild pansy) has some medicinal value, but the flowers are not scented.*

Centre Viola tricolor *with golden feverfew leaves.*

Above *Leaves of* Viola cornuta, *the horned violet, which has lightly scented flowers.*

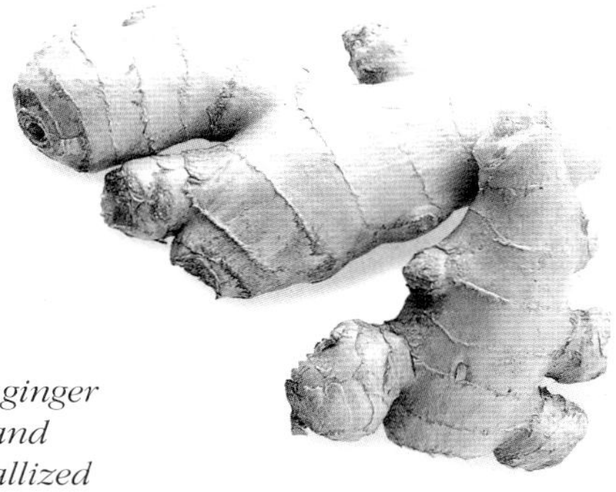

Fresh ginger root and crystallized ginger.

VERBENACEAE

Vitex agnus-castus

Chaste tree

History and traditions The association of this tree with chastity probably stems from its former use as a pepper substitute (made from the dried, powdered fruits) said to have been served in monasteries to suppress libido. The herb has, in fact, been established in recent times to have an effect on the hormonal balance of the body. It was also used in earlier times to relieve aches and pains, and other popular names for it are "Abraham's balm" and "hemp tree", because the leaves are similar in shape to those of *Cannabis sativa*.

Description A hardy deciduous shrub or small tree, up to 5 m (16 ft) tall, it has palmate leaves, dull-green on the upper surfaces, downy and greyish beneath, with long spikes of fragrant lilac flowers in summer, followed by small black fruits.

Habitat/distribution Originates in southern Europe and western Asia, also found in North and South America. Found on dry coastal sites.

Growth Grows in most soils and tolerates dry conditions well. Propagated by seed, sown in spring or autumn, or by semi-ripe cuttings taken in summer.

Parts used Fruits.

USES Medicinal A relaxant herb with pain-relieving properties, sometimes used by herbalists for hormonal complaints and imbalances.

ZINGIBERACEAE

Zingiber officinale

Ginger

History and traditions Ginger has been known in China and India since earliest times, valued for its medicinal properties and as a potent culinary flavouring. It was imported by the Greeks and Romans from the East, by way of the Red Sea, and its names in Greek, *zingiberis*, and Latin, *zingiber*, are derived from the Sanskrit, *singabera*. During the Middle Ages it was an important trading commodity, appearing on import-duty tariffs at European ports from 1170 onwards. It was known in Britain at this time and is frequently referred to in Anglo-Saxon leech-books, and in the 13th and 14th centuries it was second only to pepper as an imported spice. At the start of the 16th century, ginger was taken by the Spaniards from the East Indies to the Americas and West Indies, where it soon became established and was exported to Europe in large quantities as early as 1547. Ginger is one of the most popular culinary flavourings worldwide today. It is an important ingredient in both Chinese and Ayurvedic medicine, known in the latter as *maha-aushadi*, "the great medicine", and has an eastern tradition as an aphrodisiac, probably because it stimulates circulation and increases blood flow.

Description A perennial reed-like plant, it has thick, branching rhizomes and grows 1–1.2 m (3–4 ft) tall, with bright-green, lanceolate, alternately arranged leaves, on short, sheathed stems. The yellow-green flowers are borne in dense cones on separate stalks from the leaves.

Habitat/distribution Native to south-east Asia, introduced and widely grown in tropical zones.

Growth A tender, tropical plant, grown in fertile, humus-rich, well-drained soil with plenty of moisture and humidity. It is usually treated as an annual crop. Propagated by division.

Parts used Rhizomes – fresh, or dried, whole or ground.

USES Medicinal Ginger has antiseptic, expectorant properties, promotes sweating and is taken in decoctions for colds, chills and feverish infections. It is taken in tablet form or as a tincture for nausea, travel sickness, indigestion, stomach upsets and menstrual pain, and is said to be safe in small doses for morning sickness during pregnancy. The essential oil is taken in drops on sugar lumps for fevers, nausea and digestive upsets, and added to massage oil to ease rheumatic pain and aching joints.

Culinary Fresh ginger is grated and added to stir-fry dishes, and widely used, fresh or dried, in Chinese and Thai cuisines. Dried ground ginger is an ingredient of curry powder, pickles and chutneys and used in Western cookery in biscuits, cakes and desserts. Whole fresh ginger is crystallized in sugar syrup and made into chocolates and confectionery.

Aromatic The essential oil is used in perfumery and as a flavouring in the food industry.

GARDENING CALENDAR

Winter

AW *all winter* **EW** *early winter* **MW** *midwinter*
LW *late winter*

General

Clean and maintain tools and equipment **AW**
Plan next year's crops **AW**
Order seed and plants **AW**
Order sowing and potting composts (soil mixes) **AW**
Order manure **AW**
Continue digging soil when conditions allow **AW**
Avoid treading or working on waterlogged soil **AW**
Clean and prepare pots and propagators **AW**
Compost any organic waste **AW**

Vegetables

Sow early vegetables under glass for planting under protection **MW–LW**
Sow early vegetables for planting out **LW**
Check stored vegetables **AW**
Plant rhubarb **MW–LW**
Sow broad (fava) beans **MW–LW**
Sow parsnips if conditions allow **LW**
Plant early potatoes if conditions allow **LW**
Protect overwintering crops such as peas and broad (fava) beans with cloches **AW**
Protect brassicas from birds **AW**
Force rhubarb **LW**

Herbs

Continue to remove dead stems from herbaceous material **AW**
Continue to prepare ground when conditions allow **AW**
Use cloches for protection or to promote winter growth **AW**

Fruit

Prune fruit bushes **AW**
Prune apple and pear trees **AW**
Heel in bare-rooted trees and bushes when they arrive **AW**
Plant bushes and trees when conditions allow **AW**
Prevent birds stripping buds from fruit bushes **AW–LW**
Check stored fruit **AW**
Check supports and ties on supported trees and bushes **AW**
Take hardwood cuttings **EW**

Spring

AS *all spring* **ES** *early spring* **MS** *mid-spring*
LS *late spring*

General

Prepare seed beds **AS**
Finish winter digging and ground preparation **ES**
Keep weeds under control **AS**
Water in dry weather **LS**

Vegetables

Mulch permanent beds with manure **ES–MS**
Begin main sowing and planting of hardy vegetables **AS**
Continue successional sowings **MS–LS**
Sow tender vegetables like runner beans under glass **LS**
Plant tomatoes, aubergines (eggplants), cucumbers and peppers in heated greenhouses **ES–MS**
Plant tomatoes, aubergines (eggplants), cucumbers and peppers in unheated greenhouses **MS–LS**
Plant Jerusalem artichokes, potatoes and onions **ES–MS**
Plant permanent crops such as globe artichokes and asparagus **ES**
Plant out tender vegetables after last frosts **LS**
Protect vulnerable new growth from frosts **AS**
Erect supports for peas and beans **MS–LS**
Force rhubarb **ES**
Mulch vegetables **LS**

Herbs

Finish removing last year's dead growth **ES**
Sow seed for annuals and perennials **ES**
Sow tender herbs ready for planting out after frosts **MS–LS**
Plant out hardy herbs **AS**
Prune shrubby herbs **ES**
Plant out tender herbs after last frosts **LS**
Take basal cuttings **ES–MS**
Divide herbaceous herbs **ES–MS**

Fruit

Mulch bushes and trees with manure **ES–MS**
Finish winter pruning **ES**
Remove any winter-damaged branches **ES**
Finish planting bushes and trees **ES**
Hand-pollinate early fruit trees **ES**
Protect blossom from frosts **AS**
Prune plum trees **LS**
Thin gooseberries **LS**
Mulch strawberries with straw **LS**

Summer

AS *all summer* **ES** *early summer* **MS** *midsummer*
LS *late summer*

General

Keep weeds under control **AS**
Water when necessary **AS**
Keep an eye out for pests and diseases **AS**
Take soft and semi-ripe cuttings **MS–LS**

Vegetables

Plant out greenhouse-sown tender vegetables **ES**
Sow tender vegetables **ES**
Sow winter crops **MS–LS**
Continue successional sowings **ES–MS**
Harvest early vegetables as required **AS**
Shade and ventilate greenhouse vegetables **AS**
Dampen greenhouse floor to maintain humidity **AS**
Pick greenhouse vegetables as they ripen **AS**
Pinch out side shoots from tomatoes **AS**
Earth up vegetables that require it **AS**
Lift and dry onions, shallots and garlic **LS**

Herbs

Harvest herbs as required **AS**
Harvest herbs for storing before they flower **ES–MS**
Plant out tender herbs **ES**
Deadhead as necessary unless seed is required **AS**
Cut back herbaceous plant to stimulate new growth **AS**

Fruit

Pick early soft fruit **ES–MS**
Continue to pick soft fruit **MS–LS**
Pick cherries and early tree fruits **MS**
Net soft fruit against birds **AS**
Tie in new growth on cane fruit **AS**
Summer prune tree fruit **AS**
Thin tree fruit if necessary **ES–MS**
Remove spent raspberry canes and tie in new growth **LS**
Remove foliage and mulch from spent strawberries **LS**
Pot up or transplant strawberry runners **LS**
Tip-layer briar fruit **LS**

Autumn

AA *all autumn* **EA** *early autumn* **MA** *mid-autumn* **LA** *late autumn*

General

Continue weeding **AA**
Compost all waste vegetation **AA**
Water if necessary **EA**
Start autumn digging on heavy soils **MA–LA**
Clean and oil tools before putting away for winter **LA**

Vegetables

Lift and store potatoes **EA–MA**
Lift and store root crops in cold areas **LA**
Remove and compost finished crops **AA**
Plant garlic **LA**
Plant spring cabbage **EA**
Sow broad (fava) beans **LA**
Sow salad crops under glass **EA**
Protect globe artichokes, celeriac (celery root) and celery with straw in cold areas **LA**
Protect brassicas from birds **AA**
Check stored vegetables **LA**

Herbs

Harvest seed as it ripens **AA**
Tidy away dead material as necessary **AA**
Protect tender herbs **MA–LA**
Plant perennial and shrubby herbs **AA**
Move container herbs under protection **MA–LA**
Divide herbaceous herbs **EA**

Fruit

Pick tree fruit as it ripens **AA**
Store apples and pears **AA**
Pick late crops of strawberries and raspberries **AA**
Plant new strawberry beds **EA, MA**
Remove old fruiting canes from briar fruit and tie in the new **MA**
Finish removing old raspberry canes and tying in the new **EA**
Take hardwood cuttings **LA**
Plant new fruit trees and bushes **MA–LA**
Check stored fruit **LA**
Check all supports and ties **EA–MA**

WINTER It is advisable to protect permanent plants, such as globe artichokes, from winter cold and frost. A straw-filled box is a good source of insulation.

SPRING Leeks can be harvested between early autumn and late spring by simply digging them out with a fork. Autumn varieties are not as hardy and should be harvested before midwinter.

SUMMER Harvest globe artichokes, in summer, from the second year onwards. Take off the flower-heads before they open and while they are still green, cutting 2.5cm/1in below the head with a sharp knife or secateurs (pruners).

AUTUMN Potatoes can be harvested from early summer to autumn, depending on whether they are first earlies, second earlies or maincrop potatoes.

GLOSSARY

Salvia officinalis *'Icterina'*

Acid soil – soil with a ph value between 1 (very acid) and 7 (neutral. Vegetables are usually grown on a soils with a pH of 5.5–7.5.

Alkaline soil – soil with a pH value between 7 (neutral) and 14.

Alkaloid – a nitrogen-based compound contained in a plant, usually capable of having a powerful effect on bodily systems, such as painkilling or poisoning.

Allergen – a substance which causes an allergic reaction.

Alternate – refers to leaves arranged successively on either side of a stem.

Analgesic – pain relieving.

Annual – a plant that normally lives and grows for only one year or season.

Antiscorbutic – counteracts scurvy, a disease caused by Vitamin C deficiency.

Aphid – garden pest.

Aril – seed-covering, often fleshy and brightly coloured, of certain plants.

Astringent – has a binding, contracting effect on bodily tissue and stops bleeding.

Axil – the upper angle between a leaf or bract and the stem on which it grows.

Axillary – growing in the axil.

Basal (of leaves) – growing or forming at the base of the stem.

Biennial – a plant that has a normal life cycle of two years.

Biodegradable – capable of being decomposed by natural biological processes.

Biological pest control – the use of specific predatory insects for controlling pests, particularly in the greenhouse.

Black fly – garden pest.

Blanching – (gardening) covering part of a plant, such as celery or chicory, to deprive it of light.

Blanching – (culinary) cooking briefly in boiling water, then plunging into cold water in preparation for freezing.

Blight – a fungal disease.

Bolt – to run to seed prematurely.

Bordeaux mixture – an inorganic chemical fungicide.

Botrytis – a fungal disease.

Bract – a small, modified leaf.

Broadcasting – sowing seeds by scattering them evenly over the surface of the soil.

Bulbil – a small, bulb-like structure growing in a leaf axil or flower cluster.

Bush tree – a short, bushy-shaped tree with an open centre.

Cabbage root fly – garden pest.

Calcareous – containing lime; chalky.

Calyx (pl. **calyces**) – the outer circle of sepals, joined or divided, which surround a flower head or bud.

Carrot fly – garden pest.

Celery fly – garden pest.

Chitting – a method of encouraging early seed potatoes into growth by placing them eyes upwards in a cool, light place until short shoots appear.

Cloche – a semi-cylindrical or bell-shaped cover, made of glass or plastic, for protecting young plants.

Club root – a disease, particularly affecting leaf vegetables.

Cold frame – a structure with a frame, made from wood or aluminium, and a glass top for protecting young plants against the cold.

Below *A colourful border display.*

Below *An espaliered fruit tree.*

Below Calendula officinalis.

Companion planting – a system for using the insect-repellent properties of certain plants to protect others from pests.

Compost – recycled organic waste rotted down and used to condition the soil.

Cordon – a tree or bush consisting of a single main stem.

Corymb – a flat-topped or convex flower cluster having flower stalks arising from different points on the stem.

Crop rotation – a system of growing plants of different types in individual plots sequentially over three or four years.

Cultivar – a plant produced or selected from a natural species, its distinctive characteristics maintained by cultivation.

Cuttings (taking) – a means of propagation.

Damping off – a fungal disease.

Deciduous – describes a tree or shrub that loses its leaves annually, regrowing them the following season.

Decoction – an extraction of the water-soluble constituents of a medicinal plant, made by boiling it in water.

Derris – a non-persistent pesticide, available in liquid or powder form.

Dibber (dibble) – a pointed tool for making holes in the soil for planting seeds, bulbs and seedlings.

Dioecious – produces male and female flowers on different plants.

Disc-floret – small, often tubular floret, which, along with many, forms the centre of a compound flower head, such as a daisy.

Division – a means of propagation in which a root clump is separated into two.

Double digging – breaking up both the topsoil and the subsoil with a spade. Organic material is usually incorporated during the process.

Double cordon – a tree or bush with two main shoots that have been trained vertically, to form a U-shape.

Drill – a straight, shallow trench for planting seeds in a row.

Dropsy – (edema) a disease characterized by excessive build-up of fluid in bodily tissues.

Drupe – fleshy fruit with one or more seeds enclosed in a hard casing.

Dwarf pyramid tree – tree pruned into a pyramid.

Left *A border of purple and green sage.*

Above *A bed of mixed thymes.*

Below *Catmint and a yellow climbing rose.*

Eelworm – a garden pest.
Elliptic – oval-shaped, tapering to a point at each end.
Emetic – causes vomiting.
Emollient – softens and smooths the skin.
Entire – refers to smooth, untoothed leaf margins.
Espalier – a tree with parallel branches trained flat against a wall.
Essential oil – the volatile liquid in plants which gives them their scent.
Expectorant – encourages the ejection of phlegm from the respiratory tract.
Fan – a tree trained with its branches spreading from the top of a short trunk into a two-dimensional fan.
Flat – a wooden seed tray.
Flea beetle – garden pest.
Forcing – a technique for bringing crops to maturity faster than they would normally.
Forking – roots that branch when they should be single owing to a soil that is too rich.
Fruit cage – covering, usually made from galavanized wire, to protect fruit trees and bushes from birds and other pests.
Globose – spherical.
Green manure – crops that can be dug back into the ground to improve soil condition and add nutrients.
Growing bag – a plastic sack filled with formulated growing medium.

Above *Rhubarb pots must be put over the rhubarb just before growth begins.*

Growmore – an inorganic fertilizer (not available in the United States).
Guyot – a system for training and pruning grapevines.
Half-standard – a tree smaller than a standard and with a natural shape.
Harden off – the gradual exposure of indoor-grown seedlings to outdoor conditions to acclimatize them before planting out.
Hotbed – a method of heating a cold frame by positioning it on a heap of unrotted farm-yard manure which generates heat as it rots.
Hybrid – a plant produced by cross-fertilization between two species.
Infusion – an extraction of water-soluble constituents of a medicinal plant, made by steeping it in water that has been brought to boiling point.
Intercropping – Planting quick-growing plants among slower-growing ones.
Inorganic fertilizer – synthetic concentrated fertilizer made up of chemicals not derived from organic materials.
Lanceolate – (of leaves) narrow and tapering to a point at the tip.
Layering – a means of propagation.
Leafmould – a natural soil conditioner made from fallen leaves. It can be incorporated into the soil or used as a top-dressing.
Lime – (soil additive) calcium carbonate.
Loam – a combination of clay and sandy soils.
Mealy bug – greenhouse pest.
Modular tray – a seed tray divided into cells. Usually, two seeds are planted in each cell. It may be biodegradable.
Monoecious – bears separate male and female flowers on the same plant.
Mosaic virus – a viral infection.
Mucilage – a glutinous substance contained in a plant.
Mulch – a layer of organic or inorganic material covering the soil to protect against drought, weeds and other adverse conditions.
Neck rot – a fungal disease affecting bulbs of the onion family.
Obovate – an inverted egg-shape, narrow at the base and broader at the top.
Opposite – (of leaves) growing in pairs at the same level, on opposite sides of the stem.
Organic fertilizer – synthetic concentrated fertilizer made up of chemicals derived from organic materials.
Ovate – egg-shaped, with the broader part at the base, narrow at the top.

Above *Citrus fruits ripening in a greenhouse.*

Ovoid – a solid egg-shape with the broader end at the base, usually applied to fruit.
Palmate – describes a compound leaf with several leaflets arising from a common point.
Panicle – branched, compound flower cluster.
Pelleted seeds – seeds with a clay coating to make them easier to handle and sow.
Perennial – a plant with a lifespan of more than two years.
Permanent planting – a bed with plants that will remain in position for a number of years.
Perfoliate – describes a stalkless leaf, or leaves, which encircle and enclose the stem.
Pergola – an arbour with a trellis-work roof on which plants may be trained.
pH scale – a measure of acidity and alkalinity.
Pinnate – describes a compound leaf, made up of two rows of leaflets on either side of the central stem.
Polytunnel – plastic tunnel for protecting plants in winter and early spring.
Potager – a kitchen garden, usually with a decorative as well as practical function.
Potash – an inorganic fertilizer.
Powdery mildew – a fungal disease.
Propagation – (gardening) an artificial means of increasing the stock of plants.
Propagator – a glass or plastic box to keep a seed tray moist and warm.
Prophylactic – protects from disease.
Prune – to remove branches or other growth to improve growth and/or shape.
Purgative – strongly laxative.
Quicklime – calcium oxide.
Raceme – an unbranched, often conical-shaped, flower cluster.
Ray-floret – the usually strap-shaped outer petal (floret) of a compound flower head such as a daisy.

Red spider mite – greenhouse pest.
Rhizome – an underground, ground level, branched, swollen root-like stem, that usually grows horizontally and bears leafy shoots.
Root cuttings – a means of propagation.
Root division – a means of propagation.
Rotenone – a pesticide.
Rust – a fungal disease.
Scale insect – garden pest.
Scarification – the process of breaking up the hard outer coating of some seeds by rubbing with fine sandpaper.
Sets – small bulbs (of the onion family) grown by seed merchants from seed sown the previous season, ready for planting out.
Single digging – a method of breaking up the topsoil. Organic material is usually incorporated in the process.
Slaked lime – calcium hydroxide.
Slow-release fertilizer – coated synthetic fertilizer that is released slowly into the soil, especially useful in containers.
Soakaway – a drainage pit below the level of the planting beds.
Soil tester – commercially available kit for testing the acidity and alkalinity (pH) of soil.
Spadix – a flower spike with a thick, fleshy stem, usually encased in a spathe.
Spathe – a leaf or bract wrapped round a central spike of flowers.
Spindle bush tree – short, cone-shaped tree with the side branches tied down to make them spread.
Spit – the depth of a spade.
Spur prune – shape into which a bush tree, usually an apple, may be pruned.
Standard (tree) – a full-size tree with a natural shape.
Station sowing – sowing three seeds at the distances that will be the eventual gap between plants.
Stem cuttings – a means of propagation.
Stratification – the process of submitting certain seeds to a period of intense cold before sowing to ensure germination. Also called vernalization.
Subsoil – the layer of soil below the topsoil, which is lighter in colour and contains little organic matter.
Successional cropping – phased planting of the same or different crops.
Sulphate of ammonia – an inorganic fertilizer.
Sulphur powder – a fungicide.
Taproot – the main, downward-growing root of a plant, which is often cylindrical or a cone shape.
Thinning – the removal of unwanted and weaker plants to leave the better-developed ones spaced at regular intervals correct for the type of plant grown.
Tilth – soil broken down into fine particles to encourage plant growth.
Tincture – a solution, usually in alcohol, of the active constituents of a medicinal plant.
Top-dressing – applying a relatively thin layer of organic material to the bed after planting or around growing plants.
Topiary – the art of clipping trees and shrubs into geometric or fantastic shapes.
Topsoil – the dark, top layer of soil that contains organic material.
Trifoliate – describes leaves with three lobes or leaflets.
Tuber – swollen underground stem or root, such as a potato.
Umbel – an umbrella-shaped flower cluster.
Variety – a subdivision of species and hybrids with a distinctive difference, but only minor variations in botanical structure.
Vermifuge – expels intestinal worms.
Vernalization – the process of submitting certain seeds to a period of intense cold before sowing to ensure germination. Also called stratification.
Vulnerary – promotes the healing of wounds.
Whitefly – garden pest.
White rot – a fungal disease, particularly affecting the onion family.
Whorl – leaves or flowers arising from the same point and encircling the stem.
Vine eye – device for holding in place supporting wire for plants, such as fruit trees and bushes.

Above *A bright and colourful display of herbs.*

Above *Tomatoes can be grown in containers.*

SOURCES AND SUPPLIERS

United Kingdom

Suppliers of essential oils

Culpeper Ltd
Hadstock Road
Linton
Cambridge CB1 6NJ
Tel 01233 788196

The Fragrant Earth Co. Ltd
PO Box 182
Taunton
Somerset TA1 1YR
Tel 01823 335734 for mail order catalogue.

Neal's Yard Remedies
5 Golden Cross
Cornmarket Street
Oxford OX1 3EU
Tel 01865 245436 for mail order catalogue.

Shirley Price
Essentia House
Upper Bond Street
Hinckley
Leicestershire LE10 1RS
Tel 0455 615466 for mail order catalogue.

Medicinal and culinary herbs

G. Baldwin & Co.
171–173 Walworth Road
London SE17 1RN
Tel 020 7703 5550

Potters Herbal Supplies
Leyland Mill Lane
Lancashire WN1 2SB
Tel 01942 405100 for mail order cut herbs.

Poyntzfield Herb Nursery
Black Isle by Dingwall
Ross & Cromarty
Scotland IV7 8LX
Tel 01381 610352 for mail order plants. Informative catalogue sent on receipt of four first class stamps.

Rosemary Titterington
Iden Croft Herbs
Frittenden Road
Kent TN12 0DH
Tel 01580 891432 for mail order.

North America

Suppliers of essential oils

The Body Shop
2870 Janitell Road
Colorado Springs, CO 80906
Tel (800) 263 9746

Lorann Oils
PO Box 22009
Lansing, MI 48909–2009
Tel (800) 248 1302 for mail order.

Above left *Golden feverfew.*

Below *A deeply-coloured knot garden.*

Medicinal and culinary herbs

Caprilands Herb Farm
Silver Street
North Coventry, CT 06238

Richter's Herbs
Goodwood
Ontario
Canada LOC 1AO
Tel (905) 640 6677

Seeds Blum
HC 33 Box 2057
Boise, ID 83706
Tel (208) 342 0858
Order tel (800) 538 3658

Australia

Medicinal and culinary herbs

Bundanoon Village Nursery
71 Penrose Road
Bundanoon 2578
NSW
Tel (02) 4883-6303
e-mail: cabbage@pbq.com.au. A nursery in a garden. Classes on use of herbs, seeds and some Chinese medicinal herb tubers available by mail order.

Red spider mite – greenhouse pest.
Rhizome – an underground, ground level, branched, swollen root-like stem, that usually grows horizontally and bears leafy shoots.
Root cuttings – a means of propagation.
Root division – a means of propagation.
Rotenone – a pesticide.
Rust – a fungal disease.
Scale insect – garden pest.
Scarification – the process of breaking up the hard outer coating of some seeds by rubbing with fine sandpaper.
Sets – small bulbs (of the onion family) grown by seed merchants from seed sown the previous season, ready for planting out.
Single digging – a method of breaking up the topsoil. Organic material is usually incorporated in the process.
Slaked lime – calcium hydroxide.
Slow-release fertilizer – coated synthetic fertilizer that is released slowly into the soil, especially useful in containers.
Soakaway – a drainage pit below the level of the planting beds.
Soil tester – commercially available kit for testing the acidity and alkalinity (pH) of soil.
Spadix – a flower spike with a thick, fleshy stem, usually encased in a spathe.
Spathe – a leaf or bract wrapped round a central spike of flowers.
Spindle bush tree – short, cone-shaped tree with the side branches tied down to make them spread.

Above *Tomatoes can be grown in containers.*

Above *A bright and colourful display of herbs.*

Spit – the depth of a spade.
Spur prune – shape into which a bush tree, usually an apple, may be pruned.
Standard (tree) – a full-size tree with a natural shape.
Station sowing – sowing three seeds at the distances that will be the eventual gap between plants.
Stem cuttings – a means of propagation.
Stratification – the process of submitting certain seeds to a period of intense cold before sowing to ensure germination. Also called vernalization.
Subsoil – the layer of soil below the topsoil, which is lighter in colour and contains little organic matter.
Successional cropping – phased planting of the same or different crops.
Sulphate of ammonia – an inorganic fertilizer.
Sulphur powder – a fungicide.
Taproot – the main, downward-growing root of a plant, which is often cylindrical or a cone shape.
Thinning – the removal of unwanted and weaker plants to leave the better-developed ones spaced at regular intervals correct for the type of plant grown.
Tilth – soil broken down into fine particles to encourage plant growth.
Tincture – a solution, usually in alcohol, of the active constituents of a medicinal plant.
Top-dressing – applying a relatively thin layer of organic material to the bed after planting or around growing plants.
Topiary – the art of clipping trees and shrubs into geometric or fantastic shapes.
Topsoil – the dark, top layer of soil that contains organic material.
Trifoliate – describes leaves with three lobes or leaflets.
Tuber – swollen underground stem or root, such as a potato.
Umbel – an umbrella-shaped flower cluster.
Variety – a subdivision of species and hybrids with a distinctive difference, but only minor variations in botanical structure.
Vermifuge – expels intestinal worms.
Vernalization – the process of submitting certain seeds to a period of intense cold before sowing to ensure germination. Also called stratification.
Vulnerary – promotes the healing of wounds.
Whitefly – garden pest.
White rot – a fungal disease, particularly affecting the onion family.
Whorl – leaves or flowers arising from the same point and encircling the stem.
Vine eye – device for holding in place supporting wire for plants, such as fruit trees and bushes.

BIBLIOGRAPHY

History and Traditions

Old Herbals

Anderson, Frank J., *An Illustrated History of the Herbals* (Columbia University Press, New York, 1977)

Baker, Margaret, *Discovering the Folklore of Plants* (Shire Publications Ltd, Princes Risborough, 1969/1980)

Cockayne, Oswald, *Leechdoms, Wortcunning and Starcraft of Early England* (2 vols. London, 1864)

Encyclopaedia Britannica (New York, 1910)

Folkard, R., *Plant Lore, Legends and Lyric* (London, 1892)

Grieve, Maud, *A Modern Herbal* (Jonathan Cape, 1931, Penguin Books, London, 1980)

Griggs, Barbara, *Green Pharmacy* (Jill Norman & Hobhouse, London, 1981)

Hepper, F. N., *Bible Plants at Kew and Pharaoh's Flowers – The Botanical Treasures of Tutankhamun* (HMSO, London, 1981/1990)

Manniche, Lise, *An Ancient Egyptian Herbal* (British Museum Publications, London, 1989)

Rohde, Eleanour Sinclair, *The Old English Herbals* (Minerva Press, London, 1972)

A Garden of Herbs (P. Lee Warner & Medici Society)

Shakespeare's Wild Flowers, Fairy Lore, Gardens, Herbs, Gatherers of Simples and Bee Lore (The Medici Society, London, 1935)

Medicinal

Bakhru, H. K., *Herbs that Heal, and Foods that Heal* (Orient Paperbacks, Delhi, 1997)

Britt, Jennifer and Keen, Lesley, *Feverfew* (Century Hutchinson, London, 1987)

Buchman, Dian Dincin, *Herbal Medicine* (The Herb Society/Rider, London, 1983)

Frawley, David and Lad, Vasant, *The Yoga of Herbs: An Ayurvedic Guide to Herbal Medicine* (Lotus Press, Sante Fe, 1988)

Heyn, Birgit, *Ayurvedic Medicine* (Thorsons, London, 1987)

Kaptchuk, Ted, *Chinese Medicine -The Web that has no Weaver* (Rider, London, 1983)

Kreig, Margaret, *Green Medicine – the Search for Plants that Heal* (George Harrap, London, Toronto, Wellington, Sydney, 1965)

Leung, Albert, *Chinese Herbal Remedies* (Wildwood House, London, 1985)

Mills, Simon Y., *A Dictionary of Modern Herbalism* (Thorsons, Wellingborough, 1985)

Ody, Penelope, *The Herb Society's Complete Medicinal Herbal* (Dorling Kindersley, London, 1993)

Saynor, Reg, *The Garlic Effect* (Hodder & Stoughton, London, 1995)

Squire, Peter Wyatt, *Squire's Companion to the British Pharmacopoeia* (J. & A. Churchill, London, 1908)

Stary, Frantisek, *The Natural Guide to Medicinal Herbs and Plants* (Tiger Books International, Twickenham, 1998)

Vogel, Virgil, *American Indian Medicine* (University of Oklahoma Press, US, 1970)

Weiss, R. F., *Herbal Medicine* (Beaconsfield Publishers, Beaconsfield, 1988)

Wren, R. C., *Potter's New Encyclopaedia of Botanical Drugs and Preparations* (C.W. Daniel, Saffron Walden, 1988)

Culinary

Jaffrey, Madhur, *An Invitation to Indian Cooking* (Jonathan Cape, London, 1976)

McWhirter, Alasdair and Clasen, Liz (edş.), *Foods that Harm, Foods that Heal* (The Reader's Digest Association Ltd, London, 1996)

Richardson, Rosamund, *Hedgerow Cookery* (Penguin Books, London, 1980)

Stobart, Tom, *Herbs, Spices and Flavourings* (Penguin Books, London, 1977)

Aromatic and Essential Oils

Arctander, Steffan, *Perfume and Flavour Materials of Natural Origin* (Steffan Arctander, New York, 1960)

Day, Ivan, *Perfumery with Herbs* (Darton, Longman & Todd/The Herb Society, London, 1979)

Genders, Roy, *Scented Wild Flowers of Britain* (Collins, London, 1971)

A History of Scent (Hamish Hamilton, UK, 1972)

Poucher, William A., *Perfumes, Cosmetics and Soaps* (3 vols, Chapman and Hall, London, 1950)

Price, Shirley, *Practical Aromatherapy* (Thorsons, Wellingborough, 1983)

Rimmel, Eugene, *The Book of Perfumes* (Chapman and Hall, London, 1865)

Tisserand, Robert, *The Art of Aromatherapy* (C. W. Daniel, Saffron Walden, 1977)

Plants and Gardening

Achele, Dietmar, *A Field Guide in Colour to Wild Flowers* (Octopus Books, London, 1975)

Anthony, John, *The Renaissance Garden in Britain* (Shire Publications, Princes Risborough, 1991)

Bown, Deni, *The RHS Encyclopaedia of Herbs* (Dorling Kindersley, London, 1995)

Brickell, Christopher (Ed-in-Chief), *The RHS A–Z Encyclopaedia of Garden Plants* (Dorling Kindersley, London, 1992)

Below *A herb border flourishes in the shelter of a wall at Poyntzfield Nursery, Scotland.*

Britton, Nathaniel and Brown, Addison, *An Illustrated Flora of the Northern United States and Canada* (3 vols, Dover Publications Inc., New York, 1970)

Buczacki, Stefan, and Harris, Keith, *Pests, Diseases and Disorders of Garden Plants* (Harper Collins, London, 1981, 1988)

Davis, P.H., *Flora of Turkey and the East Aegean Islands* (Edinburgh University Press, 1965)

Harvey, John, *Restoring Period Gardens* (Shire, Princes Risborough, 1988)

Hills, Lawrence D., *Comfrey for Gardeners and Smallholders* (Henry Doubleday Research Association, Coventry, 1985)

Hooker, J.D., *The Flora of British India* (vols 1–7, Reeve & Co, London, 1872–1897)

Huxley, Anthony and Taylor, William, *Flowers of Greece and the Aegean* (Chatto and Windus, London, 1977)

Lancaster, Roy, *A Plantsman in Nepal* (Antique Collectors Club, Woodbridge, 1995)

Lord, Tony (Ed.) and Botanists of RHS Gardens, Wisley, *The Plant Finder 1998–99* (Dorling Kindersley, London, 1998)

Mabberley, D. J., *The Plant Book – A Portable Dictionary of the Vascular Plants* (Cambridge University Press, Cambridge, 1997)

McVicar, Jekka, *Jekka's Complete Herb Book* (Kyle Cathie Ltd, London, 1997)

Miller, A.G. and Morris, M, *Plants of Dhofar* (Office of the Advisor for Conservation of the Environment (Oman, 1988)

Phillips, Roger and Foy, Nicky, *Herbs* (Pan Books Ltd, London, 1990)

Polunin, Oleg, and Stainton, A., *Flowers of the Himalaya* (Oxford University Press, Delhi, 1985)

Rice, Elsie Garrett and Compton, Robert Harold, *Wild Flowers of the Cape of Good Hope* (Botanical Society of South Africa, Kirstenbosch, S.A., 1950)

Ridley, H.N., *The Flora of the Malay Peninsula* (L. Reeve & Co., London, 1922–25)

Sharma, B.D. et al (eds.) *Flora of India* (Botanical Survey of India, Calcutta, 1993)

Simonetti, Gualtiero, *The Macdonald Encyclopaedia of Herbs and Spices* (Macdonald & Co (Publishers) Ltd., London 1991)

Stodola, Jiri and Volak, Jan, *The Illustrated Book of Herbs* (Octopus Books, London and Artia, Prague, 1984)

Stuart, Malcolm (ed.), *The Colour Dictionary of Herbs and Herbalism* (Orbis Publishing, London, 1979)

Watt, J.M. and Breyer-Brankdwijk, M.G., *Medicinal and Poisonous Plants of Southern and Eastern Africa* (E. S. Livingstone, Edinburgh and London, 1962)

Periodicals and Papers

Abstracts of papers on Neem, published by the Neem Foundation, India

The Herbal Review and *Herbs* (various volumes, The Herb Society, Warmington, Oxfordshire, 1977–97)

Balandrin et al, "Plant-Derived Natural Products in Drug Discovery and Development" (*American Chemical Society*, 1993)

Buchbauer, G. and Jirovetz, L., "Aromatherapy – Use of Fragrances and Essential Oils as Medicaments" (*Flavour and Fragrance Journal*, 1994)

Deans, S. G. and Ritchie, G., "Antibacterial Properties of Plant Essential Oils" (*International Journal of Food Microbiology*, 1987)

Fellows, Linda, "Botany Breaks into the Candy Store" (*New Scientist*, 1989)

O'Neill, M.J. and Lewis, J.A., "The Renaissance of Plant Research in the Pharmaceutical Industry" (*American Chemical Society*, 1993)

Above left *Fragrant herbs surround a bench.*

Above *Chives in a raised bed.*

Below *An arched walkway of herbs.*

SOURCES AND SUPPLIERS

United Kingdom

Suppliers of essential oils

Culpeper Ltd
Hadstock Road
Linton
Cambridge CB1 6NJ
Tel 01233 788196

The Fragrant Earth Co. Ltd
PO Box 182
Taunton
Somerset TA1 1YR
Tel 01823 335734 for mail order catalogue.

Neal's Yard Remedies
5 Golden Cross
Cornmarket Street
Oxford OX1 3EU
Tel 01865 245436 for mail order catalogue.

Shirley Price
Essentia House
Upper Bond Street
Hinckley
Leicestershire LE10 1RS
Tel 0455 615466 for mail order catalogue.

Medicinal and culinary herbs

G. Baldwin & Co.
171–173 Walworth Road
London SE17 1RN
Tel 020 7703 5550

Potters Herbal Supplies
Leyland Mill Lane
Lancashire WN1 2SB
Tel 01942 405100 for mail order cut herbs.

Poyntzfield Herb Nursery
Black Isle by Dingwall
Ross & Cromarty
Scotland IV7 8LX
Tel 01381 610352 for mail order plants. Informative catalogue sent on receipt of four first class stamps.

Rosemary Titterington
Iden Croft Herbs
Frittenden Road
Kent TN12 0DH
Tel 01580 891432 for mail order.

North America

Suppliers of essential oils

The Body Shop
2870 Janitell Road
Colorado Springs, CO 80906
Tel (800) 263 9746

Lorann Oils
PO Box 22009
Lansing, MI 48909–2009
Tel (800) 248 1302 for mail order.

Above left *Golden feverfew.*

Below *A deeply-coloured knot garden.*

Medicinal and culinary herbs

Caprilands Herb Farm
Silver Street
North Coventry, CT 06238

Richter's Herbs
Goodwood
Ontario
Canada LOC 1AO
Tel (905) 640 6677

Seeds Blum
HC 33 Box 2057
Boise, ID 83706
Tel (208) 342 0858
Order tel (800) 538 3658

Australia

Medicinal and culinary herbs

Bundanoon Village Nursery
71 Penrose Road
Bundanoon 2578
NSW
Tel (02) 4883-6303
e-mail: cabbage@pbq.com.au. A nursery in a garden. Classes on use of herbs, seeds and some Chinese medicinal herb tubers available by mail order.

Above Helianthus annuus.

Above Monarda didyma *'Cambridge Scarlet'.*

Above *Wild strawberry and marjoram pot.*

Chamomile Farm
79 Monbulk Road
Emerald 3782
Victoria
Tel (03) 5968-4807. No mail order.

Darling Mills Farm
62 Francis Street
Castle Hill 2154
NSW
Tel (02) 9634-2843
Fax (02) 9894-7439
Wide variety of salad leaves and the more common herbs as well as some Asian herbs.

Herbie's Spices
745 Darling Street
Rozelle 2039
NSW
Tel (02) 9555-6035
Website:http://www.herbies.com.au
All culinary herbs and spices in one place. Huge range. Mail order for dried herbs nationally and throughout the Pacific.

House of Herbs
1 Digney Street
Sandy Bay
Tasmania 7005
Tel (03) 6224-3788. Wide range to show size and shape under Tasmanian conditions.

Right Tanacetum cinerariifolium.

Lillydale Herb Farm
Mangans Road
Lilydale 3140
Victoria
Tel (03) 9735-0486
Display gardens with medicinal, culinary, fragrant, companion and insect repellent plants. Shop with range of herbal items and books.

Renaissance Herbs
Lot 521
Hakone Road
Warnervale 2259
Tel (02) 4392-4600
Fax (02) 4393-1221
Largest range – supplies to nurseries nationally through franchised growers throughout Australia.

TLC Herbs
Lot 10
Old Coach Road
Aldinga 5173 SA
Tel (08) 8577-7161
Many varieties, including more unusual ones. Mail order.

Resource information

For information on any aspect of the herb industry in Australia, the *Australian Herb Industry Resource Guide* by Kim Fletcher is invaluable. Regularly updated. Available from:

Focus on Herbs
Consultancy & Information Service
PO Box 203, Launceston
Tasmania 7250

INDEX

ACKNOWLEDGEMENTS

The publisher would like to thank the following people for assisting with the photography for this book:

Roger and Linda Bastin
Kruidenkwekerij Herb Nursery
Trichterweg 148a
6446 AT Brunssum
Holland

Christine and Peter Bench and
Mrs Nancy Bench
The Herb Nursery
Thistleton
Oakham
Rutland LE15 7RE
Tel 01572 767658

Chris and Mandie Dennis
The Citrus Centre
Marehill Nursery
West Mare Lane
Marehill
Pulborough
Sussex RH20 2EA
Tel 01798 872786

Adam Gordon
Rochfords
Joseph Rochford Gardens Ltd
Pipers End
Letty Green
Hertford SG14 2PB
Tel 01707 261370

Henry Doubleday Research
Association
Ryton Organic Gardens
Coventry CV8 3LG
Tel 01203 303517

Simon and Judith Hopkinson
Hollington Nurseries
Woolton Hill
Newbury
Berkshire RG20 9XT
Tel 01653 253908

Victoria Ker
Bedwyn Common
Wiltshire

The Kew Gardener
4a Station Approach
Kew Gardens
Surrey TW9 3QB
Tel 020 8332 9630

Anne Marie Powell
Garden Designer
West London
Tel 020 8840 1230

Letta Proper Pranger
Castle Hex
Belgium

Sally Reed
Braxton Gardens
Braxton Courtyard
Lymore Lane
Melford-on-Sea
Hampshire SO41 0TX
Tel 01590 642008

Duncan and Susan Ross
Poyntzfield Herb Nursery
Black Isle by Dingwall
Ross & Cromarty
Scotland IV7 8LX
Tel 01381 610352

The Royal Botanic Gardens
Kew
Surrey TW9 3AB
Tel 020 8332 5000

Lord Salisbury/Michael Pickard
(Curator)
Hatfield House
Hatfield
Hertfordshire AL9 5NQ
Tel 01707 262823

Richard Scott
The Herb Farm
Peppard Road
Sonning Common
Reading
Berkshire RG4 9NJ

The Shakespeare Birthplace Trust
Shakespeare Centre
Henley Street
Stratford-upon-Avon CV37 6QW
Tel 01789 204016

The Shrewsbury Quest
Abbey Foregate
Shrewsbury
Shropshire SY2 6AH
Tel 01743 366355

Roger Souvereyns
Scholteshof Restaurant and Hotel
with Gardens
Belgium

Phillip C Stallard
Site Facilities Officer
(Tretower Court)
CADW Welsh Historic
Monuments

Peter Turner
The National Herb Centre
Banbury Road
Warmington
Near Banbury
Oxfordshire OX17 1DF
Tel 01295 690999

Stijn Vanormelingen
De Horne Restaurant and Gardens
Brugstraat 30a Vechmaal
Belgium

Susie & Kevin White
Hexham Herbs
Chesters Walled Garden
Chollerford
Hexham
Northumberland NE46 4BQ

ACKNOWLEDGEMENTS

Author's Acknowledgements

Jessica Houdret would like to thank the following people for specialist information: Alan Gear of the Henry Doubleday Research Association, on the use of comfrey in the garden; Dr. Stanley Deans on thyme oil; Duncan Ross of Poyntzfield Herb Nursery on ginseng; Dr. Rosita Arvigo and the Traditional Healers Foundation of Belize, on plants of Central America; and also to Dr. Katya Svoboda of the Scottish Agricultural College, Dr. Rosemary Cole of the National Herb Centre and Dr. Charles Hill.

Picture Credits

Pages 10 bl, 14 bl, 17 tl ET Archive; pages 14 tr, 15 bl Edimedia; pages 15 tr, 16 bl, 17br, 20 bl The Bridgeman Art Library; pages 11 tr & 123 Vaughn Fleming, 20 tr Clay Perry, 26 rc David Askham, 43 br Steven Wooster, 100 tl, 134 tr, 145 tr John Glover, 123 bc, 128 tr Brigitte Thomas, 135 tr Sunniva Harte, 136 tr Clive Boursnell, 144 tl Lamontagne, 144/5 tc Christopher Gallagher, 149 tr Ron Evans, 213 b Clive Nichols – The Garden Picture Library; pages 21t, 41 br, 53 cl, 78 tr & cr, 79, 97 bc, 98 tl, 100 br, 106 tl, 107 tl 108 tc, 113 bl, 118 tl, 119 tl, 121 tr, 122 tl, 125 tl, 129 tl, 132 tl, 143 tc, 147 bl, tr, 155 tc, 156, 157 tl, 159 bc, 164 tl, 165 tl, 171 bc, 181 tr, 197 tr, 204 tr, 208 tr, 209 tl, tr, 213 t, 214 br, 215 tr, 216 b, 218 tl, 222 tl Jessica Houdret; pages 21 bl, 40 bl, 41 bl, 102 tr Lucy Mason; pages 21 tr, 24 tr, 36 bl, 48 tr, 51 br, 59 tr Jacqui Hurst; pages 32 br, 226 tr Adrian Thomas, 44 bl Neil Joy, 57 Michael Jones, 60 tr Geoffrey S. Chapman, 124 tc K. Jayara, 127 bl Malcolm Richards, 138 tr Michael R. Chandler, 232 tl Anthony Cooper, 233 tr E. Mole, 235 tl Bjorn Svensson 235 tr – A–Z Botanical Collection Ltd; pages 34 bl, 41 tr & tl, 67, 68, 69 tl, tc, tr, 73 tr & bl, 80/81, 82 br, 85 tr, 86, 88 bc, 90 tr, 122 cr, br, 149 br, 153 br, 161 bl, 169 br, 171c, 218 tr Michelle Garrett; pages 82 bl, 83 br, 85 br & bl, 86 cl, 88 tl & tr, 89 bl, 91 cr Polly Wreford; pages 95 tr, 126 tl, 134 tc, 136 tl, 151 tr, 194 tl, 197 bl, 225 tl Harry Smith Collection; page 98 tr Brenda Szabo – Kirstenbosch Botanic Garden, South Africa; pages 99 tl, 204 tl Dr. Eckart Pott, 113 br Bob & Clara Calhoun, 185 tc, tr, 191 tl Staffen Widstrand, 191 cl N. Schwihtz, 206 tl Harald Lange, 206 cr Hans Reinhard – Bruce Coleman Ltd.; pages 116 tl, 185 tl, 192 tr Deni Bown; pages 140 tl, 142 tl, 156 br, 158 tl Dr. John Feltwell, Garden & Wildlife Matters; page 194 br Duncan Ross, Poyntzfield Nursery.

key t = top, b = bottom, c = centre, l = left, r = right

gardener's

records

Every garden is unique. They all vary in shape and size, and they have different soils, aspects and plants. They are looked after by very different people. For some people gardening is a necessary chore, but for the kitchen and herb gardener, it is a fascinating hobby, and an endless challenge to improve the garden and grow better fruit, vegetables and herbs. Through trial and error, you can create the garden of your dreams, with the certain knowledge that if something goes wrong you will definitely have another chance to get it right the following year.

ABOVE **Vegetable plots can be highly decorative and look dramatic as well as being full of healthy produce for the kitchen.**

For many gardeners the kitchen garden is the hub of the year's activities. It is perfectly possible, even with a fairly small vegetable plot, to keep a family of two adults and three children in vegetables for at least eight months of the year. With careful planning and a certain amount of deep-freezing, a family needn't spend much money on buying vegetables at all. When you see the prices charged for vegetables in most supermarkets, the saving – for the cost of a few packets of seeds and a little hard work – is well worth having. One gardening commentator says that digging is better exercise than jogging, and at the end of it you have a nice looking patch of good brown earth. He may not be correct medically, but it is a sentiment that all enthusiastic gardeners would agree with wholeheartedly.

The important thing is to plan the kitchen garden at the start of the year so that the vegetables follow in succession. It really is worth sowing seeds at fortnightly (bi-weekly) intervals throughout the summer and planning to grow winter vegetables – Brussels sprouts, winter cabbage, winter broccoli and spring greens – to eat when the glut of summer vegetables is over. You will need a good supply of organic matter, preferably well-rotted manure, to dig into the soil when one crop is over before replanting with another. You also need to be determined to defeat the birds as they descend on the tender emerging shoots. It is a good deal easier to grow peas in the centre of a city, where the multitudes of pigeons are used to feeding on scraps and are completely uneducated about fresh vegetables, than in the depths of the country.

BELOW **Although these vegetables are all green the variety of shapes, textures and size of the leaves provide a great display throughout a long planting season.**

Finally there is the question of flavour: there is absolutely nothing as good as fresh young vegetables picked and cooked straight from the garden, while the fact that you have grown them yourself makes the pleasure of eating them even greater.

VEGETABLES

Then a sentimental passion of a vegetable fashion
must excite your languid spleen,
An attachment a la Plato, for a bashfull young
potatoe, or not too French French bean!
(W. S. Gilbert *Patience*)

Today, there is a wealth of varieties of vegetables that the keen gardener can grow quite easily in a relatively small plot of land. There is no greater pleasure than picking your own produce straight from the garden and putting it straight in the pot. Those early new potatoes, and new sugar snap peas cooked in the pod, young asparagus in the spring are all quite delicious and immeasurably superior to anything you might buy at the supermarket.

ABOVE **Courgettes, or zucchini squashes, are usually harvested in their infancy, but they will mature to fine marrows with long-keeping qualities.**

Year .... Year .... Year ....

Vegetable .... Sown ....
Variety .... Thinned ....
Harvested ....

Vegetable .... Sown ....
Variety .... Thinned ....
Harvested ....

Vegetable .... Sown ....
Variety .... Thinned ....
Harvested ....

Vegetable .... Sown ....
Variety .... Thinned ....
Harvested ....

Vegetable .... Sown ....
Variety .... Thinned ....
Harvested ....

Vegetable .... Sown ....
Variety .... Thinned ....
Harvested ....

VEGETABLES

		Year	Year	Year ....
Vegetable	Sown			
Variety	Thinned			
	Harvested			
Vegetable	Sown			
Variety	Thinned			
	Harvested			
Vegetable	Sown			
Variety	Thinned			
	Harvested			
Vegetable	Sown			
Variety	Thinned			
	Harvested			
Vegetable	Sown			
Variety	Thinned			
	Harvested			
Vegetable	Sown			
Variety	Thinned			
	Harvested			

ABOVE **Tomatoes can be started off in a greenhouse and then transplanted outside.**

OPPOSITE **Each of these blocks of vegetables and herbs is about 1.2m/4ft wide, which allows access for paths.**

ABOVE **Potatoes and beetroot freshly dug from the vegetable garden. These can be peeled and cooked immediately.**

FRUIT

Go, bind thou up you dangling apricocks,
Which, like unruly children, make their sire
Stoop with oppression of their prodigal weight.
(William Shakespeare *King Richard II*)

If you have space in your garden, consider growing some fruit. This may present a challenge: to grow fruit successfully you need either plenty of space or a garden that doesn't have to double as a playing field. If you have children and a small town garden, don't plant raspberry canes (vines) or espalier apple trees along the walls: the game balls will do too much damage to make the effort worthwhile. But if you don't have any such obstacles you can certainly grow raspberries up a wall, or espalier apple and pear trees along the fence. There are many excellent varieties available grafted on to miniature rootstocks for this purpose. If you do have room you can make a fruit cage in which to grow strawberries and raspberries. You can plant currant bushes, apple, pear and plum trees, and if you live in a mild enough climate and have a south or south-west facing wall you can try growing peaches or apricots. With the help of the freezer you can again make major inroads into the family's expenditure at the supermarket. But beware of the birds: you will need to net all your fruit or the birds will eat the lot before you can.

ABOVE **Strawberries can be grown in containers for eating and for decoration. These healthy specimens are ripe for picking and enjoying.**

Fruit Trees

Year .... Year .... Year ....

Type .... Planted ....
Variety .... Pruned ....
Source .... Mulched ....
Sprayed ....
Picked ....

Type .... Planted ....
Variety .... Pruned ....
Source .... Mulched ....
Sprayed ....
Picked ....

Fruit Trees

Year .... Year .... Year

Type .... Planted ....
Variety .... Pruned ....
Source .... Mulched ....
Sprayed ....
Picked ....

Type .... Planted ....
Variety .... Pruned ....
Source .... Mulched ....
Sprayed ....
Picked ....

Type .... Planted ....
Variety .... Pruned ....
Source .... Mulched ....
Sprayed ....
Picked ....

Type .... Planted ....
Variety .... Pruned ....
Source .... Mulched ....
Sprayed ....
Picked ....

ABOVE **This pear tree has been beautifully trained into a fan. The fan is supported on wires, but it could also be grown against a wall.**

ABOVE **Ripe apples and pears picked straight from the tree. The flavour is incomparable to shop-bought fruit.**

FRUIT

Berries

Year .... Year .... Year

Type .... Planted ....
Variety .... Pruned ....
Source .... Mulched ....
Sprayed ....
Picked ....

Type .... Planted ....
Variety .... Pruned ....
Source .... Mulched ....
Sprayed ....
Picked ....

Type .... Planted ....
Variety .... Pruned ....
Source .... Mulched ....
Sprayed ....
Picked ....

Type .... Planted ....
Variety .... Pruned ....
Source .... Mulched ....
Sprayed ....
Picked ....

Type .... Planted ....
Variety .... Pruned ....
Source .... Mulched ....
Sprayed ....
Picked ....

OPPOSITE **Most fruit ripens in colour when it is ready to eat. These damsons can be made into preserves and jelly.**

HERBS

There's rosemary, that's for remembrance; pray, love, remember:

(William Shakespeare ***Hamlet***)

You should always try to find some room in your garden to grow a few herbs. Fresh herbs for the kitchen make any savoury dish taste so much better. No cook should be without a supply of fresh mint, parsley, rosemary, chives and thyme, and, if you are more ambitious, tarragon, basil and coriander (cilantro). Do not be put off growing herbs for lack of space, you can always use a pot or a window box.

Herbs can also be grown to use medicinally or aromatically. You can make infusions and poultices and dry them to scent rooms around the house.

ABOVE **You can create a formal look to a herb garden by planting herbs in blocks and encompassing them with box borders.**

Herbs

			Year	Year	Year ....
Type	....	Sown			
Variety	....	Thinned			
		Picked			
Type	....	Sown			
Variety	....	Thinned			
		Picked			
Type	....	Sown			
Variety	....	Thinned			
		Picked			
Type	....	Sown			
Variety	....	Thinned			
		Picked			
Type	....	Sown			
Variety	....	Thinned			
		Picked			

OPPOSITE **A colourful and decorative display of sunflowers and nasturtiums that is also edible.**

CREATE A COTTAGE GARDEN

HERBS

Year .... Year .... Year ....

Type .... Sown ....
Variety .... Thinned ....
Picked ....

Type .... Sown ....
Variety .... Thinned ....
Picked ....

Type .... Sown ....
Variety .... Thinned ....
Picked ....

Type .... Sown ....
Variety .... Thinned ....
Picked ....

Type .... Sown ....
Variety .... Thinned ....
Picked ....

Type .... Sown ....
Variety .... Thinned ....
Picked ....

ABOVE **You can easily grow herbs such as chives and parsley in containers or in hanging baskets.**

ABOVE **A stunning edible display of sweet violets and cowslips which can be added to salads and used as garnish.**

			Year	Year	Year
Type		Sown			
Variety		Thinned			
		Picked			
Type		Sown			
Variety		Thinned			
		Picked			
Type		Sown			
Variety		Thinned			
		Picked			
Type		Sown			
Variety		Thinned			
		Picked			
Type		Sown			
Variety		Thinned			
		Picked			
Type		Sown			
Variety		Thinned			
		Picked			

ABOVE **Nasturtium leaves are added to salads for their peppery taste and the flowers for their colour. The flowers are also used as a flavouring for vinegar.**

ABOVE **Herbs are not only useful for culinary and aromatic purposes, they can also make highly decorative gardens.**

CUTTINGS

There is no ancient gentleman
but gardeners, ditchers, and Gravemakers;
they hold up Adam's profession
(William Shakespeare ***Hamlet***)

It is relatively easy to raise new plants by taking cuttings from softwood or semi-ripe cuttings in spring and summer. Trees and shrubs can be raised from hardwood cuttings that are taken in autumn. Do not cram in too many cuttings in one pot or put one in the middle of the pot. Some herbs are better propagated by cutting roots, for example, mint; some grow better by division of roots, such as chives, or by layering, such as bay, rosemary or sage.

ABOVE **If planting herbs in summer, choose a damp spell and water well.**

Year .... Year .... Year ....

Plant .... Taken ....
Planted out ....

Plant .... Taken ....
Planted out ....

Plant .... Taken ....
Planted out ....

Plant .... Taken ....
Planted out ....

Plant .... Taken ....
Planted out ....

Plant .... Taken ....
Planted out ....

Plant .... Taken ....
Planted out ....

Plant .... Taken ....
Planted out ....

Plant .... Taken ....
Planted out ....

WEATHER YEAR

	Rainfall	Sunshine	Average Temperature	Comments
January				
February				
March				
April				
May				
June				
July				
August				
September				
October				
November				
December				

	Rainfall	Sunshine	Average Temperature	Comments
January				
February				
March				
April				
May				
June				
July				
August				
September				
October				
November				
December				

ABOVE **These healthy lettuces have been planted out in fertile soil and are ready to be picked.**

ABOVE **A greenhouse will be an invaluable aid if you wish to grow winter crops, overwinter plants and propagate your plants.**

TOOLS AND MACHINERY

Lawnmower .... Guarantee ....
Supplier ....
Telephone No. .... Serviced ....

Rotavator (Tiller) .... Guarantee ....
Supplier ....
Telephone No. .... Serviced ....

Other Machines .... Guarantee ....
Supplier ....
Telephone No. .... Serviced ....

PLANT SUPPLIERS

Name ....
Address ....
....
Telephone No. ....

Name ....
Address ....
....
Telephone No. ....

Name ....
Address ....
....
Telephone No. ....

Name ....
Address ....
....
Telephone No. ....

Name ....
Address ....
....
Telephone No. ....

Name ....
Address ....
....
Telephone No. ....

ABOVE **Always keep your equipment well-maintained and you will have fewer repair bills.**

ABOVE **If you have a large garden, you may need a shed. Think carefully about the use of the shed before you buy.**